1956	1958	1960	1962	1964	1966	1968	1970	1971	1972	1973	1974	1975	1976
271.9	296.6	332.3	363.8	411.7	481.8	558.7	648.9	702.4	770.7	852.5	932.4	1,030.3	1,149.8
72.0	64.5	78.9	88.1	102.1	131.3	141.2	152.4	178.2	207.6	244.5	249.4	230.2	292.0
91.8	106.5	113.8	132.2	145.1	174.3	212.8	237.1	251.0	270.1	287.9	322.4	361.1	384.5
2.3	0.4	2.4	2.4	5.5	1.9	-1.3	1.2	-3.0	-8.0	0.6	-3.1	13.6	-2.3
438.0	467.9	527.4	586.5	664.4	789.3	911.5	1,039.7	1,128.6	1,240.4	1,385.5	1,501.0	1,635.2	1,823.9
47.3	52.7	57.0	61.0	66.6	85.6	90.9	109.1	118.9	130.9	142.9	164.8	193.0	208.9
390.7	415.2	470.4	525.5	597.8	712.7	820.6	930.6	1,009.7	1,109.5	1,242.6	1,336.2	1,444.2	1,615.0
-2.5	-2.7	-3.2	-4.3	-5.0	-5.2	-6.2	-6.4	-7.7	-8.7	-12.7	-15.7	-13.3	-17.2
34.5	40.6	46.1	52.7	60.7	71.2	83.2	99.5	113.5	117.8	127.9	140.0	155.3	175.8
358.7	377.3	427.5	477.1	542.1	646.7	743.6	837.5	903.9	1,000.4	1,127.4	1,211.9	1,302.2	1,456.4
10.0	11.4	16.4	19.1	22.4	31.3	38.7	46.4	51.2	59.2	75.5	85.2	89.3	101.3
22.0	19.0	22.7	24.0	28.0	33.7	39.4	34.4	37.7	41.9	49.3	51.8	50.9	64.2
16.2	11.6	14.3	16.8	21.5	30.5	27.0	18.8	26.5	34.0	46.9	54.1	52.9	67.8
29.5	34.7	38.6	40.7	45.6	53.2	76.0	103.2	116.6	129.0	157.7	204.8	222.6	252.3
340.0	370.0	412.7	457.9	515.8	606.4	714.5	841.1	905.1	994.3	1,113.4	1,225.6	1,331.7	1,475.4
37.2	39.2	46.5	52.3	52.8	67.3	88.3	104.6	103.4	125.7	134.4	153.3	150.3	175.5
302.8	330.8	366.2	405.6	463.0	539.1	626.2	736.5	801.7	868.6	979.0	1,072.3	1,181.4	1,299.9

1956	1958	1960	1962	1964	1966	1968	1970	1971	1972	1973	1974	1975	1976
2,141.1	2,162.8	2,376.7	2,578.9	2,846.5	3,227.5	3,466.1	3,578.0	3,697.7	3,898.4	4,123.4	4,099.0	4,084.4	4,311.7
2.0	-1.0	2.5	6.0	5.8	6.6	4.8	0.2	3.3	5.4	5.8	-0.6	-0.4	5.6
8,930	8,922	9,210	9,666	10,456	11,417	12,196	12,823	13,218	13,692	14,496	14,268	14,393	14,873
27.2	28.9	29.6	30.2	31.0	32.4	34.8	38.8	40.5	41.8	44.4	49.3	53.8	56.9
1.5	2.8	1.7	1.0	1.3	2.9	4.2	5.7	4.4	3.2	6.2	11.0	9.1	5.8
33.6	31.9	36.5	39.8	45.0	53.8	58.1	58.7	59.5	65.3	70.6	69.6	63.4	69.3
136.0	138.4	140.7	147.8	160.3	172.0	197.4	214.3	228.2	249.1	262.7	274.0	286.8	305.9
3.77	3.83	4.82	4.50	4.50	5.63	6.30	7.91	5.72	5.25	8.03	10.81	7.86	6.84
168.9	174.9	180.7	186.5	191.9	196.6	200.7	205.1	207.7	209.9	211.9	213.9	216.0	218.0
66.6	67.6	69.6	70.6	73.1	75.8	78.7	82.8	84.4	87.0	89.4	91.9	93.8	96.2
2.8	4.6	3.9	3.9	3.8	2.9	2.8	4.1	5.0	4.9	4.4	5.2	7.9	7.4
4.1	6.8	5.5	5.5	5.2	3.8	3.6	4.9	5.9	5.6	4.9	5.6	8.5	7.7
43.4	46.0	48.8	52.9	57.5	62.0	65.4	67.0	69.9	72.2	74.5	73.2	75.8	78.5
0.1	2.9	1.9	4.6	4.6	4.1	3.1	2.0	4.4	3.3	3.2	-1.7	3.5	3.6
2.7	0.8	2.8	3.4	6.8	3.0	0.6	2.3	-1.4	-5.8	7.1	2.0	18.1	4.3
272.7	279.7	290.5	302.9	316.1	328.5	368.7	380.9	408.2	435.9	466.3	483.9	541.9	629.0

(Continued)

MACROECONOMICS

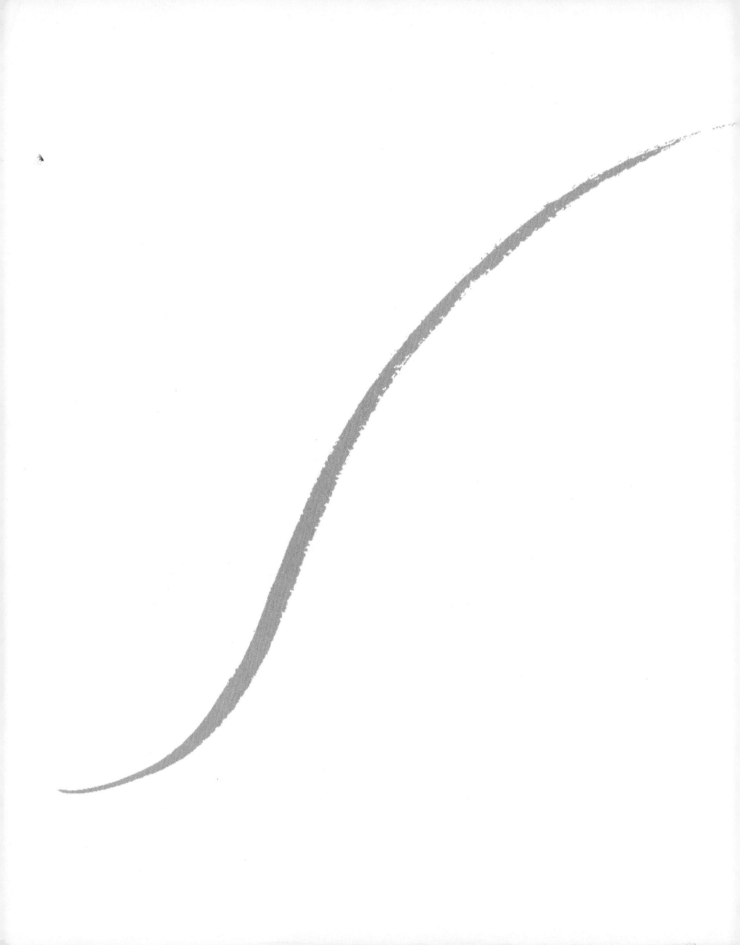

FIFTEENTH EDITION

Macroeconomics

Principles, Problems, and Policies

Campbell R. McConnell
Professor of Economics, Emeritus
University of Nebraska

Stanley L. Brue
Professor of Economics
Pacific Lutheran University

McGraw-Hill Irwin

Boston   Burr Ridge, IL   Dubuque, IA   Madison, WI   New York   San Francisco   St. Louis
Bangkok   Bogotá   Caracas   Kuala Lumpur   Lisbon   London   Madrid   Mexico City
Milan   Montreal   New Delhi   Santiago   Seoul   Singapore   Sydney   Taipei   Toronto

To *Mem* and to *Terri* and *Craig*

McGraw-Hill Higher Education
A Division of The **McGraw·Hill** Companies

MACROECONOMICS: PRINCIPLES, PROBLEMS, AND POLICIES
Published by McGraw-Hill/Irwin, an imprint of The McGraw-Hill Companies, Inc. 1221 Avenue
of the Americas, New York, NY, 10020. Copyright © 2002, 1999, 1996, 1993, 1990, 1987,
1984, 1981, 1978, 1975, 1972, 1969, 1966, 1963, 1960, by The McGraw-Hill Companies, Inc.
All rights reserved. No part of this publication may be reproduced or distributed in any form or by
any means, or stored in a database or retrieval system, without the prior written consent of
The McGraw-Hill Companies, Inc., including, but not limited to, in any network or other electronic
storage or transmission, or broadcast for distance learning.

Some ancillaries, including electronic and print components, may not be available to customers
outside the United States.

This book is printed on acid-free paper.

3 4 5 6 7 8 9 0 VNH/VNH 0 9 8 7 6 5 4 3 2

ISBN 0072340894

Publisher: *Gary Burke*
Sponsoring editor: *Lucille Sutton*
Developmental editor: *Erin Strathmann*
Marketing manager: *Martin Quinn*
Senior project manager: *Jean Lou Hess*
Senior production supervisor: *Lori Koetters*
Interior and cover designer: *Michael Warrell*
Director of design: *Keith McPherson*
Last Word illustrator: *Jacques Cournoyer*
Lead supplement coordinator: *Becky Szura*
Senior producer media technology: *Ed Przyzycki*
Compositor: *Techbooks*
Typeface: *10/12 Janson*
Printer: *Von Hoffmann Press, Inc.*

Library of Congress Cataloging-in-Publication Data

McConnell, Campbell R.
   Economics: principles, problems, and policies/Campbell R. McConnell, Stanley R. Brue.–
15th ed.
     p. cm.
   ISBN-0-07-234089-4 (alk. paper)
   Includes index.
   1. Economics. I. Brue, Stanley L., 1945- II. Title.
HB171.5 .M473 2002
339–dc21   2001037065

www.mhhe.com

Campbell R. McConnell earned his Ph.D. from the University of Iowa after receiving degrees from Cornell College and the University of Illinois. He taught at the University of Nebraska–Lincoln from 1953 until his retirement in 1990. He is also coauthor of *Contemporary Labor Economics*, 6th ed. (McGraw-Hill/Irwin) and has edited readers for the principles and labor economics courses. He is a recipient of both the University of Nebraska Distinguished Teaching Award and the James A. Lake Academic Freedom Award and is past president of the Midwest Economics Association. Professor McConnell was awarded an honorary Doctor of Laws degree from Cornell College in 1973 and received its Distinguished Achievement Award in 1994. His primary areas of interest are labor economics and economic education. He has an extensive collection of jazz recordings and enjoys reading jazz history.

Stanley L. Brue did his undergraduate work at Augustana College (SD) and received its Distinguished Achievement Award in 1991. He received his Ph.D. from the University of Nebraska–Lincoln. He is a professor at Pacific Lutheran University, where he has been honored as recipient of the Burlington Northern Faculty Achievement Award. He has also received the national Leavey Award for excellence in economic education. Professor Brue has served as national president and chair of the Board of Trustees of Omicron Delta Epsilon International Economics Honorary. He is co-author of *Economic Scenes*, *5th edition* (Prentice-Hall) and *Contemporary Labor Economics*, *6th edition* (McGraw-Hill/Irwin) and author of *The Evolution of Economic Thought*, *6th edition* (Harcourt). For relaxation, he enjoys international travel, attending sporting events, and skiing with family and friends.

LIST OF KEY GRAPHS

Welcome to the fifteenth edition of *Macroeconomics* (and its companion editions of *Economics* and *Microeconomics*), the nation's best-selling economics textbook. More than 12 million students worldwide have now used this book. It has been adapted into Canadian, Australian, Italian, and Russian editions, and translated into French, Spanish, and other languages. It continues to be the leading principles book in Russia and several other Russian-speaking countries.

The New Economy, concerns about recession, budget surpluses, Fed interest rate cuts, WTO issues, emerging technologies, the advent of the euro— what an interesting time to teach and learn economics! Clearly, those who understand economic principles will have a distinct advantage in making sense of the economy and successfully participating in it.

▋ Fundamental Objectives

We have three main goals for *Macroeconomics:*
- To help the beginning economics student comprehend the principles essential for understanding the basic economizing problem, specific economic issues, and the policy alternatives.
- To help the student understand and apply the economic perspective and to reason accurately and objectively about economic matters.
- To promote a lasting student interest in economics and the economy.

▋ What's New and Improved?

We thoroughly revised, polished, and updated this edition. The comments and suggestions of more than 100 reviewers and survey correspondents provided encouragement, motivated many improvements, and sparked innovation.

In-Text Web Buttons

We have enhanced the book substantially by linking it directly to newly created pedagogical features found at our website www.mhhe.com/economics/mcconnell15. Three types of icons appear throughout the book, indicating that additional content on a subject can be found online. The Web materials greatly enrich course content for those who wish to use it, but their design and careful placement in the text also allows for instructors to not use the information if they choose. Therefore the book remains adaptable to many teaching styles and types of courses. Button types include:

- The ▐!▌ symbol directs students to **Analogies, Anecdotes, and Insights** at our website. These short pieces, written by Stan Brue, help students understand and remember the economic ideas by connecting them to other, better-known ideas or easy-to-remember stories and examples.
- The ▐𝒫▌ symbol directs students to **Origins of the Idea.** These brief histories were written by Randy Grant of Linfield College and examine the origins of major ideas identified in the book. Students will find it interesting to learn about the economist who first developed such ideas as opportunity costs, equilibrium price, the multiplier, comparative advantage, and elasticity.
- The ▐⊿▌ symbol directs students to **Interactive Graphs.** Developed under the supervision of Norris Peterson of Pacific Lutheran University, this interactive feature depicts major graphs and instructs students to shift the curves, observe the outcomes, and derive relevant generalizations.

Streamlined Presentations

A major revision goal was to streamline presentations where possible without compromising the thoroughness of our explanations. Our efforts resulted not only in a shorter book, but in more efficient organization and greater clarity. An example is Chapter 4, The Market System, which is both shorter and better organized than before. You will find similar kinds of improvements throughout the fifteenth edition. Where needed, of course, the "extra sentence of explanation" remains a distinguishing characteristic of *Macroeconomics*. Brevity at the expense of clarity is false economy.

Improved Content

Chapter 8 (Introduction to Economic Growth and Instability) now discusses economic growth, as well as unemployment and inflation. We have simplified the presentations in Chapters 9 and 10 by focusing the graphical analysis on the aggregate expenditures-real output model rather than on both it and the leakage-injection model. This allowed us to eliminate the most difficult graphs in Chapter 10. Instead, we now develop the equilibrium condition $C + I_g + X_n + G = \text{GDP}$ graphically and then simply use our tables to demonstrate that two subsidiary equilibrium conditions are met: leakages = injections and unintended changes in inventories are zero.

Part 4 is now labeled "Long-Run Perspectives and Macroeconomic Debates." The chapters are revised and reorganized to reflect the new title and emphasis. Chapter 16 extends the analysis of aggregate supply to the long run. Chapter 17 looks at economic growth and has a complete discussion of the New Economy thesis. Chapter 18 discusses public debt and recent budget surpluses, and Chapter 19 examines disputes over macro theory and policy.

New Last Words

About one-third of the Last Words are new and others have been revised and updated. The new topics are: the remarkable organizational ability of markets (Chapter 4); the sources of the data used to construct the GDP accounts (Chapter 7); Say's Law, the Great Depression, and Keynes (Chapter 9); the diminished impact of oil prices (Chapter 16); some pleasant side-effects of the New Economy (Chapter 17); debt reduction and the U.S. trade deficit (Chapter 18); the Taylor monetary rule (Chapter 19); and the struggle for control of capital in Russia (Internet chapter).

Bonus Internet-Only Chapter

A special Internet chapter "Economies in Transition: Russia and China" is available for free use at our website. The chapter contains all the features of regular chapters, is readable in Adobe format, and can be printed if desired. This chapter is fully supported by all the ancillaries to the book.

Internet Math Notes

Although most students in the principles course have only modest math skills, a few have taken advanced mathematics courses in high school or college. For those students, seeing the algebra or calculus behind the economics is highly revealing and useful. Therefore we have placed a set of 50 math notes that are keyed to the topics in the book on our Website.

Written by Professor Norris Peterson, these notes are creative, concise, and to the point. They undoubtedly will enhance the educational experience for math-minded students.

Other New Topics and Revised Discussions
Along with the improvements just discussed, there are many other revisions. Here are some examples.

- *Part 1. Chapter 1:* Changed terminology from *material wants* to *economic wants;* revised discussion of economic methodology, focusing on the scientific method. *Chapter 2:* Reorganized section on applications of the production possibilities model; greatly consolidated section on economic systems. *Chapter 3:* Several new examples including increased demand for coffee drinks, soy-enhanced hamburger as an inferior good, increased supply of Internet service provision. *Chapter 4:* New chapter title and introduction; revised section on competition to generalize beyond pure competition; consolidation of the Five Fundamental Questions to Four, with discussion explicitly organized around each; shorter chapter. *Chapter 5:* New chapter title; new terminology: "horizontally organized firms," "vertically integrated firms," and "conglomerates"; new Figure 5-7 on government spending. *Chapter 6:* New Figure 6-1 showing the types of international flows (trade flows, resource flows, information and technology flows, and money flows); new discussion of the euro; expanded discussion of the WTO.

- *Part 2. Chapter 7:* briefer introduction; improved explanation of inventory changes as investment; revised discussion of government purchases to reflect the consumption and gross investment portions as now accounted for in GDP. *Chapter 8:* Revised Global Perspective 8-1 to show comparable growth rates since 1992, rather than since 1950; reorganized discussion of the unemployment section; Table 8-3 now includes unemployment rates for Hispanics; new Figure 8-4 shows inflation rates over the years rather than tracing out the CPI; revised discussion of redistribution and output effects of inflation. *Chapter 9:* Moved the section on the historical background of the aggregate expenditures model to a new Last Word (Say's Law, the Great Depression, and Keynes); simplified terminology and discussion of the role of inventory changes in achieving equilibrium; fuller discussion of the wealth effect. *Chapter 10:*

Consolidated the application on the Great Depression and added a new application on recession in Japan during the late 1990s. *Chapter 11:* Discussion of changes in AD and AS are now organized around specific macro outcomes; new section on simultaneous full employment, strong growth, and price stability; deleted discussion of the ratchet effect. *Chapter 12:* New Figure 12-4 and a greatly revised and simplified discussion of the full employment budget and the method of evaluating whether fiscal policy is neutral, contractionary, or expansionary.

■ *Part 3. Chapter 13:* The section on "Recent Developments" now stresses consolidation among banks, the convergence of services among financial institutions, and electronic transactions. *Chapter 14:* Changed terminology from *demand deposits* to *checkable deposits. Chapter 15:* Deleted peripheral content; *demand-deposit multiplier* is now *checkable-deposit multiplier;* new discussion of the ineffectiveness of expansionary monetary policy in Japan.

■ *Part 4. Chapter 16:* Significantly revised and condensed section on the inflation-unemployment relationship; consolidated discussion of supply-side economics. *Chapter 17:* New Figure 17-3 links shifts in the production possibilities curve and the long-run AS curve; replaced the discussion of the productivity slowdown with a new section on recent productivity growth and the New Economy; new Figure 17-7 compares trend productivity growth between 1973–1995 and 1995–2000; new Global Perspective 17-2 shows growth competitiveness rankings of countries; brought the material on "Is growth desirable?" from the Last Word of the prior edition to the body in this edition. *Chapter 18:* New discussion of budget surpluses and policy options for using them; new Figure 18-4 shows the rising percentage of the U.S. population over 65. *Chapter 19:* New discussion of the Taylor monetary rule.

■ *Part 5. Chapter 20:* Shortened this chapter; new section on the WTO. *Chapter 21:* Eliminated the balance sheets in explaining the financing of export and import transactions; updated the discussion of the managed floating system in view of significant bailouts by the IMF and currency interventions by major countries; updated discussion of U.S. trade deficits. *Chapter 22:* New Figure 22-2 on projected population growth; new Global Perspective 22-1 showing data from Transparency International's corruption index; new discussions on debt forgiveness.

▌Distinguishing Features

This text embraces a number of distinguishing features.

■ ***Comprehensive Explanations at an Appropriate Level.*** *Macroeconomics* is comprehensive, analytical, and challenging, yet fully accessible to a wide range of students. Its thoroughness and accessibility enable instructors to select topics for special classroom emphasis with confidence that students can read and comprehend independently other assigned material in the book.

■ ***Fundamentals of the Market System.*** Many economies throughout the world are making difficult transitions from planning to markets. Our detailed description of the institutions and operation of the *market system* in Chapter 4 is even more relevant than before. We pay particular attention to property rights, entrepreneurship, freedom of enterprise and choice, competition, and the role of profits because these concepts are poorly understood by beginning students.

■ ***Early Integration of International Macroeconomics.*** We give the principles and institutions of the global economy early treatment. Chapter 6 examines the growth of world trade, the major participants in world trade, specialization and comparative advantage, the foreign exchange market, tariffs and subsidies, and various trade agreements. This strong introduction to international economics permits "globalization" of later macroeconomic discussions.

■ ***Early and Extensive Treatment of Government.*** Government is an integral component of modern capitalism. This book introduces the economic functions of government early and accords them systematic treatment in Chapter 5. Government's role in promoting full employment, price-level stability, and economic growth is central to the macroeconomic policy chapters.

■ ***Building-block Approach*** We systematically present macroeconomics by

  ■ Establishing the real GDP concept and previewing economic growth, unemployment, and inflation.

  ■ Building the aggregate expenditures model (AE model).

  ■ Deriving aggregate demand from the AE model and developing the aggregate demand–aggregate supply model (AD-AS model).

- ■ Using the AD-AS model to discuss fiscal policy.
- ■ Introducing monetary considerations into the AD-AS model.
- ■ Using the AD-AS model to discuss monetary policy.
- ■ Extending the AD-AS model by distinguishing between short-run and long-run aggregate supply.
- ■ Applying the "extended AD-AS model" to macroeconomic instability, economic growth, and disagreements on macro theory and policy.

■ ***Emphasis on Technological Change and Economic Growth.*** This edition continues to emphasize economic growth. Chapter 2 uses the production possibilities curve to show the basic ingredients of growth. Chapter 8 explains how growth is measured and presents the facts of growth. Chapter 17 discusses the causes of growth, looks at productivity growth and the New Economy, and addresses some of the controversies surrounding economic growth. Chapter 22 focuses on the less developed countries and the growth obstacles they confront. The special Internet chapter looks at growth in the transition economies of Russia and China.

■ Organization and Content

Macroeconomics reflects the challenge that specific topics and concepts will likely pose for average students. For instance, macro output and price-level determination are carefully treated. Here, simplicity is correlated with comprehensiveness, not brevity.

Our experience suggests that in treating each basic topic — aggregate demand and aggregate supply, money and banking, and international economics — it is desirable to couple analysis with policy. Generally, we use a three-step development of analytical tools: (1) verbal descriptions and illustrations; (2) numerical examples, and (3) graphical presentation based on these numerical illustrations.

All these considerations prompted us to organize the book into five parts: Part 1: An Introduction to Macroeconomics and the Economy; Part 2: National Income, Employment, and Fiscal Policy; Part 3: Money, Banking, and Monetary Policy; Part 4: Long-Run Perspectives and Macroeconomic Debates; and

Part 5: International Economics and the World Economy.

■ Organizational Alternatives

Although instructors generally agree as to the content of the principles of macroeconomics course, they often differ as to how to arrange the material. *Macroeconomics* provides considerable organizational flexibility. Previous users tell us they often substantially rearrange chapters with little sacrifice of continuity.

The AD-AS model appears after two chapters on aggregate expenditures analysis. Those who want to rely exclusively on AD-AS can omit those two chapters, supplementing the AD analysis with discussions of investment demand and the multiplier implicit within shifts of the AD curve.

Also, instructors can easily take up Chapter 17 on the public debt and budget surpluses immediately after Chapter 12 on fiscal policy.

■ Pedagogical Aids

Macroeconomics has always been student oriented. The "To the Student" statement at the beginning of Part 1 details the book's many pedagogical aids. The fifteenth edition is also accompanied by a variety of high-quality supplements.

Supplements for Students

- ■ ***Study Guide*** William Walstad of the University of Nebraska at Lincoln, who is one of the world's foremost experts on economic education, has prepared the fifteenth edition of the *Study Guide*, which many students find indispensable. Each chapter contains an introductory statement, a checklist of behavioral objectives, an outline, a list of important terms, fill-in questions, problems and projects, objective questions, and discussion questions. The answers to *Economics'* end-of-chapter Key Questions appear at the end of the *Study Guide*, along with the text's glossary. The *Guide* comprises a superb "portable tutor" for the principles student.

- ■ ***DiscoverEcon*** This software by Jerry Nelson at the University of Illinois–Champaign/Urbana is available in a CD format or on the Website for those who purchase a code. This menu-driven software provides students with a complete tutorial linked to the text. Each chapter features two essay questions, interactive graphs, a multiple-choice test bank, and links to the glossary—all tied cohesively to the textbook.

- *Website* As noted, Web-button icons alert students to points in the book where they can springboard to the Website to learn more. There also are weekly news updates, an interactive glossary, and self-grading tests—all specific to *Macroeconomics*. For the math-minded student, there is a "Want to See the Math?" area where they can explore the mathematical details of the concepts in the text. There is also a bonus chapter on the Web titled "Transition Economies: Russia and China."

Supplements for Instructors

- *Instructor's Resource Manual* Janet West of the University of Nebraska at Omaha has revised and updated the *Instructor's Resource Manual*. It includes chapter summaries, listings of "what's new" in each chapter, teaching tips and suggestions, learning objectives, chapter outlines, data and visual aid sources with suggestions for classroom use, and questions and problems.

  Available again in this edition is an MS-Word version of the *Manual*. Instructors can print out portions of the *Manual*'s contents, complete with their own additions and alterations, for use as student handouts or in whatever ways they wish. This capability includes printing out answers to the end-of-chapter questions.

- *Instructor's Presentation CD-ROM* This CD-ROM contains everything the instructor needs for a multimedia lecture. Video clips, photos, PowerPoint slides, and much more are included and can be customized with personal material. The CD-ROM also contains key supplements for added flexibility and convenience.

- *Three Test Banks* Two test banks of objective, predominately multiple-choice questions and a third test bank of short-answer essay questions and problems supplement this edition of *Macroeconomics*.

Test Bank I This test bank includes more than 5900 questions, most written by the text authors.

Test Bank II Written by William Walstad, this test bank contains more than 5400 questions. All Test Bank II questions are categorized according to level of difficulty: easy, moderate, or difficult.

Test Bank III Also prepared by William Walstad, Test Bank III contains "constructive response" testing to evaluate student understanding in a manner different from conventional multiple-choice and true-false questions. Suggested answers to the essay and problem questions are included.

For all test items in Test Banks I and II, the nature of each question is identified (for example, G = graphical; C = complex, etc.) as are the numbers of the text's pages that are the basis for each. Also, each chapter in Test Banks I and II has an outline or table of contents that groups questions by topics. In all, more than 11,000 questions give instructors maximum testing flexibility while assuring the fullest possible text correlation.

Test Banks I, II and III are available in computerized Brownstone Diploma versions. These systems can produce high-quality graphs from the test banks and feature the ability to generate multiple tests, with versions "scrambled" to be distinctive. This software meets the various needs of the widest spectrum of computer users. Testbank III, the essay bank, is available in printed and MS Word formats.

- *PageOut* This software allows instructors to create a course Website via a relatively easy "paint-by-numbers" method. Simply fill in the templates, choose a design, and within minutes your syllabus will be posted on your own Website. Students can then follow your syllabus and be referred to daily assignments and postings.

- *Color transparencies* There are more than 150 new full-color transparencies for the fifteenth edition. They encompass all the figures appearing in *Macroeconomics* and are available on request to adopters.

- *PowerWeb* This online resource provides high quality, peer-reviewed content including up-to-date articles from leading periodicals and journals, current news, weekly updates with assessment, interactive exercises, Web research guide, study tips, and more. PowerWeb is available packaged with the McConnell & Brue text or for online purchase at the website www.dushkin.com/powerweb.

▌Acknowledgments

We give special thanks to Norris Peterson of Pacific Lutheran University and Randy Grant of Linfield College who teamed up with Stan Brue to create the "button" content on our Website. We again thank

James Reese of the University of South Carolina at Spartanburg, who wrote end-of-chapter Internet exercises for the previous edition. Although we have replaced many of those questions, several remain virtually unchanged in the new edition. We also thank Robert Jensen of Pacific Lutheran University for his meticulous help in proofreading the entire manuscript (twice).

The fifteenth edition has benefited from a number of perceptive reviews. The contributors, listed at the end of the Preface, were a rich source of suggestions for this revision.

We are greatly indebted to the many professionals at McGraw-Hill—in particular Gary Burke, Lucille Sutton, Erin Strathmann, Martin Quinn, Jean Lou Hess, Keith McPherson, Aric Bright, and Lori Koetters—for their publishing and marketing expertise.

We thank Ev Sims for his thorough and sensitive editing and Jacques Cournoyer for his vivid Last Word illustrations. Dean Ruggles provided the colorful cover.

We also strongly acknowledge the McGraw-Hill/Irwin sales staff, which greeted this edition with wholehearted enthusiasm.

Campbell R. McConnell
Stanley L. Brue

CONTRIBUTORS

Reviewers

Neil Alper, *Northeastern University*
Carl Bauer, *Oakton Community College*
Bernadette Chachere, *Delgado Community College*
David Chen, *North Carolina A&T State University*
Al Culver, *Chico State University*
Martin Bookbinder, *Passaic County Community College*
Ron Debeaumont, *Black Hills State College*
Mark DeHainaut, *Penn State University*
Bernice Evans, *Morgan State University*
Larry Frateschi, *College of DuPage*
Arthur Friedberg, *Mohawk Valley Community College*
J. Pat Fuller, *Brevard Community College*
Paul Harris, *Camden County College*
Mark Healy, *William Rainey Harper College*
John Ifediora, *University of Wisconsin*
Jonathan Ikoba, *Scott Community College*
Katherine Huger, *Charleston Southern University*
John Kinworthy, *Concordia University*
Shirley Kress, *Skyline Community College*
Peter Kressler, *Rowan University*
Oluseyi Kuforiji, *Albany State University*
Pat Litzinger, *Robert Morris College*
Andrew Lucassen, *Texas A&M University*
Laura Maghoney, *Solano Community College*
Stephen McGary, *Ricks College*
Barbara Moore, *University of Central Florida*
Ron O'Neal, *Camden Community College*
L. Wayne Plumly Jr., *Valdosta State University*
Henry Ryder, *Gloucester Community College*
Ray Schreffler, *Houston Community College–Northwest*
Ron Schuelke, *Santa Rosa Community College*
Virginia Shingleton, *Valparaiso University*
Dave Shorow, *Richland College*
John Sinton, *Finger Lakes Community College*
Lynn Smith, *Clarion University of Pennsylvania*
Joanne Spitz, *University of Massachusetts–Boston*
Arlena Sullivan, *Jones County Junior College*
Bill Sumrall, *Northwest Mississippi Community College*
Ross Thomas, *Albequerque TVI*
Donna Thompson, *Brookdale Community College*
Lee VanScyoc, *University of Wisconsin–Oshkosh*
Charles Wagoner, *Delta State University*
Dale Wasson, *Southwest Missouri State*
Janet Weaver, *Drake University*
Janet West, *University of Nebraska at Omaha*
Wendy Wood, *Bevill State Community College*

User Survey Respondents

Thomas Burke, *St. Joseph's University*

Christopher Lee, *Saint Ambrose University*
Kristen Monaco, *University of Wisconsin*
Tahnay Naggar, *West Chester University*
Melvin Oliver Jr., *North Carolina Wesleyan College*
Rebecca Rutz, *Mississippi Gulf Coast Community College*
Mark Schopmeyer, *Jackson Community College*
Lavern Timmer, *Alfred State College*
George Giannakouros, *Loras College*
M. Wayne Martin, *Danville Community College*
Harry Richard Call, *The American River College*
Margarita Rose, *King's College*
Marwan El Nasser, *State University of New York College at Fredonia*
Irving Richards, *Cuyahoga Community College*
Nozar Hashemzadeh, *Radford University*
Charles Reichheld, *Cuyahoga Community College*
Robert Kephart, *Corning Community College*
Kevin Schochart, *University of Northern Iowa*
Kwang-Wen Chu, *California State University–Fullerton*
Charles Link, *University of Delaware*
Janet West, *University of Nebraska at Omaha*
Barry Bomboy, *J. Sargeant Reynolds Community College*
Sarah P. Rook, *University of South Carolina at Spartanburg*
Gaminie Meepagala, *Howard University*
Jim Ciminskie, *Bay de Noc Community College*
Michael Twomy, *University of Michigan at Dearborn*
S. Gokturk, *Saint John's University*
Doug Curtis, *Northeast Community College*
Paul J. Hoyt, *Valencia Community College*
Saul Mekies, *Kirkwood Community College*
Joanna Moss, *San Francisco State University*
Timothy J. Bettner, *University of Laverne*
Lawrence B. Morse, *North Carolina A&T State University*
Frank Leroi, *College of San Mateo*
Kahtan Al Yasiri, *University of Wisconsin at Platteville*
Calvin Shipley, *Henderson State University*
Rosemary Walker, *Washburn University*
William Peek, *Niagara University*
Lee Deavours, *Mississippi Gulf Coast Community College*
Carl Bauer, *Oakton Community College*
Wayne Bartholomew, *Indiana University at South Bend*
Donna Thompson, *Brookdale Community College*
Shiv K. Gupta, *University of Findlay*
Arvnee Grow, *Mesa Community College*
Scott Simkins, *North Carolina A&T State University*
Emmanuel Asigbee, *Kirkwood Community College*
Sister Ann Coyle, *Immaculata College*
Michael McCully, *High Point University*
James Phillips, *Cypress College*
Mashid Jalilvand, *University of Wisconsin–Stout*
Marvin Burnett, *St. Louis Community College at Florissant Valley*
Thomas Kemp, *Tarrant County College*
William Walstad, *University of Nebraska at Lincoln*

Gerald Fox, *High Point University*
Julie Granthen, *Oakland University*
Norm Caldwell, *Indiana Central Community College*
Jerry McElroy, *Saint Mary's College*
Fred Hershede, *Indiana University at South Bend*
Paul Joray, *Indiana University at South Bend*
Patricia Humston, *Coastal Bend College*
John Kirk, *College of San Mateo*
Quentin Ciolfi, *Brevard Community College*
Lawrence Fratecschi, *College of DuPage*
Irwin Kellner, *Hofstra University*
Dan Berszez, *College of DuPage*
Ted Woodruff, *Saint Ambrose University*
David Chen, *North Carolina A&T State University*
C. F. Hawkins, *Lamar University*
Nina Shapiro, *Saint Peter's College*
Roy Howsep, *Western Kentucky University*
Anthony Truong, *University of Hawaii LCC*
Robert Gustavson, *Washington University*
Greg Rose, *Sacramento City College*
Wali Mondal, *Henderson State University*

David Shorow, *Richland College*
Henry Kolendzanos, *Danville Community College*
William Swift, *Hofstra University*
John Dorsey, *University of Maryland*
Martin Melkonian, *Hofstra University*
Emmanuel Nnadozie, *Truman State University*
Salim Harik, *Western Michigan University*
Connie Culbreth, *Brevard Community College*
Elizabeth Hill, *Penn State University*
William Harris, *University of Delaware*
Laddie Sula, *Loras College*
Eugene Williams, *McMurray University*
William Tabel, *South Suburban College*
Maria Gamba, *University of Findlay*
Janice Weaver, *Drake University*
Alan Kessler, *Providence College*
Ismail Shariff, *University of Wisconsin at Green Bay*
John P. Connelly, *Corning Community College*
M. B. Biery, *Tarrant County College*
Erick M. Elder, *University of Arkansas at Little Rock*
Della Sampson, *Dalton State College*

BRIEF CONTENTS

C O N T E N T S

1

An Introduction to Economics and the Economy

▍ To the Student

This book and its ancillaries contain a number of features designed to help you learn economics:

■ **In-Text Web Buttons**   A glance through the book will reveal many pages that contain small symbols at the ends of paragraphs. The "buttons" are designed to direct you to the text's Internet site: www.mhhe.com/economics/mcconnell15 The ⚠ button stands for "Analogies, Anecdotes, and Insights." These short pieces help you understand and remember the economic ideas by connecting them to other, better-known, ideas or easy to remember stories and examples. The 🔑 button stands for "Origin of the Idea." These pieces trace the particular idea to the person or persons who first developed it. The ⬔ button stands for "Interactive Graphs." Brief exercises ask you to interact with the graphs, for example, by clicking onto a specific curve and dragging it to a new location. These exercises will enhance your understanding of the underlying concepts.

   After reading a chapter, thumb back through it to note the symbols and the number that follows them. On the home page of our Internet site, click "In-Text Web Buttons" and find your way to the numbered piece. We think you will find this interactivity between the text and the Internet highly engaging and helpful.

■ **Other Internet aids**   Our Internet site contains many other aids. In the "For the Student" section you will find self-testing multiple-choice quizzes, links to relevant news articles, a student discussion room, answers to frequently asked questions, and much more. For those of you with very strong mathematics backgrounds, be sure to check out the "Want to See the Math?" section on the website. There, you will find nearly 50 notes that develop the algebra and, in some cases, the calculus that underlies the economic concepts.

■ **Appendix on graphs**   Be assured, however, that you will need only basic math skills to do well in the principles course. In particular, you will need to be comfortable with graphical analysis and a few quantitative concepts. The appendix to Chapter 1 reviews graphing, slopes of curves, and linear equations. Be sure not to skip it.

■ **Reviews**   Each chapter contains two or three Quick Reviews and an end-of-chapter summary. These reviews will help you focus on essential ideas and study for exams.

■ **Key Terms and Key Graphs**   Key terms are set in boldface type within the chapters, listed at the end of each chapter, and defined in the Glossary at the end of the book. Graphs with special relevance are labeled Key Graphs, and each includes a multiple-choice Quick Quiz. Your instructor may not emphasize all these figures, but you should pay special attention to those that are discussed in class; you can be certain that there will be exam questions on them.

■ **Last Words**   Each chapter concludes with a Last Word minireading. While it is tempting to ignore these sections, don't. Some of them are revealing applications of economic concepts; others are short case studies. Most are fun to read, and all will broaden your grasp of economics.

■ **Questions**   A comprehensive list of questions is located at the end of each chapter. Answering these questions will enhance your understanding. Several of the questions are designated as Key Questions and are answered in the *Study Guide* and also at our Internet site.

■ **Study Guide**   We enthusiastically recommend the *Study Guide* accompanying this text. This "portable tutor" contains not only a broad sampling of various kinds of questions but a host of useful learning aids. An excellent CD-ROM is also available for use with the book. Although it is not as comprehensive as the *Study Guide*, many students will find it to be very helpful.

Our overriding goal is to help you understand and apply economics. With your effort, our effort, and the effort of your instructor, you will be able to comprehend a whole range of economic, social, and political problems that otherwise would have remained puzzling and perplexing.

   Good luck with your study of economics. We think it will be well worth your effort.

1

The Nature and Method of Economics

Want is a growing giant whom the coat of Have was never large enough to cover.
Ralph Waldo Emerson, The Conduct of Life, 1860

P EOPLE'S ECONOMIC WANTS are multitudinous and diverse. Biologically, humans need only air, water, food, clothing, and shelter. But in contemporary society we also seek the many goods and services associated with a comfortable or affluent standard of living. Fortunately, society is blessed with productive resources—labor and managerial talent, tools and machinery, land and mineral deposits—that are used to produce goods and services. This production satisfies many of our economic wants and occurs through the organizational mechanism called the *economic system* or, more simply, the *economy*. ■ The blunt reality, however, is that our economic wants far exceed the productive capacity of our limited or scarce resources. So the complete satisfaction of society's economic wants is impossible. This unyielding truth provides our definition of **economics:** *It is the social science concerned with the efficient use of scarce resources to achieve the maximum satisfaction of economic wants.* ■ Numerous problems and issues are rooted in the challenge of using limited resources efficiently. Although it would be tempting to plunge into them, that sort of analysis must wait. In this chapter, we need to discuss some important preliminaries. 🔑 1.1

■ The Economic Perspective

Economists view things through a unique perspective. This **economic perspective** or *economic way of thinking* has several critical and closely interrelated features.

Scarcity and Choice

From our definition of economics, it is easy to see why economists view the world through the lens of scarcity. Since human and property resources are scarce (limited), it follows that the goods and services we produce must also be limited. Scarcity limits our options and necessitates that we make choices. Because we "can't have it all," we must decide what we will have, and what we must forgo.

At the core of economics is the idea that "there is no free lunch." You may get treated to lunch, making it "free" to you, but there is a cost to someone—ultimately to society. Scarce inputs of land, equipment, farm labor, the labor of cooks and waiters, and

3

managerial talent are required. Because these resources could be used in alternative production activities, they and the other goods and services they could have produced are sacrificed in making the lunch available. Economists call these sacrifices *opportunity costs*. To get more of one thing, you forgo the opportunity of getting something else. So the cost of that which you get is the value of that which is sacrificed to obtain it. We will say much more about opportunity costs in Chapter 2. ⚠ 1.1

Rational Behavior

Economics is grounded on the assumption of "rational self-interest." Individuals pursue actions that will enable them to achieve their greatest satisfaction. Rational behavior means that individuals will make different choices under different circumstances. For example, Jones may decide to buy Coca-Cola in bulk at a warehouse store rather than at a convenience store where it is much more expensive. That will leave him with extra money to buy something else that provides satisfaction. Yet, while driving home from work, he may stop at the convenience store to buy a single can of Coca-Cola.

Rational self-interest also means that individuals will make different choices. High school graduate Alvarez may decide to attend college to major in business. Baker may opt to take a job at a warehouse and buy a new car. Chin may accept a signing bonus and join the Navy. All three choices reflect the pursuit of self-interest and are rational, but they are based on differing preferences and circumstances.

Of course, rational decisions may change as costs and benefits change. Jones may switch to Pepsi when it is on sale. And, after taking a few business courses, Alvarez may decide to change her major to social work.

It is clear that rational self-interest is not the same as selfishness. People make personal sacrifices to help family members or friends, and they contribute to charities because they derive pleasure from doing so. Parents help pay for their children's education for the same reason. These self-interested, but unselfish, acts help maximize the givers' satisfaction as much as any personal purchase of goods or services. Self-interest behavior is simply behavior that enables a person to achieve personal satisfaction, however it may be derived.

Marginalism: Benefits and Costs

The economic perspective focuses largely on **marginal analysis**—comparisons of *marginal benefits* and *marginal costs*. (Used this way, "marginal" means "extra," "additional," or "a change in.") Most choices or decisions involve changes in the status quo (the existing state of affairs). Should you attend school for another year or not? Should you study an extra hour for an exam? Should you add fries to your fast-food order? Similarly, should a business expand or reduce its output? Should government increase or decrease its funding for a missile defense system?

Each option involves marginal benefits and, because of scarce resources, marginal costs. In making choices rationally, the decision maker must compare those two amounts. Example: You and your fiancé are shopping for an engagement ring. Should you buy a $\frac{1}{4}$-carat diamond, a $\frac{1}{2}$-carat diamond, a $\frac{3}{4}$-carat diamond, or a larger one? The marginal cost of the larger-size diamond is the added expense beyond the cost of the smaller-size diamond. The marginal benefit is the greater lifetime pleasure (utility) from the larger-size stone. If the marginal benefit of the larger diamond exceeds its marginal cost, you should buy the larger stone. But if the marginal cost is more than the marginal benefit, you should buy the smaller diamond instead.

In a world of scarcity, the decision to obtain the marginal benefit associated with some specific option always includes the marginal cost of forgoing something else. The money spent on the larger-size diamond means forgoing something else. Again, there is no free lunch!

One somewhat surprising implication of decisions based on marginal analysis is that there can be too much of a good thing. Although certain goods and services seem inherently desirable—education, health care, a pristine environment—we can in fact have too much of them. "Too much" occurs when we keep obtaining them beyond the point where their marginal cost (the value of the forgone options) equals their marginal benefit. Then we are sacrificing alternative products that are more valuable *at the margin*—the place where we consider the very last units of each. Society can have too much health care, and you can have too many CDs. **(Key Question 1)** 🔎 1.2

This chapter's Last Word provides an everyday application of the economic perspective.

▮ Why Study Economics?

Is studying economics worth your time and effort? More than half a century ago John Maynard Keynes (1883–1946), one of the most influential economists of this century, said:

> The ideas of economists and political philosophers, both when they are right and when they are wrong, are more powerful than is commonly understood. Indeed the world is ruled by little else. Practical men, who believe themselves to be quite exempt from any intellectual influences, are usually the slaves of some defunct economist.

Most of the ideologies of the modern world have been shaped by prominent economists of the past— Adam Smith, David Ricardo, John Stuart Mill, Karl Marx, and John Maynard Keynes. And current world leaders routinely solicit the advice and policy suggestions of today's economists.

For example, the president of the United States benefits from the recommendations of his Council of Economic Advisers. The broad range of economic issues facing political leaders is suggested by the contents of the annual *Economic Report of the President*. Areas covered typically include unemployment, inflation, economic growth, taxation, poverty, international trade, health care, pollution, discrimination, immigration, regulation, and education, among others. And the Federal Reserve (the U.S. central bank) relies heavily on economic analysis in shaping its monetary policies.

Economics for Citizenship

A basic understanding of economics is essential if we are to be well-informed citizens. Most of today's political problems have important economic aspects: Should we use Federal budget surpluses to pay off the public debt, expand various government programs, or reduce income taxes? How can we make the social security retirement program financially secure? Why do we continue to have large international trade deficits? What must we do to keep inflation in check? What can be done to keep income inequality from growing? How should we respond to growing market dominance by a few firms in some high-technology sectors of the economy?

As voters, we can influence the decisions of our elected officials in responding to such questions. But intelligence at the polls requires a basic working knowledge of economics. And a sound grasp of economics is even more helpful to the politicians themselves.

A survey by the National Center for Research in Economic Education suggests that economic illiteracy is widespread in the United States. The public, including high school seniors and college seniors, shows a broad lack of knowledge of the basic economics needed to understand economic events and changes in the national economy.

Professional and Personal Applications

Economics lays great stress on precise, systematic analysis. Thus, studying economics invariably helps students improve their analytical skills, which are in great demand in the workplace. Also, the study of economics helps us make sense of the everyday activity we observe around us. How is it that so many different people, in so many different places, doing so many different things, produce the goods and services we want to buy? Economics provides an answer.

Economics is also vital to business. An understanding of the basics of economic decision making and the operation of the economic system enables business managers and executives to increase profit. The executive who understands when to use new technology, when to merge with another firm, when to expand employment, and so on, will outperform the executive who is less deft at such decision making. The manager who understands the causes and consequences of recessions (downturns in the overall economy) or inflation (rising prices) can make more intelligent business decisions during these periods.

Economics helps consumers and workers make better buying and employment decisions. How can you spend your limited money income to maximize your satisfaction? How can you hedge against the reduction in the dollar's purchasing power that accompanies inflation? Is it more economical to buy or lease a car? Should you use a credit card or pay cash? Which occupations pay well; which are most immune to unemployment?

Similarly, an understanding of economics makes for better financial decisions. Someone who understands the relationship between budget surpluses and interest rates, between foreign exchange rates and exports, between interest rates and bond prices, is in a better position to successfully allocate personal savings. So, too, is someone who understands the business implications of emerging new technologies.

In spite of these practical benefits, however, you should know that economics is *mainly* an academic, not a vocational, subject. Unlike accounting, advertising, corporate finance, and marketing, economics is not primarily a how-to-make-money area of study. Knowledge of economics and mastery of the economic perspective will help you run a business or manage your personal finances, but that is not the subject's primary objective. Instead, economics ultimately examines problems and decisions from the *social*, rather than the *personal*, point of view. The production, exchange, and consumption of goods and services are discussed from the viewpoint of society's best interest, not strictly from the standpoint of one's own pocketbook.

QUICK REVIEW 1.1

■ Economics is concerned with obtaining maximum satisfaction through the efficient use of scarce resources.

■ The economic perspective stresses (a) resource scarcity and the necessity of making choices, (b) the assumption of rational behavior, and (c) comparisons of marginal benefit and marginal cost.

■ Your study of economics will help you as a voting citizen as well as benefit you professionally and personally.

■ Economic Methodology

Like the physical and life sciences, as well as other social sciences, economics relies on the **scientific method.** It consists of a number of elements:

■ The observation of facts (real-world data).

■ Based on those facts, the formulation of a possible explanation of cause and effect (hypothesis).

■ The testing of this explanation by comparing the outcomes of specific events to the outcome predicted by the hypothesis.

■ The acceptance, rejection, or modification of the hypothesis, based on these comparisons.

■ The continued testing of the hypothesis against the facts. As favorable results accumulate, the

hypothesis evolves into a *theory*. A very well tested and widely accepted theory is referred to as a *law* or *principle*. Combinations of such laws or principles are incorporated into *models*—simplified representations of how something works, such as a market or segment of the economy.

Laws, principles, and models enable the economist, like the natural scientist, to understand and explain reality and to predict the various outcomes of particular actions. But as we will soon see, economic laws and principles are usually less certain than the laws of physics or chemistry.

Theoretical Economics

Economists develop models of the behavior of individuals (consumers, workers) and institutions (businesses, governments) engaged in the production, exchange, and consumption of goods and services. They start by gathering facts about economic activities and economic outcomes. Because the world is cluttered with innumerable interrelated facts, economists, like all scientists, must select the useful information. They must determine which facts are relevant to the problem under consideration. But even when this sorting process is complete, the relevant information may at first seem random and unrelated.

The economist draws on the facts to establish cause-effect hypotheses about economic behavior. Then the hypotheses are tested against real-world observation and data. Through this process, the economist tries to discover hypotheses that rise to the level of theories and principles (or laws)—well-tested and widely accepted generalizations about how individuals and institutions behave. The process of deriving theories and principles is called **theoretical economics** (see the lower box in Figure 1.1). *The role of economic theorizing is to systematically arrange facts, interpret them, and generalize from them.* Theories and principles bring order and meaning to facts by arranging them in cause-and-effect order.

Observe that the arrow from "theories" to "facts" in Figure 1.1 moves in both directions. Some understanding of factual, real-world evidence is required to formulate meaningful hypotheses. And hypotheses are tested through gathering and organizing factual data to see if the hypotheses can be verified.

Economic theories and **principles** *are statements about economic behavior or the economy that enable prediction of the probable effects of certain actions.* Good

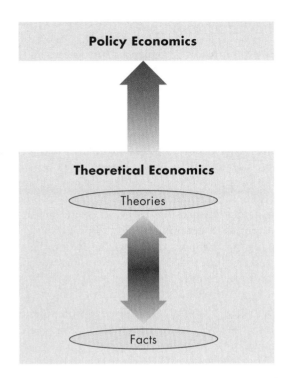

Figure 1.1

The relationship between facts, theories, and policies in economics. *Theoretical economics* involves establishing economic theories by gathering, systematically arranging, and generalizing from facts. Good economic theories are tested for validity against facts. Economists use these theories—the most reliable of which are called *laws* or *principles*—to explain and analyze the economy. *Policy economics* entails using the economic laws and principles to formulate economic policies.

theories are those that do a good job of explaining and predicting. They are supported by facts concerning how individuals and institutions actually behave in producing, exchanging, and consuming goods and services. But these facts may change in time, so economists must continually check theories against the shifting economic environment.

Theories, laws, and principles are highly useful in analyzing economic behavior and understanding how the economy operates. They are the ingredients of *analytical economics*—the ascertaining of cause and effect, of action and outcome, within the economic system.

Several other points relating to economic principles are important to know.

Terminology   Economists speak of "hypotheses," "theories," "laws," and "principles." Some of these

terms overlap, but they usually reflect a gradation of confidence in the generalizations. A hypothesis needs initial testing; a theory has been tested but needs more testing; a law or principle is a theory that has provided strong predictive accuracy, over and over. The terms "economic laws" and "principles" are useful even though they imply a degree of exactness, universal application, and even moral rightness that is rare in any social science. The word "theory" is often used in economics even though many people incorrectly believe theories have nothing to do with real-world applications. Economists often use the term "model," which combines principles into a simplified representation of reality.

In this book, custom or convenience will govern the use of "theory," "law," "principle," and "model." Thus, to describe the relationship between the price of a product and the amount of it purchased, we will use the term *law of demand*, rather than theory or principle of demand, simply because this is the custom. We will refer to the *circular flow model*, not the circular flow law, because the concept combines several ideas into a single representation.

Generalizations   As we have already mentioned, economic theories, principles, and laws are **generalizations** relating to economic behavior or to the economy itself. They are imprecise because economic facts are usually diverse; no two individuals or institutions act in exactly the same way. *Economic principles are expressed as the tendencies of typical or average consumers, workers, or business firms.* For example, when economists say that consumer spending rises when personal income increases, they are well aware that some households may save *all* of an increase in their incomes. But, on average, and for the full economy, spending goes up when income increases. Similarly, economists say that consumers buy more of a particular product when its price falls. Some consumers may increase their purchases by a large amount, others by a small amount, and a few not at all. This "price-quantity" principle, however, holds for the typical consumer and for consumers as a group.

Other-Things-Equal Assumption   Like other scientists, economists use the *ceteris paribus* or **other-things-equal assumption** to construct their generalizations. They assume that all other variables except those under immediate consideration are held constant for a particular analysis. For example,

consider the relationship between the price of Pepsi and the amount of it purchased. It helps to assume that, of all the factors that might influence the amount of Pepsi purchased (for example, the price of Pepsi, the price of Coca-Cola, and consumer incomes and preferences), only the price of Pepsi varies. The economist can then focus on the "price of Pepsi–purchases of Pepsi" relationship without being confused by changes in other variables. 🔍 1.3

Natural scientists such as chemists or physicists can usually conduct controlled experiments where "all other things" are in fact held constant (or virtually so). They can test with great precision the assumed relationship between two variables. For example, they might examine the height from which an object is dropped and the length of time it takes to hit the ground. But economics is not a laboratory science. Economists test their theories using real-world data, which are generated by the actual operation of the economy. In this rather bewildering environment, "other things" *do* change. Despite the development of complex statistical techniques designed to hold other things equal, control is less than perfect. As a result, economic principles are less certain and less precise than those of laboratory sciences. That also means they are more open to debate than many scientific theories (for example, the law of gravity).

Abstractions
Economic principles, or theories, are *abstractions*—simplifications that omit irrelevant facts and circumstances. Economic models do *not* mirror the full complexity of the real world. The very process of sorting out and analyzing facts involves simplification and removal of clutter. Unfortunately, this "abstraction" leads some people to consider economic theory impractical and unrealistic. That is simply nonsense! Economic theories are practical precisely because they are abstractions. The full scope of economic reality itself is too complex and bewildering to be understood as a whole. Economists abstract—that is, develop theories and build models—to give meaning to an otherwise overwhelming and confusing maze of facts. Theorizing for this purpose is highly practical. ❗ 1.2

Graphical Expression
Many of the economic models in this book are expressed graphically; the most important are labeled Key Graphs. Be sure to read the appendix to this chapter as a review of graphs.

Policy Economics

Policy economics recognizes that theories and data can be used to formulate *policies*—courses of action based on economic principles and intended to resolve a specific economic problem or further an economic goal. Economic theories are the foundation of economic policy, as shown in the upper part of Figure 1.1. Economic policy normally is applied to problems after they arise. However, if economic analysis can predict some undesirable event such as unemployment, inflation, or an increase in poverty, then it may be possible to avoid or moderate that event through economic policy. For example, you may read in the newspaper that the Federal Reserve has reduced interest rates to increase private spending and prevent a recession.

Economic Policy
The creation of policies to achieve specific goals is no simple matter. Here are the basic steps in policymaking:

- *State the goal.* The first step is to make a clear statement of the economic goal. If we say that we want "full employment," do we mean that everyone between, say, 16 and 65 years of age should have a job? Or do we mean that everyone who *wants* to work should have a job? Should we allow for some unemployment caused by inevitable changes in the structure of industry and workers voluntarily changing jobs? The goal must be specific.
- *Determine the policy options.* The next step is to formulate alternative policies designed to achieve the goal and determine the possible effects of each policy. This requires a detailed assessment of the economic impact, benefits, costs, and political feasibility of the alternative policies. For example, to achieve full employment, should government use fiscal policy (which involves changing government spending and taxes), monetary policy (which entails altering the supply of money), an education and training policy that enhances worker employability, or a policy of wage subsidies to firms that hire disadvantaged workers?
- *Implement and evaluate the policy that was selected.* After implementing the policy, we need to evaluate how well it worked. Only through unbiased evaluation can we improve on economic policy. Did a specific change in taxes or the money supply alter the level of employment to the extent predicted? Did deregulation of a

particular industry (for example, banking) yield the predicted beneficial results? If not, why not? What were the harmful side effects, if any? How might the policy be altered to make it work better? **(Key Question 5)**

Economic Goals   If economic policies are designed to achieve certain economic goals, then we need to recognize a number of goals that are widely accepted in the United States and many other countries. They include:

- *Economic growth*   Produce more and better goods and services, or, more simply, develop a higher standard of living.
- *Full employment*   Provide suitable jobs for all citizens who are willing and able to work.
- *Economic efficiency*   Achieve the maximum fulfillment of wants using the available productive resources.
- *Price-level stability*   Avoid large upswings and downswings in the general price level; that is, avoid inflation and deflation.
- *Economic freedom*   Guarantee that businesses, workers, and consumers have a high degree of freedom in their economic activities.
- *Equitable distribution of income*   Ensure that no group of citizens faces poverty while most others enjoy abundance.
- *Economic security*   Provide for those who are chronically ill, disabled, laid off, aged, or otherwise unable to earn minimal levels of income.
- *Balance of trade*   Seek a reasonable overall balance with the rest of the world in international trade and financial transactions.

Although most of us might accept these goals as generally stated, we might also disagree substantially on their specific meanings. What are "large" changes in the price level? What is a "high degree" of economic freedom? What is an "equitable" distribution of income? How can we measure precisely such abstract goals as "economic freedom"? These objectives are often the subject of spirited public debate.

Also, some of these goals are complementary; when one is achieved, some other one will also be realized. For example, achieving full employment means eliminating unemployment, which is a basic cause of inequitable income distribution. But other goals may conflict or even be mutually exclusive. They may entail **tradeoffs,** meaning that to achieve one we must sacrifice another. For example, efforts to equalize the distribution of income may weaken incentives to work, invest, innovate, and take business risks, all of which promote economic growth. Taxing high-income people heavily and transferring the tax revenues to low-income people is one way to equalize the distribution of income. But then the incentives to high-income individuals may diminish because higher taxes reduce their rewards for working. Similarly, low-income individuals may be less motivated to work when government stands ready to subsidize them.

When goals conflict, society must develop a system to prioritize the objectives it seeks. If more economic freedom is accompanied by less economic security and more economic security allows less economic freedom, society must assess the tradeoffs and decide on the optimal (best) balance between them.

QUICK REVIEW 1.2

- Economists use the scientific method to establish theories, laws, and principles. Economic theories (laws, principles, or models) are generalizations relating to the economic behavior of individuals and institutions; good theories are grounded in facts.
- Theoretical economics involves formulating theories (or laws and principles) and using them to understand and explain economic behavior and the economy; policy economics involves using the theories to fix economic problems or promote economic goals.
- Policymaking requires a clear statement of goals, a thorough assessment of options, and an unbiased evaluation of results.
- Some of society's economic goals are complementary, while others conflict; where conflicts exist, tradeoffs arise.

▌Macroeconomics and Microeconomics

Economists derive and apply principles about economic behavior at two levels.

Macroeconomics

Macroeconomics examines either the economy as a whole or its basic subdivisions or aggregates, such as the government, household, and business sectors. An **aggregate** is a collection of specific economic units treated as if they were one unit. Therefore, we might lump together the millions of consumers in the U.S. economy and treat them as if they were one huge unit called "consumers."

In using aggregates, macroeconomics seeks to obtain an overview, or general outline, of the structure of the economy and the relationships of its major aggregates. Macroeconomics speaks of such economic measures as *total* output, *total* employment, *total* income, *aggregate* expenditures, and the *general* level of prices in analyzing various economic problems. No or very little attention is given to specific units making up the various aggregates. Macroeconomics examines the beach, not the sand, rocks, and shells.

Microeconomics

Microeconomics looks at specific economic units. At this level of analysis, the economist observes the details of an economic unit, or very small segment of the economy, under a figurative microscope. In microeconomics we talk of an individual industry, firm, or household. We measure the price of a *specific* product, the number of workers employed by a *single* firm, the revenue or income of a *particular* firm or household, or the expenditures of a *specific* firm, government entity, or family. In microeconomics, we examine the sand, rocks, and shells, not the beach.

The macro-micro distinction does not mean that economics is so highly compartmentalized that every topic can be readily labeled as either macro or micro; many topics and subdivisions of economics are rooted in both. Example: While the problem of unemployment is usually treated as a macroeconomic topic (because unemployment relates to *aggregate* spending), economists recognize that the decisions made by *individual* workers in searching for jobs and the way *specific* product and labor markets operate are also critical in determining the unemployment rate. **(Key Question 7)**

Positive and Normative Economics

Both macroeconomics and microeconomics involve facts, theories, and policies. Each contains elements of *positive* economics and *normative* economics. **Positive economics** focuses on facts and cause-and-effect relationships. It includes description, theory development, and theory testing (theoretical economics). Positive economics avoids value judgments, tries to establish scientific statements about economic behavior, and deals with what the economy is

actually like. Such scientific-based analysis is critical to good policy analysis.

Policy economics, on the other hand, involves **normative economics,** which incorporates value judgments about what the economy should be like or what particular policy actions should be recommended to achieve a desirable goal. Normative economics looks at the desirability of certain aspects of the economy. It underlies expressions of support for particular economic policies.

Positive economics concerns *what is*, while normative economics embodies subjective feelings about *what ought to be*. Examples: Positive statement: "The unemployment rate in several European nations is higher than that in the United States." Normative statement: "European nations ought to undertake policies to reduce their unemployment rates." A second positive statement: "Other things equal, if tuition is substantially increased, college enrollment will fall." Normative statement: "College tuition should be lowered so that more students can obtain an education." Whenever words such as "ought" or "should" appear in a sentence, there is a strong chance you are encountering a normative statement.

Most of the disagreement among economists involves normative, value-based policy questions. Of course, there is often some disagreement about which theories or models best represent the economy and its parts. But economists agree on a full range of economic principles. Most economic controversy thus reflects differing opinions or value judgments about what society should be like. **(Key Question 8)**

QUICK REVIEW   1.3

■   Macroeconomics examines the economy as a whole; microeconomics focuses on specific units of the economy.

■   Positive economics deals with factual statements ("what is"); normative economics involves value judgments ("what ought to be"). Theoretical economics is "positive"; policy economics is "normative."

■ Pitfalls to Objective Thinking

Because they affect us so personally, we often have difficulty thinking objectively about economic issues. Here are some common pitfalls to avoid in successfully applying the economic perspective.

Biases

Most people bring a bundle of biases and preconceptions to the field of economics. For example, some might think that corporate profits are excessive or that lending money is always superior to borrowing money. Others might believe that government is necessarily less efficient than businesses or that more government regulation is always better than less. Biases cloud thinking and interfere with objective analysis. All of us must be willing to shed biases and preconceptions that are not supported by facts.

Loaded Terminology

The economic terminology used in newspapers and popular magazines is sometimes emotionally biased, or loaded. The writer or the interest group he or she represents may have a cause to promote or an ax to grind and may slant an article accordingly. High profits may be labeled "obscene," low wages may be called "exploitive," or self-interested behavior may be "greed." Government workers may be referred to as "mindless bureaucrats," and those favoring stronger government regulations may be called "socialists." To objectively analyze economic issues, you must be prepared to reject or discount such terminology.

Definitions

Some of the terms used in economics have precise technical definitions that are quite different from those implied by their common usage. This is generally not a problem if everyone understands these definitions and uses them consistently. For example, "investment" to the average citizen means the purchase of stocks and bonds in security markets, as when someone "invests" in Microsoft stock or government bonds. But to the economist, "investment" means the purchase of newly created real capital assets such as machinery and equipment or the construction of a new factory building. It does not mean the purely financial transaction of swapping cash for securities. ⚠ 1.3

Fallacy of Composition

Another pitfall in economic thinking is the assumption that what is true for one individual or part of a whole is necessarily true for a group of individuals or the whole. This is a logical fallacy called the **fallacy of composition;** the assumption is *not* correct. A statement that is valid for an individual or part is *not* necessarily valid for the larger group or whole.

Consider the following example from outside of economics: You are at a football game and the home team makes an outstanding play. In the excitement, you leap to your feet to get a better view. A valid statement: "If you, *an individual*, stand, your view of the game is improved." But is this also true for the group—for everyone watching the play? Not necessarily. If *everyone* stands to watch the play, probably nobody—including you—will have a better view than when all remain seated.

A second example comes from economics: An *individual* farmer who reaps a particularly large crop is likely to realize a sharp gain in income. But this statement cannot be generalized to farmers as a *group.* The individual farmer's large or "bumper" crop will not noticeably influence (reduce) crop prices because each farmer produces a negligible fraction of the total farm output. But for *all* farmers as a group, prices decline when total output increases. Thus, if all farmers reap bumper crops, the total output of farm products will rise, depressing crop prices. If the price declines are relatively large, total farm income might actually *fall*.

Recall our earlier distinction between macroeconomics and microeconomics: *The fallacy of composition reminds us that generalizations valid at one of these levels of analysis may or may not be valid at the other.*

Causation Fallacies

Causation is sometimes difficult to identify in economics. Two important fallacies often interfere with economic thinking.

Post Hoc Fallacy
You must think very carefully before concluding that because event A precedes event B, A is the cause of B. This kind of faulty reasoning is known as the *post hoc, ergo propter hoc,* or **"after this, therefore because of this," fallacy.**

Example: Suppose that early each spring the medicine man of a tribe performs a special dance. A week or so later the trees and grass turn green. Can we safely conclude that event A, the medicine man's dance, has caused event B, the landscape's turning green? Obviously not. The rooster crows before dawn, but that does not mean the rooster is responsible for the sunrise!

Fast-Food Lines: An Economic Perspective

How can the economic perspective help us understand the behavior of fast-food consumers?

You enter a fast-food restaurant. Do you immediately look to see which line is the shortest? What do you do when you are in the middle of a long line and a new serving station opens? Have you ever gone to a fast-food restaurant, seen very long lines, and then left? Have you ever become annoyed when someone in front of you in line placed an order that took a long time to fill?

The economic perspective is useful in analyzing the behavior of fast-food customers. These consumers are at the restaurant because they expect the marginal benefit from the food they buy to match or exceed its marginal cost. When customers enter the restaurant, they go to the shortest line, believing that that line will minimize their time cost of obtaining food. They are acting purposefully; time is limited, and people prefer using it in some way other than standing in line.

If one fast-food line is temporarily shorter than other lines, some people will move to that line. These movers apparently view the time saving associated with the shorter line to exceed the cost of moving from their present line. The line switching tends to equalize line lengths. No further movement of customers between lines occurs once all lines are about equal.

Fast-food customers face another cost-benefit decision when a clerk opens a new station at the counter. Should they move to the new station or stay put? Those who shift to the new line decide that the time saving from the move exceeds the extra cost of physically moving. In so deciding, customers must also consider just how quickly they can get to the new station compared with others who may be contemplating the same move. (Those who hesitate in this situation are lost!)

Customers at the fast-food establishment do not have perfect information when they select lines. For example, they do not first survey those in the lines to determine what they are ordering before deciding which line to enter. There are two reasons for this. First, most customers would tell them "It's none of your business," and therefore no information would be forthcoming. Second, even

A professional football team hires a new coach and the team's record improves. Is the new coach the cause? Maybe. But perhaps the presence of more experienced and talented players or an easier schedule is the true cause.

Correlation versus Causation Do not confuse correlation, or connection, with causation. Correlation between two events or two sets of data indicates only that they are associated in some systematic and dependable way. For example, we may find that when variable X increases, Y also increases. But this correlation does not necessarily mean that there is causation—that an increase in X is the cause of an increase in Y. The relationship could be purely coincidental or dependent on some other factor, Z, not included in the analysis.

Here is an economic example: Economists have found a positive correlation between education and income. In general, people with more education earn higher incomes than those with less education. Common sense suggests education is the cause and higher incomes are the effect; more education implies a more knowledgeable and productive worker, and such workers receive larger salaries.

But causation could also partly run the other way. People with higher incomes could buy more education, just as they buy more furniture and steaks. Or is part of the relationship explainable in still other ways? Are education and income correlated because the characteristics required to succeed in education—ability and motivation—are the same ones required to be a productive and highly paid worker? If so, then people with those traits will probably obtain more education *and* earn higher incomes. But greater education will not be the sole cause of the higher income. **(Key Question 9)**

∎ A Look Ahead

The ideas in this chapter will come into much sharper focus as you advance through Part 1, where we develop specific economic principles and models. Specifically, in Chapter 2 we build a model of the production choices facing an economy. In Chapter 3 we develop laws of demand and supply that will help you understand how prices and quantities of goods and services are established in markets. In Chapter 4 we combine all markets in the economy to see how the *market system* works. And in Chapters 5 and 6 we examine important sectors (components) of the economy, specifically, the private sector, the government sector, and the international sector.

if they could obtain the information, the amount of time necessary to get it (a cost) would most certainly exceed any time saving associated with finding the best line (the benefit). Because information is costly to obtain, fast-food patrons select lines without perfect information. Thus, not all decisions turn out as expected. For example, you might enter a short line and find someone in front of you is ordering hamburgers and fries for 40 people in the Greyhound bus parked out back (and the employee is a trainee)! Nevertheless, at the time you made your decision, you thought it was optimal.

Imperfect information also explains why some people who arrive at a fast-food restaurant and observe long lines decide to leave. These people conclude that the marginal cost (monetary plus time costs) of obtaining the fast food is too large relative to the marginal benefit. They would not have come to the restaurant in the first place had they known the lines would be so long. But getting that information by, say, employing an advance scout with a cellular phone would cost more than the perceived benefit.

Finally, customers must decide what food to order when they arrive at the counter. In making their choices, they again compare marginal costs and marginal benefits in attempting to obtain the greatest personal satisfaction or well-being for their expenditure.

Economists believe that what is true for the behavior of customers at fast-food restaurants is true for economic behavior in general. Faced with an array of choices, consumers, workers, and businesses rationally compare marginal costs and marginal benefits in making decisions.

SUMMARY

1. Economics is the study of the efficient use of scarce resources in the production of goods and services to achieve the maximum satisfaction of economic wants.

2. The economic perspective includes three elements: scarcity and choice, rational behavior, and marginalism. It sees individuals and institutions making rational decisions based on comparisons of marginal costs and marginal benefits.

3. Knowledge of economics contributes to effective citizenship and provides useful insights for politicians, consumers, and workers.

4. Economists employ the scientific method, in which they form and test hypotheses of cause-and-effect relationships to generate theories, laws, and principles. Economists often combine theories into representations called models.

5. Generalizations stated by economists are called principles, theories, laws, or models. The derivation of these principles is the object of theoretical economics. Good theories explain real-world relationships and predict real-world outcomes.

6. Because economic principles are valuable predictors, they are the bases for economic policy, which is designed to identify and solve problems to the greatest extent possible and at the least possible cost. This type of application of economics is called policy economics.

7. Our society accepts certain shared economic goals, including economic growth, full employment, economic efficiency, price-level stability, economic freedom, equity in the distribution of income, economic security, and a reasonable balance in international trade and finance. Some of these goals are complementary; others entail tradeoffs.

8. Macroeconomics looks at the economy as a whole or its major aggregates; microeconomics examines specific economic units or institutions.

9. Positive statements state facts ("what is"); normative statements express value judgments ("what ought to be").

10. In studying economics, we encounter such pitfalls as biases and preconceptions, unfamiliar or confusing terminology, the fallacy of composition, and the difficulty of establishing clear cause-effect relationships.

TERMS AND CONCEPTS

economics	principles	tradeoffs	normative economics
economic perspective	generalizations	macroeconomics	fallacy of composition
marginal analysis	other-things-equal	aggregate	"after this, therefore
scientific method	assumption	microeconomics	because of this," fallacy
theoretical economics	policy economics	positive economics	

STUDY QUESTIONS

1. **Key Question** Use the economic perspective to explain why someone who is normally a light eater at a standard restaurant may become a bit of a glutton at a buffet-style restaurant that charges a single price for all you can eat.

2. What is the scientific method, and how does it relate to theoretical economics? What is the difference between a hypothesis and an economic law or principle?

3. Why is it significant that economics is not a laboratory science? What problems may be involved in deriving and applying economic principles?

4. Explain the following statements:
   a. Good economic policy requires good economic theory.
   b. Generalization and abstraction are nearly synonymous.
   c. Facts serve to sort out good and bad hypotheses.
   d. The *other-things-equal assumption* helps isolate key economic relationships.

5. **Key Question** Explain in detail the interrelationships between economic facts, theory, and policy. Critically evaluate this statement: "The trouble with economic theory is that it is not practical. It is detached from the real world."

6. To what extent do you accept the eight economic goals stated and described in this chapter? What priorities do you assign to them?

7. **Key Question** Indicate whether each of the following statements applies to microeconomics or macroeconomics:
   a. The unemployment rate in the United States was 4.2 percent in January 2001.
   b. The Alpo dog-food plant in Bowser, Iowa, laid off 15 workers last month.
   c. An unexpected freeze in central Florida reduced the citrus crop and caused the price of oranges to rise.
   d. U.S. output, adjusted for inflation, grew by 5 percent in 2000.
   e. Last week Wells Fargo Bank lowered its interest rate on business loans by one-half of 1 percentage point.
   f. The consumer price index rose by 3.4 percent in 2000.

8. **Key Question** Identify each of the following as either a positive or a normative statement:

   a. The high temperature today was 89 degrees.
   b. It was too hot today.
   c. Other things equal, higher interest rates reduce the total amount of borrowing.
   d. Interest rates are too high.

9. **Key Question** Explain and give an example of (*a*) the fallacy of composition, and (*b*) the "after this, therefore because of this," fallacy. Why are cause-and-effect relationships difficult to isolate in economics?

10. Suppose studies show that students who study more hours receive higher grades. Does this relationship guarantee that any particular student who studies longer will get higher grades?

11. Studies indicate that married men on average earn more income than unmarried men of the same age. Why must we be cautious in concluding that marriage is the *cause* and higher income is the *effect*?

12. **(Last Word)** Use the economic perspective to explain the behavior of the *workers* (rather than the customers) observed at a fast-food restaurant. Why are these workers there, rather than, say, cruising around in their cars? Why do they work so diligently? Why do so many of them quit these jobs once they have graduated high school?

13. **Web-Based Question: *Three economic goals—are they being achieved?*** Three major economic goals are economic growth (rises in real GDP), full employment (less than 5 percent unemployment), and price-level stability (less than 2 percent inflation as measured by the consumer price index, or CPI). The White House statistical website, www.whitehouse.gov/fsbr/esbr.html, provides links to economic information produced by a number of federal agencies. Visit the separate links for Employment, Output, and Prices to assess whether the United States is currently meeting each of these three goals.

14. **Web-Based Question: *Normative economics—Republicans versus Democrats*** Visit both the Republicans' www.rnc.org/ and the Democrats' www.democrats.org/ websites. Identify an economic issue that both parties address, and compare and contrast their views on that issue. Generally speaking, how much of the disagreement is based on normative economics compared to positive economics? Give an example of loaded terminology from each site.

Graphs and Their Meaning

If you glance quickly through this text, you will find many graphs. Some seem simple, while others seem more formidable. All are included to help you visualize and understand economic relationships. Physicists and chemists sometimes illustrate their theories by building arrangements of multicolored wooden balls, representing protons, neutrons, and electrons, which are held in proper relation to one another by wires or sticks. Economists most often use graphs to illustrate their models. By understanding these "pictures," you can more readily comprehend economic relationships. Most of our principles or models explain relationships between just two sets of economic facts, which can be conveniently represented with two-dimensional graphs.

Construction of a Graph

A *graph* is a visual representation of the relationship between two variables. Table 1 is a hypothetical illustration showing the relationship between income and consumption for the economy as a whole. Without even studying economics, we would expect intuitively that people would buy more goods and services when their incomes go up. Thus we are not surprised to find in Table 1 that total consumption in the economy increases as total income increases.

The information in Table 1 is expressed graphically in Figure 1. Here is how it is done: We want to show visually or graphically how consumption

changes as income changes. Since income is the determining factor, we represent it on the **horizontal axis** of the graph, as is customary. And because consumption depends on income, we represent it on the **vertical axis** of the graph, as is also customary. Actually, what we are doing is representing the *independent variable* on the horizontal axis and the *dependent variable* on the vertical axis.

Now we arrange the vertical and horizontal scales of the graph to reflect the ranges of values of consumption and income, and we mark the scales in convenient increments. As you can see, the values marked on the scales cover all the values in Table 1. The increments on both scales are $100 for approximately each $\frac{1}{2}$ inch.

Because the graph has two dimensions, each point within it represents an income value and its associated consumption value. To find a point that represents one of the five income-consumption combinations in Table 1, we draw perpendiculars from the appropriate values on the vertical and horizontal

Table 1

The Relationship between Income and Consumption

Income per Week	Consumption per Week	Point
$ 0	$ 50	a
100	100	b
200	150	c
300	200	d
400	250	e

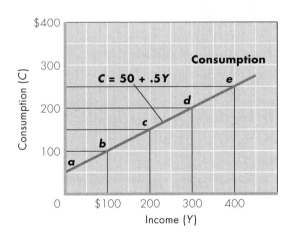

Figure 1

Graphing the direct relationship between consumption and income. Two sets of data that are positively or directly related, such as consumption and income, graph as an upsloping line.

axes. For example, to plot point *c* (the $200 income–$150 consumption point), we draw perpendiculars up from the horizontal (income) axis at $200 and across from the vertical (consumption) axis at $150. These perpendiculars intersect at point *c*, which represents this particular income-consumption combination. You should verify that the other income-consumption combinations shown in Table 1 are properly located in Figure 1. Finally, by assuming that the same general relationship between income and consumption prevails for all other incomes, we draw a line or smooth curve to connect these points. That line or curve represents the income-consumption relationship.

If the graph is a straight line, as in Figure 1, we say the relationship is *linear*.

Direct and Inverse Relationships

The line in Figure 1 slopes upward to the right, so it depicts a direct relationship between income and consumption. By a **direct relationship** (or positive relationship) we mean that two variables—in this case, consumption and income—change in the *same* direction. An increase in consumption is associated with an increase in income; a decrease in consumption accompanies a decrease in income. When two sets of data are positively or directly related, they always graph as an *upsloping* line, as in Figure 1.

In contrast, two sets of data may be inversely related. Consider Table 2, which shows the relationship between the price of basketball tickets and game attendance at Gigantic State University (GSU). Here we have an **inverse relationship** (or negative relationship) because the two variables change in *opposite* directions. When ticket prices decrease, attendance increases. When ticket prices increase, attendance decreases. The six data points in Table 2 are plotted

in Figure 2. Observe that an inverse relationship always graphs as a *downsloping* line.

Dependent and Independent Variables

Although it is not always easy, economists seek to determine which variable is the "cause" and which is the "effect." Or, more formally, they seek the independent variable and the dependent variable. The **independent variable** is the cause or source; it is the variable that changes first. The **dependent variable** is the effect or outcome; it is the variable that changes because of the change in the independent variable. As noted in our income-consumption example, income generally is the independent variable and consumption the dependent variable. Income causes consumption to be what it is rather than the other way around. Similarly, ticket prices (set in advance of the season) determine attendance at GSU basketball games; attendance at games does not determine the ticket prices for those games. Ticket price is the independent variable, and the quantity of tickets purchased is the dependent variable.

You may recall from your high school courses that mathematicians always put the independent variable (cause) on the horizontal axis and the depen-

Table 2

The Relationship between Ticket Prices and Attendance

Ticket Price	Attendance, Thousands	Point
$50	0	a
40	4	b
30	8	c
20	12	d
10	16	e
0	20	f

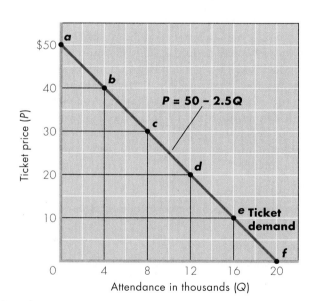

Figure 2

Graphing the inverse relationship between ticket prices and game attendance. Two sets of data that are negatively or inversely related, such as ticket price and the attendance at basketball games, graph as a downsloping line.

dent variable (effect) on the vertical axis. Economists are less tidy; their graphing of independent and dependent variables is more arbitrary. Their conventional graphing of the income-consumption relationship is consistent with mathematical presentation, but economists put price and cost data on the vertical axis. Hence, economists' graphing of GSU's ticket price–attendance data conflicts with normal mathematical procedure.

Other Things Equal

Our simple two-variable graphs purposely ignore many other factors that might affect the amount of consumption occurring at each income level or the number of people who attend GSU basketball games at each possible ticket price. When economists plot the relationship between any two variables, they employ the *ceteris paribus* (other-things-equal) assumption. Thus, in Figure 1 all factors other than income that might affect the amount of consumption are presumed to be constant or unchanged. Similarly, in Figure 2 all factors other than ticket price that might influence attendance at GSU basketball games are assumed constant. In reality, "other things" are not equal; they often change, and when they do, the relationship represented in our two tables and graphs will change. Specifically, the lines we have plotted would shift to new locations.

Consider a stock market "crash." The dramatic drop in the value of stocks might cause people to feel less wealthy and therefore less willing to consume at each level of income. The result might be a downward shift of the consumption line. To see this, you should plot a new consumption line in Figure 1, assuming that consumption is, say, $20 less at each income level. Note that the relationship remains direct; the line merely shifts downward to reflect less consumption spending at each income level.

Similarly, factors other than ticket prices might affect GSU game attendance. If GSU loses most of its games, attendance at GSU games might be less at each ticket price. To see this, redraw Figure 2, assuming that 2000 fewer fans attend GSU games at each ticket price. **(Key Appendix Question 2)**

Slope of a Line

Lines can be described in terms of their slopes. The **slope of a straight line** is the ratio of the vertical change (the rise or drop) to the horizontal change (the run) between any two points of the line.

Positive Slope   Between point b and point c in Figure 1 the rise or vertical change (the change in consumption) is +$50 and the run or horizontal change (the change in income) is +$100. Therefore:

$$\text{Slope} = \frac{\text{vertical change}}{\text{horizontal change}} = \frac{+50}{+100} = \frac{1}{2} = .5$$

Note that our slope of $\frac{1}{2}$ or .5 is positive because consumption and income change in the same direction; that is, consumption and income are directly or positively related.

The slope of .5 tells us there will be a $1 increase in consumption for every $2 increase in income. Similarly, it indicates that for every $2 decrease in income there will be a $1 decrease in consumption.

Negative Slope   Between any two of the identified points in Figure 2, say, point c and point d, the vertical change is −10 (the drop) and the horizontal change is +4 (the run). Therefore:

$$\text{Slope} = \frac{\text{vertical change}}{\text{horizontal change}} = \frac{-10}{+4}$$
$$= -2\frac{1}{2} = -2.5$$

This slope is negative because ticket price and attendance have an inverse relationship.

Note that on the horizontal axis attendance is stated in thousands of people. So the slope of −10/+4 or −2.5 means that lowering the price by $10 will increase attendance by 4000 people. This is the same as saying that a $2.50 price reduction will increase attendance by 1000 persons.

Slopes and Measurement Units   The slope of a line will be affected by the choice of units for either variable. If, in our ticket price illustration, we had chosen to measure attendance in individual people, our horizontal change would have been 4000 and the slope would have been

$$\text{Slope} = \frac{-10}{+4000} = \frac{-1}{+400} = -.0025$$

The slope depends on the way the relevant variables are measured.

Slopes and Marginal Analysis   Recall that economics is largely concerned with changes from the status quo. The concept of slope is important in economics because it reflects marginal changes—

those involving 1 more (or 1 less) unit. For example, in Figure 1 the .5 slope shows that $.50 of extra or marginal consumption is associated with each $1 change in income. In this example, people collectively will consume $.50 of any $1 increase in their incomes and reduce their consumption by $.50 for each $1 decline in income.

Infinite and Zero Slopes

Many variables are unrelated or independent of one another. For example, the quantity of wristwatches purchased is not related to the price of bananas. In Figure 3a we represent the price of bananas on the vertical axis and the quantity of watches demanded on the horizontal axis. The graph of their relationship is the line parallel to the vertical axis, indicating that the same quantity of watches is purchased no matter what the price of bananas. The slope of such a line is *infinite*.

Similarly, aggregate consumption is completely unrelated to the nation's divorce rate. In Figure 3b we put consumption on the vertical axis and the divorce rate on the horizontal axis. The line parallel to the horizontal axis represents this lack of relatedness. This line has a slope of *zero*.

Vertical Intercept

A line can be located on a graph (without plotting points) if we know its slope and its vertical intercept. The **vertical intercept** of a line is the point where the line meets the vertical axis. In Figure 1 the intercept is $50. This intercept means that if current income were zero, consumers would still spend $50. They might do this through borrowing or by selling some of their assets. Similarly, the $50 vertical intercept in Figure 2 shows that at a $50 ticket price, GSU's basketball team would be playing in an empty arena.

Equation of a Linear Relationship

If we know the vertical intercept and slope, we can describe a line succinctly in equation form. In its general form, the equation of a straight line is

$$y = a + bx$$

where y = dependent variable
a = vertical intercept
b = slope of line
x = independent variable

For our income-consumption example, if C represents consumption (the dependent variable) and Y represents income (the independent variable), we can write $C = a + bY$. By substituting the known values of the intercept and the slope, we get

$$C = 50 + .5Y$$

This equation also allows us to determine the amount of consumption C at any specific level of income. You should use it to confirm that at the $250 income level, consumption is $175.

When economists reverse mathematical convention by putting the independent variable on the vertical axis and the dependent variable on the horizontal axis, then y stands for the independent variable, rather than the dependent variable in the general form. We noted previously that this case is relevant for our GSU ticket price–attendance data. If P represents the ticket price (independent variable) and Q represents attendance (dependent variable), their relationship is given by

$$P = 50 - 2.5Q$$

where the vertical intercept is 50 and the negative slope is $-2\frac{1}{2}$ or -2.5. Knowing the value of P lets us solve for Q, our dependent variable. You should use

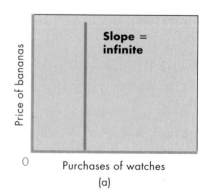

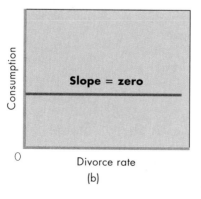

Figure 3

Infinite and zero slopes. (a) A line parallel to the vertical axis has an infinite slope. Here, purchases of watches remain the same no matter what happens to the price of bananas. (b) A line parallel to the horizontal axis has a slope of zero. Here, consumption remains the same no matter what happens to the divorce rate. In both (a) and (b), the two variables are totally unrelated to one another.

this equation to predict GSU ticket sales when the ticket price is $15. **(Key Appendix Question 3)**

Slope of a Nonlinear Curve

We now move from the simple world of linear relationships (straight lines) to the more complex world of nonlinear relationships. The slope of a straight line is the same at all its points. The slope of a line representing a nonlinear relationship changes from one point to another. Such lines are referred to as *curves*. (It is also permissible to refer to a straight line as a "curve.")

Consider the downsloping curve in Figure 4. Its slope is negative throughout, but the curve flattens as we move down along it. Thus, its slope constantly changes; the curve has a different slope at each point.

To measure the slope at a specific point, we draw a straight line tangent to the curve at that point. A line is *tangent* at a point if it touches, but does not intersect, the curve at that point. Thus line *aa* is tangent to the curve in Figure 4 at point *A*. The slope of the curve at that point is equal to the slope of the tangent line. Specifically, the total vertical change (drop) in the tangent line *aa* is −20 and the total horizontal change (run) is +5. Because the slope of the tangent line *aa* is −20/+5, or −4, the slope of the curve at point *A* is also −4.

Line *bb* in Figure 4 is tangent to the curve at point *B*. Following the same procedure, we find the slope at *B* to be −5/+15, or −$\frac{1}{3}$. Thus, in this flatter part of the curve, the slope is less negative. **(Key Appendix Question 6)**

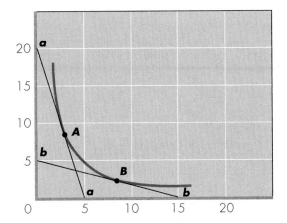

Figure 4

Determining the slopes of curves. The slope of a nonlinear curve changes from point to point on the curve. The slope at any point (say, *B*) can be determined by drawing a straight line that is tangent to that point (line *bb*) and calculating the slope of that line.

APPENDIX SUMMARY

1. Graphs are a convenient and revealing way to represent economic relationships.

2. Two variables are positively or directly related when their values change in the same direction. The line (curve) representing two directly related variables slopes upward.

3. Two variables are negatively or inversely related when their values change in opposite directions. The curve representing two inversely related variables slopes downward.

4. The value of the dependent variable (the "effect") is determined by the value of the independent variable (the "cause").

5. When the "other factors" that might affect a two-variable relationship are allowed to change, the graph of the relationship will likely shift to a new location.

6. The slope of a straight line is the ratio of the vertical change to the horizontal change between any two points. The slope of an upsloping line is positive; the slope of a downsloping line is negative.

7. The slope of a line or curve depends on the units used in measuring the variables. It is especially relevant for economics because it measures marginal changes.

8. The slope of a horizontal line is zero; the slope of a vertical line is infinite.

9. The vertical intercept and slope of a line determine its location; they are used in expressing the line—and the relationship between the two variables—as an equation.

10. The slope of a curve at any point is determined by calculating the slope of a straight line tangent to the curve at that point.

APPENDIX TERMS AND CONCEPTS

horizontal axis

vertical axis

direct relationship

inverse relationship

independent variable

dependent variable

slope of a straight line

vertical intercept

APPENDIX STUDY QUESTIONS

1. Briefly explain the use of graphs as a way to represent economic relationships. What is an inverse relationship? How does it graph? What is a direct relationship? How does it graph? Graph and explain the relationships you would expect to find between (*a*) the number of inches of rainfall per month and the sale of umbrellas, (*b*) the amount of tuition and the level of enrollment at a university, and (*c*) the popularity of an entertainer and the price of her concert tickets.

   In each case cite and explain how variables other than those specifically mentioned might upset the expected relationship. Is your graph in part *b*, above, consistent with the fact that, historically, enrollments and tuition have both increased? If not, explain any difference.

2. **Key Appendix Question** Indicate how each of the following might affect the data shown in Table 2 and Figure 2 of this appendix:
   a. GSU's athletic director schedules higher-quality opponents.
   b. An NBA team locates in the city where GSU plays.
   c. GSU contracts to have all its home games televised.

3. **Key Appendix Question** The following table contains data on the relationship between saving and income. Rearrange these data into a meaningful order and graph them on the accompanying grid. What is the slope of the line? The vertical intercept? Interpret the meaning of both the slope and the intercept. Write the equation that represents this line. What would you predict saving to be at the $12,500 level of income?

Income per Year	Saving per Year
$15,000	$1,000
0	−500
10,000	500
5,000	0
20,000	1,500

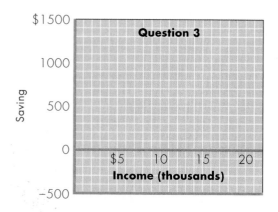

4. Construct a table from the data shown on the graph below. Which is the dependent variable and which the independent variable? Summarize the data in equation form.

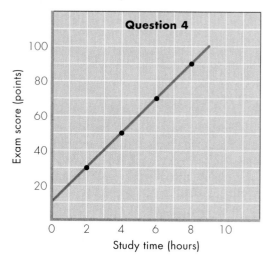

5. Suppose that when the interest rate on loans is 16 percent, businesses find it unprofitable to invest in machinery and equipment. However, when the interest rate is 14 percent, $5 billion worth of investment is profitable. At 12 percent interest, a total of $10 billion of investment is profitable. Similarly, total investment increases by $5 billion for each successive 2-percentage-point decline in the interest rate. Describe the relevant relationship between the interest rate and investment in words, in a table, on a graph, and as an equation. Put the interest rate on the vertical axis and investment on the horizontal axis. In your equation use the form $i = a + bI$, where i is the interest rate, a is the vertical intercept, b is the slope of the line (which is negative), and I is the level of investment. Comment on the advantages and disadvantages of the verbal, tabular, graphical, and equation forms of description.

6. **Key Appendix Question** The accompanying graph shows curve *XX′* and tangents at points *A*, *B*, and *C*. Calculate the slope of the curve at these three points.

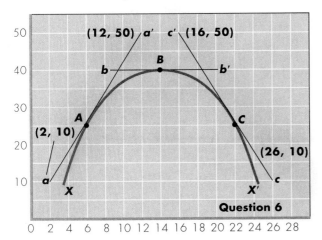

Question 6

7. In the accompanying graph, is the slope of curve *AA′* positive or negative? Does the slope increase or decrease as we move along the curve from *A* to *A′*? Answer the same two questions for curve *BB′*.

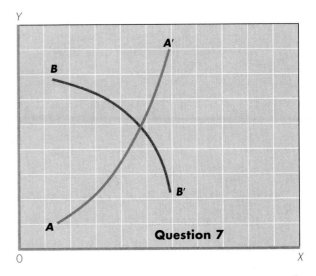

Question 7

2

The Economizing Problem

YOU MAKE DECISIONS every day that capture the essence of economics. Suppose you have $40 and are deciding how to spend it. Should you buy a new pair of jeans? Two or three compact discs? A ticket for a concert? ■ Should you forgo work while you are attending college and concentrate solely on your coursework and grades? Is that an option for you, given the high cost of college? If you decide to work, should it be full-time or part-time? Should you work on campus at lower pay or off campus at higher pay? What are the implications of your employment for your course grades? ■ Money and time are both scarce, and making decisions in the context of scarcity always means there are costs. If you choose the jeans, the cost is the forgone CDs or concert. If you work full-time, the cost might be greater stress, poorer performance in your classes, or an extra year or two in college. ■ This chapter examines the fundamentals of economics—scarcity, choices, and costs. We first examine the *economizing problem*, focusing closely on *wants* and *resources*. Next, we develop two economic models: (1) a *production possibilities model* that incorporates and illustrates several key ideas, and (2) a simple *circular flow model* that identifies the major groups of decision makers and major markets in the economy.

■ The Foundation of Economics

Two fundamental facts together constitute the **economizing problem** and provide a foundation for economics:

- Society's economic wants—that is, the economic wants of its citizens and institutions—are virtually unlimited and insatiable.
- Economic resources—the means of producing goods and services—are limited or scarce.

All that follows depends directly on these two facts.

Unlimited Wants

What do we mean by "economic wants"? We mean, first, the desires of consumers to obtain and use various goods and services that provide **utility**—that is, pleasure or satisfaction. These wants extend over a wide range of products, from *necessities* (food, shelter, clothing) to *luxuries* (perfumes, yachts, race cars).

Some wants—basic food, clothing, and shelter—have biological roots. Other wants—for example, the specific kinds of food, clothing, and shelter we seek—are rooted in the conventions and customs of society.

Over time, wants change and tend to multiply, fueled by new products. Not long ago, we did not want personal computers, Internet service, digital recorders, lattes, or pagers because they simply did not exist. Also, the satisfaction of certain wants tends to trigger others: the acquisition of a Neon or Civic has been known to whet the appetite for a Porsche or a Mercedes.

Services, as well as products, satisfy our wants. Car repair work, the removal of an inflamed appendix, legal and accounting advice, and haircuts all satisfy human wants. Actually, we buy many goods, such as automobiles and washing machines, for the services they render. The differences between goods and services are often smaller than they appear to be.

Businesses and units of government also strive to satisfy economic goals. Businesses want factories, machinery, trucks, warehouses, and phone systems to help them achieve their production goals. Government, reflecting the collective wants of its citizens or goals of its own, seeks highways, schools, and military equipment.

All these wants are *insatiable*, or *unlimited*, meaning that our desires for goods and services cannot be completely satisfied. Our desires for a *particular* good or service can be satisfied; over a short period of time we can surely get enough toothpaste or pasta. And one appendectomy is plenty. But goods *in general* are another story. We do not, and presumably cannot, get enough. Suppose all members of society were asked to list the goods and services they would buy if they had unlimited income. That list would probably never end.

In short, individuals and institutions have innumerable unfilled wants. *The objective of all economic activity is to fulfill wants.* 🔑 **2.1**

Scarce Resources

The second fundamental fact is that *economic resources are limited or scarce.* By **economic resources** we mean all natural, human, and manufactured resources that go into the production of goods and services. That includes all the factory and farm buildings and all the equipment, tools, and machinery used to produce manufactured goods and agricultural products; all transportation and communication facilities; all types of labor; and land and min-

eral resources. Economists classify all these resources as either *property* resources—land, raw materials, and capital—or *human* resources—labor and entrepreneurial ability.

Resource Categories Let's look at four specific categories of economic resources.

Land **Land** means much more to the economist than it does to most people. To the economist land includes all natural resources—all "gifts of nature"—that are used in the production process, such as arable land, forests, mineral and oil deposits, and water resources.

Capital **Capital** (or *capital goods* or *investment goods*) includes all manufactured aids used in producing consumer goods and services—that is, all tools, machinery, equipment, factory, storage, transportation, and distribution facilities. The process of producing and purchasing capital goods is known as **investment.**

Capital goods differ from *consumer goods* in that consumer goods satisfy wants directly, while capital goods do so indirectly by aiding the production of consumer goods. Note that the term "capital" as used by economists refers *not* to money but to *real capital*—tools, machinery, and other productive equipment. Money produces nothing; it is *not* an economic resource. So-called money capital or financial capital is simply a means for purchasing real capital.

Labor **Labor** is a broad term for all the physical and mental talents of individuals available and usable in producing goods and services. The services of a logger, retail clerk, machinist, teacher, professional football player, and nuclear physicist all fall under the general heading "labor."

Entrepreneurial Ability Finally, there is the special human resource, distinct from labor, that we label **entrepreneurial ability.** The entrepreneur performs several functions:

■ The entrepreneur *takes the initiative* in combining the resources of land, capital, and labor to produce a good or a service. Both a sparkplug and a catalyst, the entrepreneur is the driving force behind production and the agent who combines the other resources in what is hoped will be a successful business venture.

■ The entrepreneur *makes basic business-policy decisions*—that is, the nonroutine decisions that set the course of a business enterprise.

- The entrepreneur is an *innovator*—the one who commercializes new products, new production techniques, or even new forms of business organization.
- The entrepreneur is a *risk bearer*. The entrepreneur in a market system has no guarantee of profit. The reward for the entrepreneur's time, efforts, and abilities may be profits *or* losses. The entrepreneur risks not only his or her invested funds but those of associates and stockholders as well.

Because these four resources—land, labor, capital, and entrepreneurial ability—are combined to *produce* goods and services, they are called the **factors of production.**

Resource Payments The income received from supplying raw materials and capital equipment (the property resources) is called *rental income* and *interest income*, respectively. The income accruing to those who supply labor is called *wages*, which include salaries and all wage and salary supplements such as bonuses, commissions, and royalties. Entrepreneurial income is called *profits*, which may be negative—that is, losses.

Relative Scarcity The four types of economic resources, or factors of production, or *inputs*, have one significant characteristic in common: *They are scarce or limited in supply.* Our planet contains only finite, and therefore limited, amounts of arable land, mineral deposits, capital equipment, and labor. Their scarcity constrains productive activity and output. In the United States, one of the most affluent nations, output per person was limited to roughly $34,000 in 2000. In the poorest nations, annual output per person may be as low as $300 or $400.

▌ Economics: Employment and Efficiency

The economizing problem is at the heart of the definition of economics stated in Chapter 1: *Economics is the social science concerned with the problem of using scarce resources to attain the maximum fulfillment of society's unlimited wants.* Economics is concerned with "doing the best with what we have."

Economics is thus the social science that examines efficiency—the best use of scarce resources. Society wants to use its limited resources efficiently; it desires to produce as many goods and services as possible from its available resources, thereby maximizing total satisfaction.

Full Employment: Using Available Resources

To realize the best use of scarce resources, a society must achieve both full employment and full production. By **full employment** we mean the use of all available resources. No workers should be out of work if they are willing and able to work. Nor should capital equipment or arable land sit idle. But note that we say all *available* resources should be employed. Each society has certain customs and practices that determine what resources are available for employment and what resources are not. For example, in most countries legislation and custom provide that children and the very aged should not be employed. Similarly, to maintain productivity, farmland should be allowed to lie fallow periodically. And we should conserve some resources—fishing stocks and forest, for instance—for use by future generations.

Full Production: Using Resources Efficiently

The employment of all available resources is not enough to achieve efficiency, however. Full production must also be realized. By **full production** we mean that all employed resources should be used so that they provide the maximum possible satisfaction of our material wants. If we fail to realize full production, economists say our resources are *underemployed*.

Full production implies two kinds of efficiency—productive and allocative efficiency. **Productive efficiency** is the production of *any particular mix of goods and services in the least costly way.* When we produce, say, compact discs at the lowest achievable unit cost, we are expending the smallest amount of resources to produce CDs and are therefore making available the largest amount of resources to produce other desired products. Suppose society has only $100 worth of resources available. If we can produce a CD for only $5 of those resources, then $95 will be available to produce other goods. This is clearly better than producing the CD for $10 and having only $90 of resources available for alternative uses.

In contrast, **allocative efficiency** is the production of *that particular mix of goods and services most wanted by society.* For example, society wants resources allocated to compact discs, not to 45-rpm records. We want personal computers (PCs), not manual typewriters. Furthermore, we do not want to devote *all* our resources to producing CDs and PCs; we want to assign some of them to producing automobiles and office buildings. Allocative efficiency requires that an economy produce the "right" mix of goods and services, with each item being produced at the lowest-possible unit cost. This means apportioning limited resources among firms and industries in such a way that society obtains the combination of goods and services it wants the most. **(Key Question 5)**

QUICK REVIEW 2.1

■ People's economic wants are virtually unlimited.

■ Economic resources—land, capital, labor, and entrepreneurial ability—are scarce.

■ Economics is concerned with the efficient allocation of scarce resources to achieve the maximum fulfillment of society's economic wants.

■ Economic efficiency embodies full employment and full production.

■ Full production requires both productive and allocative efficiency.

Production Possibilities Table

Because resources are scarce, a full-employment, full-production economy cannot have an unlimited output of goods and services. Consequently, people must choose which goods and services to produce and which to forgo. The necessity and consequences of those choices can best be understood through a *production possibilities model*. We examine the model first as a table and then as a graph.

Assumptions We begin our discussion of the production possibilities model with simplifying assumptions:

■ *Full employment and productive efficiency* The economy is employing all its available resources (full employment) and is producing goods and services at least cost (productive efficiency).

■ *Fixed resources* The available supplies of the factors of production are fixed in both quantity and quality. Nevertheless, they can be reallocated, within limits, among different uses; for example, land can be used either for factory sites or for food production.

■ *Fixed technology* The state of technology—the methods used to produce output—does not change during our analysis. This assumption and the previous one imply that we are looking at an economy at a certain point in time or over a very short period of time.

■ *Two goods* The economy is producing only two goods: pizzas and industrial robots. Pizzas symbolize **consumer goods,** products that satisfy our wants *directly;* industrial robots symbolize **capital goods,** products that satisfy our wants *indirectly* by making possible more efficient production of consumer goods.

The Need for Choice Given our assumptions, we see that society must choose among alternatives. Fixed resources mean limited outputs of pizza and robots. And since all available resources are fully employed, to increase the production of robots we must shift resources away from the production of pizzas. The reverse is also true: To increase the production of pizzas, we must shift resources away from the production of robots. There is no such thing as a free pizza. This, recall, is the essence of the economizing problem.

A **production possibilities table** lists the different combinations of two products that can be produced with a specific set of resources (and with full employment *and* productive efficiency). Table 2.1 is such a table for a pizza-robot economy; the data are, of course, hypothetical. At alternative A, this economy would be devoting all its available resources to the production of robots (capital goods); at alternative E, all resources would go to pizza production (consumer goods). Those alternatives are unrealistic extremes; an economy typically produces both capital goods and consumer goods, as in B, C, and D. As we move from alternative A to E, we increase the production of pizza at the expense of robot production.

Because consumer goods satisfy our wants directly, any movement toward E looks tempting. In producing more pizzas, society increases the current satisfaction of its wants. But there is a cost: more pizzas mean fewer robots. This shift of resources to consumer goods catches up with society over time as the stock of capital goods dwindles—or at least

Table 2.1

Production Possibilities of Pizzas and Robots with Full Employment and Productive Efficiency

Type of Product	Production Alternatives				
	A	B	C	D	E
Pizzas (in hundred thousands)	0	1	2	3	4
Robots (in thousands)	10	9	7	4	0

KEY GRAPH

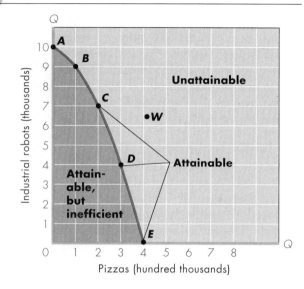

Q

10 A
9   B
8   **Unattainable**
7   C
6   •W
5
4   D   **Attainable**
3
2   **Attain-**
    able,
1   **but**
    inefficient
    E
0   1   2   3   4   5   6   7   8   Q

Industrial robots (thousands)

Pizzas (hundred thousands)

Figure 2.1

The production possibilities curve. Each point *on* the production possibilities curve represents some maximum combination of two products that can be produced if full employment and full production are achieved. When operating on the curve, more robots means fewer pizzas, and vice versa. Limited resources and a fixed technology make any combination of robots and pizzas lying outside the curve (such as at *W*) unattainable. Points inside the curve are attainable, but they indicate that full employment and productive efficiency are not being realized.

Quick Quiz 2.1

1. Production possibilities curve *ABCDE* is bowed out from the origin (concave to the origin) because:
   a. the marginal benefit of pizzas declines as more pizzas are consumed.
   b. the curve gets steeper as we move from *E* to *A*.
   c. it reflects the law of increasing opportunity costs.
   d. resources are scarce.

2. The marginal opportunity cost of the second unit of pizza is:
   a. 2 units of robots.
   b. 3 units of robots.
   c. 7 units of robots.
   d. 9 units of robots.

3. The total opportunity cost of 7 units of robots is:
   a. 1 unit of pizza.
   b. 2 units of pizza.
   c. 3 units of pizza.
   d. 4 units of pizza.

4. All points on this production possibilities curve necessarily represent:
   a. allocative efficiency.
   b. less than full use of resources.
   c. unattainable levels of output.
   d. productive efficiency.

Answers: 1. c; 2. a; 3. b; 4. d

---

ceases to expand at the current rate—with the result that some potential for greater future production is lost. By moving toward alternative E, society chooses "more now" at the expense of "much more later."

By moving toward A, society chooses to forgo current consumption, thereby freeing up resources that can be used to increase the production of capital goods. By building up its stock of capital this way, society will have greater future production and, therefore, greater future consumption. By moving toward A, society is choosing "more later" at the cost of "less now."

Generalization: *At any point in time, an economy achieving full employment and productive efficiency must sacrifice some of one good to obtain more of another good. Scarce resources prohibit such an economy from having more of both goods.*

Production Possibilities Curve

The data presented in a production possibilities table can also be shown graphically. We use a simple two-dimensional graph, arbitrarily representing the output of capital goods (here, robots) on the vertical axis and the output of consumer goods (here, pizzas) on the horizontal axis, as shown in **Figure 2.1 (Key Graph).** Following the procedure given in the appendix to Chapter 1, we can graph a **production possibilities curve.** ⌐ 2.1

Each point on the production possibilities curve represents some maximum output of the two products. The curve is a production *frontier* because it shows the limit of attainable outputs. To obtain the various combinations of pizza and robots that fall *on* the production possibilities curve, society must achieve both full employment and productive efficiency. Points lying *inside* (to the left of) the curve are also attainable, but they reflect inefficiency and therefore are not as desirable as points on the curve. Points inside the curve imply that the economy could have more of both robots and pizzas if it achieved full employment and productive efficiency. Points lying *outside* (to the right of) the production possibilities curve, like point *W*, would represent a greater output than the output at any point on the curve. Such points, however, are unattainable with the current supplies of resources and technology.

Law of Increasing Opportunity Cost

Because resources are scarce relative to the virtually unlimited wants they can be used to satisfy, people must choose among alternatives. More pizzas mean fewer robots. The amount of other products that must be forgone or sacrificed to obtain 1 unit of a specific good is called the **opportunity cost** of that good. In our case, the number of robots that must be given up to get another unit of pizza is the *opportunity cost*, or simply the *cost*, of that unit of pizza. 🔑 2.2 ❗ 2.1

In moving from alternative A to alternative B in Table 2.1, we find that the cost of 1 additional unit of pizza is 1 less unit of robots. But as we pursue the concept of cost through the additional production possibilities—B to C, C to D, and D to E—an important economic principle is revealed: The opportunity cost of each additional unit of pizza is greater than the opportunity cost of the preceding one. When we move from A to B, just 1 unit of robots is sacrificed for 1 more unit of pizza; but in going from B to C we sacrifice 2 additional units of robots for 1 more unit of pizza; then 3 more of robots for 1 more of pizza; and finally 4 for 1. Conversely, confirm that as we move from E to A, the cost of an additional robot is $\frac{1}{4}$, $\frac{1}{3}$, $\frac{1}{2}$, and 1 unit of pizza, respectively, for the four successive moves.

Note these points about these opportunity costs:
- Here opportunity costs are being measured in *real* terms, that is, in actual goods rather than in money terms.

- We are discussing *marginal* (meaning "extra") opportunity costs, rather than cumulative or total opportunity costs. For example, the marginal opportunity cost of the third unit of pizza in Table 2.1 is 3 units of robots ($=7 - 4$). But the *total* opportunity cost of 3 units of pizza is 6 units of robots ($=1$ unit of robots for the first unit of pizza *plus* 2 units of robots for the second unit of pizza *plus* 3 units of robots for the third unit of pizza).

Our example illustrates the **law of increasing opportunity costs:** The more of a product that is produced, the greater is its opportunity cost ("marginal" being implied).

Shape of the Curve   The law of increasing opportunity costs is reflected in the shape of the production possibilities curve: The curve is bowed out from the origin of the graph. Figure 2.1 shows that when the economy moves from *A* to *E*, it must give up successively larger amounts of robots (1, 2, 3, and 4) to acquire equal increments of pizza (1, 1, 1, and 1). This is shown in the slope of the production possibilities curve, which becomes steeper as we move from *A* to *E*. A curve that gets steeper as we move down it is "concave to the origin."

Economic Rationale   What is the economic rationale for the law of increasing opportunity costs? Why does the sacrifice of robots increase as we produce more pizzas? The answer is that *economic resources are not completely adaptable to alternative uses.* Many resources are better at producing one good than at producing others. Fertile farmland is highly suited to producing the ingredients needed to make pizzas, while land rich in mineral deposits is highly suited to producing the materials needed to make robots. As we step up pizza production, resources that are less and less adaptable to making pizzas must be "pushed" into pizza production. If we start at *A* and move to *B*, we can shift the resources whose productivity of pizzas is greatest in relation to their productivity of robots. But as we move from *B* to *C*, *C* to *D*, and so on, resources highly productive of pizzas become increasingly scarce. To get more pizzas, resources whose productivity of robots is great in relation to their productivity of pizzas will be needed. It will take more and more of such resources, and hence greater sacrifices of robots, to achieve each increase of 1 unit in the production of pizzas. This lack of perfect flexibility, or interchangeability, on the part of resources is the cause of increasing opportunity costs. **(Key Question 6)**

Allocative Efficiency Revisited

So far, we have assumed full employment and productive efficiency, both of which are necessary to realize *any point* on an economy's production possibilities curve. We now turn to allocative efficiency, which requires that the economy produce at the most valued, or *optimal*, point on the production possibilities curve. Of all the attainable combinations of pizzas and robots on the curve in Figure 2.1, which is best? That is, what specific quantities of resources should be allocated to pizzas and what specific quantities to robots in order to maximize satisfaction?

Our discussion of the *economic perspective* in Chapter 1 puts us on the right track. Recall that economic decisions center on comparisons of marginal benefits and marginal costs. Any economic activity—for example, production or consumption—should be expanded as long as marginal benefit exceeds marginal cost and should be reduced if marginal cost exceeds marginal benefit. The optimal amount of the activity occurs where MB = MC.

Consider pizzas. We already know from the law of increasing opportunity costs that the marginal cost (MC) of additional units of pizzas will rise as more units are produced. This can be shown by an upsloping MC curve, as in Figure 2.2. We also know

that we obtain extra or marginal benefits (MB) from additional units of pizzas. However, although material wants in the aggregate are insatiable, studies reveal that the second unit of a particular product yields less additional utility or benefit to a person than the first. And a third provides even less MB than the second. So it is for society as a whole. We therefore can portray the marginal benefits from pizzas with a downsloping MB curve, as in Figure 2.2. Although total benefits rise when society consumes more pizza, marginal benefits decline.

The optimal quantity of pizza production is indicated by the intersection of the MB and MC curves: 200,000 units in Figure 2.2. Why is this the optimal quantity? If only 100,000 pizzas were produced, the marginal benefit of pizza would exceed its marginal cost. In money terms, MB might be $15, while MC is only $5. This suggests that society would be *underallocating* resources to pizza production and that more of it should be produced.

How do we know? Because society values an additional pizza as being worth $15, while the alternative products that those resources could produce are worth only $5. Society benefits—it is better off in the sense of having a higher-valued output to enjoy—whenever it can gain something worth $15 by forgoing something worth only $5. Society would use its resources more efficiently by allocating more resources to pizza. Each additional pizza up to 200,000 would provide such a gain, indicating that allocative efficiency would be improved by that production. But when MB = MC, the benefits of producing pizzas or alternative products with the available resources are equal. Allocative efficiency is achieved where MB = MC.

The production of 300,000 pizzas would represent an *overallocation* of resources to pizza production. Here the MC of pizza is $15 and its MB is only $5. This means that 1 unit of pizza is worth only $5 to society, while the alternative products that those resources could otherwise produce are valued at $15. By producing 1 less unit, society loses a pizza worth $5. But by reallocating the freed resources, it gains other products worth $15. When society gains something worth $15 by forgoing something worth only $5, it is better off. In Figure 2.2, such net gains can be realized until pizza production has been reduced to 200,000.

Generalization: *Resources are being efficiently allocated to any product when the marginal benefit and marginal cost of its output are equal (MB = MC).* Suppose that by applying the above analysis to robots, we find

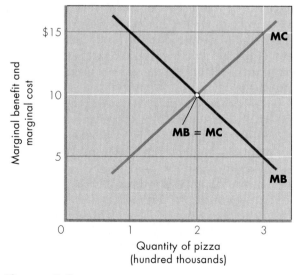

Figure 2.2

Allocative efficiency: MB = MC. Allocative efficiency requires the expansion of a good's output until its marginal benefit (MB) and marginal cost (MC) are equal. No resources beyond that point should get allocated to the product. Here, allocative efficiency occurs when 200,000 pizzas are produced.

their optimal (MB = MC) output is 7000. This would mean that alternative *C* on our production possibilities curve—200,000 pizzas and 7000 robots—would result in allocative efficiency for our hypothetical economy. **(Key Question 9)**

QUICK REVIEW 2.2

▪ The production possibilities curve illustrates four concepts: (a) *scarcity* of resources is implied by the area of unattainable combinations of output lying outside the production possibilities curve; (b) *choice* among outputs is reflected in the variety of attainable combinations of goods lying along the curve; (c) *opportunity cost* is illustrated by the downward slope of the curve; (d) the law of *increasing opportunity costs* is implied by the concavity of the curve.

▪ Full employment and productive efficiency must be realized in order for the economy to operate on its production possibilities curve.

▪ A comparison of marginal benefits and marginal costs is needed to determine allocative efficiency—the best or optimal output mix on the curve.

▪ Unemployment, Growth, and the Future

Let's now discard the first three assumptions underlying the production possibilities curve and see what happens.

Unemployment and Productive Inefficiency

The first assumption was that our economy was achieving full employment and productive efficiency. Our analysis and conclusions change if some resources are idle (unemployment) or if least-cost production is not realized. The five alternatives in Table 2.1 represent maximum outputs; they illustrate the combinations of robots and pizzas that can be produced when the economy is operating at full capacity—with full employment and productive efficiency. With unemployment or inefficient production, the economy would produce less than each alternative shown in the table.

Graphically, we represent situations of unemployment or productive inefficiency by points *inside* the original production possibilities curve (reproduced in Figure 2.3). Point *U* is one such point.

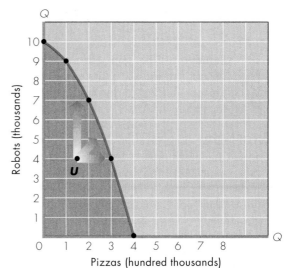

Figure 2.3

Unemployment, productive inefficiency, and the production possibilities curve. Any point inside the production possibilities curve, such as *U*, represents unemployment or a failure to achieve productive efficiency. The arrows indicate that, by realizing full employment and productive efficiency, the economy could operate on the curve. This means it could produce more of one or both products than it is producing at point *U*.

Here the economy is falling short of the various maximum combinations of pizzas and robots represented by the points *on* the production possibilities curve. The arrows in Figure 2.3 indicate three possible paths back to full-employment and least-cost production. A move toward full employment and productive efficiency would yield a greater output of one or both products.

A Growing Economy

When we drop the assumption that the quantity and quality of resources and technology are fixed, the production possibilities curve shifts positions—that is, the potential maximum output of the economy changes.

Increases in Resource Supplies   Although resource supplies are fixed at any specific moment, they can and do change over time. For example, a nation's growing population will bring about increases in the supplies of labor and entrepreneurial ability. Also, labor quality usually improves over time. Historically, the economy's stock of capital has increased at a significant, though unsteady, rate. And although we are depleting some of our energy and mineral resources, new sources are being discovered.

The development of irrigation programs, for example, adds to the supply of arable land.

The net result of these increased supplies of the factors of production is the ability to produce more of both pizzas and robots. Thus 20 years from now, the production possibilities in Table 2.2 may supersede those shown in Table 2.1. The greater abundance of resources will result in a greater potential output of one or both products at each alternative. Society will have achieved economic growth in the form of expanded potential output.

But such a favorable change in the production possibilities data does not *guarantee* that the economy will actually operate at a point on its new production possibilities curve. Some 135 million jobs will give the United States full employment now, but 10 or 20 years from now its labor force will be larger, and 135 million jobs will not be sufficient for full employment. The production possibilities curve may shift, but at the future date the economy may fail to produce at a point on that new curve.

Advances in Technology
Our second assumption is that we have constant, unchanging technology. In reality, though, technology has progressed dramatically over time. An advancing technology brings both new and better goods *and* improved ways of producing them. For now, let's think of technological advances as being only improvements in capital facilities—more efficient machinery and equipment. These advances alter our previous discussion of the economizing problem by improving productive efficiency, thereby allowing society to produce more goods with fixed resources. As with increases in resource supplies, technological advances make possible the production of more robots *and* more pizzas.

Thus, when either supplies of resources increase or an improvement in technology occurs, the pro-

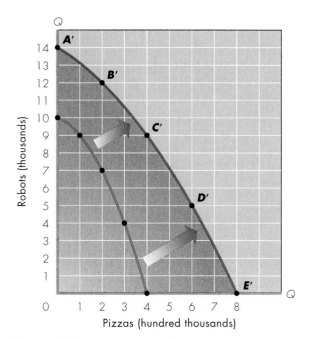

Figure 2.4

Economic growth and the production possibilities curve. The increase in supplies of resources, the improvements in resource quality, and the technological advances that occur in a dynamic economy move the production possibilities curve outward and to the right, allowing the economy to have larger quantities of both types of goods.

duction possibilities curve in Figure 2.3 shifts outward and to the right, as illustrated by curve A', B', C', D', E' in Figure 2.4. Such an outward shift of the production possibilities curve represents growth of economic capacity or, simply, **economic growth:** *the ability to produce a larger total output.* This growth is the result of (1) increases in supplies of resources, (2) improvements in resource quality, and (3) technological advances.

The consequence of growth is that our full-employment economy can enjoy a greater output of both robots and pizzas. *While a static, no-growth economy must sacrifice some of one product in order to get more of another, a dynamic, growing economy can have larger quantities of both products.*

Economic growth does not ordinarily mean proportionate increases in a nation's capacity to produce all its products. Note in Figure 2.4 that, at the maximums, the economy can produce twice as many pizzas as before but only 40 percent more robots. To reinforce your understanding of this concept, sketch in two new production possibilities curves: one show-

Table 2.2

Production Possibilities of Pizza and Robots with Full Employment and Productive Efficiency

Type of Product	Production Alternatives				
	A'	B'	C'	D'	E'
Pizzas (in hundred thousands)	0	2	4	6	8
Robots (in thousands)	14	12	9	5	0

ing the situation where a better technique for producing robots has been developed while the technology for producing pizzas is unchanged, and the other illustrating an improved technology for pizzas while the technology for producing robots remains constant.

Present Choices and Future Possibilities   An economy's current choice of positions on its production possibilities curve is a basic determinant of the future location of that curve. Let's designate the two axes of the production possibilities curve as *goods for the future* and *goods for the present*, as in Figure 2.5. Goods for the future are such things as capital goods, research and education, and preventive medicine. They increase the quantity and quality of property resources, enlarge the stock of technological information, and improve the quality of human resources. As we have already seen, goods for the future, like industrial robots, are the ingredients of economic growth. Goods for the present are pure consumer goods, such as pizza, clothing, and soft drinks.

Now suppose there are two economies, Alta and Zorn, which are initially identical in every respect except one: Alta's current choice of positions on its production possibilities curve strongly favors present

goods over future goods. Point *A* in Figure 2.5a indicates that choice. It is located quite far down the curve to the right, indicating a high priority for goods for the present, at the expense of fewer goods for the future. Zorn, in contrast, makes a current choice that stresses larger amounts of future goods and smaller amounts of present goods, as shown by point *Z* in Figure 2.5b.

Now, other things equal, we can expect the future production possibilities curve of Zorn to be farther to the right than Alta's curve. By currently choosing an output more favorable to technological advances and to increases in the quantity and quality of resources, Zorn will achieve greater economic growth than Alta. In terms of capital goods, Zorn is choosing to make larger current additions to its "national factory"—to invest more of its current output—than Alta. The payoff from this choice for Zorn is more rapid growth—greater future production capacity. The opportunity cost is fewer consumer goods in the present for Zorn to enjoy.

Is Zorn's choice thus "better" than Alta's? That, we cannot say. The different outcomes simply reflect different preferences and priorities in the two countries. **(Key Questions 10 and 11)** ✓ 2.2

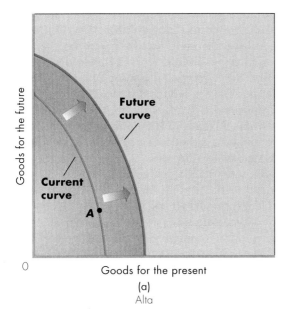
(a)
Alta

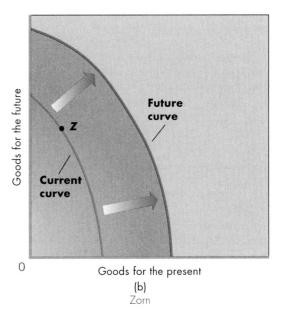
(b)
Zorn

Figure 2.5
An economy's present choice of positions on its production possibilities curve helps determine the curve's future location.   A nation's current choice favoring "present goods," as made by Alta in (a), will cause a modest outward shift of the curve in the future. A nation's current choice favoring "future goods," as made by Zorn in (b), will result in a greater outward shift of the curve in the future.

A Qualification: International Trade

Production possibilities analysis implies that an individual nation is limited to the combinations of output indicated by its production possibilities curve. *But we must modify this principle when international specialization and trade exist.*

You will see in later chapters that an economy can avoid, through international specialization and trade, the output limits imposed by its domestic production possibilities curve. *International specialization* means directing domestic resources to output that a nation is highly efficient at producing. *International trade* involves the exchange of these goods for goods produced abroad. Specialization and trade enable a nation to get more of a desired good at less sacrifice of some other good. Rather than sacrifice 3 robots to get a third unit of pizza, as in Table 2.1, a nation might be able to obtain the third unit of pizza by trading only 2 units of robots for it. Specialization and trade have the same effect as having more and better resources or discovering improved production techniques; both increase the quantities of capital and consumer goods available to society. The output gains from greater international specialization and trade are the equivalent of economic growth.

QUICK REVIEW 2.3

■ Unemployment and the failure to achieve productive efficiency cause an economy to operate at a point inside its production possibilities curve.

■ Increases in resource supplies, improvements in resource quality, and technological advance cause economic growth, which are depicted as an outward shift of the production possibilities curve.

■ An economy's present choice of capital and consumer goods helps determine the future location of its production possibilities curve. (See Global Perspective 2.1.)

■ International specialization and trade enable a nation to obtain more goods than its production possibilities curve indicates.

Examples and Applications

There are many possible applications and examples relating to the production possibilities model. We will discuss just a few of them.

Unemployment and Productive Inefficiency Almost all nations have at one point or another experienced widespread unemployment of resources. That is, they have operated inside of their production possibilities curves. In the depths of the Great Depression of the 1930s, one-quarter of U.S. workers were unemployed and one-third of U.S. production capacity was idle. In the last half of the 1990s, several countries (for example, Argentina, Japan, Mexico, and South Korea) operated inside their production possibilities curves, at least temporarily, because of substantial declines in economic activity.

Economies that experience substantial discrimination based on race, ethnicity, and gender do not achieve productive efficiency, and thus they operate inside their production possibilities curves. Because discrimination prevents those discriminated against from obtaining jobs that best use their skills, society has less output than otherwise. Eliminating discrimination would move such an economy from a point inside its production possibilities curve toward a point on its curve. Similarly, economies in which labor usage and production methods are based on custom, heredity, and caste, rather than on efficiency, operate well inside their production possibilities curves.

Tradeoffs and Opportunity Costs Many current controversies illustrate the tradeoffs and opportunity costs indicated by movements along a particular production possibilities curve. (Any two categories of "output" can be placed on the axes of production possibilities curves.) Should scenic land be used for logging and mining or be preserved as wilderness? If the land is used for logging and mining, the opportunity cost is the forgone benefits of wilderness. If the land is used for wilderness, the opportunity cost is the lost value of the wood and minerals that society forgoes.

Should society devote more resources to the criminal justice system (police, courts, and prisons) or to education (teachers, books, and schools)? If society devotes more resources to the criminal justice system, other things equal, the opportunity cost is forgone improvements in education. If more resources are allocated to education, the opportunity cost is the forgone benefits from an improved criminal justice system. If we decide to devote more resources to both, what other goods and services do we forgo? ▐ 2.2

Shifts in Production Possibilities Curves The United States has recently experienced a spurt of new technologies relating to computers, communications, and biotechnology. Technological advances have dropped the prices of computers and greatly enhanced their speed. Cellular phones and the Internet have increased communications capacity, enhancing production and improving the efficiency of markets. Advances in biotechnology, specifically genetic engineering, have resulted in important agricultural and medical discoveries. Many economists believe these new technologies are so significant that they are contributing to faster-than-normal U.S. economic growth (faster rightward shifts of the nation's production possibilities curve).

In some circumstances a nation's production possibilities curve can collapse inward. For example, in the late 1990s Yugoslavian forces began to "ethnically cleanse" Kosovo by driving out its Muslim residents. A decisive military response by the United States and its allies eventually pushed Yugoslavia out of Kosovo. The military action also devastated Yugoslavia's economy. Allied bombing inflicted great physical damage on Yugoslavia's production facilities and its system of roads, bridges, and communications. Consequently, Yugoslavia's production possibilities curve shifted inward.

GLOBAL PERSPECTIVE 2.1

Investment and Economic Growth, Selected Countries

Nations that invest large portions of their national output tend to enjoy high growth rates, measured here by output per person. Additional capital goods make workers more productive, which means greater output per person.

Source: International Monetary Fund data, as reported in *Economic Report of the President, 1994,* p. 37.

■ Economic Systems

Every society needs to develop an **economic system**—*a particular set of institutional arrangements and a coordinating mechanism*—to respond to the economizing problem. Economic systems differ as to (1) who owns the factors of production and (2) the method used to coordinate and direct economic activity. There are two general types of economic systems: the market system and the command system.

The Market System

The private ownership of resources and the use of markets and prices to coordinate and direct economic activity characterize the **market system,** or **capitalism.** In that system each participant acts in his or her own self-interest; each individual or business seeks to maximize its satisfaction or profit through its own decisions regarding consumption or production. The system allows for the private ownership of capital, communicates through prices, and coordinates economic activity through *markets*—places where buyers and sellers come together. Goods and services are produced and resources are supplied by whoever is willing and able to do so. The result is competition among independently acting buyers and sellers of each product and resource. Thus, economic decision making is widely dispersed.

In *pure* capitalism—or *laissez-faire* capitalism—government's role would be limited to protecting private property and establishing an environment appropriate to the operation of the market system. The term "laissez-faire" means "let it be," that is, keep government from interfering with the economy. The idea is that such interference will disturb the efficient working of the market system. ⚿ 2.3

But in the capitalism practiced in the United States and most other countries, government plays a substantial role in the economy. It not only provides the rules for economic activity but also promotes economic stability and growth, provides certain goods and services that would otherwise be underproduced or not produced at all, and modifies the distribution of income. The government, however, is not the dominant economic force in deciding what to produce, how to produce it, and who will get it. That force is the market.

The Command System

The alternative to the market system is the **command system,** also known as *socialism* or *communism.* In that system, government owns most property resources and economic decision making occurs through a central economic plan. A central planning board appointed by the government makes nearly all the major decisions concerning the use of resources, the composition and distribution of output, and the organization of production. The government owns most of the business firms, which produce according to government directives. A central planning board determines production goals for each enterprise and specifies the amount of resources to be allocated to each enterprise so that it can reach its production goals. The division of output between capital and consumer goods is centrally decided, and capital goods are allocated among industries on the basis of the central planning board's long-term priorities.

A *pure* command economy would rely exclusively on a central plan to allocate the government-owned property resources. But, in reality, even the preeminent command economy—the Soviet Union—tolerated some private ownership and incorporated some markets before its demise in 1992. Recent reforms in Russia and most of the eastern European nations have to one degree or another transformed their command economies to capitalistic, market-oriented systems. China's reforms have not gone as far, but they have reduced the reliance on central planning. Although there is still extensive government ownership of resources and capital in China, the nation has increasingly relied on free markets to organize and coordinate its economy. North Korea and Cuba are the last remaining examples of largely centrally planned economies.

▍The Circular Flow Model

Because nearly all the major nations now use the market system, we need to gain a good understanding of how this system operates. Our goal in the remainder of this chapter is to identify the market economy's decision makers and major markets. In Chapter 3 we will explain how prices are established in individual markets. Then in Chapter 4 we will detail the characteristics of the market system and explain how the system addresses the economizing problem.

As shown in **Figure 2.6 (Key Graph),** the market economy has two groups of decision makers: *households* and *businesses.* (We will add government as a third decision maker in Chapter 5.) It also has two broad markets: the *resource market* and the *product market.*

The upper half of the diagram represents the **resource market:** *the place where resources or the services of resource suppliers are bought and sold.* In the resource market, households sell resources and businesses demand them. Households (that is, people) own all economic resources either directly as workers or entrepreneurs or indirectly through their ownership of business corporations. They sell their resources to businesses, which buy them because they are necessary for producing goods and services. The funds that businesses pay for resources are costs to businesses but are flows of wage, rent, interest, and profit income to the households. Resources therefore flow from households to businesses, and money flows from businesses to households.

Next consider the lower part of the diagram, which represents the **product market:** *the place where goods and services produced by businesses are bought and sold.* In the product market, businesses combine the resources they have obtained to produce and sell goods and services. Households use the income they have received from the sale of resources to buy goods and services. The monetary flow of consumer spending on goods and services yields sales revenues for businesses.

The **circular flow model** suggests a complex, interrelated web of decision making and economic activity involving businesses and households. Businesses and households are both buyers and sellers. Businesses buy resources and sell products. Households buy products and sell resources. As shown in Figure 2.6, there is a counterclockwise *real flow* of economic resources and finished goods and services, and a clockwise *money flow* of income and consumption expenditures. These flows are simultaneous and repetitive. 🔑 2.4

KEY GRAPH

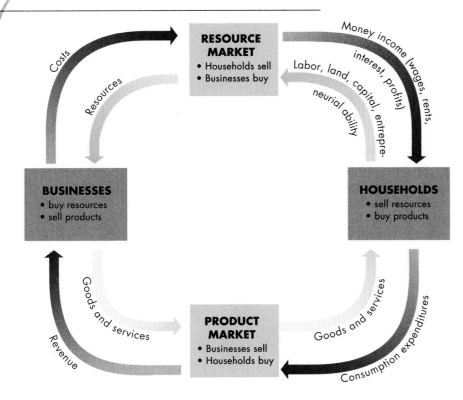

Figure 2.6

The circular flow diagram.

Resources flow from households to businesses through the resource market, and products flow from businesses to households through the product market. Opposite these real flows are monetary flows. Households receive income from businesses (their costs) through the resource market, and businesses receive revenue from households (their expenditures) through the product market.

Women and Expanded Production Possibilities

A Large Increase in the Number of Employed Women Has Shifted the U.S. Production Possibilities Curve Outward.

One of the more remarkable trends of the past half-century in the United States has been the substantial rise in the number of women working in the paid workforce. Today, 60 percent of women work full-time or part-time in paid jobs, compared to only 40 percent in 1965. There are many reasons for this increase.

Women's Rising Wage Rates Over recent years, women have greatly increased their productivity in the workplace, mostly by becoming better educated and professionally trained. As a result, they can earn higher wages. Because those higher wages have increased the opportunity costs—the forgone wage earnings—of staying at home, women have substituted employment in the labor market for more "expensive" traditional home activities. This substitution has been particularly pronounced among married women.

Women's higher wages and longer hours away from home have produced creative reallocations of time and purchasing patterns. Day care services have partly replaced personal child care. Restaurants, take-home meals, and pizza delivery often substitute for traditional home cooking. Convenience stores and catalog and Internet sales have proliferated, as have lawn-care and in-home cleaning services. Microwave ovens, dishwashers, automatic washers and dryers, and other household "capital goods" enhance domestic productivity.

Expanded Job Access Greater access to jobs is a second factor increasing the employment of women. Service industries—teaching, nursing, and clerical work, for instance—that traditionally have employed mainly women have expanded in the past several decades. Also, the population in general has shifted from farms and rural regions to urban areas, where jobs for women are more abundant and more geographically accessible. The decline in the average length of the workweek and the increased availability of part-time jobs have also made it easier for women to combine labor market employment with child-rearing and household activities.

Changing Preferences and Attitudes Women collectively have changed their preferences from household activities to employment in the labor market. Many find personal fulfillment in jobs, careers,

and earnings, as evidenced by the huge influx of women into law, medicine, business, and other professions. More broadly, most industrial societies now widely accept and encourage labor-force participation by women, including those with very young children. Today about 65 percent of American mothers with preschool children participate in the labor force, compared to only 30 percent in 1970. More than half return to work before their youngest child has reached the age of 2.

Declining Birthrates There were 3.8 lifetime births per woman in 1957 at the peak of the baby boom. Today the number is less than 2. This marked decline in the size of the typical family, the result of changing lifestyles and the widespread availability of birth control, has freed up time for greater labor-force participation by women. Not only do women now have fewer children; their children are spaced closer together in age. Thus women who leave their jobs during their children's early years can return to the labor force sooner. Higher wage rates have also been at work. On average, women with relatively high wage earnings have fewer children than women with lower earnings. The opportunity cost of children—the income sacrificed by not being employed—rises as wage earnings rise. In the language of economics, the higher "price" associated with children has reduced the "quantity" of children demanded.

Rising Divorce Rates Marital instability, as evidenced by high divorce rates, may have motivated many women to enter and remain in the labor market. Because alimony and child-support payments are often erratic or nonexistent, the economic impact of divorce on nonworking women may be disastrous. Most nonworking women enter the labor force for the first time following divorce. And many married women—perhaps even women contemplating marriage—may have joined the labor force to protect themselves against the financial difficulties of potential divorce.

Slower Growth of Male Wages The earnings of many low-wage and middle-wage male workers grew slowly or even fell in the United States over the past three decades. Many wives may have entered the labor force to ensure the rise of household living standards. The median income of couples with children grew 25 percent between 1969 and 1996. Without the mothers' incomes, that growth would have been only 2 percent. A related issue is that couples of all income levels may be concerned about their family incomes compared to those of other families. So the entry of some women into the labor force may have encouraged still other women to enter in order to maintain their families' *relative* standard of living.

Taken together, these factors have produced a rapid rise in the presence of women workers in the United States. This increase in the *quantity of resources* has helped push the U.S. production possibilities curve outward. In other words, it has contributed greatly to U.S. economic growth.

SUMMARY

1. Economics is grounded on two basic facts: (a) economic wants are virtually unlimited; (b) economic resources are scarce.

2. Economic resources may be classified as property resources—raw materials and capital—or as human resources—labor and entrepreneurial ability. These resources constitute the factors of production.

3. Economics is concerned with the problem of using or managing scarce resources to produce the goods and services that satisfy the material wants of society. Both full employment and the efficient use of available resources are essential to maximize want satisfaction.

4. Efficient use of resources consists of productive efficiency (producing all output combinations in the least costly way) and allocative efficiency (producing the specific output mix most desired by society).

5. An economy that is achieving full employment and productive efficiency—one that is operating on its production possibilities curve—must sacrifice the output of some types of goods and services in order to increase the production of others. Because resources are not equally productive in all possible uses, shifting resources from one use to another brings the law of increasing opportunity costs into play. The production of additional units of one product requires the sacrifice of *increasing* amounts of the other product.

6. Allocative efficiency means operating at the optimal point on the production possibilities curve. That point

represents the highest-valued mix of goods and is determined by expanding the production of each good until its marginal benefit (MB) equals its marginal cost (MC).

7. Over time, technological advances and increases in the quantity and quality of resources enable the economy to produce more of all goods and services—that is, to experience economic growth. Society's choice as to the mix of consumer goods and capital goods in current output is a major determinant of the future location of the production possibilities curve and thus of economic growth.

8. The market system and the command system are the two broad types of economic systems used to address the economizing problem. In the market system (or capitalism) private individuals own most resources and markets coordinate most economic activity. In the command system (or socialism or communism), government owns most resources and central planners coordinate most economic activity.

9. The circular flow model locates the product and resource markets and shows the major real and money flows between businesses and households. Businesses are on the buying side of the resource market and the selling side of the product market. Households are on the selling side of the resource market and the buying side of the product market.

TERMS AND CONCEPTS

economizing problem	factors of production	production possibilities table	economic system
utility	full employment	production possibilities curve	market system
economic resources	full production	opportunity cost	capitalism
land	productive efficiency	law of increasing opportunity costs	command system
capital	allocative efficiency	economic growth	resource market
investment	consumer goods		product market
labor	capital goods		circular flow model
entrepreneurial ability			

STUDY QUESTIONS

1. Explain this statement: "If resources were unlimited and were freely available, there would be no subject called *economics.*"

2. Comment on the following statement from a newspaper article: "Our junior high school serves a splen-

did hot meal for $1 without costing the taxpayers anything, thanks in part to a government subsidy."

3. Critically analyze: "Wants aren't insatiable. I can prove it. I get all the coffee I want to drink every morning at breakfast." Explain: "Goods and services

are scarce because resources are scarce." Analyze: "It is the nature of all economic problems that absolute solutions are denied to us."

4. What are economic resources? What are the major functions of the entrepreneur?

5. **Key Question** Why is the problem of unemployment part of the subject matter of economics? Distinguish between productive efficiency and allocative efficiency. Give an illustration of achieving productive, but not allocative, efficiency.

6. **Key Question** Here is a production possibilities table for war goods and civilian goods:

Type of Production	Production Alternatives				
	A	B	C	D	E
Automobiles	0	2	4	6	8
Rockets	30	27	21	12	0

 a. Show these data graphically. Upon what specific assumptions is this production possibilities curve based?

 b. If the economy is at point C, what is the cost of one more automobile? One more rocket? Explain how the production possibilities curve reflects the law of increasing opportunity costs.

 c. What must the economy do to operate at some point on the production possibilities curve?

7. What is the opportunity cost of attending college? In 2000 nearly 80 percent of college-educated Americans held jobs, whereas only about 40 percent of those who did not finish high school held jobs. How might this difference relate to opportunity costs?

8. Suppose you arrive at a store expecting to pay $100 for an item but learn that a store 2 miles away is charging $50 for it. Would you drive there and buy it? How does your decision benefit you? What is the opportunity cost of your decision? Now suppose you arrive at a store expecting to pay $6000 for an item but discover that it costs $5950 at the other store. Do you make the same decision as before? Perhaps surprisingly, you should! Explain why.

9. **Key Question** Specify and explain the shapes of the marginal-benefit and marginal-cost curves. How are these curves used to determine the optimal allocation of resources to a particular product? If current output is such that marginal cost exceeds marginal benefit, should more or fewer resources be allocated to this product? Explain.

10. **Key Question** Label point G inside the production possibilities curve you drew in question 6. What does it indicate? Label point H outside the curve. What does that point indicate? What must occur before the

economy can attain the level of production shown by point H?

11. **Key Question** Referring again to question 6, suppose improvement occurs in the technology of producing rockets but not in the technology of producing automobiles. Draw the new production possibilities curve. Now assume that a technological advance occurs in producing automobiles but not in producing rockets. Draw the new production possibilities curve. Now draw a production possibilities curve that reflects technological improvement in the production of both products.

12. Explain how, if at all, each of the following events affects the location of the production possibilities curve:
 a. Standardized examination scores of high school and college students decline.
 b. The unemployment rate falls from 9 to 6 percent of the labor force.
 c. Defense spending is reduced to allow government to spend more on health care.
 d. A new technique improves the efficiency of extracting copper from ore.

13. Explain: "Affluence tomorrow requires sacrifice today."

14. Suppose that, on the basis of a nation's production possibilities curve, an economy must sacrifice 10,000 pizzas domestically to get the 1 additional industrial robot it desires but that it can get the robot from another country in exchange for 9000 pizzas. Relate this information to the following statement: "Through international specialization and trade, a nation can reduce its opportunity cost of obtaining goods and thus 'move outside its production possibilities curve.'"

15. Contrast how a market system and a command economy try to cope with economic scarcity.

16. Distinguish between the resource market and the product market in the circular flow model. In what way are businesses and households both *sellers and buyers* in this model? What are the flows in the circular flow model?

17. **(Last Word)** Which two of the six reasons listed in the Last Word do you think are the *most important* in explaining the rise in participation of women in the workplace? Explain your reasoning.

18. **Web-Based Question: *More labor resources— What is the evidence for the United States and France?*** Go to the Bureau of Labor Statistics' website at www.bls.gov/ and click Data and then Most Requested Data. Retrieve U.S. employment data (CPS) for the period of the last 10 years. How many more workers were there at the end of the 10-year period than at the beginning? Next, return to Most Requested Data and click Foreign Labor Statistics. Find the total employment growth of France over the

last 10 years. In which of the two countries did "more labor resources" have the greatest impact on the nation's production possibilities curve over the 10 years?

19. **Web-Based Question:** *Relative size of the military—who's incurring the largest opportunity cost?* To obtain military goods, a nation must sacrifice civilian goods. Of course, that sacrifice may be worthwhile in terms of national defense and protection of national interests. Go to the Central Intelligence Agency's website, www.odci.gov/cia/publications/factbook/index.html, to determine the amount of military expenditures and military expenditures as a percentage of GDP for each of the following five nations: Brazil, Japan, North Korea, Russia, and the United States. Which one is bearing the greatest opportunity cost?

3

Individual Markets
Demand and Supply

A CCORDING TO AN old joke, if you teach a parrot to say "demand and supply," you have an economist. There is an element of truth in this quip. The tools of demand and supply can take us far in understanding both specific economic issues and how the entire economy works. 🔑 3.1 ▦ With our circular flow model in Chapter 2, we identified the participants in the product market and resource market. We asserted that prices are determined by the "interaction" between buyers and sellers in those markets. In this chapter we examine that interaction in detail and explain how prices and output quantities are determined.

▌ Markets

Recall from Chapter 2 that a **market** is *an institution or mechanism that brings together buyers ("demanders") and sellers ("suppliers") of particular goods, services, or resources.* Markets exist in many forms. The corner gas station, e-commerce sites, the local music store, a farmer's roadside stand—all are familiar markets. The New York Stock Exchange and the Chicago Board of Trade are markets where buyers and sellers of stocks and bonds and farm commodities from all over the world communicate with one another to buy and sell. Auctioneers bring together potential buyers and sellers of art, livestock, used farm equipment, and, sometimes, real estate. In labor markets, the quarterback and his agent bargain with the owner of an NFL team. A graduating finance major interviews with Citicorp or Wells Fargo at the university placement office.

All situations that link potential buyers with potential sellers are markets. Some markets are local, while others are national or international. Some are highly personal, involving face-to-face contact between demander and supplier; others are impersonal, with buyer and seller never seeing or knowing each other.

To keep things simple, we will focus in this chapter on markets consisting of large numbers of independently acting buyers and sellers of standardized products. These are the highly competitive markets such as a central grain exchange, a stock market, or a market for foreign currencies in which the price is "discovered" through the interacting decisions of buyers and sellers. They are *not* the markets in which one or a handful of producers "set" prices, such as the markets for commercial airplanes or operating software for personal computers.

▌Demand

Demand is *a schedule or a curve that shows the various amounts of a product that consumers are willing and able to purchase at each of a series of possible prices during a specified period of time.*[1] Demand shows the quantities of a product that will be purchased at various possible prices, *other things equal*. Demand can easily be shown in table form. Table 3.1 is a hypothetical **demand schedule** for a *single consumer* purchasing bushels of corn.

Table 3.1 reveals the relationship between the various prices of corn and the quantity of corn a particular consumer would be willing and able to purchase at each of these prices. We say "willing and able" because willingness alone is not effective in the market. You may be willing to buy a digital camera, but if that willingness is not backed by the necessary dollars, it will not be effective and, therefore, will not be reflected in the market. In Table 3.1, if the price of corn were $5 per bushel, our consumer would be willing and able to buy 10 bushels per week; if it were $4, the consumer would be willing and able to buy 20 bushels per week; and so forth.

Table 3.1 does not tell us which of the five possible prices will actually exist in the corn market. That depends on demand and supply. Demand is simply a statement of a buyer's plans, or intentions, with respect to the purchase of a product.

To be meaningful, the quantities demanded at each price must relate to a specific period—a day, a week, a month. Saying "A consumer will buy 10 bushels of corn at $5 per bushel" is meaningless. Saying "A consumer will buy 10 bushels of corn per week at $5 per bushel" is meaningful. Unless a specific time period is stated, we do not know whether the demand for a product is large or small.

Table 3.1

An Individual Buyer's Demand for Corn

Price per Bushel	Quantity Demanded per Week
$5	10
4	20
3	35
2	55
1	80

---

[1]This definition obviously is worded to apply to product markets. To adjust it to apply to resource markets, substitute the word "resource" for "product" and the word "businesses" for "consumers."

Law of Demand

A fundamental characteristic of demand is this: *All else equal, as price falls, the quantity demanded rises, and as price rises, the quantity demanded falls.* In short, there is a negative or *inverse* relationship between price and quantity demanded. Economists call this inverse relationship the **law of demand.** 🔑 3.2

The other-things-equal assumption is critical here. Many factors other than the price of the product being considered affect the amount purchased. The quantity of Nikes purchased will depend not only on the price of Nikes but also on the prices of such substitutes as Reeboks, Adidas, and Filas. The law of demand in this case says that fewer Nikes will be purchased if the price of Nikes rises *and if the prices of Reeboks, Adidas, and Filas all remain constant.* In short, if the *relative price* of Nikes rises, fewer Nikes will be bought. However, if the price of Nikes and the prices of all other competing shoes increase by some amount—say, $5—consumers might buy more, less, or the same amount of Nikes.

Why the inverse relationship between price and quantity demanded? Let's look at three explanations, beginning with the simplest one:

- The law of demand is consistent with common sense. People ordinarily *do* buy more of a product at a low price than at a high price. Price is an obstacle that deters consumers from buying. The higher that obstacle, the less of a product they will buy; the lower the price obstacle, the more they will buy. The fact that businesses have "sales" is evidence of their belief in the law of demand.

- In any specific time period, each buyer of a product will derive less satisfaction (or benefit, or utility) from each successive unit of the product consumed. The second Big Mac will yield less satisfaction to the consumer than the first, and the third still less than the second. That is, consumption is subject to **diminishing marginal utility.** And because successive units of a particular product yield less and less marginal utility, consumers will buy additional units only if the price of those units is progressively reduced. 🔑 3.3

- We can also explain the law of demand in terms of income and substitution effects. The **income effect** indicates that a lower price increases the purchasing power of a buyer's money income, enabling the buyer to purchase more of the product than she or he could buy before. A higher price has the opposite effect. The **substitution effect** suggests that at a lower price buyers have the incentive to substitute what is now a less expensive product for similar products that are now *relatively* more expensive. The product whose price has fallen is now "a better deal" relative to the other products.

For example, a decline in the price of chicken will increase the purchasing power of consumer incomes, enabling people to buy more chicken (the income effect). At a lower price, chicken is relatively more attractive and consumers tend to substitute it for pork, mutton, beef, and fish (the substitution effect). The income and substitution effects combine to make consumers able and willing to buy more of a product at a low price than at a high price. 🔑 **3.4**

The Demand Curve

The inverse relationship between price and quantity demanded for any product can be represented on a simple graph, in which, by convention, we measure *quantity demanded* on the horizontal axis and *price* on the vertical axis. In Figure 3.1 we have plotted the five price-quantity data points listed in Table 3.1 and connected the points with a smooth curve, labeled *D*. Such a curve is called a **demand curve.** Its downward slope reflects the law of demand—people buy more of a product, service, or resource as its price falls. The relationship between price and quantity demanded is inverse.

Table 3.1 and Figure 3.1 contain exactly the same data and reflect the same relationship between price and quantity demanded. But the graph shows that relationship more simply and clearly than a table or a description in words.

Market Demand

So far, we have concentrated on just one consumer. But competition requires that more than one buyer be present in each market. By adding the quantities demanded by all consumers at each of the various possible prices, we can get from *individual* demand to *market* demand. If there are just three buyers in the market, as represented in Table 3.2, it is relatively easy to determine the total quantity demanded at each price. Figure 3.2 shows the graphical summing procedure: At each price we add the individual quantities demanded to obtain the total quantity demanded at that price; we then plot the price and the total quantity demanded as one point of the market demand curve.

Competition, of course, ordinarily entails many more than three buyers of a product. To avoid hundreds or thousands or millions of additions, we suppose that all the buyers in a market are willing and able to buy the same amounts at each of the possible prices. Then we just multiply those amounts by the number of buyers to obtain the market demand. This is the way we arrived at curve D_1 in Figure 3.3, for a market with 200 corn buyers whose demand is

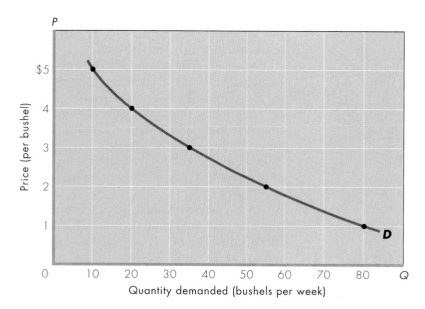

Figure 3.1

An individual buyer's demand for corn. Because price and quantity demanded are inversely related, an individual's demand schedule graphs as a downsloping curve such as *D*. Specifically, the law of demand says that, other things equal, consumers will buy more of a product as its price declines. Here and in later figures, *P* stands for price, and *Q* stands for quantity (either demanded or supplied).

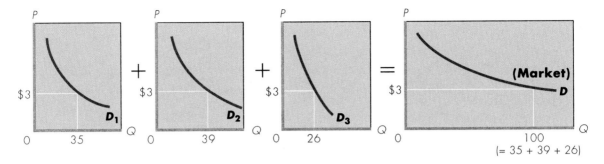

Figure 3.2

Market demand for corn, three buyers. We establish the market demand curve D by adding horizontally the individual demand curves (D₁, D₂, and D₃) of all the consumers in the market. At the price of $3, for example, the three individual curves yield a total quantity demanded of 100 bushels.

that shown in Table 3.1. Table 3.3 shows the calculations.

In constructing a demand curve such as D_1 in Figure 3.3, economists assume that price is the most important influence on the amount of any product purchased. But economists know that other factors can and do affect purchases. These factors, called **determinants of demand,** are assumed to be constant when a demand curve like D_1 is drawn. They are the "other things equal" in the relationship between price and quantity demanded. When any of these determinants changes, the demand curve will shift to the right or left. For this reason, determinants of demand are sometimes referred to as *demand shifters.*

The basic determinants of demand are (1) consumers' tastes (preferences), (2) the number of consumers in the market, (3) consumers' incomes, (4) the prices of related goods, and (5) consumer expectations about future prices and incomes.

Change in Demand

A change in one or more of the determinants of demand will change the demand data (the demand schedule) in Table 3.3 and therefore the location of the demand curve in Figure 3.3. A change in the demand schedule or, graphically, a shift in the demand curve is called a *change in demand.*

If consumers desire to buy more corn at each possible price than is reflected in column 4 in Table 3.3, that *increase in demand* is shown as a shift of the demand curve to the right, say, from D_1 to D_2. Conversely, a *decrease in demand* occurs when consumers buy less corn at each possible price than is indicated in column 4, Table 3.3. The leftward shift of the demand curve from D_1 to D_3 in Figure 3.3 shows that situation.

Now let's see how changes in each determinant affect demand.

Table 3.2
Market Demand for Corn, Three Buyers

Price per Bushel	Quantity Demanded — First Buyer		Second Buyer		Third Buyer		Total Quantity Demanded per Week
$5	10	+	12	+	8	=	30
4	20	+	23	+	17	=	60
3	35	+	39	+	26	=	100
2	55	+	60	+	39	=	154
1	80	+	87	+	54	=	221

Table 3.3
Market Demand for Corn, 200 Buyers

(1) Price per Bushel	(2) Quantity Demanded per Week, Single Buyer		(3) Number of Buyers in the Market		(4) Total Quantity Demanded per Week
$5	10	×	200	=	2,000
4	20	×	200	=	4,000
3	35	×	200	=	7,000
2	55	×	200	=	11,000
1	80	×	200	=	16,000

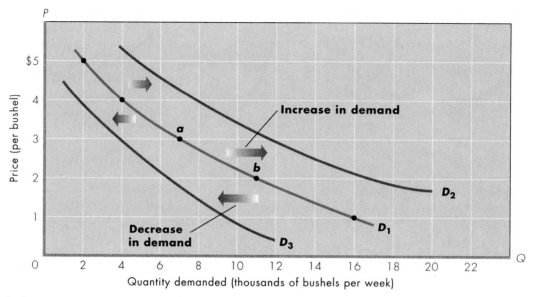

Figure 3.3

Changes in the demand for corn.   A change in one or more of the determinants of demand causes a change in demand. An increase in demand is shown as a shift of the demand curve to the right, as from D_1 to D_2. A decrease in demand is shown as a shift of the demand curve to the left, as from D_1 to D_3. These changes in demand are to be distinguished from a change in quantity demanded, which is caused by a change in the price of the product, as shown by a movement from, say, point a to point b on fixed demand curve D_1.

Tastes

A favorable change in consumer tastes (preferences) for a product—a change that makes the product more desirable—means that more of it will be demanded at each price. Demand will increase; the demand curve will shift rightward. An unfavorable change in consumer preferences will decrease demand, shifting the demand curve to the left.

New products may affect consumer tastes; for example, the introduction of compact discs greatly decreased the demand for cassette tapes. Consumers' concern over the health hazards of cholesterol and obesity have increased the demand for broccoli, low-calorie sweeteners, and fresh fruit while decreasing the demand for beef, veal, eggs, and whole milk. Over the past several years, the demand for coffee drinks, bottled water, and sports utility vehicles has greatly increased, driven by a change in tastes. So, too, has the demand for leather jackets and fleece outerwear.

Number of Buyers

An increase in the number of buyers in a market increases demand. A decrease in the number of buyers in a market decreases demand. For example, improvements in communications have given financial markets international range

and have thus increased the demand for stocks and bonds. And the baby boom after the Second World War increased demand for diapers, baby lotion, and the services of obstetricians. When the baby boomers reached their twenties in the 1970s, the demand for housing increased. Conversely, the aging of the baby boomers in the 1980s and 1990s was a factor in the relative slump in the demand for housing in those decades. Also, an increase in life expectancy has increased the demand for medical care, retirement communities, and nursing homes. And international trade agreements have reduced foreign trade barriers to American farm commodities, thus increasing the demand for those products.

Income

How changes in income affect demand is a more complex matter. For most products, a rise in income causes an increase in demand. Consumers typically buy more steaks, furniture, and computers as their incomes increase. Conversely, the demand for such products declines as their incomes fall. Products whose demand varies *directly* with money income are called *superior goods*, or **normal goods.**

Although most products are normal goods, there are some exceptions. As incomes increase beyond some point, the demand for used clothing, retread tires, and third-hand automobiles may decrease, because the higher incomes enable consumers to buy new versions of those products. Rising incomes may also decrease the demand for soy-enhanced hamburger. Similarly, rising incomes may cause the demand for charcoal grills to decline as wealthier consumers switch to gas grills. Goods whose demand varies *inversely* with money income are called **inferior goods.**

Prices of Related Goods

A change in the price of a related good may either increase or decrease the demand for a product, depending on whether the related good is a substitute or a complement:

- A **substitute good** is one that can be used in place of another good.
- A **complementary good** is one that is used together with another good.

Substitutes Beef and chicken are examples of substitute goods or, simply, *substitutes*. When the price of beef rises, consumers buy less beef, increasing the demand for chicken. Conversely, as the price of beef falls, consumers buy more beef, decreasing the demand for chicken. *When two products are substitutes, the price of one and the demand for the other move in the same direction.* So it is with pairs such as Nikes and Reeboks, Colgate and Crest, Toyotas and Hondas, and Coke and Pepsi. So-called *substitution in consumption* occurs when the price of one good rises relative to the price of a similar good.

Complements Complementary goods (or, simply, *complements*) are goods that are used together and are usually demanded together. If the price of gasoline falls and, as a result, you drive your car more often, the extra driving increases your demand for motor oil. Thus, gas and motor oil are jointly demanded; they are complements. So it is with ham and eggs, tuition and textbooks, movies and popcorn, cameras and film. *When two products are complements, the price of one good and the demand for the other good move in opposite directions.*

Unrelated Goods The vast majority of goods that are not related to one another are called *independent goods*. Examples are butter and golf balls, potatoes and automobiles, and bananas and wristwatches. A change in the price of one does not affect the demand for the other.

Expectations Changes in consumer expectations may shift demand. A newly formed expectation of higher future prices may cause consumers to buy now in order to "beat" the anticipated price rises, thus increasing current demand. For example, when freezing weather destroys much of Florida's citrus crop, consumers may reason that the price of orange juice will rise. They may stock up on orange juice by purchasing large quantities now. In contrast, a newly formed expectation of falling prices or falling income may decrease current demand for products.

Similarly, a change in expectations relating to future product availability may affect current demand. In late December 1999 there was a substantial increase in the demand for gasoline. Reason? Motorists became concerned that the Y2K computer problem might disrupt fuel pumps or credit card systems.

Finally, a change in expectations concerning future income may prompt consumers to change their current spending. For example, first-round NFL draft choices may splurge on new luxury cars in anticipation of a lucrative professional football contract. Or workers who become fearful of losing their jobs may reduce their demand for, say, vacation travel.

In summary, an *increase* in demand—the decision by consumers to buy larger quantities of a product at each possible price—may be caused by:

- A favorable change in consumer tastes.
- An increase in the number of buyers.
- Rising incomes if the product is a normal good.
- Falling incomes if the product is an inferior good.
- An increase in the price of a substitute good.
- A decrease in the price of a complementary good.
- A new consumer expectation that either prices or income will be higher in the future.

You should "reverse" these generalizations to explain a *decrease* in demand. Table 3.4 provides additional illustrations of the determinants of demand. **(Key Question 2)**

Changes in Quantity Demanded

A *change in demand* must not be confused with a *change in quantity demanded.* A **change in demand** is a shift of the entire demand curve to the right (an increase in demand) or to the left (a decrease in

Table 3.4

Determinants of Demand: Factors That Shift the Demand Curve

Determinant	Examples
Change in buyer tastes	Physical fitness rises in popularity, increasing the demand for jogging shoes and bicycles; Latin American music becomes more popular, increasing the demand for Latin CDs.
Change in number of buyers	A decline in the birthrate reduces the demand for childrens' toys.
Change in income	A rise in incomes increases the demand for such normal goods as butter, lobster, and filet mignon while reducing the demand for such inferior goods as cabbage, turnips, and inexpensive wine.
Change in the prices of related goods	A reduction in airfares reduces the demand for bus transportation (substitute goods); a decline in the price of compact disc players increases the demand for compact discs (complementary goods).
Change in expectations	Inclement weather in South America creates an expectation of higher future prices of coffee beans, thereby increasing today's demand for coffee beans.

demand). It occurs because the consumer's state of mind about purchasing the product has been altered in response to a change in one or more of the determinants of demand. Recall that "demand" is a schedule or a curve; therefore, a "change in demand" means a change in the entire schedule and a shift of the entire curve.

In contrast, a **change in quantity demanded** is a movement from one point to another point—from one price-quantity combination to another—on a fixed demand schedule or demand curve. The cause of such a change is an increase or decrease in the price of the product under consideration. In Table 3.3, for example, a decline in the price of corn from $5 to $4 will increase the quantity of corn demanded from 2000 to 4000 bushels.

In Figure 3.3 the shift of the demand curve D_1 to either D_2 or D_3 is a change in demand. But the movement from point a to point b on curve D_1 rep-

resents a change in quantity demanded: *demand has not changed; it is the entire curve, and it remains fixed in place.*

QUICK REVIEW 3.1

■ A market is any arrangement that facilitates the purchase and sale of goods, services, or resources.

■ Demand is a schedule or a curve showing the amount of a product that buyers are willing and able to purchase, in a particular time period, at each possible price in a series of prices.

■ The law of demand states that, other things equal, the quantity of a good purchased varies inversely with its price.

■ The demand curve shifts because of changes in (a) consumer tastes, (b) the number of buyers in the market, (c) consumer income, (d) the prices of substitute or complementary goods, and (e) consumer expectations.

■ A change in demand is a shift of the entire demand curve; a change in quantity demanded is a movement from one point to another on a demand curve.

■ Supply

Supply is *a schedule or curve showing the amounts of a product that producers are willing and able to make available for sale at each of a series of possible prices during a specific period.*[2] Table 3.5 is a hypothetical **supply schedule** for a single producer of corn. It shows the quantities of corn that will be supplied at various prices, other things equal.

Table 3.5

An Individual Producer's Supply of Corn

Price per Bushel	Quantity Supplied per Week
$5	60
4	50
3	35
2	20
1	5

[2]This definition is worded to apply to product markets. To adjust it to apply to resource markets, substitute "resource" for "product" and "owners" for "producers."

Law of Supply

Table 3.5 shows a positive or direct relationship that prevails between price and quantity supplied. *As price rises, the quantity supplied rises; as price falls, the quantity supplied falls.* This relationship is called the **law of supply.** A supply schedule tells us that firms will produce and offer for sale more of their product at a high price than at a low price. This, again, is basically common sense.

Price is an obstacle from the standpoint of the consumer, who is on the paying end. The higher the price, the less the consumer will buy. But the supplier is on the receiving end of the product's price. To a supplier, price represents *revenue*, which serves as an incentive to produce and sell a product. The higher the price, the greater this incentive and the greater the quantity supplied.

Consider a farmer who can shift resources among alternative products. As price moves up, as shown in Table 3.5, the farmer finds it profitable to take land out of wheat, oats, and soybean production and put it into corn. And the higher corn prices enable the farmer to cover the increased costs associated with more intensive cultivation and the use of more seed, fertilizer, and pesticides. The overall result is more corn.

Now consider a manufacturer. Beyond some quantity of production, manufacturers usually encounter increasing costs per added unit of output. Certain productive resources—in particular, the firm's plant and machinery—cannot be expanded quickly, so the firm uses more of other resources, such as labor, to produce more output. But as time passes, the existing plant becomes increasingly crowded and congested. As a result, each added worker produces less added output, and the cost of successive units of output rises accordingly. The firm will not produce the more costly units unless it receives a higher price for them. Again, price and quantity supplied are directly related.

The Supply Curve

As with demand, it is convenient to represent supply graphically. In Figure 3.4, curve S_1 is a graph of the market supply data given in Table 3.6. Those data assume there are 200 suppliers in the market,

Table 3.6

Market Supply of Corn, 200 Producers

(1) Price per Bushel	(2) Quantity Supplied per Week, Single Producer		(3) Number of Sellers in the Market		(4) Total Quantity Supplied per Week
$5	60	×	200	=	12,000
4	50	×	200	=	10,000
3	35	×	200	=	7,000
2	20	×	200	=	4,000
1	5	×	200	=	1,000

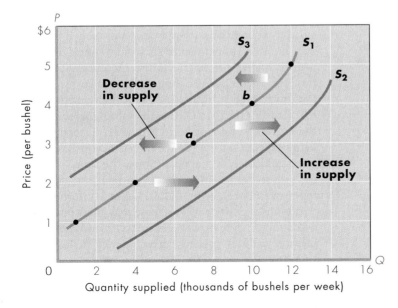

Figure 3.4

Changes in the supply of corn. A change in one or more of the determinants of supply causes a change in supply. An increase in supply is shown as a rightward shift of the supply curve, as from S_1 to S_2. A decrease in supply is depicted as a leftward shift of the curve, as from S_1 to S_3. In contrast, a change in the *quantity supplied* is caused by a change in the product's price and is shown by a movement from one point to another, as from *a* to *b*, on a fixed supply curve.

each willing and able to supply corn according to Table 3.5. We obtain the market **supply curve** by horizontally adding the supply curves of the individual producers. Note that the axes in Figure 3.4 are the same as those used in our graph of market demand (Figure 3.3), except for the change from "quantity demanded" to "quantity supplied" on the horizontal axis.

Determinants of Supply

In constructing a supply curve, we assume that price is the most significant influence on the quantity supplied of any product. But other factors (the "other things equal") can and do affect supply. The supply curve is drawn on the assumption that these other things are fixed and do not change. If one of them does change, a *change in supply* will occur, meaning that the entire supply curve will shift.

The basic **determinants of supply** are (1) resource prices, (2) technology, (3) taxes and subsidies, (4) prices of other goods, (5) price expectations, and (6) the number of sellers in the market. A change in any one or more of these determinants of supply, or *supply shifters*, will move the supply curve for a product either right or left. A shift to the *right*, as from S_1 to S_2 in Figure 3.4, signifies an *increase* in supply: Producers supply larger quantities of the product at each possible price. A shift to the *left*, as from S_1 to S_3, indicates a *decrease* in supply: Producers offer less output at each price.

Changes in Supply

Let's consider how changes in each of the determinants affect supply. The key idea is that costs are a major factor underlying supply curves; anything that affects costs (other than changes in output itself) usually shifts the supply curve.

Resource Prices   The prices of the resources used in the production process help determine the costs of production incurred by firms. Higher *resource* prices raise production costs and, assuming a particular *product* price, squeeze profits. That reduction in profits reduces the incentive for firms to supply output at each product price. For example, an increase in the prices of iron ore and coke will increase the cost of producing steel and reduce its supply.

In contrast, lower *resource* prices reduce production costs and increase profits. So when resource prices fall, firms supply greater output at each product price. For example, a decrease in the prices of seed and fertilizer will increase the supply of corn.

Technology   Improvements in technology (techniques of production) enable firms to produce units of output with fewer resources. Because resources are costly, using fewer of them lowers production costs and increases supply. Example: Recent improvements in the fuel efficiency of aircraft engines have reduced the cost of providing passenger air service. Thus, airlines now offer more flights than previously at each ticket price; the supply of air service has increased.

Taxes and Subsidies   Businesses treat most taxes as costs. An increase in sales or property taxes will increase production costs and reduce supply. In contrast, subsidies are "taxes in reverse." If the government subsidizes the production of a good, it in effect lowers the producers' costs and increases supply.

Prices of Other Goods   Firms that produce a particular product, say, soccer balls, can sometimes use their plant and equipment to produce alternative goods, say, basketballs and volleyballs. The higher prices of these "other goods" may entice soccer ball producers to switch production to those other goods in order to increase profits. This *substitution in production* results in a decline in the supply of soccer balls. Alternatively, when the prices of basketballs and volleyballs decline relative to the price of soccer balls, producers of those goods may decide to produce more soccer balls instead, increasing their supply.

Price Expectations   Changes in expectations about the future price of a product may affect the producer's current willingness to supply that product. It is difficult, however, to generalize about how a new expectation of higher prices affects the present supply of a product. Farmers anticipating a higher corn price in the future might withhold some of their current corn harvest from the market, thereby causing a decrease in the current supply of corn. Similarly, if people suddenly expect that the price of Amazon.com stock will rise significantly in the near future, the supply offered for sale today might decrease. In contrast, in many types of manufacturing industries, newly formed expectations that price will increase may induce firms to add another shift of workers or to expand their production facilities, causing current supply to increase.

Number of Sellers   Other things equal, the larger the number of suppliers, the greater the market supply. As more firms enter an industry, the supply curve shifts to the right. Conversely, the smaller the number of firms in the industry, the less the market supply. This means that as firms leave an industry, the supply curve shifts to the left. Example: The United States and Canada have imposed restrictions on haddock fishing to replenish dwindling stocks. As part of that policy, the Federal government has bought the boats of some of the haddock fishers as a way of putting them out of business and decreasing the catch. The result has been a decline in the market supply of haddock.

Table 3.7 is a checklist of the determinants of supply, along with further illustrations. (**Key Question 5**)

Table 3.7

Determinants of Supply: Factors That Shift the Supply Curve

Determinant	Examples
Change in resource prices	A decrease in the price of microchips increases the supply of computers; an increase in the price of crude oil reduces the supply of gasoline.
Change in technology	The development of more effective wireless technology increases the supply of cell phones.
Changes in taxes and subsidies	An increase in the excise tax on cigarettes reduces the supply of cigarettes; a decline in subsidies to state universities reduces the supply of higher education.
Change in prices of other goods	An increase in the price of cucumbers decreases the supply of watermelons.
Change in expectations	An expectation of a substantial rise in future log prices decreases the supply of logs today.
Change in number of suppliers	An increase in the number of Internet service providers increases the supply of such services; the formation of women's professional basketball leagues increases the supply of women's professional basketball games.

Changes in Quantity Supplied

The distinction between a *change in supply* and a *change in quantity supplied* parallels the distinction between a change in demand and a change in quantity demanded. Because supply is a schedule or curve, a **change in supply** means a change in the entire schedule and a shift of the entire curve. An increase in supply shifts the curve to the right; a decrease in supply shifts it to the left. The cause of a change in supply is a change in one or more of the determinants of supply.

In contrast, a **change in quantity supplied** is a movement from one point to another on a fixed supply curve. The cause of such a movement is a change in the price of the specific product being considered. In Table 3.6, a decline in the price of corn from $5 to $4 decreases the quantity of corn supplied per week from 12,000 to 10,000 bushels. This is a change in quantity supplied, not a change in supply. *Supply is the full schedule of prices and quantities shown, and this schedule does not change when price changes.*

QUICK REVIEW 3.2

■ A supply schedule or curve shows that, other things equal, the quantity of a good supplied varies directly with its price.

■ The supply curve shifts because of changes in (a) resource prices, (b) technology, (c) taxes or subsidies, (d) prices of other goods, (e) expectations of future prices, and (f) the number of suppliers.

■ A change in supply is a shift of the supply curve; a change in quantity supplied is a movement from one point to another on a fixed supply curve.

▌ Supply and Demand: Market Equilibrium

We can now bring together supply and demand to see how the buying decisions of households and the selling decisions of businesses interact to determine the price of a product and the quantity actually bought and sold. In Table 3.8, columns 1 and 2 repeat the market supply of corn (from Table 3.6), and columns 2 and 3 repeat the market demand for corn (from Table 3.3). We assume that this is a competitive market—neither buyers nor sellers can set the price.

Table 3.8

Market Supply of and Demand for Corn

(1) Total Quantity Supplied per Week	(2) Price per Bushel	(3) Total Quantity Demanded per Week	(4) Surplus (+) or Shortage (−)*
12,000	$5	2,000	+10,000 ↓
10,000	4	4,000	+6,000 ↓
7,000	**3**	**7,000**	**0**
4,000	2	11,000	−7,000 ↑
1,000	1	16,000	−15,000 ↑

*Arrows indicate the effect on price.

Surpluses

We have limited our example to only five possible prices. Of these, which will actually prevail as the market price for corn? We can find an answer through trial and error. For no particular reason, let's start with $5. We see immediately that this cannot be the prevailing market price. At the $5 price, producers are willing to produce and offer for sale 12,000 bushels of corn, but buyers are willing to buy only 2000 bushels. The $5 price encourages farmers to produce lots of corn but discourages most consumers from buying it. The result is a 10,000-bushel **surplus** or *excess supply* of corn. This surplus, shown in column 4 of Table 3.8, is the excess of quantity supplied over quantity demanded at $5. Corn farmers would find themselves with 10,000 unsold bushels of output.

A price of $5, even if it existed temporarily in the corn market, could not persist over a period of time. The very large surplus of corn would prompt competing sellers to lower the price to encourage buyers to take the surplus off their hands.

Suppose the price goes down to $4. The lower price encourages consumers to buy more corn and, at the same time, induces farmers to offer less of it for sale. The surplus diminishes to 6000 bushels. Nevertheless, since there is still a surplus, competition among sellers will once again reduce the price. Clearly, then, the prices of $5 and $4 will not survive because they are "too high." The market price of corn must be less than $4.

Shortages

Let's jump now to $1 as the possible market price of corn. Observe in column 4 of Table 3.8 that at this price, quantity demanded exceeds quantity supplied

by 15,000 units. The $1 price discourages farmers from devoting resources to corn production and encourages consumers to attempt to buy more than is available. The result is a 15,000-bushel **shortage** of, or *excess demand* for, corn. The $1 price cannot persist as the market price. Many consumers who want to buy at this price will not get corn. They will express a willingness to pay more than $1 to get some of the available output. Competition among these buyers will drive up the price to something greater than $1.

Suppose the competition among buyers boosts the price to $2. This higher price will reduce, but will not eliminate, the shortage of corn. For $2, farmers devote more resources to corn production, and some buyers who were willing to pay $1 per bushel will not want to buy corn at $2. But a shortage of 7000 bushels still exists at $2. This shortage will push the market price above $2.

Equilibrium Price and Quantity

By trial and error we have eliminated every price but $3. At $3, *and only at this price*, the quantity of corn that farmers are willing to produce and supply is identical with the quantity consumers are willing and able to buy. There is neither a shortage nor a surplus of corn at that price.

With no shortage or surplus at $3, there is no reason for the price of corn to change. Economists call this price the *market-clearing* or **equilibrium price**, "equilibrium" meaning "in balance" or "at rest." At $3, quantity supplied and quantity demanded are in balance at the **equilibrium quantity** of 7000 bushels. So $3 is the only stable price of corn under the supply and demand conditions shown in Table 3.8.

The price of corn, or of any other product bought and sold in competitive markets, will be established where the supply decisions of producers and the demand decisions of buyers are mutually consistent. Such decisions are consistent only at the equilibrium price (here, $3) and equilibrium quantity (here, 7000 bushels). At any higher price, suppliers want to sell more than consumers want to buy and a surplus results; at any lower price, consumers want to buy more than producers make available for sale and a shortage results. Such discrepancies between the supply and demand intentions of sellers and buyers then prompt price changes that bring the two sets of intentions into accord.

A graphical analysis of supply and demand should yield the same conclusions. **Figure 3.5 (Key**

KEY GRAPH

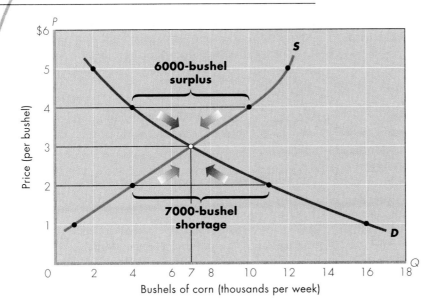

Figure 3.5
Equilibrium price and quantity.
The intersection of the downsloping demand curve D and the upsloping supply curve S indicates the equilibrium price and quantity, here $3 and 7000 bushels of corn. The shortages of corn at below-equilibrium prices (for example, 7000 bushels at $2) drive up price. The higher prices increase the quantity supplied and reduce the quantity demanded until equilibrium is achieved. The surpluses caused by above-equilibrium prices (for example, 6000 bushels at $4) push price down. As price drops, the quantity demanded rises and the quantity supplied falls until equilibrium is established. At the equilibrium price and quantity, there are neither shortages nor surpluses of corn.

Quick Quiz 3.5

1. Demand curve D is downsloping because:
   a. producers offer less of a product for sale as the price of the product falls.
   b. lower prices of a product create income and substitution effects that lead consumers to purchase more of it.
   c. the larger the number of buyers in a market, the lower the product price.
   d. price and quantity demanded are directly (positively) related.

2. Supply curve S:
   a. reflects an inverse (negative) relationship between price and quantity supplied.
   b. reflects a direct (positive) relationship between price and quantity supplied.
   c. depicts the collective behavior of buyers in this market.
   d. shows that producers will offer more of a product for sale at a low product price than at a high product price.

3. At the $3 price:
   a. quantity supplied exceeds quantity demanded.
   b. quantity demanded exceeds quantity supplied.
   c. the product is abundant and a surplus exists.
   d. there is no pressure on price to rise or fall.

4. At price $5 in this market:
   a. there will be a shortage of 10,000 units.
   b. there will be a surplus of 10,000 units.
   c. quantity demanded will be 12,000 units.
   d. quantity demanded will equal quantity supplied.

Answers: 1. b; 2. b; 3. d; 4. b

Graph) shows the market supply and demand curves for corn on the same graph. (The horizontal axis now measures both quantity demanded and quantity supplied.)

Graphically, the intersection of the supply curve and the demand curve for a product indicates the market equilibrium. Here, equilibrium price and quantity are $3 per bushel and 7000 bushels. At any above-equilibrium price, quantity supplied exceeds quantity demanded. This surplus of corn causes price re-ductions by sellers who are eager to rid themselves of their surplus. The falling price causes less corn to be offered and simultaneously encourages consumers to buy more. The market moves to its equilibrium.

Any price below the equilibrium price creates a shortage; quantity demanded then exceeds quantity supplied. Buyers try to obtain the product by offer-ing to pay more for it; this drives the price upward toward its equilibrium level. The rising price simul-taneously causes producers to increase the quantity supplied and prompts many buyers to leave the market, thus eliminating the shortage. Again the market moves to its equilibrium. ⬐ 3.1 ⯒ 3.1

Rationing Function of Prices

The ability of the competitive forces of supply and demand to establish a price at which selling and buying decisions are consistent is called the **rationing function of prices.** In our case, the equilibrium price of $3 clears the market, leaving no burdensome surplus for sellers and no inconvenient shortage for potential buyers. And it is the combination of freely made individual decisions that sets this market-clearing price. In effect, the market outcome says that all buyers who are willing and able to pay $3 for a bushel of corn will obtain it; all buyers who cannot or will not pay $3 will go without corn. Similarly, all producers who are willing and able to offer corn for sale at $3 a bushel will sell it; all producers who cannot or will not sell for $3 per bushel will not sell their product. **(Key Question 7)**

Changes in Supply, Demand, and Equilibrium

We know that demand might change because of fluctuations in consumer tastes or incomes, changes in consumer expectations, or variations in the prices of related goods. Supply might change in response to changes in resource prices, technology, or taxes. What effects will such changes in supply and demand have on equilibrium price and quantity?

Changes in Demand Suppose that supply is constant and demand increases, as shown in Figure 3.6a. As a result, the new intersection of the supply and demand curves is at higher values on both the price and the quantity axes. Clearly, an increase in demand raises both equilibrium price and equilibrium quantity. Conversely, a decrease in demand, such as that shown in Figure 3.6b, reduces both equilibrium price and equilibrium quantity. (The value of graphical analysis is now apparent: We need not fumble with columns of figures to determine the outcomes; we need only compare the new and the old points of intersection on the graph.)

Changes in Supply Now suppose that demand is constant but supply increases, as in Figure 3.6c. The new intersection of supply and demand is located at a lower equilibrium price but at a higher

equilibrium quantity. An increase in supply reduces equilibrium price but increases equilibrium quantity. In contrast, if supply decreases, as in Figure 3.6d, the equilibrium price rises while the equilibrium quantity declines.

Complex Cases When both supply and demand change, the effect is a combination of the individual effects.

Supply Increase; Demand Decrease What effect will a supply increase and a demand decrease have on equilibrium price? Both changes decrease price, so the net result is a price drop greater than that resulting from either change alone.

What about equilibrium quantity? Here the effects of the changes in supply and demand are opposed: the increase in supply increases equilibrium quantity, but the decrease in demand reduces it. The direction of the change in quantity depends on the relative sizes of the changes in supply and demand. If the increase in supply is larger than the decrease in demand, the equilibrium quantity will increase. But if the decrease in demand is greater than the increase in supply, the equilibrium quantity will decrease.

Supply Decrease; Demand Increase A decrease in supply and an increase in demand both increase price. Their combined effect is an increase in equilibrium price greater than that caused by either change separately. But their effect on equilibrium quantity is again indeterminate, depending on the relative sizes of the changes in supply and demand. If the decrease in supply is larger than the increase in demand, the equilibrium quantity will decrease. In contrast, if the increase in demand is greater than the decrease in supply, the equilibrium quantity will increase.

Supply Increase; Demand Increase What if supply and demand both increase? A supply increase drops equilibrium price, while a demand increase boosts it. If the increase in supply is greater than the increase in demand, the equilibrium price will fall. If the opposite holds, the equilibrium price will rise.

The effect on equilibrium quantity is certain: The increases in supply and in demand each raise equilibrium quantity. Therefore, the equilibrium quantity will increase by an amount greater than that caused by either change alone.

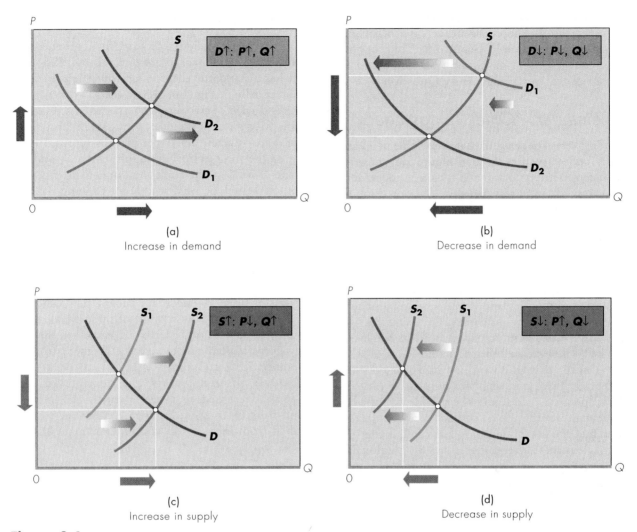

Figure 3.6

Changes in demand and supply and the effects on price and quantity. The increase in demand from D_1 to D_2 in (a) increases both equilibrium price and equilibrium quantity. The decrease in demand from D_1 to D_2 in (b) decreases both equilibrium price and equilibrium quantity. The increase in supply from S_1 to S_2 in (c) decreases equilibrium price and increases equilibrium quantity. The decline in supply from S_1 to S_2 in (d) increases equilibrium price and decreases equilibrium quantity. The boxes in the top right corners summarize the respective changes and outcomes. The upward arrows in the boxes signify increases in demand (D), supply (S), equilibrium price (P), and equilibrium quantity (Q); the downward arrows signify decreases in these items.

Supply Decrease; Demand Decrease What about decreases in both supply and demand? If the decrease in supply is greater than the decrease in demand, equilibrium price will rise. If the reverse is true, equilibrium price will fall. Because decreases in supply and in demand each reduce equilibrium quantity, we can be sure that equilibrium quantity will fall.

Table 3.9 summarizes these four cases. To understand them fully, you should draw supply and demand diagrams for each case to confirm the effects listed in Table 3.9.

Table 3.9

Effects of Changes in Both Supply and Demand

Change in Supply	Change in Demand	Effect on Equilibrium Price	Effect on Equilibrium Quantity
1. Increase	Decrease	Decrease	Indeterminate
2. Decrease	Increase	Increase	Indeterminate
3. Increase	Increase	Indeterminate	Increase
4. Decrease	Decrease	Indeterminate	Decrease

Special cases arise when a decrease in demand and a decrease in supply, or an increase in demand and an increase in supply, exactly cancel out. In both cases, the net effect on equilibrium price will be zero; price will not change. **(Key Question 8)**

A Reminder: "Other Things Equal"

We must stress once again that specific demand and supply curves (such as those in Figure 3.6) show relationships between prices and quantities demanded and supplied, *other things equal*. The downsloping demand curves tell us that price and quantity demanded are inversely related, other things equal. The upsloping supply curves imply that price and quantity supplied are directly related, other things equal.

If you forget the other-things-equal assumption, you can encounter situations that *seem* to be in conflict with these basic principles. For example, suppose salsa manufacturers sell 1 million bottles of salsa at $4 a bottle in 1 year; 2 million bottles at $5 in the next year; and 3 million at $6 in the year thereafter. Price and quantity purchased vary directly, and these data seem to be at odds with the law of demand. But there is no conflict here; the data do not refute the law of demand. The catch is that the law of demand's other-things-equal assumption has been violated over the 3 years in the example. Specifically, because of changing tastes and rising incomes, the demand for salsa has increased sharply, as in Figure 3.6a. The result is higher prices *and* larger quantities purchased.

Another example: The price of coffee occasionally has shot upward at the same time that the quantity of coffee produced has declined. These events seemingly contradict the direct relationship between price and quantity denoted by supply. The catch again is that the other-things-equal assumption underlying the upsloping supply curve was violated. Poor coffee harvests decreased supply, as in Figure 3.6d, increasing the equilibrium price of coffee and reducing the equilibrium quantity.

These examples emphasize the importance of our earlier distinction between a change in quantity demanded (or supplied) and a change in demand (supply). In Figure 3.6a a change in demand causes a change in the quantity supplied. In Figure 3.6d a change in supply causes a change in quantity demanded.

Application: Pink Salmon

To reinforce these ideas, let's briefly examine a real-world market: the market for pink salmon. This market has a standardized product, for which price has substantially declined in recent years.

A decade or two ago, fishers earned a relatively high price for each pound of pink salmon brought to the dock. In Figure 3.7 that price is represented as P_1, at the intersection of supply curve S_1 and demand curve D_1. The corresponding quantity of pink salmon—the type used mainly for canning—is represented as Q_1 pounds.

Over the past few decades, supply and demand shifted in the market for pink salmon. On the supply side, improved technology in the form of larger, more efficient fishing boats greatly increased the catch and lowered the cost of obtaining it. Also, high profits at price P_1 encouraged many new fishers to enter the industry. As a result of these changes, the supply of pink salmon greatly increased and the supply curve shifted to the right, as from S_1 to S_2 in Figure 3.7.

Over the same years, the demand for pink salmon decreased, as represented by the leftward shift from D_1 to D_2 in Figure 3.7. That decrease resulted from increases in consumer income and re-

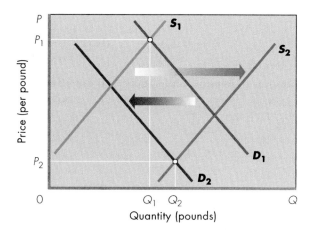

Figure 3.7

The market for pink salmon. In the last two decades, the supply of pink salmon has increased and the demand for pink salmon has decreased. As a result, the price of pink salmon has declined, here from P_1 to P_2 a pound. Since supply has increased more than demand has declined, the equilibrium quantity of pink salmon has increased, here from Q_1 to Q_2.

Ticket Scalping: A Bum Rap?

Some Market Transactions Get a Bad Name That Is Not Warranted.

Tickets to athletic and artistic events are sometimes resold at higher-than-original prices—a market transaction known by the term "scalping." For example, the original buyer may resell a $50 ticket to a college bowl game for $200, $250, or more. The media often denounce scalpers for "ripping off" buyers by charging "exorbitant" prices. Scalping and extortion are synonymous in some people's minds.

But is scalping really sinful? We must first recognize that such ticket resales are voluntary transactions. Both buyer and seller expect to gain from the exchange. Otherwise, it would not occur! The seller must value the $200 more than seeing the event, and the buyer must value seeing the event more than the $200.

So there are no losers or victims here: Both buyer and seller benefit from the transaction. The "scalping" market simply redistributes assets (game or concert tickets) from those who value them less to those who value them more.

Does scalping impose losses or injury on other parties, in particular the sponsors of the event? If the sponsors are injured, it is because they initially priced tickets below the equilibrium level. In so doing, they suffer an economic loss in the form of less revenue and profit than they might have otherwise received. But the loss is self-inflicted because of their pricing error. That mistake is quite separate and distinct from the fact that some tickets are later resold at a higher price.

What about spectators? Does scalping deteriorate the enthusiasm of the audience? Usually not! People who have the greatest interest in the event will pay the scalper's high prices. Ticket scalping also benefits the teams and performing artists, because they will appear before more dedicated audiences—ones that are more likely to buy souvenir items or CDs.

So is ticket scalping undesirable? Not on economic grounds. Both seller and buyer of a "scalped" ticket benefit, and a more interested audience results. Event sponsors may sacrifice revenue and profits, but that stems from their own misjudgment of the equilibrium price.

---

ductions in the price of substitute products. As buyers' incomes increased, consumers shifted demand away from canned fish and toward higher-quality fresh or frozen fish, including higher-quality species of salmon such as Atlantic, Chinook, and Coho salmon. Moreover, the emergence of fish farming, in which salmon are raised in net pens, lowered the prices of these substitute species. That, too, reduced the demand for pink salmon.

The increased supply of, and decreased demand for, pink salmon greatly reduced the price, as represented by the drop from P_1 to P_2 in Figure 3.7. Both the supply increase and the demand decrease helped reduce the equilibrium price. However, the equilibrium *quantity* of pink salmon increased, as represented by the move from Q_1 to Q_2. Both shifts of the curves reduced the equilibrium price, but equilibrium quantity increased because the increase in supply exceeded the decrease in demand.

QUICK REVIEW 3.3

◼ In competitive markets, prices adjust to the equilibrium level at which quantity demanded equals quantity supplied.

◼ The equilibrium price and quantity are those indicated by the intersection of the supply and demand curves for any product or resource.

◼ An increase in demand increases equilibrium price and quantity; a decrease in demand decreases equilibrium price and quantity.

◼ An increase in supply reduces equilibrium price but increases equilibrium quantity; a decrease in supply increases equilibrium price but reduces equilibrium quantity.

◼ Over time, equilibrium price and quantity may change in directions that seem at odds with the laws of demand and supply because the other-things-equal assumption is violated.

SUMMARY

1. A market is any institution or arrangement that brings together buyers and sellers of a product, service, or resource.

2. Demand is a schedule or curve representing the willingness of buyers in a specific period to purchase a particular product at each of various prices. The law of demand implies that consumers will buy more of a product at a low price than at a high price. Therefore, other things equal, the relationship between price and quantity demanded is negative or inverse and is graphed as a downsloping curve. Market demand curves are found by adding horizontally the demand curves of the many individual consumers in the market.

3. Changes in one or more of the determinants of demand (consumer tastes, the number of buyers in the market, the money incomes of consumers, the prices of related goods, and price expectations) shift the market demand curve. A shift to the right is an increase in demand; a shift to the left is a decrease in demand. A change in demand is different from a change in the quantity demanded, the latter being a movement from one point to another point on a fixed demand curve because of a change in the product's price.

4. Supply is a schedule or curve showing the amounts of a product that producers are willing to offer in the market at each possible price during a specific period. The law of supply states that, other things equal, producers will offer more of a product at a high price than at a low price. Thus, the relationship between price and quantity supplied is positive or direct, and supply is graphed as an upsloping curve. The market supply curve is the horizontal summation of the supply curves of the individual producers of the product.

5. Changes in one or more of the determinants of supply (resource prices, production techniques, taxes or subsidies, the prices of other goods, price expectations, or the number of sellers in the market) shift the supply curve of a product. A shift to the right is an increase in supply; a shift to the left is a decrease in supply. In contrast, a change in the price of the product being considered causes a change in the quantity supplied, which is shown as a movement from one point to another point on a fixed supply curve.

6. The equilibrium price and quantity are established at the intersection of the supply and demand curves. The interaction of market demand and market supply adjusts the price to the point at which the quantities demanded and supplied are equal. This is the equilibrium price. The corresponding quantity is the equilibrium quantity.

7. The ability of market forces to synchronize selling and buying decisions to eliminate potential surpluses and shortages is known as the rationing function of prices.

8. A change in either demand or supply changes the equilibrium price and quantity. Increases in demand raise both equilibrium price and equilibrium quantity; decreases in demand lower both equilibrium price and equilibrium quantity. Increases in supply lower equilibrium price and raise equilibrium quantity; decreases in supply raise equilibrium price and lower equilibrium quantity.

9. Simultaneous changes in demand and supply affect equilibrium price and quantity in various ways, depending on their direction and relative magnitudes.

TERMS AND CONCEPTS

market	determinants of demand	supply	surplus
demand	normal goods	supply schedule	shortage
demand schedule	inferior goods	law of supply	equilibrium price
law of demand	substitute good	supply curve	equilibrium quantity
diminishing marginal utility	complementary good	determinants of supply	rationing function of prices
income effect	change in demand	change in supply	
substitution effect	change in quantity demanded	change in quantity supplied	
demand curve			

STUDY QUESTIONS

1. Explain the law of demand. Why does a demand curve slope downward? What are the determinants of demand? What happens to the demand curve when each of these determinants changes? Distinguish between a change in demand and a change in the quantity demanded, noting the cause(s) of each.

2. **Key Question** What effect will each of the following have on the demand for product B?

a. Product B becomes more fashionable.

b. The price of substitute product C falls.

c. Income declines and product B is an inferior good.

d. Consumers anticipate that the price of B will be lower in the near future.

e. The price of complementary product D falls.

f. Foreign tariff barriers on product B are eliminated.

3. Explain the following news dispatch from Hull, England: "The fish market here slumped today to what local commentators called 'a disastrous level'—all because of a shortage of potatoes. The potatoes are one of the main ingredients in a dish that figures on almost every café-menu—fish and chips [French fries]."

4. Explain the law of supply. Why does the supply curve slope upward? What are the determinants of supply? What happens to the supply curve when each of these determinants changes? Distinguish between a change in supply and a change in the quantity supplied, noting the cause(s) of each.

5. **Key Question** What effect will each of the following have on the supply of product B?

a. A technological advance in the methods of producing product B.

b. A decline in the number of firms in industry B.

c. An increase in the prices of resources required in the production of B.

d. The expectation that the equilibrium price of B will be lower in the future than it is currently.

e. A decline in the price of product A, a good whose production requires substantially the same techniques and resources as does the production of B.

f. The levying of a specific sales tax on B.

g. The granting of a 50-cent-per-unit subsidy for each unit of B produced.

6. "In the corn market, demand often exceeds supply and supply sometimes exceeds demand." "The price of corn rises and falls in response to changes in supply and demand." In which of these two statements are the terms "supply" and "demand" used correctly? Explain.

7. **Key Question** Suppose the total demand for wheat and the total supply of wheat per month in the Kansas City grain market are as follows:

Thousands of Bushels Demanded	Price per Bushel	Thousands of Bushels Supplied	Surplus (+) or Shortage (−)
85	$3.40	72	_____
80	$3.70	73	_____
75	$4.00	75	_____
70	$4.30	77	_____
65	$4.60	79	_____
60	$4.90	81	_____

a. What is the equilibrium price? What is the equilibrium quantity? Fill in the surplus-shortage column and use it to explain why your answers are correct.

b. Graph the demand for wheat and the supply of wheat. Be sure to label the axes of your graph correctly. Label equilibrium price *P* and equilibrium quantity *Q*.

c. Why will $3.40 not be the equilibrium price in this market? Why not $4.90? "Surpluses drive prices up; shortages drive them down." Do you agree?

d. Now suppose that the government establishes a ceiling (maximum legal) price of, say, $3.70 for wheat. Explain carefully the effects of this ceiling price. Demonstrate your answer graphically. What might prompt the government to establish a ceiling price?

8. **Key Question** How will each of the following changes in demand and/or supply affect equilibrium price and equilibrium quantity in a competitive market; that is, do price and quantity rise, fall, or remain unchanged, or are the answers indeterminate because they depend on the magnitudes of the shifts? Use supply and demand diagrams to verify your answers.

a. Supply decreases and demand is constant.

b. Demand decreases and supply is constant.

c. Supply increases and demand is constant.

d. Demand increases and supply increases.

e. Demand increases and supply is constant.

f. Supply increases and demand decreases.

g. Demand increases and supply decreases.

h. Demand decreases and supply decreases.

9. "Prices are the automatic regulator that tends to keep production and consumption in line with each other." Explain.

10. Explain: "Even though parking meters may yield little or no net revenue, they should nevertheless be retained because of the rationing function they perform."

11. Use two market diagrams to explain how an increase in state subsidies to public colleges might affect tuition and enrollments in both public and private colleges.

12. Critically evaluate: "In comparing the two equilibrium positions in Figure 3.6a, I note that a larger amount is actually purchased at a higher price. This refutes the law of demand."

13. Suppose you go to a recycling center and are paid $.25 per pound for your aluminum cans. However, the recycling firm charges you $.20 per bundle to accept your old newspapers. Use demand and supply diagrams to portray both markets. Explain how different government policies with respect to the recycling of aluminum and paper might account for these different market outcomes.

14. **Advanced Analysis** Assume that demand for a commodity is represented by the equation $P = 10 - .2Q_d$ and supply by the equation $P = 2 + .2Q_s$, where Q_d and Q_s are quantity demanded and quantity supplied, respectively, and P is price. Using the equilibrium condition $Q_s = Q_d$, solve the equations to determine equilibrium price. Now determine equilibrium quantity. Graph the two equations to substantiate your answers.

15. **(Last Word)** Discuss the economic aspects of ticket scalping, specifying gainers and losers.

16. **Web-Based Question:** *Farm commodity prices— supply and demand in action* The U.S. Department of Agriculture, www.usda.gov/nass, publishes charts on the prices of farm products. Go to the USDA home page and select Graphics. Choose three farm products of your choice and determine whether their prices (as measured by "prices received by farmers") have generally increased, decreased, or stayed the same over the past three years. In which of the three cases, if any, do you think that supply has increased more rapidly than demand? In which of the three cases, if any, do you think that demand has increased more rapidly than supply? Explain your reasoning.

17. **Web-Based Question:** *Changes in demand—baby diapers and retirement villages* Other things equal, an increase in the number of buyers for a product or service will increase demand. Baby diapers and retirement villages are two products designed for different population groups. The U.S. Census Bureau website, www.census.gov/ipc/www/idbpyr.html, provides population pyramids (graphs that show the distribution of population by age and sex) for countries for the current year, 2025, and 2050. View the population pyramids for Mexico, Japan, and the United States. Which country do you think will have the greatest percentage increase in demand for baby diapers in the year 2050? For retirement villages? Which country do you think will have the greatest absolute increase in demand for baby diapers? For retirement villages?

CHAPTER

4

The Market System

Suppose that you were assigned to compile a list of all the individual goods and services available at a large regional shopping mall, including the different brands and variations of each type of product. We think you would agree that this task would be daunting and the list would be long! Although a single shopping mall contains a remarkable quantity and variety of goods, it is only a minuscule part of the national economy. ■ Who decided that the particular goods and services available at the mall and in the broader economy should be produced? How did the producers determine which technology and types of resources to use in producing these particular goods? Who will obtain these products? What accounts for the new and improved products among these goods? ■ In Chapter 3 we saw how equilibrium prices and quantities are established in *individual* product and resource markets. We now widen our focus to take in *all* product markets and resource markets—*capitalism*, also called the *private-enterprise system* or simply the *market system*. In this chapter we examine the characteristics of the market system and how that system answers questions such as those posed above.

■ Characteristics of the Market System

The market system, as practiced in industrially advanced economies, has several notable characteristics. Let's look at them in some detail.

Private Property

In a market system, private individuals and firms, not the government, own most of the property resources (land and capital). In fact, it is this extensive private ownership of capital that gives capitalism its name. This right of **private property,** coupled with the freedom to negotiate binding legal contracts, enables individuals and businesses to obtain, use, and dispose of property resources as they see fit. The right to bequeath—the right of property owners to designate who will receive their property when they die—sustains the institution of private property.

Property rights encourage investment, innovation, exchange, maintenance of property, and economic growth. Why would anyone stock a store, build a factory, or clear land for farming if someone else, or the government itself, could take that property for his or her own benefit?

Property rights also extend to intellectual property through patents, copyrights, and trademarks. Such long-term protection encourages people to write books, music, and computer programs and to invent new products and production processes without fear that others will steal them and the rewards they may bring.

Property rights also facilitate exchange. The title to an automobile or the deed to a cattle ranch assures the buyer that the seller is the legitimate owner. Moreover, property rights encourage owners to maintain or improve their property so as to preserve or increase its value. Finally, property rights enable people to use their time and resources to produce more goods and services, rather than using them to protect and retain the property they have already produced or acquired. !4.1

Freedom of Enterprise and Choice

Closely related to private ownership of property is freedom of enterprise and choice. The market system requires that various economic units make certain choices, which are expressed and implemented in the economy's markets:

- **Freedom of enterprise** ensures that entrepreneurs and private businesses are free to obtain and use economic resources to produce their choice of goods and services and to sell them in their chosen markets.
- **Freedom of choice** enables owners to employ or dispose of their property and money as they see fit. It also allows workers to enter any line of work for which they are qualified. Finally, it ensures that consumers are free to buy the goods and services that best satisfy their wants.

These choices are free only within broad legal limitations, of course. Illegal choices such as selling human organs or buying illicit drugs are punished through fines and imprisonment. (Global Perspective 4.1 reveals that the degree of economic freedom varies greatly from nation to nation.)

Self-Interest

In the market system, **self-interest** is the motivating force of all the various economic units as they express their free choices. Self-interest means that each economic unit tries to do what is best for itself. Entrepreneurs try to maximize profit or minimize

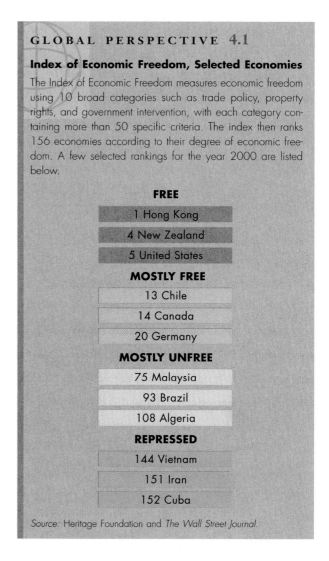

GLOBAL PERSPECTIVE 4.1

Index of Economic Freedom, Selected Economies

The Index of Economic Freedom measures economic freedom using 10 broad categories such as trade policy, property rights, and government intervention, with each category containing more than 50 specific criteria. The index then ranks 156 economies according to their degree of economic freedom. A few selected rankings for the year 2000 are listed below.

FREE
1 Hong Kong
4 New Zealand
5 United States

MOSTLY FREE
13 Chile
14 Canada
20 Germany

MOSTLY UNFREE
75 Malaysia
93 Brazil
108 Algeria

REPRESSED
144 Vietnam
151 Iran
152 Cuba

Source: Heritage Foundation and *The Wall Street Journal.*

loss. Property owners try to get the highest price for the sale or rent of their resources. Workers try to maximize their utility (satisfaction) by finding jobs that offer the best combination of wages, hours, fringe benefits, and working conditions. Consumers try to obtain the products they want at the lowest possible price and apportion their expenditures to maximize their utility. The motive of self-interest gives direction and consistency to what might otherwise be a chaotic economy.

Recall that the pursuit of self-interest is not the same as selfishness. Self-interest involves maximizing some benefit, and it does not preclude helping others. A stockholder may invest to receive maximum corporate dividends and then donate a portion of them to the United Way or give them to grandchildren. A worker may take a second job to help pay college tuition for her or his children. An entrepreneur may make a fortune and donate much of it to a charitable foundation. 🔑 4.1

Competition

The market system depends on **competition** among economic units. The basis of this competition is freedom of choice exercised in pursuit of a monetary return. Very broadly defined, *competition* requires:

- Independently acting sellers and buyers operating in a particular product or resource market.
- Freedom of sellers and buyers to enter or leave markets, on the basis of their economic self-interest.

Competition diffuses economic power within the businesses and households that make up the economy. When there are independently acting sellers and buyers in a market, no one buyer or seller is able to dictate the price of the product.

Consider the supply side of the product market. When a product becomes scarce, its price rises. An unseasonable frost in Florida may seriously reduce the supply of citrus crops and sharply increase the price of oranges. Similarly, if a single producer can somehow restrict the total output of a product, it can raise the product's price. By controlling market supply, a firm can "rig the market" to its own advantage. But that is not possible in markets where suppliers compete. A firm that raises its price will lose part or all of its business to competitors.

The same reasoning applies to the demand side of the market. Because there are multiple buyers, single buyers cannot manipulate the market to their own advantage by refusing to pay the market price.

Competition also implies that producers can enter or leave an industry; there are no insurmountable barriers to an industry's expanding or contracting. This freedom of an industry to expand or contract provides the economy with the flexibility needed to remain efficient over time. Freedom of entry and exit enables the economy to adjust to changes in consumer tastes, technology, and resource availability.

The diffusion of economic power inherent in competition limits the potential abuse of that power. A producer that charges more than the competitive market price will lose sales to other producers. An employer who pays less than the competitive market wage rate will lose workers to other employers. A firm that fails to exploit new technology will lose profits to firms that do. Competition is the basic regulatory force in the market system.

Markets and Prices

Markets and prices are key characteristics of the market system. They give the system its ability to coordinate millions of daily economic decisions. We know from Chapters 2 and 3 that a market is a mechanism that brings buyers (demanders) and sellers (suppliers) into contact. A market system is necessary to convey the decisions made by buyers and sellers of products and resources. The decisions made on each side of the market determine a set of product and resource prices that guide resource owners, entrepreneurs, and consumers as they make and revise their free choices and pursue their self-interest.

Just as competition is the regulatory mechanism of the market system, the market system itself is the organizing mechanism. It serves as an elaborate communication network through which innumerable individual free choices are recorded, summarized, and balanced. Those who respond to market signals and obey market dictates are rewarded with greater profit and income; those who do not respond to these signals and choose to ignore market dictates are penalized. Through this mechanism society decides what the economy should produce, how production can be organized efficiently, and how the fruits of production are to be distributed among the various units that make up the economy.

> **QUICK REVIEW 4.1**
>
> - The market system rests on the private ownership of property and on freedom of enterprise and freedom of choice.
> - The market system permits economic entities—businesses, resource suppliers, and consumers—to pursue and further their self-interest. It prevents any single economic entity from dictating the prices of products or resources.
> - The coordinating mechanism of the market system is a system of markets and prices.

Reliance on Technology and Capital Goods

Another characteristic of the market system is the extensive use of capital goods. In the market system, competition, freedom of choice, self-interest, and personal reward provide the opportunity and motivation for technological advance. The monetary rewards for new products or production techniques accrue directly to the innovator. The market system therefore encourages extensive use and rapid development of complex capital goods: tools, machinery, large-scale factories, and facilities for storage, communication, transportation, and marketing.

Advanced technology and capital goods are important because the most direct methods of production are often the least efficient. The only way to avoid that inefficiency is to rely on **roundabout production.** It would be ridiculous for a farmer to go at production with bare hands. There are huge benefits—in the form of more efficient production and, therefore, more abundant output—to be derived from creating and using such tools of production (capital equipment) as plows, tractors, storage bins, and so on.

Specialization

The extent to which market economies rely on **specialization** is extraordinary. The majority of consumers produce virtually none of the goods and services they consume, and they consume little or nothing of what they produce. The worker who devotes 8 hours a day to installing windows in Fords may own a Honda. Many farmers sell their milk to the local dairy and then buy margarine at the local grocery store. Society learned long ago that self-sufficiency breeds inefficiency. The jack-of-all-trades may be a very colorful individual but is certainly not an efficient producer.

Division of Labor   Human specialization—called the **division of labor**—contributes to a society's output in several ways:

- *Specialization makes use of differences in ability.* Specialization enables individuals to take advantage of existing differences in their abilities and skills. If caveman A is strong and swift and good at tracking animals, and caveman B is weak and slow but patient, their distribution of talents can be most efficiently used if A hunts and B fishes.
- *Specialization fosters learning by doing.* Even if the abilities of A and B are identical, specialization may still be advantageous. By devoting all your time to a single task, you are more likely to develop the skills it requires and to devise improved techniques than you would by working at a number of different tasks. You

learn to be a good hunter by going hunting every day.

- *Specialization saves time.* By devoting all your time to a single task, you avoid the loss of time incurred in shifting from one job to another.

For all these reasons, specialization increases the total output society derives from limited resources.

Geographic Specialization   Specialization also works on a regional and international basis. It is conceivable that oranges could be grown in Nebraska, but because of the unsuitability of the land, rainfall, and temperature, the costs would be very high. And it is conceivable that wheat could be grown in Florida. But for similar reasons such production would be costly. So Nebraskans produce products—wheat in particular—for which their resources are best suited, and Floridians do the same, producing oranges and other citrus fruits. By specializing, both economies produce more than is needed locally. Then, very sensibly, Nebraskans and Floridians swap some of their surpluses—wheat for oranges, oranges for wheat.

Similarly, on an international scale, the United States specializes in producing such items as commercial aircraft and computers, which it sells abroad in exchange for video recorders from Japan, bananas from Honduras, and woven baskets from Thailand. Both human specialization and geographical specialization are needed to achieve efficiency in the use of limited resources. 🔑 4.2

Use of Money

A rather obvious characteristic of the market system is the extensive use of money. Money performs several functions, but first and foremost it is a **medium of exchange.** It makes trade easier.

A convenient means of exchanging goods is required for specialization. Exchange can, and sometimes does, occur through **barter**—swapping goods for goods, say, wheat for oranges. But barter poses serious problems for the economy because it requires a *coincidence of wants* between the buyer and the seller. In our example, we assumed that Nebraskans had excess wheat to trade and wanted oranges. And we assumed that Floridians had excess oranges to trade and wanted wheat. So an exchange occurred. But if such a coincidence of wants is missing, trade is stymied.

Suppose that Nebraska has no interest in Florida's oranges but wants potatoes from Idaho.

And suppose that Idaho wants Florida's oranges but not Nebraska's wheat. And, to complicate matters, suppose that Florida wants some of Nebraska's wheat but none of Idaho's potatoes. We summarize the situation in Figure 4.1.

In none of the cases shown in the figure is there a coincidence of wants. Trade by barter clearly would be difficult. Instead, people in each state use **money,** which is simply a convenient social invention to facilitate exchanges of goods and services. Historically, people have used cattle, cigarettes, shells, stones, pieces of metal, and many other commodities, with varying degrees of success, as a medium of exchange. But to serve as money, an item needs to pass only one test: *It must be generally acceptable to sellers in exchange for their goods and services.* Money is socially defined; whatever society accepts as a medium of exchange *is* money.

Most economies use pieces of paper as money. The use of paper dollars (currency) as a medium of exchange is what enables Nebraska, Florida, and Idaho to overcome their trade stalemate, as demonstrated in Figure 4.1.

On a global basis the fact that different nations have different currencies complicates specialization and exchange. However, markets in which currencies are bought and sold make it possible for U.S. residents, Japanese, Germans, Britons, and Mexicans, through the swapping of dollars, yen, euros, pounds, and pesos, one for another, to exchange goods and services. ! 4.2

Active, but Limited, Government

The final characteristic of the market system, as evidenced in modern economies, is an active, but limited, government. Although a market system promotes a high degree of efficiency in the use of its resources, it has certain shortcomings. We will discover in Chapter 5 that government can increase the overall effectiveness of the economic system in several ways.

> **QUICK REVIEW 4.2**
>
> ■ The market systems of modern industrial economies are characterized by extensive use of technologically advanced capital goods. Such goods help these economies achieve greater efficiency in production.
>
> ■ Specialization is extensive in market systems; it enhances efficiency and output by enabling individuals, regions, and nations to produce the goods and services for which their resources are best suited.
>
> ■ The use of money in market systems facilitates the exchange of goods and services that specialization requires.

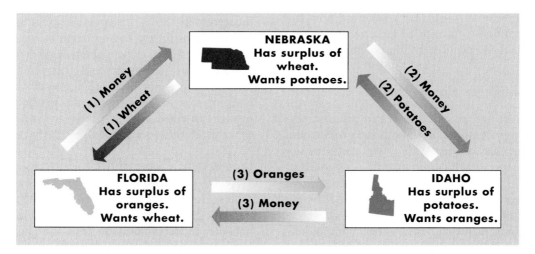

Figure 4.1

Money facilitates trade when wants do not coincide. The use of money as a medium of exchange permits trade to be accomplished despite a noncoincidence of wants. (1) Nebraska trades the wheat that Florida wants for money from Floridians; (2) Nebraska trades the money it receives from Florida for the potatoes it wants from Idaho; (3) Idaho trades the money it receives from Nebraska for the oranges it wants from Florida.

▌The Market System at Work

We have noted that a market system is characterized by competition, freedom of enterprise, and choice. Consumers are free to buy what they choose; entrepreneurs and firms are free to produce and sell what they choose; and resource suppliers are free to make their property and human resources available in whatever use or occupation they choose. We may wonder why such an economy does not collapse in chaos. If consumers want breakfast cereal but businesses choose to produce aerobic shoes and resource suppliers decide to manufacture computer software, production would seem to be deadlocked by the apparent inconsistency of these free choices.

In reality, the millions of decisions made by households and businesses are highly consistent with one another. Firms *do* produce the goods and services that consumers want, and households *do* provide the kinds of labor that businesses want.

To understand the operation of the market system, you must first recognize that every economy must respond to Four Fundamental Questions:

- What goods and services will be produced?
- How will the goods and services be produced?
- Who will get the goods and services?
- How will the system accommodate change?

The **Four Fundamental Questions** highlight the economic choices underlying the production possibilities curve discussed in Chapter 2. These questions are relevant because of scarce resources in a world of unlimited wants. Let's examine how the market system answers each of these questions and thus addresses the economizing problem.

What Will Be Produced?

With product and resource prices in place, established through competition in both the product and the resource markets, how will a market system decide on the specific types and quantities of goods to be produced? *Because businesses seek profits and avoid losses, the goods and services produced at a continuing profit* will *be produced and those produced at a continuing loss* will not. Profits and losses depend on the difference between the total revenue a firm receives from selling its product and the total cost of producing the product:

Economic profit = total revenue − total cost

Total revenue (TR) is found by multiplying the product price by the quantity of the product sold. Total cost (TC) is found by multiplying the price of each resource used by the amount employed and summing the results.

Economic Costs and Profits Saying that the products that can be produced profitably *will* be produced and those that cannot *will not* is an accurate generalization only if the meaning of **economic costs** is clearly understood.

Let's think of businesses as simply organizational charts—that is, businesses "on paper," as distinct from the capital, raw materials, labor, and entrepreneurial ability that make them function. To become actual producing firms, these "on-paper" businesses must secure all four types of resources. *Economic costs are the payments that must be made to secure and retain the needed amounts of those resources.* The per-unit size of those costs—the resource prices—are determined by supply and demand in the resource market. As with land, labor, and capital, entrepreneurial ability is a scarce resource that carries a price tag. Consequently, costs must include not only wage and salary payments to labor, and interest and rental payments for capital and land, but also payments to the entrepreneur for organizing and combining the other resources to produce a commodity. The payment for (cost of) the entrepreneur's contributions is called **normal profit.**

A product is produced only if total revenue is large enough to pay wages, interest, rent, and a normal profit (a cost) to the entrepreneur. That way all the economic costs are covered, including the opportunity cost of the entrepreneur's time and talent. If the total revenue from the sale of a product exceeds all these economic costs, the remainder goes to the entrepreneur as an added reward. That return is called *pure profit* or **economic profit.** Economic profit is an above-normal profit, and it *is* what lures other producers to a particular industry.

Profits and Expanding Industries An example will help explain how the market system determines what goods will be produced. With current technology, suppose the most favorable relationship between total revenue and total cost in producing product X occurs when a firm's output is 15 units. Assume, too, that the least-cost combination of resources in producing 15 units of X is 2 units of labor, 3 units of land, 1 unit of capital, and 1 unit of entrepreneurial ability, selling at prices of $2, $1, $3, and $3, respectively. Finally, suppose that the 15 units of X that these resources produce can be sold for $1 per unit, or $15 total. Will firms produce X? Yes, because each firm will be able to pay wages, rent, interest, and normal profit (a cost) of $13 [= (2 × $2) + (3 × $1) + (1 × $3) + (1 × $3)]. The difference between total revenue of $15 and total cost of $13 is an economic profit of $2.

This economic profit is evidence that industry X is prosperous. It will become an **expanding industry** as new firms, attracted by the above-normal profits, are formed or shift from less profitable industries.

But the entry of new firms will be self-limiting. As new firms enter industry X, the market supply of product X will increase relative to the market demand. This will lower the market price of X, as in Figure 3.6c, and economic profit will gradually diminish and finally disappear. The market supply and demand conditions prevailing when economic profit reaches zero will determine the total amount of X produced. At this point the industry will be at its "equilibrium size," at least until a further change in market demand or supply upsets that equilibrium.

Losses and Declining Industries

But what if the initial market situation for product X were less favorable? Suppose that demand conditions in the product market were such that a firm could sell the 15 units of X at a price of just $.75 per unit. Total revenue would then be $11.25 (= 15 × $.75). After paying wage, rental, and interest costs of $10, and figuring in the normal profit (a cost) of $3, the firm's total cost would again be $13. But because its total revenue is only $11.25, it would incur a loss of $1.75 (= $11.25 − $13).

Certainly, firms would not be attracted to this unprofitable **declining industry.** In fact, if these losses persisted, some of the firms in industry X would go out of business or migrate to more prosperous industries where normal or even economic profits prevailed. However, as that happened, the market supply of X would fall relative to the market demand. Product price would rise (as in Figure 3.6d), and the losses in industry X would eventually disappear. The industry would then stop shrinking. The supply and demand situation that prevailed when economic profit became zero would determine the total output of product X. Again, the industry would for the moment reach its equilibrium size.

Consumer Sovereignty and Dollar Votes

In the market system, consumers are sovereign (in command). **Consumer sovereignty** works through consumer demand, and consumer demand is crucial in determining the types and quantities of goods produced. Consumers spend the income they earn from the sale of their resources on the goods they are most willing and able to buy. Through these **"dollar votes"** consumers register their wants via the demand side of the product market. If the dollar votes for a certain product are great enough to provide a normal profit, businesses will produce that product. If there is an increase in consumer demand, so that enough dollar votes are cast to provide an economic profit, the industry will expand, as will the output of the product.

Conversely, a decrease in consumer demand—meaning fewer dollar votes cast for the product—will result in losses, and, in time, the industry will contract. As firms leave the industry, the output of the product will decline. Indeed, the industry may even cease to exist. Again, the consumers are sovereign; they collectively direct resources away from industries that are not meeting consumer wants.

The dollar votes of consumers determine not only which industries will continue to exist but also which products will survive or fail. Example: In 1991, responding to doctors and nutritionists, McDonald's introduced its low-fat McLean burger. Good idea? Not really. Most consumers found the new product "too dry" and "not tasty," so sales were meager. In 1996 McDonald's quietly dropped the McLean burger from its menu at the same time that it introduced its higher-fat Arch Deluxe burger. In effect, consumers had collectively "voted out" the McLean burger. ▮ 4.3

Market Restraints on Freedom

In short, firms are not really free to produce whatever they wish. Consumers' buying decisions make the production of some products profitable and the production of other products unprofitable, thus restricting the choice of businesses in deciding what to produce. Businesses must match their production choices with consumer choices or else face losses and eventual bankruptcy.

The same holds true for resource suppliers. The demand for resources is a **derived demand**— derived, that is, from the demand for the goods and services that the resources help produce. There is a demand for autoworkers because there is a demand for automobiles. There is no demand for buggy-whip braiders because there is no demand for buggy whips. Resource suppliers are not free to allocate their resources to the production of goods that consumers do not value highly. Consumers register their preferences on the demand side of the product market; producers and resource suppliers, prompted by their own self-interest, respond appropriately.

How Will the Goods and Services Be Produced?

The market system steers resources to the industries whose products consumers want—simply because those industries survive, are profitable, and pay for resources. Within each industry, the firms that survive to do the producing also are the ones that are profitable. Because competition weeds out high-cost producers, continued profitability requires that firms produce their output at minimum cost. Achieving least-cost production necessitates, for example, that firms locate their production facilities optimally, considering such factors as resource prices, resource productivity, and transportation costs.

Least-cost production also means that firms must employ the most economically efficient technique of production in producing their output. The most efficient production technique depends on:

- The available technology, that is, the various combinations of resources that will produce the desired results.
- The prices of the needed resources.

A technique that requires just a few inputs of resources to produce a specific output may be highly *in*efficient economically *if* those resources are valued very highly in the market. *Economic efficiency means obtaining a particular output of product with the least input of scarce resources, when both output and resource inputs are measured in dollars and cents.* The combination of resources that will produce, say, $15 worth of product X at the lowest possible cost is the most efficient.

Suppose there are three possible techniques for producing the desired $15 worth of product X.

Suppose also that the quantity of each resource required by each production technique and the prices of the required resources are as shown in Table 4.1. By multiplying the required quantities of each resource by its price in each of the three techniques, we can determine the total cost of producing $15 worth of X by means of each technique.

Technique 2 is economically the most efficient, because it is the least costly. It enables society to obtain $15 worth of output by using a smaller amount of resources—$13 worth—than the $15 worth required by the two other techniques. Competition will dictate that producers use technique 2. Thus, the question of how goods will be produced is answered. They will be produced in a least-cost way.

A change in either technology *or* resource prices, however, may cause a firm to shift from the technology it is using. If the price of labor falls to $.50, technique 1 becomes more desirable than technique 2. Firms will find they can lower their costs by shifting to a technology that uses more of the resource whose price has fallen. Exercise: Would a new technique involving 1 unit of labor, 4 of land, 1 of capital, and 1 of entrepreneurial ability be preferable to the techniques listed in Table 4.1, assuming the resource prices shown there? **(Key Question 7)**

Who Will Get the Goods and Services?

The market system enters the picture in two ways when solving the problem of distributing total output. Generally, any product will be distributed to consumers on the basis of their ability and willingness to pay its existing market price. If the price of some product, say, a pocket calculator, is $15, then buyers who are able and willing to pay that price will

Table 4.1
Three Techniques for Producing $15 Worth of Product X

Resource	Price per Unit of Resource	Units of Resource					
		Technique 1		Technique 2		Technique 3	
		Units	Cost	Units	Cost	Units	Cost
Labor	$2	4	$ 8	2	$ 4	1	$ 2
Land	1	1	1	3	3	4	4
Capital	3	1	3	1	3	2	6
Entrepreneurial ability	3	1	3	1	3	1	3
Total cost of $15 worth of X			$15		$13		$15

get a pocket calculator; those who are not, will not. This is the rationing function of equilibrium prices.

The ability to pay the equilibrium prices for pocket calculators and other products depends on the amount of income that consumers have along with their preferences for various goods. If they have sufficient income and want to spend their money on a particular good, they can have it. And the amount of income they have depends on (1) the quantities of the property and human resources they supply and (2) the prices those resources command in the resource market. Resource prices (wages, interest, rent, profit) are key in determining the size of each household's income and therefore each household's ability to buy part of the economy's output.

How Will the System Accommodate Change?

Market systems are dynamic: Consumer preferences, technology, and supplies of resources all change. This means that the particular allocation of resources that is now the most efficient for a *specific* pattern of consumer tastes, range of technological alternatives, and amount of available resources will become obsolete and inefficient as consumer preferences change, new techniques of production are discovered, and resource supplies change over time. Can the market economy adjust to such changes and still use resources efficiently?

Guiding Function of Prices   Suppose consumer tastes change. For instance, assume that consumers decide they want more fruit juice and less milk than the economy currently provides. Those changes in consumer tastes will be communicated to producers through an increase in demand for fruit and a decline in demand for milk. Fruit prices will rise and milk prices will fall.

Now, assuming that firms in both industries were enjoying precisely normal profits before these changes in consumer demand set in, the higher fruit prices will mean economic profit for the fruit industry and the lower milk prices will mean losses for the milk industry. Self-interest will induce new competitors to enter the prosperous fruit industry and will in time force firms to leave the depressed milk industry.

The economic profit that initially follows the increase in demand for fruit will not only induce that industry to expand but will also give it the revenue needed to obtain the resources essential to its growth. Higher fruit prices will permit fruit producers to pay

higher prices for resources, thereby increasing resource demand and drawing resources from less urgent alternative employment. The reverse occurs in the milk industry, where resource demand declines and fewer workers and other resources are employed. These adjustments in the economy are appropriate responses to the changes in consumer tastes. This is consumer sovereignty at work.

The market system is a gigantic communications system. Through changes in prices it communicates changes in such basic matters as consumer tastes and elicits appropriate responses from businesses and resource suppliers. By affecting product prices and profits, changes in consumer tastes direct the expansion of some industries and the contraction of others. Those adjustments are conveyed to the resource market as expanding industries demand more resources and contracting industries demand fewer; the resulting changes in resource prices guide resources from the contracting industries to the expanding industries.

This *directing* or **guiding function of prices** is a core element of the market system. Without such a system, some administrative agency such as a government planning board would have to direct businesses and resources into the appropriate industries. A similar analysis shows that the system can and does adjust to other fundamental changes—for example, to changes in technology and in the availability of various resources.

Role in Promoting Progress   Adjusting to changes is one thing; initiating desirable changes is another. How does the market system promote technological improvements and capital accumulation—two changes that lead to greater productivity and a higher level of material well-being for society?

Technological Advance   The market system provides a strong incentive for technological advance and enables better products and processes to brush aside inferior ones. An entrepreneur or firm that introduces a popular new product will gain revenue and economic profit. Technological advance also includes new and improved methods that reduce production or distribution costs. By passing part of its cost reduction on to the consumer through a lower product price, the firm can increase sales and obtain economic profit at the expense of rival firms. Moreover, the market system is conducive to the *rapid spread* of technological advance throughout an industry. Rival firms must follow the lead of the most innovative firm or else suffer immediate losses and

eventual failure. In some cases, the result is **creative destruction:** The creation of new products and production methods completely destroys the market positions of firms that are wedded to existing products and older ways of doing business. Example: The advent of personal computers and word processing software demolished the market for electric typewriters.

Capital Accumulation   Most technological advances require additional capital goods. The market system provides the resources necessary to produce those goods by adjusting the product market and the resource market through increased dollar votes for capital goods. In other words, the market system acknowledges dollar voting for capital goods as well as for consumer goods.

But who will register votes for capital goods? Entrepreneurs and owners of businesses, as receivers of profit income, often use part of that income to purchase capital goods. Doing so yields even greater profit income in the future if the technological innovation is successful. Also, by paying interest or selling ownership shares, the entrepreneur and firm can attract some of the income of households to cast dollar votes for the production of more capital goods. **(Key Question 9)**

▌Competition and the "Invisible Hand"

In his 1776 book *The Wealth of Nations*, Adam Smith first noted that the operation of a market system creates a curious unity between private interests and social interests. Firms and resource suppliers, seeking to further their own self-interest and operating within the framework of a highly competitive market system, will simultaneously, as though guided by an **"invisible hand,"** promote the public or social interest. For example, we have seen that in a competitive environment, businesses use the least-costly combination of resources to produce a specific output because it is in their self-interest to do so. To act otherwise would be to forgo profit or even to risk business failure. But, at the same time, to use scarce resources in the least-costly (most efficient) way is clearly in the social interest as well.

In our more fruit juice–less milk illustration, it is self-interest, awakened and guided by the competitive market system, that induces responses appropriate to the change in society's wants. Businesses seeking to make higher profits and to avoid losses, and resource suppliers pursuing greater monetary rewards, negotiate changes in the allocation of resources

and end up with the output that society demands. Competition controls or guides self-interest in such a way that it automatically, and quite unintentionally, furthers the best interests of society. The invisible hand ensures that when firms maximize their profits, they also maximize society's output and income.

Of the many virtues of the market system three merit special emphasis:

- **Efficiency**   The basic economic argument for the market system is that it promotes the efficient use of resources, by guiding them into the production of the goods and services most wanted by society. It forces the use of the most efficient techniques in organizing resources for production, and it encourages the development and adoption of new and more efficient production techniques.
- **Incentives**   The market system encourages skill acquisition, hard work, and innovation. Greater work skills and effort mean greater production and higher incomes, which usually translate into a higher standard of living. Similarly, the assuming of risks by entrepreneurs can result in substantial profit incomes. Successful innovations generate economic rewards.
- **Freedom**   The major noneconomic argument for the market system is its emphasis on personal freedom. In contrast to central planning, the market system coordinates economic activity without coercion. The market system permits—indeed, it thrives on—freedom of enterprise and choice. Entrepreneurs and workers are free to further their own self-interest, subject to the rewards and penalties imposed by the market system itself.

> **QUICK REVIEW 4.3**
>
> ■ The output mix of the market system is determined by profits, which in turn depend heavily on consumer preferences. Economic profits cause efficient industries to expand; losses cause inefficient industries to contract.
>
> ■ Competition forces industries to use the least-costly (most efficient) production methods.
>
> ■ In a market economy consumer income and product prices determine how output will be distributed.
>
> ■ Competitive markets reallocate resources in response to changes in consumer tastes, technological advances, and changes in supplies of resources.
>
> ■ The "invisible hand" of the market system channels the pursuit of self-interest to the good of society.

Shuffling the Deck

Economist Donald Boudreaux Marvels at the Way the Market System Systematically and Purposefully Arranges the World's Tens of Billions of Individual Resources.

In *The Future and Its Enemies,* Virginia Postrel notes the astonishing fact that if you thoroughly shuffle an ordinary deck of 52 playing cards, chances are practically 100 percent that the resulting arrangement of cards has never before existed. *Never.* Every time you shuffle a deck, you produce an arrangement of cards that exists for the first time in history.

The arithmetic works out that way. For a very small number of items, the number of possible arrangements is small. Three items, for example, can be arranged only six different ways. But the number of possible arrangements grows very large very quickly. The number of different ways to arrange five items is 120 . . . for ten items it's 3,628,800 . . . for fifteen items it's 1,307,674,368,000.

The number of different ways to arrange 52 items is 8.066×10^{67}. This is a *big* number. No human can comprehend its enormousness. By way of comparison, the number of possible ways to arrange a mere 20 items is 2,432,902,008,176,640,000— a number larger than the total number of seconds that have elapsed since the beginning of time ten billion years ago—and this number is Lilliputian compared to 8.066×10^{67}.

What's the significance of these facts about numbers? Consider the number of different resources available in the world— my labor, your labor, your land, oil, tungsten, cedar, coffee beans, chickens, rivers, the Empire State Building, Windows 2000, the wharves at Houston, the classrooms at Oxford, the airport at Miami, and on and on and on. No one can possibly count all of the different productive resources available for our use. But we can be sure that this number is at least in the tens of billions.

When you reflect on how incomprehensibly large is the number of ways to arrange a deck containing a mere 52 cards, the mind boggles at the number of different ways to arrange all the world's resources.

If our world were random—if resources combined together haphazardly, as if a giant took them all into his hands and tossed them down like so many [cards]—it's a virtual certainty that the resulting combination of resources would be useless. Unless this chance arrangement were quickly rearranged according to some productive logic, nothing worthwhile would be produced. We would all starve to death. Because only a tiny fraction of possible arrangements serves human ends, any arrangement will be useless if it is chosen randomly or with inadequate knowledge of how each and every resource might be productively combined with each other.

And yet, we witness all around us an arrangement of resources that's productive and serves human goals. Today's arrangement of resources might not be perfect, but it is vastly superior to most of the trillions upon trillions of other possible arrangements.

How have we managed to get one of the minuscule number of arrangements that works? The answer is private property—a social institution that encourages mutual accommodation.

Private property eliminates the possibility that resource arrangements will be random, for each resource owner chooses a course of action only if it promises rewards to the owner that exceed the rewards promised by all other available courses.

[The result] is a breathtakingly complex and productive arrangement of countless resources. This arrangement emerged over time (and is still emerging) as the result of billions upon billions of individual, daily, small decisions made by people seeking to better employ their resources and labor in ways that other people find helpful.

Source: Abridged from Donald J. Boudreaux, "Mutual Accommodation," *Ideas on Liberty,* May 2000, pp. 4–5. Reprinted with permission.

SUMMARY

1. The market system—known also as the private-enterprise system or capitalism—is characterized by the private ownership of resources, including capital, and the freedom of individuals to engage in economic activities of their choice to advance their material well-being. Self-interest is the driving force of such an economy, and competition functions as a regulatory or control mechanism.

2. In the market system, markets and prices organize and make effective the many millions of individual decisions that determine what is produced, the methods of production, and the sharing of output.

3. Specialization, use of advanced technology, and the extensive use of capital goods are common features of market systems.

4. Functioning as a medium of exchange, money eliminates the problems of bartering and permits easy trade and greater specialization, both domestically and internationally.

5. Every economy faces Four Fundamental Questions: (a) What goods and services will be produced? (b) How will the goods and services be produced? (c) Who will get the goods and services? (d) How will the system used accommodate changes in consumer tastes, resource supplies, and technology?

6. The market system produces products whose production and sale yield total revenue sufficient to cover all costs, including a normal profit (a cost). It does not produce products that do not yield a normal profit, or more.

7. Economic profit indicates that an industry is prosperous and promotes its expansion. Losses signify that an industry is not prosperous and hasten its contraction.

8. Consumer sovereignty means that both businesses and resource suppliers are subject to the wants of consumers. Through their dollar votes, consumers decide on the composition of output.

9. Competition forces firms to use the lowest-cost and therefore the most economically efficient production techniques.

10. The prices that a household receives for the resources it supplies to the economy determine that household's income. This income determines the household's claim on the economy's output. Those who have income to spend get the products produced in the market system.

11. By communicating changes in consumer tastes to resource suppliers and entrepreneurs, the market system prompts appropriate adjustments in the allocation of the economy's resources. The market system also encourages technological advance and capital accumulation.

12. Competition, the primary mechanism of control in the market economy, promotes a unity of self-interest and social interests; as though directed by an invisible hand, competition harnesses the self-interest motives of businesses and resource suppliers to further the social interest.

TERMS AND CONCEPTS

private property	division of labor	normal profit	guiding function of
freedom of enterprise	medium of exchange	economic profit	prices
freedom of choice	barter	expanding industry	creative destruction
self-interest	money	declining industry	"invisible hand"
competition	Four Fundamental	consumer sovereignty	
roundabout production	Questions	dollar votes	
specialization	economic costs	derived demand	

STUDY QUESTIONS

1. Explain each of the following statements:
   a. The market system not only accepts self-interest as a fact of human existence; it relies on self-interest to achieve society's material goals.
   b. The market system provides such a variety of desired goods and services precisely because no single individual or small group is deciding what the economy will produce.
   c. Entrepreneurs and businesses are at the helm of the economy, but their commanders are consumers.

2. Why is private property, and the protection of property rights, so critical to the success of the market system?

3. What are the advantages of "roundabout" production? What is meant by the term "division of labor"?

What are the advantages of specialization in the use of human and material resources? Explain: "Exchange is the necessary consequence of specialization."

4. What problem does barter entail? Indicate the economic significance of money as a medium of exchange. What is meant by the statement "We want money only to part with it."?

5. Evaluate and explain the following statements:
   a. The market system is a profit-and-loss system.
   b. Competition is the indispensable disciplinarian of the market economy.
   c. Production methods that are inferior in the engineering sense may be the most efficient methods in the economic sense, once resource prices are considered.

6. Explain the meaning and implications of the following quotation:

   The beautiful consequence of the market is that it is its own guardian. If output or prices or certain kinds of remuneration stray away from their socially ordained levels, forces are set into motion to bring them back to the fold. A curious paradox thus ensues: the market, which is the acme of individual economic freedom, is the strictest taskmaster of all. One may appeal the ruling of a planning board or win the dispensation of a [government] minister; but there is no appeal, no dispensation, from the anonymous pressures of the market mechanism. Economic freedom is thus more illusory than at first appears. One can do as one pleases in the market. But if one pleases to do what the market disapproves, the price of individual freedom is economic ruination.[1]

7. **Key Question** Assume that a business firm finds that its profit will be at a maximum when it produces $40 worth of product A. Suppose also that each of the three techniques shown in the following table will produce the desired output:

		Resource Units Required		
Resource	Price per Unit of Resource	Technique 1	Technique 2	Technique 3
Labor	$3	5	2	3
Land	4	2	4	2
Capital	2	2	4	5
Entrepreneurial ability	2	4	2	4

a. With the resource prices shown, which technique will the firm choose? Why? Will production entail profit or losses? Will the industry expand or contract? When will a new equilibrium output be achieved?

b. Assume now that a new technique, technique 4, is developed. It combines 2 units of labor, 2 of land, 6 of capital, and 3 of entrepreneurial ability. In view of the resource prices in the table, will the firm adopt the new technique? Explain your answer.

c. Suppose that an increase in the labor supply causes the price of labor to fall to $1.50 per unit, all other resource prices remaining unchanged. Which technique will the producer now choose? Explain.

d. "The market system causes the economy to conserve most in the use of resources that are particularly scarce in supply. Resources that are scarcest relative to the demand for them have the highest prices. As a result, producers use these resources as sparingly as is possible." Evaluate this statement. Does your answer to part *c*, above, bear out this contention? Explain.

8. Suppose the demand for bagels rises dramatically while the demand for breakfast cereal falls. Briefly explain how the competitive market economy will make the needed adjustments to reestablish an efficient allocation of society's scarce resources.

9. **Key Question** Some large hardware stores such as Home Depot boast of carrying as many as 20,000 different products in each store. What motivated the producers of those products—everything from screwdrivers to ladders to water heaters—to make them and offer them for sale? How did the producers decide on the best combinations of resources to use? Who made those resources available, and why? Who decides whether these particular hardware products should continue to get produced and offered for sale?

10. In a single sentence, describe the meaning of the phrase "invisible hand."

11. **(Last Word)** What explains why millions of economic resources tend to get arranged logically and productively rather than haphazardly and unproductively?

12. **Web-Based Question:** *Sparkly things—interested in buying one?* Go to the Internet auction site eBay at www.ebay.com/index.html and click the category Jewelry and Gemstones. How many diamonds are for sale at the moment? How many rubies, sapphires, and opals? Note the wide array of sizes and prices of the gemstones. In what sense is there competition among the sellers in these markets? How does that competition influence prices? In what sense is there

---

[1]Robert L. Heilbroner, *The Worldly Philosophers*, 7th ed. (New York: Simon & Schuster, 1999), pp. 57–58.

competition among buyers? How does that competition influence prices? Do you see something interesting there or elsewhere on eBay? Go ahead and buy it!

13. **Web-Based Question:** *Barter and the IRS* Bartering occurs when goods or services are exchanged without the exchange of money. For some, barter's popularity is that it enables them to avoid paying taxes to the government. How might such avoidance occur? Does the Internal Revenue Service (IRS), www.irs.ustreas.gov/, treat barter as taxable or nontaxable income? (Click Taxpayer Help and Education, then Tele-Tax Topics, and then Types of Income.) How is the value of a barter transaction determined? What are some IRS barter examples? What does the IRS require of the members of so-called barter exchanges?

C H A P T E R

The U.S. Economy
Private and Public Sectors

W E N O W M O V E from the general characteristics of the market system to specific information about the U.S. economy. For convenience, we divide the economy into two sectors: the *private sector*, which includes *households* and *businesses*, and the *public sector*, or simply *government*.

▌Households as Income Receivers

The U.S. economy currently has about 105 million households. These households consist of one or more persons occupying a housing unit and are both the ultimate suppliers of all economic resources *and* the major spenders in the economy. We can categorize the income received by households by how it was earned and by how it was divided among households.

The Functional Distribution of Income

The **functional distribution of income** indicates how the nation's earned income is apportioned among wages, rents, interest, and profits, that is, according to the function performed by the income receiver. Wages are paid to labor; rents and interest are paid to owners of property resources; and profits are paid to the owners of corporations and unincorporated businesses.

Figure 5.1 shows the functional distribution of U.S. income earned in 2000. The largest source of income for households is the wages and salaries paid to workers. Notice that the bulk of total U.S. income goes to labor, not to capital. Proprietors' income—the income of doctors, lawyers, small-business owners, farmers, and owners of other unincorporated enterprises—also has a "wage" element. Some of this income is payment for one's own labor, and some of it is profit from one's own business.

The other three types of income are self-evident: Some households own corporate stock and receive dividend incomes on their holdings. Many households also own bonds and savings accounts that yield interest income. And some households receive rental income by providing buildings and natural resources (including land) to businesses and other individuals.

The Personal Distribution of Income

The **personal distribution of income** indicates how the nation's money income is divided among individual households. In Figure 5.2 households are

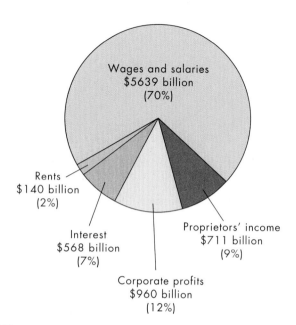

Figure 5.1

The functional distribution of U.S. income, 2000.
More than two-thirds of national income is received as wages
and salaries. Income to property owners—corporate profit, interest, and rents—accounts for about one-fifth of total income.
Source: Bureau of Economic Analysis.

divided into five numerically equal groups or quintiles; the heights of the bars show the percentage of
total income received by each group. In 1999 the
poorest 20 percent of all households received about
4 percent of total personal income, and the richest
20 percent received almost 50 percent. Clearly there
is considerable inequality in the personal distribution of U.S. income. **(Key Question 2)**

▌Households as Spenders

How do households dispose of their income? Part of
it flows to government as taxes, and the rest is divided between personal savings and personal consumption expenditures. In 2000, households disposed
of their total personal income as shown in Figure 5.3.

Personal Taxes

In 2000 households paid $1293 billion in personal
taxes, or 16 percent of $8274 billion total income.
Personal taxes, of which the personal income tax is the
major component, have risen in relative terms since
the Second World War. In 1941, households paid just
3 percent of their total income in personal taxes.

Personal Saving

Economists define "saving" as that part of after-tax
income that is not spent; hence, households have
just two choices about what to do with their income
after taxes—use it to consume, or save it. Saving is
the portion of income that is not paid in taxes or
used to purchase consumer goods but instead flows
into bank accounts, insurance policies, bonds and
stocks, mutual funds, and other financial assets.

Saving has been very low in the United States in
recent years, probably because of the dramatic increase in household wealth caused by the record increases in the value of common stock between 1996
and 1999. Feeling wealthier, households consumed
more and saved less. As indicated in Figure 5.3, saving was less than 1 percent of household income in
2000.

Usually, U.S. households save between 5 and 8
percent of their income. Reasons for saving center
on *security* and *speculation*. Households save to provide a nest egg for coping with unforeseen contin-

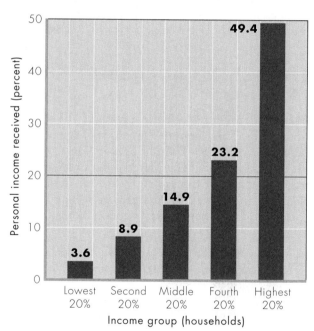

Figure 5.2

**The personal distribution of income among U.S.
households, 1999.** Personal income is unequally distributed
in the United States, with the top 20 percent of households receiving about one-half of the total income. In an equal distribution, all five vertical bars would be as high as the horizontal line
drawn at 20 percent; then each 20 percent of families would receive 20 percent of the nation's total income.
Source: U.S. Bureau of the Census.

gencies (sickness, accident, and unemployment), for retirement from the workforce, to finance the education of children, or simply for financial security. They may also channel part of their income to purchase stocks, speculating that their investments will increase in value.

The desire to save is not enough in itself, however. You must be able to save, and that depends on the size of your income. If your income is low, you may not be able to save any money at all. If your income is very, very low you may *dissave*—that is, spend more than your after-tax income. You do this by borrowing or by digging into savings you may have accumulated in years when your income was higher.

Both saving and consumption vary directly with income; as households garner more income, they save more and consume more. In fact, the top 10 percent of income receivers account for most of the personal saving in the U.S. economy.

Personal Consumption Expenditures

As Figure 5.3 shows, more than four-fifths of the total income of households flows back into the business sector as personal consumption expenditures—money spent on consumer goods.

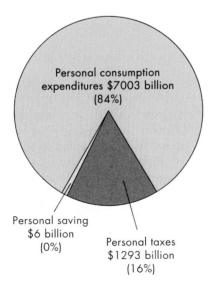

Figure 5.3

The disposition of household income, 2000.

Households apportion their income among taxes, saving, and consumption, with most going to consumption. (The way income is defined in this figure differs slightly from that used in Figure 5.1, accounting for the quantitative discrepancies between the "total income" amounts in the two figures.)
Source: Bureau of Economic Analysis.

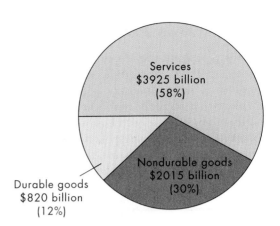

Figure 5.4

The composition of consumer expenditures, 2000.

Consumers divide their spending among durable goods (goods that have lives of 3 years or more), nondurable goods, and services. About 58 percent of consumer spending is for services.
Source: Bureau of Economic Analysis.

Figure 5.4 shows how consumers divide their expenditures among durable goods, nondurable goods, and services. Twelve percent of consumer expenditures are on **durable goods**—products that have expected lives of 3 years or more. Such goods include automobiles, furniture, and personal computers. Another 30 percent of consumer expenditures are on **nondurable goods**—products that have lives of less than 3 years. Included are such goods as food, clothing, and gasoline. About 58 percent of consumer expenditures are on **services**—the work done for consumers by lawyers, barbers, doctors, lodging personnel, and so on. This high percentage is the reason that the United States is often referred to as a *service-oriented economy*.

QUICK REVIEW 5.1

The functional distribution of income indicates how income is apportioned among wages, rents, interest, and profits; the personal distribution of income indicates how income is divided among families.

Wages and salaries are the major component of the functional distribution of income. The personal distribution of income reveals considerable inequality.

More than 80 percent of household income is consumed; the rest is saved or paid in taxes.

Consumer spending is directed to durable goods, nondurable goods, and services, with nearly 60 percent going to services.

■ The Business Population

Businesses constitute the second major part of the private sector. It will be useful to distinguish among a plant, a firm, and an industry:

■ A **plant** is a physical establishment—a factory, farm, mine, store, or warehouse—that performs one or more functions in fabricating and distributing goods and services.

■ A **firm** is a business organization that owns and operates plants. Some firms operate only one plant, but many own and operate several.

■ An **industry** is a group of firms that produce the same, or similar, products.

The organizational structures of firms are often complex and varied. *Multiplant firms* may be organized horizontally, with several plants performing much the same function. Examples are the multiple bottling plants of Coca-Cola and the many individual Wal-Mart stores. Firms also may be *vertically integrated*, meaning they own plants that perform different functions in the various stages of the production process. For example, oil companies such as Texaco own oil fields, refineries, and retail gasoline stations. Some firms are *conglomerates*, so named because they have plants that produce products in several industries. For example, Pfizer makes not only prescription medicines (Lipitor, Viagra) but also chewing gum (Trident, Dentyne), razors (Schick), cough drops (Halls), breath mints (Clorets, Certs), and antacids (Rolaids).

■ Legal Forms of Businesses

The business population is extremely diverse, ranging from giant corporations such as General Motors, with 1999 sales of $189 billion and more than 600,000 employees, to neighborhood specialty shops and "mom-and-pop" groceries with one or two employees and sales of only $200 to $300 per day. There are three major legal forms of businesses:

■ A **sole proprietorship** is a business owned and operated by one person. Usually, the proprietor (the owner) personally supervises its operation.

■ The **partnership** form of business organization is a natural outgrowth of the sole proprietorship. In a partnership, two or more individuals (the partners) agree to own and operate a business together. Usually they pool their financial

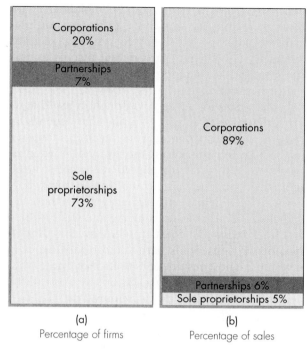

Figure 5.5

The business population and shares of domestic output. (a) Sole proprietorships dominate the business population numerically, but (b) corporations account for almost 90 percent of total sales (output).

resources and business skills. Consequently, they share the risks and the profits or losses.

■ A **corporation** is a legal creation that can acquire resources, own assets, produce and sell products, incur debts, extend credit, sue and be sued, and perform the functions of any other type of enterprise. A corporation is distinct and separate from the individual stockholders who own it. Hired managers run most corporations.

Figure 5.5a shows how the business population is distributed among the three major legal forms. About 73 percent of firms are sole proprietorships, whereas only 20 percent are corporations. But as Figure 5.5b indicates, corporations account for nearly 90 percent of all sales (output).

Advantages and Disadvantages

There are advantages and disadvantages to each form of business enterprise.

Sole Proprietorship

Sole proprietorships are very numerous because they are so easy to set up and organize; there is virtually no complex paper work or legal expense. The proprietor is one's own boss and has substantial freedom of action. Because the proprietor's profit income depends on the enterprise's success, there is strong incentive to manage the business efficiently.

But there are also several disadvantages of sole proprietorships. With rare exceptions, the financial resources of a sole proprietorship are insufficient to permit the firm to grow into a large enterprise. Finances are usually limited to what the proprietor has in the bank and what he or she can borrow. Since proprietorships often fail, commercial banks are not eager to extend them credit.

Also, being totally in charge of an enterprise necessitates that the proprietor carry out all management functions. A proprietor must make decisions on buying, selling, and the hiring and training of personnel, as well as decisions on producing, advertising, and distributing the firm's product. In short, the potential benefits of specialization in business management are not available to the typical small-scale proprietorship.

Finally, and most important, the proprietor is subject to *unlimited liability*. Individuals in business for themselves risk not only the assets of the firm but their personal assets as well. If the assets of an unsuccessful sole proprietorship are insufficient to pay the firm's bills, creditors can file claims against the proprietor's personal property.

Partnership

Like the sole proprietorship, a partnership is easy to organize. Although the partners usually sign a written agreement, there is not much legal red tape or legal expense. Also, greater specialization in management is possible because there are two or more participants. And because there is more than one owner, the financial resources of a partnership are likely to be greater than the resources of a sole proprietorship. Consequently, commercial banks regard partnerships as somewhat better risks than sole proprietorships.

But partnerships have some of the shortcomings of the proprietorship as well as some of their own. Whenever several people participate in management, the divided authority may lead to inconsistent policies or to inaction when action is required. Worse, the partners may disagree on basic policy. And although the finances of partnerships are generally superior to those of sole proprietorships, partnerships are still severely limited. The combined financial resources of three or four partners may not be enough to ensure the growth of a successful enterprise.

The continuity of a partnership is precarious. Generally, when one partner dies or withdraws, the partnership must be dissolved and reorganized, with inevitable disruption of its operations. Finally, unlimited liability plagues a partnership, just as it does a proprietorship. Each partner is liable for all business debts incurred, not only as a result of his or her own performance but also as a result of the performance of any other partner. A wealthy partner risks his or her wealth on the prudence of less affluent partners.

Corporation

The advantages of the corporate form of business enterprise have catapulted it into a dominant position in the United States. Although corporations are relatively small in number, many of them are large in size and in scale of operations. The corporation is by far the most effective form of business organization for raising financial capital (money). The corporation employs unique methods of finance—the selling of stocks and bonds—that enable it to pool the financial resources of large numbers of people. **Stocks** are shares of ownership of a corporation, whereas **bonds** are promises to repay a loan, usually at a set rate of interest. (See the Last Word.)

Financing via sales of stocks and bonds also provides advantages to those who purchase these *securities*. Such financing makes it possible for a household to own a part of the business and to share the expected monetary rewards without actively managing the firm. Moreover, an individual investor can spread risks by buying the securities of several corporations. And it is usually easy for holders of corporate securities to sell their holdings. Organized stock exchanges simplify the transfer of securities from sellers to buyers. This "ease of sale" increases the willingness of savers to make financial investments in corporate securities. Also, corporations have easier access to bank credit than do other types of business organizations. Corporations are better risks and are more likely to become profitable clients of banks. ⚠ 5.1

Corporations have the distinct advantage of **limited liability**. The owners (stockholders) of a corporation risk only what they paid for their stock. Their personal assets are not at stake if the corporation defaults on its debts. Creditors can sue the corporation as a legal person but cannot sue the owners of the corporation as individuals.

Because of their ability to attract financial capital, successful corporations can easily expand the scope of their operations and realize the benefits of expansion. For example, they can take advantage of mass-production technologies and division of labor. A corporation can hire specialists in production, accounting, and marketing functions and thus improve efficiency.

As a legal entity, the corporation has a life independent of its owners and its officers. Legally, at least, corporations are immortal. The transfer of corporate ownership through inheritance or the sale of stock does not disrupt the continuity of the corporation. Corporations have permanence that is conducive to long-range planning and growth.

The corporation's advantages are of tremendous significance and typically override any associated disadvantages. Yet there are certain drawbacks to the corporate form. Some red tape and legal expense are involved in obtaining a corporate charter. And from the social point of view, the corporate form of enterprise lends itself to certain abuses. Because the corporation is a legal entity, unscrupulous business owners can sometimes avoid personal responsibility for questionable business activities by adopting the corporate form of enterprise.

A disadvantage to the owners of corporations is the **double taxation** of some corporate income. Corporate profit that is shared among stockholders as *dividends* is taxed twice—once as corporate profit and again as stockholders' personal income.

Hybrid Structures   A number of states have passed legislation authorizing "hybrid" business structures that extend some of the advantages of corporations to firms with one or relatively few owners. Two such structures are the *limited-liability company (LLC)* and the *S corporation*.

The LLC is like an ordinary partnership for tax purposes but resembles a corporation in matters of liability. Like a partnership, an LLC distributes all profit directly to its owners and investors. But like a corporation, an LLC shields the personal assets of owners from liability claims. LLCs have a limited life, typically 30 or 40 years.

The S corporation is a corporation with 75 or fewer shareholders. Because the profit from the corporation passes directly to the owners as if the firm were a sole proprietorship or a partnership, the owners avoid the double taxation on distributed profit. They also enjoy the benefit of limited liability.

The Principal-Agent Problem

Many U.S. corporations are extremely large. In 1999 some 80 U.S. corporations had annual sales of more than $20 billion, and 170 firms had sales of more than $10 billion. General Motors alone sold $189 billion of output in 1999. Only 22 nations in the world had a total annual output that exceeded GM's annual sales!

Large size creates a potential problem. In sole proprietorships and partnerships, the owners of the real and financial assets of the firm enjoy direct control of those assets. But ownership of large corporations is spread over tens or hundreds of thousands of stockholders. The owners of a corporation usually do not manage it—they hire others to do so.

That practice can create a **principal-agent problem.** The *principals* are the stockholders who own the corporation and who hire executives as their agents to run the business on their behalf. But the interests of these managers (the agents) and the wishes of the owners (the principals) do not always coincide. The owners typically want maximum company profit and stock price. The agents, however, may want the power, prestige, and pay that usually accompany control over a large enterprise, independent of its profitability and stock price.

So a conflict of interest may develop. For example, executives may build expensive office buildings, enjoy excessive perks such as corporate jets, and pay too much to acquire other corporations. Consequently, the firm will have bloated costs. Profits and stock prices will not be maximized for the owners. 🔑 5.1

Many corporations have addressed the principal-agent problem by providing a substantial part of executive pay as shares of the companies' stock. The idea is to align the interests of the executives more closely with those of the broader corporate owners. By pursuing high profits and share prices—which benefit the broader owners—the executives enhance their own incomes. On average, high-level U.S. managers now own about 20 percent of their companies' stock. **(Key Question 4)**

∎ The Public Sector: Government's Role

The economic activities of the *public sector*—Federal, state, and local government—are extensive. We begin by discussing the economic functions of governments. What is government's role in the economy?

Providing the Legal Structure

Government provides the legal framework and the services needed for a market economy to operate effectively. The legal framework sets the legal status of business enterprises, ensures the rights of private ownership, and allows the making and enforcement of contracts. Government also establishes the legal "rules of the game" that control relationships among businesses, resource suppliers, and consumers. Discrete units of government referee economic relationships, seek out foul play, and impose penalties.

Government intervention is presumed to improve the allocation of resources. By supplying a medium of exchange, ensuring product quality, defining ownership rights, and enforcing contracts, the government increases the volume and safety of exchange. This widens the market and fosters greater specialization in the use of property and human resources. Such specialization promotes a more efficient allocation of resources.

Like the optimal amount of any "good," the optimal amount of regulation is that at which the marginal benefit and marginal cost are equal. Thus, there can be either too little regulation (MB exceeds MC) or too much regulation (MB is less than MC). The task is deciding on the right amount.

Maintaining Competition

Competition is the basic regulatory mechanism in the market system. It is the force that subjects producers and resource suppliers to the dictates of consumer sovereignty. With competition, buyers are the boss, the market is their agent, and businesses are their servants.

It is a different story where a single seller—a **monopoly**—controls an industry. By controlling supply, a monopolist can charge a higher-than-competitive price. Producer sovereignty then supplants consumer sovereignty. In the United States, government has attempted to control monopoly through *regulation* and through *antitrust*.

A few industries are natural monopolies—industries in which technology is such that only a single seller can achieve the lowest possible costs. In some cases government has allowed these monopolies to exist but has also created public commissions to regulate their prices and set their service standards. Examples of *regulated monopolies* are some firms that provide local electricity, telephone, and transportation services.

In nearly all markets, however, efficient production can best be attained with a high degree of competition. The Federal government has therefore enacted a series of antitrust (antimonopoly) laws, beginning with the Sherman Act of 1890, to prohibit certain monopoly abuses and, if necessary, break monopolists up into competing firms.

Redistributing Income

The market system is impersonal and may distribute income more inequitably than society desires. It yields very large incomes to those whose labor, by virtue of inherent ability and acquired education and skills, command high wages. Similarly, those who, through hard work or inheritance, possess valuable capital and land, receive large property incomes.

But many other members of society have less productive ability, have received only modest amounts of education and training, and have accumulated or inherited no property resources.

Moreover, some of the aged, the physically and mentally disabled, and the poorly educated earn small incomes or, like the unemployed, no income at all. Thus society chooses to redistribute a part of total income through a variety of government policies and programs. They are:

■ **Transfer payments** *Transfer payments*, for example, in the form of welfare checks and food stamps, provide relief to the destitute, the dependent, the disabled, and older citizens; unemployment compensation payments provide aid to the unemployed.

■ **Market intervention** Government also alters the distribution of income through *market intervention*, that is, by acting to modify the prices that are or would be established by market forces. Providing farmers with above-market prices for their output and requiring that firms pay minimum wages are illustrations of government interventions designed to raise the income of specific groups.

■ **Taxation** Since the 1930s, government has used the personal income tax to take a larger proportion of the income of the rich than of the poor, thus narrowing the after-tax income difference between high-income and low-income earners.

The *extent* to which government should redistribute income is subject to lively debate. Redistribution involves both benefits and costs. The alleged benefits are greater "fairness," or "economic justice"; the alleged costs are reduced incentives to work, save, invest, and produce, and therefore a loss of total output and income.

Reallocating Resources

Market failure occurs when the competitive market system (1) produces the "wrong" amounts of certain goods and services or (2) fails to allocate any resources whatsoever to the production of certain goods and services whose output is economically justified. The first type of failure results from what economists call *spillovers*, and the second type involves *public goods*. Both kinds of market failure can be corrected by government action.

Spillovers or Externalities When we say that competitive markets automatically bring about the efficient use of resources, we assume that all the benefits and costs for each product are fully reflected in the market demand and supply curves. That is not always the case. In some markets certain benefits or costs may escape the buyer or seller.

A spillover occurs when some of the costs or the benefits of a good are passed on to or "spill over to" someone other than the immediate buyer or seller. Spillovers are also called *externalities*, because they are benefits or costs that accrue to some third party that is external to the market transaction. 🔑 5.2

Spillover Costs Production or consumption costs inflicted on a third party without compensation are called **spillover costs.** Environmental pollution is an example. When a chemical manufacturer or a meatpacking plant dumps its wastes into a lake or river, swimmers, fishers, and boaters—and perhaps those who drink the water—suffer spillover costs. When a petroleum refinery pollutes the air with smoke or a paper mill creates obnoxious odors, the community experiences spillover costs for which it is not compensated.

What are the economic effects? Recall that costs determine the position of the firm's supply curve. When a firm avoids some costs by polluting, its supply curve lies farther to the right than it does when the firm bears the full costs of production. As a result, the price of the product is too low and the output of the product is too large to achieve allocative efficiency. A market failure occurs in the form of an overallocation of resources to the production of the good.

Correcting for Spillover Costs Government can do two things to correct the overallocation of resources. Both solutions are designed to internalize external costs, that is, to make the offending firm pay the costs rather than shift them to others:

■ **Legislation** In cases of air and water pollution, the most direct action is legislation prohibiting or limiting the pollution. Such legislation forces potential polluters to pay for the proper disposal of industrial wastes—here, by installing smoke-abatement equipment or water-purification facilities. The idea is to force potential offenders, under the threat of legal action, to bear *all* the costs associated with production.

■ **Specific taxes** A less direct action is based on the fact that taxes are a cost and therefore a determinant of a firm's supply curve. Government might levy a *specific tax*—that is, a tax confined to a particular product—on each unit of the polluting firm's output. The amount of this tax would roughly equal the estimated amount of the spillover cost arising from the production of each unit of output. Through this tax, government would pass back to the offending firm a cost equivalent to the spillover cost the firm is avoiding. This would shift the firm's supply curve to the left, reducing equilibrium output and eliminating the overallocation of resources.

Spillover Benefits   Sometimes spillovers appear as benefits. The production or consumption of certain goods and services may confer spillover or external benefits on third parties or on the community at large without compensating payment. Immunization against measles and polio results in direct benefits to the immediate consumer of those vaccines. But it also results in widespread substantial spillover benefits to the entire community.

Education is another example of **spillover benefits.** Education benefits individual consumers: Better-educated people generally achieve higher incomes than less well educated people. But education also provides benefits to society, in the form of a more versatile and more productive labor force, on the one hand, and smaller outlays for crime prevention, law enforcement, and welfare programs, on the other.

Spillover benefits mean that the market demand curve, which reflects only private benefits, understates total benefits. The demand curve for the product lies farther to the left than it would if the market took all benefits into account. As a result, a smaller amount of the product will be produced, or, alternatively, there will be an *underallocation* of resources to the product—again a market failure.

Correcting for Spillover Benefits   How might the underallocation of resources associated with spillover benefits be corrected? The answer is either to subsidize consumers (to increase demand), to subsidize producers (to increase supply), or, in the extreme, to have government produce the product:

■ *Subsidize consumers*   To correct the underallocation of resources to higher education, the U.S. government provides low-interest loans to students so that they can afford more education. Those loans increase the demand for higher education.

■ *Subsidize suppliers*   In some cases government finds it more convenient and administratively simpler to correct an underallocation by subsidizing suppliers. For example, in higher education, state governments provide substantial portions of the budgets of public colleges and universities. Such subsidies lower the costs of producing higher education and increase its supply. Publicly subsidized immunization programs, hospitals, and medical research are other examples.

■ *Provide goods via government*   A third policy option may be appropriate where spillover benefits are extremely large: Government may finance or, in the extreme, own and operate the industry that is involved. Examples are the U.S. Postal Service and Federal aircraft control systems.

Public Goods and Services

Certain goods called *private goods* are produced through the competitive market system and are said to be *divisible* because they are produced in units small enough to be purchased and used by individual buyers. Examples are the myriad items sold in stores. Private goods are also subject to the **exclusion principle.** Buyers who are willing and able to pay the equilibrium price of the product obtain it, but those who are unable or unwilling to pay are *excluded* from acquiring the product and its benefits.

Certain other goods and services called **public goods** have the opposite characteristics. Public goods are *indivisible;* they must be produced in such large units that they cannot ordinarily be sold to individual buyers. Individuals can buy hamburgers, computers, and automobiles through the market, but they cannot buy aircraft carriers, highways, or space telescopes.

The exclusion principle does not apply to public goods since there is no effective way of excluding individuals from their benefits once such goods come into existence. Obtaining the benefits of private goods requires that they be *purchased;* obtaining the benefits of public goods requires only that they be *available.*

The classic example of a public good is a proposed lighthouse on a treacherous coast. The construction of the lighthouse would be economically justified if its benefits (fewer shipwrecks) exceeded its cost. But the benefits accruing to a single user would not be great enough to justify the purchase of such an indivisible product. Moreover, once it was in operation, the warning light would be a guide to *all* ships; there would be no practical way to exclude any captain from using the light. Economists call this the

free-rider problem, in which people receive benefits from a good without contributing to its cost.

Because the services of the lighthouse cannot be priced and sold, it would be unprofitable for a private firm to devote resources to it. So here we have a service that could yield substantial benefits but to which the market system would allocate no resources. It is a public good, much like national defense, flood control, and public health. Society signals its desire for such goods by voting for particular political candidates who support their provision. The goods themselves must be provided by the public sector and financed by compulsory charges in the form of taxes. ⚠ 5.2

Quasi-Public Goods

Government provides many goods that fit the economist's definition of a public good. However, it also provides other goods and services that could be produced and delivered in such a way that the exclusion principle would apply. Such goods, called **quasi-public goods,** include education, streets and highways, police and fire protection, libraries and museums, preventive medicine, and sewage disposal. They could all be priced and provided by private firms through the market system. But, as we noted earlier, because they all have substantial spillover benefits, they would be underproduced by the market system. Therefore, government often provides them to avoid the underallocation of resources that would otherwise occur.

The Reallocation Process

How are resources reallocated from the production of private goods to the production of public and quasi-public goods? If the resources of the economy are fully employed, government must free up resources from the production of private goods and make them available for the production of public and quasi-public goods. It does so by reducing private demand for them. And it does that by levying taxes on households and businesses, taking some of their income out of the circular flow. With lower incomes and hence less purchasing power, households and businesses are obliged to curtail their consumption and investment spending. As a result, the private demand for goods and services declines, as does the private demand for resources. So by diverting purchasing power from private spenders to government, taxes remove resources from private use. (Global Perspective 5.1 shows the extent to which various countries divert labor from the private sector to the public sector.)

GLOBAL PERSPECTIVE 5.1

Government Employment as a Percentage of Total Employment, Selected Nations

The ratio of government employment to total employment measures the extent to which government diverts labor resources from the private sector to the production of public goods and quasi-public goods. The ratio varies greatly among nations.

Government Employment as Percentage of Total Employment, 1999

Sweden, Denmark, France, Canada, Italy, Germany, Switzerland, Netherlands, United States, Japan

Source: Organization for Economic Cooperation and Development, www.oecd.org.

Government then spends the tax proceeds to provide public and quasi-public goods and services. Taxation releases resources from the production of private consumer goods (food, clothing, television sets) and private investment goods (printing presses, boxcars, warehouses). Government shifts those resources to the production of public and quasi-public goods (post offices, submarines, parks), changing the composition of the economy's total output. **(Key Questions 9 and 10)**

Promoting Stability

An economy's level of output depends on its level of total spending relative to its production capacity. When the level of total spending matches the economy's production capacity, human and property resources are fully employed and prices in general are stable. But sometimes total spending is either inadequate or excessive and the result is either unemployment or inflation. Government promotes stability by addressing these two problems:

■ *Unemployment*   When private sector spending is too low, government may try to augment it so that total spending—private plus public—is sufficient to achieve full employment. It does this by increasing government spending or by lowering taxes to stimulate private spending. Also, it often takes actions to lower interest rates, thereby stimulating private borrowing and spending.

■ *Inflation*   Inflation is a general increase in the level of prices. Prices of goods and services rise when spenders try to buy more than the economy's capacity to produce. When total spending is excessive and becomes inflationary, government may try to reduce total spending by cutting its own expenditures or by raising taxes to curtail private spending. It may also take actions to increase interest rates to reduce private borrowing and spending.

QUICK REVIEW 5.3

■ Government enhances the operation of the market system by providing an appropriate legal foundation and promoting competition.

■ Transfer payments, direct market intervention, and taxation are among the ways in which government can lessen income inequality.

■ Government can correct for the overallocation of resources associated with spillover costs through legislation or taxes; it can offset the underallocation of resources associated with spillover benefits by granting government subsidies.

■ Government provides certain public goods because they are indivisible and free-riders can obtain them without payment; government also provides many quasi-public goods because of their large spillover benefits.

■ Government can stabilize the economy by adjusting spending, tax revenues, and interest rates.

■ The Circular Flow Revisited

In Figure 5.6 we integrate government into the circular flow model first shown in Figure 2.6. Here flows (1) through (4) are the same as the corresponding flows in that figure. Flows (1) and (2) show business expenditures for the resources provided by households. These expenditures are costs to busi-

nesses but represent wage, rent, interest, and profit income to households. Flows (3) and (4) show household expenditures for the goods and services produced by businesses.

Now consider what happens when we add government. Flows (5) through (8) illustrate that government makes purchases in both product and resource markets. Flows (5) and (6) represent government purchases of such products as paper, computers, and military hardware from private businesses. Flows (7) and (8) represent government purchases of resources. The Federal government employs and pays salaries to members of Congress, the armed forces, Justice Department lawyers, meat inspectors, and so on. State and local governments hire and pay teachers, bus drivers, police, and firefighters. The Federal government might also lease or purchase land to expand a military base, and a city might buy land on which to build a new elementary school.

Government then provides public goods and services to both households and businesses, as shown by flows (9) and (10). To finance those public goods and services, businesses and households are required to pay taxes, as shown by flows (11) and (12). These flows are labeled as *net* taxes to indicate that they also include "taxes in reverse" in the form of transfer payments to households and subsidies to businesses. Thus, flow (11) entails various subsidies to farmers, shipbuilders, and airlines as well as income, sales, and excise taxes paid by businesses to government. Most subsidies to business are "concealed" in the form of low-interest loans, loan guarantees, tax concessions, or public facilities provided at prices below their cost. Similarly, flow (12) includes both taxes (personal income taxes, payroll taxes) collected by government directly from households and transfer payments such as welfare payments and social security benefits paid by government.

We can use Figure 5.6 to review how government alters the distribution of income, reallocates resources, and changes the level of economic activity. The structure of taxes and transfer payments significantly affects income distribution. In flow (12) a tax structure that draws tax revenues primarily from well-to-do households, combined with a system of transfer payments to low-income households, reduces income inequality.

Flows (5) through (8) imply that government diverts goods and resources away from private sector consumption or use and directs them to the public

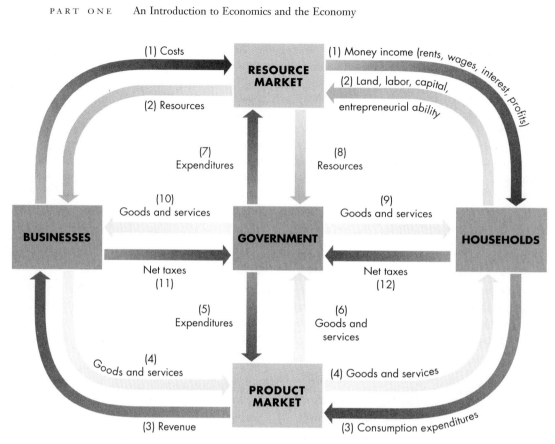

Figure 5.6

The circular flow and the public sector.   Government buys products from the product market and employs resources from the resource market to provide public goods and services to households and businesses. Government finances its expenditures through the net tax revenues (taxes minus transfer payments) it receives from households and businesses.

sector. This resource reallocation is required to produce public goods and services.

Finally, the governmental flows suggest how government might try to stabilize the economy. For example, if the economy had widespread unemployment, government might increase its spending to increase total spending, output, and employment. Similarly, government might reduce taxes or increase transfer payments to increase income available for spending. That would boost private spending and employment. To fight inflation, the opposite policies would be in order: reduced government spending, increased taxes, and reduced transfers.

▎ Government Finance

How large is the U.S. public sector? What are the main expenditure categories of Federal, state, and local governments? How are these expenditures financed?

Government Purchases and Transfers

We can get an idea of the size of government's economic role by examining government purchases of goods and services and government transfer payments. There is a significant difference between these two kinds of outlays:

- **Government purchases** are *exhaustive;* the products purchased directly absorb (require the use of) resources and are part of the domestic output. For example, the purchase of a missile absorbs the labor of physicists and engineers along with steel, explosives, and a host of other inputs.

- **Transfer payments** are *nonexhaustive;* they do not directly absorb resources or create output. Social security benefits, welfare payments, veterans' benefits, and unemployment compensation are examples of transfer payments. Their key characteristic is that recipients make no current contribution to domestic output in return for them.

Federal, state, and local governments spent $2779 billion in 2000. Of that total, government purchases were $1740 billion and government transfers were $1039 billion. Figure 5.7 shows these amounts as percentages of U.S. domestic output for 2000 and compares them to percentages for 1960. Government purchases have declined from about 22 to 17 percent of output since 1960. But transfer payments have doubled as a percentage of output—from 5 percent in 1960 to 10 percent in 2000. Relative to U.S. output, total government spending is thus slightly higher today than it was 40 years ago. This means that the tax revenues required to finance government expenditures are also slightly higher. Today, government spending and the tax revenues needed to finance it are nearly 28 percent of U.S. output.

In 2000 the so-called Tax Freedom Day in the United States was May 3. On that day the average worker had earned enough (from the start of the year) to pay his or her share of the taxes required to finance government spending for the year. Tax Freedom Day arrives even later in several other countries, as implied in Global Perspective 5.2.

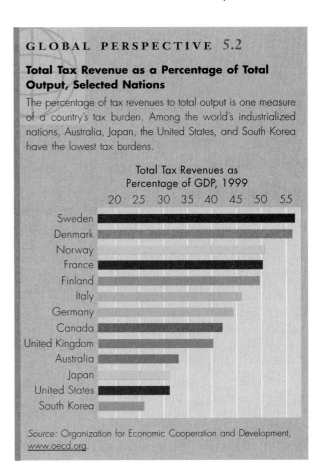

GLOBAL PERSPECTIVE 5.2

Total Tax Revenue as a Percentage of Total Output, Selected Nations

The percentage of tax revenues to total output is one measure of a country's tax burden. Among the world's industrialized nations, Australia, Japan, the United States, and South Korea have the lowest tax burdens.

Total Tax Revenues as Percentage of GDP, 1999

Source: Organization for Economic Cooperation and Development, www.oecd.org.

Federal Finance

Now let's look separately at each of the Federal, state, and local units of government in the United States and compare their expenditures and taxes. Figure 5.8 tells the story for the Federal government.

Federal Expenditures

Four areas of Federal spending stand out: (1) pensions and income security, (2) national defense, (3) health, and (4) interest on the public debt. The *pensions and income security* category includes the many income-maintenance programs for the aged, persons with disabilities or handicaps, the unemployed, the retired, and families with no breadwinner. *National defense* accounts for about 16 percent of the Federal budget, underscoring the high cost of military preparedness. *Health* reflects the cost of government health programs for the retired and poor. *Interest on the public debt* is high because the public debt itself is large.

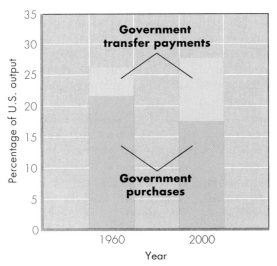

Figure 5.7

Government purchases, transfers, and total spending as percentages of U.S. output, 1960 and 2000.   Government purchases have declined as a percent of U.S. output since 1960. Transfer payments, however, have increased, so total government spending (purchases plus transfers) is now about 28 percent of U.S. output.

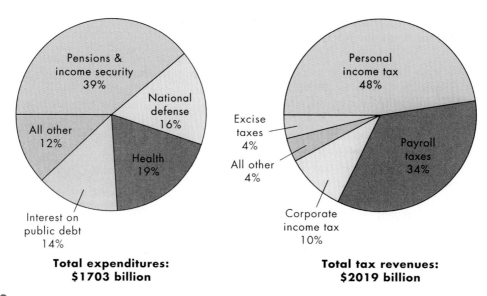

Total expenditures: $1703 billion

Total tax revenues: $2019 billion

Figure 5.8

Federal expenditures and tax revenues, 1999.   Federal expenditures are dominated by spending for pensions and income security and by spending for national defense. A full 82 percent of Federal tax revenue is derived from just two sources: the personal income tax and payroll taxes. The $316 billion difference between revenues and expenditures reflects a budget surplus. *Source:* U.S. Office of Management and Budget.

Federal Tax Revenues

The revenue side of Figure 5.8 shows that the personal income tax, payroll taxes, and the corporate income tax are the basic revenue sources, accounting respectively for 48, 34, and 10 cents of each dollar collected.

Personal Income Tax   The **personal income tax** is the kingpin of the Federal tax system and merits special comment. This tax is levied on *taxable income*, that is, on the incomes of households and unincorporated businesses after certain exemptions ($2800 for each household member) and deductions (business expenses, charitable contributions, home mortgage interest payments, certain state and local taxes) are taken into account.

The Federal personal income tax is a *progressive tax*, meaning that people with higher incomes pay a larger percentage of their incomes as taxes than do people with lower incomes. The progressivity is achieved by applying higher tax rates to successive layers or brackets of income.

Columns 1 and 2 in Table 5.1 show the mechanics of the income tax for a married couple filing a joint return in 2000. Note that a 15 percent tax rate applies to all taxable income up to $43,850, a 28 percent rate applies to additional income up to $105,950, and even

greater rates apply for three more layers of additional income, the highest rate being 39.6 percent.

The tax rates shown in column 2 in Table 5.1 are marginal tax rates. A **marginal tax rate** is the rate at which the tax is paid on each *additional* unit of taxable income. Thus, if a couple's taxable income is $60,000, they will pay the marginal tax rate of 15 percent on each dollar from $1 to $43,850 and the marginal tax rate of 28 percent on each dollar from $43,851 to $60,000. You should confirm that their total income tax is $11,100.

The marginal tax rates in column 2 overstate the personal income tax bite because the rising rates in that column apply only to the income within each successive tax bracket. To get a better idea of the tax burden, we must consider average tax rates. The **average tax rate** is the total tax paid divided by total taxable income. The couple in our previous example is in the 28 percent tax bracket because they pay a top marginal tax rate of 28 percent on some of their income. But their *average* tax rate is 18.5 percent (=$11,100/$60,000).

A tax whose average rate rises as income increases is a progressive tax. Such a tax claims both a larger absolute amount and a larger proportion of income as income rises. Thus we can say that the Federal personal income tax is progressive. **(Key Question 15)**

Table 5.1
Federal Personal Income Tax Rates, 2000*

(1) Total Taxable Income	(2) Marginal Tax Rate, %	(3) Total Tax on Highest Income in Bracket	(4) Average Tax Rate on Highest Income in Bracket, % (3) ÷ (1)
$1–$43,850	15.0	$ 6,578	15.0
$43,851–$105,950	28.0	23,966	22.6
$105,951–$161,450	31.0	41,171	25.5
$161,451–$288,350	36.0	86,855	30.1
Over $288,350	39.6		

*Data are for a married couple filing a joint return.

Payroll Taxes   Social security contributions are **payroll taxes**—taxes based on wages and salaries—used to finance two compulsory Federal programs for retired workers: social security (an income-enhancement program) and Medicare (which pays for medical services). Employers and employees pay these taxes equally. Improvements in, and extensions of, the social security programs, plus growth of the labor force, have resulted in significant increases in these payroll taxes in recent years. In 2000, employees and employers each paid 7.65 percent on the first $76,200 of an employee's annual earnings and 1.45 percent on all additional earnings.

Corporate Income Tax   The Federal government also taxes corporate income. The **corporate income tax** is levied on a corporation's profit—the difference between its total revenue and its total expenses. For almost all corporations, the tax rate is 35 percent.

Excise Taxes   Taxes on commodities or on purchases take the form of **sales and excise taxes.** The difference between the two is mainly one of coverage. Sales taxes fall on a wide range of products, whereas excises are levied individually on a small, select list of commodities. As Figure 5.8 suggests, the Federal government collects excise taxes (on the sale of such commodities as alcoholic beverages, tobacco, and gasoline) but does not levy a general sales tax; sales taxes are the primary revenue source of most state governments.

State and Local Finance

State and local governments have different mixes of revenues and expenditures than the Federal government has.

State Finances

Note in Figure 5.9 that the primary source of tax revenue for state governments is sales and excise taxes, which account for about 48 percent of all their tax revenue. State personal income taxes, which have much lower rates than the Federal income tax, are the second most important source of state revenue. A tax on corporate income and license fees account for most of the remainder of state tax revenue.

The major expenditures of state governments are for (1) education, (2) public welfare, (3) health and hospitals, and (4) highway maintenance and construction.

Figure 5.9 contains aggregated data, so it tells us little about the finances of individual states. And states vary significantly in the taxes levied. Thus, although personal income taxes are a major source of revenue for all state governments combined, seven states do not levy a personal income tax. Also, there are great variations in the size of tax receipts and disbursements among the states. Thirty-six states augment their tax revenues with state-run lotteries to help close the gap between their tax receipts and expenditures.

The huge gap between state tax revenues and expenditures in Figure 5.9 is largely eliminated when we take nontax sources of income into account. In 1998 the states received $240 billion in intergovernmental grants from the Federal government. They also received significant revenue from miscellaneous sources such as state-owned utilities and liquor stores.

Local Finances

The local level of government includes counties, municipalities, townships, and school districts as well as cities and towns. It is clear from the receipts and expenditures shown in Figure 5.10 that local governments rely heavily on **property taxes.** And they spend most of their revenues on education.

The tax revenues of local governments cover less than one-half of their expenditures. The remaining revenue comes from intergovernmental grants from the Federal and state governments.

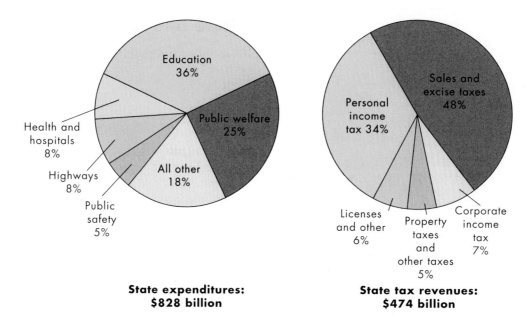

**State expenditures:
$828 billion**

**State tax revenues:
$474 billion**

Figure 5.9

State expenditures and tax revenues, 1998. State governments spend mainly on education and public welfare. Their primary source of tax revenue is sales and excise taxes.
Source: U.S. Bureau of the Census.

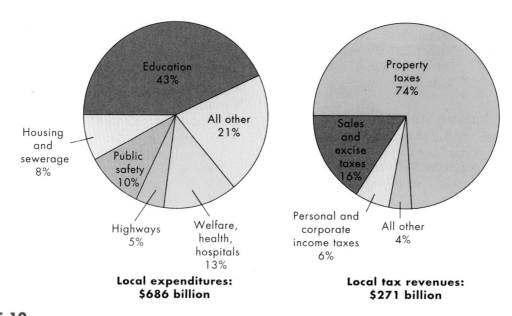

**Local expenditures:
$686 billion**

**Local tax revenues:
$271 billion**

Figure 5.10

Local expenditures and tax revenues, 1996. The expenditures of local governments are largely for education and are financed by property taxes.
Source: U.S. Bureau of the Census.

The Financing of Corporate Operations

One Advantage of Corporations Is Their Ability to Finance Their Operations through the Sale of Stocks and Bonds.

Generally, corporations finance their activities in three ways. First, a very large portion of a corporation's activities is financed internally out of undistributed corporate profits. Second, as do individuals or unincorporated businesses, corporations may borrow from financial institutions. For example, a small corporation planning to build a new plant may obtain the needed funds from a commercial bank, a savings and loan association, or an insurance company. Third, unique to corporations, they can issue common stocks and bonds.

Stocks versus Bonds A common stock represents a share in the ownership of a corporation. The purchaser of a stock certificate has the right to vote for corporate officers and to share in dividends. If you buy 1000 of the 100,000 shares issued by OutTell, Inc. (hereafter OT), then you own 1 percent of the company, are entitled to 1 percent of any dividends declared by the board of directors, and control 1 percent of the votes in the annual election of corporate officials.

In contrast, a bond does not bestow any corporate ownership on the purchaser. A bond purchaser is simply lending money to a corporation. A bond is an IOU, in acknowledgment of a loan, whereby the corporation promises to pay the holder a fixed amount set forth on the bond at some specified future date and other fixed amounts (interest payments) every year up to the bond's maturity date. For example, you might purchase a 10-year OT bond with a face value of $1000 and a 10 percent rate of interest. This means that, in exchange for your $1000, OT guarantees you a $100 interest payment for each of the next 10-years and then repays your $1000 principal at the end of that period.

Differences There are clearly important differences between stocks and bonds. First, as noted above, the bondholder is only a lender,

not an owner of the company. Second, bonds are considered to be less risky than stocks, for two reasons. On the one hand, bondholders have a "legal prior claim" on a corporation's earnings. Dividends cannot be paid to stockholders until all interest payments that are due to bondholders have been paid. On the other hand, holders of OT stock do not know how much their dividends will be or how much they might get for their stock if they decide to sell. If OutTell falls on hard times, stockholders may receive no dividends at all, and the value of their stock may plummet. Provided the corporation does not go bankrupt, the holder of an OT bond is guaranteed a $100 interest payment each year and the return of his or her $1000 at the end of 10 years.

Bond Risks This is not to imply that the purchase of corporate bonds is without risk. The market value of your OT bond may vary over time in accordance with the financial health of the corporation. If OT encounters economic misfortunes that raise questions about its financial integrity, the market value of your bond may fall. Should you sell the bond prior to maturity, you may receive only $600 or $700 for it (rather than $1000) and thereby incur a capital loss.

Changes in the interest rate paid on a bond will also affect the market prices of bonds. An increase in the interest rate will cause the bond price to fall and a decrease in the interest rate will cause the bond price to rise. Assume you purchase a $1000 ten-year OT bond this year when the interest rate is 10 percent. That means that your bond will provide a $100 fixed interest payment each year. But suppose that next year the interest rate jumps to 15 percent. Now OT must guarantee a $150 fixed annual payment on its new $1000 ten-year bonds. Clearly, no sensible person will pay you $1000 for your bond, which pays only $100 of interest income per year, when a new bond can be purchased for $1000 and will pay the holder $150 per year. Hence, if you sell your original bond before it reaches maturity, you may suffer a capital loss.

Bondholders face another source of risk: inflation. If substantial inflation occurs over the 10-year period during which you hold an OT bond, the $1000 principal repaid to you at the end of that period will represent substantially less purchasing power than the $1000 you lent OT 10 years earlier. You will have lent "dear" dollars but will be repaid in "cheap" dollars.

These grants totaled $270 billion in 1996. Also, local governments received $115 billion in proprietary income, that is, revenue from government-owned utilities providing water, electricity, natural gas, and transportation.

Fiscal Federalism

Over the years, the tax collections of both state and local governments have fallen substantially short of their expenditures. Such shortfalls are largely filled by Federal transfers or grants. It is not uncommon for 20 to 25 percent of all revenue received by state and local governments to come from the Federal government. In addition to Federal grants to state and local governments, the states also make grants to local governmental units. This system of intergovernmental transfers is called **fiscal federalism.**

> **QUICK REVIEW 5.4**
>
> ▪ Government purchases account for about 17 percent of U.S. output; the addition of transfers increases government spending to nearly 28 percent of domestic output.
>
> ▪ Income security and national defense are the main categories of Federal spending; personal income, payroll, and corporate income taxes are the primary sources of Federal revenue.
>
> ▪ States rely on sales and excise taxes for revenue; their spending is largely for education and public welfare.
>
> ▪ Education is the main expenditure for local governments, most of whose revenue comes from property taxes.

SUMMARY

1. The functional distribution of income shows how society's total income is divided among wages, rents, interest, and profit; the personal distribution of income shows how total income is divided among individual households.

2. Households use all their income to pay personal taxes, for saving, and to buy consumer goods. Over half of their consumption expenditures are for services.

3. Sole proprietorships are firms owned and usually operated by single individuals. Partnerships are firms owned and usually operated by just a handful of individuals. Corporations are legal entities, distinct and separate from the individuals who own them. They often have thousands, or even millions, of owners—the stockholders.

4. Government improves the operation of the market system by (a) providing an appropriate legal and social framework and (b) acting to maintain competition.

5. Government alters the distribution of income through the tax-transfer system and through market intervention.

6. Spillovers, or externalities, cause the equilibrium output of certain goods to vary from the socially efficient output. Spillover costs result in an overallocation of resources, which can be corrected by legislation or by specific taxes. Spillover benefits are accompanied by an underallocation of resources, which can be corrected by government subsidies to consumers or producers.

7. Only government is willing to provide public goods, which are indivisible and entail benefits from which nonpaying consumers (free riders) cannot be excluded. Private firms will not produce public goods. Quasi-public goods have some of the characteristics of public goods and some of the characteristics of private goods; government provides them because the private sector would underallocate resources to their production.

8. Government reduces unemployment and inflation by altering its taxation, spending, and interest-rate policies.

9. Government purchases exhaust (use up or absorb) resources; transfer payments do not. Government purchases have declined from about 22 percent of domestic output in 1960 to 17 percent today. Transfer payments, however, have grown significantly. Total government spending now amounts to almost 28 percent of domestic output.

10. The main categories of Federal spending are pensions and income security, national defense, health, and interest on the public debt; Federal revenues come primarily from personal income taxes, payroll taxes, and corporate income taxes.

11. States derive their revenue primarily from sales and excise taxes and personal income taxes; major state expenditures go to education, public welfare, health and hospitals, and highways.

12. Local communities derive most of their revenue from property taxes; education is their most important expenditure.

13. Under the U.S. system of fiscal federalism, state and local tax revenues are supplemented by sizable revenue grants from the Federal government.

TERMS AND CONCEPTS

functional distribution of income	industry	monopoly	personal income tax
personal distribution of income	sole proprietorship	spillover costs	marginal tax rate
durable goods	partnership	spillover benefits	average tax rate
nondurable goods	corporation	exclusion principle	payroll taxes
services	stocks	public goods	corporate income tax
plant	bonds	free-rider problem	sales and excise taxes
firm	limited liability	quasi-public goods	property taxes
	double taxation	government purchases	fiscal federalism
	principal-agent problem	transfer payments	

STUDY QUESTIONS

1. Distinguish between the functional distribution and personal distribution of income.

2. **Key Question** Assume that the five residents of Econoville receive incomes of $50, $75, $125, $250, and $500. Present the resulting personal distribution of income as a graph similar to Figure 5.2. Compare the incomes of the lowest fifth and the highest fifth of the income receivers.

3. Distinguish between a plant, a firm, and an industry. Contrast a vertically integrated firm, a horizontally organized firm, and a conglomerate.

4. **Key Question** What are the major legal forms of business organization? Briefly state the advantages and disadvantages of each. How do you account for the dominant role of corporations in the U.S. economy?

5. "The legal form an enterprise assumes is dictated primarily by the financial requirements of its particular line of production." Do you agree?

6. Enumerate and briefly discuss the main economic functions of government. Which function do you think is the most controversial? Why?

7. What divergences arise between equilibrium output and efficient output when (*a*) spillover costs and (*b*) spillover benefits are present? How might government correct for these divergences? "The presence of spillover costs suggests the underallocation of resources to a particular product and the need for governmental subsidies." Do you agree? Why or why not? Explain how zoning and seat belt laws might be used to deal with a problem of spillover costs.

8. Researchers have concluded that injuries caused by firearms cost more than $500 million a year in hospital expenses alone. Because the majority of persons shot are poor and without insurance, roughly 85 percent of these expenses must be borne by taxpayers. Use your understanding of externalities to recommend appropriate policies.

9. **Key Question** What are the characteristics of public goods? Explain the significance of the exclusion principle. By what means does government provide public goods?

10. **Key Question** Draw a production possibilities curve with public goods on the vertical axis and private goods on the horizontal axis. Assuming the economy is initially operating *on the curve*, indicate how the production of public goods might be increased. How might the output of public goods be increased if the economy is initially operating at a point *inside the curve*?

11. Use your understanding of the characteristics of private and public goods to determine whether the following should be produced through the market system or provided by government: (*a*) bread; (*b*) street lighting; (*c*) bridges; (*d*) parks; (*e*) swimming pools; (*f*) medical care; (*g*) mail delivery; (*h*) housing; (*i*) air traffic control; (*j*) libraries. State why you answered as you did in each case.

12. Explain how government can manipulate its expenditures and tax revenues to reduce (*a*) unemployment and (*b*) the rate of inflation.

13. "Most government actions simultaneously affect the distribution of income, the allocation of resources, and the levels of unemployment and prices." Use the circular flow model to confirm this assertion for each of the following:
    a. The construction of a new high school in Blackhawk County.
    b. A 2 percent reduction in the Federal corporate income tax.
    c. An expansion of preschool programs for disadvantaged children.
    d. A $50 million increase in spending for space research.
    e. The levying of a tax on air polluters.
    f. A $1 increase in the legally required minimum wage.

14. What is the most important source of revenue and the major type of expenditure at the Federal level? At the state level? At the local level?

15. **Key Question** Suppose in Fiscalville there is no tax on the first $10,000 of income, but a 20 percent tax on earnings between $10,000 and $20,000 and a 30 percent tax on income between $20,000 and $30,000. Any income above $30,000 is taxed at 40 percent. If your income is $50,000, how much will you pay in taxes? Determine your marginal and average tax rates. Is this a progressive tax? Explain.

16. **(Last Word)** Describe three ways to finance corporate activity. Make a case arguing that stocks are more risky than bonds for the financial investor.

17. **Web-Based Question:** *Personal distribution of income—what is the trend?* Visit the U.S. Census Bureau website at www.census.gov/hhes/income/midclass/index.html and select Data. Since 1969, how has the share of aggregate household income received by the lowest and highest income quintiles (fifths) changed?

18. **Web-Based Question:** *States taxes and expenditures per capita—where does your state rank?* Go to the Census Bureau site, www.census.gov/govs/www/state.html, and find the table that ranks the states by tax revenue and expenditures per capita for the latest year. Where does your home state rank in each category? Where does the state in which you are attending college, if different, rank? Speculate as to why there is such a gap between the high-ranking and low-ranking states.

C H A P T E R

The United States in the Global Economy

BACKPACKERS IN THE wilderness like to think they are "leaving the world behind," but, like Atlas, they carry the world on their shoulders. Much of their equipment is imported—knives from Switzerland, rain gear from South Korea, cameras from Japan, aluminum pots from England, miniature stoves from Sweden, sleeping bags from China, and compasses from Finland. Moreover, they may have driven to the trailheads in Japanese-made Toyotas or Swedish-made Volvos, sipping coffee from Brazil or snacking on bananas from Honduras. ▪ International trade and the global economy affect all of us daily, whether we are hiking in the wilderness, driving our cars, listening to music, or working at our jobs. We cannot "leave the world behind." We are enmeshed in a global web of economic relationships—trading of goods and services, multinational corporations, cooperative ventures among the world's firms, and ties among the world's financial markets. That web is so complex that it is difficult to determine just what is—or isn't—an American product. A Finnish company owns Wilson sporting goods; a Swiss company owns Gerber baby food; and a British corporation owns Burger King. The Buick Regal sedan is manufactured in Canada. Many "U.S." products are made with components from abroad, and, conversely, many "foreign" products contain numerous U.S.-produced parts. (This point is treated humorously in this chapter's Last Word.)

▪ International Linkages

Several economic flows link the U.S. economy and the economies of other nations. As identified in Figure 6.1, these flows are:

- *Goods and services flows* or simply *trade flows.* The United States exports goods and services to other nations and imports goods and services from them.

- *Capital and labor flows* or simply *resource flows.* U.S. firms establish production facilities—new capital—in foreign countries, and foreign firms establish production facilities in the United States. Labor also moves between nations. Each

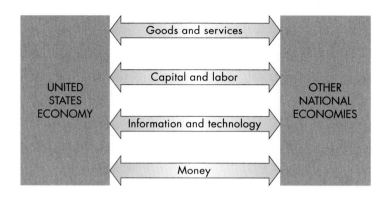

Figure 6.1

International linkages. The U.S. economy is intertwined with other national economies through goods and services flows (trade flows), capital and labor flows (resource flows), information and technology flows, and financial flows.

year many foreigners immigrate to the United States and some Americans move to other nations.

- **Information and technology flows.** The United States transmits information to other nations about U.S. products, prices, interest rates, and investment opportunities and receives such information from abroad. Firms in other countries use technology created in the United States, and U.S. businesses incorporate technology developed abroad.
- **Financial flows.** Money is transferred between the United States and other countries for several purposes, for example, paying for imports, buying foreign assets, paying interest on debt, and providing foreign aid.

■ The United States and World Trade

Our main goal in this chapter is to examine trade flows and the financial flows that pay for them. What is the extent and pattern of international trade, and how much has that trade grown? Who are the major participants?

Volume and Pattern

Table 6.1 suggests the importance of world trade for selected countries. Many countries, with restricted resources and limited domestic markets, cannot efficiently produce the variety of goods their citizens want. So they must import goods from other nations. That, in turn, means that they must export, or

sell abroad, some of their own products. For such countries, exports may run from 25 to 35 percent or more of their gross domestic product (GDP)—the market value of all goods and services produced in an economy. Other countries, the United States, for example, have rich and diversified resource bases and large internal markets. Although the total volume of trade is huge in the United States, it constitutes a smaller percentage of GDP than it does in a number of other nations.

Volume   For the United States and for the world as a whole the volume of international trade has been increasing both absolutely and relative to their GDPs. A comparison of the boxed data in Figure 6.2 reveals substantial growth in the dollar amount of

Table 6.1

Exports of Goods and Services as a Percentage of GDP, Selected Countries, 1999

Country	Exports as Percentage of GDP
Netherlands	56
Canada	41
New Zealand	29
United Kingdom	29
France	27
Italy	27
Germany	27
United States	12
Japan	11

Source: IMF, International Financial Statistics, 2000.

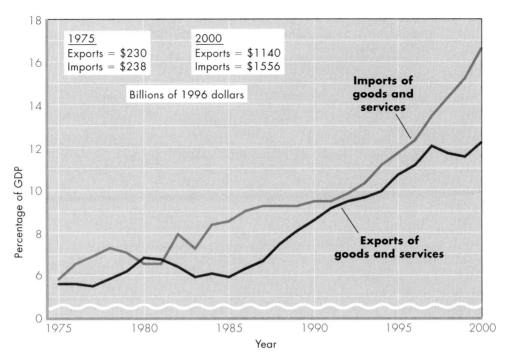

Figure 6.2

U.S. trade as percentage of GDP. U.S. imports and exports have increased in volume and have greatly increased as a percentage of GDP since 1975.

Source: Bureau of Economic Analysis. Data are from the national income accounts and are adjusted for inflation (1996 dollars).

U.S. exports and imports over the past several decades. The graph shows the rapid growth of U.S. exports and imports of goods and services as percentages of GDP. In 2000, U.S. exports and imports were 12 and 17 percent of GDP, respectively.

Even so, the United States now accounts for a diminished percentage of total world trade. In 1947 it supplied about one-third of the world's total exports, compared with about one-eighth today. World trade has increased more rapidly for other nations than it has for the United States. *But in terms of absolute volumes of imports and exports, the United States is still the world's leading trading nation.*

Dependence The United States is almost entirely dependent on other countries for bananas, cocoa, coffee, spices, tea, raw silk, nickel, tin, natural rubber, and diamonds. Imported goods compete with U.S. goods in many of our domestic markets: Japanese cameras and cars, French and Italian wines, and Swiss and Austrian snow skis are a few examples. Even the "great American pastime" of baseball relies heavily on imported gloves and baseballs.

Of course, world trade is a two-way street. Many U.S. industries rely on foreign markets. Almost all segments of U.S. agriculture rely on sales abroad; for example, exports of rice, wheat, cotton, and tobacco vary from one-fourth to more than one-half of the total output of those crops. The U.S. computer, chemical, semiconductor, aircraft, automobile, machine tool, and coal industries, among many others, sell significant portions of their output in international markets. Table 6.2 shows some of the major commodity exports and imports of the United States.

Trade Patterns The following facts will give you an overview of U.S. international trade:

- The United States has a *trade deficit* in goods. In 1999 U.S. imports of goods exceeded U.S. exports of goods by $346 billion.
- The United States has a *trade surplus* in services (such as accounting services and financial services). In 1999 U.S. exports of services exceeded U.S. imports of services by $81 billion.
- The United States imports some of the same categories of goods that it exports, specifically,

Table 6.2

**Principal U.S. Exports and Imports of Goods, 1999
(in Billions of Dollars)**

Exports	Amount	Imports	Amount
Semiconductors	$47.0	Automobiles	$96.3
Computers	46.7	Computers	81.5
Chemicals	46.0	Petroleum	67.8
Consumer durables	37.8	Clothing	55.9
Generating equipment	29.4	Household appliances	44.3
Aircraft	29.0	Semiconductors	37.6
Telecommunications	26.6	Chemicals	30.1
Automobiles	16.5	Consumer electronics	26.2
Grains	13.9	Telecommunications	23.9
Nonferrous metals	13.5	Iron and steel	18.1

Source: Consolidated from Department of Commerce data.

automobiles, computers, chemicals, semiconductors, and telecommunications equipment. (see Table 6.2).

- As Table 6.3 implies, most U.S. export and import trade is with other industrially advanced nations, not with developing countries. (Although the data in this table are for *goods* only, the same general pattern applies to *services*).
- Canada is the United States' most important trading partner quantitatively. In 1999, 24 percent of U.S. exported goods were sold to Canadians, who in turn provided 20 percent of U.S. imports of goods (see Table 6.3).

- The United States has sizable trade deficits with Japan and China. In 1999, U.S. imported goods from Japan exceeded U.S. exported goods to Japan by $75 billion, and U.S. imported goods from China exceeded U.S. exported goods to China by $69 billion (see Table 6.3).
- The U.S. dependence on foreign oil is reflected in its trade with members of the Organization of Petroleum Exporting Countries (OPEC). In 1999, the United States imported $24 billion of goods (mainly oil) from OPEC members, while exporting $12 billion of goods to those countries (see Table 6.3).

Table 6.3

U.S. Exports and Imports of Goods by Area, 1999*

Exports to	Value, Billions of Dollars	Percentage of Total	Imports from	Value, Billions of Dollars	Percentage of Total
Industrial countries	$398	58	Industrial countries	$ 552	54
Canada	$167	24	Canada	$201	20
Japan	56	8	Japan	131	13
Western Europe	163	24	Western Europe	215	21
Australia	12	2	Australia	5	1
Developing countries	286	42	Developing countries	$ 478	46
Mexico	87	13	Mexico	111	11
China	13	2	China	82	8
Eastern Europe	6	1	Eastern Europe	12	1
OPEC countries	12	2	OPEC countries	24	2
Other	168	24	Other	249	24
Total	$684	100	Total	$1030	100

*Data are on an international transactions basis and exclude military shipments. The import numbers do not add to 100 percent because of rounding.
Source: Survey of Current Business, October 2000.

■ In terms of volume, the most significant U.S. export of *services* is airline transportation provided by U.S. carriers for foreign passengers.

Financial Linkages

International trade requires complex financial linkages among nations. How does a nation such as the United States obtain more goods from others than it provides to them? How does the United States finance its goods and services trade deficit of $265 billion (= +81 in services − $346 in goods)? The answer is by either borrowing from foreigners or by selling real assets (for example, factories, real estate) to them. The United States is the world's largest borrower of foreign funds. Moreover, nations with which the United States has large trade deficits, such as Japan, often "recycle their excess dollars" by buying U.S. real assets.

Rapid Trade Growth

Several factors have propelled the rapid growth of international trade since the Second World War.

Transportation Technology

High transportation costs are a barrier to any type of trade, particularly among traders who are distant from one another. But improvements in transportation have shrunk the globe and have fostered world trade. Airplanes now transport low-weight, high-value items such as diamonds and semiconductors swiftly from one nation to another. We now routinely transport oil in massive tankers, significantly lowering the cost of transportation per barrel. Grain is loaded onto oceangoing ships at modern, efficient grain silos at Great Lakes and coastal ports. Natural gas flows through large-diameter pipelines from exporting to importing countries—for instance, from Russia to Germany and from Canada to the United States.

Communications Technology

Dramatic improvements in communications technology have also advanced world trade. Computers, the Internet, telephones, and fax (facsimile) machines now directly link traders around the world, enabling exporters to access overseas markets and to carry out trade deals. A distributor in New York can get a price quote on 1000 woven baskets in Thailand as quickly as a quotation on 1000 laptop computers in Texas. Money moves around the world in the blink of an eye. Exchange rates, stock prices, and interest rates flash onto computer screens nearly simultaneously in Los Angeles, London, and Lisbon.

General Decline in Tariffs

Tariffs are excise taxes (duties) on imported products. They have had their ups and downs over the years, but since 1940 they have generally fallen. A glance ahead to Figure 6.5 shows that U.S. tariffs as a percentage of imports (on which duties are levied) are now about 4 percent, down from 37 percent in 1940. Many nations still maintain barriers to free trade, but, on average, tariffs have fallen significantly, thus increasing international trade.

Participants in International Trade

All the nations of the world participate to some extent in international trade.

United States, Japan, and Western Europe

As Global Perspective 6.1 indicates, the top participants in world trade by total volume are the United States, Germany, and Japan. In 1999 those three nations had combined exports of $1.6 trillion. Along with Germany, other western European nations such as France, Britain, and Italy

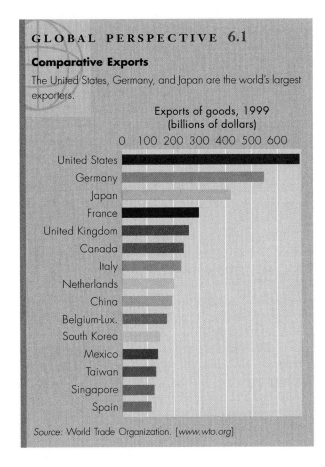

GLOBAL PERSPECTIVE 6.1

Comparative Exports

The United States, Germany, and Japan are the world's largest exporters.

Exports of goods, 1999
(billions of dollars)

Source: World Trade Organization. [www.wto.org]

are major exporters and importers. The United States, Japan, and the western European nations also form the heart of the world's financial system and provide headquarters for most of the world's large **multinational corporations**—firms that have sizable production and distribution activities in other countries. Examples of such firms are Unilever (Netherlands), Nestlé (Switzerland), Coca-Cola (United States), Bayer Chemicals (Germany), and Mitsubishi (Japan).

New Participants

Important new participants have arrived on the world trade scene. One group is made up of the newly industrializing Asian economies of Hong Kong (now part of China), Singapore, South Korea, and Taiwan. Although these Asian economies experienced economic difficulties in the 1990s, they have expanded their share of world exports from about 3 percent in 1972 to more than 10 percent today. Together, they export about as much as either Germany or Japan and much more than France, Britain, or Italy. Other economies in southeast Asia, particularly Malaysia and Indonesia, also have expanded their international trade.

China, with its increasing reliance on the market system, is an emerging major trader. Since initiating market reforms in 1978, its annual growth of output has averaged 9 percent (compared with about 3 percent annually over that period in the United States). At this remarkable rate, China's total output nearly doubles every 8 years! An upsurge of exports and imports has accompanied that expansion of output. In 1989 Chinese exports and imports were each about $50 billion. In 1999 each topped $200 billion, with 33 percent of China's exports going to the United States. Also, China has been attracting substantial foreign investment (more than $800 billion since 1990).

The collapse of communism in eastern Europe and the former Soviet Union in the early 1990s has altered world trade patterns. Before that collapse, the eastern European nations of Poland, Hungary, Czechoslovakia, and East Germany traded mainly with the Soviet Union and such political allies as North Korea and Cuba. Today, East Germany is reunited with West Germany, and Poland, Hungary, and the Czech Republic have established new trade relationships with western Europe and the United States.

Russia itself has initiated far-reaching market reforms, including widespread privatization of industry, and has made major trade deals with firms around the globe. Although its transition to capitalism has been far from smooth, Russia may one day be a major trading nation. Other former Soviet republics—now independent nations—such as Estonia and Azerbaijan also have opened their economies to international trade and finance.

QUICK REVIEW 6.1

■ There are four main categories of economic flows linking nations: goods and services flows, capital and labor flows, information and technology flows, and financial flows.

■ World trade has increased globally and nationally. In terms of volume, the United States is the world's leading international trader. But with exports and imports of only about 12 to 17 percent of GDP, the United States is not as dependent on international trade as some other nations.

■ Advances in transportation and communications technology and declines in tariffs have all helped expand world trade.

■ The United States, Japan, and the western European nations dominate world trade. Recent new traders are the Asian economies of Singapore, South Korea, Taiwan, and China (including Hong Kong), the eastern European nations, and the former Soviet states.

■ Specialization and Comparative Advantage

Given the presence of an *open economy*—one that includes the international sector—the United States produces more of certain goods (exports) and fewer of other goods (imports) than it would otherwise. Thus U.S. labor and other resources are shifted toward export industries and away from import industries. For example, the United States uses more resources to make commercial aircraft and to grow wheat and less to make autos and clothing. So we ask: "Do shifts of resources like these make economic sense? Do they enhance U.S. total output and thus the U.S. standard of living?"

The answers are affirmative. *Specialization and international trade increase the productivity of a nation's resources and allow for greater total output than would otherwise be possible.* This idea is not new. Adam Smith had this to say in 1776:

It is the maxim of every prudent master of a family, never to attempt to make at home what it will cost him more to make than to buy. The taylor does not attempt to make his own shoes, but buys them of the shoemaker. The shoemaker does not attempt to make his own clothes, but employs a taylor. The farmer attempts to make neither the one nor the other, but employs those different artificers. . . .

What is prudence in the conduct of every private family, can scarce be folly in that of a great kingdom. If a foreign country can supply us with a commodity cheaper than we can make it, better buy it of them with some part of the produce of our own industry, employed in a way in which we have some advantage.[1]

Nations specialize and trade for the same reasons as individuals: Specialization and exchange result in greater overall output and income.

Basic Principle

In the early 1800s British economist David Ricardo expanded on Smith's idea by observing that it pays for a person or a country to specialize and trade even if some potential trading partner is more productive in *all* economic activities.

Consider the certified public accountant (CPA) who is also a skilled house painter. Suppose the CPA is a swifter painter than the professional painter she is thinking of hiring. Also suppose she can earn $50 per hour but would have to pay the painter $15 per hour. And say it would take the accountant 30 hours to paint her house but the painter would take 40 hours.

Should the CPA take time from her accounting to paint her own house, or should she hire the painter? The CPA's opportunity cost of painting her house is $1500 (=30 hours of sacrificed CPA time × $50 per CPA hour). The cost of hiring the painter is only $600 (=40 hours of painting × $15 per hour of painting). Although the CPA is better at both accounting and painting, she *will get her house painted at lower cost by specializing in accounting and using some of her earnings from accounting to hire a house painter.*

Similarly, the house painter can reduce his cost of obtaining accounting services by specializing in painting and using some of his income to hire the CPA to prepare his income tax forms. Suppose it would take the painter 10 hours to prepare his tax return, while the CPA could handle the task in 2 hours. The house painter would sacrifice $150 of income (=10 hours of painting time × $15 per hour) to do something he could hire the CPA to do for $100 (=2 hours of CPA time × $50 per CPA hour).

[1]Adam Smith, *The Wealth of Nations* (New York: Modern Library, 1937), p. 424. (Originally published in 1776.)

Table 6.4
Mexico's Production Possibilities Table (in Tons)

Product	Production Alternatives				
	A	B	C	D	E
Avocados	0	20	24	40	60
Soybeans	15	10	9	5	0

By using the CPA to prepare his tax return, the painter *lowers the cost of getting his tax return prepared.*

What is true for our CPA and house painter is also true for nations. Specializing enables nations to reduce the cost of obtaining the goods and services they desire.

Comparative Costs

Our simple example shows that the reason specialization is economically desirable is that it results in more efficient production. Now let's put specialization into the context of trading nations and use the familiar concept of the production possibilities table for our analysis. Suppose the production possibilities for one product in Mexico and for one product in the United States are as shown in Tables 6.4 and 6.5. In both tables we assume constant costs. Each country must give up a constant amount of one product to secure a certain increment of the other product. (This assumption simplifies our discussion without impairing the validity of our conclusions.)

Specialization and trade are mutually beneficial or "profitable" to the two nations if the comparative costs of producing the two products within the two nations differ. What are the comparative costs of avocados and soybeans in Mexico? By comparing production alternatives A and B in Table 6.4, we see that 5 tons of soybeans (=15 − 10) must be sacrificed to produce 20 tons of avocados (=20 − 0). Or, more simply, in Mexico it costs 1 ton of soybeans (S) to produce 4 tons of avocados (A); that is, $1S \equiv 4A$. Because we assumed constant costs, this domestic

Table 6.5
U.S. Production Possibilities Table (in Tons)

Product	Production Alternatives				
	R	S	T	U	V
Avocados	0	30	33	60	90
Soybeans	30	20	19	10	0

comparative-cost ratio will not change as Mexico expands the output of either product. This is evident from production possibilities B and C, where we see that 4 more tons of avocados (=24 − 20) cost 1 unit of soybeans (=10 − 9).

Similarly, in Table 6.5, comparing U.S. production alternatives R and S reveals that in the United States it costs 10 tons of soybeans (=30 − 20) to obtain 30 tons of avocados (=30 − 0). That is, the domestic comparative-cost ratio for the two products in the United States is 1S ≡ 3A. Comparing production alternatives S and T reinforces this conclusion: an extra 3 tons of avocados (=33 − 30) comes at the sacrifice of 1 ton of soybeans (=20 − 19).

The comparative costs of the two products within the two nations are obviously different. Economists say that the United States has a domestic comparative advantage or, simply, a **comparative advantage** over Mexico in soybeans. The United States must forgo only 3 tons of avocados to get 1 ton of soybeans, but Mexico must forgo 4 tons of avocados to get 1 ton of soybeans. In terms of domestic opportunity costs, soybeans are relatively cheaper in the United States. *A nation has a comparative advantage in some product when it can produce that product at a lower domestic opportunity cost than can a potential trading partner.* Mexico, in contrast, has a comparative advantage in avocados. While 1 ton of avocados costs $\frac{1}{3}$ ton of soybeans in the United States, it costs only $\frac{1}{4}$ ton of soybeans in Mexico. Comparatively speaking, avocados are cheaper in Mexico. We summarize the situation in Table 6.6.

Because of these differences in domestic comparative costs, if both nations specialize, each according to its comparative advantage, each can achieve a larger total output with the same total input of resources. Together they will be using their scarce resources more efficiently. 🔑 6.1

Table 6.6
Comparative-Advantage Example: A Summary

Soybeans	Avocados
Mexico: Must give up 4 tons of avocados to get 1 ton of soybeans	*Mexico:* Must give up $\frac{1}{4}$ ton of soybeans to get 1 ton of avocados
United States: Must give up 3 tons of avocados to get 1 ton of soybeans	*United States:* Must give up $\frac{1}{3}$ ton of soybeans to get 1 ton of avocados
Comparative advantage: United States	Comparative advantage: Mexico

Terms of Trade

The United States can shift production between soybeans and avocados at the rate of 1S for 3A. Thus, the United States would specialize in soybeans only if it could obtain *more than* 3 tons of avocados for 1 ton of soybeans by trading with Mexico. Similarly, Mexico can shift production at the rate of 4A for 1S. So it would be advantageous to Mexico to specialize in avocados if it could get 1 ton of soybeans for *less than* 4 tons of avocados.

Suppose that through negotiation the two nations agree on an exchange rate of 1 ton of soybeans for $3\frac{1}{2}$ tons of avocados. These **terms of trade** are mutually beneficial to both countries, since each can "do better" through such trade than through domestic production alone. The United States can get $3\frac{1}{2}$ tons of avocados by sending 1 ton of soybeans to Mexico, while it can get only 3 tons of avocados by shifting its own resources domestically from soybeans to avocados. Mexico can obtain 1 ton of soybeans at a lower cost of $3\frac{1}{2}$ tons of avocados through trade with the United States, compared to the cost of 4 tons if Mexico produced the ton of soybeans itself.

Gains from Specialization and Trade

Let's pinpoint the gains in total output from specialization and trade. Suppose that, before specialization and trade, production alternative C in Table 6.4 and alternative T in 6.5 were the optimal product mixes for the two countries. That is, Mexico preferred 24 tons of avocados and 9 tons of soybeans (Table 6.4) and the United States preferred 33 tons of avocados and 19 tons of soybeans (Table 6.5) to all other available domestic alternatives. These outputs are shown in column 1 in Table 6.7.

Now assume that both nations specialize according to their comparative advantage, with Mexico producing 60 tons of avocados and no soybeans (alternative E) and the United States producing no avocados and 30 tons of soybeans (alternative R). These outputs are shown in column 2 in Table 6.7. Using our 1S ≡ $3\frac{1}{2}$A terms of trade, assume that Mexico exchanges 35 tons of avocados for 10 tons of U.S. soybeans. Column 3 in Table 6.7 shows the quantities exchanged in this trade, with a minus sign indicating exports and a plus sign indicating imports. As shown in column 4, after the trade Mexico has 25 tons of avocados and 10 tons of soybeans, while the United States has 35 tons of avocados and 20 tons of

Table 6.7

Specialization According to Comparative Advantage and the Gains from Trade (in Tons)

Country	(1) Outputs before Specialization	(2) Outputs after Specialization	(3) Amounts Traded	(4) Outputs Available after Trade	(5) Gains from Specialization and Trade (4) − (1)
Mexico	24 avocados	60 avocados	−35 avocados	25 avocados	1 avocados
	9 soybeans	0 soybeans	+10 soybeans	10 soybeans	1 soybeans
United States	33 avocados	0 avocados	+35 avocados	35 avocados	2 avocados
	19 soybeans	30 soybeans	−10 soybeans	20 soybeans	1 soybeans

soybeans. Compared with their optimum product mixes before specialization and trade (column 1), *both* nations now enjoy more avocados and more soybeans! Specifically, Mexico has gained 1 ton of avocados and 1 ton of soybeans. The United States has gained 2 tons of avocados and 1 ton of soybeans. These gains are shown in column 5.

Specialization based on comparative advantage improves global resource allocation. The same total inputs of world resources and technology result in a larger global output. If Mexico and the United States allocate all their resources to avocados and soybeans, respectively, the same total inputs of resources can produce more output between them, indicating that resources are being allocated more efficiently.

We noted in Chapter 2 that through specialization and international trade a nation can overcome the production constraints imposed by its domestic production possibilities table and curve. Our discussion of Tables 6.4, 6.5, and 6.7 has shown just how this is done. The domestic production possibilities data (Tables 6.4 and 6.5) of the two countries have not changed, meaning that neither nation's production possibilities curve has shifted. But specialization and trade mean that citizens of both countries can enjoy increased consumption (column 5 of Table 6.7). Thus specialization and trade have the same effect as an increase in resources or in technological progress: they make more goods available to an economy. **(Key Question 4)** ⚑ 6.1

▮ The Foreign Exchange Market

Buyers and sellers, whether individuals, firms, or nations, use money to buy products or to pay for the use of resources. Within the domestic economy, prices are stated in terms of the domestic currency and buyers use that currency to purchase domestic products. In Mexico, for example, buyers have pesos, and that is what sellers want.

International markets are different. Sellers set their prices in terms of their domestic currencies, but buyers often possess entirely different currencies. How many dollars does it take to buy a truckload of Mexican avocados selling for 3000 pesos, a German automobile selling for 50,000 euros, or a Japanese motorcycle priced at 300,000 yen? Producers in Mexico, Germany, and Japan want payment in pesos, euros, and yen, respectively, so that they can pay their wages, rent, interest, dividends, and taxes. A **foreign exchange market,** *a market in which various national currencies are exchanged for one another,* serves this need. The equilibrium prices in these markets are called **exchange rates.** An exchange rate is the rate at which the currency of one nation can be exchanged for the currency of another nation. (See Global Perspective 6.2.) Two points about the foreign exchange market are particularly noteworthy:

■ *A competitive market*   Real-world foreign exchange markets conform closely to the markets discussed in Chapter 3. They are competitive markets characterized by large numbers of buyers and sellers dealing in standardized products such as the American dollar, the European euro, the British pound, and the Japanese yen.

■ *Linkages to all domestic and foreign prices*   The market price or exchange rate of a nation's currency is an unusual price; it links all domestic prices with all foreign prices. Exchange rates enable consumers in one country to translate prices of foreign goods into units of their own currency: they need only multiply the foreign product price by the exchange rate. If the U.S.

Exchange Rates: Foreign Currency per U.S. Dollar

The amount of foreign currency that a dollar will buy varies greatly from nation to nation and fluctuates in response to supply and demand changes in the foreign exchange market. The amounts shown here are for January 2001.

$1 Will Buy

| 28.54 Russian rubles |
| .67 British pounds |
| 1.50 Canadian dollars |
| 9.64 Mexican pesos |
| 1.61 Swiss francs |
| 1.06 European euros |
| 114 Japanese yen |
| 1265 South Korean won |
| 9.41 Swedish krona |

dollar–yen exchange rate is $.01 (1 cent) per yen, a Sony television set priced at ¥20,000 will cost $200 (=20,000 × $.01) in the United States. If the exchange rate rises to $.02 (2 cents) per yen, it will cost $400 (=20,000 × $.02) in the United States. Similarly, all other Japanese products would double in price to U.S. buyers in response to the altered exchange rate. As you will see, a change in exchange rates has important implications for a nation's level of domestic production and employment. **!** 6.2

Dollar-Yen Market

How does the foreign exchange market work? Let's look briefly at the market for dollars and yen. U.S. firms exporting goods to Japan want payment in dollars, not yen; but the Japanese importers of those U.S. goods possess yen, not dollars. So the Japanese importers supply their yen in exchange for dollars in the foreign exchange market. At the same time, there are U.S. importers of Japanese goods who need to pay the Japanese exporters in yen, not dollars. These importers go to the foreign exchange market as demanders of yen. We then have a market in which the "price" is in dollars and the "product" is yen.

Figure 6.3 shows the supply of yen (by Japanese importers) and the demand for yen (by U.S. importers). The intersection of demand curve D_y and supply curve S_y establishes the equilibrium dollar price of yen. Here the equilibrium price of 1 yen— the dollar-yen exchange rate—is 1 cent per yen, or $.01 = ¥1. At this price, the market for yen clears; there is neither a shortage nor a surplus of yen. The equilibrium $.01 price of 1 yen means that $1 will buy 100 yen or ¥100 worth of Japanese goods. Conversely, 100 yen will buy $1 worth of U.S. goods. **↙** 6.1

Changing Rates: Depreciation and Appreciation

What might cause the exchange rate to change? The determinants of the demand for and supply of yen are similar to the determinants of demand and supply for almost any product. In the United States, several things might increase the demand for—and therefore the dollar price of—yen. Incomes might rise in the United States, enabling residents to buy not only more domestic goods but also more Sony televisions, Nikon cameras, and Nissan automobiles

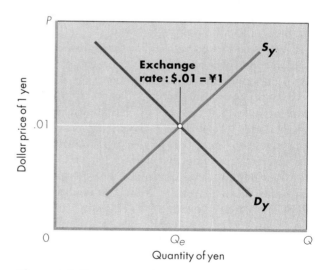

Figure 6.3
The market for yen. U.S. imports from Japan create a demand D_y for yen, while U.S. exports to Japan (Japan's imports) create a supply S_y of yen. The dollar price of 1 yen—the exchange rate—is determined at the intersection of the supply and demand curves. In this case the equilibrium price is $.01, meaning that 1 cent will buy 1 yen.

from Japan. So people in the United States would need more yen, and the demand for yen would increase. Or a change in people's tastes might enhance their preferences for Japanese goods. When gas prices soared in the 1970s, many auto buyers in the United States shifted their demand from gas-guzzling domestic cars to gas-efficient Japanese compact cars. The result was an increased demand for yen.

The point is that an increase in the U.S. demand for Japanese goods will increase the demand for yen and raise the dollar price of yen. Suppose the dollar price of yen rises from $.01 = ¥1 to $.02 = ¥1. When the dollar price of yen increases, we say a **depreciation** of the dollar relative to the yen has occurred. It then takes more dollars (pennies in this case) to buy a single yen. Alternatively stated, the *international value of the dollar* has declined. A depreciated dollar buys fewer yen and therefore fewer Japanese goods; the yen and all Japanese goods have become more expensive to U.S. buyers. Result: Consumers in the United States shift their expenditures from Japanese goods to now less expensive American goods. The Ford Taurus becomes relatively more attractive than the Honda Accord to U.S. consumers. Conversely, because each yen buys more dollars—that is, because the international value of the yen has increased—U.S. goods become cheaper to people in Japan and U.S. exports to Japan rise.

If the opposite event occurred—if the Japanese demanded more U.S. goods—then they would supply more yen to pay for these goods. The increase in the supply of yen relative to the demand for yen would decrease the equilibrium price of yen in the foreign exchange market. For example, the dollar price of yen might decline from $.01 = ¥1 to $.005 = ¥1. A decrease in the dollar price of yen is called an **appreciation** of the dollar relative to the yen. It means that the international value of the dollar has increased. It then takes fewer dollars (or pennies) to buy a single yen; the dollar is worth more because it can purchase more yen and therefore more Japanese goods. Each Sony Walkman becomes less expensive in terms of dollars, so people in the United States purchase more of them. In general, U.S. imports rise. Meanwhile, because it takes more yen to get a dollar, U.S. exports to Japan fall.

Figure 6.4 summarizes these currency relationships. **(Key Question 6)**

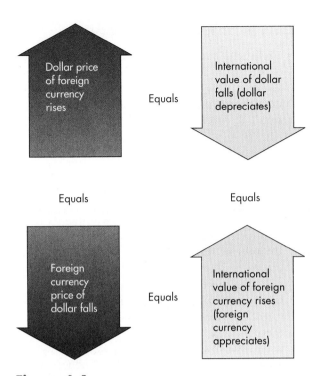

Figure 6.4

Currency appreciation and depreciation. Suppose the dollar price of a certain foreign currency rises (as illustrated by the upper left arrow). That means the international value of the dollar depreciates (upper right arrow). It also means that the foreign currency price of the dollar has declined (lower left arrow) and that the international value of the foreign currency has appreciated (lower right arrow).

QUICK REVIEW 6.2

A country has a comparative advantage when it can produce a product at a lower domestic opportunity cost than a potential trading partner can.

Specialization based on comparative advantage increases the total output available for nations that trade with one another.

The foreign exchange market is a market in which foreign currencies are exchanged.

An appreciation of the dollar is an increase in the international value of the dollar relative to the currency of some other nation; after appreciation a dollar buys more units of that currency. A depreciation of the dollar is a decrease in the international value of the dollar relative to some other currency; after depreciation a dollar buys fewer units of that currency.

▮ Government and Trade

If people and nations benefit from specialization and international exchange, why do governments sometimes try to restrict the free flow of imports or encourage exports? What kinds of world trade barriers can governments erect, and why would they do so?

Trade Impediments and Subsidies

There are four means by which governments commonly interfere with free trade:

- **Protective tariffs** are excise taxes or duties placed on imported goods. Protective tariffs are designed to shield domestic producers from foreign competition. They impede free trade by causing a rise in the prices of imported goods, thereby shifting demand toward domestic products. An excise tax on imported shoes, for example, would make domestically produced shoes more attractive to consumers.
- **Import quotas** are limits on the quantities or total value of specific items that may be imported. Once a quota is "filled," further imports of that product are choked off. Import quotas are more effective than tariffs in retarding international commerce. With a tariff, a product can go on being imported in large quantities; with an import quota, however, all imports are prohibited once the quota is filled.
- **Nontariff barriers** (and, implicitly, *nonquota* barriers) include onerous licensing requirements, unreasonable standards pertaining to product quality, or simply bureaucratic red tape in customs procedures. Some nations require that importers of foreign goods obtain licenses and then restrict the number of licenses issued. Although many nations carefully inspect imported agricultural products to prevent the introduction of potentially harmful insects, some countries use lengthy inspections to impede imports.
- **Export subsidies** consist of government payments to domestic producers of export goods. By reducing production costs, the subsidies enable producers to charge lower prices and thus to sell more exports in world markets. Two examples: Some European governments have

heavily subsidized Airbus Industries, a European firm that produces commercial aircraft, to help Airbus to compete against the American firm Boeing. The United States and other nations have subsidized domestic farmers to boost the domestic food supply. Such subsidies have lowered the market price of food and have artificially lowered export prices on agricultural produce.

Why Government Trade Interventions?

What accounts for the impulse to impede imports, boost exports, and create trade surpluses through government policy when free trade is beneficial to a nation? Why would a nation want to send more output abroad for consumption there than it gains as imported output in return? There are several reasons—some legitimate, most not.

Misunderstanding the Gains from Trade   It is a commonly accepted myth that the greatest benefit to be derived from international trade is greater domestic employment in the export sector. This suggests that exports are "good" because they increase domestic employment, whereas imports are "bad" because they deprive people of jobs at home. Actually, the true benefit created by international trade is the overall increase in output obtained through specialization and exchange. A nation can fully employ its resources, including labor, with or without international trade. International trade, however, enables society to use its resources in ways that increase its total output and therefore its overall well-being.

A nation does not need international trade to operate *on* its production possibilities curve. A closed (nontrading) national economy can have full employment without international trade. However, through world trade an economy can reach a point *beyond* its domestic production possibilities curve. The gain from trade is the extra output obtained from abroad—the imports obtained for less cost than the cost if they were produced at home.

Political Considerations   While a nation as a whole gains from trade, trade may harm particular domestic industries and particular groups of resource suppliers. In our earlier comparative-advantage example, specialization and trade adversely affected the U.S. avocado industry and the Mexican soybean industry. Those industries might seek to preserve their economic positions by persuading their respective governments to protect them from imports—perhaps through tariffs or import quotas.

Those who directly benefit from import protection are few in number but have much at stake. Thus, they have a strong incentive to pursue political activity to achieve their aims. However, the overall cost of tariffs and quotas typically greatly exceeds the benefits. It is not uncommon to find that it costs the public $100,000 or more a year to protect a domestic job that pays less than half that amount. Moreover, because these costs are buried in the price of goods and spread out over millions of citizens, the cost born by each individual citizen is quite small. In the political arena, the voice of the relatively few producers demanding *protectionism* is loud and constant, whereas the voice of those footing the bill is soft or nonexistent.

Indeed, the public may be won over by the apparent plausibility ("Cut imports and prevent domestic unemployment") and the patriotic ring ("Buy American!") of the protectionist arguments. The alleged benefits of tariffs are immediate and clear-cut to the public, but the adverse effects cited by economists are obscure and dispersed over the entire economy. When political deal making is added in—"You back tariffs for the apparel industry in my state, and I'll back tariffs on the auto industry in your state"—the outcome can be a network of protective tariffs, import quotas, and export subsidies.

Costs to Society

Tariffs and quotas benefit domestic producers of the protected products, but they harm domestic consumers, who must pay higher than world prices for the protected goods. They also hurt domestic firms that use the protected goods as inputs in their production processes. For example, a tariff on imported steel would boost the price of steel girders, thus hurting firms that construct large buildings. Also, tariffs and quotas reduce competition in the protected industries. With less competition from foreign producers, domestic firms may be slow to design and implement cost-saving production methods and introduce new or improved products.

■ Multilateral Trade Agreements and Free-Trade Zones

When one nation enacts barriers against imports, the nations whose exports suffer may retaliate with trade barriers of their own. In such a *trade war*, escalating tariffs choke world trade and reduce everyone's economic well-being. The **Smoot-Hawley Tariff Act** of 1930 is a classic example. Although that act was meant to reduce imports and stimulate U.S. production, the high tariffs it authorized prompted adversely affected nations to retaliate with tariffs equally high. International trade fell, lowering the output and income of all nations. Economic historians generally agree that the Smoot-Hawley Tariff Act was a contributing cause of the Great Depression. Aware of that fact, nations have worked to lower tariffs worldwide. Their pursuit of free trade has been aided by powerful domestic interest groups: Exporters of goods and services, importers of foreign components used in "domestic" products, and domestic sellers of imported products all strongly support lower tariffs.

Figure 6.5 makes clear that while the United States has been a high-tariff nation over much of its history, U.S. tariffs have generally declined during the past half-century.

Reciprocal Trade Agreements Act

The **Reciprocal Trade Agreements Act** of 1934 started the downward trend of tariffs. Aimed at reducing tariffs, this act had two main features:

■ *Negotiating authority* It authorized the president to negotiate with foreign nations agreements that would reduce existing U.S. tariffs by up to 50 percent. Those reductions were contingent on the actions other nations took to lower tariffs on U.S. exports.

■ *Generalized reductions* The specific tariff reductions negotiated between the United States and any particular nation were generalized through most-favored-nation clauses, which often accompany such agreements. These clauses

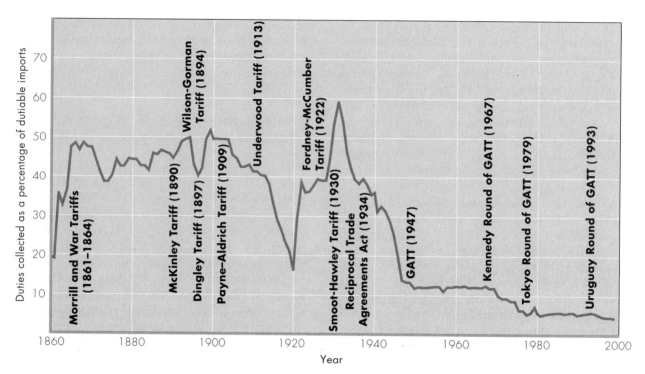

Figure 6.5

U.S. tariff rates, 1860–1999. Historically, U.S. tariff rates have fluctuated. But beginning with the Reciprocal Trade Agreements Act of 1934, the trend has been downward.

Source: U.S. Department of Commerce data.

stipulate that any subsequently reduced U.S. tariffs, resulting from negotiation with any other nation, would apply equally to any nation that signed the original agreement. So if the United States negotiates a reduction in tariffs on wristwatches with, say, France, the lower U.S. tariffs on imported French watches also apply to the imports of the other nations having most-favored-nation status, say, Japan and Switzerland. This way, the reductions in U.S. tariffs automatically apply to many nations.

General Agreement on Tariffs and Trade

The Reciprocal Trade Agreements Act provided only bilateral (between two nations) negotiations. Its approach was broadened in 1947 when 23 nations, including the United States, signed the **General Agreement on Tariffs and Trade (GATT).** GATT was based on three principles: (1) equal, nondis-

criminatory trade treatment for all member nations, (2) the reduction of tariffs by multilateral negotiation, and (3) the elimination of import quotas. Basically, GATT provided a forum for the negotiation of reduced trade barriers on a multilateral basis among nations.

Since the Second World War, member nations have completed eight "rounds" of GATT negotiations to reduce trade barriers. The eighth and most recent round of negotiations began in Uruguay in 1986. After 7 years of wrangling, in 1993 the 128 member nations reached a new agreement. The *Uruguay Round* agreement took effect on January 1, 1995, and its provisions are to be phased in through 2005.

Under this agreement, tariffs on thousands of products have been eliminated or reduced, with overall tariffs eventually dropping by 33 percent. The agreement also liberalized government rules that in the past impeded the global market for such services as advertising, legal services, tourist services, and financial services. Quotas on imported textiles and apparel were phased out and replaced with tariffs. Other provisions reduced agricultural subsidies paid to farmers and protected intellectual property (patents, trademarks, copyrights) against piracy.

When fully implemented, the Uruguay Round agreement will boost the world's GDP by an estimated $6 trillion, or 8 percent. Consumers in the United States will save more than $30 billion annually.

World Trade Organization

The Uruguay Round agreement established the **World Trade Organization (WTO)** as GATT's successor. Some 140 nations belong to the WTO, with China being one of the latest entrants. The WTO oversees trade agreements reached by the member nations and rules on trade disputes among them. It also provides forums for further rounds of trade negotiations.

GATT and the WTO have been positive forces in the trend toward liberalized world trade. The trade rules agreed upon by the member nations provide a strong and necessary bulwark against the protectionism called for by the special-interest groups in the various nations.

For that reason and others, the WTO is highly controversial. Critics are concerned that rules crafted to expand international trade and investment enable firms to circumvent national laws that protect workers and the environment. What good are minimum-wage laws, worker safety laws, collective bargaining rights, and environmental laws if firms can easily shift their production to nations that have weaker laws or consumers can buy goods produced in those countries?

Proponents of the WTO respond that labor and environmental protections should be pursued directly in nations that have low standards and via international organizations other than the WTO. These issues should not be linked to the process of trade liberalization, which confers widespread economic benefits across nations. Moreover, say proponents of the WTO, many environmental and labor concerns are greatly overblown. Most world trade is among advanced industrial countries, not between them and countries that have lower environmental and labor standards. Moreover, the free flow of goods and resources raises output and income in the developing nations. Historically, such increases in living standards have engendered stronger, not weaker, protections for the environment and for workers.

The European Union

Countries have also sought to reduce tariffs by creating regional *free-trade zones*—also called *trade blocs*. The most dramatic example is the **European Union (EU)**, formerly called the European Economic Community. Initiated as the Common Market in 1958, the EU now comprises 15 western European nations—France, Germany, Italy, Belgium, the Netherlands, Luxembourg, Denmark, Ireland, United Kingdom, Greece, Spain, Portugal, Austria, Finland, and Sweden.

The EU Trade Bloc   The EU has abolished tariffs and import quotas on nearly all products traded among the participating nations and established a common system of tariffs applicable to all goods received from nations outside the EU. It has also liberalized the movement of capital and labor within the EU and has created common policies in other economic matters of joint concern, such as agriculture, transportation, and business practices. The EU is now a strong **trade bloc:** a group of countries having common identity, economic interests, and trade rules.

EU integration has achieved for Europe what the U.S. constitutional prohibition on tariffs by individual states has achieved for the United States: increased regional specialization, greater productivity, greater output, and faster economic growth. The free flow of goods and services has created large markets for EU industries. The resulting economies of large-scale production have enabled these industries to achieve much lower costs than they could have achieved in their small, single-nation markets.

The effects of EU success on nonmember nations, such as the United States, have been mixed. A peaceful and increasingly prosperous EU makes its members better customers for U.S. exports. But U.S. firms and other nonmember firms have been faced with tariffs and other barriers that make it difficult for them to compete against firms within the EU trade bloc. For example, autos produced in Germany and sold in Spain or France face no tariffs, whereas U.S. and Japanese autos sold in those EU countries do. This puts U.S. and Japanese firms at a serious disadvantage. Similarly, EU trade restrictions hamper eastern European exports of metals, textiles, and farm products, goods that the eastern Europeans produce in abundance.

By giving preferences to countries within their free-trade zone, trade blocs such as the EU tend to reduce their members' trade with non-bloc members. Thus, the world loses some of the benefits of a completely open global trading system. Eliminating that disadvantage has been one of the motivations for liberalizing global trade through the World Trade Organization.

The Euro One of the most significant recent accomplishments of the EU is the establishment of the so-called Euro Zone. In 2000, 11 of the 15 EU members shared a common currency—the **euro.** Greece becomes the twelfth member of the Euro Zone on January 1, 2002. Great Britain, Denmark, and Sweden have opted out of the common currency, at least for now.

On January 1, 1999, the euro made its debut for electronic payments such as credit card purchases and transfer of funds among banks. On January 1, 2002, euro notes and coins will begin circulating alongside the existing currencies, and on July 1, 2002, only the euro will be accepted for payment.

Economists expect the euro to raise the standard of living of the Euro Zone members over time. By ending the inconvenience and expense of exchanging currencies, the euro will enhance the free flow of goods, services, and resources among the Euro Zone members. It will also enable consumers and businesses to comparison shop for outputs and inputs, and this will increase competition, reduce prices, and lower costs.

North American Free Trade Agreement

In 1993 Canada, Mexico, and the United States formed a major trade bloc. The **North American Free Trade Agreement (NAFTA)** established a free-trade zone that has about the same combined output as the EU but encompasses a much larger geographic area. NAFTA has greatly reduced tariffs and other trade barriers between Canada, Mexico, and the United States and will eliminate them entirely by 2008.

Critics of NAFTA feared that it would cause a massive loss of U.S. jobs as firms moved to Mexico

to take advantage of lower wages and weaker regulations on pollution and workplace safety. Also, there was concern that Japan and South Korea would build plants in Mexico and transport goods tariff-free to the United States, further hurting U.S. firms and workers.

In retrospect, the critics were much too pessimistic. Employment has increased in the United States by more than 14 million workers since passage of NAFTA, and the unemployment rate has sunk from 6.9 to 4.2 percent. Increased trade between Canada, Mexico, and the United States has enhanced the standard of living in all three countries. **(Key Question 10)**

QUICK REVIEW 6.3

■ Governments curtail imports and promote exports through protective tariffs, import quotas, nontariff barriers, and export subsidies.

■ The General Agreement on Tariffs and Trade (GATT) established multinational reductions in tariffs and import quotas. The Uruguay Round of GATT (1993) reduced tariffs worldwide, liberalized international trade in services, strengthened protections for intellectual property, and reduced agricultural subsidies.

■ The World Trade Organization (WTO)—GATT's successor—rules on trade disputes and provides forums for negotiations on further rounds of trade liberalization.

■ The European Union (EU) and the North American Free Trade Agreement (NAFTA) have reduced internal trade barriers among their members by establishing large free-trade zones. Of the 15 EU members, 11 now have a common currency—the euro.

■ Increased Global Competition

Freer international trade has brought intense competition both within the United States and across the globe. In the United States, imports have gained major shares of many markets, including those for cars, steel, car tires, clothing, sporting goods, electronics, motorcycles, outboard motors, and toys. Nevertheless, hundreds of U.S. firms have prospered in the global marketplace. Such firms as Boeing, McDonald's, Dow Chemicals, Intel, Coca-Cola, Microsoft, AT&T, Monsanto, Procter & Gamble, and Hewlett-Packard have continued to retain high market shares at home and have dramatically expanded their sales abroad. Of course, not all U.S. firms have been so successful. Some have not been able to compete, either because their international competitors make better-quality products, have lower production costs, or both.

Is the heightened competition that accompanies the global economy a good thing? Although some domestic producers *do* get hurt and their workers must find employment elsewhere, foreign competition clearly benefits consumers and society in general. Imports break down the monopoly power of existing firms, thereby lowering product prices and providing consumers with a greater variety of goods. Foreign competition also forces domestic producers to become more efficient and to improve product quality; that has already happened in several U.S. industries, including steel and autos. Most U.S. firms can and do compete quite successfully in the global marketplace.

What about the U.S. firms that cannot compete successfully in open markets? The harsh reality is that they should go out of business, much like an unsuccessful corner boutique. Persistent economic losses mean that scarce resources are not being used efficiently. Shifting those resources to alternative, profitable uses will increase total U.S. output. It will be far less expensive for the United States to provide training and, if necessary, relocation assistance to laid-off workers than to try to protect these jobs from foreign competition.

Buy American: The Global Refrigerator

Humorist Art Buchwald Looks at the Logic of the "Buy American" Campaign.

"There is only one way the country is going to get on its feet," said Baleful.

"How's that?" I asked, as we drank coffee in his office at the Baleful Refrigerator Company.

"The consumer has to start buying American," he said, slamming his fist down on the desk. "Every time an American buys a foreign refrigerator it costs one of my people his job. And every time one of my people is out of work it means he or she can't buy refrigerators."

"It's a vicious circle," I said.

Baleful's secretary came in. "Mr. Thompson, the steel broker is on the phone."

My friend grabbed the receiver. "Thompson, where is that steel shipment from Japan that was supposed to be in last weekend? . . . I don't care about weather. We're almost out of steel, and I'll have to close down the refrigerator assembly line next week. If you can't deliver when you promise, I'll find myself another broker."

"You get your steel from Japan?" I asked Baleful.

"Even with shipping costs, their price is still lower than steel made in Europe. We used to get all our sheets from Belgium, but the Japanese are now giving them a run for their money."

The buzzer on the phone alerted Baleful. He listened for a few moments and then said, "Excuse me, I have a call from Taiwan. Mark Four? Look, R&D designed a new push-button door handle and we're going to send the specs to you. Tell Mr. Chow if his people send us a sample of one and can make it for us "at the same price as the old handle, we'll give his company the order."

A man came in with a plastic container and said, "Mr. Baleful, you said you wanted to see one of these before we ordered them. They are the containers for the ice maker in the refrigerator."

Baleful inspected it carefully and banged it on the floor a couple of times. "What's the price on it?"

"Hong Kong can deliver it at $2 a tray, and Dong-Fu Plastics in South Korea said they can make it for $1.70."

"It's just a plastic tray. Take the South Korea bid. We'll let Hong Kong supply us with the shelves for the freezer. Any word on the motors?"

"There's a German company in Brazil that just came out with a new motor, and it's passed all our tests, so Johnson has ordered 50,000."

"Call Cleveland Motors and tell them we're sorry, but the price they quoted us was just too high."

"Yes, sir," the man said and departed.

The secretary came in again and said, "Harry telephoned and wanted to let you know the defroster just arrived from Finland. They're unloading the box cars now."

"Good. Any word on the wooden crates from Singapore?"

"They're at the dock in Hoboken."

"Thank heaven. Cancel the order from Boise Cascade."

"What excuse should I give them?"

"Tell them we made a mistake in our inventory, or we're switching to plastic. I don't care what you tell them."

Baleful turned to me. "Where were we?"

"You were saying that if the consumer doesn't start buying American, this country is going to be in a lot of trouble."

"Right. It's not only his patriotic duty, but his livelihood that's at stake. I'm going to Washington next week to tell the Senate Commerce Committee that if they don't get on the stick, there isn't going to be a domestic refrigerator left in this country. We're not going to stay in business for our health."

"Pour it to them," I urged him.

Baleful said, "Come out with me into the showroom."

I followed him. He went to his latest model, and opened the door. "This is an American refrigerator made by the American worker, for the American consumer. What do you have to say to that?"

"It's beautiful," I said. "It puts foreign imports to shame."

Source: Art Buchwald, "Being Bullish on Buying American." Reprinted by permission. We discovered this article in *Master Curriculum Guide in Economics: Teaching Strategies for International Trade* (New York: Joint Council on Economic Education, 1988).

SUMMARY

1. Goods and services flows, capital and labor flows, information and technology flows, and financial flows link the United States and other countries.

2. International trade is growing in importance globally and for the United States. World trade is significant to the United States in two respects: (a) The absolute volumes of U.S. imports and exports exceed those of any other single nation. (b) The United States is completely dependent on trade for certain commodities and materials that cannot be obtained domestically.

3. Principal U.S. exports include semiconductors, computers, chemicals, consumer durables, generating equipment, and aircraft; principal U.S. imports include automobiles, computers, petroleum, clothing, and household appliances. Quantitatively, Canada is the United States' most important trading partner.

4. Global trade has been greatly facilitated by (a) improvements in transportation technology, (b) improvements in communications technology, and (c) general declines in tariffs. Although the United States, Japan, and the western European nations dominate the global economy, the total volume of trade has been increased by the contributions of several new trade participants. They include the Asian economies of Singapore, South Korea, Taiwan, and China (including Hong Kong), the eastern European countries (such as the Czech Republic, Hungary, and Poland), and the newly independent countries of the former Soviet Union (such as Estonia, Ukraine, and Azerbaijan).

5. Specialization based on comparative advantage enables nations to achieve higher standards of living through trade with other countries. A trading partner should specialize in products and services for which its domestic opportunity costs are lowest. The terms of trade must be such that both nations can obtain more of some product via trade than they could obtain by producing it at home.

6. The foreign exchange market sets exchange rates between currencies. Each nation's imports create a supply of its own currency and a demand for foreign currencies. The resulting supply–demand equilibrium sets the exchange rate that links the currencies of all nations. Depreciation of a nation's currency reduces its imports and increases its exports; appreciation increases its imports and reduces its exports.

7. Governments influence trade flows through (a) protective tariffs, (b) quotas, (c) nontariff barriers, and (d) export subsidies. Such impediments to free trade result from misunderstandings about the advantages of free trade and from political considerations. By artificially increasing product prices, trade barriers cost U.S. consumers billions of dollars annually.

8. The Reciprocal Trade Agreements Act of 1934 marked the beginning of a trend toward lower U.S. tariffs. Most-favored-nation status allows a nation to export goods into the United States at the United States' lowest tariff level, then or at any later time.

9. In 1947 the General Agreement on Tariffs and Trade (GATT) was formed to encourage nondiscriminatory treatment for all member nations, to reduce tariffs, and to eliminate import quotas. The Uruguay Round of GATT negotiations (1993) reduced tariffs and quotas, liberalized trade in services, reduced agricultural subsidies, reduced pirating of intellectual property, and phased out quotas on textiles.

10. GATT's successor, the World Trade Organization (WTO), has 140 member nations. It implements WTO agreements, rules on trade disputes between members, and provides forums for continued discussions on trade liberalization.

11. Free-trade zones (trade blocs) liberalize trade within regions but may at the same time impede trade with non-bloc members. Two examples of free-trade arrangements are the 15-member European Union (EU) and the North American Free Trade Agreement (NAFTA), comprising Canada, Mexico, and the United States. Eleven of the EU nations have agreed to abandon their national currencies for a common currency called the euro.

12. The global economy has created intense foreign competition in many U.S. product markets, but most U.S. firms are able to compete well both at home and globally.

TERMS AND CONCEPTS

multinational corporations
comparative advantage
terms of trade
foreign exchange market
exchange rates
depreciation

appreciation
protective tariffs
import quotas
nontariff barriers
export subsidies
Smoot-Hawley Tariff Act
Reciprocal Trade Agreements Act

most-favored-nation clauses
General Agreement on Tariffs and Trade (GATT)
World Trade Organization (WTO)

European Union (EU)
trade bloc
euro
North American Free Trade Agreement (NAFTA)

STUDY QUESTIONS

1. Describe the four major economic flows that link the United States with other nations. Provide a specific example to illustrate each flow. Explain the relationships between the top and bottom flows in Figure 6.1.

2. How important is international trade to the U.S. economy? In terms of volume, does the United States trade more with the industrially advanced economies or with developing economies? What country is the United States' most important trading partner, quantitatively?

3. What factors account for the rapid growth of world trade since the Second World War? Who are the major players in international trade today? Besides Japan, what other Asian nations play significant roles in international trade?

4. **Key Question** The following are production possibilities tables for South Korea and the United States. Assume that before specialization and trade the optimal product mix for South Korea is alternative B and for the United States is alternative U.

	South Korea's Production Possibilities					
Product	A	B	C	D	E	F
Radios (in thousands)	30	24	18	12	6	0
Chemicals (in tons)	0	6	12	18	24	30

	U.S. Production Possibilities				
Product	R	S	T	U	V	W
Radios (in thousands)	10	8	6	4	2	0
Chemicals (in tons)	0	4	8	12	16	20

   a. Are comparative-cost conditions such that the two areas should specialize? If so, what product should each produce?

   b. What is the total gain in radio and chemical output that would result from such specialization?

   c. What are the limits of the terms of trade? Suppose actual terms of trade are 1 unit of radios for $1\frac{1}{2}$ units of chemicals and that 4 units of radios are exchanged for 6 units of chemicals. What are the gains from specialization and trade for each nation?

   d. Can you conclude from this illustration that specialization according to comparative advantage results in more efficient use of world resources? Explain.

5. Suppose that the comparative-cost ratios of two products—baby formula and tuna fish—are as follows in the hypothetical nations of Canswicki and Tunata:

   Canswicki: 1 can baby formula ≡ 2 cans tuna fish

   Tunata:　　1 can baby formula ≡ 4 cans tuna fish

   In what product should each nation specialize? Explain why terms of trade of 1 can baby formula ≡ $2\frac{1}{2}$ cans tuna fish would be acceptable to both nations.

6. **Key Question** True or False? "U.S. exports create a demand for foreign currencies; foreign imports of U.S. goods create a supply of foreign currencies." Explain. Would a decline in U.S. consumer income or a weakening of U.S. preferences for foreign products cause the dollar to depreciate or to appreciate? Other things equal, what would be the effects of that depreciation or appreciation on U.S. exports and imports?

7. If the European euro were to decline in value (depreciate) in the foreign exchange market, would it be easier or harder for the French to sell their wine in the United States? Suppose you were planning a trip to Paris. How would depreciation of the euro change the dollar cost of your trip?

8. True or False? "An increase in the American dollar price of the South Korean won implies that the South Korean won has depreciated in value." Explain.

9. What measures do governments take to promote exports and restrict imports? Who benefits and who loses from protectionist policies? What is the net outcome for society?

10. **Key Question** Identify and state the significance of each of the following: (a) WTO; (b) EU; (c) euro; (d) NAFTA. What commonality do they share?

11. Explain: "Free-trade zones such as the EU and NAFTA lead a double life: They can promote free trade among members, but they pose serious trade obstacles for nonmembers." Do you think the net effects of trade blocs are good or bad for world trade? Why? How do the efforts of the WTO relate to these trade blocs?

12. Speculate as to why some U.S. firms strongly support trade liberalization while other U.S. firms favor protectionism. Speculate as to why some U.S. labor unions strongly support trade liberalization while other U.S. labor unions strongly oppose it.

13. **(Last Word)** What point is Art Buchwald making in his humorous essay on the Baleful Refrigerator Company? Why might Mr. Baleful *oppose* tariffs on imported goods even though he wants consumers to buy "American" refrigerators?

14. **Web-Based Question:** *Trade balances with partner countries* The U.S. Census Bureau, at www.census.gov/foreign-trade/www/statistics.html, lists the top trading partners of the United States (imports and exports added together) as well as the top 10 countries with which the United States has a trade surplus and a trade deficit. Using the current year-to-date data, compare the top 10 deficit and surplus countries with the top 10 trading partners. Are deficit and surplus countries equally represented in the top 10 trading partners list, or does one group dominate the list? The top 10 trading partners represent what percent of U.S. imports and what percent of U.S. exports?

15. **Web-Based Question:** *Foreign exchange rates—the yen for dollars* The Federal Reserve System website, www.federalreserve.gov/releases/H10/hist/, provides historical foreign-exchange-rate data for a wide variety of currencies. The information is based on data collected by the Federal Reserve Bank of New York from a sample of market participants. Look at the data for the Japanese yen from 1990 to the present. Assume that you were in Tokyo every New Year's from January 1, 1990, to this year and bought a *bento* (box lunch) for 1000 yen each year. Convert this amount to dollars using the yen-dollar exchange rate for each January since 1990, and plot the dollar price of the *bento* over time. Has the dollar appreciated or depreciated against the yen? What was the least amount in dollars that your box lunch cost? The most?

2

National Income, Employment, and Fiscal Policy

CHAPTER

7

Measuring Domestic Output, National Income, and the Price Level

"**D**ISPOSABLE INCOME FLAT." "Personal Consumption Surges." "Investment Spending Stagnates." "GDP Up 4 Percent." "CPI Data Indicate Inflation Is in Check." ■ These headlines, typical of those in *The Wall Street Journal,* give economists valuable information on the state of the economy. To beginning economics students, however, they may be gibberish. This chapter will help you learn the language of macroeconomics and national income accounting and will provide you with a basic understanding that you can build on in the next several chapters.

■ Assessing the Economy's Performance

National income accounting measures the economy's overall performance. It does for the economy as a whole what private accounting does for the individual firm or for the individual household.

A business firm measures its flows of income and expenditures regularly—usually every 3 months or once a year. With that information in hand, the firm can gauge its economic health. If things are going well and profits are good, the accounting data can be used to explain that success. Were costs down? Was output up? Have market prices risen? If things are going badly and profits are poor, the firm may be able to identify the reason by studying the

record over several accounting periods. All this information helps the firm's managers plot their future strategy.

National income accounting operates in much the same way for the economy as a whole. The Bureau of Economic Analysis (an agency of the Commerce Department) compiles the national income accounts for the U.S. economy. This accounting enables economists and policymakers to:

■ Assess the health of the economy by comparing levels of production at regular intervals.

■ Track the long-run course of the economy to see whether it has grown, been constant, or declined.

■ Formulate policies that will safeguard and improve the economy's health.

▌Gross Domestic Product

The primary measure of the economy's performance is its annual total output of goods and services or, as it is called, its *aggregate output*. Aggregate output is labeled **gross domestic product (GDP):** *the total market value of all final goods and services produced in a given year.* GDP includes all goods and services produced by either citizen-supplied or foreign-supplied resources employed within the country. The U.S. GDP includes the market value of Fords produced by an American-owned factory in Michigan and the market value of Hondas produced by a Japanese-owned factory in Ohio.

A Monetary Measure

If the economy produces three sofas and two computers in year 1 and two sofas and three computers in year 2, in which year is output greater? We can't answer that question until we attach a price tag to each of the two products to indicate how society evaluates their relative worth.

That's what GDP does. It is a *monetary measure.* Without such a measure we would have no way of comparing the relative values of the vast number of goods and services produced in different years. In Table 7.1 the price of sofas is $500 and the price of computers is $2000. GDP would gauge the output of year 2 ($7000) as greater than the output of year 1 ($5500), because society places a higher monetary value on the output of year 2. Society is willing to pay $1500 more for the combination of goods produced in year 2 than for the combination of goods produced in year 1.

Avoiding Multiple Counting

To measure aggregate output accurately, all goods and services produced in a particular year must be counted once and only once. Because most products go through a series of production stages before they reach the market, some of their components are bought and sold many times. To avoid counting those components each time, GDP includes only the market value of *final goods* and ignores *intermediate goods* altogether.

Intermediate goods are goods and services that are purchased for resale or for further processing or manufacturing. **Final goods** are goods and services that are purchased for final use by the consumer, not for resale or for further processing or manufacturing.

Why is the value of final goods included in GDP but the value of intermediate goods excluded? Because the value of final goods already includes the value of all the intermediate goods that were used in producing them. Including the value of intermediate goods would amount to **multiple counting,** and that would distort the value of GDP.

To see why, suppose that there are five stages involved in manufacturing a wool suit and getting it to the consumer—the final user. Table 7.2 shows that firm A, a sheep ranch, sells $120 worth of wool to firm B, a wool processor. Firm A pays out the $120 in wages, rent, interest, and profit. Firm B processes the wool and sells it to firm C, a suit manufacturer, for $180. What does firm B do with the $180 it receives? It pays $120 to firm A for the wool and uses the remaining $60 to pay wages, rent, interest, and profit for the resources used in processing the wool. Firm C, the manufacturer, sells the suit to firm D, a wholesaler, which sells it to firm E, a retailer. Then at last a consumer, the final user, comes in and buys the suit for $350.

How much of these amounts should we include in GDP to account for the production of the suit? Just $350, the value of the final product. The $350 includes all the intermediate transactions leading up to the product's final sale. Including the sum of all the intermediate sales, $1140, in GDP would amount to multiple counting. The production and sale of the final suit generated just $350 of output, not $1140.

Table 7.1

Comparing Heterogeneous Output by Using Money Prices

Year	Annual Output	Market Value
1	3 sofas and 2 computers	3 at $500 + 2 at $2000 = $5500
2	2 sofas and 3 computers	2 at $500 + 3 at $2000 = $7000

Table 7.2

Value Added in a Five-Stage Production Process

(1) Stage of Production	(2) Sales Value of Materials or Product	(3) Value Added
Firm A, sheep ranch	$ 0	$120 (= $120 − $ 0)
Firm B, wool processor	120	60 (= 180 − 120)
Firm C, suit manufacturer	180	40 (= 220 − 180)
Firm D, clothing wholesaler	220	50 (= 270 − 220)
Firm E, retail clothier	270	80 (= 350 − 270)
	350	
Total sales values	$1140	
Value added (total income)		**$350**

Alternatively, we could avoid multiple counting by measuring and cumulating only the *value added* at each stage. **Value added** is the market value of a firm's output *less* the value of the inputs the firm has bought from others. At each stage, the difference between what a firm pays for a product and what it receives from selling the product is paid out as wages, rent, interest, and profit. Column 3 of Table 7.2 shows that the value added by firm B is $60, the difference between the $180 value of its output and the $120 it paid for the input from firm A. We find the total value of the suit by adding together all the values added by the five firms. Similarly, by calculating and summing the values added to all the goods and services produced by all firms in the economy, we can find the market value of the economy's total output—its GDP.

GDP Excludes Nonproduction Transactions

Although many monetary transactions in the economy involve final goods and services, many others do not. Those nonproduction transactions must be excluded from GDP because they have nothing to do with the generation of final goods. *Nonproduction transactions* are of two types: purely financial transactions and secondhand sales.

Financial Transactions   Purely financial transactions include the following:

- **Public transfer payments**   These are the social security payments, welfare payments, and veterans' payments that the government makes directly to households. Since the recipients contribute nothing to *current production* in return, to

include such payments in GDP would be to overstate the year's output.

- **Private transfer payments**   Such payments include, for example, the money that parents give children or the cash gifts given at Christmas time. They produce no output. They simply transfer funds from one private individual to another and consequently do not enter into GDP.
- **Stock market transactions**   The buying and selling of stocks (and bonds) is just a matter of swapping bits of paper. Stock market transactions create nothing in the way of current production and are not included in GDP. Payments for the services of a security broker *are* included, however, because those services do contribute to current output.

Secondhand Sales   Secondhand sales contribute nothing to current production and for that reason are excluded from GDP. Suppose you sell your 1965 Ford Mustang to a friend; that transaction would be ignored in reckoning this year's GDP because it generates no current production. The same would be true if you sold a brand-new Mustang to a neighbor a week after you purchased it. **(Key Question 3)**

Two Ways of Looking at GDP: Spending and Income

Let's look again at how the market value of total output—or of any single unit of total output—is measured. Given the data listed in Table 7.2, how can we measure the market value of a suit?

One way is to see how much the final user paid for it. That will tell us the market value of the final product. Or we can add up the entire wage, rental, interest, and profit incomes that were created in producing the suit. The second approach is the value-added technique used in Table 7.2.

The final-product approach and the value-added approach are two ways of looking at the same thing. *What is spent on making a product is income to those who helped make it.* If $350 is spent on manufacturing a suit, then $350 is the total income derived from its production.

We can look at GDP in the same two ways. We can view GDP as the sum of all the money spent in buying it. That is the *output approach*, or **expenditures approach.** Or we can view GDP in terms of the income derived or created from producing it. That is the *earnings* or *allocations approach*, or the **income approach.**

As illustrated in Figure 7.1, we can determine GDP for a particular year either by adding up all that was spent to buy total output or by adding up all the money that was derived as income from its production. Buying (spending money) and selling (receiving income) are two aspects of the same transaction. On the expenditures side of GDP, all final goods produced by the economy are bought either by three domestic sectors (households, businesses, and government) or by foreign buyers. On the income side (once certain statistical adjustments are made), the total receipts acquired from the sale of that total output are allocated to the suppliers of resources as wage, rent, interest, and profit income.

∎ The Expenditures Approach

To determine GDP using the expenditures approach, we add up all the spending on final goods and services that has taken place throughout the year. National income accountants use precise terms for the types of spending listed on the left side of Figure 7.1.

Personal Consumption Expenditures (C)

What we have called "consumption expenditures by households," the national income accountants call **personal consumption expenditures.** That term covers all expenditures by households on *durable consumer goods* (automobiles, refrigerators, video recorders), *nondurable consumer goods* (bread, milk, vitamins, pencils, toothpaste), and *consumer expenditures for services* (of lawyers, doctors, mechanics, barbers). The accountants use the symbol C to designate this component of GDP.

Gross Private Domestic Investment (Ig)

Under the heading **gross private domestic investment,** the accountants include the following items:

- All final purchases of machinery, equipment, and tools by business enterprises.
- All construction.
- Changes in inventories.

Expenditures, or output, approach

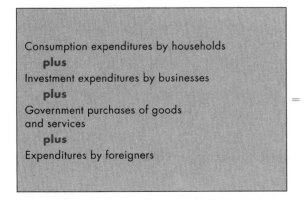

Income, or allocations, approach

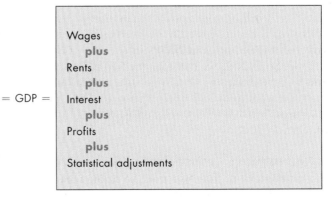

Figure 7.1

The expenditures and income approaches to GDP. There are two general approaches to measuring gross domestic product. We can determine GDP as the value of output by summing all expenditures on that output. Alternatively, with some modifications, we can determine GDP by adding up all the components of income arising from the production of that output.

Notice that this list, except for the first item, includes more than we have meant by "investment" so far. The second item includes residential construction as well as the construction of new factories, warehouses, and stores. Why do the accountants regard residential construction as investment rather than consumption? Because apartment buildings and houses, like factories and stores, earn income when they are rented or leased. Owner-occupied houses are treated as investment goods because they *could be* rented to bring in an income return. So the national income accountants treat all residential construction as investment. Finally, increases in inventories (unsold goods) are considered to be investment because they represent, in effect, "unconsumed output." And, as we know from production possibilities analysis, that is precisely what investment is.

Positive and Negative Changes in Inventories

Let's look at changes in inventories more closely. Inventories can either increase or decrease over some period. Suppose they increased by $10 billion between December 31, 1999, and December 31, 2000. That means the economy produced $10 billion more output than was purchased in 2000. We need to count all output produced in 2000 as part of that year's GDP, even though some of it remained unsold at the end of the year. This is accomplished by including the $10 billion increase in inventories as investment in 2000. That way the expenditures in 2000 will correctly measure the output produced that year.

Alternatively, suppose that inventories decreased by $10 billion in 2000. This "drawing down of inventories" means that the economy sold $10 billion more of output in 2000 than it produced that year. It did this by selling goods produced in prior years—goods already counted as GDP in those years. Unless corrected, expenditures in 2000 will overstate GDP for 2000. So in 2000 we consider the $10 billion decline in inventories as "negative investment" and subtract it from total investment that year. Thus, expenditures in 2000 will correctly measure the output produced in 2000.

Noninvestment Transactions

So much for what investment is. You also need to know what it isn't. Investment does *not* include the transfer of paper assets (stocks, bonds) or the resale of tangible assets (houses, jewelry, boats). Such transactions merely transfer the ownership of existing assets. Investment has to do with the creation of *new* capital assets—

assets that create jobs and income. The mere transfer (sale) of claims to existing capital goods does not create new capital.

Gross Investment versus Net Investment As we have seen, the category gross private domestic investment includes (1) all final purchases of machinery, equipment, and tools; (2) all construction; and (3) changes in inventories. The words "private" and "domestic" mean that we are speaking of spending by private businesses, not by government (public) agencies, and that the investment is taking place inside the country, not abroad.

The word "gross" means that we are referring to all investment goods—both those that replace machinery, equipment, and buildings that were used up (worn out or made obsolete) in producing the current year's output and any net additions to the economy's stock of capital. Gross investment includes investment in replacement capital *and* in added capital.

In contrast, **net private domestic investment** includes *only* investment in the form of added capital. The amount of capital that is used up over the course of a year is called *depreciation*. So

$$\text{Net investment} = \text{gross investment} - \text{depreciation}$$

In typical years, gross investment exceeds depreciation. Thus net investment is positive and the nation's stock of capital rises, as illustrated in Figure 7.2. Such increases in capital shift the U.S. production possibilities curve outward and thus expand the nation's production capacity.

Gross investment need not always exceed depreciation, however. When gross investment and depreciation *are equal*, net investment is zero and there is no change in the size of the capital stock. When gross investment *is less than* depreciation, net investment is negative. The economy then is *disinvesting*—using up more capital than it is producing—and the nation's stock of capital shrinks. That happened in the Great Depression of the 1930s.

National income accountants use the symbol I for private domestic investment spending, along with the subscript g to signify gross investment. They use the subscript n to signify net investment. But it is gross investment, I_g, that they use in determining GDP. **!** 7.1

Government Purchases (G)

The third category of expenditures in the national income accounts is **government purchases,** officially labeled "government consumption expendi-

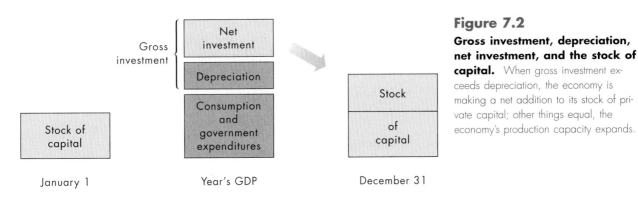

Figure 7.2

Gross investment, depreciation, net investment, and the stock of capital. When gross investment exceeds depreciation, the economy is making a net addition to its stock of private capital; other things equal, the economy's production capacity expands.

tures and gross investment." These expenditures have two components: (1) expenditures for goods and services that government consumes in providing public services and (2) expenditures for *social capital* such as schools and highways, which have long lifetimes. Government purchases (Federal, state, and local) include all government expenditures on final goods and all direct purchases of resources, including labor. It does *not* include government transfer payments, because, as we have seen, they merely transfer government receipts to certain households and generate no production of any sort. National income accountants use the symbol G to signify government purchases.

Net Exports (X_n)

International trade transactions are a significant item in national income accounting. We know that GDP records all spending on goods and services produced in the United States, including spending on U.S. output by people abroad. So we must include the value of exports when we are using the expenditures approach to determine GDP.

At the same time, we know that Americans spend a great deal of money on imports—goods and services produced abroad. That spending shows up in other nations' GDP. We must subtract the value of imports from U.S. spending to avoid overstating total production in the United States.

Rather than add exports and then subtract imports, national income accountants use "exports less imports," or **net exports**. We designate exports as X, imports as M, and net exports as X_n:

$$\text{Net exports } (X_n) = \text{exports } (X) - \text{imports } (M)$$

Table 7.3 shows that in 2000 Americans spent $370 billion more on imports than foreigners spent on U.S. exports. That is, net exports in 2000 were a *minus* $370 billion.

Table 7.3

Accounting Statement for the U.S. Economy, 2000 (in billions)

Receipts: Expenditures Approach		Allocations: Income Approach	
Personal consumption expenditures (C)	$6759	Compensation of employees	$5639
Gross private domestic investment (I_g)	1834	Rents	140
Government purchases (G)	1743	Interest	571
Net exports (X_n)	−370	Proprietors' income	711
		Corporate income taxes	286
		Dividends	397
		Undistributed corporate profits	274
		National income	$8018
		Indirect business taxes	682
		Consumption of fixed capital	1257
		Net foreign factor income earned in the U.S.	9
Gross domestic product	$9966	Gross domestic product	$9966

Source: Bureau of Economic Analysis. Preliminary 2000 data.

Putting It All Together: GDP = C + I$_g$ + G + X$_n$

Taken together, these four categories of expenditures provide a measure of the market value of a given year's total output—its GDP. For the United States in 2000 (Table 7.3),

$$GDP = \$6759 + 1834 + 1743 - 370 = \$9966$$

Global Perspective 7.1 lists the GDPs of several countries.

■ The Income Approach

Table 7.3 shows how 2000's expenditures of $9966 billion were allocated as income to those responsible for producing the output. It would be simple if we could say that the entire amount flowed back to them in the form of wages, rent, interest, and profit. But

we have to make a few adjustments to balance the expenditures and income sides of the account. We look first at the items that make up *national income*, shown on the right side of the table. Then we turn to the adjustments.

Compensation of Employees

By far the largest share of national income—$5639 billion—was paid as wages and salaries by business and government to their employees. That figure also includes wage and salary supplements, in particular, payments by employers into social insurance and into a variety of private pension, health, and welfare funds for workers.

Rents

Rents consist of the income received by the households and businesses that supply property resources. They include the monthly payments tenants make to landlords and the lease payments corporations pay for the use of office space. The figure used in the national accounts is *net* rent—gross rental income minus depreciation of the rental property.

Interest

Interest consists of the money paid by private businesses to the suppliers of money capital. It also includes such items as the interest households receive on savings deposits, certificates of deposit (CDs), and corporate bonds.

Proprietors' Income

What we have loosely termed "profits" is broken down by the national income accountants into two accounts: proprietors' income, which consists of the net income of sole proprietorships, partnerships, and other unincorporated businesses, and corporate profits. Proprietors' income flows to the proprietors.

Corporate Profits

Corporate profits are the earnings of owners of corporations. National income accountants subdivide corporate profits into three categories:

■ *Corporate income taxes* These taxes are levied on corporations' net earnings and flow to the government.

GLOBAL PERSPECTIVE 7.1

Comparative GDPs in Trillions of Dollars, Selected Nations, 1999

The United States, Japan, and Germany have the world's highest GDPs. The GDP data charted below have been converted to dollars via international exchange rates.

GDP in Trillions of Dollars

Source: World Bank. [www.worldbank.org]

■ *Dividends* These are the part of corporate profits that are paid to the corporate stockholders and thus flow to households—the ultimate owners of all corporations.

■ *Undistributed corporate profits* These are money saved by corporations to be invested later in new plants and equipment. They are also called *retained earnings*.

From National Income to GDP

The national income accountants add together employee compensation, rents, interest, proprietors' income, and corporate profits and get **national income**—*all the income that flows to American-supplied resources, whether here or abroad*. But notice that the figure for national income shown in Table 7.3—$8018 billion—is less than GDP as reckoned by the expenditures approach shown on the left side of the table. The account is balanced by adding three items to national income.

Indirect Business Taxes **Indirect business taxes** include general sales taxes, excise taxes, business property taxes, license fees, and customs duties. Why do we add indirect business taxes to national income as a way of balancing expenditures and income?

Assume that a firm produces a product that sells for $1. The production and sale of that product create $1 of wage, rent, interest, and profit income. But now the government imposes a 5 percent sales tax on all products sold at retail. The retailer adds the tax to the price of the product and shifts it along to consumers, and this becomes part of consumption expenditures. But the $.05 is clearly not earned income because the government contributes nothing to the production of the product in return for it. Only $1 of what consumers pay goes out as wage, rent, interest, and profit income. So the national income accountants need to add the $.05 to the $1.00 of national income in calculating GDP and make the same adjustment for the entire economy.

Consumption of Fixed Capital The useful lives of private capital equipment (such as bakery ovens or automobile assembly lines) extend far beyond the year in which they were produced. To avoid understating profit and income in the year of purchase and to avoid overstating profit and income in succeeding years, the cost of such capital

must be allocated over its lifetime. The amount allocated is an estimate of how much of the capital is being used up each year. It is called *depreciation*. A bookkeeping entry, the depreciation allowance results in a more accurate statement of profit and income for the economy each year. Social capital, such as courthouses and bridges, also requires a depreciation allowance in the national income accounts.

The huge depreciation charge made against private and social capital each year is called **consumption of fixed capital** because it is the allowance for capital that has been "consumed" in producing the year's GDP. It is the portion of GDP that is set aside to pay for the ultimate replacement of those capital goods.

The money allocated to consumption of fixed capital (the depreciation allowance) is a cost of production and thus included in the gross value of output. But this money is not available for other purposes, and, unlike other costs of production, it does not add to anyone's income. So it is not included in national income. We must therefore add it to national income to achieve balance with the economy's expenditures, as in Table 7.3.

Net Foreign Factor Income The last step in balancing the national account is to make a slight adjustment in "national" income versus "domestic" income. National income is *the total income of Americans, whether it was earned in the United States or abroad*. But GDP is a measure of domestic output—total output produced within the United States regardless of the nationality of those who provide the resources. So in moving from national income to GDP, we must consider the income Americans gain from supplying resources abroad and the income foreigners gain by supplying resources in the United States. In 2000, foreign-owned resources earned $9 billion more in the United States than American-owned resources earned abroad. That difference is called *net foreign factor income*. For that reason it is not included in U.S. national income. We must *add* it to national income in determining the value of U.S. domestic output (output produced within the U.S. borders).

Table 7.3 summarizes the expenditures approach and income approach to GDP. The left side shows what the U.S. economy produced in 2000 and what was spent to produce it. The right side shows how those expenditures, when appropriately adjusted, were allocated as income.

Other National Accounts

Several other national accounts provide additional useful information about the economy's performance. We can derive these accounts by making various adjustments to GDP.

Net Domestic Product

As a measure of total output, GDP does not make allowances for replacing the capital goods used up in each year's production. As a result, it does not tell us how much new output was available for consumption and for additions to the stock of capital. To determine that, we must subtract from GDP the capital that was consumed in producing the GDP and that had to be replaced. That is, we need to subtract consumption of fixed capital (depreciation) from GDP. The result is a measure of **net domestic product (NDP):**

NDP = GDP − consumption of fixed capital (depreciation)

For the United States in 2000:

	Billions
Gross domestic product	$9966
Consumption of fixed capital	−1257
Net domestic product	$8709

NDP is simply GDP adjusted for depreciation. It measures the total annual output that the entire economy—households, businesses, government, and foreigners—can consume without impairing its capacity to produce in ensuing years.

National Income

Sometimes it is useful to know how much Americans earned for their contributions of land, labor, capital, and entrepreneurial talent. Recall that U.S. national income (NI) includes all income earned through the use of American-owned resources, whether they are located at home or abroad. To derive NI from NDP, we must make two adjustments:

■ **Subtract net foreign factor income from NDP** Net foreign factor income is factor (resource) income earned by foreigners in the United States in excess of factor income earned by Americans abroad. Since foreigners earn this income, it is not included in U.S. national income.

■ **Subtract indirect business taxes from NDP** Because government is not an economic resource, the indirect business taxes it collects do not qualify as payments to productive resources and thus are not included in national income.

For the United States in 2000:

	Billions
Net domestic product	$8709
Net foreign factor income earned	−9
Indirect business taxes	−682
National income	$8018

We know, too, that we can calculate national income through the income approach by simply adding up employee compensation, rent, interest, proprietors' income, and corporate profit.

Personal Income

Personal income (PI) includes all income received whether earned or unearned. It is likely to differ from national income (income earned) because some income earned—social security taxes (payroll taxes), corporate income taxes, and undistributed corporate profits—is not received by households. Conversely, some income received—such as social security payments, unemployment compensation payments, welfare payments, disability and education payments to veterans, and private pension payments—is not earned. These transfer payments must be added to obtain PI.

In moving from national income to personal income, we must subtract the income that is earned but not received and add the income that is received but not earned. For the United States in 2000:

	Billions
National income	$8018
Social security contributions	−706
Corporate income taxes	−286
Undistributed corporate profits	−274
Transfer payments	+1530*
Personal income	$8282

*Includes a statistical discrepancy.

Disposable Income

Disposable income (DI) is personal income less personal taxes. Personal taxes include personal income taxes, personal property taxes, and inheritance taxes. Disposable income is the amount of income that households have left over after paying their personal taxes. They are free to divide that income between consumption (*C*) and saving (*S*):

$$DI = C + S$$

For the United States in 2000:

	Billions
Personal income	$8282
Personal taxes	−1292
Disposable income	$6990

QUICK REVIEW 7.2

▪ Net domestic product (NDP) is the market value of GDP minus consumption of fixed capital (depreciation).

▪ National income (NI) is all income earned through the use of American-owned resources, whether located at home or abroad.

▪ Personal income (PI) is all income received by households, whether earned or not.

▪ Disposable income (DI) is all income received by households minus personal taxes.

Table 7.4

The Relationships between GDP, NDP, NI, PI, and DI in the United States, 2000

	Billions
Gross domestic product (GDP)	$9966
Consumption of fixed capital	−1257
Net domestic product (NDP)	$8709
Net foreign factor income earned in the U.S.	−9
Indirect business taxes	−682
National income (NI)	$8018
Social security contributions	−706
Corporate income taxes	−286
Undistributed corporate profits	−274
Transfer payments	+1530
Personal income (PI)	$8282
Personal taxes	−1292
Disposable income (DI)	$6990

Table 7.4 summarizes the relationships among GDP, NDP, NI, PI, and DI. **(Key Question 8)**

The Circular Flow Revisited

Figure 7.3 is an elaborate flow diagram that shows the economy's four main sectors along with the flows of expenditures and allocations that determine GDP, NDP, NI, and PI. The green arrows represent the spending flows—$C + I_g + G + X_n$—that together measure gross domestic product. To the right of the GDP rectangle are gold arrows that show first the allocations of GDP and then the adjustments needed to derive NDP, NI, PI, and DI.

The diagram illustrates the adjustments necessary to determine each of the national income accounts. For example, net domestic product is smaller than GDP because consumption of fixed capital flows away from GDP in determining NDP. National income is smaller than NDP because indirect business taxes and net foreign factor income earned in the United States flow away from NDP in determining NI. And so on.

Note the three domestic sectors of the economy: households, government, and businesses. The household sector has an inflow of disposable income and outflows of consumption spending and saving. The government sector has an inflow of revenue in the form of types of taxes and an outflow of government disbursements in the form of purchases and

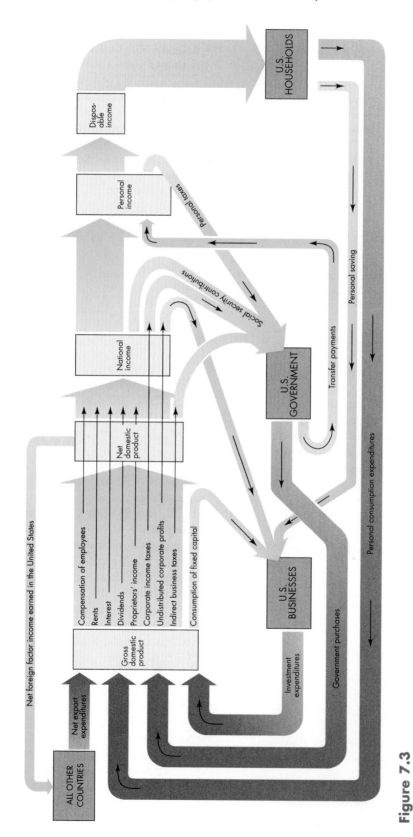

Figure 7.3

U.S. domestic output and the flows of expenditure and income. This figure is an elaborate circular flow diagram that fits the expenditures and allocations sides of GDP to one another. The expenditures flows are shown in green; the allocations or income flows are shown in gold. You should trace through the income and expenditures flows, relating them to the five basic national income accounting measures.

transfers. The business sector has inflows of three major sources of funds for business investment and an outflow of investment expenditures.

Finally, note the foreign sector (all other countries) in the flow diagram. Spending by foreigners on U.S. exports adds to U.S. GDP, but some of U.S. consumption, government, and investment expenditures buy imported products. The flow from foreign markets shows that we handle this complication by calculating net exports (U.S. exports minus U.S. imports). The net export flow may be a positive or negative amount, adding to or subtracting from U.S. GDP.

Figure 7.3 shows that flows of expenditures and income are part of a continuous, repetitive process. Cause and effect are intermingled: Expenditures create income, and from this income arise expenditures, which again flow to resource owners as income.

▌Nominal GDP versus Real GDP

Recall that GDP is a measure of the market or money value of all final goods and services produced by the economy in a given year. We use money or nominal values as a common denominator in order to sum that heterogeneous output into a meaningful total. But that creates a problem: How can we compare the market values of GDP from year to year if the value of money itself changes in response to inflation or deflation? After all, we determine the value of GDP by multiplying total output by market prices.

Whether there is a 5 percent increase in output with no change in prices or a 5 percent increase in prices with no change in output, the change in the value of GDP will be the same. And yet it is the

quantity of goods that get produced and distributed to households that affects our standard of living, not the price of the goods. The hamburger that sold for $2 in 2000 yields the same satisfaction as an identical hamburger that sold for 50 cents in 1970.

The way around this problem is to *deflate* GDP when prices rise and to *inflate* GDP when prices fall. These adjustments give us a measure of GDP for various years as if the value of the dollar had always been the same as it was in some reference year. A GDP based on the prices that prevailed when the output was produced is called unadjusted GDP, or **nominal GDP.** A GDP that has been deflated or inflated to reflect changes in the price level is called adjusted GDP, or real GDP.

Adjustment Process in a One-Product Economy

There are two ways we can adjust nominal GDP to reflect price changes. For simplicity, let's assume that the economy produces only one good, pizza, in the amount indicated in Table 7.5 for years 1, 2, and 3. Suppose that we gather revenue data directly from the financial reports of the pizza businesses to measure nominal GDP in various years. After completing our effort, we will have determined nominal GDP for each year, as shown in column 4 of Table 7.5. We will have no way of knowing to what extent changes in price and/or changes in quantity of output have accounted for the increases or decreases in nominal GDP that we observe.

GDP Price Index How can we determine real GDP in our pizza economy? One way is to assemble data on the price changes that occurred over

Table 7.5
Calculating Real GDP

Year	(1) Units of Output	(2) Price of Pizza per Unit	(3) Price Index (Year 1 = 100)	(4) Unadjusted, or Nominal, GDP (1) × (2)	(5) Adjusted, or Real, GDP
1	5	$10	100	$ 50	$50
2	7	20	200	140	70
3	8	25	250	200	80
4	10	30	——	——	——
5	11	28	——	——	——

various years (column 2) and use them to establish an overall price index for the entire period. Then we can use the index in each year to adjust nominal GDP to real GDP for that year.

A **price index** is *a measure of the price of a specified collection of goods and services, called a "market basket," in a given year as compared to the price of an identical (or highly similar) collection of goods and services in a reference year.* That point of reference, or benchmark, is known as the base period or base year. More formally,

$$\text{Price index in given year} = \frac{\text{price of market basket in specific year}}{\text{price of same market basket in base year}} \times 100 \quad (1)$$

By convention, the price ratio between a given year and the base year is multiplied by 100 to facilitate computation. For example, a price ratio of $2/1 (= 2)$ is expressed as a price index of 200. A price ratio of $1/3 (= .33)$ is expressed as a price index of 33.

In our pizza-only example, of course, our market basket consists of only one product. Column 2 of Table 7.5 reveals that the price of pizza was $10 in year 1, $20 in year 2, $25 in year 3, and so on. Let's select year 1 as our base year. Now we can express the successive prices of the contents of our market basket in, say, years 2 and 3 as compared to the price of the market basket in year 1:

$$\text{Price index, year 2} = \frac{\$20}{\$10} \times 100 = 200$$

$$\text{Price index, year 3} = \frac{\$25}{\$10} \times 100 = 250$$

For year 1 the index has to be 100, since that year and the base year are identical.

The index numbers tell us that the price of pizza rose from year 1 to year 2 by 100 percent $\{= [(200 - 100)/100] \times 100\}$ and from year 1 to year 3 by 150 percent $\{= [(250 - 100)/100] \times 100\}$.

Dividing Nominal GDP by the Price Index

We can now use the index numbers shown in column 3 to deflate the nominal GDP figures in column 4. The simplest and most direct method of deflating is to express the index numbers as hundredths—in decimal form—and then to divide them into corresponding nominal GDP. That gives us **real GDP:**

$$\text{Real GDP} = \frac{\text{nominal GDP}}{\text{price index (in hundredths)}} \quad (2)$$

Column 5 shows the results. These figures for real GDP measure the market value of the output of pizza in years 1, 2, and 3 as if the price of pizza had been a constant $10 throughout the 3-year period. In short, real GDP reveals the market value of each year's output measured in terms of dollars that have the same purchasing power as dollars had in the base year.

To test your understanding, extend Table 7.5 to years 4 and 5, using equations (1) and (2). Then run through the entire deflating procedure, using year 3 as the base period. This time you will have to inflate some of the nominal GDP data, using the same procedure as we used in the examples. 🔑 **7.1**

An Alternative Method

Another way to establish real GDP is to gather separate data on physical outputs (as in column 1) and their prices (as in column 2) of Table 7.5. We could then determine the market value of outputs in successive years *if the base-year price ($10) had prevailed.* In year 2, the 7 units of pizza would have a value of $70 (= 7 units × $10). As column 5 confirms, that $70 worth of output is year 2's real GDP. Similarly, we could determine the real GDP for year 3 by multiplying the 8 units of output that year by the $10 price in the base year.

Once we have determined real GDP through this method, we can identify the price index for a given year simply by dividing the nominal GDP by the real GDP for that year:

$$\text{Price index (in hundredths)} = \frac{\text{nominal GDP}}{\text{real GDP}} \quad (3)$$

Example: In year 2 we get a price index of 200—or, in hundredths, 2.00—which equals the nominal GDP of $140 divided by the real GDP of $70. Note that equation 3 is simply a rearrangement of equation 2. Table 7.6 summarizes the two methods of determining real GDP in our single-good economy. **(Key Question 11)**

Real-World Considerations and Data

In the real world of many goods and services, of course, determining GDP and constructing a reliable price index are far more complex matters than in our pizza-only economy. The government accountants must assign a "weight" to each of several

Table 7.6

Steps for Deriving Real GDP from Nominal GDP

Method 1

1. Find nominal GDP for each year.
2. Compute a GDP price index.
3. Divide each year's nominal GDP by that year's price index (in hundredths) to determine real GDP.

Method 2

1. Break down nominal GDP into physical quantities of output and prices for each year.
2. Find real GDP for each year by determining the dollar amount that each year's physical output would have sold for if base-year prices had prevailed. (The GDP price index can then be found by dividing nominal GDP by real GDP.)

categories of goods and services based on the relative proportion of each category in total output. They update the weights annually as expenditure patterns change and roll the base year forward year by year using a moving average of expenditure patterns. The GDP price index used in the United States is called the *chain-type annual-weights price index*—which hints at its complexity. We spare you the details.

Table 7.7 shows some of the real-world relationships between nominal GDP, real GDP, and the GDP price index. Here the reference year is 1996, where the value of the index is set at 100. Because the price level has been rising over the long run, the pre-1996 values of real GDP (column 3) are higher than the nominal values of GDP for those years (column 2). This upward adjustment acknowledges that prices were lower in the years before 1996, and thus

Table 7.7

Nominal GDP, Real GDP, and GDP Price Index, Selected Years

(1) Year	(2) Nominal GDP, Billions of $	(3) Real GDP, Billions of $	(4) GDP Price Index* (1996 = 100)
1975	1635.2	4084.4	____
1980	2795.6	____	57.05
1985	4213.0	5717.1	73.69
1990	5803.2	6707.9	____
1995	7400.5	____	98.10
1996	7813.2	7813.2	100.00
1999	9299.2	8875.8	104.77

*Chain-type annual-weights price index.
Source: Bureau of Economic Analysis, www.bea.doc.gov.

nominal GDP understated the real output of those years and must be inflated.

Conversely, the rising price level of the post-1996 years caused nominal GDP figures for those years to overstate real output. So the statisticians deflate those figures to determine what real GDP would have been in other years if 1996 prices had prevailed. Doing so reveals that real GDP has been less than nominal GDP since 1996.

By inflating the nominal pre-1996 GDP data and deflating the post-1996 data, government accountants determine annual real GDP, which can then be compared with the real GDP of any other year in the series of years. So the real GDP values in column 3 are directly comparable with one another.

Once we have determined nominal GDP and real GDP, we can fashion the price index. And once we have determined nominal GDP and the price index, we can calculate real GDP. Example: Nominal GDP in 1999 was $9299.2 billion and real GDP was $8875.8 billion. So the price level in 1999 was 104.77 (= $9299.2/$8875.8 × 100), or 4.8 percent higher than in 1996. To find real GDP for 1999, we divide the nominal GDP of $9299.2 by the 1999 GDP price index, expressed in hundredths (1.0477).

To test your understanding of the relationships between nominal GDP, real GDP, and the price level, determine the values of the price index for 1975 and 1990 in Table 7.7 and determine real GDP for 1980 and 1995. We have left those figures out on purpose. **(Key Question 12)**

▮ The Consumer Price Index

A different sort of price index is the **consumer price index (CPI),** compiled by the Bureau of Labor Statistics (BLS). This is the price index that is often in the news because it is the index that the government uses to measure the rate of inflation from month to month. It is also the index the government uses to adjust social security benefits and income tax brackets for inflation. The CPI reports the price of a market basket of some 300 consumer goods and services that presumably are purchased by a typical urban consumer. (The GDP index is much broader since it includes not only consumer goods and services but also capital goods, goods and services purchased by the government, and goods and services that enter world trade.)

The current composition of the market basket is based on spending patterns of urban consumers between 1993 and 1995. But the BLS sets the CPI equal to 100 for 1982–1984 (not 1993–1995). So, in any given year, the CPI is found as follows:

$$CPI = \frac{\text{Price of 1993–1995 market basket in any given year}}{\text{Price of the same market basket in 1982–1984}} \times 100 \quad (4)$$

Unlike the GDP price index, in which the relative weights of various goods and services are annually adjusted, the CPI is a fixed-weight price index. If consumers spent 20 percent of their incomes on housing in 1993–1995, it is assumed that they spent 20 percent on housing in all years in the index series. The BLS updates the composition of the market basket only periodically. The purpose of this fixed-weight approach is to measure changes in the cost of a constant market basket of purchases. Changes in the CPI thus are designed to measure the rate of inflation facing consumers. For example, the CPI (1984 = 100) increased from 166.6 in 1999 to 172.2 in 2000, indicating that the inflation rate for 2000 was 3.4 percent [= (172.2 − 166.6)/166.6].

QUICK REVIEW 7.3

■ Nominal GDP is output valued at current prices. Real GDP is output valued at constant base-year prices.

■ The GDP price index compares the price (market value) of all the goods and services included in GDP in a given year to the price of the same market basket in a reference year.

■ Nominal GDP can be transformed into real GDP by dividing the nominal GDP by the GDP price index expressed in hundredths.

■ The consumer price index (CPI) measures changes in the prices of a fixed market basket of some 300 goods bought by the typical urban consumer.

■ Shortcomings of GDP

GDP is a reasonably accurate and extremely useful measure of how well or how poorly the economy is performing. But it has several shortcomings as a measure of both total output and well-being (total utility).

Nonmarket Transactions

Certain production transactions do not take place in any market—the services of homemakers, for example, and the labor of carpenters who repair their own homes. Such transactions never show up in GDP, which measures only the *market value* of output. Consequently, GDP understates a nation's total output. There is one exception: The portion of farmers' output that farmers consume themselves *is* estimated and included in GDP.

Leisure

The workweek in the United States has declined since the turn of the century—from about 53 hours to about 36 hours. Moreover, the greater frequency of paid vacations, holidays, and leave time has shortened the work year itself. This increase in leisure time has clearly had a positive effect on overall well-being. But our system of national income accounting understates well-being by ignoring leisure's value. Nor does the system accommodate the satisfaction—the "psychic income"—that many people derive from their work.

Improved Product Quality

Because GDP is a quantitative measure rather than a qualitative measure, it fails to take into account the value of improvements in product quality. There is a very real difference in quality between a $3000 personal computer purchased today and a computer that cost the same amount just a decade ago. Today's computer has far more speed and storage capacity, a clearer monitor, and enhanced multimedia capabilities.

Obviously quality improvement has a great effect on economic well-being, as does the quantity of goods produced. But again GDP ignores that effect entirely.

The Underground Economy

Embedded in our economy is a flourishing, productive underground sector. Some of the people who conduct business there are gamblers, smugglers, prostitutes, "fences" of stolen goods, drug growers, and drug dealers. They have good reason to conceal their incomes.

Most participants in the underground economy however, engage in perfectly legal activities but choose not to report their full incomes to the Internal Revenue Service (IRS). A bell captain at a hotel may report just a portion of the tips received from customers. Storekeepers may report only a portion of their sales receipts. Workers who want to hold on to their unemployment compensation benefits may take

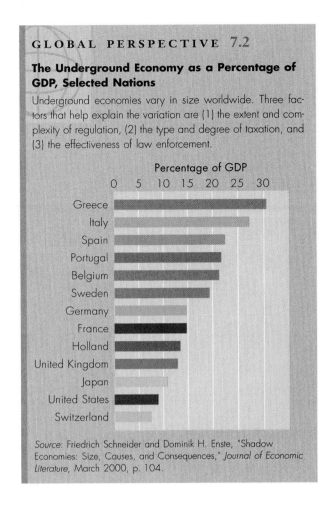

GLOBAL PERSPECTIVE 7.2

The Underground Economy as a Percentage of GDP, Selected Nations

Underground economies vary in size worldwide. Three factors that help explain the variation are (1) the extent and complexity of regulation, (2) the type and degree of taxation, and (3) the effectiveness of law enforcement.

Percentage of GDP
0   5   10   15   20   25   30

Greece
Italy
Spain
Portugal
Belgium
Sweden
Germany
France
Holland
United Kingdom
Japan
United States
Switzerland

Source: Friedrich Schneider and Dominik H. Enste, "Shadow Economies: Size, Causes, and Consequences," *Journal of Economic Literature,* March 2000, p. 104.

an "off-the-books" or "cash-only" job. A brick mason may agree to rebuild a neighbor's fireplace in exchange for the neighbor's repairing his boat engine. The value of none of these transactions shows up in GDP.

The value of underground transactions is estimated to be about 8 percent of the recorded GDP in the United States. That would mean that GDP in 2000 was understated by about $798 billion. Global Perspective 7.2 shows estimates of the relative sizes of underground economies in selected nations.

GDP and the Environment

The growth of GDP is inevitably accompanied by "gross domestic by-products," including dirty air and polluted water, toxic waste, congestion, and noise. The social costs of the negative by-products reduce our economic well-being. And since those costs are not deducted from total output, GDP over-

states our national well-being. Ironically, when money is spent to clean up pollution and reduce congestion, those expenses are added to the GDP!

Composition and Distribution of Output

The composition of output is undoubtedly important for well-being. But GDP does not tell us whether the mix of goods and services is enriching or potentially detrimental to society. GDP assigns equal weight to an assault rifle and a set of encyclopedias, as long as both sell for the same price. Moreover, GDP reveals nothing about the way output is distributed. Does 90 percent of the output go to 10 percent of the households, for example, or is the output more evenly distributed? The distribution of output may make a big difference for society's overall well-being.

Per Capita Output

For many purposes, the most meaningful measure of economic performance is **per capita output,** found by dividing real GDP by population. Because GDP measures only the magnitude of total output, it conceals changes in the standard of living of individuals and households. If GDP and population rise simultaneously, the per-person standard of living may be constant or even declining.

That is the plight of some low-income developing countries. For example, Madagascar's GDP grew at a rate of 1.3 percent per year from 1990 to 1998. But over the same period its annual population growth was 2.8 percent, resulting in a decline in per capita output of about 1.5 percent per year.

Noneconomic Sources of Well-Being

Finally, the connection between GDP and well-being is problematic for another reason. Just as a household's income does not measure its total happiness, a nation's GDP does not measure its total well-being. There are many things that could make a society better off without necessarily raising GDP: a reduction of crime and violence, peaceful relations with other countries, people's greater civility toward one another, better understanding between parents and children, and a reduction of drug and alcohol abuse.

Feeding the GDP Accounts

The Bureau of Economic Analysis (BEA), an Agency of the Department of Commerce, Compiles the GDP Accounts. Where Does It Get the Actual Data?

Discussions of national income accounting often leave the impression that a handful of economic sorcerers collect the data for the national income accounts from some mysterious place. Let's see where the accountants get their data.

Consumption The BEA derives the data for the consumption component of the GDP accounts from four main sources:

■ The Census Bureau's *Retail Trade Survey*, which gains sales information from a sample of 22,000 firms.

■ The Census Bureau's *Survey of Manufacturers*, which gathers information on shipments of consumer goods from 50,000 establishments.

■ The Census Bureau's *Service Survey*, which collects sales data from 30,000 service businesses.

■ Industry trade sources. For example, data on auto sales and aircraft are collected directly from auto and aircraft manufacturers.

Investment The sources of the data for the investment component of GDP include:

■ All the sources above used to determine consumption. Purchases of capital goods are separated from purchases of consumer goods. For example, estimates of investment in equipment and software are based on manufacturer's ship-

ments reported in the *Survey of Manufacturers*, the *Service Survey*, and industry sources.

■ Census construction surveys. The Census Bureau's *Housing Starts Survey* and *Housing Sales Survey* produce the data used to measure the amount of housing construction, and the *Construction Progress Reporting Survey* is the source of data on nonresidential construction. The BEA determines changes in business inventories through the *Retail Trade Survey*, the *Wholesale Trade Survey* (of 7100 wholesale firms), and the *Survey of Manufacturing*.

Government Purchases The data for government purchases (officially "government consumption and investment expenditures") are obtained through the following sources:

■ The U.S. Office of Personnel Management, which collects data on wages and benefits, broken out by the private and public sector. Wages and benefits of government employees are the single largest "purchase" by Federal, state, and local government.

■ The previously mentioned Census Bureau's construction surveys, which break out private and public sector construction expenditures.

■ The Census Bureau's *Survey of Government Finance*, which provides data on government consumption and investment expenditures.

Net Exports The BEA determines net exports through two main sources:

■ The U.S. Customs Service, which collects data on exports and imports of goods.

■ BEA surveys of potential domestic exporters and importers of services, which collect data on exports and imports of services.

Mystery solved!

Source: Based on Joseph A. Ritter, "Feeding the National Accounts," Federal Reserve Bank of St. Louis *Review* March–April 2000, pp. 11–20. For those interested, this article also provides information on the sources of data for the income side of the national accounts.

SUMMARY

1. Gross domestic product (GDP), a basic measure of an economy's economic performance, is the market value of all final goods and services produced within the borders of a nation in a year.

2. Intermediate goods, nonproduction transactions, and secondhand sales are purposely excluded in calculating GDP.

3. GDP may be calculated by summing total expenditures on all final output or by summing the income derived from the production of that output.

4. By the expenditures approach, GDP is determined by adding consumer purchases of goods and services, gross investment spending by businesses, government purchases, and net exports: GDP = $C + I_g + G + X_n$.

5. Gross investment is divided into (a) replacement investment (required to maintain the nation's stock of capital at its existing level) and (b) net investment (the net increase in the stock of capital). In most years, net investment is positive and therefore the economy's stock of capital and production capacity increase.

6. By the income or allocations approach, GDP is calculated as the sum of compensation to employees, rents, interest, proprietors' income, corporate profits plus consumption of fixed capital, indirect business taxes, and net foreign factor income earned in the United States.

7. Other national accounts are derived from GDP. Net domestic product (NDP) is GDP less the consumption of fixed capital. National income (NI) is total income earned by a nation's resource suppliers; it is found by subtracting net foreign factor income earned in the United States and indirect business taxes from NDP. Personal income (PI) is the total income paid to households prior to any allowance for personal taxes. Disposable income (DI) is personal income after personal taxes have been paid. DI measures the amount of income available to households to consume or save.

8. Price indexes are computed by dividing the price of a specific collection or market basket of output in a particular period by the price of the same market basket in a base period and multiplying the result (the quotient) by 100. The GDP price index is used to adjust nominal GDP for inflation or deflation and thereby obtain real GDP.

9. Nominal (current-dollar) GDP measures each year's output valued in terms of the prices prevailing in that year. Real (constant-dollar) GDP measures each year's output in terms of the prices that prevailed in a selected base year. Because real GDP is adjusted for price-level changes, differences in real GDP are due only to differences in production activity.

10. The consumer price index (CPI) measures changes in the price of a market basket of some 300 goods and services purchased by urban consumers. Unlike the GDP price index, in which the weights of the goods change annually with spending patterns, the CPI is a fixed-weight price index, meaning that each year the items in the market basket remain the same as those in the base period (1993–1995).

11. GDP is a reasonably accurate and very useful indicator of a nation's economic performance, but it has its limitations. It fails to account for nonmarket and illegal transactions, changes in leisure and in product quality, the composition and distribution of output, and the environmental effects of production. The link between GDP and well-being is tenuous.

TERMS AND CONCEPTS

national income accounting

gross domestic product (GDP)

intermediate goods

final goods

multiple counting

value added

expenditures approach

income approach

personal consumption expenditures (C)

gross private domestic investment (I_g)

net private domestic investment

government purchases (G)

net exports (X_n)

national income

indirect business taxes

consumption of fixed capital

net domestic product (NDP)

personal income (PI)

disposable income (DI)

nominal GDP

price index

real GDP

consumer price index (CPI)

per capita output

STUDY QUESTIONS

1. In what ways are national income statistics useful?

2. Explain why an economy's output, in essence, is also its income.

3. **Key Question** Why do national income accountants include only final goods in measuring GDP for a particular year? Why don't they include the value of the stocks and bonds bought and sold? Why don't they include the value of the used furniture bought and sold?

4. What is the difference between gross private domestic investment and net private domestic investment? If you were to determine net domestic product (NDP) through the expenditures approach, which of these two measures of investment spending would be appropriate? Explain.

5. Why are changes in inventories included as part of investment spending? Suppose inventories declined by $1 billion during 2001. How would this affect the size of gross private domestic investment and gross domestic product in 2001? Explain.

6. Use the concepts of gross investment and net investment to distinguish between an economy that has a rising stock of capital and one that has a falling stock of capital. "In 1933 net private domestic investment was minus $6 billion. This means that in that particular year the economy produced no capital goods at all." Do you agree? Why or why not? Explain: "Though net investment can be positive, negative, or zero, it is quite impossible for gross investment to be less than zero."

7. Define net exports. Explain how U.S. exports and imports each affect domestic production. Suppose foreigners spend $7 billion on U.S. exports in a given year and Americans spend $5 billion on imports from abroad in the same year. What is the amount of the United States' net exports? Explain how net exports might be a negative amount.

8. **Key Question** Below is a list of domestic output and national income figures for a given year. All figures are in billions. The questions that follow ask you to determine the major national income measures by both the expenditures and the income approaches. The results you obtain with the different methods should be the same.

Personal consumption expenditures	$245
Net foreign factor income earned in the U.S.	4
Transfer payments	12
Rents	14
Consumption of fixed capital (depreciation)	27
Social security contributions	20
Interest	13

Proprietors' income	33
Net exports	11
Dividends	16
Compensation of employees	223
Indirect business taxes	18
Undistributed corporate profits	21
Personal taxes	26
Corporate income taxes	19
Corporate profits	56
Government purchases	72
Net private domestic investment	33
Personal saving	20

a. Using the above data, determine GDP by both the expenditures and the income approaches. Then determine NDP.

b. Now determine NI in two ways: first, by making the required additions or subtractions from NDP; and second, by adding up the types of income that make up NI.

c. Adjust NI (from part *b*) as required to obtain PI.

d. Adjust PI (from part *c*) as required to obtain DI.

9. Using the following national income accounting data, compute (*a*) GDP, (*b*) NDP, and (*c*) NI. All figures are in billions.

Compensation of employees	$194.2
U.S. exports of goods and services	17.8
Consumption of fixed capital	11.8
Government purchases	59.4
Indirect business taxes	14.4
Net private domestic investment	52.1
Transfer payments	13.9
U.S. imports of goods and services	16.5
Personal taxes	40.5
Net foreign factor income earned in the U.S.	2.2
Personal consumption expenditures	219.1

10. Why do national income accountants compare the market value of the total outputs in various years rather than actual physical volumes of production? What problem is posed by any comparison over time of the market values of various total outputs? How is this problem resolved?

11. **Key Question** Suppose that in 1984 the total output in a single-good economy was 7000 buckets of chicken. Also suppose that in 1984 each bucket of chicken was priced at $10. Finally, assume that in 1996 the price per bucket of chicken was $16 and that 22,000 buckets were purchased. Determine the GDP price index for 1984, using 1996 as the base year. By what percentage did the price level, as measured by

this index, rise between 1984 and 1996? Use the two methods listed in Table 7.6 to determine real GDP for 1984 and 1996.

12. **Key Question** The following table shows nominal GDP and an appropriate price index for a group of selected years. Compute real GDP. Indicate in each calculation whether you are inflating or deflating the nominal GDP data.

Year	Nominal GDP, Billions	Price Index (1996 = 100)	Real GDP, Billions
1960	$ 527.4	22.19	$_____
1968	911.5	26.29	$_____
1978	2295.9	48.22	$_____
1988	4742.5	80.22	$_____
1998	8790.2	103.22	$_____

13. Which of the following are included in this year's GDP? Explain your answer in each case.
    a. Interest on an AT&T bond.
    b. Social security payments received by a retired factory worker.
    c. The services of a painter in painting the family home.
    d. The income of a dentist.
    e. The money received by Smith when she sells her economics textbook to a book buyer.
    f. The monthly allowance a college student receives from home.
    g. Rent received on a two-bedroom apartment.
    h. The money received by Mac when he resells his current-year-model Plymouth Prowler to Stan.
    i. Interest received on corporate bonds.
    j. A 2-hour decrease in the length of the work-week.
    k. The purchase of an AT&T bond.
    l. A $2 billion increase in business inventories.
    m. The purchase of 100 shares of GM common stock.
    n. The purchase of an insurance policy.

14. **(Last Word)** What government agency compiles the U.S. GDP accounts? In what U.S. Department is it located? Of the several specific sources of information, name one source for each of the four components of GDP: consumption, investment, government purchases, and net exports.

15. **Web-Based Question:** *Nominal and real GDP— visit the BEA* Visit the Bureau of Economic Analysis website, www.bea.doc.gov, and select GDP and Related Data. Under "Time Series Estimates," identify the current-dollar GDP (nominal GDP) and real GDP data for the past four quarters. Why was current-dollar GDP higher than real GDP in each of those quarters? What were the percentage changes in current-dollar GDP and real GDP for the most recent quarter? How do those percentage changes compare to those for the prior three quarters?

16. **Web-Based Question:** *Per capita gross domestic product* The OECD (Organization for Economic Cooperation and Development), at www.oecd.org/std/nahome.htm, provides through its "Selected On-Line Statistics" an annual comparison of levels of GDP per capita based on both exchange rates and purchasing power parities (PPPs). Rank the current top 10 countries using each method. According to information at this website, how do the rankings differ? Which method do you think is a more realistic indicator of "output per person"? What explains the difference in Canada's per capita income calculated by using exchange rates and that calculated by using PPPs?

Introduction to Economic Growth and Instability

B ET W E E N 1 9 9 6 AND 2 0 0 0 , real GDP in the United States expanded briskly and the price level rose only slowly. The economy experienced neither significant unemployment nor inflation. But if the past is any guide, this desirable set of outcomes will not continue forever. Within the past three decades real GDP in the United States has declined in four periods: 1973–1975, 1980, 1981–1982, and 1990–1991. At times high unemployment or inflation has been a problem. For example, between 1990 and 1992 the number of unemployed persons increased by 2.6 million. The U.S. rate of inflation was 13.5 percent in 1980 and 5.4 percent in 1990. Also, Japan and a number of other countries suffered recessions in the last half of the 1990s. Further, the U.S. economy slowed substantially in early 2001, raising concerns of a possible decline in real GDP. So macroeconomic instability is a continuing concern. ▪ In this chapter we provide an *introductory* look at the trend of real GDP growth in the United States and the macroeconomic problems that have occasionally accompanied it. Our specific topics are economic growth, the business cycle, unemployment, and inflation.

▌Economic Growth

Economists define and measure **economic growth** as either:

- An increase in real GDP occurring over some time period.
- An increase in real GDP *per capita* occurring over some time period.

For measuring growth in military potential or in political preeminence, the first definition is more use-

ful. For comparing living standards, however, the second definition is superior. While China's GDP was $980 billion in 1999 compared with Denmark's $170 billion, Denmark's GDP per capita was $32,030 compared with China's meager $780.

With either definition, economic growth is calculated as a percentage rate of growth per year. For example, if real GDP was $200 billion in some country last year and $210 billion this year, the rate of growth would be 5 percent {= [($210 billion − $200 billion)/$200 billion] × 100}. **(Key Question 2)**

Growth as a Goal

Growth is a widely held economic goal. The expansion of total output relative to population results in rising real wages and incomes and thus higher standards of living. An economy that is experiencing economic growth is better able to meet people's wants and resolve socioeconomic problems. Rising real wages and income provide richer opportunities to individuals and families—a vacation trip, a personal computer, a higher education—without sacrificing other opportunities and pleasures. A growing economy can undertake new programs to alleviate poverty and protect the environment without impairing existing levels of consumption, investment, and public goods production.

In short, *growth lessens the burden of scarcity.* A growing economy, unlike a static economy, can consume more today while increasing its capacity to produce more in the future. By easing the burden of scarcity—by relaxing society's constraints on production—economic growth enables a nation to attain its economic goals more readily and to undertake new endeavors that require goods and services to be accomplished.

Arithmetic of Growth

Why do economists pay so much attention to small changes in the rate of economic growth? Because those changes really matter! For the United States, with a current real GDP of about $10 trillion, the difference between a 3 percent and a 4 percent rate of growth is about $100 billion of output each year. For a poor country, a difference of one-half a percentage point in the rate of growth may mean the difference between starvation and mere hunger.

The mathematical approximation called the **rule of 70** provides a quantitative grasp of the effect of economic growth. It tells us that we can find the number of years it will take for some measure to double, given its annual percentage increase, by dividing that percentage increase into the number 70. So

$$\begin{array}{l}\text{Approximate} \\ \text{number of years} \\ \text{required to double} \\ \text{real GDP}\end{array} = \dfrac{70}{\begin{array}{c}\text{annual percentage rate} \\ \text{of growth}\end{array}}$$

Examples: A 3 percent annual rate of growth will double real GDP in about 23 (= 70 ÷ 3) years. Growth of 8 percent per year will double real GDP in about 9 (= 70 ÷ 8) years. The rule of 70 is generally applicable. For example, it works for estimating how long it will take the price level, or a savings account to double at various percentage rates of inflation or interest. When compounded over many years, an apparently small difference in the rate of growth thus becomes highly significant. Suppose Alta and Zorn have identical GDPs, but Alta grows at a 4 percent yearly rate, while Zorn grows at 2 percent. Alta's GDP would double in about 18 years, while Zorn's GDP would double in 35 years.

Main Sources of Growth

There are two fundamental ways society can increase its real output and income: (1) by increasing its inputs of resources, and (2) by increasing the productivity of those inputs. Other things equal, increases in land, labor, capital, and entrepreneurial resources yield additional output. But economic growth also occurs through increases in **productivity**—measured broadly as real output per unit of input. Productivity rises when the health, training, education, and motivation of workers are improved; when workers have more and better machinery and natural resources with which to work; when production is better organized and managed; and when labor is reallocated from less efficient industries to more efficient industries. About one-third of U.S. growth comes from more inputs. The remaining two-thirds results from improved productivity.

Growth in the United States

Table 8.1 gives an overview of economic growth in the United States over past periods. Column 2 reveals strong growth as measured by increases in real GDP. Note that between 1940 and 2000 real GDP increased about tenfold. But the U.S. population also increased. Nevertheless, in column 4 we find that real GDP per capita rose nearly fivefold over these years.

What has been the *rate* of U.S. growth? Real GDP grew at an annual rate of about 3.5 percent between 1950 and 2000. Real GDP per capita increased about 2.3 percent per year over that time. But we must qualify these raw numbers in several ways:

■ *Improved products and services* Since the numbers in Table 8.1 do not fully account for

Table 8.1
Real GDP and Per Capita GDP, 1929–2000

(1) Year	(2) GDP, Billions of 1996 $	(3) Population, Millions	(4) Per Capita GDP, 1996 $ (2) ÷ (3)
1929	$ 822	122	$ 6,738
1933	603	126	4,786
1940	981	132	7,432
1945	1693	140	12,093
1950	1687	152	11,099
1955	2100	166	12,651
1960	2377	181	13,133
1965	3029	194	15,613
1970	3578	205	17,454
1975	4084	214	19,084
1980	4901	228	21,496
1985	5717	239	23,921
1990	6708	250	26,832
1995	7544	263	28,684
2000	9320	275	33,891

Source: Data are from the Bureau of Economic Analysis [www.bea.doc.gov] and the U.S. Census Bureau [www.census.gov].

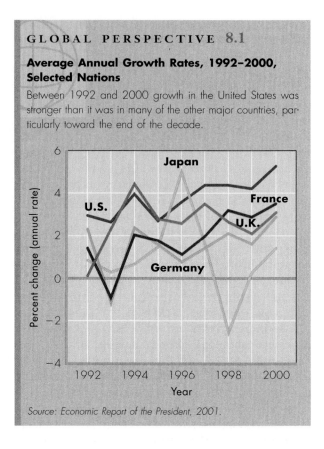

GLOBAL PERSPECTIVE 8.1

Average Annual Growth Rates, 1992–2000, Selected Nations

Between 1992 and 2000 growth in the United States was stronger than it was in many of the other major countries, particularly toward the end of the decade.

Source: Economic Report of the President, 2001.

the improvements in products and services, they understate the growth of economic well-being. Such purely quantitative data do not fully compare an era of iceboxes and LPs with an era of refrigerators and CDs.

- *Added leisure*   The increases in real GDP and per capita GDP identified in Table 8.1 were accomplished despite large increases in leisure. The standard workweek, once 50 hours, is now about 40 hours. Again the raw growth numbers understate the gain in economic well-being.

- *Other impacts*   These measures of growth do not account for any effects growth may have had on the environment and the quality of life. If growth debases the physical environment and creates a stressful work environment, the bare growth numbers will overstate the gains in well-being that result from growth. On the other hand, if growth leads to stronger environmental protections and greater human security, these numbers will understate the gains in well-being.

Relative Growth Rates

Viewed from the perspective of the last half-century, economic growth in the United States lagged behind that in Japan, Germany, Italy, Canada, and France.

Japan's annual growth rate, in fact, averaged twice that of the United States. But the 1990s were quite another matter. As shown in Global Perspective 8.1, the U.S. growth rate surged ahead of the rates of other industrial nations. (This fact has led some economists to conclude that the United States has achieved a "New Economy" of faster economic growth. We will examine that somewhat controversial viewpoint in detail in Chapter 17.)

▌ The Business Cycle

Long-run economic growth in the United States has been interrupted by periods of economic instability. At various times, growth has given way to recession and depression—that is, to declines in real GDP and significant increases in unemployment. At other times, rapid economic growth has been marred by rapid inflation. Both unemployment and inflation often are associated with *business cycles*. 🔑 **8.1**

Phases of the Business Cycle

The term **business cycle** refers to alternating rises and declines in the level of economic activity, sometimes extending over several years. Individual cycles (one "up" followed by one "down") vary substantially in duration and intensity. Yet all display certain phases, to which economists have assigned various labels. Figure 8.1 shows the four phases of a generalized business cycle.

- *Peak*   At a **peak,** such as the middle peak shown in Figure 8.1, business activity has reached a temporary maximum. Here the economy is at full employment and the level of real output is at or very close to the economy's capacity. The price level is likely to rise during this phase.
- *Recession*   A peak is followed by a **recession**—a period of decline in total output, income, employment, and trade. This downturn, which lasts 6 months or more, is marked by the widespread contraction of business activity in many sectors of the economy. But because many prices are downwardly inflexible, the price level is likely to fall only if the recession is severe and prolonged—that is, only if a depression occurs.
- *Trough*   In the **trough** of the recession or depression, output and employment "bottom out" at their lowest levels. The trough phase may be either short-lived or quite long.
- *Recovery*   In the expansion or **recovery** phase, output and employment rise toward full employment. As recovery intensifies, the price level may begin to rise before full employment and full-capacity production return.

Table 8.2
U.S. Recessions since 1950

Period	Duration, Months	Depth (Decline in Real Output)
1953–54	10	−3.7%
1957–58	8	−3.9
1960–61	10	−1.6
1969–70	11	−1.0
1973–75	16	−4.9
1980	6	−2.3
1981–82	16	−3.3
1990–91	8	−1.8

Source: Economic Report of the President, 1993, updated.

Although business cycles all pass through the same phases, they vary greatly in duration and intensity. Many economists prefer to talk of business "fluctuations" rather than cycles because cycles imply regularity while fluctuations do not. The Great Depression of the 1930s resulted in a 40 percent decline in real GDP over a 3-year period in the United States and seriously impaired business activity for a decade. By comparison, more recent U.S. recessions, detailed in Table 8.2, were relatively mild in both intensity and duration.

Recessions, of course, occur in other countries, too. At one time or another during the 1990s Argentina, Brazil, Canada, Colombia, Japan, Indonesia, Mexico, and South Korea experienced recessions.

Causation: A First Glance

Economists have suggested many theories to explain fluctuations in business activity. Some say that momentous innovations, such as the railroad, the automobile, synthetic fibers, and microchips, have great impact on investment and consumption spending and therefore on output, employment, and the price level. Such major innovations occur irregularly and thus contribute to the variability of economic activity.

Some economists see major changes in productivity as causes of business cycles. When productivity expands, the economy booms; when productivity falls, the economy recedes. Still others view the business cycle as a purely monetary phenomenon. When government creates too much money, they say, an inflationary boom occurs. Too little money triggers

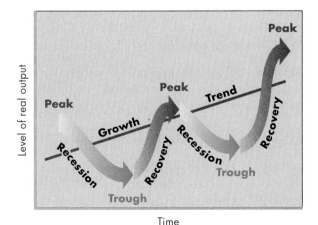

Figure 8.1
The business cycle. Economists distinguish four phases of the business cycle; the duration and strength of each phase may vary.

a decline in output and employment and, eventually, in the price level.

Most economists, however, believe that the immediate cause of cyclical changes in the levels of real output and employment is changes in the level of total spending. In a market economy, businesses produce goods or services only if they can sell them at a profit. If total spending sinks, many businesses find that it is no longer profitable to go on producing their current volume of goods and services. As a consequence, output, employment, and incomes all fall. When the level of spending rises, an increase in production becomes profitable, and output, employment, and incomes will rise accordingly. Once the economy nears full employment, however, further gains in real output become more difficult to achieve. Continued increases in spending may raise the price level as consumers bid for the limited amount of goods available.

We have seen that the long-run growth trend of the U.S. economy is one of expansion. Note that the stylized cycle in Figure 8.1 is drawn against a trend of economic growth.

Cyclical Impact: Durables and Nondurables

Although the business cycle is felt everywhere in the economy, it affects different segments in different ways and to different degrees.

Firms and industries producing *capital goods* (for example, housing, commercial buildings, heavy equipment, and farm implements) and *consumer durables* (for example, automobiles, personal computers, refrigerators) are affected most by the business cycle. Within limits, firms can postpone the purchase of capital goods. As the economy recedes, producers frequently delay the purchase of new equipment and the construction of new plants. The business outlook simply does not warrant increases in the stock of capital goods. In good times, capital goods are usually replaced before they depreciate completely. But when recession strikes, firms patch up their old equipment and make do. As a result, investment in capital goods declines sharply. Firms that have excess plant capacity may not even bother to replace all the capital that is depreciating. For them, net investment may be negative. The pattern is much the same for consumer durables such as automobiles and major appliances. When recession occurs and households must trim their budgets, purchases of these goods are often deferred. Families repair their old cars and appliances

rather than buy new ones, and the firms producing these products suffer. (Of course, producers of capital goods and consumer durables also benefit most from expansions.)

In contrast, *service* industries and industries that produce *nondurable consumer goods* are somewhat insulated from the most severe effects of recession. People find it difficult to cut back on needed medical and legal services, for example. And a recession actually helps some service firms, such as pawnbrokers and law firms that specialize in bankruptcies. Nor are the purchases of many nondurable goods such as food and clothing easy to postpone. The quantity and quality of purchases of nondurables will decline, but not so much as will purchases of capital goods and consumer durables. **(Key Question 4)**

> **QUICK REVIEW 8.1**
>
> ■ Economic growth can be measured as (a) an increase in real GDP over time or (b) an increase in real GDP per capita over time.
>
> ■ Real GDP in the United States has grown at an average annual rate of about 3.5 percent since 1950; real GDP per capita has grown at roughly a 2.3 percent annual rate over that same period.
>
> ■ The typical business cycle goes through four phases: peak, recession, trough, and recovery.
>
> ■ During recession, industries that produce capital goods and consumer durables normally suffer greater output and employment declines than do service and nondurable consumer goods industries.

▮ Unemployment

The twin problems that arise from economic instability are unemployment and inflation. Let's look at unemployment first.

Measurement of Unemployment

To measure the unemployment rate, we must first determine who is eligible and available to work. Figure 8.2 provides a helpful starting point. It divides the total U.S. population into three groups. One group is made up of people less than 16 years of age and people who are institutionalized, for example, in mental hospitals or correctional institutions. Such people are not considered potential members of the labor force.

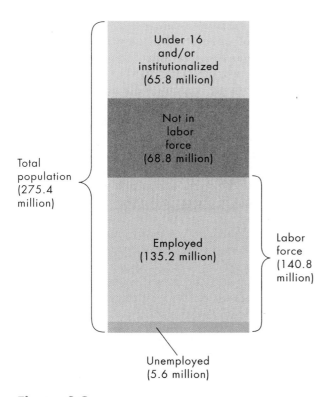

Figure 8.2

The labor force, employment, and unemployment, 2000. The labor force consists of persons 16 years of age or older who are not in institutions and who are (1) employed or (2) unemployed but seeking employment.

A second group, labeled "Not in labor force," is composed of adults who are potential workers but are not employed and are not seeking work. For example, they are homemakers, full-time students, or retirees.

The third group is the **labor force,** which constituted about 50 percent of the total population in 2000. The labor force consists of people who are able and willing to work. Both those who are employed and those who are unemployed but actively seeking work are counted as being in the labor force. The **unemployment rate** is the percentage of the labor force unemployed:

$$\text{Unemployment rate} = \frac{\text{unemployed}}{\text{labor force}} \times 100$$

The statistics included in Figure 8.2 show that in 2000 the unemployment rate averaged

$$\frac{5,655,000}{140,863,000} \times 100 = 4.0\%$$

Unemployment rates for selected years between 1929 and 2000 appear on the inside covers of this book.

The U.S. Bureau of Labor Statistics (BLS) conducts a nationwide random survey of some 60,000 households each month to determine who is employed and who is not employed. In a series of questions it asks which members of the household are working, unemployed and looking for work, not looking for work, and so on. From the answers it determines an unemployment rate for the entire nation. Despite the use of scientific sampling and interviewing techniques, the data collected in this survey are subject to criticism:

■ ***Part-time employment***   The BLS lists all part-time workers as fully employed. In 2000 about 18.7 million people worked part-time as a result of personal choice. But another 3.2 million part-time workers either wanted to work full-time and could not find suitable full-time work or worked fewer hours because of a temporary slack in consumer demand. These last two groups were, in effect, partially employed and partially unemployed. By counting them as fully employed, say critics, the official BLS data understate the unemployment rate.

■ ***Discouraged workers***   You must be actively seeking work in order to be counted as unemployed. An unemployed individual who is not actively seeking employment is classified as "not in the labor force." The problem is that many workers, after unsuccessfully seeking employment for a time, become discouraged and drop out of the labor force. The number of such **discouraged workers** is larger during recession than during prosperity; an estimated 1.25 million people fell into this category in recession year 1991. By not counting discouraged workers as unemployed, say critics, the official BLS data understate the unemployment rate. **(Key Question 6)**

Types of Unemployment

There are three *types* of unemployment: frictional, structural, and cyclical.

Frictional Unemployment

At any given time some workers are "between jobs." Some of them will be moving voluntarily from one job to another. Others will have been fired and will be seeking reemployment. Still others will have been laid off temporarily because of seasonal demand. In addition to those between jobs, many young workers will be searching for their first jobs.

As these unemployed people find jobs or are called back from temporary layoffs, other job seekers and laid-off workers will replace them in the "unemployment pool." So even though the workers who are unemployed for such reasons change from month to month, this type of unemployment persists.

Economists use the term **frictional unemployment**—consisting of *search unemployment* and *wait unemployment*—for workers who are either searching for jobs or waiting to take jobs in the near future. The word "frictional" implies that the labor market does not operate perfectly and instantaneously (without friction) in matching workers and jobs.

Frictional unemployment is inevitable and, at least in part, desirable. Many workers who are voluntarily between jobs are moving from low-paying, low-productivity jobs to higher-paying, higher-productivity positions. That means greater income for the workers, a better allocation of labor resources, and a larger real GDP for the economy.

Structural Unemployment Frictional unemployment blurs into a category called **structural unemployment.** Here, economists use "structural" in the sense of "compositional." Changes over time in consumer demand and in technology alter the "structure" of the total demand for labor, both occupationally and geographically.

Occupationally, the demand for certain skills (for example, sewing clothes or working on farms) may decline or even vanish. The demand for other skills (for example, designing software or maintaining computer systems) will intensify. Unemployment results because the composition of the labor force does not respond immediately or completely to the new structure of job opportunities. Workers who find that their skills and experience have become obsolete or unneeded thus find that they have no marketable talents. They are structurally unemployed until they adapt or develop skills that employers want.

Geographically, the demand for labor also changes over time. An example: migration of industry and thus of employment opportunities from the Snow Belt to the Sun Belt over the past few decades. Another example is the movement of jobs from inner-city factories to suburban industrial parks. As job opportunities shift from one place to another, some workers become structurally unemployed.

The distinction between frictional and structural unemployment is hazy at best. The key difference is that *frictionally* unemployed workers have salable skills and either live in areas where jobs exist or are able to move to areas where they do. *Structurally* unemployed workers find it hard to obtain new jobs without retraining, gaining additional education, or relocating. Frictional unemployment is short-term; structural unemployment is more likely to be long-term and consequently more serious.

Cyclical Unemployment Cyclical unemployment is caused by a decline in total spending and is likely to occur in the recession phase of the business cycle. As the demand for goods and services decreases, employment falls and unemployment rises. For this reason, **cyclical unemployment** is sometimes called *deficient-demand unemployment.* The 25 percent unemployment rate in the depth of the Great Depression in 1933 reflected mainly cyclical unemployment, as did significant parts of the 9.7 percent unemployment rate during the recession year 1982 and the 6.7 percent rate in the recession year 1991.

Cyclical unemployment is a very serious problem when it occurs. We will say more about its high costs later, but first we need to define "full employment." 8.1

Definition of Full Employment

Because frictional and structural unemployment are largely unavoidable in a dynamic economy, *full employment* is something less than 100 percent employment of the labor force. Economists say that the economy is "fully employed" when it is experiencing only frictional and structural unemployment. That is, full employment occurs when there is no cyclical unemployment.

Economists describe the unemployment rate that is consistent with full employment as the **full-employment rate of unemployment,** or the **natural rate of unemployment (NRU).** At the NRU, the economy is said to be producing its **potential output.** This is the real GDP that occurs when the economy is "fully employed."

The NRU occurs when the number of *job seekers* equals the number of *job vacancies.* Even when labor markets are in balance, however, the NRU is some positive percentage because it takes time for frictionally unemployed job seekers to find open jobs they can fill. Also, it takes time for the structurally unemployed to achieve the skills and geographic relocation needed for reemployment.

"Natural" does not mean, however, that the economy will always operate at this rate and thus realize its potential output. When cyclical unemployment occurs, the economy has much more unemployment than that which would occur at the NRU. Moreover, the economy can operate for a while at an unemployment rate *below* the NRU. At times, the demand for labor may be so great that firms take a stronger initiative to hire and train the structurally unemployed. Also, some homemakers, teenagers, college students, and retirees who were casually looking for just the right part-time or full-time jobs may quickly find them. Thus the unemployment rate temporarily falls below the natural rate.

Also, the NRU can vary over time. In the 1980s, the NRU was about 6 percent. Today, it is 4 to 5 percent. Why the decline?

- The growing proportion of younger workers in the labor force has declined as the baby-boom generation has aged. The labor force now has a larger proportion of middle-aged workers, who traditionally have lower unemployment rates.
- The growth of temporary-help agencies and the improved information resulting from the Internet have lowered the NRU by enabling workers to find jobs more quickly.
- The work requirements under the new welfare laws have moved many people from the ranks of the unemployed to the ranks of the employed.
- The doubling of the U.S. prison population since 1985 has removed relatively high unemployment individuals from the labor force and thus lowered the overall unemployment rate.

A decade ago, a 4 to 5 percent rate of unemployment would have reflected excessive spending, an unbalanced labor market, and rising inflation; today, the same rate is consistent with a balanced labor market and a stable, low rate of inflation.

Economic Cost of Unemployment

Unemployment that is above the natural rate involves great economic and social costs.

GDP Gap and Okun's Law

The basic economic cost of unemployment is forgone output. *When the economy fails to create enough jobs for all who are able and willing to work, potential production of goods and services is irretrievably lost.* In terms of Chapter 2's analysis, unemployment above the natural rate means that society is operating at some point inside its production possibilities curve. Economists measure this sacrificed output as the **GDP gap**—the amount by which *actual* GDP falls short of *potential* GDP.

Potential GDP is determined by assuming that the natural rate of unemployment prevails. The growth of potential GDP is simply projected forward on the basis of the economy's "normal" growth rate of real GDP. Figure 8.3 shows the GDP gap for recent years in the United States. It also indicates the close correlation between the actual unemployment rate (Figure 8.3b) and the GDP gap (Figure 8.3a). The higher the unemployment rate, the larger is the GDP gap.

Macroeconomist Arthur Okun was the first to quantify the relationship between the unemployment rate and the GDP gap. On the basis of recent estimates, **Okun's law** indicates that *for every 1 percentage point by which the actual unemployment rate exceeds the natural rate, a GDP gap of about 2 percent occurs*. With this information, we can calculate the absolute loss of output associated with any above-natural unemployment rate. For example, in 1992 the unemployment rate was 7.4 percent, or 1.4 percentage points above the 6.0 percent natural rate of unemployment then existing. Multiplying this 1.4 percent by Okun's 2 indicates that 1992's GDP gap was 2.8 percent of potential GDP (in real terms). By applying this 2.8 percent loss to 1992's potential GDP of $6300 billion, we find that the economy sacrificed $176 billion of real output because the natural rate of unemployment was not achieved. **(Key Question 8)**

As you can see in Figure 8.3, sometimes the economy's actual output will exceed its potential output. Figure 8.3 reveals that an economic expansion caused actual GDP to exceed potential GDP in 1999 and 2000, creating a "negative" GDP gap. Potential GDP can occasionally be exceeded, but the excess of actual over potential GDP typically causes inflation and cannot be sustained indefinitely.

Unequal Burdens

An increase in the unemployment rate from 5 to, say, 7 or 8 percent might be more tolerable to society if every worker's hours of work and wage income were reduced proportionally. But this is not the case. Part of the burden of unemployment is that its cost is unequally distributed.

Table 8.3 examines unemployment rates for various labor market groups for 2 years. The 1990–1991 recession pushed the 1992 unemployment rate to 7.4 percent. In 1999, the economy achieved full employment, with a 4.2 percent unemployment rate. By observing the large variance in unemployment

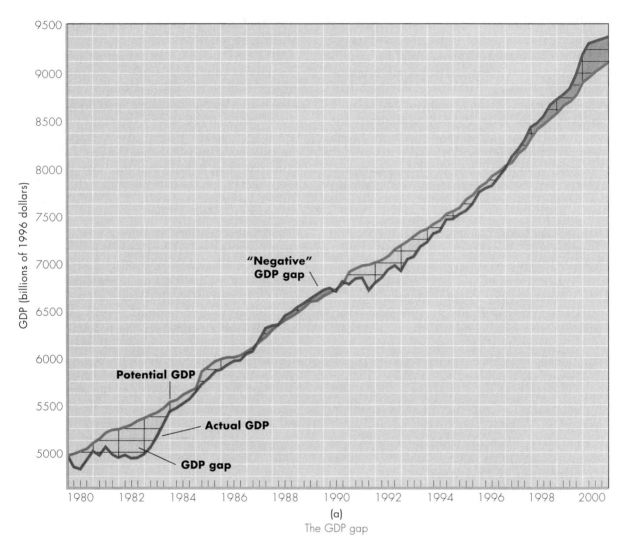

(a)
The GDP gap

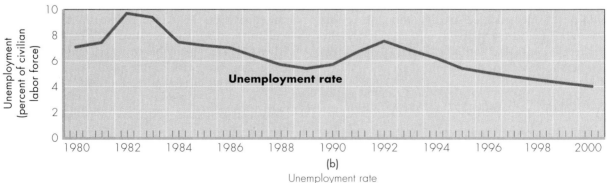

(b)
Unemployment rate

Figure 8.3

Potential and actual GDP and the unemployment rate.   (a) The difference between potential GDP and actual GDP is the GDP gap. The GDP gap measures the output that the economy sacrifices when it fails to achieve its full production potential. (b) A high unemployment rate means a large GDP gap, and a low unemployment rate means a small or even negative GDP gap.

(*Source:* Data are from the Federal Reserve Bank of St. Louis, www.stls.frb.org/index.html, and the Bureau of Economic Analysis, www.bea.doc.gov.)

Table 8.3

Unemployment Rates by Demographic Group: Recession (1992) and Full Employment (1999)*

Demographic Group	Unemployment Rate	
	1992	1999
Overall	7.4%	4.2%
Occupation:		
Managerial and professional	3.1	1.9
Operators, fabricators, and laborers	11.0	6.3
Age:		
16–19	20.2	13.9
Black male, 16–19	42.0	30.9
White male, 16–19	18.5	12.6
Male, 20+	7.0	3.5
Female, 20+	6.3	3.8
Race and ethnicity:		
Black	14.1	8.0
Hispanic	11.6	6.4
White	6.5	3.7
Gender:		
Women	6.9	4.3
Men	7.8	4.2
Education:**		
Less than high school diploma	11.3	6.0
High school diploma only	6.8	3.5
College degree or more	2.9	1.8
Duration:		
15 or more weeks	2.7	1.1

*Civilian labor-force data. In 1992 the economy was suffering the lingering unemployment effects of the 1990–1991 recession.
**People age 25 or over.
Source: Economic Report of the President; Employment and Earnings; Census Bureau, www.census.gov.

rates for the different groups within each year and comparing the rates between the two years, we can generalize as follows:

■ **Occupation** Workers in lower-skilled occupations (for example, laborers) have higher unemployment rates than workers in higher-skilled occupations (for example, professionals). Lower-skilled workers have more and longer spells of structural unemployment than higher-skilled workers. They also are less likely to be self-employed than are higher-skilled workers. Moreover, lower-skilled workers usually bear the brunt of recessions. Businesses generally retain most of their higher-skilled workers, in whom they have invested the expense of training.

■ **Age** Teenagers have much higher unemployment rates than adults. Teenagers have lower skill levels, quit their jobs more frequently, are more frequently "fired," and have less geographic mobility than adults. Many unemployed teenagers are new in the labor market, searching for their first jobs. Male black teenagers, in particular, have very high unemployment rates.

■ **Race and ethnicity** The unemployment rate for blacks and Hispanics is higher than that for whites. The causes of the higher rates include lower rates of educational attainment, greater concentration in lower-skilled occupations, and discrimination in the labor market. In general, the unemployment rate for blacks is twice that of whites.

■ **Gender** The unemployment rates for men and women are very similar. (The lower unemployment rate for women in 1992 occurred because of the greater incidence of male workers in such cyclically vulnerable industries as automobiles, steel, and construction.)

■ **Education** Less educated workers, on average, have higher unemployment rates than workers with more education. Less education is usually associated with lower-skilled, less permanent jobs, more time between jobs, and jobs that are more vulnerable to cyclical layoff.

■ **Duration** The number of persons unemployed for long periods—15 weeks or more—as a percentage of the labor force is much lower than the overall unemployment rate. But that percentage rises significantly during recessions.

Noneconomic Costs

Severe cyclical unemployment is more than an economic malady; it is a social catastrophe. Depression means idleness. And idleness means loss of skills, loss of self-respect, plummeting morale, family disintegration, and sociopolitical unrest. Widespread joblessness increases poverty, heightens racial and ethnic tensions, and reduces hope for material advancement.

History demonstrates that severe unemployment can lead to rapid and sometimes violent social and political change. Witness Hitler's ascent to power against a background of unemployment in Germany. Furthermore, relatively high unemployment among some racial and ethnic minorities has contributed to the unrest and violence that has periodically plagued some cities in the United States and abroad. At the individual level, research links increases in suicide, homicide, fatal heart attacks and strokes, and mental illness to high unemployment.

International Comparisons

Unemployment rates differ greatly among nations at any given time. One reason is that nations have different natural rates of unemployment. Another is that nations may be in different phases of their business cycles. Global Perspective 8.2 shows unemployment rates for five industrialized nations in recent years. Between 1990 and 2000, the U.S. unemployment rate was considerably lower than the rates in the United Kingdom, Germany, and France.

QUICK REVIEW 8.2

◾ Unemployment is of three general types: frictional, structural, and cyclical.

◾ The natural unemployment rate (frictional plus structural) is presently 4 to 5 percent.

◾ Society loses real GDP when cyclical unemployment occurs; according to Okun's law, for each 1 percentage point of unemployment above the natural rate, the U.S. economy suffers a 2 percent decline in real GDP below its potential GDP.

◾ Lower-skilled workers, teenagers, blacks and Hispanics, and less well educated workers bear a disproportionate burden of unemployment.

GLOBAL PERSPECTIVE 8.2

Unemployment Rates in Five Industrial Nations, 1990–2000

Compared with France, the United Kingdom, and Germany, the United States had a low unemployment rate throughout most of the 1990s.

Source: Economic Report of the President, 2001.

◾ Inflation

We now turn to inflation, another aspect of macroeconomic instability. The problems inflation poses are subtler than those posed by unemployment.

Meaning of Inflation

Inflation is a rise in the *general level of prices.* This does not mean that *all* prices are rising. Even during periods of rapid inflation, some prices may be relatively constant while others are falling. For example, although the United States experienced high rates of inflation in the 1970s and early 1980s, the prices of video recorders, digital watches, and personal computers declined. As you will see, one troublesome aspect of inflation is that prices rise unevenly. Some shoot upward; others rise slowly; still others do not rise at all.

Measurement of Inflation

Price-index numbers (such as those we described in Chapter 7) measure inflation. Recall that a price index measures the general level of prices in any year relative to prices in a base period. In 2000 the CPI was about 172, which means that the price level was 72 percent higher in 2000 than in the base period of 1982–1984, when the CPI was 100.

The rate of inflation for any given year (say, 2000) is found by subtracting the preceding year's (1999) price index from that year's (2000) index, dividing by the preceding year's index, and multiplying by 100 to express the result as a percentage. As an example, the CPI was 166.6 in 1999 and 172.2 in 2000, so the rate of inflation for 2000 is calculated as follows:

$$\text{Rate of inflation} = \frac{172.2 - 166.6}{166.6} \times 100 = 3.4\%$$

Recall that the mathematical approximation called the *rule of 70* tells us that we can find the number of years it will take for some measure to double, given its annual percentage increase, by dividing that percentage increase into the number 70. So a 3 percent annual rate of inflation will double the price level in about 23 (= 70 ÷ 3) years. Inflation of 8 percent per year will double the price level in about 9 (= 70 ÷ 8) years. **(Key Question 10)**

Facts of Inflation

Figure 8.4 shows the annual rates of inflation in the United States between 1960 and 2000. Observe that inflation reached double-digit rates in the 1970s and

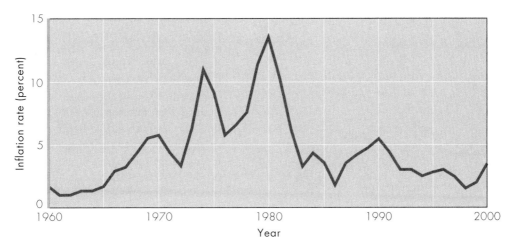

Figure 8.4

Annual inflation rates in the United States, 1960–2000. The major periods of inflation in the United States in the past forty years were in the 1970s and 1980s.
Source: Bureau of Labor Statistics, stats.bls.gov.

early 1980s, but has since declined and has been relatively mild recently.

In recent years U.S. inflation has been neither unusually high nor low relative to inflation in several other industrial countries (see Global Perspective 8.3). Some nations (not shown) have had double-digit or even higher annual rates of inflation in recent years. In 1999, for example, the annual inflation rate in Venezuela was 29 percent; in Turkey, 52 percent; in Russia, 56 percent; and in Ecuador, 60 percent.

Types of Inflation

Economists distinguish between two types of inflation: *demand-pull inflation* and *cost-push inflation*.

Demand-Pull Inflation   Usually, changes in the price level are caused by an excess of total spending beyond the economy's capacity to produce. When resources are already fully employed, the business sector cannot respond to this excess demand by expanding output. So the excess demand bids up the prices of the limited real output, causing **demand-pull inflation.** The essence of this type of inflation is "too much spending chasing too few goods." 🔳 8.2

But the relationship between total spending, on the one hand, and output, employment, and the price level, on the other, is not so simple. Figure 8.5 will help us unravel the complications. This figure is a

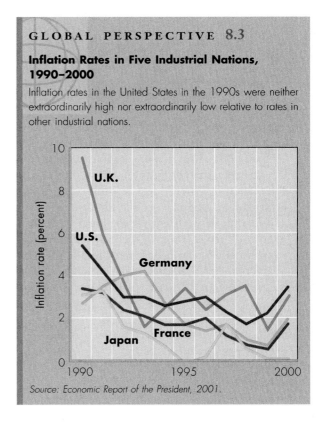

GLOBAL PERSPECTIVE 8.3

Inflation Rates in Five Industrial Nations, 1990–2000

Inflation rates in the United States in the 1990s were neither extraordinarily high nor extraordinarily low relative to rates in other industrial nations.

Source: Economic Report of the President, 2001.

graph of the price level and real GDP, with the full-employment level of output (potential output) designated Q_f. The three ranges marked on the curve are ranges of changes in price level and real output.

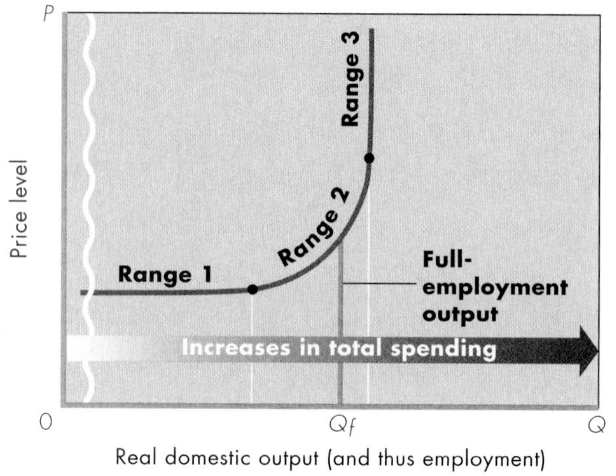

Figure 8.5

The price level and the level of real GDP (and thus employment). As total spending increases, the price level first stays constant as real output expands (range 1); then the price level rises as real output approaches, reaches, and exceeds the full-employment level (range 2); finally it jumps sharply as real output nears and attains its maximum capacity (range 3). Demand-pull inflation occurs in ranges 2 and 3.

The left-to-right arrow near the bottom of the diagram represents increases in total spending. Let's use the figure to see where demand-pull inflation arises:

- **Range 1** Toward the left in range 1, output is very low relative to the economy's full-employment output. This implies a very low level of total spending and a substantial GDP gap. Unemployment rates are high, and businesses have much idle production capacity.

  Assume now that total spending increases. As it does, real GDP will increase, and the unemployment rate will fall. But there is little or no increase in the price level within range 1. Since firms have excess production capacity, their costs and thus their prices do not rise as they increase their output. Large amounts of idle human and property resources will be put back to work at their existing prices. An unemployed worker does not ask for a wage increase when called back to work.

- **Range 2** As output continues to expand in response to further increases in total spending, the economy enters range 2. Here it approaches and eventually surpasses its full-employment output.

  Even before full employment is achieved, the price level may begin to rise. Workplaces become increasingly congested as more workers are em-

ployed, and each added worker contributes less to output. Labor costs therefore begin to rise, forcing up product prices. Also, as production expands, supplies of idle resources disappear at different rates in various sectors and industries. Some input-supplying industries are able to reach their full-production capacity before others and thus cannot respond to further increases in total spending for their products. These shortages of inputs cause resource prices to rise, boosting the production costs and product prices of industries that still have excess capacity.

As total spending in range 2 increases beyond output Q_f, still higher prices induce some businesses to demand, and some households to supply, resources beyond the full-employment level of output. Firms may employ additional work shifts and use overtime to achieve greater output. Households may supply additional workers such as teenagers and spouses, who previously had chosen not to enter the labor force. In this part of range 2, the part to the right of Q_f, the rate of unemployment falls below the natural rate and the actual GDP exceeds potential GDP. Here, the pace of inflation usually quickens.

- **Range 3** As total spending increases into range 3, the economy simply cannot supply more resources. Firms cannot respond to increases in demand by increasing output. Real domestic output is at an absolute maximum. So, in effect, further increases in demand raise the price level. The rate of inflation may be high and still rising because total demand greatly exceeds society's absolute capacity to produce. There is no increase in real output to absorb some of the increased spending.

Cost-Push Inflation Inflation may also arise on the supply, or cost, side of the economy. During some periods in U.S. economic history, including the mid-1970s, the price level increased even though aggregate demand was not excessive. These were periods when output and employment were both *declining* (evidence that total demand was not excessive) while the general price level was *rising*.

The theory of **cost-push inflation** explains rising prices in terms of factors that raise **per-unit production costs** at each level of spending. A per-unit production cost is the average cost of a particular level of output. This average cost is found by dividing the total cost of all resource inputs by the amount of output produced. That is,

$$\text{Per-unit production cost} = \frac{\text{total input cost}}{\text{units of output}}$$

Rising per-unit production costs squeeze profits and reduce the amount of output firms are willing to supply at the existing price level. As a result, the economy's supply of goods and services declines and the price level rises. In this scenario, costs are *pushing* the price level upward, whereas in demand-pull inflation demand is *pulling* it upward.

The major source of cost-push inflation has been so-called *supply shocks*. Specifically, abrupt increases in the costs of raw materials or energy inputs have on occasion driven up per-unit production costs and thus product prices. The rocketing prices of imported oil in 1973–1974 and again in 1979–1980 are good illustrations. As energy prices surged upward during these periods, the costs of producing and transporting virtually every product in the economy rose. Rapid cost-push inflation ensued.

Complexities

The real world is more complex than the distinction between demand-pull and cost-push inflation suggests. It is difficult to distinguish between demand-pull inflation and cost-push inflation unless the original source of inflation is known. For example, suppose a significant increase in total spending occurs in a fully employed economy, causing demand-pull inflation. But as the demand-pull stimulus works its way through various product and resource markets, individual firms find their wage costs, material costs, and fuel prices rising. From their perspective they must raise their prices because production costs (someone else's prices) have risen. Although this inflation is clearly demand-pull in origin, it may mistakenly appear to be cost-push inflation to business firms and to government. Without proper identification of the source of the inflation, government may be slow to enact policies to reduce excessive total spending.

Another complexity is that cost-push inflation and demand-pull inflation differ in their sustainability. Demand-pull inflation will continue as long as there is excess total spending. Cost-push inflation is automatically self-limiting; it will die out by itself. Increased per-unit costs will reduce supply, and this means lower real output and employment. Those decreases will constrain further per-unit cost increases. In other words, cost-push inflation generates a recession. And in a recession, households and businesses concentrate on keeping their resources employed, not on pushing up the prices of those resources.

QUICK REVIEW 8.3

■ Inflation is a rising general level of prices and is measured as a percentage change in a price index such as the CPI.

■ For the past several years, the U.S. inflation rate has been within the middle range of the rates of other advanced industrial nations and far below the rates experienced by some nations.

■ Demand-pull inflation occurs when total spending exceeds the economy's ability to provide goods and services at the existing price level; total spending *pulls* the price level upward.

■ Cost-push inflation occurs when factors such as excessive wage increases and rapid increases in raw-material prices drive up per-unit production costs at each level of output; higher costs *push* the price level upward.

■ Redistribution Effects of Inflation

Inflation hurts some people, leaves others unaffected, and actually helps still others. That is, inflation redistributes real income from some people to others. Who gets hurt? Who benefits? Before we can answer, we need some terminology.

Nominal and Real Income   There is a difference between money (or nominal) income and real income. **Nominal income** is the number of dollars received as wages, rent, interest, or profits. **Real income** is a measure of the amount of goods and services nominal income can buy; it is the purchasing power of nominal income, or income adjusted for inflation. That is,

$$\text{Real income} = \frac{\text{nominal income}}{\text{price index (in hundredths)}}$$

Inflation need not alter an economy's overall real income—its purchasing power. It is evident from the above equation that real income will remain the same when nominal income rises at the same percentage rate as does the price index.

But when inflation occurs, not everyone's nominal income rises at the same pace as the price level. Therein lies the potential for redistribution of real income from some to others. If the change in the price level differs from the change in a person's nominal income, his or her real income will be affected.

The following rule tells us approximately by how much real income will change:

$$\begin{array}{ccc} \text{Percentage} & \text{percentage} & \text{percentage} \\ \text{change in} \cong & \text{change in} - & \text{change in} \\ \text{real income} & \text{nominal income} & \text{price level} \end{array}$$

For example, suppose that the price level rises by 6 percent in some period. If Bob's nominal income rises by 6 percent, his real income will *remain unchanged.* But if his nominal income instead rises by 10 percent, his real income will *increase* by about 4 percent. And if Bob's nominal income rises by only 2 percent, his real income will *decline* by about 4 percent.[1]

Anticipations The redistribution effects of inflation depend on whether or not it is expected. With fully expected or **anticipated inflation,** an income receiver may be able to avoid or lessen the adverse effects of inflation on real income. The generalizations that follow assume **unanticipated inflation**— inflation whose full extent was not expected.

Who Is Hurt by Inflation?

Unanticipated inflation hurts fixed-income recipients, savers, and creditors. It redistributes real income away from them and toward others.

Fixed-Income Receivers People whose incomes are fixed see their real incomes fall when inflation occurs. The classic case is the elderly couple living on a private pension or annuity that provides a fixed amount of nominal income each month. They may have retired in, say, 1990 on what appeared to be an adequate pension. However, by 2000 they would have discovered that inflation had cut the purchasing power of that pension—their real income— by one-fourth.

Similarly, landlords who receive lease payments of fixed dollar amounts will be hurt by inflation as they receive dollars of declining value over time. Likewise, public sector workers whose incomes are

---

[1]A more precise calculation uses our equation for real income. In our first illustration above, if nominal income rises by 10 percent from $100 to $110 and the price level (index) rises by 6 percent from 100 to 106, then real income has increased as follows:

$$\frac{\$110}{1.06} = \$103.77$$

The 4 percent increase in real income shown by the simple formula in the text is a reasonable approximation of the 3.77 percent yielded by our more precise formula.

---

dictated by fixed pay schedules may suffer from inflation. The fixed "steps" (the upward yearly increases) in their pay schedules may not keep up with inflation. Minimum-wage workers and families living on fixed welfare incomes will also be hurt by inflation.

Savers Unanticipated inflation hurts savers. As prices rise, the real value, or purchasing power, of an accumulation of savings deteriorates. Paper assets such as savings accounts, insurance policies, and annuities that were once adequate to meet rainy-day contingencies or provide for a comfortable retirement decline in real value during inflation. The simplest case is the person who hoards money as a cash balance. A $1000 cash balance would have lost one-half its real value between 1981 and 2000. Of course, most forms of savings earn interest. But the value of savings will still decline if the rate of inflation exceeds the rate of interest.

Example: A household may save $1000 in a certificate of deposit (CD) in a commercial bank or savings and loan association at 6 percent annual interest. But if inflation is 13 percent (as it was in 1980), the real value or purchasing power of that $1000 will be cut to about $938 by the end of the year. Although the saver will receive $1060 (equal to $1000 plus $60 of interest), deflating that $1060 for 13 percent inflation means that its real value is only about $938 (= $1060 ÷ 1.13).

Creditors Unanticipated inflation harms creditors (lenders). Suppose Chase Bank lends Bob $1000, to be repaid in 2 years. If in that time the price level doubles, the $1000 that Bob repays will have only half the purchasing power of the $1000 he borrowed. True, if we ignore interest charges, the same number of dollars will be repaid as was borrowed. But because of inflation, each of those dollars will buy only half as much as it did when the loan was negotiated. As prices go up, the value of the dollar goes down. Thus, the borrower is lent "dear" dollars but, because of inflation, pays back "cheap" dollars. The owners of Chase Bank suffer a loss of real income.

Who Is Unaffected or Helped by Inflation?

Some people are unaffected by inflation and others are actually helped by it. For the second group, inflation redistributes real income toward them and away from others.

Flexible-Income Receivers People who have flexible incomes may escape inflation's harm or even benefit from it. For example, individuals who derive their incomes solely from social security are largely unaffected by inflation, because social security payments are *indexed* to the CPI. Benefits automatically increase when the CPI increases, preventing erosion of benefits from inflation. Some union workers also get automatic **cost-of-living adjustments (COLAs)** in their pay when the CPI rises, although such increases rarely equal the full percentage rise in inflation.

Some flexible-income receivers and all borrowers are helped by unanticipated inflation. The strong product demand and labor shortages implied by rapid demand-pull inflation may cause some nominal incomes to spurt ahead of the price level, thereby enhancing real incomes. For some, the 3 percent increase in nominal income that occurs when inflation is 2 percent may become a 7 percent increase when inflation is 5 percent. As an example, property owners faced with an inflation-induced real estate boom may be able to boost flexible rents more rapidly than the rate of inflation. Also, some business owners may benefit from inflation. If product prices rise faster than resource prices, business revenues will increase more rapidly than costs. In those cases, the growth rate of profit incomes will outpace the rate of inflation.

Debtors Unanticipated inflation benefits debtors (borrowers). In our earlier example, Chase Bank's loss of real income from inflation is Bob's gain of real income. Debtor Bob borrows "dear" dollars but, because of inflation, pays back the principal and interest with "cheap" dollars whose purchasing power has been eroded by inflation. Real income is redistributed away from the owners of Chase Bank toward borrowers such as Bob.

As a historical example, the inflation of the 1970s and 1980s created a windfall of capital gains for people who purchased homes in earlier periods with low, fixed-interest-rate mortgages. Inflation greatly reduced the real burden of their mortgage indebtedness. They also benefited because the nominal value of housing in that period increased much more rapidly than the overall price level.

The Federal government, which had amassed $5.6 trillion of public debt through 2000, has also benefited from inflation. Historically, the Federal government regularly paid off its loans by taking out new ones. Inflation permitted the Treasury to pay off its loans with dollars of less purchasing power than the dollars originally borrowed. Nominal national income and therefore tax collections rise with inflation; the amount of public debt owed does not. Thus, inflation reduces the real burden of the public debt to the Federal government.

Anticipated Inflation

The redistribution effects of inflation are less severe or are eliminated altogether if people anticipate inflation and can adjust their nominal incomes to reflect the expected price-level rises. The prolonged inflation that began in the late 1960s prompted many labor unions in the 1970s to insist on labor contracts with cost-of-living adjustment clauses.

Similarly, if inflation is anticipated, the redistribution of income from lender to borrower may be altered. Suppose a lender (perhaps a commercial bank or a savings and loan institution) and a borrower (a household) both agree that 5 percent is a fair rate of interest on a 1-year loan provided the price level is stable. But assume that inflation has been occurring and is expected to be 6 percent over the next year. If the bank lends the household $100 at 5 percent interest, the bank will be paid back $105 at the end of the year. But if 6 percent inflation does occur during that year, the purchasing power of the $105 will have been reduced to about $99. The lender will, in effect, have paid the borrower $1 for the use of the lender's money for a year.

The lender can avoid this subsidy by charging an *inflation premium*—that is, by raising the interest rate by 6 percent, the amount of the anticipated inflation. By charging 11 percent, the lender will receive back $111 at the end of the year. Adjusted for the 6 percent inflation, that amount will have the purchasing power of today's $105. The result then will be a mutually agreeable transfer of purchasing power from borrower to lender of $5, or 5 percent, for the use of $100 for 1 year. Financial institutions have also developed variable-interest-rate mortgages to protect themselves from the adverse effects of inflation. (Incidentally, this example points out that, rather than being a *cause* of inflation, high nominal interest rates are a *consequence* of inflation.)

Our example reveals the difference between the real rate of interest and the nominal rate of interest. The **real interest rate** is the percentage increase in *purchasing power* that the borrower pays the lender. In our example the real interest rate is 5 percent. The **nominal interest rate** is the percentage increase in *money* that the borrower pays the lender, including that resulting from the built-in expectation of inflation, if any. In equation form:

Nominal interest rate = real interest rate +
inflation premium
(the expected rate
of inflation)

As illustrated in Figure 8.6, the nominal interest rate in our example is 11 percent. 🔑 8.2

Addenda

We end our discussion of the redistribution effects of inflation by making three final points:

- **Deflation** The effects of unanticipated **deflation**—declines in the price level—are the reverse of those of inflation. People with fixed nominal incomes will find their real incomes enhanced. Creditors will benefit at the expense of debtors. And savers will discover that the purchasing power of their savings has grown because of the falling prices.
- **Mixed effects** A person who is an income earner, a holder of financial assets, and an owner of real assets simultaneously will probably find that the redistribution impact of inflation is cushioned. If the person owns fixed-value monetary assets (savings accounts, bonds, and insurance policies), inflation will lessen their real value. But that same inflation may increase the real value of any property assets (a house, land)

that the person owns. In short, many individuals are simultaneously hurt and benefited by inflation. All these effects must be considered before we can conclude that any particular person's net position is better or worse because of inflation.
- **Arbitrariness** The redistribution effects of inflation occur regardless of society's goals and values. Inflation lacks a social conscience and takes from some and gives to others, whether they are rich, poor, young, old, healthy, or infirm.

QUICK REVIEW 8.4

■ Inflation harms those who receive relatively fixed nominal incomes and either leaves unaffected or helps those who receive flexible nominal incomes.

■ Unanticipated inflation hurts savers and creditors while benefiting debtors.

■ The nominal interest rate equals the real interest plus the inflation premium (the expected rate of inflation).

■ Effects of Inflation on Output

Thus far, our discussion has focused on how inflation redistributes a given level of total real income. But inflation may also affect an economy's level of real output (and thus its level of real income). The direction and significance of this effect on output depends on the type of inflation and its severity.

Cost-Push Inflation and Real Output

Recall that abrupt and unexpected rises in key resource prices such as oil can sufficiently drive up overall production costs to cause cost-push inflation. As prices rise, the quantity of goods and services demanded falls. So firms respond by producing less output, and unemployment goes up.

Economic events of the 1970s provide an example of how inflation can reduce real output. In late 1973 the Organization of Petroleum Exporting Countries (OPEC), by exerting its market power, managed to quadruple the price of oil. The cost-push inflationary effects generated rapid price-level increases in the 1973–1975 period. At the same time, the U.S. unemployment rate rose from slightly less

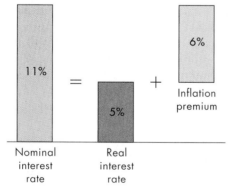

Figure 8.6
The inflation premium and nominal and real interest rates. The inflation premium—the expected rate of inflation—gets built into the nominal interest rate. Here, the nominal interest rate of 11 percent comprises the real interest rate of 5 percent plus the inflation premium of 6 percent.

than 5 percent in 1973 to 8.5 percent in 1975. Similar outcomes occurred in 1979–1980 in response to a second OPEC oil supply shock.

In short, cost-push inflation reduces real output. It redistributes a decreased level of real income.

Demand-Pull Inflation and Real Output

Economists do not fully agree on the effects of mild inflation (less than 3 percent) on real output. One perspective is that even low levels of inflation reduce real output, because inflation diverts time and effort toward activities designed to hedge against inflation. Examples:

- Businesses must incur the cost of changing thousands of prices on their shelves and in their computers simply to reflect inflation.
- Households and businesses must spend considerable time and effort obtaining the information they need to distinguish between real and nominal values such as prices, wages, and interest rates.
- To limit the loss of purchasing power from inflation, people try to limit the amount of money they hold in their billfolds and checking accounts at any one time and instead put more money into interest-bearing accounts and stock and bond funds. But cash and checks are needed in even greater amounts to buy the higher-priced goods and services. So more frequent trips, phone calls, or Internet visits to financial institutions are required to transfer funds to checking accounts and billfolds, when needed. **!** 8.3

Without inflation, these uses of resources, time, and effort would not be needed, and they could be diverted toward producing more valuable goods and services. Proponents of "zero inflation" bolster their case by pointing to cross-country studies that indicate that lower rates of inflation are associated with higher rates of economic growth. Even mild inflation, say these economists, is detrimental to economic growth.

In contrast, other economists point out that full employment and economic growth depend on strong levels of total spending. Such spending creates high profits, strong demand for labor, and a powerful incentive for firms to expand their plants and equipment. In this view, the mild inflation that is a byproduct of strong spending is a small price to pay for full-employment and continued economic growth.

Moreover, a little inflation may have positive effects because it makes it easier for firms to adjust real wages downward when the demands for their products fall. With mild inflation, firms can reduce real wages by holding nominal wages steady. With zero inflation firms would need to cut nominal wages to reduce real wages. Such cuts in nominal wages are highly visible and may cause considerable worker resistance and labor strife.

Finally, defenders of mild inflation say that it is much better for an economy to err on the side of strong spending, full employment, economic growth, and mild inflation than on the side of weak spending, unemployment, recession, and deflation.

Hyperinflation and Breakdown

All economists agree that the nation's policymakers must carefully monitor mild inflation so that it does not snowball into higher rates of inflation or even into **hyperinflation.** The latter is an extremely rapid inflation whose impact on real output and employment usually is devastating. When inflation begins to escalate, consumers, workers, and businesses assume that it will rise even further. So, rather than let their idle savings and current incomes depreciate, consumers "spend now" to beat the anticipated price rises. Businesses do the same by buying capital goods. Workers demand and receive higher nominal wages to recoup lost purchasing power and to maintain future purchasing power in the face of expected higher inflation. Actions based on these inflationary expectations then intensify the pressure on prices, and inflation feeds on itself.

Aside from its disruptive redistribution effects, hyperinflation may cause economic collapse. Severe inflation encourages speculative activity. Businesses, anticipating further price increases, may find it profitable to hoard both materials and finished products. But restricting the availability of materials and products intensifies the inflationary pressure. Also, rather than invest in capital equipment, businesses and individual savers may decide to purchase nonproductive wealth—jewels, gold and other precious metals, real estate, and so forth—as a hedge against inflation.

In the extreme, as prices shoot up sharply and unevenly, normal economic relationships are disrupted. Business owners do not know what to charge for their products. Consumers do not know what to pay. Resource suppliers want to be paid with actual output, rather than with rapidly depreciating money.

Creditors avoid debtors to keep them from repaying their debts with cheap money. Money eventually becomes almost worthless and ceases to do its job as a medium of exchange. The economy may be thrown into a state of barter, and production and exchange drop dramatically. The net result is economic, social, and possibly political chaos. The hyperinflation has precipitated monetary collapse, depression, and sociopolitical disorder.

History reveals a number of examples that fit this scenario. Consider the effects of the Second World War on price levels in Hungary and Japan:

> The inflation in Hungary exceeded all known records of the past. In August 1946, 828 octillion (1 followed by 27 zeros) depreciated pengös equaled the value of 1 prewar pengö. The price of the American dollar reached a value of 3×10^{22} (3 followed by 22 zeros) pengös. Fishermen and farmers in 1947 Japan used scales to weigh currency and change, rather than bothering to count it. Prices rose some 116 times in Japan, 1938 to 1948.[2]

The German inflation of the 1920s also was catastrophic. The German Weimar Republic printed so much money to pay its bills that

> during 1922, the German price level went up 5,470 percent. In 1923, the situation worsened; the German price level rose 1,300,000,000,000 times. By October of 1923, the postage on the lightest letter sent from Germany to the United States was 200,000 marks. . . . Prices increased so rapidly that waiters changed the prices on the menu several times during the course of a lunch. Sometimes customers had to pay double the price listed on the menu when they ordered.[3]

Less extreme hyperinflation also has occurred more recently. Argentina, Bolivia, Brazil, and Zaire, for example, experienced inflation rates of 2000 percent or more for 1 or more years during the 1980s or 1990s. Such dramatic hyperinflations are almost invariably the consequence of highly imprudent expansions of the money supply by government. The results are highly exorbitant total spending and severe demand-pull inflation.

---

[2]Theodore Morgan, *Income and Employment*, 2d ed. (Englewood Cliffs, N.J.: Prentice-Hall, 1952), p. 361.

[3]Raburn M. Williams, *Inflation! Money, Jobs, and Politicians* (Arlington Heights, Ill.: AHM Publishing, 1980), p. 2.

The Stock Market and the Economy

How, If at All, Do Changes in Stock Prices Relate to Macroeconomic Instability?

Every day, the individual stocks (ownership shares) of thousands of corporations are bought and sold in the stock market. The owners of the individual stocks receive dividends—a portion of the firm's profit. Supply and demand in the stock market determine the price of each firm's stock, with individual stock prices generally rising and falling in concert with the collective expectations for each firm's profits. Greater profits normally result in higher dividends to the stock owners, and, in anticipation of higher dividends, people are willing to pay a higher price for the stock.

The media closely monitor and report stock market averages such as the Dow Jones Industrial Average (DJIA)—the weighted-average price of the stocks of 30 major U.S. industrial firms. It is common for these price averages to change over time or even to rise or fall sharply during a single day. On "Black Monday," October 19, 1987, the DJIA fell by 20 percent. A sharp drop in stock prices also occurred in October 1997, mainly in response to rapid declines in stock prices in Hong Kong and other Southeast Asia stock markets. In contrast, the stock market averages rose spectacularly in 1998 and 1999, with the DJIA rising 17 and 25 percent in those two years. In 2000, the DJIA fell 6 percent.

The volatility of the stock market raises this question: Do changes in stock price averages and thus stock market wealth cause macroeconomic instability? There are linkages between the stock market and the economy that might lead us to answer "yes." Consider a sharp increase in stock prices. Feeling wealthier, stock

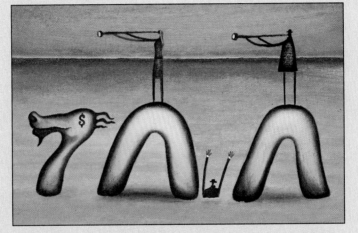

owners respond by increasing their spending (the *wealth effect*). Firms react by increasing their purchases of new capital goods, because they can finance such purchases through issuing new shares of high-valued stock (the *investment effect*). Of course, sharp declines in stock prices would produce the opposite results.

Studies find that changes in stock prices do affect consumption and investment but that these consumption and investment impacts are relatively weak. For example, a 10 percent sustained increase in stock market values in 1 year is associated with a 4 percent increase in consumption spending over the next 3 years. The investment response is even weaker. So typical day-to-day and year-to-year changes in stock market values have little impact on the macroeconomy.

In contrast, *stock market bubbles* can be detrimental to an economy. Such bubbles are huge run-ups of overall stock prices, caused by excessive optimism and frenzied buying. The rising stock values are unsupported by realistic prospects of the future strength of the economy and the firms operating in it. Rather than slowly decompress, such bubbles may burst and cause harm to the economy. The free fall of stock values, if long-lasting, causes reverse wealth effects. The stock market crash may also create an overall pessimism about the economy that undermines consumption and investment spending even further.

A related question: Even though typical changes in stock prices do not cause recession or inflation, might they predict such maladies? That is, since stock market values are based on expected profits, wouldn't we expect rapid changes in stock price averages to forecast changes in future business conditions? Indeed, stock prices often do fall prior to recessions and rise prior to expansions. For this reason stock prices are among a group of 10 variables that constitute an index of leading indicators (Last Word, Chapter 12). Such an index may provide a useful clue to the future direction of the economy. But taken alone, stock market prices are not a reliable predictor of changes in GDP. Stock prices have fallen rapidly in some instances with no recession following. Black Monday itself did not produce a recession during the following 2 years. In other instances, recessions have occurred with no prior decline in stock market prices.

SUMMARY

1. Economic growth may be defined as either (a) an increase of real GDP over time or (b) an increase in real GDP per capita over time. Growth lessens the burden of scarcity and provides increases in real GDP that can be used to resolve socioeconomic problems. Since the Second World War, real GDP growth in the United States has been about 3.5 percent annually; real GDP per capita has grown at about a 2.3 percent annual rate.

2. The United States and other industrial economies have gone through periods of fluctuations in real GDP, employment, and the price level. Although they have certain phases in common—peak, recession, trough, recovery—business cycles vary greatly in duration and intensity.

3. Although economists explain the business cycle in terms of such causal factors as major innovations, political events, and money creation, they generally agree that the level of total spending is the immediate determinant of real output and employment.

4. The business cycle affects all sectors of the economy, though in varying ways and degrees. The cycle has greater effects on output and employment in the capital goods and durable consumer goods industries than in the services and nondurable goods industries.

5. Economists distinguish between frictional, structural, and cyclical unemployment. The full-employment or natural rate of unemployment, which is made up of frictional and structural unemployment, is currently between 4 and 5 percent. The presence of part-time and discouraged workers makes it difficult to measure unemployment accurately.

6. The economic cost of unemployment, as measured by the GDP gap, consists of the goods and services forgone by society when its resources are involuntarily idle. Okun's law suggests that every 1-percentage-point increase in unemployment above the natural rate causes an additional 2 percent GDP gap.

7. Unemployment rates and inflation rates vary widely globally. Unemployment rates differ because nations have different natural rates of unemployment and often are in different phases of their business cycles. Inflation and unemployment rates in the United States recently have been in the middle to low range compared with rates in other industrial nations.

8. Economists discern both demand-pull and cost-push (supply-side) inflation. Demand-pull inflation results from an excess of total spending relative to the economy's capacity to produce. The main source of cost-push inflation is abrupt and rapid increases in the prices of key resources. These supply shocks push up per-unit production costs and ultimately the prices of consumer goods.

9. Unanticipated inflation arbitrarily redistributes real income at the expense of fixed-income receivers, creditors, and savers. If inflation is anticipated, individuals and businesses may be able to take steps to lessen or eliminate adverse redistribution effects.

10. When inflation is anticipated, lenders add an inflation premium to the interest rate charged on loans. The nominal interest rate thus reflects the real interest rate plus the inflation premium (the expected rate of inflation).

11. Cost-push inflation reduces real output and employment. Proponents of zero inflation argue that even mild demand-pull inflation (1 to 3 percent) reduces the economy's real output. Other economists say that mild inflation may be a necessary by-product of the high and growing spending that produces high levels of output, full employment, and economic growth. Hyperinflation, usually associated with injudicious government policy, may undermine the monetary system and cause severe declines in real output.

TERMS AND CONCEPTS

economic growth

rule of 70

productivity

business cycle

peak

recession

trough

recovery

labor force

unemployment rate

discouraged workers

frictional unemployment

structural unemployment

cyclical unemployment

full-employment rate of unemployment

natural rate of unemployment (NRU)

potential output

GDP gap

Okun's law

inflation

demand-pull inflation

cost-push inflation

per-unit production costs

nominal income

real income

anticipated inflation

unanticipated inflation

cost-of-living adjustments (COLAs)

real interest rate

nominal interest rate

deflation

hyperinflation

STUDY QUESTIONS

1. Why is economic growth important? Why could the difference between a 2.5 percent and a 3 percent annual growth rate be of great significance over several decades?

2. **Key Question** Suppose an economy's real GDP is $30,000 in year 1 and $31,200 in year 2. What is the growth rate of its real GDP? Assume that population is 100 in year 1 and 102 in year 2. What is the growth rate of GDP per capita?

3. Briefly describe the growth record of the United States. Compare the rates of growth of real GDP and real GDP per capita, explaining any differences. Compare the average growth rates of Japan and the United States between 1950 and 2000 and between 1990 and 2000. To what extent might growth rates understate or overstate economic well-being?

4. **Key Question** What are the four phases of the business cycle? How long do business cycles last? How do seasonal variations and long-run trends complicate measurement of the business cycle? Why does the business cycle affect output and employment in capital goods industries and consumer durable goods industries more severely than in industries producing consumer nondurables?

5. What factors make it difficult to determine the unemployment rate? Why is it difficult to distinguish between frictional, structural, and cyclical unemployment? Why is unemployment an economic problem? What are the consequences of a GDP gap? What are the noneconomic effects of unemployment?

6. **Key Question** Use the following data to calculate (a) the size of the labor force and (b) the official unemployment rate: total population, 500; population under 16 years of age or institutionalized, 120; not in labor force, 150; unemployed, 23; part-time workers looking for full-time jobs, 10.

7. Since the United States has an unemployment compensation program that provides income for those out of work, why should we worry about unemployment?

8. **Key Question** Assume that in a particular year the natural rate of unemployment is 5 percent and the actual rate of unemployment is 9 percent. Use Okun's law to determine the size of the GDP gap in percentage-point terms. If the potential GDP is $500 billion in that year, how much output is being forgone because of cyclical unemployment?

9. Explain how an increase in your nominal income and a decrease in your real income might occur simultaneously. Who loses from inflation? Who loses from unemployment? If you had to choose between (a) full employment with a 6 percent annual rate of inflation and (b) price stability with an 8 percent unemployment rate, which would you choose? Why?

10. **Key Question** If the price index was 110 last year and is 121 this year, what is this year's rate of inflation? What is the "rule of 70"? How long would it take for the price level to double if inflation persisted at (a) 2, (b) 5, and (c) 10 percent per year?

11. Describe the relationship between total spending and the level of output and employment. Explain what happens to the price level as increases in total spending move the economy from substantial unemployment to moderate unemployment, to full employment, and finally to full-capacity output.

12. Explain how hyperinflation might lead to a severe decline in total output.

13. Evaluate as accurately as you can how each of the following individuals would be affected by unanticipated inflation of 10 percent per year:
    a. A pensioned railroad worker.
    b. A department-store clerk.
    c. A unionized automobile assembly-line worker.
    d. A heavily indebted farmer.
    e. A retired business executive whose current income comes entirely from interest on government bonds.
    f. The owner of an independent small-town department store.

14. A noted television comedian once defined inflation as follows: "Inflation? That means your money today won't buy as much as it would have during the Depression when you didn't have any." Was his definition accurate? Explain.

15. **(Last Word)** Suppose that stock prices were to fall by 10 percent in the stock market. All else equal, would the lower stock prices be likely to cause a decrease in real GDP? How might they predict a decline in real GDP?

16. **Web-Based Question:** *The employment situation —write the news release* Visit the U.S. Department of Labor website, stats.bls.gov/news. release/empsit.toc.htm, and look at the current employment situation summary for the latest month. Then rewrite the following paragraph. See also stats.bls.gov/cps_faq.htm for the site's FAQs (frequently asked questions).

    Employment (rose/fell/remained unchanged), and the unemployment rate edged (up/down/stayed unchanged) to (?) percent in the latest month. The jobless rate had (risen/ fallen/stayed unchanged) from (?) percent in (previous month) to (?) percent in (latest month). The number of payroll jobs (increased/ decreased/ was unchanged) by (? thousand) in the latest month, with widespread (gains/losses) in the (?) sector of the economy. Average weekly hours (declined/increased/ were unchanged), and average hourly earnings were (lower/higher/unchanged) over the month.

17. **Web-Based Question:** *Inflation and the "official CPI"* Each month, the BLS releases thousands of detailed CPI numbers to the press. However, the press generally focuses on the broadest, most comprehensive CPI, called the *official CPI.* Go to the U.S. Department of Labor's CPI FAQs (frequently asked questions) page at <u>stats.bls.gov/cpifaq.htm</u>. Which index is the official CPI reported in the media? Look at <u>stats.bls.gov/news.release/cpi.toc.htm</u> and find the current figures for the official CPI: (*a*) index level (for example, December 2000 = 174.0); (*b*) 12-month percentage change (for example, December 1999 to December 2000 = 3.4 percent); and (*c*) 1-month percentage change on a seasonally adjusted basis (for example, from November 2000 to December 2000 = .2 percent).

9

Building the Aggregate Expenditures Model

Two of the most critical questions in macroeconomics are, (1) What determines the level of GDP, given a nation's production capacity? (2) What causes real GDP to rise in one period and to fall in another? To answer these questions, we construct the aggregate expenditures model. Recall that to economists "aggregate" means "total" or "combined," so "aggregate expenditures" refers to the economy's total spending. As we explain in this chapter's Last Word, the aggregate expenditures model has its origins in the writings of John Maynard Keynes (pronounced "Caines"). ■ Our strategy in this chapter is to analyze the consumption and investment components of aggregate expenditures and derive a simple private (no-government) closed (no-international-trade) model of equilibrium GDP and employment.

▮ Simplifications

Because we initially want to develop a model of a "private closed economy," we will defer the complications arising from government expenditures, taxes, exports, and imports to Chapter 10. Also, to keep things simple, we will assume that all saving consists of personal saving and that depreciation and net foreign factor income are zero. That is, there is no business saving, gross investment equals net investment, and Americans earn as much abroad as foreigners earn in the United States.

These simplifying assumptions have two implications. First, aggregate spending initially consists of only *consumption* and *investment*. Second, gross domestic product (GDP), national income (NI), personal in-

come (PI), and disposable income (DI) are equal. All the items that in practice distinguish them from one another result from depreciation, net foreign factor income earned in the United States, government (taxes and transfer payments), and business saving (see Table 7.4). So if $500 billion of output is produced as GDP, households will receive exactly $500 billion of disposable income to consume or to save.

Tools of the Aggregate Expenditures Model

The basic premise of the aggregate expenditures model is that the amount of goods and services produced and therefore the level of employment depend directly on the level of aggregate expenditures (total spending). Businesses will produce only a level of output that they think they can profitably sell. They will idle their workers and machinery when there are no markets for their goods and services. When aggregate expenditures fall, total output and employment decrease; when aggregate expenditures rise, total output and employment increase.

As we begin, we assume that the economy has excess production capacity and unemployed labor (unless specified otherwise). Hence, an increase in aggregate expenditures will increase real output and employment but will not raise the price level. *In fact, unless stated otherwise, we will assume that the price level is constant.* 🔑 9.1

▮ Consumption and Saving

Because consumption is the largest component of aggregate expenditures, we need to understand the determinants of consumption spending. Recall that economists define personal saving as "not spending" or "that part of disposable income not consumed." In other words, saving (S) equals disposable income (DI) *minus* consumption (C). So in examining the determinants of consumption we are also exploring the determinants of saving.

Income-Consumption and Income-Saving Relationships

Many factors determine the level of consumer spending, but the most significant determinant is income—in particular, disposable income. And, since saving is the part of disposable income not consumed, DI is also the basic determinant of personal saving.

Consider some recent historical data. In Figure 9.1 each green dot represents consumption and disposable income for 1 year between 1980 and 2000. The green line that is fitted to these points shows that consumption is directly related to disposable income; moreover, in most years households spend most of their incomes.

But we can say more. The black 45° (degree) line serves as a reference line. Because this line bisects the 90° angle formed by the vertical and horizontal axes of the graph, each point on the line must be equidistant from the two axes. That is, each point on the line represents a situation in which consumption equals disposable income, or $C = $ DI. We can therefore regard the vertical distance from any point on the horizontal axis to the 45° line as measuring either consumption or disposable income. If we regard it as measuring disposable income, then the vertical distance by which

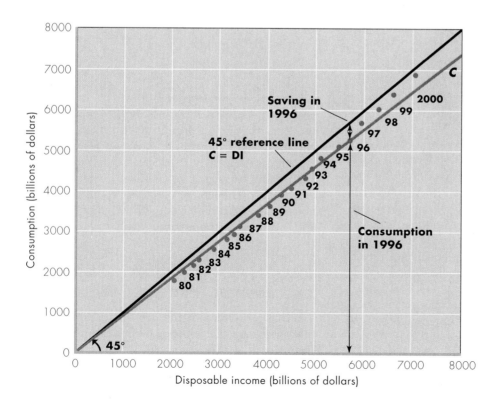

Figure 9.1

Consumption and disposable income, 1980–2000.
Each dot in this figure shows consumption and disposable income in a specific year. The line C, which generalizes the relationship between consumption and disposable income, indicates a direct relationship and shows that households consume most of their incomes.

actual consumption in any year falls short of the 45° line represents the amount of saving in that year—(DI − C = S). For example, in 1996 disposable income was $5678 billion and consumption was $5238 billion, so saving was $440 billion in 1996. By observing the vertical distances between the 45° line and the consumption line as we move to the left or to the right in Figure 9.1, we see that saving also varies directly with the level of disposable income: As DI rises, saving increases; as DI falls, saving decreases.

Figure 9.1 thus suggests that (1) households consume most of their disposable income and (2) both consumption and saving are directly related to the income level.

The Consumption Schedule

The dots in Figure 9.1 represent historical data—the actual amounts of DI, C, and S over a period of years. Those data help us understand the relationship between DI and consumption and saving. But to build our model, we need a schedule that shows the various amounts that households would plan to consume at each of the various levels of disposable income that might prevail at some specific time. Columns 1 and 2 of Table 9.1, represented in **Figure 9.2a (Key Graph)**, shows a hypothetical consumption schedule of the type that we require.

This **consumption schedule** reflects the direct consumption–disposable income relationship suggested by the data in Figure 9.1, and it is consistent with many household budget studies. Households tend to spend a larger proportion of a small disposable income than of a large disposable income. 🔑 9.2

The Saving Schedule

It is relatively simple to derive a **saving schedule**. Because saving equals disposable income less consumption (S = DI − C), we need only subtract consumption (Table 9.1, column 2) from disposable income (column 1) to find the amount saved (column 3) at each DI. Thus, columns 1 and 3 in Table 9.1 are the saving schedule, presented in Figure 9.2b. The graph shows that there is a direct relationship between saving and DI but that saving is a smaller proportion of a small DI than of a large DI. If households consume a smaller and smaller proportion of DI as DI increases, then they must be saving a larger and larger proportion.

Remembering that at each point on the 45° line consumption equals DI, we see that dissaving (consuming in excess of after-tax income) will occur at relatively low DIs, such as $370 billion (row 1, Table 9.1), at which consumption is $375 billion. Households can consume more than their incomes

Table 9.1

Consumption and Saving Schedules (in billions) and Propensities to Consume and Save

(1) Level of Output and Income (GDP = DI)	(2) Consumption (C)	(3) Saving (S), (1) − (2)	(4) Average Propensity to Consume (APC), (2)/(1)	(5) Average Propensity to Save (APS), (3)/(1)	(6) Marginal Propensity to Consume (MPC), Δ(2)/Δ(1)*	(7) Marginal Propensity to Save (MPS), Δ(3)/Δ(1)*
(1) $370	$375	$−5	1.01	−.01	.75	.25
(2) 390	390	0	1.00	.00	.75	.25
(3) 410	405	5	.99	.01	.75	.25
(4) 430	420	10	.98	.02	.75	.25
(5) 450	435	15	.97	.03	.75	.25
(6) 470	450	20	.96	.04	.75	.25
(7) 490	465	25	.95	.05	.75	.25
(8) 510	480	30	.94	.06	.75	.25
(9) 530	495	35	.93	.07	.75	.25
(10) 550	510	40	.93	.07	.75	.25

*The Greek letter Δ, delta, means "the change in."

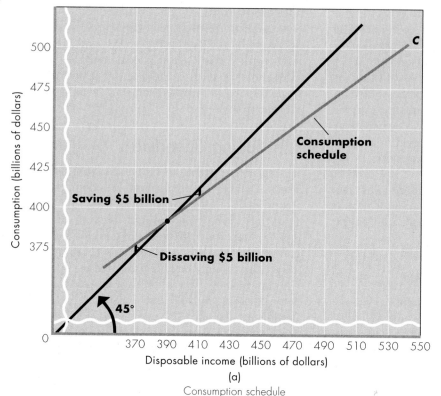

(a)
Consumption schedule

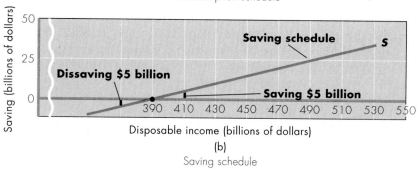

(b)
Saving schedule

Figure 9.2

(a) Consumption and (b) saving schedules. The two parts of this figure show the income-consumption and income-saving relationships in Table 9.1 graphically. The saving schedule in (b) is found by subtracting the consumption schedule in (a) vertically from the 45° line. Consumption equals disposable income (and saving thus equals zero) at $390 billion for these hypothetical data.

Quick Quiz 9.2

1. The slope of the consumption schedule in this figure is .75. Thus the:
   a. slope of the saving schedule is 1.33.
   b. marginal propensity to consume is .75.
   c. average propensity to consume is .25.
   d. slope of the saving schedule is also .75.

2. In this figure, when consumption is a positive amount, saving:
   a. must be a negative amount.
   b. must also be a positive amount.
   c. can be either a positive or a negative amount.
   d. is zero.

3. In this figure:
   a. the marginal propensity to consume is constant at all levels of income.
   b. the marginal propensity to save rises as disposable income rises.
   c. consumption is inversely (negatively) related to disposable income.
   d. saving is inversely (negatively) related to disposable income.

4. When consumption equals disposable income:
   a. the marginal propensity to consume is zero.
   b. the average propensity to consume is zero.
   c. consumption and saving must be equal.
   d. saving must be zero.

Answers: 1. b; 2. c; 3. a; 4. d

by liquidating (selling for cash) accumulated wealth or by borrowing. Graphically, dissaving is shown as the vertical distance of the consumption schedule above the 45° line or as the vertical distance of the saving schedule below the horizontal axis. We have marked the dissaving at the $370 billion level of income in both panels of Figure 9.2. Both vertical distances measure the $5 billion of dissaving that occurs at $370 billion of income.

In our example, the **break-even income** is $390 billion (row 2). This is the income level at which households plan to consume their entire incomes ($C = DI$). Graphically, the consumption schedule cuts the 45° line, and the saving schedule cuts the horizontal axis (saving is zero) at the break-even income level.

At all higher incomes, households plan to save part of their incomes. Graphically, the vertical distance that the consumption schedule lies below the 45° line measures this saving, as does the vertical distance that the saving schedule lies above the horizontal axis. For example, at the $410 billion level of income (row 3), both these distances indicate $5 billion worth of saving (see Figure 9.2a and 9.2b).

Average and Marginal Propensities

Columns 4 to 7 in Table 9.1 show additional characteristics of the consumption and saving schedules.

APC and APS

The fraction, or percentage, of total income that is consumed is called the **average propensity to consume (APC)**. The fraction of total income that is saved is the **average propensity to save (APS)**. That is,

$$\text{APC} = \frac{\text{consumption}}{\text{income}}$$

and

$$\text{APS} = \frac{\text{saving}}{\text{income}}$$

For example, at $470 billion of income (row 6) in Table 9.1, the APC is $\frac{450}{470} = \frac{45}{47}$, or about 96 percent, while the APS is $\frac{20}{470} = \frac{2}{47}$, or about 4 percent. Columns 4 and 5 in Table 9.1 show the APC and APS at each of the 10 levels of DI; note in the table that the APC falls and the APS rises as DI increases, as was implied in our previous comments.

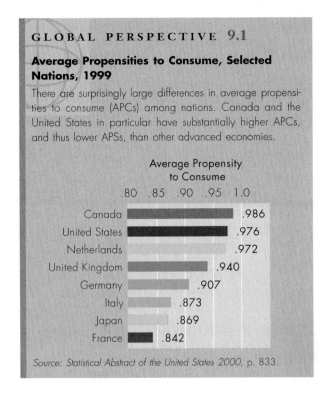

GLOBAL PERSPECTIVE 9.1

Average Propensities to Consume, Selected Nations, 1999

There are surprisingly large differences in average propensities to consume (APCs) among nations. Canada and the United States in particular have substantially higher APCs, and thus lower APSs, than other advanced economies.

Average Propensity to Consume

.80   .85   .90   .95   1.0

Canada .986
United States .976
Netherlands .972
United Kingdom .940
Germany .907
Italy .873
Japan .869
France .842

Source: Statistical Abstract of the United States 2000, p. 833.

Because disposable income is either consumed or saved, the fraction of any DI consumed plus the fraction saved (not consumed) must exhaust that income. Mathematically, APC + APS = 1 at any level of disposable income, as columns 4 and 5 in Table 9.1 illustrate.

Global Perspective 9.1 shows APCs for several countries.

MPC and MPS

The fact that households consume a certain proportion of a particular total income—for example, $\frac{45}{47}$ of a $470 billion disposable income—does not guarantee that they will consume the same proportion of any change in income they might receive. The proportion, or fraction, of any change in income consumed is called the **marginal propensity to consume (MPC)**, "marginal" meaning "extra" or "a change in." Equivalently, the MPC is the ratio of a change in consumption to a change in the income that caused the consumption change:

$$\text{MPC} = \frac{\text{change in consumption}}{\text{change in income}}$$

Similarly, the fraction of any change in income saved is the **marginal propensity to save (MPS)**. The

MPS is the ratio of a change in saving to the change in income that brought it about:

$$\text{MPS} = \frac{\text{change in saving}}{\text{change in income}}$$

If disposable income is $470 billion (row 6 in Table 9.1) and household income rises by $20 billion to $490 billion (row 7), households will consume $\frac{15}{20}$, or $\frac{3}{4}$, and save $\frac{5}{20}$, or $\frac{1}{4}$, of that increase in income. In other words, the MPC is $\frac{3}{4}$ or .75, and the MPS is $\frac{1}{4}$ or .25, as shown in columns 6 and 7.

The sum of the MPC and the MPS for any change in disposable income must always be 1. Consuming or saving out of extra income is an either-or proposition; the fraction of any change in income not consumed is, by definition, saved. Therefore, the fraction consumed (MPC) plus the fraction saved (MPS) must exhaust the whole change in income:

$$\text{MPC} + \text{MPS} = 1$$

In our example, .75 plus .25 equals 1.

MPC and MPS as Slopes

The MPC is the numerical value of the slope of the consumption schedule, and the MPS is the numerical value of the slope of the saving schedule. We know from the appendix to Chapter 1 that the slope of any line is the ratio of the vertical change to the horizontal change occasioned in moving from one point to another on that line.

In Figure 9.3 we measure the slopes of the consumption and saving lines, using enlarged portions of Figure 9.2a and 9.2b. Observe that consumption changes by $15 billion (vertical change) for each $20 billion change in disposable income (horizontal change). The slope of the consumption line is thus .75 (= $15/$20)—the value of the MPC. Saving changes by $5 billion (vertical change) for every $20 billion change in disposable income (horizontal change). The slope of the saving line therefore is .25 (= $5/$20), which is the value of the MPS. **(Key Question 5)**

Nonincome Determinants of Consumption and Saving

The amount of disposable income is the basic determinant of the amounts households will consume and save. But certain determinants other than income might cause households to consume more or less at each possible level of income and thereby change

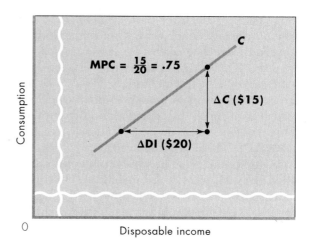

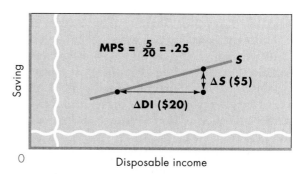

Figure 9.3

The marginal propensity to consume and the marginal propensity to save. The MPC is the slope (ΔC/ΔDI) of the consumption schedule, and the MPS is the slope (ΔS/ΔDI) of the saving schedule. The Greek letter delta (Δ) means "the change in."

the locations of the consumption and saving schedules. Those other determinants are wealth, expectations, indebtedness, and taxation.

Wealth

Other things equal, the greater the wealth households have accumulated, the larger is their collective consumption at any level of current income. By "wealth" we mean both real assets (a house, automobiles, television sets, and other durables) and financial assets (cash, savings accounts, stocks, bonds, insurance policies, pensions) that households own. Households save to accumulate wealth. When some other factor boosts household wealth, households reduce their saving and increase their spending. This so-called **wealth effect** *shifts the saving schedule downward and shifts the consumption schedule upward.* Example: In the late 1990s, dramatic increases in U.S. stock values ballooned household wealth. Predictably, households saved less and spent more.

Expectations   Household expectations about future prices and income may affect current spending and saving. For example, expectations of rising prices tomorrow may trigger more spending and less saving today. Thus, the current consumption schedule shifts up, and the current saving schedule shifts down. Or expectations of lower income in the future may result in less consumption and more saving today. If so, the consumption schedule will shift down and the saving schedule will shift up.

Taxation   When government is considered, changes in taxes shift the consumption and saving schedules. Taxes are paid partly at the expense of consumption and partly at the expense of saving. So an increase in taxes will shift both the consumption and the saving schedules downward. Conversely, a tax reduction will be partly consumed and partly saved by households. A tax decrease will shift both the consumption and the saving schedules upward.

Household Debt   In drawing a particular consumption schedule, we hold household debt as a percentage of DI constant. But when consumers as a group increase their household debt, they can increase current consumption. The consumption schedule thus shifts upward. In contrast, when levels of household debt get abnormally high, households may decide to reduce their consumption to pay off some of their loans. At that time, the consumption schedule shifts downward.

Terminology, Shifts, and Stability

There are several additional points we need to make regarding the consumption and saving schedules:

■ *Terminology*   The movement from one point to another on a consumption schedule (for example, from *a* to *b* on C_0 in Figure 9.4a)—a *change in the amount consumed*—is caused solely by a change in disposable income (or GDP). On the other hand, an upward or downward shift of the entire schedule (for example, a shift from C_0 to C_1 or C_2 in Figure 9.4a) is caused by changes in any one or more of the four *nonincome* determinants of consumption just discussed.

A similar distinction in terminology applies to the saving schedule in Figure 9.4b.

■ *Schedule shifts*   Changes in wealth, expectations, and household debt will shift the consumption schedule in one direction and the saving schedule in the opposite direction. If households decide to consume more at each possible level of disposable income, they want to save less, and vice versa. (Even when they spend more by borrowing, they are, in effect, reducing their current saving by the amount borrowed.) Graphically, if the consumption schedule shifts upward from C_0 to C_1 in Figure 9.4a, the saving schedule will shift downward, from S_0 to S_1 in Figure 9.4b. Similarly, a

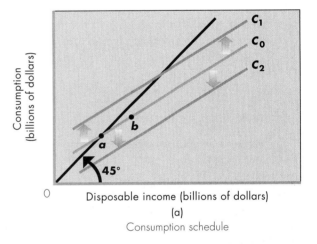

(a)
Consumption schedule

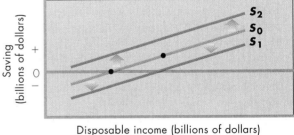

(b)
Saving schedule

Figure 9.4

Shifts in the (a) consumption and (b) saving schedules.   Normally, if households consume more at each level of DI, they are necessarily saving less. Graphically this means that an upward shift of the consumption schedule (C_0 to C_1) entails a downward shift of the saving schedule (S_0 to S_1). If households consume less at each level of DI, they are saving more. A downward shift of the consumption schedule (C_0 to C_2) is reflected in an upward shift of the saving schedule (S_0 to S_2). (This pattern breaks down, however, when taxes change; then the consumption and saving schedules move in the *same* direction—opposite to the direction of the tax change.)

downward shift of the consumption schedule from C_0 to C_2 means an upward shift of the saving schedule from S_0 to S_2.

In contrast, a change in taxes will result in the consumption and saving schedules' moving in the same direction. A tax increase causes both schedules to shift downward, and a tax decrease does just the opposite.

- *Stability* Although changes in nonincome determinants can shift the consumption and saving schedules, usually these schedules are relatively stable. Their stability may be because consumption-saving decisions are strongly influenced by long-term considerations such as saving to meet emergencies or saving for retirement. It may also be because changes in the nonincome determinants frequently work in opposite directions and therefore may cancel each other.

QUICK REVIEW 9.1

■ Both consumption spending and saving rise when disposable income increases; both fall when disposable income decreases.

■ The average propensity to consume (APC) is the fraction of any specific level of disposable income that is spent on consumer goods; the average propensity to save (APS) is the fraction of any specific level of disposable income that is saved. The APC falls and the APS rises as disposable income increases.

■ The marginal propensity to consume (MPC) is the fraction of a change in disposable income that is consumed; it is the slope of the consumption schedule. The marginal propensity to save (MPS) is the fraction of a change in disposable income that is saved; it is the slope of the saving schedule.

■ Changes in consumer wealth, consumer expectations, household debt, and taxes can shift the consumption and saving schedules.

■ Investment

We now turn to investment, the second component of private spending. Recall that investment consists of expenditures on new plants, capital equipment, machinery, inventories, and so on. The investment decision is a marginal-benefit–marginal-cost decision: The marginal benefit from investment is the expected rate of return businesses hope to realize. The marginal cost is the interest rate that must be paid for borrowing funds. We will see that businesses will invest in all projects for which the expected rate of return exceeds the interest rate. Expected returns (profits) and the interest rate therefore are the two basic determinants of investment spending.

Expected Rate of Return

Investment spending is guided by the profit motive; businesses buy capital goods only when they conclude that such purchases will be profitable. Suppose the owner of a woodworking shop is considering whether or not to invest in a new sanding machine that costs $1000 and has a useful life of only 1 year. The new machine will presumably increase the firm's output and sales revenue. Suppose the net expected revenue from the machine (that is, after such operating costs as power, lumber, labor, and certain taxes have been subtracted) is $1100. Then, after operating costs have been accounted for, the remaining expected net revenue is sufficient to cover the $1000 cost of the machine and leave a profit of $100. Comparing this $100 profit with the $1000 cost of the machine, we find that the **expected rate of return,** r, on the machine is 10 percent (= $100/$1000). (The computation gets more complex when the return occurs over several years, but the concept remains the same.)

The Real Interest Rate

One important cost associated with investing that our example has ignored is interest—the financial cost of borrowing the *money* "capital" required to purchase the *real* capital (the sanding machine).

The interest cost is computed by applying the interest rate, i, to the amount borrowed—the cost of the machine. The cost of the machine is the same as the amount we used to compute the rate of return, r. So we can generalize as follows: If the expected rate of return (say, 10 percent) exceeds the interest rate (say, 7 percent), the investment will be profitable. But if the interest rate (say, 12 percent) exceeds the expected rate of return (10 percent), the investment will be unprofitable. The firm should undertake all profitable investment projects. That means it should invest to where $r = i$, because then it has undertaken all investment for which r exceeds i.

But what if the firm, instead of borrowing, finances the investment internally out of funds saved from past profits? The role of the interest rate in investing in real capital does not change. When the firm uses money from savings to invest in the sander, it incurs an opportunity cost because it forgoes the interest income it could have earned by lending the funds to someone else.

The *real* rate of interest, rather than the *nominal* rate, is crucial in making investment decisions. Recall from Chapter 8 that the nominal interest rate is expressed in dollars of current value, while the real interest rate is stated in dollars of constant or inflation-adjusted value. The **real interest rate** is the nominal rate less the rate of inflation. In our sanding machine illustration our implicit assumption of a constant price level ensures that all our data, including the interest rate, are in real terms.

But what if inflation *is* occurring? Suppose a $1000 investment is expected to yield a real (inflation-adjusted) rate of return of 10 percent and the nominal interest rate is 15 percent. At first, we would say the investment would be unprofitable. But assume there is ongoing inflation of 10 percent per year. This means the investing firm will pay back dollars with approximately 10 percent less in purchasing power. While the nominal interest rate is 15 percent, the real rate is only 5 percent (= 15 percent − 10 percent). By comparing this 5 percent real interest rate with the 10 percent expected real rate of return, we find that the investment is profitable and should be undertaken.

Investment Demand Curve

We now move from a single firm's investment decision to total demand for investment goods by the entire business sector. Assume that every firm has estimated the expected rates of return from all investment projects and has recorded those data. We can cumulate—successively sum—these data by asking: What is the dollar value of investment projects that have an expected rate of return of, say, 16 percent or more? Of 14 percent or more? Of 12 percent or more? And so on.

Suppose there are no prospective investments that are yielding an expected return of 16 percent or more. But suppose there are $5 billion of investment opportunities with expected rates of return between 14 and 16 percent; another $5 billion yielding between 12 and 14 percent; still another $5 billion yielding between 10 and 12 percent; and an additional $5 billion in each successive 2 percent range of yield down to and including the 0 to 2 percent range.

Table 9.2

Rates of Expected Return and Investment

Expected Rate of Return (r)	Cumulative Amount of Investment Having This Rate of Return or Higher, Billions per Year
16%	$ 0
14	5
12	10
10	15
8	20
6	25
4	30
2	35
0	40

To cumulate these figures for each rate of return, r, we add the amounts of investment that will yield each particular rate of return r or higher. This way, we obtain the data in Table 9.2, shown graphically in **Figure 9.5 (Key Graph).** In Table 9.2 the number opposite 12 percent, for example, tells us there are $10 billion of investment opportunities that will yield an expected rate of return of 12 percent or more. The $10 billion includes the $5 billion of investment expected to yield a return of 14 percent or more plus the $5 billion expected to yield between 12 and 14 percent.

We know from our example of the sanding machine that an investment project will be profitable, and will be undertaken, if its expected rate of return, r, exceeds the real interest rate, i. Let's first suppose i is 12 percent. Businesses will undertake all investments for which r exceeds 12 percent. That is, they will invest until the 12 percent rate of return equals the 12 percent interest rate. Figure 9.5 reveals that $10 billion of investment spending will be undertaken at a 12 percent interest rate; that means investment projects worth $10 billion have an expected rate of return of 12 percent or more.

Put another way: At a financial "price" of 12 percent, $10 billion of investment goods will be demanded. If the interest rate is lower, say, 8 percent, the amount of investment for which r equals or exceeds i is $20 billion. Thus, firms will demand $20 billion of investment goods at an 8 percent real interest rate. At 6 percent, they will demand $25 billion of investment goods.

By applying the marginal-benefit–marginal-cost rule that investment projects should be undertaken up to the point where $r = i$, we see that we can add

KEY GRAPH

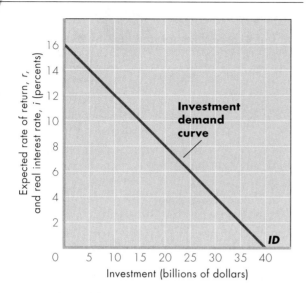

Figure 9.5

The investment demand curve. The investment demand curve is constructed by arraying all potential investment projects in descending order of their expected rates of return. The curve slopes downward, reflecting an inverse relationship between the real interest rate (the financial "price" of each dollar of investing) and the quantity of investment demanded.

Quick Quiz 9.5

1. The investment demand curve:
   a. reflects a direct (positive) relationship between the real interest rate and investment.
   b. reflects an inverse (negative) relationship between the real interest rate and investment.
   c. shifts to the right when the real interest rate rises.
   d. shifts to the left when the real interest rate rises.

2. In this figure:
   a. greater cumulative amounts of investment are associated with lower expected rates of return on investment.
   b. lesser cumulative amounts of investment are associated with lower expected rates of return on investment.
   c. higher interest rates are associated with higher expected rates of return on investment, and therefore greater amounts of investment.
   d. interest rates and investment move in the same direction.

3. In this figure, if the real interest rate falls from 6 to 4 percent:
   a. investment will increase from 0 to $30 billion.
   b. investment will decrease by $5 billion.
   c. the expected rate of return will rise by $5 billion.
   d. investment will increase from $25 billion to $30 billion.

4. In this figure, investment will be:
   a. zero if the real interest rate is zero.
   b. $40 billion if the real interest rate is 16 percent.
   c. $30 billion if the real interest rate is 4 percent.
   d. $20 billion if the real interest rate is 12 percent.

Answers: 1. b; 2. a; 3. d; 4. c

the real interest rate to the vertical axis in Figure 9.5. The curve in Figure 9.5 not only shows rates of return; it shows the quantity of investment demanded at each "price" *i* (interest rate) of investment. The vertical axis in Figure 9.5 shows the various possible real interest rates, and the horizontal axis shows the corresponding quantities of investment demanded. The inverse (downsloping) relationship between the interest rate (price) and the dollar quantity of investment demanded conforms with the law of demand discussed in Chapter 3. The curve *ID* in Figure 9.5 is the economy's **investment demand curve.**

It shows the amount of investment forthcoming at each real interest rate. **(Key Question 7)** 9.3

Shifts in the Investment Demand Curve

Figure 9.5 shows the relationship between the interest rate and the amount of investment demanded, other things equal. When other things change, the investment demand curve shifts. In general, any factor that leads businesses collectively to expect greater

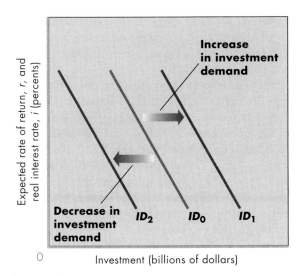

Figure 9.6

Shifts in the investment demand curve. Increases in investment demand are shown as rightward shifts in the investment demand curve; decreases in investment demand are shown as leftward shifts in the investment demand curve.

rates of return on their investments increases investment demand; that factor shifts the investment demand curve to the right, as from ID_0 to ID_1 in Figure 9.6. Any factor that leads businesses collectively to expect lower rates of return on their investments shifts the curve to the left, as from ID_0 to ID_2. What are those non-interest-rate determinants of investment demand?

Acquisition, Maintenance, and Operating Costs

As revealed by the sanding machine example, the initial costs of capital goods and the estimated costs of operating those goods affect the expected rate of return on investment. When costs fall, the expected rate of return from prospective investment projects rises, shifting the investment demand curve to the right. Example: Higher electricity costs associated with operating equipment shift the investment demand curve to the left. Lower costs, in contrast, shift the curve to the right.

Business Taxes

When government is considered, firms look to expected returns *after taxes* in making their investment decisions. An increase in business taxes lowers the expected profitability of investments and shifts the investment demand curve to the left; a reduction of business taxes shifts it to the right.

Technological Change

Technological progress —the development of new products, improvements in existing products, and the creation of new machinery and production processes—stimulates investment. The development of a more efficient machine, for example, lowers production costs or improves product quality and thus increases the expected rate of return from investing in the machine. Profitable new products (for example, cholesterol medications, Internet services, high-resolution televisions, cellular phones, and so on) induce a flurry of investment as firms tool up for expanded production. A rapid rate of technological progress shifts the investment demand curve to the right.

Stock of Capital Goods on Hand

The stock of capital goods on hand, relative to output and sales, influences investment decisions by firms. When the economy is overstocked with production facilities and when firms have excessive inventories of finished goods, the expected rate of return on new investment declines. Firms with excess production capacity have little incentive to invest in new capital. Therefore, the investment demand curve shifts leftward. In contrast, when firms are selling their output quickly and find their production facilities strained, the expected rate of return on new investment increases and the investment demand curve shifts rightward.

Expectations

We noted that business investment is based on expected returns (expected additions to profit). Most capital goods are durable, with a life expectancy of 10 or 20 years. So the expected rate of return on capital investment depends on the firm's expectations of future sales, future operating costs, and future profitability of the product that the capital helps produce. These expectations are based on forecasts of future business conditions as well as on such elusive and difficult-to-predict factors as changes in the domestic political climate, the thrust of foreign affairs, population growth, and consumer tastes. If executives become more optimistic about future sales, costs, and profits, the investment demand curve will shift to the right; a pessimistic outlook will shift it to the left.

Global Perspective 9.2 compares investment spending relative to GDP for several nations in a recent year. Domestic real interest rates and investment demand determine the levels of investment relative to GDP.

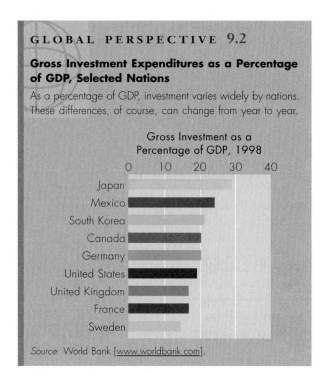

QUICK REVIEW 9.2

■ A specific investment will be undertaken if the expected rate of return, r, equals or exceeds the real interest rate, i.

■ The investment demand curve shows the total monetary amounts that will be invested by an economy at various possible real interest rates.

■ The investment demand curve shifts when changes occur in (a) the costs of acquiring, operating, and maintaining capital goods, (b) business taxes, (c) technology, (d) the stock of capital goods on hand, and (e) business expectations.

Investment Schedule

To add the investment decisions of businesses to the consumption plans of households, we must express investment plans in terms of the level of disposable income (DI) or gross domestic product (GDP). That is, we need to construct an investment schedule showing the amounts business firms collectively intend to invest at each possible level of GDP. Such a schedule represents the investment plans of businesses in the same way the consumption schedule represents the consumption plans of

households. In developing the investment schedule, we will assume that this **planned investment** is independent of the level of current disposable income or real output.

Suppose the investment demand curve is as shown in Figure 9.7a and the current real interest rate is 8 percent. This means that firms will find it profitable to spend $20 billion on investment goods. Our assumption tells us that this $20 billion of investment will occur at both low and high levels of GDP. The line I_g (*gross* investment) in Figure 9.7b shows this graphically; it is the economy's **investment schedule.** You should not confuse investment schedule I_g with the investment demand curve *ID* in Figure 9.7a. The investment schedule shows the amount of investment forthcoming at each level of GDP. As indicated in Figure 9.7, this amount ($20 billion) is determined by the interest rate together with the location of the investment demand curve. Table 9.3 shows the investment schedule in tabular form for the GDP levels in Table 9.1.

Instability of Investment

In contrast to the consumption schedule, the investment schedule is unstable; it shifts significantly upward or downward quite often. Investment, in fact, is the most volatile component of total spending. Figure 9.8 shows just how volatile investment has been. Note that its swings are much greater than those of GDP.

Several factors explain the variability of investment.

Table 9.3
The Investment Schedule (in Billions)

(1) Level of Real Output and Income	(2) Investment (I_g)
$370	$20
390	20
410	20
430	20
450	20
470	20
490	20
510	20
530	20
550	20

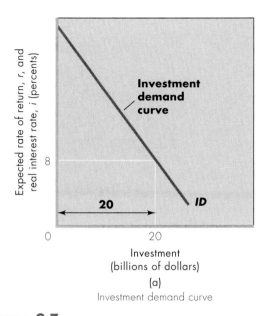

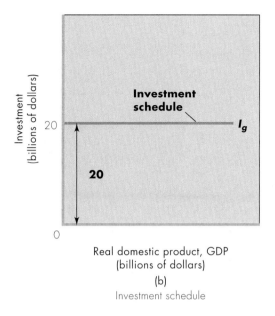

Figure 9.7

(a) The investment demand curve and (b) the investment schedule. (a) The level of investment spending (here, $20 billion) is determined by the real interest rate (here, 8 percent) together with the investment demand curve *ID*. (b) The investment schedule I_g relates the amount of investment ($20 billion) determined in (a) to the various levels of GDP.

Durability of Capital and Variability of Expectations

Because of their durability, capital goods have an indefinite useful life. Within limits, purchases of capital goods are discretionary and therefore can be postponed. Firms can scrap or replace older equipment and buildings, or they can patch them up and use them for a few more years. Optimism about the future may prompt firms to replace their older facilities, and such modernizing will call for a high level of investment. A less optimistic view, however, may lead to smaller amounts of investment as firms repair older facilities and keep them in use.

The degree of business optimism or pessimism is influenced by a whole host of factors. The expectation of future profitability is influenced to some degree by the size of current profits. Current profits, however, are themselves highly variable. Thus, the variability of profits contributes to the volatile nature of the incentive to invest.

Moreover, changes in exchange rates, changes in the outlook for international peace, court decisions in key labor or antitrust cases, legislative actions, changes in trade barriers, changes in governmental economic policies, and a host of similar considerations may cause substantial shifts in business expectations.

The stock market can influence business expectations because firms look to it as one of several indicators of society's overall confidence in future business conditions. Rising stock prices tend to signify public confidence in the business future, while falling stock prices may imply a lack of confidence. The stock market, however, is quite speculative. Some participants buy when stock prices begin to rise and sell as soon as prices begin to fall. This behavior can magnify what otherwise would be modest changes in stock prices. By creating swings in optimism and pessimism, the stock market may add to the instability of investment spending.

Irregularity of Innovation

We know that technological progress is a major determinant of investment. New products and processes stimulate investment. But history suggests that major innovations—railroads, electricity, automobiles, microchips, and the Internet—occur quite irregularly. When they do happen, they induce a vast upsurge or "wave" of investment spending that in time recedes.

A contemporary example is the widespread acceptance of new information technology, which has caused a wave of investment in computers, computer software, Internet service, cell phones, and electronic commerce. This wave of investment may last for a decade or more, but at some time it will surely level off.

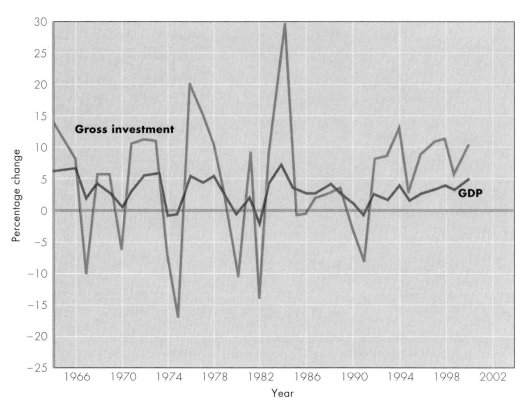

Figure 9.8

The volatility of investment. Annual percentage changes in investment spending are often several times greater than the percentage changes in GDP. (Data are in real terms.)

For all these reasons, changes in investment cause most of the fluctuations in output and employment. We can think of the volatility of investment as occasional and substantial changes in investment caused by shifts in the investment demand schedule in Figure 9.7a. In turn, these changes in investment are depicted as upward and downward shifts of the investment schedule in Figure 9.7b.

▌ Equilibrium GDP

Now let's combine the consumption and investment schedules to explain the equilibrium levels of output, income, and employment.

Tabular Analysis

Columns 2 through 5 in Table 9.4 repeat the consumption and saving schedules in Table 9.1 and the investment schedule in Table 9.3.

Real Domestic Output   Column 2 in Table 9.4
lists the various possible levels of total output—of real GDP—that the private sector might produce.

Producers are willing to offer any of these 10 levels of output if they can expect to receive an identical level of income from the sale of that output. For example, firms will produce $370 billion of output, incurring $370 billion of costs (wages, rents, interest, and normal profit costs) only if they believe they can sell that output for $370 billion. Firms will offer $390 billion of output if they think they can sell that output for $390 billion. And so it is for all the other possible levels of output.

Aggregate Expenditures   In the assumed private closed economy of Table 9.4, aggregate expenditures consist of consumption (column 3) plus investment (column 5). The sum is shown in column 6, which with column 2 makes up the **aggregate expenditures schedule** for the economy. This schedule shows the amount $(C + I_g)$ that will be spent at each possible output or income level.

At this point we are working with *planned investment*—the data in column 5, Table 9.4. These data show the amounts firms intend to invest, not the amounts they actually will invest if there are un-

Table 9.4
Determination of the Equilibrium Levels of Employment, Output, and Income: A Closed Private Economy

(1) Possible Levels of Employment, Millions	(2) Real Domestic Output (and Income) (GDP= DI),* Billions	(3) Consumption (C), Billions	(4) Saving (S), Billions	(5) Investment (I_g), Billions	(6) Aggregate Expenditures (C + I_g), Billions	(7) Unplanned Changes in Inventories, (+ or −)	(8) Tendency of Employment, Output, and Incomes
(1) 40	$370	$375	$−5	$20	$395	$−25	Increase
(2) 45	390	390	0	20	410	−20	Increase
(3) 50	410	405	5	20	425	−15	Increase
(4) 55	430	420	10	20	440	−10	Increase
(5) 60	450	435	15	20	455	−5	Increase
(6) **65**	**470**	**450**	**20**	**20**	**470**	**0**	**Equilibrium**
(7) 70	490	465	25	20	485	+5	Decrease
(8) 75	510	480	30	20	500	+10	Decrease
(9) 80	530	495	35	20	515	+15	Decrease
(10) 85	550	510	40	20	530	+20	Decrease

*If depreciation and net foreign factor income are zero, government is ignored, and it is assumed that all saving occurs in the household sector of the economy, GDP as a measure of domestic output is equal to NI, PI, and DI. This means that households receive a DI equal to the value of total output.

planned changes in inventories. More about that shortly.

Equilibrium
Of the 10 possible levels of GDP in Table 9.4, which is the equilibrium level? Which total output is the economy capable of sustaining?

The equilibrium output is that output whose production creates total spending just sufficient to purchase that output. So the equilibrium level of GDP is the level at which the total quantity of goods produced (GDP) equals the total quantity of goods purchased (C + I_g). If you look at the domestic output levels in column 2 and the aggregate expenditures levels in column 6, you will see that this equality exists only at $470 billion of GDP (row 6). That is the only output at which the economy is willing to spend precisely the amount needed to move that output off the shelves. At $470 billion of GDP, the annual rates of production and spending are in balance. There is no overproduction, which would result in a piling up of unsold goods and, consequently, cutbacks in the production rate. Nor is there an excess of total spending, which would draw down inventories of goods and prompt increases in the rate of production. In short, there is no reason for businesses to alter this rate of production; $470 billion is the **equilibrium GDP.**

Disequilibrium
No level of GDP other than the equilibrium level of GDP can be sustained. At levels of GDP *below* equilibrium, the economy wants to

spend at higher levels than the levels of GDP the economy is willing to produce. If, for example, firms produced $410 billion of GDP (row 3 in Table 9.4), they would find it would yield $405 billion in consumer spending. Supplemented by $20 billion of planned investment, aggregate expenditures (C + I_g) would be $425 billion, as shown in column 6. The economy would provide an annual rate of spending more than sufficient to purchase the $410 billion of annual production. Because buyers would be taking goods off the shelves faster than firms could produce them, an unintended decline in business inventories of $15 billion would occur (column 7) if this situation continued. But businesses can adjust to such an imbalance between aggregate expenditures and real output by stepping up production. Greater output will increase employment and total income. This process will continue until the equilibrium level of GDP is reached ($470 billion).

The reverse is true at all levels of GDP *above* the $470 billion equilibrium level. Businesses will find that these total outputs fail to generate the spending needed to clear the shelves of goods. Being unable to recover their costs, businesses will cut back on production. To illustrate: At the $510 billion output (row 8), business managers would find there is insufficient spending to permit the sale of all that output. Of the $510 billion of income that this output creates, $480 billion would be received back by businesses as consumption spending. Though supplemented by $20 billion of planned investment spending, total expenditures ($500 billion) would still be $10 billion below the $510 billion quantity produced. If this imbalance persisted, $10 billion of inventories would pile up (column 7). But businesses can adjust to this unintended accumulation of unsold goods by cutting back on the rate of production. The resulting decline in output would mean fewer jobs and a decline in total income.

The equilibrium level of GDP occurs where the total output, measured by GDP, and aggregate expenditures, $C + I_g$, are equal. Any excess of total spending over total output will drive GDP upward. Any deficiency of total spending will pull GDP downward.

Graphical Analysis

We can demonstrate the same analysis by means of a graph. In **Figure 9.9 (Key Graph)** the **45° line** now takes on increased significance. Recall that at any point on this line, the value of what is being measured on the horizontal axis (here, GDP) is equal to the value of what is being measured on the vertical axis (here, aggregate expenditures, or $C + I_g$). Having discovered in our tabular analysis that the equilibrium level of domestic output is determined where $C + I_g$ equals GDP, we can say that the 45° line in Figure 9.9 is a graphical statement of that equilibrium condition.

Now we must graph the aggregate expenditures schedule onto Figure 9.9. One way to do this is to duplicate the consumption schedule C in Figure 9.2a and add to it vertically the constant $20 billion amount of investment I_g from Figure 9.7b. This $20 billion is the amount we assumed firms plan to invest at all levels of GDP. Or, more directly, we can plot the $C + I_g$ data from column 6, Table 9.4.

Observe in Figure 9.9 that the aggregate expenditures line $C + I_g$ shows that total spending rises with income and output (GDP) but not as much as income rises, because the marginal propensity to consume—the slope of line C—is less than 1. A part of any increase in income will be saved rather than spent. And because the aggregate expenditures line $C + I_g$ is parallel to the consumption line C, the slope of the aggregate expenditures line also equals the MPC for the economy and is less than 1. For our particular data, aggregate expenditures rise by $15 billion for every $20 billion increase in real output and income because $5 billion of each $20 billion increment is saved. Therefore, in numerical terms the slope of the aggregate expenditures line is .75 (= $\Delta\$15/\Delta\$20$).

The equilibrium level of GDP is the GDP that corresponds to the intersection of the aggregate expenditures schedule and the 45° line. This intersection locates the only point at which aggregate expenditures (on the vertical axis) are equal to GDP (on the horizontal axis). Because Figure 9.9 is based on the data in Table 9.4, we once again find that equilibrium output is $470 billion. Observe that consumption at this output is $450 billion and investment is $20 billion.

It is evident from Figure 9.9 that no levels of GDP *above* the equilibrium level are sustainable because at those levels $C + I_g$ falls short of GDP. Graphically, the aggregate expenditures schedule lies below the 45° line in those situations. At the $510 billion GDP level, for example, $C + I_g$ is only $500 billion. This underspending causes inventories to rise, prompting firms to readjust production downward in the direction of the $470 billion output level.

Conversely, at levels of GDP *below* $470 billion, the economy wants to spend in excess of what businesses are producing. Then $C + I_g$ exceeds total output. Graphically, the aggregate expenditures schedule lies above the 45° line. At the $410 billion GDP level, for example, $C + I_g$ totals $425 billion. This overspending causes inventories to decline, prompting firms to raise production toward the $470 billion GDP. Unless there is some change in the location of the aggregate expenditures line, the $470 billion level of GDP will be sustained indefinitely. ◢ 9.1

■ Other Features of Equilibrium GDP

At equilibrium GDP, $C + I_g$ = GDP. A closer look at Table 9.4 reveals two more characteristics of equilibrium GDP:

■ Saving and planned investment are equal.
■ There are no unplanned changes in inventories.

Saving Equals Planned Investment

As shown by row 6 in Table 9.4, saving and planned investment are both $20 billion at the $470 billion equilibrium level of GDP.

Saving represents a **leakage** or withdrawal of spending from the income-expenditures stream. Saving is what causes consumption to be less than total output or GDP. As a result of saving, consumption by itself is insufficient to take all domestic

KEY GRAPH

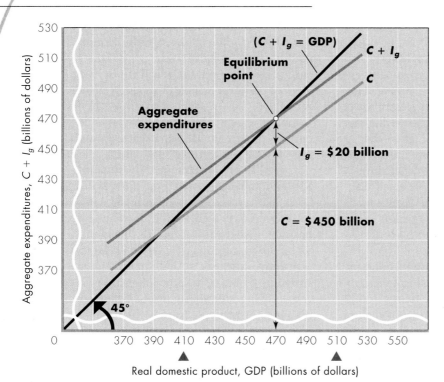

Figure 9.9

Equilibrium GDP. The aggregate expenditures schedule, $C + I_g$, is determined by adding the investment schedule I_g to the upsloping consumption schedule C. Since investment is assumed to be the same at each level of GDP, the vertical distances between C and $C + I_g$ do not change. Equilibrium GDP is determined where the aggregate expenditures schedule intersects the 45° line, in this case at $470 billion.

output off the shelves. This would seem to set the stage for a decline in total output.

However, firms do not intend to sell their entire output to consumers; some domestic output will consist of capital goods sold within the business sector. Investment can therefore be thought of as an **injection** of spending into the income-expenditures stream; investment is an adjunct to consumption. Investment is thus a potential replacement for the leakage of saving.

If, at a certain level of GDP, the leakage of saving exceeds the injection of investment, then $C + I_g$ will fall short of GDP and that level of GDP is too high to be sustained. Any GDP for which saving exceeds investment is an above-equilibrium GDP. For example, at a GDP of $510 billion (row 8 in Table 9.4), households will save $30 billion. Firms, however, will plan to invest only $20 billion. The $10 billion excess of saving over planned investment will reduce total spending to $10 billion below the value

175

of total output. Specifically, aggregate expenditures will be $500 billion, while real GDP is $510 billion. This spending deficiency will reduce real GDP.

Conversely, if the injection of investment exceeds the leakage of saving, then $C + I_g$ will be greater than GDP and GDP will be driven upward. Any GDP for which investment exceeds saving is a below-equilibrium GDP. For example, at a GDP of $410 billion (row 3) households will save only $5 billion, but firms will invest $20 billion. Hence, investment exceeds saving by $15 billion. The small leakage of saving at this relatively low GDP level is more than compensated for by the larger injection of investment spending. That causes $C + I_g$ to exceed GDP and drives GDP upward.

In this model of a private closed economy, aggregate expenditures will equal real output only where $S = I_g$—where the leakage of saving of $20 billion is exactly offset by the injection of investment of $20 billion. And that $C + I_g$ = GDP condition is what defines the equilibrium GDP. **(Key Question 9)** ⚠ 9.1

No Unplanned Changes in Inventories

As part of their investment plans, firms may decide to increase or decrease their inventories. But, as confirmed in row 6 of Table 9.4, there are no **unplanned changes in inventories** at equilibrium GDP. This fact, along with $C + I_g$ = GDP, and $S = I$, is a characteristic of equilibrium GDP in the private closed economy.

Unplanned changes in inventories play a major role in achieving equilibrium GDP. Consider, as an example, the $490 billion *above-equilibrium* GDP shown in row 7 of Table 9.4. What happens if firms produce that output, thinking they can sell it? Households save $25 billion of their $490 billion DI, so consumption is only $465 billion. Planned investment (column 5) is $20 billion. This means that aggregate expenditures $(C + I_g)$ are $485 billion and sales fall short of production by $5 billion. Firms retain that extra $5 billion of goods as an unplanned increase in inventories (column 7). It results from the failure of total spending to remove total output from the shelves.

Because changes in inventories are a part of investment, we note that **actual investment** is $25 billion. It consists of $20 billion of planned investment *plus* the $5 billion unplanned increase in inventories. Actual investment exactly equals the saving of $25

billion, even though saving exceeds planned investment by $5 billion. Because firms cannot earn profits by accumulating unwanted inventories, they will cut back production. GDP will fall to its equilibrium level of $470, at which changes in inventories are zero.

Now look at the *below-equilibrium* $450 billion output (row 5, Table 9.4). Because households save only $15 billion of their $450 billion DI, consumption is $435 billion. Planned investment by firms is $20 billion, so aggregate expenditures are $455 billion. Sales exceed production by $5 billion. This is so only because a $5 billion unplanned decrease in business inventories occurred. Firms must *disinvest* $5 billion in inventories (column 7). Note again that actual investment is $15 billion ($20 billion planned *minus* the $5 billion decline in inventory investment) and is equal to the saving of $15 billion, even though planned investment exceeds saving by $5 billion. The unplanned decline in inventories, resulting from the excess of sales over production, will encourage firms to expand production. GDP will rise to $470 billion, at which unplanned changes in inventories are zero.

When economists say differences between investment and saving can occur and bring about changes in equilibrium GDP, they are referring to planned investment and saving. Equilibrium occurs only when planned investment and saving are equal. *But when unplanned changes in inventories are considered, investment and saving are always equal, regardless of the level of GDP.* That is true because actual investment consists of planned investment and unplanned investment (unplanned changes in inventories). Unplanned changes in inventories act as a balancing item that equates the actual amounts saved and invested in any period. **(Key Question 10)**

QUICK REVIEW 9.3

▪ In a private closed economy, equilibrium GDP occurs where aggregate expenditures equal real domestic output $(C + I_g$ = GDP$)$.

▪ At equilibrium GDP, saving equals planned investment $(S = I_g)$.

▪ At equilibrium GDP, unplanned changes in inventories are zero.

▪ Actual investment consists of planned investment plus unplanned changes in inventories (+ or −) and is always equal to saving in a private closed economy.

Say's Law, the Great Depression, and Keynes

The Aggregate Expenditures Theory Emerged as a Critique of Classical Economics and as a Response to the Great Depression.

Until the Great Depression of the 1930s, many prominent economists, including David Ricardo (1772–1823) and John Stuart Mill (1806–1873), believed that the market system would ensure full employment of an economy's resources. These so-called *classical economists* acknowledged that now and then abnormal circumstances such as wars, political upheavals, droughts, speculative crises, and gold rushes would occur, deflecting the economy from full-employment status. But when such deviations occurred, the economy would automatically adjust and soon return to full-employment output. For example, a slump in output and employment would result in lower prices, wages, and interest rates, which in turn would increase consumer spending, employment, and investment spending. Any excess supply of goods and workers would soon be eliminated.

Classical macroeconomists denied that the level of spending in an economy could be too low to bring about the purchase of the entire full-employment output. They based their denial of inadequate spending in part on *Say's law*, attributed to the nineteenth-century French economist J. B. Say (1767–1832). This law is the disarmingly simple idea that the very act of producing goods generates income equal to the value of the goods produced. The production of any output automatically provides the income needed to buy that output. More succinctly stated, *supply creates its own demand*.

Say's law can best be understood in terms of a barter economy. A woodworker, for example, produces or supplies furniture as a means of buying or demanding the food and clothing produced by other workers. The woodworker's supply of furniture is the income that he will "spend" to satisfy his demand for other goods. The goods he buys (demands) will have a total value exactly equal to the goods he produces (supplies). And so it is for other producers and for the entire economy. Demand must be the same as supply!

Assuming that the composition of output is in accord with consumer preferences, all markets would be cleared of their outputs. It would seem that all firms need to do to sell a full-employment output is to produce that level of output. Say's law guarantees there will be sufficient spending to purchase it all. 🔑 **9.4**

The Great Depression of the 1930s called into question the theory that supply creates its own demand (Say's law). In the United States, real GDP declined by 40 percent and the unemployment rate rocketed to nearly 25 percent. Other nations experienced similar impacts. And cyclical unemployment lingered for a decade. An obvious inconsistency exists between a theory that says that unemployment is virtually impossible and the actual occurrence of a 10-year siege of substantial unemployment.

In 1936 British economist John Maynard Keynes (1883–1946) explained why cyclical unemployment could occur in a market economy. In his *General Theory of Employment, Interest, and Money*, Keynes attacked the foundations of classical theory and developed the ideas underlying the aggregate expenditures model. Keynes disputed Say's law, pointing out that not all income need be spent in the same period that it is produced. Investment spending, in particular, is volatile, said Keynes. A substantial decline in investment will lead to insufficient total spending. Unsold goods will accumulate in producers' warehouses, and producers will respond by reducing their output and discharging workers. A recession or depression will result, and widespread cyclical unemployment will occur. Moreover, said Keynes, recessions or depressions are not likely to correct themselves. In contrast to the more laissez-faire view of the classical economists, Keynes argued that government should play an active role in stabilizing the economy.

SUMMARY

1. The basic tools of the aggregate expenditures model are the consumption, saving, and investment schedules, which show the various amounts that households intend to consume and save and that firms plan to invest at the various income and output levels, assuming a fixed price level.

2. The *average* propensities to consume and save show the fractions of any total income that are consumed and saved; APC + APS = 1. The *marginal* propensities to consume and save show the fractions of any change in total income that are consumed and saved; MPC + MPS = 1.

3. The locations of the consumption and saving schedules are determined by (a) the amount of wealth owned by households; (b) expectations of future income, future prices, and product availability; (c) the relative size of household debt; and (d) taxation. The consumption and saving schedules are relatively stable.

4. The immediate determinants of investment are (a) the expected rate of return and (b) the real rate of interest. The economy's investment demand curve is found by cumulating investment projects, arraying them in descending order according to their expected rates of return, graphing the result, and applying the rule that investment will be profitable up to the point at which the real interest rate, i, equals the expected rate of return, r. The investment demand curve reveals an inverse relationship between the interest rate and the level of aggregate investment.

5. Shifts in the investment demand curve can occur as the result of changes in (a) the acquisition, maintenance, and operating costs of capital goods; (b) business taxes; (c) technology; (d) the stocks of capital goods on hand; and (e) expectations.

6. The investment schedule shows the amount of investment forthcoming at each level of real GDP. Either changes in interest rates or shifts in the investment demand curve can shift the investment schedule. We assume that the level of investment does not vary with the level of real GDP.

7. The durability of capital goods, the variability of expectations, and the irregular occurrence of major innovations all contribute to the instability of investment spending.

8. For a private closed economy the equilibrium level of GDP occurs when aggregate expenditures and real output are equal or, graphically, where the $C + I_g$ line intersects the 45° line. At any GDP greater than equilibrium GDP, real output will exceed aggregate spending, resulting in unintended investment in inventories and eventual declines in output and income (GDP). At any below-equilibrium GDP, aggregate expenditures will exceed real output, resulting in unintended declines in inventories and eventual increases in GDP.

9. At equilibrium GDP, the amount households save (leakages) and the amount businesses plan to invest (injections) are equal. Any excess of saving over planned investment will cause a shortage of total spending, forcing GDP to fall. Any excess of planned investment over saving will cause an excess of total spending, inducing GDP to rise. The change in GDP will in both cases correct the discrepancy between saving and planned investment.

10. At equilibrium GDP, there are no unplanned changes in inventories. When aggregate expenditures diverge from real GDP, an unplanned change in inventories occurs. Unplanned increases in inventories are followed by a cutback in production and a decline of real GDP. Unplanned decreases in inventories result in an increase in production and a rise of GDP.

11. Actual investment consists of planned investment plus unplanned changes in inventories and is always equal to saving.

TERMS AND CONCEPTS

consumption schedule	marginal propensity to consume (MPC)	investment demand curve	leakage
saving schedule		planned investment	injection
break-even income	marginal propensity to save (MPS)	investment schedule	unplanned changes in inventories
average propensity to consume (APC)	wealth effect	aggregate expenditures schedule	actual investment
average propensity to save (APS)	expected rate of return	equilibrium GDP	
	real interest rate	45° line	

STUDY QUESTIONS

1. Explain what relationships are shown by (*a*) the consumption schedule, (*b*) the saving schedule, (*c*) the investment demand curve, and (*d*) the investment schedule.

2. Precisely how are the APC and the MPC different? Why must the sum of the MPC and the MPS equal 1? What are the basic determinants of the consumption and saving schedules? Of your own level of consumption?

3. Explain how each of the following will affect the consumption and saving schedules or the investment schedule, other things equal:
   a. A large increase in the value of real estate, including private houses.
   b. The threat of limited, nonnuclear war, leading the public to expect future shortages of consumer durables.
   c. A decline in the real interest rate.
   d. A sharp, sustained decline in stock prices.
   e. An increase in the rate of population growth.
   f. The development of a cheaper method of manufacturing computer chips.
   g. A sizable increase in the retirement age for collecting social security benefits.
   h. The expectation that mild inflation will persist in the next decade.
   i. An increase in the Federal personal income tax.

4. Explain why an upward shift of the consumption schedule typically involves an equal downshift of the saving schedule. What is the exception to this relationship?

5. **Key Question** Complete the following table:

   a. Show the consumption and saving schedules graphically.
   b. Find the break-even level of income. Explain how it is possible for households to dissave at very low income levels.
   c. If the proportion of total income consumed (APC) decreases and the proportion saved (APS) increases as income rises, explain both verbally and graphically how the MPC and MPS can be constant at various levels of income.

6. What are the basic determinants of investment? Explain the relationship between the real interest rate and the level of investment. Why is the investment schedule less stable than the consumption and saving schedules?

7. **Key Question** Assume there are no investment projects in the economy that yield an expected rate of return of 25 percent or more. But suppose there are $10 billion of investment projects yielding expected returns of between 20 and 25 percent; another $10 billion yielding between 15 and 20 percent; another $10 billion, between 10 and 15 percent; and so forth. Cumulate these data and present them graphically, putting the expected rate of return on the vertical axis and the amount of investment on the horizontal axis. What will be the equilibrium level of aggregate investment if the real interest rate is (*a*) 15 percent, (*b*) 10 percent, and (*c*) 5 percent? Explain why this curve is the investment demand curve.

8. Explain graphically the determination of the equilibrium GDP for a private closed economy. Explain why the intersection of the aggregate expenditures schedule and the 45° line determines the equilibrium GDP.

Level of Output and Income (GDP = DI)	Consumption	Saving	APC	APS	MPC	MPS
$240	$_____	$−4	___	___	___	___
260	_____	0	___	___	___	___
280	_____	4	___	___	___	___
300	_____	8	___	___	___	___
320	_____	12	___	___	___	___
340	_____	16	___	___	___	___
360	_____	20	___	___	___	___
380	_____	24	___	___	___	___
400	_____	28	___	___	___	___

9. **Key Question** Assuming the level of investment is $16 billion and independent of the level of total output, complete the following table and determine the equilibrium levels of output and employment that this private closed economy would provide. What are the sizes of the MPC and MPS?

Possible Levels of Employment, Millions	Real Domestic Output (GDP = DI), Billions	Consumption, Billions	Saving, Billions
40	$240	$244	$____
45	260	260	____
50	280	276	____
55	300	292	____
60	320	308	____
65	340	324	____
70	360	340	____
75	380	356	____
80	400	372	____

10. **Key Question** Using the consumption and saving data in question 9 and assuming investment is $16 billion, what are saving and planned investment at the $380 billion level of domestic output? What are saving and actual investment at that level? What are saving and planned investment at the $300 billion level of domestic output? What are the levels of saving and actual investment? Use the concept of unplanned investment to explain adjustments toward equilibrium from both the $380 billion and the $300 billion levels of domestic output.

11. Why is saving called a *leakage*? Why is planned investment called an *injection*? Why must saving equal planned investment at equilibrium GDP? Are unplanned changes in inventories rising, falling, or constant at equilibrium GDP? Explain.

12. "Planned investment is equal to saving at all levels of GDP; actual investment equals saving only at the equilibrium GDP." Do you agree or disagree? Explain. Critically evaluate: "The fact that households may save more than firms want to invest is of no consequence, because events will in time force households and firms to save and invest at the same rates."

13. **Advanced Analysis** Linear equations for the consumption and saving schedules take the general form $C = a + bY$ and $S = -a + (1 - b) Y$, where C, S, and Y are consumption, saving, and national income, respectively. The constant a represents the vertical intercept, and b the slope of the consumption schedule.

a. Use the following data to substitute numerical values for a and b in the consumption and saving equations:

National Income (Y)	Consumption (C)
$ 0	$ 80
100	140
200	200
300	260
400	320

b. What is the economic meaning of b? Of $(1 - b)$?

c. Suppose the amount of saving that occurs at each level of national income falls by $20 but the values of b and $(1 - b)$ remain unchanged. Restate the saving and consumption equations for the new numerical values, and cite a factor that might have caused the change.

14. **Advanced Analysis** Suppose that the linear equation for consumption in a hypothetical economy is $C = 40 + .8Y$. Also suppose that income (Y) is $400. Determine (*a*) the marginal propensity to consume, (*b*) the marginal propensity to save, (*c*) the level of consumption, (*d*) the average propensity to consume, (*e*) the level of saving, and (*f*) the average propensity to save.

15. **Advanced Analysis** Assume that the linear equation for consumption in a hypothetical private closed economy is $C = 10 + .9Y$, where Y is total real income (output). Also suppose that the equation for investment is $I_g + I_{g0} = 40$, meaning that I_g is 40 at all levels of total real income. Using the equation $Y = C + I_g$, determine the equilibrium level of Y. What are the total amounts of consumption, saving, and investment at equilibrium Y?

16. **(Last Word)** What is Say's law? How does it relate to the view held by classical economists that the economy generally will operate at a position on its production possibilities curve (Chapter 2). Use production possibilities analysis to demonstrate Keynes' view on this matter.

17. **Web-Based Question:** *The Beige Book and current consumer spending* The Beige Book, at www.federalreserve.gov/FOMC/BeigeBook/2001, is a report on economic conditions published eight times a year by the Federal Reserve System. Each Federal Reserve Bank gathers anecdotal information on current economic conditions in its district through reports from bank and branch directors and interviews with key executives, economists, market

experts, and others. Locate the Beige Book report for the most recent year and period. Compare consumer spending for the entire U.S. economy with consumer spending in your Federal Reserve District. What are the economic strengths and weaknesses for both? Are retailers reporting that recent sales have met their expectations? What are the expectations for the future?

18. **Web-Based Question:** *Investment instability— changes in real private nonresidential fixed investment* Investment is the most volatile component of total spending. Real private nonresidential fixed investment is made up of two components: structures and producers' durable equipment. The Bureau of Economic Analysis provides data for real private nonresidential fixed investment in table form at www.bea.doc.gov/briefrm/tables/ebr2.htm and shows the data graphically through Chart Nonresidential Investment at that site. Has recent investment been volatile? Which is the largest component of investment, structures or producers' durable equipment? Which component has been more volatile (as measured by percentage change from previous quarter)? Looking at the investment graph, what investment forecast would you make for the forthcoming year?

10

Aggregate Expenditures

The Multiplier, Net Exports, and Government

I N   C H A P T E R   **9** we saw that a private closed economy may achieve a particular equilibrium level of real GDP. But, as we saw in Chapter 8, the U.S. GDP is not always stable; instead, there sometimes are cyclical fluctuations. We now turn to why and how the equilibrium real GDP might fluctuate. And since the public sector and the foreign sector influence real GDP, later in this chapter we will bring those two sectors into the aggregate expenditures model in order to make it more realistic. That is, we will "open" our simplified "closed" economy to show how exports and imports affect it. We will also convert our "private" economy to a more realistic "mixed" economy that includes government purchases and taxes.

■ Changes in Equilibrium GDP and the Multiplier

In the private closed economy, the equilibrium GDP will change in response to changes in either the investment schedule or the consumption schedule. Because changes in the investment schedule usually are the main source of instability, we will direct our attention toward them.

Figure 10.1 shows the effect of changes in investment spending on the equilibrium real GDP. Suppose that the expected rate of return on investment rises or that the real interest rate falls. In either case, investment spending will rise—let's say by $5 billion. We would show this increase as an upward shift of the I_g schedule depicted in Figure

9.7b. In Figure 10.1, the $5 billion increase of investment will shift the aggregate expenditures schedule upward from $(C + I_g)_0$ to $(C + I_g)_1$. Equilibrium real GDP will rise from $470 billion to $490 billion.

If the expected rate of return on investment decreases or if the real interest rate rises, investment spending will decline by, say, $5 billion. That would be shown as a downward shift of the investment schedule in Figure 9.7b and a downward shift of the aggregate expenditures schedule from $(C + I_g)_0$ to $(C + I_g)_2$ in Figure 10.1. Equilibrium GDP will fall from $470 billion to $450 billion.

You should verify these conclusions by substituting first $25 billion and then $15 billion for the $20 billion planned investment amount in column 5

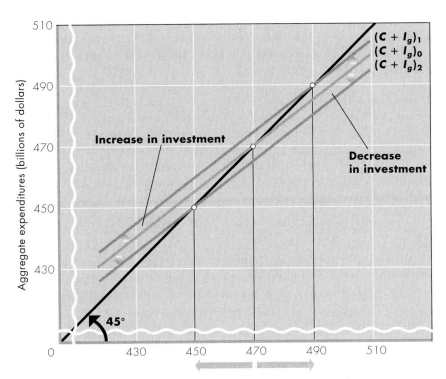

Figure 10.1
Changes in the equilibrium GDP caused by shifts in the aggregate expenditures schedule and the investment schedule. An upward shift of the aggregate expenditures schedule from $(C + I_g)_0$ to $(C + I_g)_1$ will increase the equilibrium GDP. Conversely, a downward shift from $(C + I_g)_0$ to $(C + I_g)_2$ will lower the equilibrium GDP.

of Table 9.4. When you do, you will see that $C + I_g$ equals GDP first at $490 billion (row 7) and then at $450 billion (row 5). These are the altered equilibrium values of GDP indicated in Figure 10.1.

The Multiplier Effect

You may have noticed that in our example a $5 billion change in investment spending led to a $20 billion change in output and income. That surprising result is called the *multiplier effect:* a change in a component of aggregate expenditures leads to a larger change in equilibrium GDP. The **multiplier** determines how much larger that change will be; it is the ratio of a change in equilibrium GDP to the initial change in spending (in this case, investment). Stated generally,

$$\text{Multiplier} = \frac{\text{change in real GDP}}{\text{initial change in spending}}$$

Here the multiplier is 4 (= $20/$5). By rearranging this equation, we can also say that

$$\text{Change in GDP} = \text{multiplier} \times \text{initial change in spending}$$

Note these three points about the multiplier:
- The "initial change in spending" is usually associated with investment spending because of investment's volatility. But changes in consumption, net exports, and government purchases also lead to the multiplier effect.
- The "initial change in spending" refers to an upward or downward shift of the aggregate expenditures schedule caused by the change of one of its components. In Figure 10.1 we find that real GDP has increased by $20 billion because investment increased by $5 billion. That is, the investment schedule—shown previously as Figure 9.7b—has shifted upward.
- Implicit in the preceding point is that the multiplier works in both directions. An increase in initial spending may create a multiple increase in GDP, and a decrease in spending may be multiplied into a larger decrease in GDP.

Rationale   The multiplier effect follows from two facts. First, the economy supports repetitive, continuous flows of expenditures and income through which dollars spent by Smith are received as income by Chin, then spent by Chin and received as income by Gonzales, and so on. Second, any change in income will cause both consumption and saving to vary in the same direction as, and by a fraction of, the change in income.

It follows that an initial change in spending will set off a spending chain throughout the economy. That chain of spending, although of diminishing importance at each successive step, will cumulate to a multiple change in GDP.

Table 10.1 illustrates the rationale underlying the multiplier effect. Suppose that a $5 billion increase in investment spending occurs. This is the upward shift of the aggregate expenditures schedule by $5 billion in Figure 10.1. Because we are still using the data in Table 9.1, we assume that the MPC is .75 and the MPS is .25. Also, we assume that the economy is initially in equilibrium at a GDP of $470 billion.

The initial increase in investment spending generates an equal amount of wage, rent, interest, and profit income, because spending income and receiving income are two sides of the same transaction. How much consumption will be induced by this $5 billion increase in the incomes of households? We find the answer by applying the marginal propensity to consume of .75 to this change in income. Thus, the $5 billion increase in income initially raises consumption by $3.75 (= .75 × $5) billion and saving by $1.25 (= .25 × $5) billion, as shown in columns 2 and 3 in Table 10.1.

Other households receive as income (second round) the $3.75 billion of consumption spending. Those households consume .75 of this $3.75 billion,

or $2.81 billion, and save .25 of it, or $0.94 billion. The $2.81 billion that is consumed flows to still other households as income to be spent or saved (third round). And the process continues.

Figure 10.2, derived from Table 10.1, shows the cumulative effects of this process. Each round adds a gold block to national income and GDP. The accumulation of the additional income in each round—the sum of the gold blocks—is the total change in income or GDP. Although the spending and respending effects of the increase in investment diminish with each successive round of spending, the cumulative increase in output and income will be $20 billion. The $5 billion increase in investment will therefore increase the equilibrium GDP by $20 billion, from $470 billion to $490 billion. Thus, the multiplier is 4 (= $20 billion ÷ $5 billion).

It is no coincidence that the multiplier effect ends at the point where exactly enough saving has been generated to offset the initial $5 billion increase in investment spending. Only then will the disequilibrium created by the investment increase be corrected. In other words, GDP and total income must rise by $20 billion to create $5 billion in additional saving to balance the $5 billion increase in investment spending. Income must increase by four times the initial excess of investment over saving, because households save one-fourth of any increase in their income (that is, the MPS is .25).

The Multiplier and the Marginal Propensities
You may have sensed from Table 10.1 a relationship between the MPS and the multiplier. The fraction of an increase in income saved (the MPS)

Table 10.1
The Multiplier: A Tabular Illustration (in Billions)

	(1) Change in Income	(2) Change in Consumption (MPC = .75)	(3) Change in Saving (MPS = .25)
Increase in investment of **$5.00**	$5.00	$3.75	$1.25
Second round	3.75	2.81	.94
Third round	2.81	2.11	.70
Fourth round	2.11	1.58	.53
Fifth round	1.58	1.19	.39
All other rounds	4.75	3.56	1.19
Total	**$20.00**	$15.00	**$5.00**

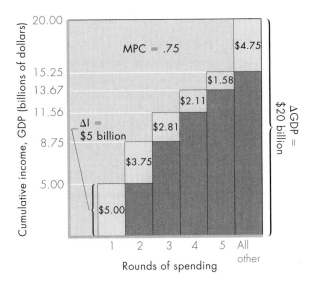

Figure 10.2

The multiplier process (MPC = .75). An initial change in investment spending of $5 billion creates an equal $5 billion of new income in round 1. Households spend $3.75 (= .75 × $5) billion of this new income, creating $3.75 of added income in round 2. Of this $3.75 of new income, households spend $2.81 (= .75 × $3.75) billion, and income rises by that amount in round 3. The cumulation of such income increments over the entire process eventually results in a total change of income and GDP of $20 billion. The multiplier therefore is 4 (= $20 billion ÷ $5 billion).

determines the cumulative respending effects of any initial change in spending and therefore determines the multiplier. *The MPS and the multiplier are inversely related.* The smaller the fraction of any change in income saved, the greater the respending at each round and, therefore, the greater the multiplier. If the MPS is .25, as in our example, the multiplier is 4. If the MPS were .33, the multiplier would be 3. If the MPS were .2, the multiplier would be 5. Let's see why.

This time we assume that the MPS is .33. Initially the economy is in equilibrium at the $470 billion level of GDP (Table 9.4). Now businesses increase investment by $5 billion, so aggregate expenditures are $475 billion at the $470 billion level of GDP. This means $470 billion is no longer the equilibrium GDP. By how much must output and income rise to restore equilibrium? By enough to generate $5 billion of additional saving to offset the $5 billion increase in investment. Because households save $1 out of every $3 of additional income they receive (MPS = .33), GDP must rise by $15 billion—

three times the increase in investment—to create the $5 billion of extra saving necessary to restore equilibrium. Thus, when the MPS is .33 rather than .25, the multiplier is 3 rather than 4.

But if the MPS were .2, GDP would have to rise by $25 billion (five times the increase in investment) to generate $5 billion of additional saving and restore equilibrium, and therefore the multiplier would be 5.

We can summarize by saying the multiplier is equal to the reciprocal of the MPS. The reciprocal of any number is the quotient you obtain by dividing 1 by that number:

$$\text{Multiplier} = \frac{1}{\text{MPS}}$$

This formula is a quick way to determine the multiplier. To do so, all you need to know is the MPS.

Recall, too, from Chapter 9 that MPC + MPS = 1; it follows, then, that MPS = 1 − MPC. Therefore, we can also write the multiplier formula as

$$\text{Multiplier} = \frac{1}{1 - \text{MPC}}$$

Significance of the Multiplier   The significance of the multiplier is that a small change in the investment plans of businesses or in the consumption and saving plans of households can trigger a larger change in the equilibrium GDP. The multiplier magnifies the fluctuations in business activity initiated by changes in spending.

As illustrated in Figure 10.3, the larger the MPC (the smaller the MPS), the greater the

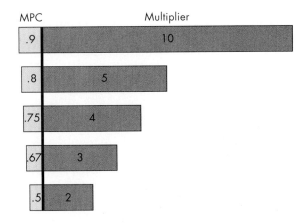

Figure 10.3

The MPC and the multiplier. The larger the MPC (the smaller the MPS), the greater the size of the multiplier.

multiplier. If the MPC is .75, the multiplier is 4; a $10 billion decline in planned investment will reduce the equilibrium GDP by $40 billion. But if the MPC is only .67, the multiplier is 3; the same $10 billion drop in investment will reduce the equilibrium GDP by only $30 billion. This makes sense intuitively: A large MPC means the succeeding rounds of consumption spending shown in Figure 10.2 diminish slowly and thereby cumulate to a large change in income. Conversely, a small MPC (a large MPS) causes the increases in consumption to decline quickly, so the cumulative change in income is small.

Generalizing the Multiplier   The multiplier we have just described is called the *simple multiplier*, because it is based on a simple model of the economy. When it is computed as 1/MPS, the multiplier reflects only the leakage of income into saving. In the real world, successive rounds of income and spending may also be diminished by leakages into imports and taxes. As with the leakage into saving, some part of income at each round will be used to purchase additional goods from abroad, and another part siphoned off as additional taxes. The result of these added leakages is that the 1/MPS statement of the multiplier can be generalized. Specifically, we can change the denominator to read "fraction of the change in income that is not spent on domestic output" or "fraction of the change in income that leaks, or is diverted, from the income-expenditures stream." The more realistic multiplier that results when all leakages—saving, taxes, and imports—are included is called the *complex multiplier*. The Council of Economic Advisers, which advises the U.S. president on economic matters, has estimated that the complex multiplier for the United States is about 2. **(Key Question 2)** ⚠ 10.1

International Trade and Equilibrium Output

Thus far, we have ignored international trade by assuming a closed economy. We now acknowledge the existence of exports and imports and note that **net exports** (exports minus imports) may be either positive or negative. Item 4 on the inside covers of this book reveals that net exports in some years have been positive (exports > imports) and in other years negative (imports > exports).

Net Exports and Aggregate Expenditures

Like consumption and investment, exports (X) create domestic production, income, and employment for a nation. Even though U.S. goods and services produced for export are sent abroad, foreign spending on those goods and services increases production and creates jobs and incomes in the United States. Exports must therefore be added as a component of each nation's aggregate expenditures.

Conversely, when an economy is open to international trade, part of its spending will be for imports (M)—goods and services produced abroad rather than in domestic industries. To avoid overstating the value of domestic production, we must adjust total spending by the amount spent on imported goods. In measuring aggregate expenditures for domestic goods and services, we must subtract expenditures on imports.

In short, for a private closed economy, aggregate expenditures are $C + I_g$. But for an open economy with international trade, aggregate expenditures are $C + I_g + (X - M)$. Or, recalling that net exports (X_n) equal $(X - M)$, we can say that aggregate expenditures for a private open economy are $C + I_g + X_n$.

The Net Export Schedule

Table 10.2 shows two possible net export schedules for the hypothetical economy in Tables 9.1 and 9.4. Similar to consumption and investment schedules, a net export schedule lists the amount of a particular expenditure—in this case, net exports—that will occur at each level of GDP. In net export schedule X_{n1} (columns 1 and 2), exports exceed imports by $5 billion at each level of GDP. Perhaps exports are $15 billion while imports are $10 billion. In schedule X_{n2} (columns 1 and 3), imports are $5 billion higher than exports. Perhaps imports are $20 billion while exports are $15

Table 10.2

Two Net Export Schedules (in Billions)

(1) Level of GDP	(2) Net Exports X_{n1} $(X > M)$	(3) Net Exports X_{n2} $(X < M)$
$370	$+5	$−5
390	+5	−5
410	+5	−5
430	+5	−5
450	+5	−5
470	+5	−5
490	+5	−5
510	+5	−5
530	+5	−5
550	+5	−5

billion. To simplify our discussion, we assume in both schedules that net exports are independent of GDP.[1]

The two net export schedules in Table 10.2 are plotted in Figure 10.4b. Schedule X_{n1} reveals that a positive $5 billion of net exports is associated with each level of GDP. Conversely, X_{n2} is below the horizontal axis and thus shows net exports of a negative $5 billion at all GDPs.

Net Exports and Equilibrium GDP

The aggregate expenditures schedule labeled $C + I_g$ in Figure 10.4a is identical to that in Table 9.4 and Figure 9.9. That is, $C + I_g$ reflects the combined consumption and gross investment expenditures occurring at each level of GDP. With no foreign sector, the equilibrium GDP will be $470 billion. This equilibrium real output is determined at the intersection of the $C + I_g$ schedule and the 45° reference line. Only there will aggregate expenditures equal GDP.

But net exports can be either positive or negative. Let's see how each of the net export schedules in Figure 10.4b affects equilibrium GDP.

Positive Net Exports   Suppose the net export schedule is X_{n1}. The $5 billion of additional net export expenditures by the rest of the world is accounted

for by adding that $5 billion to the $C + I_g$ schedule in Figure 10.4a. Aggregate expenditures at each level of GDP are then $5 billion higher than $C + I_g$ alone. The aggregate expenditures schedule for the open economy thus becomes $C + I_g + X_{n1}$. It shows that international trade in this case increases equilibrium GDP from $470 billion in the private closed economy to $490 billion in the private open economy.

Verify that the new equilibrium GDP is $490 billion by adding $X_n = 5 billion to each level of aggregate expenditures in Table 9.4 and then determining the GDP for which $C + I_g + X_n$ equals GDP.

Generalization: *Other things equal, positive net exports increase aggregate expenditures and GDP beyond what they would be in a closed economy.* Adding net exports of $5 billion has increased GDP by $20 billion, in this case implying a multiplier of 4.

Negative Net Exports   An extension of our reasoning enables us to determine the effect of negative net exports on equilibrium GDP. If net exports are X_{n2} in Figure 10.4b, net exports are a negative $5 billion. This means that our hypothetical economy is importing $5 billion more of goods than it is exporting. The aggregate expenditures schedule shown as $C + I_g$ in Figure 10.4a therefore overstates the expenditures on domestic output at each level of GDP. We must reduce the sum of expenditures by the $5 billion net amount spent on imported goods. We must subtract the $5 billion of net imports from $C + I_g$.

After we subtract $5 billion from the $C + I_g$ schedule in Figure 10.4a, the relevant aggregate expenditures schedule becomes $C + I_g + X_{n2}$. It shows that equilibrium GDP falls from $470 to $450. Again, a change in net exports of $5 billion has resulted in a fourfold change in GDP, reminding us that the multiplier is 4. Confirmation of the new equilibrium GDP can be obtained by subtracting $5 billion from aggregate expenditures at each level of GDP in Table 9.4 and ascertaining the new equilibrium GDP for which $C + I_g + X_n$ equals GDP.

This gives us a corollary to our first generalization: *Negative net exports reduce aggregate expenditures and GDP below what they would be in a closed economy.* Imports add to the stock of goods available in the economy, but they diminish real GDP by reducing expenditures on domestically produced products.

Our generalizations of the effects of X_n on GDP mean that a decline in net exports—a decrease in exports or an increase in imports—reduces aggregate expenditures and contracts a nation's GDP. Conversely, an increase in net exports—the result of

---

[1]In reality, although our exports depend on foreign incomes and are thus independent of U.S. GDP, our imports do vary directly with our own domestic national income. Just as our domestic consumption varies directly with our GDP, so do our purchases of foreign goods. As our GDP rises, U.S. households buy not only more Pontiacs and more Pepsi but also more Porsches and more Perrier. However, for now we will ignore the complications of the positive relationship between imports and U.S. GDP.

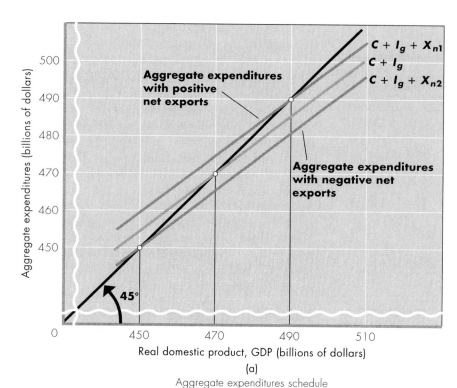

(a)
Aggregate expenditures schedule

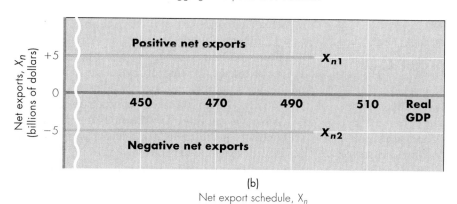

(b)
Net export schedule, X_n

Figure 10.4

Net exports and equilibrium GDP. Positive net exports such as shown by the net export schedule X_{n1} in (b) elevate the aggregate expenditures schedule in (a) from the closed-economy level of $C + I_g$ to the open-economy level of $C + I_g + X_{n1}$. Negative net exports such as depicted by the net export schedule X_{n2} in (b) lower the aggregate expenditures schedule in (a) from the closed-economy level of $C + I_g$ to the open-economy level of $C + I_g + X_{n2}$.

either an increase in exports or a decrease in imports—increases aggregate expenditures and expands GDP.

As is shown in Global Perspective 10.1, net exports vary greatly among the major industrial nations. **(Key Question 5)**

International Economic Linkages

Our analysis of net exports and real GDP reveals how circumstances or policies abroad can affect U.S. GDP.

Prosperity Abroad A rising level of real output and thus income among U.S. foreign trading part-

ners permits the United States to sell more goods abroad, thus raising U.S. net exports and increasing its real GDP (assuming initially there is excess capacity). There is good reason for us to be interested in the prosperity of our trading partners, because their good fortune enables them to buy more of our exports, increasing our income and enabling us to buy more of their imports. Prosperity abroad transfers some of that prosperity to us.

Tariffs Suppose foreign trading partners impose high tariffs on U.S. goods to reduce their imports from the United States and thus to increase production in their own economies. Their imports are U.S.

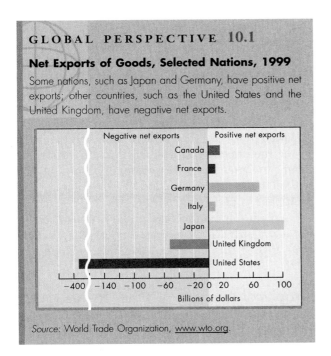

GLOBAL PERSPECTIVE 10.1

Net Exports of Goods, Selected Nations, 1999

Some nations, such as Japan and Germany, have positive net exports; other countries, such as the United States and the United Kingdom, have negative net exports.

Negative net exports | Positive net exports

Canada
France
Germany
Italy
Japan
United Kingdom
United States

-400 -140 -100 -60 -20 0 20   60   100
Billions of dollars

Source: World Trade Organization, www.wto.org.

exports. So when they restrict their imports to stimulate *their* economies, they are reducing U.S. exports and depressing *our* economy. We may retaliate by imposing trade barriers on their products. If so, their exports to us will decline and their net exports may fall. It is not at all clear, then, whether tariffs increase or decrease a nation's net exports. In the Great Depression of the 1930s various nations, including the United States, imposed trade barriers as a way of reducing domestic unemployment. But rounds of retaliation simply throttled world trade, worsened the Depression, and increased unemployment.

Exchange Rates Depreciation of the dollar relative to other currencies (discussed in Chapter 6) enables people abroad to obtain more dollars per unit of their own currencies. The price of U.S. goods in terms of those currencies will fall, stimulating purchases of U.S. exports. Also, U.S. customers will find they need more dollars to buy foreign goods and, consequently, will reduce their spending on imports. The increased exports and decreased imports will increase U.S. net exports and thus expand the nation's GDP.

Whether depreciation of the dollar will actually raise real GDP or produce inflation depends on the initial position of the economy relative to its full-employment output. If the economy is operating below its full-employment level, depreciation of the dollar and the resulting rise in net exports will increase aggregate expenditures and thus expand real

GDP. But if the economy is already fully employed, the increase in net exports and aggregate expenditures will cause demand-pull inflation. Because resources are already fully employed, the increased spending cannot expand real output; but it can and does increase the prices of the existing output.

This last example has been cast only in terms of depreciation of the dollar. Now think through the impact that appreciation of the dollar would have on net exports and equilibrium GDP.

QUICK REVIEW 10.2

- Positive net exports increase aggregate expenditures relative to the closed economy and increase equilibrium GDP.
- Negative net exports decrease aggregate expenditures relative to the closed economy and reduce equilibrium GDP.
- In the open economy, U.S. net exports and therefore aggregate expenditures and equilibrium GDP can be affected by changes in prosperity abroad, changes in tariffs, and changes in exchange rates.

■ Adding the Public Sector

Our final step in constructing the full aggregate expenditures model is to move the analysis from that of a private (no-government) open economy to a mixed open economy that has a public sector. This means adding government spending and taxes to the model.

Simplifying Assumptions

For clarity, we will make the following simplifying assumptions.

- Levels of investment and net exports are independent of the level of GDP.
- Government purchases neither depress nor stimulate private spending. They do not cause any upward or downward shifts in the consumption and investment schedules.
- Government's net tax revenues—total tax revenues less "negative taxes" in the form of transfer payments—are derived entirely from personal taxes. Although disposable income (DI) will fall short of personal income (PI) by the amount of the government's tax revenues, GDP, national income (NI), and PI will remain equal.

- A fixed amount of taxes is collected regardless of the level of GDP.
- Unless otherwise indicated, the price level is constant.

These assumptions will give us a simple and uncluttered view of how government spending and taxes fit within the aggregate expenditures model. We will drop most of these assumptions in Chapter 12 when we discuss how government uses changes in its expenditures and taxes to alter equilibrium GDP and the rate of inflation.

Government Purchases and Equilibrium GDP

Suppose the government decides to purchase $20 billion of goods and services regardless of the level of GDP.

Tabular Example Table 10.3 shows the impact of this purchase on the equilibrium GDP. Columns 1 through 4 are carried over from Table 9.4 for the private closed economy, in which the equilibrium GDP was $470 billion. The only new items are exports and imports in column 5 and government purchases in column 6. (Observe in column 5 that net exports are zero.) By adding government purchases to private spending $(C + I_g + X_n)$, we get a new, higher level of aggregate expenditures $(C + I_g + X_n + G)$, as shown in column 7. Comparing columns 1 and 7, we find that aggregate expenditures and real

output are equal at a higher level of GDP. Without government spending, equilibrium GDP was $470 billion (row 6); *with* government spending, aggregate expenditures and real output are equal at $550 billion (row 10). *Increases in public spending, like increases in private spending, shift the aggregate expenditures schedule upward and result in a higher equilibrium GDP.*

Note, too, that government spending is subject to the multiplier. A $20 billion increase in government purchases has increased equilibrium GDP by $80 billion (from $470 billion to $550 billion). The multiplier in this example is 4.

This $20 billion increase in government spending is *not* financed by increased taxes. In a moment you will find that increased taxes *reduce* equilibrium GDP.

Graphical Analysis In Figure 10.5 we add $20 billion of government purchases, G, vertically to the level of private spending, $C + I_g + X_n$. That increases the aggregate expenditures schedule (private plus public) to $C + I_g + X_n + G$, resulting in the $80 billion increase in equilibrium GDP from $470 billion to $550 billion.

A decline in government spending, G, will lower the aggregate expenditures schedule in Figure 10.5 and result in a multiplied decline in the equilibrium GDP. Verify in Table 10.3 that if government spending were to decline from $20 billion to $10 billion, the equilibrium GDP would fall by $40 billion— that is, from $550 billion to $510 billion. ◢ **10.1**

Table 10.3

The Impact of Government Purchases on Equilibrium GDP

(1) Real Domestic Output and Income (GDP = DI), Billions	(2) Consumption (C), Billions	(3) Savings (S), Billions	(4) Investment (I_g), Billions	(5) Net Exports (X_n), Billions		(6) Government Purchases (G), Billions	(7) Aggregate Expenditures (C + I_g + X_n + G), Billions (2) + (4) + (5) + (6)
				Exports (X)	Imports (M)		
(1) $370	$375	$−5	$20	$10	$10	$20	$415
(2) 390	390	0	20	10	10	20	430
(3) 410	405	5	20	10	10	20	445
(4) 430	420	10	20	10	10	20	460
(5) 450	435	15	20	10	10	20	475
(6) 470	450	20	20	10	10	20	490
(7) 490	465	25	20	10	10	20	505
(8) 510	480	30	20	10	10	20	520
(9) 530	495	35	20	10	10	20	535
(10) **550**	**510**	**40**	**20**	**10**	**10**	**20**	**550**

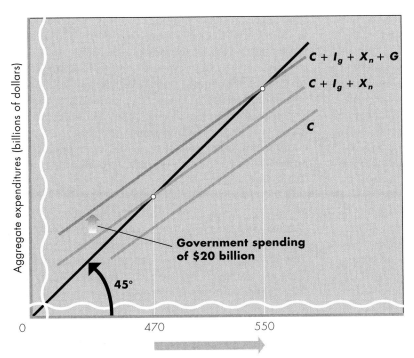

Figure 10.5
**Government spending and equilib-
rium GDP.** The addition of government expenditures of G to our analysis raises the aggregate expenditures ($C + I_g + X_n + G$)
schedule and increases the equilibrium level of
GDP, as would an increase in C, I_g, or X_n.

Taxation and Equilibrium GDP

The government also collects taxes. Suppose it imposes a **lump-sum tax,** which is *a tax of a constant
amount or, more precisely, a tax yielding the same amount
of tax revenue at each level of GDP.* Suppose this tax is
$20 billion, so that the government obtains $20 billion of tax revenue at each level of GDP.

Tabular Example   In Table 10.4, which continues our example, we find taxes in column 2, and we
see in column 3 that disposable (after-tax) income is
lower than GDP (column 1) by the $20 billion
amount of the tax. Because disposable income is used
for consumer spending and saving, the tax lowers
both consumption and saving relative to their levels

Table 10.4

Determination of the Equilibrium Levels of Employment, Output, and Income: Private and Public Sectors

(1) Real Domestic Output and Income (GDP = NI = PI), Billions	(2) Taxes (T), Billions	(3) Disposable Income (DI), Billions, (1) − (2)	(4) Consumption (C_a), Billions	(5) Saving (S_a), Billions, (3) − (4)	(6) Investment (I_g), Billions	(7) Net Exports (X_n), Billions — Exports (X)	Imports (M)	(8) Government Purchases (G), Billions	(9) Aggregate Expenditures ($C_a + I_g + X_n + G$), Billions, (4) + (6) + (7) + (8)
(1) $370	$20	$350	$360	$−10	$20	$10	$10	$20	$400
(2) 390	20	370	375	−5	20	10	10	20	415
(3) 410	20	390	390	0	20	10	10	20	430
(4) 430	20	410	405	5	20	10	10	20	445
(5) 450	20	430	420	10	20	10	10	20	460
(6) 470	20	450	435	15	20	10	10	20	475
(7) **490**	**20**	**470**	**450**	**20**	**20**	**10**	**10**	**20**	**490**
(8) 510	20	490	465	25	20	10	10	20	505
(9) 530	20	510	480	30	20	10	10	20	520
(10) 550	20	530	495	35	20	10	10	20	535

in the private economy. But by how much will each decline as a result of the $20 billion in taxes? The MPC and MPS hold the answer: The MPC tells us what fraction of a decline in disposable income will come out of consumption, and the MPS indicates what fraction will come out of saving. Since the MPC is .75, if government collects $20 billion in taxes at each possible level of GDP, the amount of consumption at each level of GDP will drop by $15 billion (= .75 × $20 billion). Since the MPS is .25, the amount of saving at each level of GDP will drop by $5 billion (= .25 × $20 billion).

Columns 4 and 5 in Table 10.4 list the amounts of consumption and saving *at each level of GDP;* note that they are $15 billion and $5 billion smaller, respectively, than those in Table 10.3. For example, before taxes, where GDP equaled DI, consumption was $420 billion and saving $10 billion at the $430 billion level of GDP (row 4 in Table 10.3). After taxes are imposed, DI is $410 billion ($20 billion short of the $430 billion GDP), with the result that consumption is only $405 billion and saving is $5 billion (row 4, Table 10.4).

Taxes cause disposable income to fall short of GDP by the amount of the taxes. This decline in DI reduces both consumption and saving at each level of GDP. The MPC and the MPS determine the declines in C and S.

What is the effect of taxes on equilibrium GDP? To find out, we calculate aggregate expenditures again as shown in column 9, Table 10.4. Note there

that aggregate spending is $15 billion less at each level of GDP than it was in Table 10.3. The reason is that after-tax consumption, designated by C_a, is $15 billion less at each level of GDP. Comparing real output and aggregate expenditures in columns 1 and 9, we see that the aggregate amounts produced and purchased are equal only at $490 billion of GDP (row 7). The $20 billion lump-sum tax has caused equilibrium GDP to fall by $60 billion from $550 billion (row 10, Table 10.3) to $490 billion (row 7, Table 10.4).

Graphical Analysis In Figure 10.6 the $20 billion increase in taxes shows up as a $15 (not $20) billion decline in the aggregate expenditures ($C_a + I_g + X_n + G$) schedule. Under our assumption that all taxes are personal income taxes, this decline in aggregate expenditures results solely from a decline in the consumption C component of the aggregate expenditures schedule. The equilibrium GDP changes from $550 billion to $490 billion because of this tax-caused drop in consumption. *Increases in taxes lower the aggregate expenditures schedule relative to the 45° line and reduce the equilibrium GDP.*

In contrast to our previous case, a *decrease* in existing taxes will raise the aggregate expenditures schedule in Figure 10.6 as a result of an increase in consumption at all GDP levels. You should confirm that a tax reduction of $10 billion (from the present

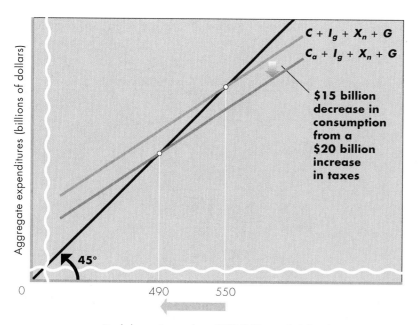

$C + I_g + X_n + G$

$C_a + I_g + X_n + G$

$15 billion decrease in consumption from a $20 billion increase in taxes

45°

0   490   550

Real domestic product, GDP (billions of dollars)

Aggregate expenditures (billions of dollars)

Figure 10.6

Taxes and equilibrium GDP. If the MPC is .75, the $20 billion of taxes will lower the consumption schedule by $15 billion and cause a decline in the equilibrium GDP. In the open economy with government, equilibrium GDP occurs where C_a (after-tax income) + I_g + X_n + G = GDP.

$20 billion to $10 billion) would increase the equilibrium GDP from $490 billion to $520 billion. **(Key Question 8)**

Injections, Leakages, and Unplanned Changes in Inventories

Table 10.4 and Figure 10.6 constitute the full aggregate expenditures model for an open economy with government. Equilibrium GDP occurs where $C_a + I_g + X_n + G =$ GDP. Moreover, the related characteristics of equilibrium that we noted for the private closed economy also apply to the expanded model. Injections into the income-expenditures stream equal leakages from the income stream. For the private closed economy, $S = I_g$. For the expanded economy, imports and taxes are added leakages. Saving, importing, and paying taxes are all uses of income that do not involve domestic consumption. Consumption will now be less than GDP—creating a potential spending gap—in the amount of after-tax saving (S_a), imports (M), and taxes (T). But exports (X) and government purchases (G), along with investment (I_g), are injections into the income-expenditures stream. At the equilibrium GDP, the sum of the leakages equals the sum of injections. In symbols:

$$S_a + M + T = I_g + X + G$$

You should use the data in Table 10.4 to confirm this equality between leakages and injections at the equilibrium GDP of $490 billion. Also, substantiate that a lack of such an equality exists at all other possible levels of GDP.

Although not directly shown in Table 10.4, the equilibrium characteristic of "no unplanned changes in inventories" will also be fulfilled at the $490 billion GDP. Because aggregate expenditures equal GDP, all the goods and services produced will be purchased. There will be no unplanned increase in inventories, so firms will have no incentive to reduce their employment and production. Nor will they experience an unplanned decline in their inventories, which would prompt them to expand their employment and output in order to replenish their inventories.

Balanced-Budget Multiplier

There is a curious thing about our tabular and graphical illustrations. *Equal increases in government spending and in taxation increase the equilibrium GDP. If G* and T *are each increased by a particular amount, the equilibrium level of real output will rise by the same amount.* In our example the $20 billion increase in G and the $20 billion rise in T cause the equilibrium GDP to increase by $20 billion (from $470 billion to $490 billion).

The rationale for this **balanced-budget multiplier** is revealed in our example. A change in government spending affects aggregate expenditures more powerfully than a tax change of the same size.

Government spending has a *direct* and unadulterated impact on aggregate expenditures. Government spending is a *direct* component of aggregate expenditures. So when government purchases increase by $20 billion, as in our example, the aggregate expenditures schedule shifts upward by the entire $20 billion.

But a change in taxes affects aggregate expenditures *indirectly* by changing disposable income and thereby changing consumption. Specifically, our lump-sum tax increase shifts the aggregate expenditures schedule downward only by the amount of the tax times the MPC. A $20 billion tax increase shifts the aggregate expenditures schedule downward by $15 billion (= $20 billion × .75).

The overall result is a *net* upward shift of the aggregate expenditures schedule of $5 billion that, subject to a multiplier of 4, boosts GDP by $20 billion. This $20 billion increase in GDP is equal to the size of the initial increase in government expenditures and taxes. Hence, *the balanced-budget multiplier is 1.*

Figure 10.7 clarifies that point. With an MPC of .75, the tax increase of $20 billion reduces disposable income by $20 billion and decreases consumption expenditures by $15 billion. The $15 billion decline in consumption expenditures *reduces* GDP by $60 billion (= $15 billion × the multiplier of 4). But observe in Figure 10.7 that the increase in government expenditures of $20 billion *increases* GDP by $80 billion (= $20 billion × the multiplier of 4). The equal increases of taxes and government expenditures of $20 billion thus yield a *net* increase in GDP of $20 billion (= $80 billion − $60 billion). *Equal increases in G and T expand GDP by an amount equal to those increases.*

This balanced-budget multiplier effect is not limited to situations in which the multiplier is 4. It holds no matter what the multiplier is—a fact that you should verify by experimenting with different MPCs and MPSs. The balanced-budget multiplier is always 1.

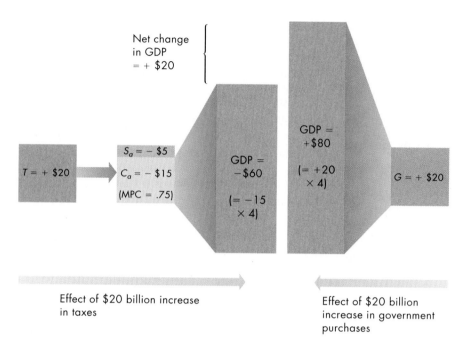

Figure 10.7

The balanced-budget multiplier. The balanced-budget multiplier is 1. An equal increase in taxes and government expenditures will increase GDP by an amount equal to the increase in the amount of government expenditures and taxes. Given an MPC of .75, a tax increase of $20 billion will reduce disposable income by $20 billion and will lower consumption expenditures by $15 billion. Because the multiplier is 4, GDP will therefore decline by $60 billion. The $20 billion increase in government expenditures, however, will produce an increase in GDP of $80 billion. The net increase in GDP will be $20 billion, which equals the amount of the increase in government expenditures and taxes.

■ Equilibrium versus Full-Employment GDP

Now that we have the complete aggregate expenditures model at our disposal, we can use it to evaluate the equilibrium GDP.

The $490 billion equilibrium GDP in our complete analysis (Table 10.4 and Figure 10.6) may or may not provide full employment. Indeed, our assumption thus far has been that the economy is operating at less than full employment.

Recessionary Gap

Assume in Figure 10.8a that the full-employment level of GDP is $510 billion and the aggregate expenditures schedule is AE_1. (For brevity, we will now dispense with the $C_a + I_g + X_n + G$ labeling.) This schedule intersects the 45° line to the left of the economy's full-employment output, so the economy's equilibrium GDP of $490 billion is $20 billion short of its full-employment output of $510 billion. According to column 1 in Table 9.4 of the previous chapter, total employment at the full-employment GDP is 75 million workers. But the economy depicted in Figure 10.8a is employing only 70 million workers; 5 million available workers are not employed. For that reason, the economy is sacrificing $20 billion of output.

The **recessionary gap** is the amount by which aggregate expenditures *at the full-employment GDP*

fall short of those required to achieve the full-employment GDP. This deficiency of spending contracts or depresses the economy. Table 10.4 shows that at the full-employment level of $510 billion (column 1), the corresponding level of aggregate expenditures is only $505 billion (column 9). The recessionary gap is thus $5 billion, the amount by which the aggregate expenditures curve would have to shift upward to realize equilibrium at the full-employment GDP. Graphically, the recessionary gap is the *vertical* distance (measured at the full-employment GDP) by which the actual aggregate expenditures schedule AE_1 lies below the hypothetical full-employment aggregate expenditures schedule AE_0. In Figure 10.8a this recessionary gap is $5 billion. Because the multiplier is 4, there is a $20 billion differential (the recessionary gap of $5 billion times the multiplier of 4) between the equilibrium GDP and the full-employment GDP. This $20 billion difference is the *GDP gap*—an idea we first developed when discussing cyclical unemployment (Figure 8.3).

Inflationary Gap

The **inflationary gap** is the amount by which an economy's aggregate expenditures *at the full-employment GDP* exceed those just necessary to achieve the full-employment GDP. In Figure 10.8b,

KEY GRAPH

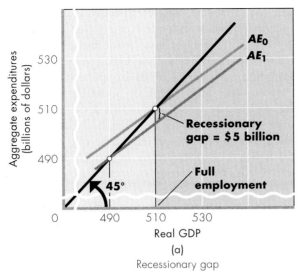

(a)
Recessionary gap

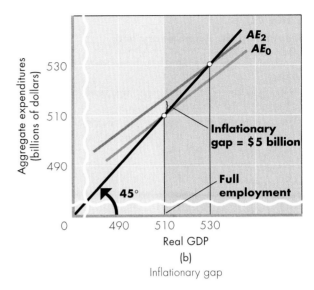

(b)
Inflationary gap

Figure 10.8

Recessionary and inflationary gaps. The equilibrium and full-employment GDPs may not coincide. (a) A recessionary gap is the amount by which aggregate expenditures at the full-employment GDP fall short of those needed to achieve the full-employment GDP. Here, the $5 billion recessionary gap causes a $20 billion GDP gap. (b) An inflationary gap is the amount by which aggregate expenditures at the full-employment GDP exceed those just sufficient to achieve the full-employment GDP. Here the inflationary gap is $5 billion; this overspending produces demand-pull inflation.

there is a $5 billion inflationary gap at the $510 billion full-employment GDP. This is shown by the vertical distance between the actual aggregate expenditures schedule AE_2 and the hypothetical schedule AE_0, which would be just sufficient to achieve the $510 billion full-employment GDP. Thus, the inflationary gap is the amount by which the aggregate expenditures schedule would have to shift downward to realize equilibrium at the full-employment GDP.

The effect of this inflationary gap—this excessive spending—is that it will pull up output prices. Since businesses cannot respond to the $5 billion in excessive spending by expanding their real output, demand-pull inflation will occur. Nominal GDP will rise because of a higher price level, but real GDP will not. Table 10.5 summarizes the steps for determining recessionary and inflationary gaps. (**Key Question 10**)

Table 10.5

Determining the Recessionary and Inflationary Gaps

Steps:

1. Determine the economy's full-employment GDP.
2. Look at the economy's current aggregate expenditures schedule, and from that schedule find the amount of expenditures that would be forthcoming at the economy's full-employment GDP.
3. Find the amount of expenditures just necessary to achieve the full-employment GDP.
4. Subtract the amount determined in step 2 from the amount determined in step 3. A negative difference reflects a recessionary gap; a positive difference reflects an inflationary gap.

QUICK REVIEW 10.3

▪ Government purchases shift the aggregate expenditures schedule upward and raise the equilibrium GDP.

▪ Taxes reduce disposable income, lower consumption spending and saving, shift the aggregate expenditures schedule downward, and reduce the equilibrium GDP.

▪ The balanced-budget multiplier is 1.

▪ A recessionary gap is the amount by which an economy's aggregate expenditures schedule must shift upward to achieve the full-employment GDP; the inflationary gap is the amount by which the economy's aggregate expenditures schedule must shift downward to eliminate demand-pull inflation and still achieve the full-employment GDP.

▪ Applications of the Model

Let's see how the ideas of recessionary and inflationary gaps apply to three major historical events, two in the United States and the other in Japan.

The Great Depression in the United States

In 1930 the most severe and prolonged depression of modern times began. In the United States, real GDP plummeted by nearly 40 percent in the first several years of the 1930s, and the unemployment rate rose from 3 to 25 percent. As late as 1939, real GDP was still only slightly above its level of 10 years before, and the unemployment rate was still 17 per-

cent. (As shown in Global Perspective 10.2, the Great Depression was worldwide.)

A sagging level of investment spending was the major factor that pushed the U.S. economy into the economic chaos of the 1930s. In real terms, gross investment spending shrank by about 90 percent. In Figure 10.8, we would depict this decline in investment as a large downward shift in the nation's aggregate expenditures schedule. The outcome in the 1930s was a historic decline in real GDP and a severe recessionary (depressionary) gap.

Several factors caused this steep decline in investment. Flush with the prosperity of the 1920s, businesses had overexpanded their production capacity. In particular, there was tremendous expansion of the automobile industry—and the related petroleum, rubber, steel, glass, and textile industries—that ended as the market for new autos became saturated. Business indebtedness also increased rapidly during the 1920s. So by the late 1920s much of the income of businesses was committed for the payment of interest and principal on past capital purchases and thus was not available for expenditures on new capital.

The 1920s experienced a boom in residential construction in response to population growth and to the housing demand that had been deferred because of the First World War. That investment spending began to level off as early as 1926, and by the late 1920s the construction industry had virtually collapsed.

The most striking aspect of the Great Depression was the stock market crash of October 1929. The optimism of the prosperous 1920s had elevated stock prices to the point where they did not reflect financial reality; they rose far beyond the profit-making potential of the firms they represented. A downward adjustment was necessary, and it came suddenly and quickly in 1929. The stock market crash did not *cause* the Great Depression—industrial production had begun its slide 2 months before the stock market crash. But the crash did have major repercussions. The falling stock market reduced household wealth and created a wave of consumer and business pessimism, which added to the decline in aggregate expenditures.

Moreover, the nation's money supply plummeted by 30 percent between 1929 and 1933. This shrinkage resulted from forces operating both abroad and at home, including inappropriate policies adopted by the Federal Reserve Banks. This drastic reduction of

Changes in Industrial Production, Selected Countries, 1929–1930 and 1937–1938

The Great Depression of the 1930s was global, with large declines in industrial output occurring in most countries. The Depression began in 1929–1930 for many countries. Precipitous declines in industrial output occurred again in some nations in 1937–1938.

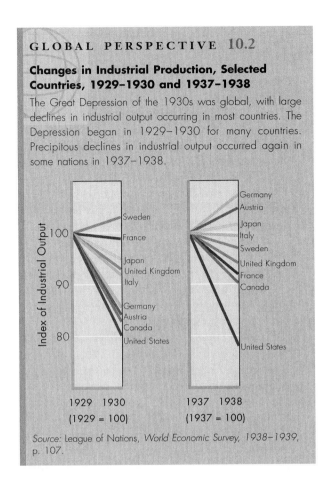

Source: League of Nations, *World Economic Survey, 1938–1939,* p. 107.

the money supply contributed heavily to a sharp decline in aggregate expenditures, including investment, which occurred in the early 1930s.

Vietnam War Inflation

The 1960s in the United States were a period of prolonged expansion of real GDP, fueled by increases in consumption spending and investment. A factor in that expansion was the revolution in economic policy that occurred during the Kennedy and Johnson administrations. This new policy called for the government to manipulate its tax collections and expenditures in such a way as to elevate aggregate expenditures, increasing employment and real GDP. For example, in 1962 legislation was enacted that provided for a 7 percent tax credit on investment in new machinery and equipment, thus strengthening the incentives of businesses to invest. In 1964 the government cut personal and corporate income taxes, boosting consumption spending and further increas-

ing investment spending. The unemployment rate fell from 5.2 percent in 1964 to 4.5 percent in 1965.

At this time another expansionary force came into play. The escalation of the war in Vietnam resulted in a 40 percent increase in government spending on national defense between 1965 and 1967. There was another 15 percent increase in war-related spending in 1968. Simultaneously, the draft drew more and more young people from the ranks of the unemployed.

The unemployment rate fell below 4 percent during the entire 1966–1969 period. But the increased government expenditures, imposed on an already booming economy, also brought about the worst inflation in two decades. Inflation jumped from 1.6 percent in 1965 to 5.7 percent by 1970. In terms of Figure 10.8, the rising investment and government expenditures shifted the aggregate expenditures schedule sharply upward, creating a sizable inflationary gap.

The End of the Japanese Growth "Miracle"

In the 1980s Japan was showing signs of replacing the United States as the world's leading economic power. For example, it had surpassed the United States in production of automobiles, televisions, motorcycles, electronics equipment, industrial robots, and cameras. Japan's extraordinarily high saving rate of nearly 15 percent, compared to 4 percent in the United States, diverted substantial amounts of resources from consumption to investment. The resulting rapid expansion of plant and equipment produced growth rates averaging 9.7 percent annually between 1966 and 1974 and 3.9 percent annually between 1974 and 1990. Very low rates of unemployment accompanied Japan's fast-growing economy. Its high growth and low unemployment were all the more miraculous because its infrastructure was destroyed in the Second World War, its population is large relative to its landmass, and its natural resource base is very limited.

But Japan's rapid economic growth ended in the 1990s when its economy slowed to a near halt and then became mired in its longest and deepest recession since the Second World War. Japan's real GDP grew very slowly in the first half of the 1990s and fell by 2.8 percent in 1998.

What happened? Although the answer is multifaceted, the main reason relates to the same high saving rate that enabled Japan's earlier fast growth.

As explained previously, it is imperative that all savings be borrowed and spent on current output. If planned investment spending is less than saving (and there are no compensating increases in net exports or government spending), aggregate expenditures $(AE = C_a + I_g + X_n + G)$ will be insufficient to purchase the output that is produced. Inventories will rise, firms will cut back production, and real GDP will fall. In short, there will be a recessionary gap such as that in Figure 10.8a.

That is exactly what happened in Japan. Although its high saving rates boosted long-run economic growth, they presented a short-run problem. Because of collapsing real estate prices, a failing financial system, and surging opportunities for investment in the United States and Europe, Japan was unable to sustain the high levels of domestic investment needed to "soak up" its large volume of saving. Hence, aggregate expenditures were insufficient to achieve the full-employment level of real output, meaning that a recessionary gap developed in the Japanese economy. Only in late 1999 did Japan show signs of recovery. Most economists believe that it will be many years before Japan can restore its historically high growth rates.

▌ Limitations of the Model

Our analysis and examples demonstrate the power of the aggregate expenditures model to help us understand how the economy works, how recessions or depressions can occur, and how demand-pull inflation can arise. But this model has four well-known limitations:

- **▪ *The model does not show price-level changes.*** It can account for demand-pull inflation, as in Figure 10.8b, but it does not indicate how much the price level will rise when aggregate expenditures are excessive relative to the economy's capacity. Will the $5 billion inflationary gap of Figure 10.8b cause a 3 percent, a 5 percent, a 10

percent, or some other rate of inflation? By how much will the GDP price index rise for each $1 billion of the inflationary gap? The aggregate expenditures model has no way of measuring the rate of inflation.

- **▪ *The model ignores premature demand-pull inflation.*** In Chapter 8, specifically Figure 8-5, we noted that mild demand-pull inflation can occur before an economy reaches its full-employment level of output. The aggregate expenditures model does not explain why that can happen. In Figure 10.8 the economy could move from $490 billion of expenditures and real GDP to the $510 billion full-employment level of GDP without inflation occurring. According to the aggregate expenditures model, inflation occurs only after the economy reaches its full-employment level of output—but that is not what always happens in reality.

- **▪ *The model bars real GDP beyond the full-employment level of output.*** We also know from prior discussions that for a time an actual economy can expand beyond its full-employment real GDP. The aggregate expenditures model does not allow for that possibility. In Figure 10.8b, the economy's real output cannot expand beyond the full-employment level of $510 billion, even though the aggregate expenditures schedule is AE_2. This high level of spending does not generate additional real output; according to the model, spending simply drives up inflation.

- **▪ *The model does not deal with cost-push inflation.*** We know from Chapter 8 that there are two general types of inflation: demand-pull inflation and cost-push inflation. The aggregate expenditures model does not address cost-push inflation.

In Chapter 11 we remedy these deficiencies while preserving the many valuable insights of the aggregate expenditures model.

Squaring the Economic Circle

Humorist Art Buchwald examines the multiplier.

WASHINGTON—The recession hit so fast that nobody knows exactly how it happened. One day we were the land of milk and honey and the next day we were the land of sour cream and food stamps.

This is one explanation.

Hofberger, the Chevy salesman in Tomcat, Va., a suburb of Washington, called up Littleton, of Littleton Menswear & Haberdashery, and said, "Good news, the new [Fords] have just come in and I've put one aside for you and your wife."

Littleton said, "I can't, Hofberger, my wife and I are getting a divorce."

"I'm sorry," Littleton said, "but I can't afford a new car this year. After I settle with my wife, I'll be lucky to buy a bicycle."

Hofberger hung up. His phone rang a few minutes later.

"This is Bedcheck the painter," the voice on the other end said. "When do you want us to start painting your house?"

"I changed my mind," said Hofberger, "I'm not going to paint the house."

"But I ordered the paint," Bedcheck said. "Why did you change your mind?"

"Because Littleton is getting a divorce and he can't afford a new car."

That evening when Bedcheck came home his wife said, "The new color television set arrived from Gladstone's TV Shop."

"Take it back," Bedcheck told his wife.

"Why?" she demanded.

"Because Hofberger isn't going to have his house painted now that the Littletons are getting a divorce."

The next day Mrs. Bedcheck dragged the TV set in its carton back to Gladstone. "We don't want it."

Gladstone's face dropped. He immediately called his travel agent, Sandstorm. "You know that trip you had scheduled for me to the Virgin Islands?"

"Right, the tickets are all written up."

"Cancel it. I can't go. Bedcheck just sent back the color TV set because Hofberger didn't sell a car to Littleton because they're going to get a divorce and she wants all his money."

Sandstorm tore up the airline tickets and went over to see his banker, Gripsholm. "I can't pay back the loan this month because Gladstone isn't going to the Virgin Islands."

Gripsholm was furious. When Rudemaker came in to borrow money for a new kitchen he needed for his restaurant, Gripsholm turned him down cold. "How can I loan you money when Sandstorm hasn't repaid the money he borrowed?"

Rudemaker called up the contractor, Eagleton, and said he couldn't put in a new kitchen. Eagleton laid off eight men.

Meanwhile, General Motors announced it was giving a rebate on its new models. Hofberger called up Littleton immediately. "Good news," he said, "even if you are getting a divorce, you can afford a new car."

"I'm not getting a divorce," Littleton said. "It was all a misunderstanding and we've made up."

"That's great," Hofberger said. "Now you can buy the [Ford]."

"No way," said Littleton. "My business has been so lousy I don't know why I keep the doors open."

"I didn't realize that," Hofberger said.

"Do you realize I haven't seen Bedcheck, Gladstone, Sandstorm, Gripsholm, Rudemaker or Eagleton for more than a month? How can I stay in business if they don't patronize my store?"

Source: Art Buchwald, "Squaring the Economic Circle," *Cleveland Plain Dealer*, Feb. 22, 1975. Reprinted by permission.

SUMMARY

1. A shift in the investment schedule (caused by a change in the expected rate of return or a change in the interest rate) shifts the aggregate expenditures curve and alters the equilibrium level of real GDP. Real GDP changes by more than the amount of the initial change in investment. This multiplier effect ($\Delta \text{GDP}/\Delta I_g$) accompanies both increases and decreases in aggregate expenditures and also applies to changes in net exports (X_n) and government purchases (G).

2. The multiplier is equal to the reciprocal of the marginal propensity to save: The greater is the marginal propensity to save, the smaller is the multiplier. Also, the greater is the marginal propensity to consume, the larger is the multiplier.

3. The net export schedule relates net exports (exports minus imports) to levels of real GDP. For simplicity, we assume that the level of net exports is the same at all levels of real GDP.

4. Positive net exports increase aggregate expenditures to a higher level than they would be if the economy were "closed" to international trade. They raise equilibrium real GDP by a multiple of the net exports. Negative net exports decrease aggregate expenditures relative to those in a closed economy, decreasing equilibrium real GDP by a multiple of their amount. Increases in exports or decreases in imports have an expansionary effect on real GDP, while decreases in exports or increases in imports have a contractionary effect.

5. Government purchases shift the aggregate expenditures schedule upward and raise GDP.

6. Taxation reduces disposable income, lowers consumption spending *and* saving, shifts the aggregate expenditures curve downward, and reduces equilibrium GDP.

7. In the complete aggregate expenditures model, equilibrium GDP occurs where $C_a + I_g + X_n + G =$ GDP. At the equilibrium GDP, *leakages* of after-tax saving (S_a), imports (M), and taxes (T) equal *injections* of investment (I_g), exports (X), and government purchases (G). Also, there are no unplanned changes in inventories.

8. The equilibrium GDP and the full-employment GDP may differ. The recessionary gap is the amount by which aggregate expenditures at the full-employment GDP fall short of those needed to achieve the full-employment GDP. This gap produces a magnified GDP gap (actual GDP minus potential GDP). The inflationary gap is the amount by which aggregate expenditures at the full-employment GDP exceed those just sufficient to achieve the full-employment GDP. This gap causes demand-pull inflation.

9. The Great Depression of the 1930s resulted from a precipitous decline in aggregate expenditures that produced a severe and long-lasting recessionary (depressionary) gap. In the Vietnam war period, an abrupt increase in aggregate expenditures caused by war spending led to a sizable inflationary gap, with its accompanying demand-pull inflation. In the 1990s, aggregate expenditures in Japan fell short of those needed to achieve full-employment real GDP. The result was a sizable recessionary gap.

10. The aggregate expenditures model provides many insights into the macroeconomy, but it does not (a) show price-level changes, (b) account for premature demand-pull inflation, (c) allow for real GDP to temporarily expand beyond the full-employment output, or (d) account for cost-push inflation.

TERMS AND CONCEPTS

multiplier	lump-sum tax	balanced-budget multiplier	recessionary gap
net exports			inflationary gap

STUDY QUESTIONS

1. What effect will each of the changes listed in Study Question 3 of Chapter 9 have on the equilibrium level of GDP? Explain your answers.

2. **Key Question** What is the multiplier effect? What relationship does the MPC bear to the size of the multiplier? The MPS? What will the multiplier be when the MPS is 0, .4, .6, and 1? What will it be when the MPC is 1, .90, .67, .50, and 0? How much of a change in GDP will result if firms increase their

level of investment by $8 billion and the MPC is .80? If the MPC is .67? Explain the difference between the simple multiplier and the complex multiplier.

3. Depict graphically the aggregate expenditures model for a private closed economy. Now show a decrease in the aggregate expenditures schedule, and explain why the decline in real GDP in your diagram is greater than the initial decline in aggregate expenditures. What would be the ratio of a decline in real GDP to

the initial drop in aggregate expenditures if the slope of your aggregate expenditures schedule was .8?

4. Suppose that Zumo has an MPC of .9 and a real GDP of $400 billion. If its investment spending decreases by $4 billion, what will be its new real GDP?

5. **Key Question** The data in columns 1 and 2 in the accompanying table are for a private closed economy:

a. Graph this consumption schedule and determine the MPC.

b. Assume now that a lump-sum tax is imposed such that the government collects $10 billion in taxes at all levels of GDP. Graph the resulting consumption schedule, and compare the MPC and the multiplier with those of the pretax consumption schedule.

(1) Real Domestic Output (GDP = DI), Billions	(2) Aggregate Expenditures, Private Closed Economy, Billions	(3) Exports, Billions	(4) Imports, Billions	(5) Net Exports, Billions	(6) Aggregate Expenditures, Private Open Economy, Billions
$200	$240	$20	$30	$_____	$_____
250	280	20	30	_____	_____
300	320	20	30	_____	_____
350	360	20	30	_____	_____
400	400	20	30	_____	_____
450	440	20	30	_____	_____
500	480	20	30	_____	_____
550	520	20	30	_____	_____

a. Use columns 1 and 2 to determine the equilibrium GDP for this hypothetical economy.

b. Now open up this economy to international trade by including the export and import figures of columns 3 and 4. Fill in columns 5 and 6 and determine the equilibrium GDP for the open economy. Explain why this equilibrium GDP differs from that of the closed economy.

c. Given the original $20 billion level of exports, what would be the equilibrium GDP if imports were $10 billion greater at each level of GDP? Or $10 billion less at each level of GDP? What generalization concerning the level of imports and the equilibrium GDP do these examples illustrate?

d. What is the multiplier in these examples?

6. Assume that, without taxes, the consumption schedule of an economy is as follows:

GDP, Billions	Consumption, Billions
$100	$120
200	200
300	280
400	360
500	440
600	520
700	600

7. Explain graphically the determination of equilibrium GDP for a private economy through the aggregate expenditures model. Now add government spending (any amount you choose) to your graph, showing its impact on equilibrium GDP. Finally, add taxation (any amount of lump-sum tax that you choose) to your graph and show its effect on equilibrium GDP. Looking at your graph, determine whether equilibrium GDP has increased, decreased, or stayed the same given the sizes of the government spending and taxes that you selected.

8. **Key Question** Refer to columns 1 and 6 in the table for question 5. Incorporate government into the table by assuming that it plans to tax and spend $20 billion at each possible level of GDP. Also assume that the tax is a personal tax and that government spending does not induce a shift in the private aggregate expenditures schedule. Compute and explain the change in equilibrium GDP caused by the addition of government.

9. What is the balanced-budget multiplier? Demonstrate the balanced-budget multiplier in terms of your answer to question 8. Explain: "Equal increases in government spending and tax revenues of *n* dollars will increase the equilibrium GDP by *n* dollars." Does this hold true regardless of the size of the MPS? Why or why not?

10. **Key Question** Refer to the table below in answering the questions that follow:

(1) Possible Levels of Employment, Billions	(2) Real Domestic Output, Billions	(3) Aggregate Expenditures $(C_a + I_g + X_n + G)$, Billions
90	$500	$520
100	550	560
110	600	600
120	650	640
130	700	680

a. If full employment in this economy is 130 million, will there be an inflationary or a recessionary gap? What will be the consequence of this gap? By how much would aggregate expenditures in column 3 have to change at each level of GDP to eliminate the inflationary or the recessionary gap? Explain.

b. Will there be an inflationary or a recessionary gap if the full-employment level of output is $500 billion? Explain the consequences. By how much would aggregate expenditures in column 3 have to change at each level of GDP to eliminate the inflationary or the recessionary gap?

c. Assuming that investment, net exports, and government expenditures do not change with changes in real GDP, what are the sizes of the MPC, the MPS, and the multiplier?

11. **Advanced Analysis** Assume that the consumption schedule for a private open economy is such that consumption $C = 50 + 0.8Y$. Assume further that planned investment I_g and net exports X_n are independent of the level of real GDP and constant at $I_g = 30$ and $X_n = 10$. Recall that, in equilibrium, the real output produced (Y) is equal to aggregate expenditures: $Y = C + I_g + X_n$.

a. Calculate the equilibrium level of income or real GDP for this economy. Check your work by expressing the consumption, investment, and net export schedules in tabular form and determining the equilibrium GDP.

b. What happens to equilibrium Y if I_g changes to 10? What does this outcome reveal about the size of the multiplier?

12. **(Last Word)** What is the central economic idea humorously illustrated in Art Buchwald's piece, "Squaring the Economic Circle"?

13. **Web-Based Question:** *The multiplier—calculate a hypothetical change in GDP* Go to the Bureau of Economic Analysis website at www.bea.doc.gov and select GDP and Related Data and Selected NIPA Tables to find the most recent values for real GDP = $C_a + I_g + G + (X - M)$. Assume that the MPC is .75 and that, for each of the following, the values of the initial variables are those you just discovered. Determine the new value of GDP if, other things equal:

a. Investment increased by 5 percent.

b. Imports increased by 5 percent while exports increased by 5 percent.

c. Consumption increased by 5 percent.

d. Government spending increased by 5 percent. Which of the changes, *a* through *d*, caused the greatest change in GDP in absolute dollars?

14. **Web-Based Question:** *Of GDP gaps and recessionary gaps* The St. Louis Federal Reserve Bank website, www.stls.frb.org/fred/index.html, provides data on both real GDP and potential real GDP for the United States. Both are located as links under "Gross Domestic Product and Components." What was potential GDP for the fourth quarter of 1991? (Tip: Potential GDP is at the very bottom of the listing.) What was the actual level of real GDP for that quarter? What was the size difference between the two—the GDP gap? Assuming that the multiplier was 2.5 in that period, determine the size of the economy's recessionary gap.

CHAPTER 11

Aggregate Demand and Aggregate Supply

IN EARLY 2000, Alan Greenspan, chair of the Federal Reserve Board, stated:

> Through the so-called wealth effect, [huge gains in the stock market] have tended to foster increases in aggregate demand beyond the increases in supply. It is this imbalance . . . that contains the potential seeds of rising inflationary . . . pressures that could undermine the current expansion. . . . Our goal [at the Federal Reserve] is to extend the expansion by containing its imbalances and avoiding the very recession that would complete the business cycle.[1]

This is precisely the language of the **aggregate demand–aggregate supply (AD-AS) model** that we will develop in this chapter. The aggregate expenditures model of Chapters 9 and 10 is a *fixed-price-level model*—it emphasizes changes in real GDP. The AD-AS model is a *variable-price-level model* that enables us to analyze changes in both real GDP and the price level simultaneously. The AD-AS model builds on the aggregate expenditures model and provides numerous insights on inflation, unemployment, and economic growth. In later chapters, we will see that it also explains the logic of macroeconomic stabilization policies.

[1]Alan Greenspan, speech to the New York Economics Club, Jan. 13, 2000.

Aggregate Demand

Aggregate demand is a schedule or curve that shows the amounts of real output that buyers collectively desire to purchase at each possible price level. The relationship between the price level and the amount of real GDP demanded is inverse or negative: When the price level rises, the quantity of real GDP demanded decreases; when the price level falls, the quantity of real GDP demanded increases.

Aggregate Demand Curve

The inverse relationship between the price level and real GDP is shown in Figure 11.1, where the aggregate demand curve AD slopes downward, as does the demand curve for an individual product.

Why the downward slope? *The explanation is not the same as that for why the demand for a single product slopes downward.* That explanation centered on the income effect and the substitution effect. When the

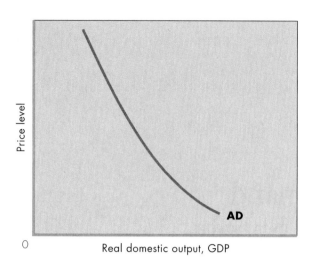

Figure 11.1

The aggregate demand curve. The downsloping aggregate demand curve AD indicates an inverse relationship between the price level and the amount of real output purchased.

price of an *individual* product falls, the consumer's (constant) nominal income allows a larger purchase of the product (the income effect). And, as price falls, the consumer wants to buy more of the product because it becomes relatively less expensive than other goods (the substitution effect).

But these explanations do not work for aggregates. In Figure 11.1, when the economy moves down its aggregate demand curve, it moves to a lower general price level. But our circular flow model tells us that when consumers pay lower prices for goods and services, less nominal income flows to resource suppliers in the form of wages, rents, interest, and profits. As a result, a decline in the price level does not necessarily mean an increase in the nominal income of the economy as a whole. Thus, a decline in the price level need not produce an income effect, where more output is purchased because lower prices leave buyers with greater real income.

Similarly, in Figure 11.1 prices in general are falling as we move down the aggregate demand curve, so the rationale for the substitution effect (where more of a product is purchased because it becomes cheaper relative to all other products) is not applicable. There is no *overall* substitution effect among domestically produced goods when the price level falls.

If the conventional substitution and income effects do not explain the downward slope of the aggregate demand curve, what does? That explanation rests on three effects of a price-level change. 🔑 11.1

Real-Balances Effect A change in the price level produces a **real-balances effect.** Here is how it works: A higher price level reduces the real value or purchasing power of the public's accumulated saving balances. In particular, the real value of assets with fixed money values, such as savings accounts or bonds, diminishes. Because of the erosion of the purchasing power of such assets, the public is poorer in real terms and will reduce its spending. A household might buy a new car or a sailboat if the purchasing power of its financial asset balances is, say, $50,000. But if inflation erodes the purchasing power of its asset balances to $30,000, the family may defer its purchase. So a higher price level means less consumption spending.

Interest-Rate Effect The aggregate demand curve also slopes downward because of the **interest-rate effect.** When we draw an aggregate demand curve, *we assume that the supply of money in the economy is fixed.* But when the price level rises, consumers need more money for purchases and businesses need more money to meet their payrolls and to buy other resources. A $10 bill will do when the price of an item is $10, but a $10 bill plus a $1 bill is needed when the item costs $11. In short, a higher price level increases the demand for money. So, given a fixed supply of money, an increase in money demand will drive up the price paid for its use. That price is the interest rate.

Higher interest rates curtail investment spending and interest-sensitive consumption spending. Firms that expect a 6 percent rate of return on a potential purchase of capital will find that investment profitable when the interest rate is, say, 5 percent. But the investment will be unprofitable and will not be made when the interest rate has risen to 7 percent. Similarly, consumers may decide not to purchase a new house or new automobile when the interest rate on loans goes up. So, by increasing the demand for money and consequently the interest rate, a higher price level reduces the amount of real output demanded.

Foreign Purchases Effect The final reason why the aggregate demand curve slopes downward is the **foreign purchases effect.** When the U.S. price level rises relative to foreign price levels, foreigners buy fewer U.S. goods and Americans buy more foreign goods. Therefore U.S. exports fall and U.S. imports rise. In short, the rise in the price level reduces the quantity of U.S. goods demanded as net exports.

These three effects, of course, work in the opposite direction for a decline in the price level. Then the quantity demanded of consumption goods, investment goods, and net exports rises.

Derivation of the Aggregate Demand Curve from the Aggregate Expenditures Model[2]

We can derive the downward-sloping aggregate demand curve of Figure 11.1 directly from the aggregate expenditures model discussed in Chapters 9 and 10. We simply need to relate the various possible price levels to corresponding equilibrium GDPs.

---

[2]This section presumes knowledge of the aggregate expenditures model discussed in Chapters 9 and 10 and may be skipped by readers who were not assigned those chapters.

Note that in Figure 11.2 we have stacked the aggregate expenditures model (Figure 11.2a) and the aggregate demand curve (Figure 11.2b) vertically. We can do this because the horizontal axes of both models measure real GDP. Now let's derive the AD curve in three distinct steps. (Throughout this discussion, keep in mind that price level P_1 < price level P_2 < price level P_3.)

- First suppose that the economy's price level is P_1 and its aggregate expenditures schedule is AE_1, the top schedule in Figure 11.2a. The equilibrium GDP is then GDP_1 at point 1. So in Figure 11.2b we can plot the equilibrium real-output GDP_1 and the corresponding price level P_1. This gives us point 1′ in Figure 11.2b.

- Now assume the price level rises from P_1 to P_2. Other things equal, this higher price level will (1) decrease the value of wealth, decreasing

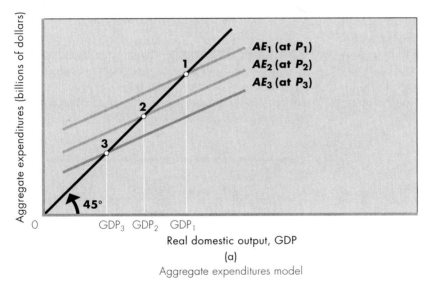

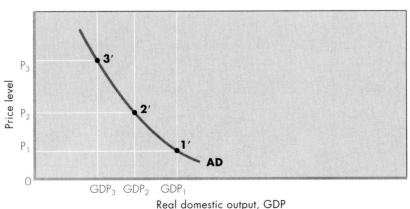

Figure 11.2

Deriving the aggregate demand curve from the expenditures-output model. Through the real-balances, interest-rate, and foreign purchases effects, the aggregate expenditures schedule will fall when the price level rises and will rise when the price level falls. If the aggregate expenditures schedule is AE_1 when the price level is P_1, the equilibrium output is GDP_1; then P_1 and GDP_1 determine one point (1′) on the aggregate demand curve. A higher price level such as P_2 reduces aggregate expenditures to AE_2, providing point 2′ on the aggregate demand curve. Similarly, an increase in the price level from P_2 to P_3 drops aggregate expenditures to AE_3, so P_3 and GDP_3 yield another point on the aggregate demand curve at 3′.

consumption expenditures; (2) increase the interest rate, reducing investment and interest-sensitive consumption expenditures; and (3) increase imports and decrease exports, reducing net export expenditures. The aggregate expenditures schedule will fall from AE_1 to, say, AE_2 in Figure 11.2a, giving us equilibrium GDP_2 at point 2. In Figure 11.2b we plot this new price-level–real-output combination, P_2 and GDP_2, as point 2'.

■   Finally, suppose the price level rises from P_2 to P_3. The value of real balances falls, the interest rate rises, exports fall, and imports rise. Consequently, the consumption, investment, and net export schedules fall, shifting the aggregate expenditures schedule downward from AE_2 to AE_3, which gives us equilibrium GDP_3 at point 3. In Figure 11.2b, this enables us to locate point 3', where the price level is P_3 and real output is GDP_3.

In summary, increases in the economy's price level will successively shift its aggregate expenditures schedule downward and will reduce real GDP. The resulting price-level–real GDP combinations will yield various points such as 1', 2', and 3' in Figure 11.2b. Together, such points locate the downward-sloping aggregate demand curve for the economy.

Determinants of Aggregate Demand

Other things equal, a change in the price level will change the amount of aggregate spending and therefore change the amount of real GDP demanded by the economy. Movements along a fixed aggregate demand curve represent these changes in real GDP. However, if one or more of those "other things" change, the entire aggregate demand curve will shift. We call these other things **determinants of aggregate demand** or, less formally, *aggregate demand shifters.*

In Figure 11.3, the rightward shift of the curve from AD_1 to AD_2 shows an increase in aggregate demand. At each price level, the amount of real goods and services demanded is larger than before. The leftward shift of the curve from AD_1 to AD_3 shows a decrease in aggregate demand, the lesser amount of real GDP demanded at each price level.

Let's examine each of the determinants of aggregate demand that are listed in Figure 11.3.

Consumer Spending
Even when the U.S. price level is constant, domestic consumers may alter their purchases of U.S.-produced real output. If consumers decide to buy more output at each price level, the aggregate demand curve will shift to the right, as

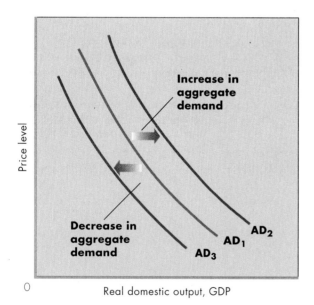

Determinants of Aggregate Demand: Factors that Shift the Aggregate Demand Curve

1. Change in consumer spending
   a. Consumer wealth
   b. Consumer expectations
   c. Household indebtedness
   d. Taxes
2. Change in investment spending
   a. Interest rates
   b. Expected returns
      ■ Expected future business conditions
      ■ Technology
      ■ Degree of excess capacity
      ■ Business taxes
3. Change in government spending
4. Change in net export spending
   a. National income abroad
   b. Exchange rates

Figure 11.3

Changes in aggregate demand.   A change in one or more of the listed determinants of aggregate demand will change aggregate demand. An increase in aggregate demand is shown as a rightward shift of the AD curve, here from AD_1 to AD_2; a decrease in aggregate demand is shown as a leftward shift, here from AD_1 to AD_3.

from AD$_1$ to AD$_2$ in Figure 11.3. If they decide to buy less output, the aggregate demand curve will shift to the left, as from AD$_1$ to AD$_3$.

Several factors other than a change in the price level may change consumer spending and thus shift the aggregate demand curve. As Figure 11.3 shows, those factors are real consumer wealth, consumer expectations, household indebtedness, and taxes.

Consumer Wealth   Consumer wealth includes both financial assets, such as stocks and bonds, and physical assets, such as houses and land. A sharp increase in the real value of consumer wealth (for example, because of a rise in stock market values) prompts people to save less and buy more products. The resulting increase in consumer spending—called the *wealth effect*—will shift the aggregate demand curve to the right. In contrast, a major decrease in the real value of consumer wealth at each price level will reduce consumption spending and thus shift the aggregate demand curve to the left.

Consumer Expectations   Changes in expectations about the future may alter consumer spending. When people expect their future real incomes to rise, they spend more of their current incomes. Thus current consumption spending increases (current saving falls), and the aggregate demand curve shifts to the right. Similarly, a widely held expectation of surging inflation in the near future may increase aggregate demand today because consumers will want to buy products before their prices escalate. Conversely, expectations of lower future income or lower future prices may reduce current consumption and shift the aggregate demand curve to the left.

Household Indebtedness   Households finance some of their spending by borrowing. If household indebtedness from past spending rises beyond normal levels, consumers may be forced to cut current spending in order to pay the interest and principle on their debt. Consumption spending will then decline, and the aggregate demand curve will shift to the left. Alternatively, when household indebtedness is unusually low, consumers have considerable leeway to borrow and spend today. Then the aggregate demand curve may shift to the right.

Taxes   A reduction in personal income tax rates raises take-home income and increases consumer purchases at each possible price level. Tax cuts shift

the aggregate demand curve to the right. Tax increases reduce consumption spending and shift the curve to the left.

Investment Spending   Investment spending (the purchase of capital goods) is a second major determinant of aggregate demand. A decline in investment spending at each price level will shift the aggregate demand curve to the left. An increase in investment spending will shift it to the right. In Chapter 9 we saw that investment spending depends on the real interest rate and the expected return from the investment.

Real Interest Rates   Other things equal, an increase in interest rates will lower investment spending and reduce aggregate demand. We are not referring here to the "interest-rate effect" resulting from a change in the price level. Instead, we are identifying a change in the interest rate resulting from, say, a change in the nation's money supply. An increase in the money supply lowers the interest rate, thereby increasing investment and aggregate demand. A decrease in the money supply raises the interest rate, reduces investment, and decreases aggregate demand.

Expected Returns   Higher expected returns on investment projects will increase the demand for capital goods and shift the aggregate demand curve to the right. Alternatively, declines in expected returns will decrease investment and shift the curve to the left. Expected returns, in turn, are influenced by several factors:

- ***Expectations about future business conditions*** If firms are optimistic about future business conditions, they are more likely to forecast high rates of return on current investment and therefore may invest more today. On the other hand, if they think the economy will deteriorate in the future, they will forecast low rates of return and perhaps will invest less today.
- ***Technology*** New and improved technologies enhance expected returns on investment and thus increase aggregate demand. For example, recent advances in microbiology have motivated pharmaceutical companies to establish new labs and production facilities.
- ***Degree of excess capacity*** A rise in excess capacity—unused capital—will reduce the expected return on new investment and hence decrease aggregate demand. Other things equal,

firms operating factories at well below capacity have little incentive to build new factories. But when firms discover that their excess capacity is dwindling or has completely disappeared, their expected returns on new investment in factories and capital equipment rises. Thus, they increase their investment spending, and the aggregate demand curve shifts to the right.

- **Business taxes** An increase in business taxes will reduce after-tax profits from capital investment and will lower expected returns. So investment and aggregate demand will decline. A decrease in business taxes will have the opposite effects.

Government Spending Government purchases are the third determinant of aggregate demand. An increase in government purchases (for example, more computers for government agencies) will shift the aggregate demand curve to the right, as long as tax collections and interest rates do not change as a result. In contrast, a reduction in government spending (for example, a cutback in orders for military hardware) will shift the curve to the left.

Net Export Spending The final determinant of aggregate demand is net export spending. A greater level of U.S. *exports* constitutes an increased foreign demand for U.S. goods, whereas a lesser level of U.S. *imports* implies that American consumers have increased their demand for U.S.-produced products. So a rise in net exports (higher exports and/or lower imports) shifts the aggregate demand curve to the right. In contrast, a decrease in U.S. net exports shifts the aggregate demand curve leftward. (These changes in net exports are *not* those prompted by a change in the U.S. price level—those associated with the foreign purchases effect. The changes here explain shifts in the curve, not movements along the curve.)

What might cause net exports to change, other than the price level? Two possibilities are changes in national income abroad and changes in exchange rates.

National Income Abroad Rising national income abroad encourages foreigners to buy more products, some of which are made in the United States. U.S. net exports thus rise, and the U.S. aggregate demand curve shifts to the right. Declines in national income abroad, of course, do the opposite:

They reduce U.S. net exports and shift the U.S. aggregate demand curve to the left.

Exchange Rates Changes in exchange rates (Chapter 6) may affect U.S. net exports and therefore aggregate demand. Suppose the dollar depreciates in terms of the euro (the euro appreciates in terms of the dollar). The new relative lower value of dollars and higher value of euros enable European consumers to obtain more dollars with each euro. From their perspective, U.S. goods are now less expensive; it takes fewer euros to obtain them. So European consumers buy more U.S. goods and U.S. exports rise. But American consumers can now obtain fewer euros for each dollar. Because they must pay more dollars to buy European goods, Americans reduce their imports. U.S. exports rise and U.S. imports fall. *Depreciation* of the dollar increases U.S. net exports, thereby shifting the U.S. aggregate demand curve to the right.

Think through the opposite scenario, in which the dollar *appreciates* and the euro depreciates.

Aggregate Demand Shifts and the Aggregate Expenditures Model[3]

The determinants of aggregate demand listed in Figure 11.3 are the components of the aggregate expenditures model discussed in Chapter 10. When one of those determinants changes, the aggregate expenditures schedule shifts too. We can easily link such shifts in the aggregate expenditures schedule to shifts of the aggregate demand curve.

Let's suppose that the price level is constant. In Figure 11.4 we begin with the aggregate expenditures schedule at AE_1 in the top diagram, yielding real output of GDP_1. Assume now that investment spending increases in response to more optimistic business expectations, so the aggregate expenditures schedule rises from AE_1 to AE_2. (The notation "at P_1" reminds us that the price level is assumed to be constant.) The result will be a multiplied increase in real output from GDP_1 to GDP_2.

In the lower graph the increase in investment spending is reflected in the horizontal distance between AD_1 and the broken curve to its right. The immediate effect of the increase in investment is an increase in aggregate demand by the exact amount

---

[3]This section presumes knowledge of the aggregate expenditures model (Chapters 9 and 10).

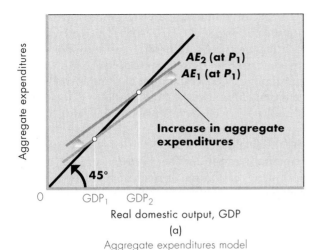

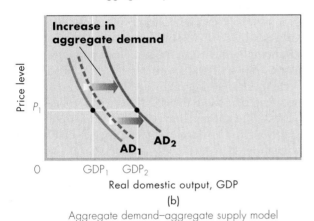

Figure 11.4

Shifts in the aggregate expenditures schedule and in the aggregate demand curve. (a) A change in some determinant of consumption, investment, or net exports (other than the price level) shifts the aggregate expenditures schedule up-ward from AE_1 to AE_2. The multiplier increases real output from GDP_1 to GDP_2. (b) The counterpart of this change is an initial rightward shift of the aggregate demand curve by the amount of initial new spending (from AD_1 to the broken curve). This leads to a multiplied rightward shift of the curve to AD_2, which is just sufficient to show the same increase in GDP as in the aggregate expenditures model.

of the new spending. But then the multiplier process magnifies the initial increase in investment into successive rounds of consumption spending and an ultimate multiplied increase in aggregate demand from AD_1 to AD_2. Equilibrium real output rises from GDP_1 to GDP_2, the same multiplied increase in real GDP as that in the top graph. The initial increase in investment in the top graph has shifted the AD curve in the lower graph by a horizontal distance equal to the change in investment times the

multiplier. This particular change in real GDP is still associated with the constant price level P_1. To generalize,

$$\text{Shift of AD curve} = \text{initial change in spending} \times \text{multiplier}$$

QUICK REVIEW 11.1

■ Aggregate demand reflects an inverse relationship between the price level and the amount of real output demanded.

■ Changes in the price level create real-balances, interest-rate, and foreign purchases effects that explain the downward slope of the aggregate demand curve.

■ Changes in one or more of the determinants of aggregate demand (Figure 11.3) alter the amounts of real GDP demanded at each price level; they shift the aggregate demand curve.

■ An increase in aggregate demand is shown as a rightward shift of the aggregate demand curve; a decrease, as a leftward shift of the curve.

■ Aggregate Supply

Aggregate supply is a schedule or a curve showing the level of real domestic output that firms will produce at each price level. Higher price levels create an incentive for firms to produce and sell more output, while lower price levels prompt them to reduce output. As a result, there is a direct or positive relationship between the price level and the amount of real output that firms offer for sale.

Aggregate Supply Curve

For now, think of the aggregate supply curve as having three distinct segments or ranges: (1) the horizontal range, (2) the intermediate (upsloping) range, and (3) the vertical range. The shape of the aggregate supply curve reflects what happens to the per-unit production cost as GDP expands or contracts. Recall from Chapter 8 that the per-unit production cost is found by dividing the total cost of all the resources used in production by the total quantity of output. That is, the per-unit production cost of a particular level of output is the average cost of that output. And the average cost of output establishes that output's price level because the price level must cover all the costs of production, including profit "costs."

With that background, let's examine the three ranges shown in Figure 11.5 and see what each represents. (Until later chapters, we assume the aggregate supply curve itself does not shift when the price level changes.)

Horizontal Range   In Figure 11.5 we designate the full-employment real output as Q_f. That is the output at which the *natural rate of unemployment* (Chapter 8) occurs. Observe in the figure that the **horizontal range** (*ab*) of aggregate supply includes only levels of real output that are substantially less than the full-employment output Q_f. Thus, the horizontal range implies that the economy is in a recession or depression and has large amounts of unused machinery and equipment and unemployed workers available for production. Firms can put these idle human and property resources back to work with no upward pressure on the price level. As output expands over this range from *a* to *b*, no shortages or production bottlenecks will arise to raise prices. Workers unemployed for 2 or 3 months will hardly expect a wage increase when recalled to their jobs. Because producers can acquire labor and other inputs at stable prices, per-unit production costs will stay constant as firms expand output up to Q_u. So firms will have no reason to raise product prices.

This horizontal range also implies that if real output falls, product and resource prices will not move downward. So, although real output and employment may fall, product prices and wages will remain rigid. Indeed, real output and employment will decline in this range because prices and wages are inflexible. We will say more about this later.

Intermediate (Upsloping) Range   In the **intermediate range** (*bc*) between Q_u and Q_c, an expansion of real output is accompanied by a rising price level. The aggregate economy is made up of innumerable product and resource markets, and full employment is not reached evenly or simultaneously in all the industries. Example: As the economy expands in real-output range *bc*, the high-tech computer industry may encounter shortages of skilled workers while the steel industry still faces substantial unemployment. At the same time, in certain industries raw-material shortages or other production bottlenecks may begin to appear. Expansion may also mean that some firms will be forced to use older and less efficient machinery as they approach capacity production. And adding employees may create congestion in workplaces, reducing each worker's output. Perhaps, too, less capable workers may be hired as output expands. All these factors tend to increase per-unit production costs and boost prices as production increases in range *bc*.

Once the full-employment level of GDP is reached at Q_f, further price-level increases may bring forth added real output for a time. We know from Chapter 8 that employment and real GDP can expand beyond the full-employment level of output until the economy reaches its maximum capacity. That is, actual GDP can occasionally exceed full-employment GDP. In a prosperous economy, the size of the labor force, daily working hours, and the workweek can be extended. Workers can also "moonlight"—hold more than one job. But once the economy's full capacity is reached at Q_c, the aggregate supply curve becomes vertical.

In the intermediate range of aggregate supply, per-unit production costs rise and firms must receive higher product prices for their output in order to be profitable. In this range a rising price level accompanies rising real output.

Vertical Range   The economy reaches its full-capacity real output at Q_c. Increases of the price level in the **vertical range** (*cd*) will produce no additional real output since the economy already is operating

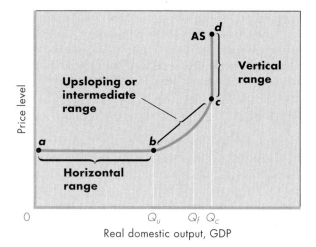

Figure 11.5
The aggregate supply curve. The aggregate supply curve shows the levels of real output that firms will produce at various price levels. It has three ranges: a horizontal range *ab*, where the price level remains constant as real output varies; an intermediate range *bc*, where both real output and the price level are variable; and a vertical range *cd*, where real output is constant at the full-capacity level and only the price level can vary.

at its full capacity. Individual firms may try to expand production by bidding resources away from other firms. But the resources and additional production that one firm gains will be lost by some other firm. The bidding will raise resource prices (costs) and ultimately boost product prices, but real output will remain unchanged.

Determinants of Aggregate Supply

From our discussion of the shape of the aggregate supply curve, we see that real output rises as the economy moves from left to right through the horizontal and intermediate ranges of aggregate supply. These increases in output result from movements along the aggregate supply curve and must be distinguished from shifts of the curve itself.

An existing aggregate supply curve identifies the relationship between the price level and real output, other things equal. But when one or more of the "other things" change, the curve itself shifts. The rightward shift of the curve from AS_1 to AS_2 in Figure 11.6 represents an increase in aggregate supply, indicating that firms are willing to produce and sell more real output at each price level. The leftward shift of the curve from AS_1 to AS_3 represents a decrease in aggregate supply. Firms will not produce as much output as before at each price level.

Figure 11.6 lists the other things that shift the aggregate supply curve. Called the **determinants of aggregate supply** or *aggregate supply shifters,* they collectively determine the location of the aggregate supply curve and shift the curve when they change. Changes in these determinants cause per-unit production costs to be either higher or lower than before *at each price level.* The change in production costs affects profits and leads firms to alter their output at each price level. Hence, when one of the determinants listed in Figure 11.6 changes, the aggregate supply curve shifts. Changes that decrease per-unit production costs shift the aggregate supply curve to the right, as from AS_1 to AS_2; changes that increase per-unit production costs shift it to the left, as from AS_1 to AS_3. *When per-unit production costs change for reasons other than changes in real output, firms collectively alter the amount of output they produce at each price level.*

Let's examine the aggregate supply determinants listed in Figure 11.6 in more detail.

Input Prices

Input or resource prices—to be distinguished from the output prices that make up the price level—are a major determinant of aggregate supply. Other things equal, higher input prices increase per-unit production costs and reduce aggregate supply. Lower input prices do just the opposite. Several factors influence input prices.

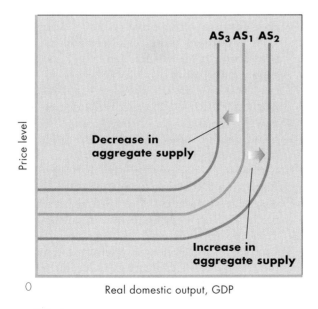

Determinants of Aggregate Supply: Factors that Shift the Aggregate Supply Curve

1. Change in input prices
   a. Domestic resource availability
      ▪ Land
      ▪ Labor
      ▪ Capital
      ▪ Entrepreneurial ability
   b. Prices of imported resources
   c. Market power
2. Change in productivity
3. Change in legal-institutional environment
   a. Business taxes and subsidies
   b. Government regulations

Figure 11.6

Changes in aggregate supply. A change in one or more of the listed determinants of aggregate supply will shift the aggregate supply curve. The rightward shift of the aggregate supply curve from AS_1 to AS_2 represents an increase in aggregate supply; the leftward shift of the curve from AS_1 to AS_3 shows a decrease in aggregate supply.

Domestic Resource Availability   Increases in the supply of domestic resources will lower resource prices, reduce per-unit production costs, and shift the aggregate supply curve to the right. Conversely, declines in resource supplies will raise input prices, increase per-unit production costs, and shift the aggregate supply curve to the left.

How might changes in the availability of land, labor, capital, and entrepreneurial resources serve to shift the aggregate supply curve? Here are several examples, grouped by resource category:

- *Land*   Land resources might expand through discoveries of mineral deposits, irrigation of land, or technical innovations that transform what were previously "nonresources" (say, vast desert lands) into valuable factors of production (productive lands). An increase in the supply of land resources lowers the price of land inputs, reduces per-unit production costs, and shifts the aggregate supply curve to the right.

   Land resources might also *decline*, say, by depletion of underground water reserves through irrigation or loss of topsoil through intensive farming. Then the aggregate supply curve will shift to the left.

- *Labor*   Wages and salaries make up about 75 percent of all business costs. Other things equal, changes in wages affect per-unit production costs and thus may shift the aggregate supply curve. An increase in the availability of labor resources reduces the price of labor and increases aggregate supply; a decrease has the opposite effect. For example, the influx of women into the labor force during the past two decades put downward pressure on wages and expanded U.S. aggregate supply. Emigration of employable workers from abroad also has increased the availability of labor in the United States and expanded the amount of output available at each price level.

   Conversely, the AIDS epidemic has reduced the supply of labor and has thus diminished aggregate supply.

- *Capital*   Aggregate supply usually increases when society improves or adds to its stock of capital goods. For example, firms have increased aggregate supply by replacing poor-quality equipment with new, superior equipment. On the other hand, aggregate supply declines when the quantity or quality of the nation's stock of capital diminishes. This can happen, for example, as a result of destruction of production facilities through war.

- *Entrepreneurial ability*   The amount of entrepreneurial ability in the economy may change, shifting the aggregate supply curve. Recent media focus on the entrepreneurs relating to the Internet revolution might increase the number of people with entrepreneurial aspirations. If so, the aggregate supply curve might shift rightward.

Prices of Imported Resources   Just as foreign demand for U.S. goods contributes to U.S. aggregate demand, resources imported from abroad (such as oil, tin, and coffee beans) add to U.S. aggregate supply. Added resources—whether domestic or imported—boost production capacity. Generally, a decrease in the price of imported resources increases U.S. aggregate supply and an increase in their price reduces U.S. aggregate supply.

Exchange-rate fluctuations are one factor that may alter the price of imported resources. Suppose that the dollar appreciates, enabling U.S. firms to obtain more foreign currency with each dollar. This means that domestic producers face a lower *dollar* price of imported resources. U.S. firms would respond by increasing their imports of foreign resources, thereby lowering their per-unit production costs at each level of output. Falling per-unit production costs would shift the U.S. aggregate supply curve to the right.

A depreciation of the dollar, in contrast, will raise the price of imported resources. Consequently, U.S. imports of these resources will fall, per-unit production costs will rise, and the U.S. aggregate supply curve will move leftward.

Market Power   A change in the degree of market power—the ability to set above-competitive prices—held by sellers of major inputs also can affect input prices and aggregate supply. An example is the fluctuating market power held by the Organization of Petroleum Exporting Countries (OPEC) over the past several decades. The 10-fold increase in the price of oil that OPEC achieved during the 1970s drove up per-unit production costs and jolted the U.S. aggregate supply curve leftward. Then, a steep reduction in OPEC's market power during the mid-1980s resulted in a sharp decline in oil prices and a rightward shift of the U.S. aggregate supply curve. In 1999 OPEC reasserted its market power, creating higher oil prices that pushed up costs for some U.S. producers (for example, airlines and truckers).

Productivity   The second major determinant of aggregate supply is **productivity,** which is a measure of the relationship between a nation's level of real output and the amount of resources used to produce it. Productivity is a measure of average real output, or of real output per unit of input:

$$\text{Productivity} = \frac{\text{total output}}{\text{total inputs}}$$

An increase in productivity enables the economy to obtain more real output from its limited resources. It does this by reducing the per-unit cost of output (per-unit production cost). Suppose, for example, that real output is 10 units, that 5 units of input are needed to produce that quantity, and that the price of each input unit is $2. Then

$$\text{Productivity} = \frac{\text{total output}}{\text{total inputs}} = \frac{10}{5} = 2$$

and

$$\text{Per-unit production cost} = \frac{\text{total input cost}}{\text{total output}}$$
$$= \frac{\$2 \times 5}{10} = \$1$$

Note that we obtain the total input cost by multiplying the unit input cost by the number of inputs used.

Now suppose productivity increases and that real output doubles to 20 units, while the price and quantity of the input remain constant at $2 and 5 units. Using the above equations, we see that productivity rises from 2 to 4 and that the per-unit production cost of the output falls from $1 to $.50. The doubled productivity has reduced the per-unit production cost by half.

By reducing the per-unit production cost, an increase in productivity shifts the aggregate supply curve to the right. The main source of productivity advance is improved production technology, often embodied within new plant and equipment that replaces old plant and equipment. Other sources of productivity increases are a better-educated and trained workforce, improved forms of business enterprises, and the reallocation of labor resources from lower- to higher-productivity uses.

Legal-Institutional Environment   Changes in the legal-institutional setting in which businesses operate are the final determinant of aggregate supply. Such changes may alter the per-unit costs of

output and, if so, shift the aggregate supply curve. Two changes of this type are changes in taxes and subsidies and changes in the extent of regulation.

Business Taxes and Subsidies   Higher business taxes, such as sales, excise, and payroll taxes, increase per-unit costs and reduce aggregate supply in much the same way as a wage increase does. An increase in such taxes paid by businesses will increase per-unit production costs and shift the aggregate supply to the left.

Similarly, a business subsidy—a payment or tax break by government to producers—lowers production costs and increases aggregate supply. For example, the Federal government subsidizes firms that blend ethanol (derived from corn) with gasoline to increase the U.S. gasoline supply. This reduces the per-unit production cost of making blended gasoline. To the extent that this and other subsidies are successful, the aggregate supply curve shifts rightward.

Government Regulation   It is usually costly for businesses to comply with government regulations. More regulation therefore tends to increase per-unit production costs and shift the aggregate supply curve to the left. "Supply-side" proponents of deregulation of the economy have argued forcefully that, by increasing efficiency and reducing the paperwork associated with complex regulations, deregulation will reduce per-unit costs and shift the aggregate supply curve to the right.

QUICK REVIEW 11.2

The aggregate supply curve has three distinct ranges: a horizontal range, an upsloping intermediate range, and a vertical range.

In the intermediate range, per-unit production costs and therefore the price level rise as output expands toward and beyond its full-employment level.

By altering the per-unit production cost independent of changes in the level of output, changes in one or more of the determinants of aggregate supply (Figure 11.6) shift the aggregate supply curve.

An increase in aggregate supply is shown as a rightward shift of the aggregate supply curve; a decrease is shown as a leftward shift of the curve.

KEY GRAPH

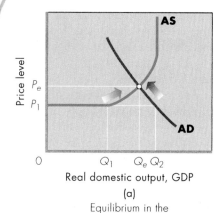

(a)
Equilibrium in the
intermediate range
of aggregate supply

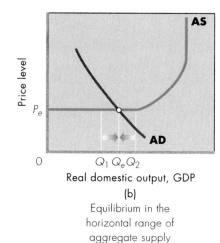

(b)
Equilibrium in the
horizontal range of
aggregate supply

Figure 11.7

The equilibrium price level and equilibrium real GDP. The intersection of the aggregate demand curve and the aggregate supply curve determines the equilibrium price level and equilibrium real output. In (a), where the aggregate demand curve intersects the aggregate supply curve in its intermediate range, the price level will change to eliminate underproduction or overproduction of output; in (b), where the aggregate demand curve intersects the aggregate supply curve in its horizontal range, the move toward equilibrium real output occurs without a change in the price level.

Quick Quiz 11.7

1. The AD curve slopes downward because:
   a. per-unit production costs fall as real GDP increases.
   b. the income and substitution effects are at work.
   c. changes in the determinants of AD alter the amounts of real GDP demanded at each price level.
   d. decreases in the price level give rise to real-balances effects, interest-rate effects, and foreign purchases effects that increase the amounts of real GDP demanded.

2. The AS curve slopes upward in the intermediate range because:
   a. per-unit production costs rise as real GDP expands toward and beyond its full-employment level.
   b. the income and substitution effects are at work.
   c. changes in the determinants of AS alter the amounts of real GDP supplied at each price level.
   d. increases in the price level give rise to real-balances effects, interest-rate effects, and foreign purchases effects that increase the amounts of real GDP supplied.

3. At price level P_1 in graph (a):
   a. a GDP surplus of Q_2 minus Q_1 occurs that drives the price level up to P_e.
   b. a GDP shortage of Q_2 minus Q_1 occurs that drives the price level up to P_e.
   c. the aggregate amount of real GDP demanded is less than the aggregate amount of GDP supplied.
   d. the economy is in an "unemployment equilibrium."

4. Suppose the business sector has produced real GDP Q_2 in graph (b). We would expect:
   a. the price level to fall below P_e.
   b. the AD curve to shift to the right until it intersects AS at real GDP Q_2.
   c. the price level to rise above P_e.
   d. inventories to increase, compelling firms to reduce production to Q_e.

Answers: 1. d; 2. a; 3. b; 4. d

■ Equilibrium: Real Output and the Price Level

As Figure 11.7 (Key Graph) shows, the intersection of the aggregate demand curve and the aggregate supply curve determines the economy's **equilibrium price level** and **equilibrium real output.**

In Figure 11.7a, where the aggregate demand curve crosses the aggregate supply curve in its inter-mediate range, the equilibrium price level and level of real output are P_e and Q_e, respectively. To illustrate why, suppose the price level were P_1 rather than P_e. Price level P_1 would encourage businesses to produce (at most) real output Q_1. But the aggregate demand curve tells us that buyers would want to purchase only Q_2 real output at price level P_1. Competition among buyers to purchase the lesser available real output Q_1 will pull up the price level to P_e.

214

As the arrows in Figure 11.7a indicate, the rise in the price level from P_1 to P_e (1) encourages producers to increase their real output from Q_1 to Q_e and (2) causes buyers to scale back their purchases from Q_2 to Q_e. When equality occurs between the amount of real output produced and the amount purchased, as it does at P_e, the economy has achieved equilibrium.

In Figure 11.7b the aggregate demand curve intersects the aggregate supply curve in the horizontal range of the aggregate supply curve. Here the price level does not play a role in bringing about the equilibrium level of real output. To understand why, first observe that the equilibrium price and real-output levels in Figure 11.7b are P_e and Q_e. If firms produce a larger output, such as Q_2, they cannot sell it all. Aggregate demand is insufficient to take all that output off the shelves. Faced with higher inventories of goods, businesses will reduce their production to Q_e, as shown by the leftward-pointing arrow, and the market will then clear.

If firms produce only smaller output Q_1, they will find their inventory of goods quickly diminishing, because the quantity of output demanded Q_e is greater than the output produced. Firms will step up their production, and, as shown by the rightward-pointing arrow, real output will increase from Q_1 to the equilibrium level Q_e. ⊿ 11.1

▌Changes in Equilibrium

Now let's see how shifts in the AD and AS curves affect the economy.

Increases in AD: Demand-Pull Inflation

Suppose households and businesses decide to increase their consumption and investment spending—an action that shifts the aggregate demand curve to the right. Our list of determinants of aggregate demand (Figure 11.3) provides several reasons why this shift might occur. Perhaps consumers feel wealthier because of large gains in their stock holdings. As a result, consumers would consume more (save less) of their current incomes. Perhaps firms boost their investment spending because they anticipate higher future profits from investments in new capital. Those profits are predicated on having new equipment and facilities that incorporate a number of new technologies.

As shown in Figure 11.8, the inflationary effects of an increase in aggregate demand depend on whether the economy is currently in the horizontal, intermediate, or vertical range of the aggregate supply curve.

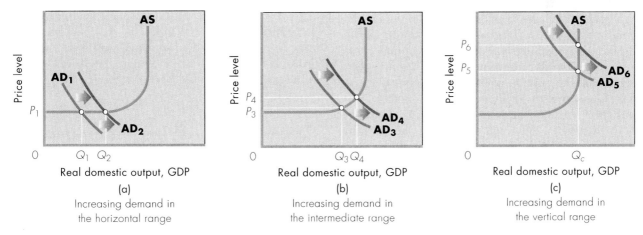

Figure 11.8

Increases in aggregate demand and demand-pull inflation. The inflationary effects of an increase in aggregate demand depend on the range of the aggregate supply curve in which it occurs. (a) An increase in aggregate demand in the horizontal range increases real output but leaves the price level unaffected. (b) An increase in demand in the intermediate range increases both real output and the level of prices. (c) In the vertical range, an increase in aggregate demand increases the price level, but real output cannot increase beyond the full-capacity level. Demand-pull inflation occurs in (b) and (c).

- In the horizontal range of Figure 11.8a, where there tends to be substantial unemployment and much unused production capacity, an increase in aggregate demand (from AD_1 to AD_2) creates a large increase in real output (Q_1 to Q_2). Unemployment falls because more workers are needed to produce the greater output. The price level remains at P_1, so there is no inflation.

- In the intermediate range of Figure 11.8b, an increase in aggregate demand (AD_3 to AD_4) raises both real output (Q_3 to Q_4) and the price level (P_3 to P_4). Output expands but there is some inflation.

- In the vertical range of Figure 11.8c, where labor and capital are at their full capacities, an increase in aggregate demand (AD_5 to AD_6) affects the price level only, raising it from P_5 to P_6. Real output remains at Q_c.

Rising price levels in the intermediate and vertical ranges of the aggregate supply curve (Figure 11.8b and 11.8c) constitute *demand-pull inflation*, which results because shifts in aggregate demand pull up the price level. **(Key Question 4)**

Multiplier with Price-Level Changes

Close inspection reveals that real GDP does not increase as much in Figure 11.8b as it does in Figure 11.8a, although the shifts in aggregate demand are of equal magnitudes. In Figure 11.9, which combines panels (a) and (b) of Figure 11.8, we see that the shift in aggregate demand from AD_1 to AD_2 occurs in the horizontal range of the aggregate supply curve. Businesses are willing to produce more output *at existing prices*. In this range, any initial change in spending, and in the multiple change in aggregate demand that results, transmits fully into a change in real GDP and employment. The price level remains constant. In the horizontal range of aggregate supply the "full-strength" multiplier outcome of Chapter 10 occurs.

In contrast, if the economy is in the intermediate or vertical range of the aggregate supply curve, part or all of any initial increase in aggregate demand will be dissipated in inflation and therefore will not be reflected in increased real output. In Figure 11.9 the shift of aggregate demand from AD_2 to AD_3 is of the same magnitude as the shift from AD_1 to AD_2. But look what happens. Because a portion of the increase in aggregate demand is absorbed as inflation as the price level rises from P_1 to P_2, real GDP rises only to GDP'. If the aggregate supply curve had been horizontal, then the shift from AD_2

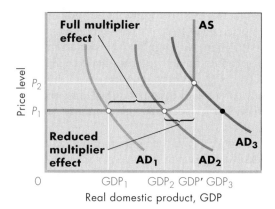

Figure 11.9

Inflation and the multiplier. The aggregate demand–aggregate supply model shows how inflation reduces the size of the multiplier effect. For the increase in aggregate demand from AD_1 to AD_2, the price level is constant and the multiplier is at full strength; output increases from GDP$_1$ to GDP$_2$. Although the increase in aggregate demand from AD_2 to AD_3 is of the same magnitude, the impact is partly dissipated in inflation (from P_1 to P_2), and real output increases only from GDP$_2$ to GDP'.

to AD_3 would have increased real output to GDP$_3$. But inflation has reduced the multiplier effect to only about half as much as otherwise.

We conclude that *for any initial increase in aggregate demand, the resulting increase in real GDP will be smaller the greater the increase in the price level.* Price-level increases weaken the multiplier effect.

To confirm that this increase in spending would be entirely absorbed as inflation, sketch an increase in aggregate demand equal to the shift from AD_2 to AD_3 in the vertical range of aggregate supply. The multiplier effect would be zero, because real GDP would not change.

Decreases in AD: Recession and Cyclical Unemployment

Decreases in aggregate demand in the horizontal range of aggregate supply describe the opposite end of the business cycle: recession and cyclical unemployment (rather than above-full employment and demand-pull inflation). Suppose, for example, that firms greatly reduce their investment spending because of substantially higher interest rates and that foreigners simultaneously reduce their purchases of U.S. products and thus U.S. net exports plunge. In Figure 11.10 we show the resulting decline in aggregate demand as a shift from AD_1 to AD_2. The

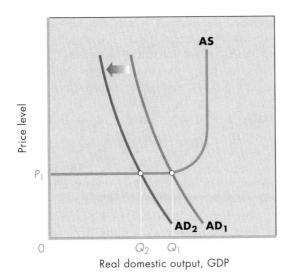

Figure 11.10

A decrease in aggregate demand that causes a recession. A shift of the aggregate demand curve from AD_1 to AD_2 along the horizontal range of the aggregate supply curve reduces real GDP from Q_1 to Q_2. The result is idle production capacity and cyclical unemployment.

outcome is a decline of real output from Q_1 to Q_2, with no change in the price level. This decline of real output constitutes a *recession*, and since fewer workers are needed to produce the lower output, *cyclical unemployment* arises.

Real output takes the full brunt of the decline in aggregate demand because it occurs in the horizontal range of the aggregate supply curve. This range owes its existence to resource prices and product prices that are "sticky" or inflexible in a downward direction for a considerable time. There are numerous reasons for downward price inflexibility.

- **Wage contracts** Wage rates often are inflexible downward, and it usually is not profitable for firms to cut their product prices if they cannot also cut their wage rates. Wages tend to be inflexible downward because large parts of the labor force work under contracts prohibiting wage cuts for the duration of the contract. (It is not uncommon for collective bargaining agreements in major industries to run for 3 years.) Similarly, the wages and salaries of nonunion workers are usually adjusted once a year, rather than quarterly or monthly.

- **Morale, effort, and productivity** Wage inflexibility downward is reinforced by the reluctance of many employers to reduce wage rates. Current wages may be so-called **efficiency wages**— *wages that elicit maximum work effort and thus*

minimize labor cost per unit of output. Lower wages might impair worker morale and work effort, thereby reducing labor productivity (output per worker). While lower wage rates *do* reduce labor costs per hour of work, lower worker productivity means less output on an hourly basis. If the latter more than counterbalances the former, then a lower wage rate will increase, not reduce, labor costs per unit of production. In such situations, firms will resist lowering wages when faced with a decline in aggregate demand. 🔑 11.2

- **Minimum wage** The minimum wage imposes a legal floor under the wages of the least skilled workers. Firms cannot reduce that wage rate when aggregate demand declines.

- **Menu costs** Firms that think a recession will be relatively short-lived may be reluctant to cut their prices. One reason is so-called **menu costs**, named after their most obvious example: the cost of printing new menus when a restaurant changes its prices. But changes in prices create other costs as well. There are the costs of (1) estimating the magnitude and duration of the shift in demand to determine whether prices should be lowered, (2) repricing items held in inventory, (3) printing and mailing new catalogs, and (4) communicating new prices to customers, perhaps through advertising. When menu costs are substantial, firms may choose to avoid them by retaining current prices. That is, they will wait to see if the decline in aggregate demand is permanent.

- **Fear of price wars** Some firms may be concerned that if they reduce their prices, rivals not only will match their price cuts but may retaliate by making even deeper cuts. An initial price cut may touch off an unwanted *price war:* successively deeper and deeper rounds of price cuts. In such a situation, all the firms end up with far less profit than would be the case if they had simply maintained their prices. For this reason, each firm may resist making the initial price cut, choosing instead to reduce production and lay off workers.

Not all economists, however, think that wages and prices are as inflexible downward as the horizontal range of the aggregate supply curve suggests. They point to the declining power of unions in the United States and the large wage cuts that occurred in several basic industries following the 1981–1982 and 1990–1991 recessions as evidence of increased downward wage flexibility. They also note that growing foreign competition has undermined monopoly power and the accompanying ability of firms to resist price cuts when faced with falling demand. But most economists question whether these recent changes are sufficient to have altered the basic historical pattern. Since 1950 the U.S. economy has experienced eight recessions (listed in Table 8.1) but only one yearly decline in the price level (1955).

Decreases in AS: Cost-Push Inflation

Suppose that a war in the Middle East severely disrupts world oil supplies and drives up oil prices by 500 percent. Higher energy prices would spread through the economy, driving up production and distribution costs on a wide variety of goods. The U.S. aggregate supply curve would shift to the left, say, from AS_1 to AS_2 in Figure 11.11. The resulting increase in the price level would be *cost-push inflation* (Chapter 8).

The effects of a leftward shift in aggregate supply are doubly bad. When aggregate supply shifts from AS_1 to AS_2, the economy moves from point *a* to point *b*. Real output declines from Q_1 to Q_2, and the price level rises from P_1 to P_2. Along with the cost-push inflation, a recession occurs. That is exactly what happened in the United States in the mid-

1970s when the price of oil rocketed upward. Then, oil expenditures were about 10 percent of U.S. GDP, compared to only 3 percent today. So the U.S. economy is now less vulnerable to cost-push inflation arising from such "aggregate supply shocks."

Increases in AS: Full Employment with Price-Level Stability

In the last half of the 1990s and 2000 the United States experienced full employment, strong economic growth, and very low inflation. Specifically, the unemployment rate fell to 4 percent and real GDP grew nearly 4 percent annually, *without igniting inflation*. At first thought, this "macroeconomic bliss" seems to be incompatible with the AD-AS model. The intermediate range of the aggregate supply curve suggests that increases in aggregate demand that are sufficient for full employment (or overfull employment) will raise the price level (see Figure 11.8b). Higher inflation, so it would seem, is the inevitable price paid for expanding output to and beyond the full-employment level.

But inflation remained very mild in the late 1990s and early 2000s. Figure 11.12 helps explain why. Let's first suppose that aggregate demand increased from AD_1 to AD_2 along the intermediate range of aggregate supply curve AS_1. Taken alone, that increase in aggregate demand would move the economy from *a* to *b*. Real output would rise from less-than-full-employment real output Q_1 to full-capacity real output Q_2. The economy would experience inflation, as shown by the increase in the price level from P_1 to P_3. Such inflation occurred at the end of previous vigorous expansions of aggregate demand.

In the more recent period, however, larger-than-usual increases in productivity occurred due to a burst of new technology relating to computers, the Internet, inventory management systems, electronic commerce, and so on. The quickened productivity growth in the so-called New Economy reduced per-unit production costs and shifted the aggregate supply curve to the right, as from AS_1 to AS_2 in Figure 11.11. The relevant aggregate demand and aggregate supply curves thus became AD_2 and AS_2, not AD_2 and AS_1. Instead of moving from *a* to *b*, the economy moved from *a* to *c*. Real output increased from Q_1 to Q_3, and the price level rose only modestly (from P_1 to P_2). The shift of the aggregate supply curve from AS_1 to AS_2 increased the economy's full-employment output and its full-capacity output.

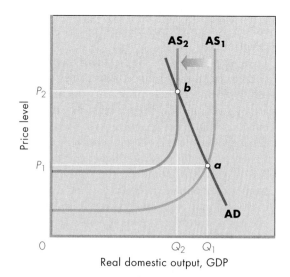

Figure 11.11

A decrease in aggregate supply that causes cost-push inflation. A leftward shift of aggregate supply from AS_1 to AS_2 raises the price level from P_1 to P_2 and thus produces cost-push inflation. Real output falls from Q_1 to Q_2.

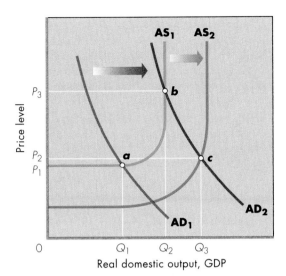

Figure 11.12

Growth, full employment, and relative price stability. Normally, an increase in aggregate demand from AD_1 to AD_2 would move the economy from a to b along AS_1. Real output would expand to its full-capacity level (Q_2) and inflation would result $(P_1$ to $P_3)$. But in the late 1990s and early 2000s, significant increases in productivity shifted the aggregate supply curve, as from AS_1 to AS_2. The economy moved not from a to b but from a to c. It experienced strong economic growth $(Q_1$ to $Q_3)$, full employment, and only very mild inflation $(P_1$ to $P_2)$.

That accommodated the increase in aggregate demand without causing inflation.

Can this happy scenario of rapid productivity growth, rapid real GDP growth, full employment, and price stability continue indefinitely? Is the business cycle dead? Economists doubt it. If increases in aggregate demand at any point exceed the increases in aggregate supply, demand-pull inflation will emerge. That was the concern expressed by Federal Reserve Chair Greenspan in the quotation that opened this chapter. To guard against demand-pull inflation, the Fed raised interest rates several times in 2000. Those high interest rates, along with a reverse wealth effect resulting from a major decline in stock market values, threatened to end the economic expansion. In early 2001 the Fed lowered interest rates to try to prevent a recession. We will examine government stabilization policies, such as those carried out by the Federal Reserve, in the chapters that follow. We will also examine the characteristics of the New Economy in more detail. **(Key Questions 5, 7, and 8)**

QUICK REVIEW 11.3

■ The equilibrium price level and amount of real output are determined at the intersection of the aggregate demand curve and the aggregate supply curve.

■ Increases in aggregate demand in the upsloping and vertical ranges of the aggregate supply curve cause demand-pull inflation.

■ Because the price level tends to be "sticky" or inflexible in a downward direction, decreases in aggregate demand cause recessions and cyclical unemployment.

■ Decreases in aggregate supply cause cost-push inflation.

■ Full employment, high economic growth, and price stability are compatible with one another if productivity-driven increases in aggregate supply are sufficient to balance growing aggregate demand.

Why Is Unemployment in Europe So High?

Are the High Unemployment Rates in Europe the Result of Structural Problems or of Deficient Aggregate Demand?

Several European economies have had high unemployment rates in the past several years. For example, in 2000 France had an unemployment rate of 9.7 percent; Italy, 10.7 percent; Belgium, 8.5 percent; Germany, 8.3 percent; and Spain, 14.7 percent. These rates compare to the 4.0 percent unemployment rate in the United States in 2000.

Why are European unemployment rates so high? There are two views on this question.

High Natural Rates of Unemployment Many economists believe the high unemployment rates in Europe largely reflect high natural rates of unemployment. They envision a situation as in Figure 11.7a, where aggregate demand and aggregate

supply have produced the full-employment level of real output Q_e. But high levels of frictional and structural unemployment accompany such a level of output. In this view, the recent extensive unemployment in Europe has resulted from a high natural rate of unemployment, not from deficient aggregate demand. An increase in aggregate demand would push these economies beyond their full-employment levels of output, causing demand-pull inflation.

The sources of the high natural rates of unemployment are government policies and union contracts that have increased the costs of hiring workers and have reduced the cost of being unemployed. Examples: High minimum wages have discouraged employers from hiring low-skilled workers; generous welfare benefits have weakened incentives for people to take available jobs; restrictions against firings have discouraged firms from employing workers; 30 to 40 days per year of paid vacations and holidays have boosted the cost of hiring workers; high worker absenteeism has reduced productivity; and high employer costs of health, pension, disability, and other benefits have discouraged hiring.

Deficient Aggregate Demand Not all economists agree that government and union policies have pushed up Europe's natural rate of unemployment. Instead, they point to insufficient aggregate demand as the problem. They see the European economies in terms of Figure 11.7b, where the equilibrium real output Q_e is less than it would be if aggregate demand were stronger. The argument is that the European governments have been so fearful of inflation that they have not undertaken appropriate fiscal and monetary policies (discussed in Chapters 12 and 15) to increase aggregate demand. In this view, increases in aggregate demand would not be inflationary, since these economies have considerable excess capacity. If they are operating in the horizontal range of their aggregate supply curves, a rightward shift of their aggregate demand curves would expand output and employment without increasing inflation.

Conclusion: The debate over high unemployment in Europe reflects disagreement on where European aggregate demand curves lie relative to full-employment levels of output. If these curves are at the full-employment real GDP, as in Figure 11.7a, then the high levels of unemployment are "natural." Public policies should focus on lowering minimum wages, reducing vacation time, reducing welfare benefits, easing restrictions on layoffs, and so on. But if the aggregate demand curves in the European nations lie to the left of their full-employment levels of output, as in Figure 11.7b, then expansionary government policies such as reduced interest rates or tax cuts may be in order.

SUMMARY

1. The aggregate demand–aggregate supply (AD-AS) model is a variable-price model that enables analysis of simultaneous changes of real GDP and the price level.

2. The aggregate demand curve shows the level of real output that the economy will purchase at each price level.

3. The aggregate demand curve is downsloping because of the real-balances effect, the interest-rate effect, and the foreign purchases effect. The real-balances effect indicates that inflation reduces the real value or purchasing power of fixed-value financial assets held by households, causing cutbacks in consumer spending. The interest-rate effect means that with a specific

supply of money, a higher price level increases the demand for money, thereby raising the interest rate and reducing investment purchases. The foreign purchases effect suggests that an increase in one country's price level relative to the price levels in other countries reduces the net export component of that nation's aggregate demand.

*4. A change in the price level alters the location of the aggregate expenditures schedule through the real-balances, interest-rate, and foreign purchases effects. The aggregate demand curve is derived from the aggregate expenditures model by allowing the price level to change and observing the effect on the aggregate expenditures schedule and thus on equilibrium GDP.

5. Aggregate demand is determined by the spending of domestic consumers, businesses, government, and foreign buyers. Changes in the factors listed in Figure 11.3 alter the spending by these groups and shift the aggregate demand curve.

*6. With the price level held constant, increases in consumption, investment, and net export expenditures shift the aggregate expenditures schedule upward and the aggregate demand curve to the right. Decreases in these spending components produce the opposite effects.

7. The aggregate supply curve shows the levels of real output that businesses will produce at various possible price levels.

8. The shape of the aggregate supply curve depends on what happens to per-unit production costs, and hence to the prices that the firms must receive, as real output expands. In the horizontal range of aggregate supply, there is substantial unemployment and thus firms can increase production without experiencing rising per-unit costs or prices. In the intermediate range, per-unit costs increase as production bottlenecks appear and less efficient equipment and workers are employed. Prices must therefore rise as real output is expanded. The vertical range coincides with full capacity; real output is at a maximum and cannot be increased, but the price level will rise in response to an increase in aggregate demand.

9. Figure 11.6 lists the determinants of aggregate supply: input prices, productivity, and the legal-institutional environment. A change in any one of these factors will change per-unit production costs at each level of output and therefore will shift the aggregate supply curve.

10. The intersection of the aggregate demand and aggregate supply curves determines an economy's equilibrium price level and real GDP.

11. Increases in aggregate demand (a) increase real output and employment but do not alter the price level in the horizontal range of aggregate supply, (b) increase both real output and the price level in the intermediate range, and (c) increase the price level but not real output in the vertical range.

12. In the intermediate and vertical ranges of the aggregate supply curve, the aggregate demand–aggregate supply model shows that the multiplier is weakened because a portion of any increase in aggregate demand is dissipated in inflation.

13. Leftward shifts of the aggregate supply curve in the horizontal range of aggregate supply cause recession and cyclical unemployment. The horizontal range of aggregate supply implies inflexible prices downward. The inflexibility results from wage contracts, efficiency wages, menu costs, minimum wages, and fears of price wars.

14. Leftward shifts of the aggregate supply curve reflect increases in per-unit production costs and cause cost-push inflation. Rightward shifts of the aggregate supply curve result from decreases in per-unit costs and produce an expansion of real output.

15. Rightward shifts of the aggregate supply curve, caused by improvements in productivity, help explain the simultaneous achievement of full employment, economic growth, and price stability that the United States achieved in the late 1990s and early 2000s.

---

*Starred summary items presume knowledge of the aggregate expenditures model presented in Chapters 9 and 10.

TERMS AND CONCEPTS

aggregate demand–
   aggregate supply
   (AD-AS) model
aggregate demand
real-balances effect
interest-rate effect

foreign purchases effect
determinants of aggregate demand
aggregate supply
horizontal range
   (of AS curve)

intermediate range
   (of AS curve)
vertical range
   (of AS curve)
determinants of aggregate supply

productivity
equilibrium price level
equilibrium real output
efficiency wages
menu costs

STUDY QUESTIONS

1. Why is the aggregate demand curve downsloping? Specify how your explanation differs from the explanation for the downsloping demand curve for a single product.

2. Explain the shape of the aggregate supply curve, and account for the horizontal, intermediate, and vertical ranges of the curve.

*3. Explain: "A change in the price level shifts the aggregate expenditures curve but not the aggregate demand curve."

4. Key Question Suppose that the aggregate demand and supply schedules for a hypothetical economy are as shown below:

Amount of Real GDP Demanded, Billions	Price Level (Price Index)	Amount of Real GDP Supplied, Billions
$100	300	$400
200	250	400
300	200	300
400	150	200
500	150	100

a. Use these sets of data to graph the aggregate demand and aggregate supply curves. What are the equilibrium price level and the equilibrium level of real output in this hypothetical economy? Is the equilibrium real output also the full-capacity real output? Explain.

b. Why will a price level of 150 not be an equilibrium price level in this economy? Why not 250?

c. Suppose that buyers desire to purchase $200 billion of extra real output at each price level. Sketch in the new aggregate demand curve as AD_1. What factors might cause this change in aggregate demand? What are the new equilibrium price level and level of real output? Over which range of the aggregate supply curve—horizontal, intermediate, or vertical—has equilibrium changed?

5. Key Question Suppose that the hypothetical economy in question 4 has the following relationship between its real output and the input quantities necessary for producing that output:

Input Quantity	Real GDP
150.0	$400
112.5	300
75.0	200

a. What is productivity in this economy?

b. What is the per-unit cost of production if the price of each input unit is $2?

c. Assume that the input price increases from $2 to $3 with no accompanying change in productivity. What is the new per-unit cost of production? In what direction would the $1 increase in input price push the aggregate supply curve? What effect would this shift in aggregate supply have on the price level and the level of real output?

d. Suppose that the increase in input price does not occur but, instead, that productivity increases by 100 percent. What would be the new per-unit cost of production? What effect would this change in per-unit production cost have on the aggregate supply curve? What effect would this shift of aggregate supply have on the price level and the level of real output?

6. Distinguish between the "real-balances effect" and the "wealth effect," as the terms are used in this chapter. How does each relate to the aggregate demand curve?

7. Key Question What effects would each of the following have on aggregate demand or aggregate supply? In each case use a diagram to show the expected effects on the equilibrium price level and level of real output. Assume that all other things remain constant.

a. A widespread fear of depression on the part of consumers.

b. A large purchase of U.S. wheat by Russia.

c. A $1 increase in the excise tax on cigarettes.

d. A reduction in interest rates at each price level.

e. A major cut in Federal spending for health care.

f. The expectation of a rapid rise in the price level.

g. The complete disintegration of OPEC, causing oil prices to fall by one-half.

h. A 10 percent reduction in personal income tax rates.

i. An increase in labor productivity.

j. A 12 percent increase in nominal wages (with no change in productivity).

k. Depreciation in the international value of the dollar.

---

*Questions with an asterisk presume knowledge of the aggregate expenditures model (Chapters 9 and 10).

l. A sharp decline in the national incomes of our western European trading partners.

m. A sizable increase in U.S. immigration.

8. **Key Question** Other things equal, what effect will each of the following have on the equilibrium price level and level of real output?

   a. An increase in aggregate demand in the vertical range of aggregate supply.

   b. An increase in aggregate supply, with no change in aggregate demand (assume that prices and wages are flexible upward and downward).

   c. Equal increases in aggregate demand and aggregate supply.

   d. A reduction in aggregate demand in the horizontal range of aggregate supply.

   e. An increase in aggregate demand and a decrease in aggregate supply.

   f. A decrease in aggregate demand in the intermediate range of aggregate supply.

*9. Suppose that the price level is constant and that investment spending increases sharply. How would you show this increase in the aggregate expenditures model? What would be the outcome? How would you show this rise in investment in the aggregate demand–aggregate supply model? What range of the aggregate supply curve is involved?

*10. Explain how an upsloping aggregate supply curve weakens the multiplier.

11. Why does a reduction in aggregate demand reduce real output, rather than the price level?

12. Explain: "Unemployment can be caused by a decrease of aggregate demand or a decrease of aggregate supply." In each case, specify the price-level outcomes.

13. Use shifts in the AD and AS curves to explain (*a*) the U.S. experience of strong economic growth, full employment, and price stability in the late 1990s and early 2000s; (*b*) how a strong positive wealth effect could cause demand-pull inflation even though productivity growth is surging; and (*c*) how a strong negative wealth effect from, say, a precipitous drop in the stock market could cause a recession even though productivity is surging.

14. **(Last Word)** State the alternative views on why unemployment in Europe has recently been so high. Discuss the policy implications of each view.

15. **Web-Based Question:** *Aggregate demand and supply—equilibrium prices and GDPs* Actual data showing aggregate demand and supply curves do not exist. However, data for prices (CPI) and GDP do exist for several countries. Go to www.oecd.org/std/fas.htm and look at the data for the United States, Japan, and Germany. Assume that the CPI and GDP figures shown represent the equilibrium price levels and real GDPs for their respective years. Plot the price/GDP levels for the past 3 years for each country, using a graph similar to Figure 11.12. Are there any similarities across countries? What changes in aggregate demand and aggregate supply do the equilibrium points imply?

16. **Web-Based Question:** *Feeling wealthier; spending more* At the St. Louis Federal Reserve Bank website, www.stls.frb.org/fred/data/gdp.html, find the levels of real GDP and real consumption for 1996 and 1999. Did consumption increase more rapidly or less rapidly in percentage terms than disposable income? At averages.dowjones.com/home.html select Dow Data and then Historical Queries to find the level of the Dow Jones Industrial Average (DJIA) for June 28, 1996, and June 30, 1999. What was the percentage change in the DJIA over that period? How might that change help explain your findings about the growth of consumption versus real GDP between 1996 and 1999?

CHAPTER 12

Fiscal Policy

IN THE PREVIOUS chapter we saw that a significant decline in aggregate demand can cause recession and cyclical unemployment, whereas an excessive increase in aggregate demand can cause demand-pull inflation. For those reasons, central governments sometimes use budgetary actions to try to "stimulate the economy" or "reign in inflation." Such so-called **fiscal policy** consists of deliberate changes in government spending and tax collections to achieve full employment, control inflation, and encourage economic growth. 🔑 12.1 ▪ With varying degrees of success, the U.S. government has used fiscal policy in several circumstances. In the early 1960s it cut taxes to increase sluggish economic growth. In 1970 it placed a 10 percent surcharge (a tax on top of existing taxes) on both corporate and personal income taxes to reduce aggregate demand and curb inflation. In the early 1980s it cut personal income taxes by 25 percent over 3 years to increase work incentives and encourage economic growth. In the early 1990s it increased taxes to reduce large Federal budget deficits, which were thought to be causing high real interest rates, low levels of investment, and slow economic growth. ▪ Other nations, too, have used fiscal policy to help cope with recession or inflation. For example, in recent years Japan launched a series of government spending programs designed to increase aggregate demand and extract its economy from major recession. ▪ What is the legal mandate for fiscal policy in the United States? What is the logic behind such policy? Why do some economists question its effectiveness?

▪ Legislative Mandates

In the United States, the idea that government fiscal actions can exert a stabilizing influence on the economy emerged out of the Depression of the 1930s and the ascension of Keynesian economics. Since then, macroeconomic theory has played a major role both in the design of fiscal policy and in an improved understanding of its limitations.

Employment Act of 1946 In 1946, when the end of the Second World War raised anew the specter of unemployment, the Federal government passed the **Employment Act of 1946.** It commits the Federal government to use all practicable means, consistent with the market system, "to create economic conditions under which there will be . . . employment opportunities, including self-employment, for those able, willing, and seeking to work, and to promote maximum employment, production, and purchasing power."

The Employment Act of 1946 is a landmark in American economic legislation. In effect, it commits the Federal government to take action through monetary and fiscal policy in order to maintain economic stability.

CEA and JEC   The executive branch is responsible for fulfilling the purposes of the act; the president must submit an annual report to Congress that describes the current state of the economy and recommends policies to stabilize it. The act also established the **Council of Economic Advisers (CEA)** to assist and advise the president on economic matters and the *Joint Economic Committee (JEC)* of Congress, which has since investigated a wide range of economic problems of national interest.

▮ Fiscal Policy and the AD-AS Model

The fiscal policy that we have been describing is *discretionary* (or "active"). The changes in government spending and taxes are *at the option* of the Federal government. They do not occur automatically, independent of congressional action. The latter changes are *nondiscretionary* (or "passive" or "automatic"), and we will examine them later in this chapter.

Expansionary Fiscal Policy

When recession occurs, an **expansionary fiscal policy** may be in order. Consider Figure 12.1, where we suppose that a sharp decline in investment spending has shifted the economy's aggregate demand curve to the left from AD_1 to AD_2. (Disregard the arrows and the dashed line for now.) The cause of the recession may be that profit expectations on investment projects have dimmed, curtailing investment spending and reducing aggregate demand. As a result, real GDP has fallen from $505 billion to $485 billion. This $20 billion decline in real GDP is accompanied by an increase in unemployment, since fewer workers are needed to produce the reduced output. In short, the economy is experiencing both recession and cyclical unemployment.

What fiscal policy should the Federal government adopt in order to stimulate the economy? It has three main options: (1) increase government spending, (2) reduce taxes, or (3) use some combination of the two. If the Federal budget is balanced at the outset, expansionary fiscal policy will create a government **budget deficit**—government spending in excess of tax revenues.

Increased Government Spending   Other things equal, an increase in government spending will shift an economy's aggregate demand curve to the right, from AD_2 to AD_1 in Figure 12.1. To see why, suppose that the recession prompts the

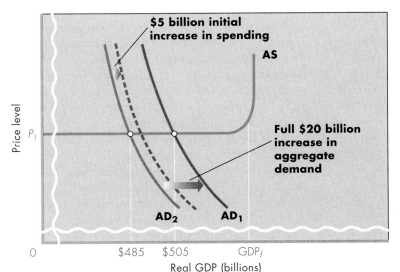

Figure 12.1

Expansionary fiscal policy. Expansionary fiscal policy uses increases in government spending or tax cuts to push the economy out of recession. In an economy with an MPC of .75, a $5 billion increase in government spending or a $6.67 billion decrease in personal taxes (producing a $5 billion initial increase in consumption) expands aggregate demand from AD_2 to the dashed curve. The multiplier then magnifies this initial increase in spending to AD_1. Hence, real GDP rises by $20 billion.

government to initiate $5 billion of new spending on highways, education, and health care. We represent this new $5 billion of government spending as the horizontal distance between AD_2 and the dashed line immediately to its right. At each price level, the amount of real output that is demanded is now $5 billion greater than that demanded before the expansion of government spending.

But the initial increase in aggregate demand is not the end of the story. Through the multiplier effect, the aggregate demand curve shifts to AD_1, a distance that exceeds that represented by the originating $5 billion increase in government purchases. This greater shift occurs because the multiplier process magnifies the initial change in spending into successive rounds of new consumption spending. If the economy's MPC is .75, then the simple multiplier is 4. So the aggregate demand curve shifts rightward by four times the distance between AD_2 and the broken line. Because this *particular* increase in aggregate demand occurs within the horizontal range of aggregate supply, real output rises by the full extent of the multiplier. Observe that real output rises to $505 billion, up $20 billion from its recessionary level of $485 billion. Concurrently, unemployment falls as firms increase their employment back to levels that existed before the recession.

Tax Reductions

Alternatively, the government could reduce taxes to shift the aggregate demand curve rightward, as from AD_2 to AD_1. Suppose the government cuts personal income taxes by $6.7 billion, which increases disposable income by the same amount. Consumption will rise by $5 billion (= MPC of .75 × $6.67 billion), and saving will go up by $1.67 billion (= MPS of .25 × $6.67 billion). In this case the horizontal distance between AD_2 and the dashed line in Figure 12.1 represents only the $5 billion initial increase in consumption spending. Again, we call it "initial" consumption spending because the multiplier process yields successive rounds of increased consumption spending. The aggregate demand curve eventually shifts rightward by four times the $5 billion initial increase in consumption produced by the tax cut. Real GDP rises by $20 billion, from $485 billion to $505 billion, implying a multiplier of 4. Employment increases accordingly.

You may have noted that a tax cut must be somewhat larger than the proposed increase in government spending if it is to achieve the same amount of rightward shift in the aggregate demand curve. This is because part of a tax reduction increases saving, rather than consumption. To increase initial consumption by a specific amount, the government must reduce taxes by more than that amount. With an MPC of .75, taxes must fall by $6.67 billion for $5 billion of new consumption to be forthcoming, because $1.67 billion is saved (not consumed). If the MPC had instead been, say, .6, an $8.33 billion reduction in tax collections would have been necessary to increase initial consumption by $5 billion. The smaller the MPC, the greater the tax cut needed to accomplish a specific initial increase in consumption and a specific shift in the aggregate demand curve.

Combined Government Spending Increases and Tax Reductions The government may combine spending increases and tax cuts to produce the desired initial increase in spending and the eventual increase in aggregate demand and real GDP. In the economy depicted in Figure 12.1, the government might increase its spending by $1.25 billion while reducing taxes by $5 billion. As an exercise, you should explain why this combination will produce the targeted $5 billion initial increase in new spending.

If you were assigned Chapters 9 and 10, think through these three fiscal policy options in terms of the recessionary-gap analysis associated with the aggregate expenditures model (Figure 10.8). And recall from Chapter 11 that rightward shifts of the aggregate demand curve relate directly to upward shifts of the aggregate expenditures schedule. **(Key Question 2)**

Contractionary Fiscal Policy

When demand-pull inflation occurs, a restrictive or **contractionary fiscal policy** may help control it. Figure 12.2 emphasizes the vertical range of aggregate supply. Suppose that a shift of the aggregate demand curve from AD_3 to AD_4 in the vertical range of aggregate supply has boosted the price level from P_3 to P_4. (Ignore the dashed line for now.) This increase in aggregate demand might have resulted from a sharp increase in, say, investment or net export spending. If the government looks to fiscal policy to control this inflation, its options are the opposite of those used to combat recession. It can (1) decrease government spending, (2) raise taxes, or (3) use some combination of those two policies. When the economy faces demand-pull inflation, fiscal policy should move toward a government **budget surplus**—tax revenues in excess of government spending.

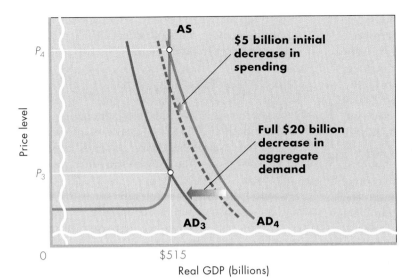

Figure 12.2

Contractionary fiscal policy. Contractionary fiscal policy uses decreases in government spending or increases in taxes to reduce demand-pull inflation. In an economy with an MPC of .75, a $5 billion decline in government spending or a $6.67 billion increase in taxes (producing a $5 billion initial decrease in consumption) shifts the aggregate demand curve from AD_4 to the dashed line. The multiplier effect then shifts the curve farther leftward to AD_3. The overall decrease in aggregate demand halts the demand-pull inflation.

Decreased Government Spending Reduced government spending shifts the aggregate demand curve leftward to control demand-pull inflation. In Figure 12.2, the horizontal distance between AD_4 and the dashed line represents a $5 billion reduction in government spending. Once the multiplier process is complete, this spending cut will have shifted the aggregate demand curve leftward from AD_4 all the way to AD_3. Assuming downward price flexibility, the price level will return to P_3, where it was before demand-pull inflation occurred. Real output will remain at its full-capacity level of $515 billion of real GDP.

As we have seen, in the real world prices tend to be inflexible downward. So stopping inflation is a matter of halting the rise in the price level, not trying to lower it to some previous level. Demand-pull inflation usually is experienced as a continual shifting of the aggregate demand curve to the right. Fiscal policy is designed to stop a shift, not to restore a lower price level. Nevertheless, Figure 12.2 displays the basic principle: Reductions in government expenditures can halt demand-pull inflation.

Increased Taxes Just as government can use tax cuts to increase consumption spending, it can use tax *increases* to *reduce* consumption spending. If the economy in Figure 12.2 has an MPC of .75, the government must raise taxes by $6.67 billion to reduce consumption by $5 billion. The $6.67 billion tax reduces saving by $1.67 billion (= the MPS of .25 × $6.67 billion). This $1.67 billion reduction in saving, by definition, is not a reduction in spending. But the $6.67 billion tax increase also reduces consumption spending by $5 billion (= the MPC of .75 × $6.67

billion), as shown by the distance between AD_4 and the dashed line to its left in Figure 12.2. After the multiplier process is complete, aggregate demand will have shifted leftward by $20 billion at each price level (= multiplier of 4 × $5 billion) and the price level will have fallen from P_4 to P_3. Demand-pull inflation will have been controlled.

Combined Government Spending Decreases and Tax Increases The government may choose to combine spending decreases and tax increases in order to reduce aggregate demand and check inflation. To check your understanding, determine why a $2 billion decline in government spending with a $4 billion increase in taxes would shift the aggregate demand curve from AD_4 to AD_3.

Also, if you were assigned Chapters 9 and 10, explain the three fiscal policy options for fighting inflation by referring to the inflationary-gap concept developed with the aggregate expenditures model (Figure 10.8). And recall from Chapter 11 that leftward shifts of the aggregate demand curve are associated with downshifts of the aggregate expenditures schedule. **(Key Question 3)**

Financing of Deficits and Disposing of Surpluses

The expansionary effect of deficit spending on the economy depends on the method used to finance the deficit. Similarly, the anti-inflationary effect of a budget surplus depends on what is done with the surplus.

Borrowing versus New Money

There are two ways the government can finance a deficit: borrowing from (selling interest-bearing bonds to) the public and, with the help of its monetary authorities, issuing new money to its creditors. The two methods have different effects on aggregate demand:

- **Borrowing from the public** If the government enters the money market and borrows, it will compete for funds with private business borrowers. This added demand for funds might drive up the interest rate and crowd out some private investment spending and interest-sensitive consumer spending. Any decline in private spending will weaken the expansionary effect of the deficit spending.

- **Money creation** If the central bank supports the deficit spending by creating new money, the crowding out of private spending can be avoided. In that case, federal spending can increase without adversely affecting investment or consumption. The creation of new money is more expansionary (but potentially more inflationary) than borrowing as a way of financing deficit spending.

Debt Retirement versus Idle Surplus

Demand-pull inflation calls for fiscal action that will result in a budget surplus. But the anti-inflationary effect of the surplus depends on what the government does with it:

- **Debt reduction** Because the Federal government has a large public debt, it is logical to think that it should use the surplus to reduce the debt. Using the surplus to pay off debt, however, may reduce the anti-inflationary impact of the surplus. To retire its debt, the government buys back some of its bonds; by doing so, it transfers its surplus tax revenues back into the money market, causing interest rates to fall and thus private borrowing and spending to rise. The increase in private spending somewhat offsets the contractionary fiscal policy that created the budget surplus.

- **Impounding** The government can realize a greater anti-inflationary effect from its creation of a budget surplus by impounding the surplus funds—that is, by allowing them to stand idle. When a surplus is impounded, the government is extracting and withholding purchasing power from the economy. If surplus tax revenues are not put back into the economy, no portion of that surplus can be spent. Consequently, there is no chance that the surplus funds will create inflationary pressure to offset the anti-inflationary impact of the

contractionary fiscal policy. Impounding a budget surplus is more anti-inflationary than using the surplus to retire public debt.

Policy Options: G or T?

Which is preferable as a means of eliminating recession and inflation? The use of government spending or the use of taxes? The answer depends largely on one's view as to whether the government is too large or too small.

Economists who believe there are many unmet social and infrastructure needs usually recommend that government spending be increased during recessions. In times of demand-pull inflation, they usually recommend tax increases. Both actions either expand or preserve the size of government.

Economists who think that the government is too large and inefficient usually advocate tax cuts during recessions and cuts in government spending during times of demand-pull inflation. Both actions either restrain the growth of government or reduce its size.

The point is that discretionary fiscal policy designed to stabilize the economy can be associated with either an expanding government or a contracting government.

QUICK REVIEW 12.1

- The Employment Act of 1946 commits the Federal government to promoting "maximum employment, production, and purchasing power."

- Discretionary fiscal policy is the purposeful change of government expenditures and tax collections by government to promote full employment, price stability, and economic growth.

- The government uses expansionary fiscal policy to shift the aggregate demand curve rightward in order to expand real output. This policy entails increases in government spending, reductions in taxes, or some combination of the two.

- The government uses contractionary fiscal policy to shift the aggregate demand curve leftward in an effort to halt demand-pull inflation. This policy entails reductions in government spending, tax increases, or some combination of the two.

- The expansionary effect of fiscal policy is greater when the budget deficit is financed through money creation rather than through borrowing; the contractionary effect of the creation of a budget surplus is greater when the budget surplus is impounded rather than used for debt reduction.

▌ Built-In Stability

To some degree, government tax revenues change automatically over the course of the business cycle and in ways that stabilize the economy. This automatic response, or built-in stability, constitutes nondiscretionary (or "passive" or "automatic") budgetary policy and results from the makeup of most tax systems. We did not include this built-in stability in our discussion of fiscal policy because we implicitly assumed that the same amount of tax revenue was being collected at each level of GDP. But the actual U.S. tax system is such that *net tax revenues* vary directly with GDP. (Net taxes are tax revenues less transfers and subsidies. From here on, we will use the simpler "taxes" to mean "net taxes.")

Virtually any tax will yield more tax revenue as GDP rises. In particular, personal income taxes have progressive rates and thus generate more-than-proportionate increases in tax revenues as GDP expands. Furthermore, as GDP rises and more goods and services are purchased, revenues from corporate income taxes and from sales taxes and excise taxes also increase. And, similarly, revenues from payroll taxes rise as economic expansion creates more jobs. Conversely, when GDP declines, tax receipts from all these sources also decline.

Transfer payments (or "negative taxes") behave in the opposite way from tax revenues. Unemployment compensation payments, welfare payments, and subsidies to farmers all decrease during economic expansion and increase during economic contraction.

Automatic or Built-In Stabilizers

A **built-in stabilizer** is anything that increases the government's budget deficit (or reduces its budget surplus) during a recession and increases its budget surplus (or reduces its budget deficit) during inflation without requiring explicit action by policymakers. As Figure 12.3 reveals, this is precisely what the U.S. tax system does. Government expenditures *G* are fixed and assumed to be independent of the level of GDP. Congress decides on a particular level of spending, but it does not determine the magnitude of tax revenues. Instead, it establishes tax rates, and the tax revenues then vary directly with the level of GDP that the economy achieves. Line *T* represents that direct relationship between tax revenues and GDP.

Economic Importance   The economic importance of the direct relationship between tax receipts and GDP becomes apparent when we consider that:
- Taxes reduce spending and aggregate demand.
- Reductions in spending are desirable when the economy is moving toward inflation, whereas increases in spending are desirable when the economy is slumping.

As shown in Figure 12.3, tax revenues automatically increase as GDP rises during prosperity, and since taxes reduce household and business spending, they restrain the economic expansion. That is, as the economy moves toward a higher GDP, tax revenues automatically rise and move the budget from deficit toward surplus. In Figure 12.3, observe that the high and perhaps inflationary income level GDP$_3$ automatically generates a contractionary budget surplus.

Conversely, as GDP falls during recession, tax revenues automatically decline, increasing spending and cushioning the economic contraction. With a falling GDP, tax receipts decline and move the government's budget from surplus toward deficit. In Figure 12.3, the low level of income GDP$_1$ will automatically yield an expansionary budget deficit.

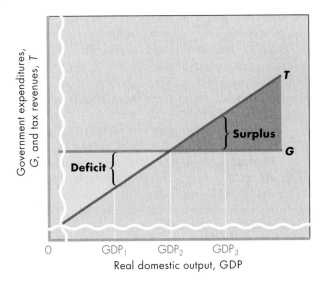

Figure 12.3

Built-in stability. Tax revenues *T* vary directly with GDP, and government spending *G* is assumed to be independent of GDP. As GDP falls in a recession, deficits occur automatically and help alleviate the recession. As GDP rises during expansion, surpluses occur automatically and help offset possible inflation.

Tax Progressivity   Figure 12.3 reveals that the size of the automatic budget deficits or surpluses—and therefore built-in stability—depends on the responsiveness of tax revenues to changes in GDP. If tax revenues change sharply as GDP changes, the slope of line T in the figure will be steep and the vertical distances between T and G (the deficits or surpluses) will be large. If tax revenues change very little when GDP changes, the slope will be gentle and built-in stability will be low.

The steepness of T in Figure 12.3 depends on the tax system itself. In a **progressive tax system,** the average tax rate (= tax revenue/GDP) rises with GDP. In a **proportional tax system,** the average tax rate remains constant as GDP rises. In a **regressive tax system,** the average tax rate falls as GDP rises. The progressive tax system has the steepest tax line T of the three. However, tax revenues will rise with GDP under both the progressive and the proportional tax systems, and they may rise, fall, or stay the same under a regressive tax system. The main point is this: *The more progressive the tax system, the greater the economy's built-in stability.*

So changes in public policies or laws that alter the progressivity of the tax system affect the degree of built-in stability. For example, in 1993 the Clinton administration increased the highest marginal tax rate on personal income from 31 to 39.6 percent and boosted the corporate income tax 1 percentage point, to 35 percent. These increases in tax rates raised the overall progressivity of the tax system, bolstering the economy's built-in stability. As the economy expanded vigorously in the late 1990s, the Federal budget swung from deficit to surplus. That swing helped dampen private spending and forestall demand-pull inflation.

The built-in stability provided by the U.S. tax system has reduced the severity of business fluctuations. But built-in stabilizers can only diminish, not eliminate, swings in real GDP. Discretionary fiscal policy (changes in tax rates and expenditures) or monetary policy (central bank–caused changes in interest rates) may be needed to correct recession or inflation of any appreciable magnitude.

∎ Evaluating Fiscal Policy

How can we determine whether discretionary fiscal policy is expansionary, neutral, or contractionary in a particular period? We cannot simply examine changes in the actual budget deficits or surpluses, because those changes may reflect automatic changes in tax revenues that accompany changes in GDP, not changes in discretionary fiscal policy. Moreover, the strength of any deliberate change in government spending or taxes depends on how large it is relative to the size of the economy. So, in evaluating the status of fiscal policy, we must:

- Adjust deficits and surpluses to eliminate automatic changes in tax revenues.
- Compare the sizes of the adjusted budget deficits (or surpluses) to the levels of GDP.

Full-Employment Budget

Economists use the **full-employment budget** (also called the *standardized budget*) to adjust the actual Federal budget deficits and surpluses to eliminate the automatic changes in tax revenues. The full-employment budget measures what the Federal budget deficit or surplus would be with existing tax rates and government spending levels if the economy had achieved its full-employment level of GDP (its potential output) in each year. The idea is to compare *actual* government expenditures for each year with the tax revenues *that would have occurred* in that year if the economy had achieved full-employment GDP. That procedure removes budget deficits or surpluses that arise simply because of changes in GDP and thus tell us nothing about changes in discretionary fiscal policy.

Consider Figure 12.4a, where line G represents government expenditures and line T represents tax revenues. In full-employment year 1, government expenditures of $500 billion equal tax revenues of $500 billion, as indicated by the intersection of lines G and T at point a. The full-employment budget deficit in year 1 is zero—government expenditures equal the tax revenues forthcoming at the full-employment output GDP_1. Obviously, the full-employment deficit *as a percentage of GDP* is also zero.

Now suppose that a recession occurs and GDP falls from GDP_1 to GDP_2, as shown in Figure 12.4a. Let's also assume that the government takes no discretionary action, so lines G and T remain as shown in the figure. Tax revenues automatically fall to $450 billion (point c) at GDP_2, while government spending remains unaltered at $500 billion (point b). A $50 billion budget deficit (represented by distance

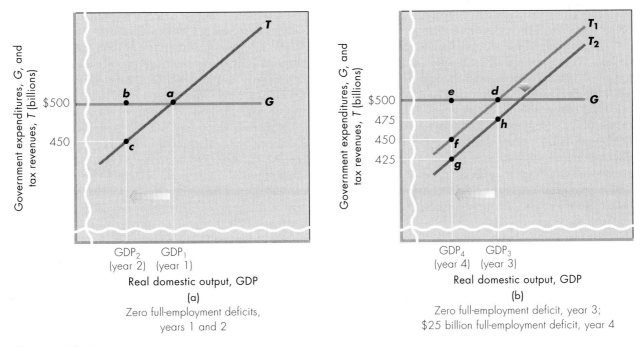

Figure 12.4

Full-employment deficits. (a) In the left-hand graph the full-employment deficit is zero at the full-employment output GDP$_1$. But it is also zero at the recessionary output GDP$_2$, because the $500 billion of government expenditures at GDP$_2$ equals the $500 of tax revenues that would be forthcoming at the full-employment GDP$_1$. There has been no change in fiscal policy. (b) In the right-hand graph, discretionary fiscal policy, as reflected in the downward shift of the tax line from T_1 to T_2, has increased the full-employment budget deficit from zero in year 3 to $25 billion in year 4. This is found by comparing the $500 billion of government spending in year 4 with the $475 billion of taxes that would accrue at the full-employment GDP$_3$. Such a rise in the full-employment deficit (as a percentage of GDP) identifies an expansionary fiscal policy.

bc) arises. But this **cyclical deficit** is simply a by-product of the economy's slide into recession, not the result of discretionary fiscal actions by the government. We would be wrong to conclude from this deficit that the government is engaging in an expansionary fiscal policy.

That fact is highlighted when we consider the full-employment budget deficit for year 2 in Figure 12.4a. The $500 billion of government expenditures in year 2 are shown by *b* on line *G*. And, as shown by *a* on line *T*, $500 billion of tax revenues would have occurred if the economy had achieved its full-employment GDP. Because both *b* and *a* represent $500 billion, the full-employment budget deficit in year 2 is zero, as is this deficit as a percentage of GDP. Since the full-employment deficits are zero in both years, we know that government did not change its discretionary fiscal policy, even though a recession occurred and an actual deficit of $50 billion resulted.

Next, consider Figure 12.4b. Suppose that real output declined from full-employment GDP$_3$ to GDP$_4$. But also suppose that the Federal government responded to the recession by reducing tax rates in year 4, as represented by the downward shift of the tax line from T_1 to T_2. What has happened to the size of the full-employment deficit? Government expenditures in year 4 are $500 billion, as shown by *e*. We compare that amount with the $475 billion of tax revenues that would occur if the economy achieved its full-employment GDP. That is, we compare position *e* on line *G* with position *h* on line T_2. The $25 billion of tax revenues by which *e* exceeds *h* is the full-employment budget deficit for year 4. (It is equal to the actual deficit of *eg* in year 4 *minus* the cyclical deficit of *ef*.) As a percentage of GDP, the full-employment budget deficit has increased from zero in year 3 (before the tax-rate cut) to some positive percent [= ($25 *billion*/GDP$_4$) × 100] in year 4. This increase in the relative size of the full-employment deficit between the two years reveals that fiscal policy is *expansionary*.

In contrast, if we observed a full-employment deficit (as a percentage of GDP) of zero in one year, followed by a full-employment budget surplus in the next, we could conclude that fiscal policy is contractionary. Because the full-employment budget adjusts for automatic changes in tax revenues, the increase in the full-employment budget surplus reveals that government either decreased its spending (*G*) or increased tax rates such that tax revenues (*T*) increased. These changes in *G* and *T* are precisely the discretionary actions that we have identified as elements of a *contractionary* fiscal policy.

Recent U.S. Fiscal Policy

Table 12.1 lists the actual Federal budget deficits and surpluses (column 2) and the full-employment deficits and surpluses (column 3), as percentages of GDP, for recent years. Observe that the full-employment deficits are generally smaller than the actual deficits. This is because the actual deficits include cyclical deficits, whereas the full-employment deficits do not. The latter deficits provide the information needed to assess discretionary fiscal policy.

Column 3 shows that fiscal policy was expansionary in the early 1990s but became contractionary in the later years shown. In this regard, the full-employment budget moved from a deficit of 1.9 percent of GDP in 1995 to a surplus of 1.1 percent in 2000. This contractionary fiscal policy was appropriate in light of the fully employed, rapidly growing U.S. economy over that period. This policy undoubtedly dampened the rapid growth of aggregate demand and contributed to price-level stability. Actual deficits have given way to actual surpluses, and full-employment deficits have given way to full-employment surpluses. Because of these surpluses, the Federal government was well positioned to move toward an expansionary fiscal policy when the economy significantly weakened in 2001. **(Key Question 7)**

Global Perspective 12.1 shows the extent of the actual budget deficits or surpluses of a number of countries in a recent year.

Table 12.1
Federal Deficits (−) and Surpluses (+) as Percentages of GDP, 1991–2000

(1) Year	(2) Actual Deficit or Surplus	(3) Full-Employment Deficit or Surplus
1990	−3.9%	−2.1%
1991	−4.5	−2.6
1992	−4.7	−3.0
1993	−3.9	−2.6
1994	−2.9	−2.0
1995	−2.2	−1.9
1996	−1.4	−1.2
1997	−0.3	−0.9
1998	+0.8	−0.4
1999	+1.4	+0.3
2000	+2.4	+1.1

Source: Congressional Budget Office, www.cbo.gov.

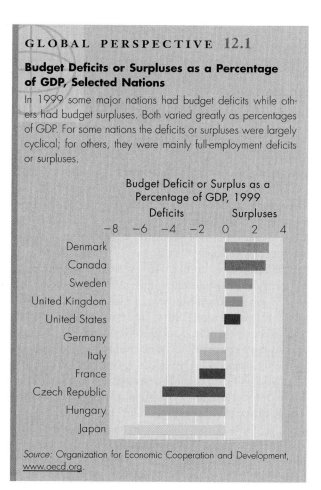

GLOBAL PERSPECTIVE 12.1

Budget Deficits or Surpluses as a Percentage of GDP, Selected Nations

In 1999 some major nations had budget deficits while others had budget surpluses. Both varied greatly as percentages of GDP. For some nations the deficits or surpluses were largely cyclical; for others, they were mainly full-employment deficits or surpluses.

Source: Organization for Economic Cooperation and Development, www.oecd.org.

Problems, Criticisms, and Complications

Economists recognize that governments may encounter a number of significant problems in enacting and applying fiscal policy.

Problems of Timing

Several problems of timing may arise in connection with fiscal policy:

■ *Recognition lag* The recognition lag is the time between the beginning of recession or inflation and the certain awareness that it is actually happening. This lag arises because of the difficulty in predicting the future course of economic activity. Although forecasting tools such as the index of leading indicators (see this chapter's Last Word) provide clues to the direction of the economy, the economy may be 4 or 6 months into a recession or inflation before that fact appears in relevant statistics and is acknowledged. Meanwhile, the economic downslide or the inflation may become more serious than it would have if the situation had been identified and acted on sooner.

■ *Administrative lag* The wheels of democratic government turn slowly. There will typically be a significant lag between the time the need for fiscal action is recognized and the time action is taken. The U.S. Congress has on occasion taken so much time in adjusting fiscal policy that the economic situation has changed in the interim, rendering the belated policy action inappropriate.

■ *Operational lag* A lag also occurs between the time fiscal action is taken and the time that action affects output, employment, or the price level. Although changes in tax rates can be put into effect relatively quickly, government spending on public works—new dams, interstate highways, and so on—requires long planning periods and even longer periods of construction. Such spending is of questionable use in offsetting short (for example, 6- to 18-month) periods of recession. Consequently, discretionary fiscal policy has increasingly relied on tax changes rather than on changes in spending as its main tool.

A Political Business Cycle?

Fiscal policy is conducted in a political arena. Some economists think that political considerations—such as getting reelected—may swamp economic considerations in the conduct of fiscal policy. At the extreme, politicians might manipulate fiscal policy to maximize voter support, even though their fiscal decisions destabilize the economy. In this view, fiscal policy, as we have described it, may be corrupted for political purposes and actually cause economic fluctuations. The result may well be a **political business cycle.**

The populace, it is assumed, takes economic conditions into account in voting. Incumbents are penalized at the polls if the economy is depressed; they are rewarded if it is prosperous. As an election approaches, the incumbent administration (aided by an election-minded Congress) cuts taxes and increases government spending. Not only are these actions popular; they push all the critical economic indicators in positive directions. Output and real incomes rise; unemployment falls; and the price level is relatively stable. As a result, incumbents enjoy a very cordial economic environment for reelection.

But after the election, continued expansion of the economy will be reflected in demand-pull inflation. Growing public concern over inflation may then prompt politicians to enact a contractionary fiscal policy. Crudely put, a "made-in-Washington" recession is engineered by trimming government spending and raising taxes in order to restrain inflation. A mild recession will not hurt an incumbent administration, because the next election is still 2 or 3 years away, and the critical consideration for most voters is how the economy is performing the year or so before the election. Indeed, the recession provides a new starting point from which fiscal policy can be used to generate another expansion in time for the next election campaign.

Such a scenario is difficult to document, and empirical tests of this hypothesis are inconclusive. Nevertheless, there is little doubt that political considerations weigh heavily in the formulation of fiscal policy in election years. The question is how often those political considerations run counter to "sound economics."

Offsetting State and Local Finance

The fiscal policies of state and local governments are frequently *pro-cyclical*, meaning that they worsen rather than correct recession or inflation. Unlike the Federal government, most state and local governments face constitutional or other legal requirements to balance their budgets. Like households and private businesses, state and local governments increase their expenditures during prosperity and cut them during recession. During the Great Depression of the 1930s, most of the increase in Federal spending was offset by decreases in state and local spending. During the recession of 1990–1991, many state and local governments had to increase tax rates, impose new taxes, and reduce spending to offset falling tax revenues resulting from the reduced personal income and spending of their citizens.

Crowding-Out Effect

We now move from the practical problems that arise in implementing fiscal policy to a criticism of fiscal policy itself. That criticism is based on the so-called **crowding-out effect:** An expansionary fiscal policy (deficit spending) will increase the interest rate and reduce private spending, thereby weakening or canceling the stimulus of the expansionary policy. In this view, fiscal policy may be largely or totally ineffective!

Suppose the economy is in recession and government enacts a discretionary fiscal policy in the form of increased government spending. Also suppose that the monetary authorities hold the supply of money constant. To finance its budget deficit, the government borrows funds in the money market. The re-

sulting increase in the demand for money raises the price paid for borrowing money: the interest rate. Because investment spending varies inversely with the interest rate, some investment will be choked off or crowded out. (Some interest-sensitive consumption spending such as purchases of automobiles on credit may also be crowded out). 🔑 12.2

Graphical Presentation Figure 12.5 shows the crowding-out effect graphically. Suppose the economy is enjoying a noninflationary full-capacity level of real GDP at $515 billion, as shown in Figure 12.5a. For simplicity, our aggregate supply curve here has no real-world intermediate range. Up to the $515 billion full-capacity output, the price level is constant. After the economy achieves full capacity, the vertical range of AS prevails, so any additional increase in aggregate demand would be purely inflationary.

We begin in Figure 12.5a with aggregate demand at AD_1, which gives us equilibrium at real GDP of $495 billion. Assume now that government enacts an expansionary fiscal policy that shifts the aggregate demand curve rightward by $20 billion to AD_2. The economy thus achieves full-capacity output without inflation at $515 billion of GDP. Assuming an MPC of .75 and thus a simple multiplier of 4, we know that an increase in government spending of $5 billion or a decrease in taxes of $6.67 billion would create this expansionary effect. With no offsetting or complicating factors, this "pure and simple" expansionary fiscal policy moves the economy from recession to its full-capacity output.

Figure 12.5b shows the complication of crowding out. While fiscal policy is expansionary and designed to shift aggregate demand from AD_1 to AD_2, the borrowing needed to finance the deficit spending presumably increases the interest rate and crowds out some investment spending. The aggregate demand curve thus shifts only to AD_2', not to AD_2. Equilibrium real GDP expands to $505 billion, not to the desired $515 billion. Lesson: The crowding-out effect may greatly weaken expansionary fiscal policy.

Criticisms of the Crowding-Out Effect Nearly all economists agree that a full-employment deficit is inappropriate when the economy has achieved full-employment. Such a deficit will surely crowd out private investment. But there is disagreement on whether crowding out exists under all circumstances. Many economists believe that little crowding out will occur when fiscal policy is used

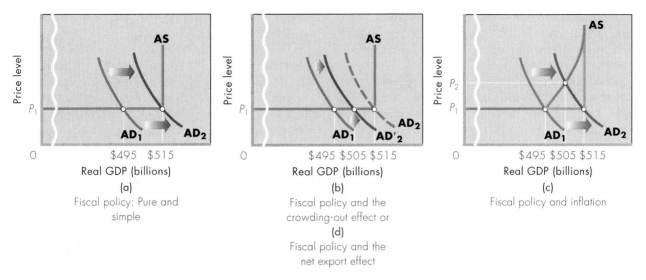

Figure 12.5

Fiscal policy: The effects of crowding out, the net export effect, and inflation.   With a simplified aggregate supply curve, we observe in (a) that fiscal policy is uncomplicated and works at full strength to produce full-employment at a GDP of $515 billion. In (b) it is assumed that some amount of private investment is crowded out by the expansionary fiscal policy and thus fiscal policy is weakened, achieving a GDP of only $505 billion. In (c) a more realistic aggregate supply curve reminds us that when the economy is in the intermediate range of the aggregate supply curve, part of the impact of an expansionary fiscal policy will be reflected in inflation (the price-level rise to P_2). In (d)—the same graph as (b)—we assume that fiscal policy increases the interest rate, thereby attracting foreign financial capital to the United States. The dollar therefore appreciates and U.S. net exports fall, weakening the expansionary fiscal policy. GDP again rises only to $505 billion.

during a severe recession. Both increased government spending and increased consumption spending resulting from tax cuts will likely improve the profit expectations of businesses. The greater expected returns on private investment may encourage more of it. Thus, private investment need not fall, even though interest rates rise. (In terms of Figure 9.7a, the investment demand curve *ID* may shift rightward sufficiently to offset a higher interest rate. So the investment schedule I_g in Figure 9.7b need not decline.)

Critics also point out that policymakers (specifically the Federal Reserve) can counteract the crowding-out effect by increasing the supply of money just enough to offset the deficit-caused increase in the demand for money. Then the equilibrium interest rate would not change, and the crowding-out effect would be zero.

Fiscal Policy, Aggregate Supply, and Inflation

Aggregate supply can also complicate fiscal policy. Suppose there is no crowding-out effect and expansionary fiscal policy shifts the aggregate demand

curve from AD₁ to AD₂, as depicted in Figure 12.5c. If the aggregate supply curve were horizontal as in Figure 12.5a and 12.5b, the price level would remain at P_1 and the economy would achieve full-employment at $515 billion of GDP. But when the aggregate supply curve slopes upward, part of the increase in aggregate demand is dissipated in higher prices. In Figure 12.5c, the price level rises from P_1 to P_2, and real GDP increases from $495 billion to $505 billion, not to $515 billion. Fiscal policy faces the realities imposed by the upward-sloping portion of the aggregate supply curve. It may cause some inflation along with declines in unemployment and increases in real GDP.

Fiscal Policy in the Open Economy

Additional complications arise from the fact that each national economy is a component of the world economy.

Shocks Originating from Abroad   Events and policies abroad that affect a nation's net exports also affect its own economy. National economies are vulnerable to unforeseen international aggregate demand shocks that can alter domestic GDP and make current domestic fiscal policy inappropriate.

Suppose the United States is in a recession and has enacted an expansionary fiscal policy to increase aggregate demand and GDP without igniting inflation (as from AD_1 to AD_2 in Figure 12.5a). Now suppose the economies of the major trading partners of the United States unexpectedly expand rapidly. Greater employment and rising incomes in those nations mean more purchases of U.S. goods. In the United States, net exports rise, and aggregate demand increases so rapidly that the nation experiences demand-pull inflation. If U.S. policymakers had known in advance that net exports might rise significantly, they would have enacted a less expansionary fiscal policy. Participation in the world economy inevitably brings with it the complications of mutual interdependence along with the gains derived from specialization and trade.

Net Export Effect

The **net export effect** may also work through international trade to reduce the effectiveness of fiscal policy. We concluded in our discussion of the crowding-out effect that an expansionary fiscal policy might boost interest rates, thereby reducing investment and weakening current fiscal policy. Now we ask what effect an interest-rate increase might have on a nation's net exports (exports minus imports).

Suppose the United States undertakes an expansionary fiscal policy that causes a higher U.S. interest rate. The higher interest rate will attract financial capital from abroad, where interest rates are unchanged. But foreign financial investors must acquire U.S. dollars in order to invest in U.S. securities. We know that an increase in the demand for a commodity (in this case, dollars) will cause its price to rise. So the price of dollars rises in terms of foreign currencies—that is, the dollar appreciates.

What will be the impact of that dollar appreciation on U.S. net exports? Because more units of foreign currencies are needed to buy goods from the United States, the rest of the world will see U.S. exports as being more expensive. Hence, U.S. exports will decline. Americans, who can now exchange their dollars for more units of foreign currencies, will buy more imports. Consequently, with U.S. exports falling and imports rising, net export expenditures in the United States will diminish. This is a contractionary change, so the expansionary fiscal policy of the United States will be partially negated.[1]

A return to our aggregate demand and supply analysis in Figure 12.5b, now labeled "d", will clarify this point. An expansionary fiscal policy aimed at increasing aggregate demand from AD_1 to AD_2 may hike the domestic interest rate and ultimately reduce net exports through the process just described. The decline in the net export component of aggregate demand will partially offset the expansionary fiscal policy. The aggregate demand curve will shift rightward from AD_1 to AD_2', *not* to AD_2, and equilibrium GDP will increase from $495 billion to $505 billion, *not* to $515 billion. Thus, the net export effect of fiscal policy joins the problems of timing, politics, crowding out, and inflation in complicating the "management" of aggregate demand.

Table 12.2 summarizes the net export effect resulting from fiscal policy. Column 1 reviews the analysis just discussed (Figure 12.5d). But note that the net export effect works in both directions. By reducing the domestic interest rate, a contractionary fiscal policy increases net exports. With that in mind, follow through the analysis in column 2 in Table 12.2 and relate it to the aggregate demand–aggregate supply model. **(Key Question 10)**

Supply-Side Fiscal Policy

We have seen how movements along the aggregate supply curve can complicate the operation of fiscal policy. We now turn to the possibility of a more direct link between fiscal policy and aggregate supply. Economists recognize that **supply-side fiscal policy,** particularly tax changes, may alter aggregate supply and affect the results of a change in fiscal policy.

For simplicity, let's generalize the aggregate supply as an upward-sloping curve, without its distinct segments. Suppose that in Figure 12.6 aggregate demand and aggregate supply are AD_1 and AS_1 and thus the equilibrium level of real GDP is Q_1 and the price level is P_1. Assume also that the government concludes that the level of unemployment associated with Q_1 is too high and therefore enacts an expansionary fiscal policy in the form of a tax cut. The

---

[1]The appreciation of the dollar will also reduce the dollar price of foreign resources such as oil imported into the United States. As a result, aggregate supply will increase and part of the contractionary net export effect described here may be offset.

Table 12.2

Fiscal Policy and the Net Export Effect

(1) Expansionary Fiscal Policy	(2) Contractionary Fiscal Policy
Problem: Recession, slow growth	Problem: Inflation
↓	↓
Expansionary fiscal policy	Contractionary fiscal policy
↓	↓
Higher domestic interest rate	Lower domestic interest rate
↓	↓
Increased foreign demand for dollars	Decreased foreign demand for dollars
↓	↓
Dollar appreciates	Dollar depreciates
↓	↓
Net exports decline (aggregate demand decreases, partially offsetting the expansionary fiscal policy)	Net exports increase (aggregate demand increases, partially offsetting the contractionary fiscal policy)

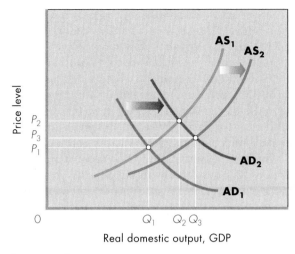

Figure 12.6

Supply-side effects of fiscal policy.   The traditional view is that tax cuts will increase aggregate demand, as from AD_1 to AD_2, increasing both real domestic output (Q_1 to Q_2) and the price level (P_1 to P_2). If the tax reductions induce favorable supply-side effects, aggregate supply will shift rightward, as from AS_1 to AS_2. This allows the economy to realize an even larger output (Q_3 compared with Q_2) and a smaller price-level increase (P_3 compared with P_2).

demand-side effect is an increase in aggregate demand from AD_1 to, say, AD_2. That rightward shift of the aggregate demand curve increases real GDP to Q_2 but also pulls up the price level to P_2.

How might tax cuts affect aggregate supply? "Supply-side economists" contend that tax reductions will shift the aggregate supply curve to the right, negating the inflation and increasing economic growth. They give three main reasons for these effects:

- **Saving and investment**   Lower taxes will increase disposable income and increase household saving. Similarly, tax reductions on businesses will increase the profitability of investment. In brief, lower taxes will increase both saving and investment, thereby increasing the nation's stock of capital. The size of our "national factory"—our production capacity—will grow more rapidly.
- **Work incentives**   Lower personal income tax rates increase after-tax wages and thus encourage work. As a result, any people not already in the labor force will offer their services, and those

already in the labor force will want to work more hours and take fewer vacations.

- **Risk taking**   Lower tax rates encourage risk takers. Entrepreneurs and businesses will be more willing to risk their energies and financial capital on new production methods and new products when lower tax rates promise a larger potential after-tax reward.

Through all these avenues, lower taxes will shift aggregate supply to the right, say, from AS_1 to AS_2 in Figure 12.6, reducing inflation and further increasing real GDP.

Some supply-side economists also say that lower tax rates will not result in lower tax revenues. In fact, they say that lower tax rates that cause a substantial expansion of output and income may generate increases in tax revenues. This enlarged tax base may enhance total tax revenues even though tax rates are lower. (The mainstream view is that a reduction in U.S. tax rates will reduce tax revenues.)

Mainstream Skepticism   Most economists are skeptical about the effectiveness of supply-side tax cuts, particularly in view of evidence gleaned from the supply-side tax cuts of the 1980s. First, they doubt that the positive effects of a tax reduction on incentives to work, to save and invest, and to bear risks are nearly as strong as supply-siders believe. Indeed, the U.S. economy has boomed even though personal income tax rates were significantly raised in 1995. Second, most economists think that any rightward shifts of the aggregate supply curve would occur only over an extended period of time, whereas the demand-side impact would be much more immediate, and therefore potentially inflationary.

Such criticisms aside, however, mainstream economists now agree with supply-side economists that government needs to consider potential aggregate supply effects when formulating its discretionary fiscal policy.

QUICK REVIEW 12.3

- Time lags and political problems complicate fiscal policy.

- The crowding-out effect indicates that an expansionary fiscal policy may increase the interest rate and reduce investment spending.

- The upward-sloping range of the aggregate supply curve means that part of an expansionary fiscal policy may be dissipated in inflation.

- Fiscal policy may be weakened by the net export effect, which works through changes in (a) the interest rate, (b) exchange rates, and (c) exports and imports.

The Leading Indicators

One of several tools policymakers use to forecast the future direction of real GDP is a monthly index of 10 variables that in the past have provided advance notice of changes in GDP.

The Conference Board's *index of leading indicators* has historically reached a peak or a trough in advance of corresponding turns in the business cycle.* Thus changes in this composite index of 10 economic variables provide a clue to the future direction of the economy. Such advance warning helps policymakers formulate appropriate macroeconomic policy.

Here is how each of the 10 components of the index would change if it were predicting a decline in real GDP. The opposite changes would forecast a rise in real GDP.

1. Average workweek Decreases in the length of the average workweek of production workers in manufacturing foretell declines in future manufacturing output and possible declines in real GDP.

2. Initial claims for unemployment insurance Higher first-time claims for unemployment insurance are associated with falling employment and subsequently sagging real GDP.

3. New orders for consumer goods Decreases in the number of orders received by manufacturers for consumer goods portend reduced future production—a decline in real GDP.

4. Vendor performance Somewhat ironically, better on-time delivery by sellers of inputs indicates slackening business demand and potentially falling real GDP.

5. New orders for capital goods A drop in orders for capital equipment and other investment goods implies reduced future aggregate demand and thus lower real GDP.

6. Building permits for houses Decreases in the number of building permits issued for new homes imply future declines in investment and therefore the possibility that real GDP will fall.

7. Stock prices Declines in stock prices often are reflections of expected declines in corporate sales and profits. Also, lower stock

prices diminish consumer wealth, leading to possible cutbacks in consumer spending. Lower stock prices also make it less attractive for firms to issue new shares of stock as a way of raising funds for investment. Thus, declines in stock prices can bring forth declines in aggregate demand and real GDP.

8. Money supply Decreases in the nation's money supply are associated with falling real GDP.

9. Interest-rate spread Increases in short-term nominal interest rates typically reflect monetary policies designed to slow the economy. Such policies have much less effect on long-term interest rates, which usually are higher than short-term rates. So a smaller difference between short-term interest rates and long-term interest rates suggests restrictive monetary policies and potentially a future decline in GDP.

10. Consumer expectations Less favorable consumer attitudes about future economic conditions, measured by an index of consumer expectations, foreshadow lower consumption spending and potential future declines in GDP.

None of these factors alone consistently predicts the future course of the economy. It is not unusual in any month, for example, for one or two of the indicators to be decreasing while the other indicators are increasing. Rather, changes in the composite of the 10 components are what in the past have provided advance notice of a change in the direction of GDP. The rule of thumb is that three successive monthly declines or increases in the index indicate the economy will soon turn in that same direction.

Although the composite index has correctly signaled business fluctuations on numerous occasions, it has not been infallible. At times the index has provided false warnings of recessions that never happened. In other instances, recessions have so closely followed the downturn in the index that policymakers have not had sufficient time to make use of the "early" warning. Moreover, changing structural features of the economy have, on occasion, rendered the existing index obsolete and necessitated its revision.

Given these caveats, the index of leading indicators can best be thought of as a useful but not totally reliable signaling device that authorities must employ with considerable caution in formulating macroeconomic policy.

*The Conference Board is a private, nonprofit research and business membership group, with more than 2700 corporate and other members in 60 nations. See www.conference-board.org.

SUMMARY

1. Government responsibility for achieving and maintaining full-employment is specified in the Employment Act of 1946. The Council of Economic Advisers (CEA) was established to advise the president on policies to fulfill the goals of the act.

2. Other things equal, increases in government spending expand, and decreases contract, aggregate demand and equilibrium GDP. Increases in taxes reduce, and decreases expand, aggregate demand and equilibrium GDP. Fiscal policy therefore calls for increases in government spending and decreases in taxes—a budget deficit—to correct for recession. Decreases in government spending and increases in taxes—a budget surplus—are appropriate fiscal policy for correcting demand-pull inflation.

3. Built-in stability arises from net tax revenues, which vary directly with the level of GDP. During recession, the Federal budget automatically moves toward a stabilizing deficit; during expansion, the budget automatically moves toward an anti-inflationary surplus. Built-in stability lessens, but does not fully correct, undesired changes in the real GDP.

4. The full-employment budget or standardized budget measures the Federal budget deficit or surplus that would occur if the economy operated at full

employment throughout the year. Cyclical deficits or surpluses are those that result from changes in GDP.

5. Changes in the full-employment deficit or surplus provide meaningful information as to whether the government's fiscal policy is expansionary, neutral, or contractionary. Changes in the actual budget deficit or surplus do not, since such deficits or surpluses can include cyclical deficits or surpluses.

6. The enactment and application of appropriate fiscal policy are subject to certain problems and questions, such as these: (a) Can fiscal policy be better timed to maximize its effectiveness in heading off economic fluctuations? (b) Can the economy rely on Congress to enact appropriate fiscal policy? (c) An expansionary fiscal policy may be weakened if it crowds out some private investment spending. (d) Some of the effect of an expansionary fiscal policy may be dissipated in inflation. (e) Fiscal policy may be rendered ineffective or inappropriate by unforeseen events occurring within the borders of international trading partners. Also, fiscal policy may precipitate changes in exchange rates that weaken its effects. (f) Supply-side economists contend that traditional fiscal policy fails to consider the effects of tax changes on aggregate supply.

TERMS AND CONCEPTS

fiscal policy

Employment Act of 1946

Council of Economic
    Advisers (CEA)

expansionary fiscal policy

budget deficit

contractionary fiscal
    policy

budget surplus

built-in stabilizer

progressive tax system

proportional tax system

regressive tax system

full-employment budget

cyclical deficit

political business cycle

crowding-out effect

net export effect

supply-side fiscal policy

STUDY QUESTIONS

1. What is the central thrust of the Employment Act of 1946? What is the role of the Council of Economic Advisers (CEA) in response to this law? Class assignment: Determine the names and educational backgrounds of the present members of the CEA.

2. **Key Question** Assume that a hypothetical economy with an MPC of .8 is experiencing severe recession. By how much would government spending have to increase to shift the aggregate demand curve rightward by $25 billion? How large a tax cut would be needed to achieve the same increase in aggregate demand? Why the difference? Determine one possible combination of government spending increases and tax decreases that would accomplish the same goal.

3. **Key Question** What are government's fiscal policy options for ending severe demand-pull inflation? Use the aggregate demand–aggregate supply model to show the impact of these policies on the price level. Which of these fiscal policy options do you think a "conservative" economist might favor? A "liberal" economist?

4. (For students who were assigned Chapters 9 and 10) Use the aggregate expenditures model to show how government fiscal policy could eliminate either a recessionary gap or an inflationary gap (Figure 10.8). Use the concept of the balanced-budget multiplier to explain how equal increases in G and T could eliminate a recessionary gap and how equal decreases in G and T could eliminate an inflationary gap.

5. Designate each of the following statements as true or false and justify your answer:
   a. Expansionary fiscal policy during a depression will have a greater positive effect on real GDP if the government borrows the money to finance the budget deficit than if it creates new money to finance the deficit.
   b. Contractionary fiscal policy during severe demand-pull inflation will be more effective if the government impounds the budget surplus rather than using the surplus to pay off some of its debt.

6. Explain how built-in (or automatic) stabilizers work. What are the differences between proportional, progressive, and regressive tax systems as they relate to an economy's built-in stability?

7. **Key Question** Define the full-employment budget, explain its significance, and state why it may differ from the actual budget. Suppose the full-employment, noninflationary level of real output is GDP$_3$ (not GDP$_2$) in the economy depicted in Figure 12.3. If the economy is operating at GDP$_2$, instead of GDP$_3$, what is the status of it full-employment budget? Of its current fiscal policy? What change in fiscal policy would you recommend? How would you accomplish that in terms of the G and T lines in the figure?

8. As shown in Table 12.1, between 1990 and 1991 the actual budget deficit (as a percentage of GDP) grew more rapidly than the full-employment budget deficit. What could explain this fact?

9. Some politicians have suggested that the United States enact a constitutional amendment requiring that the Federal government balance its budget annually. Explain why such an amendment, if strictly enforced, would force the government to enact a *contractionary* fiscal policy whenever the economy experienced a severe recession.

10. **Key Question** Briefly state and evaluate the problem of time lags in enacting and applying fiscal policy. Explain the notion of a political business cycle. What is the crowding-out effect, and why is it relevant to fiscal policy? In what respect is the net export effect similar to the crowding-out effect?

11. In view of your answers to question 10, explain the following statement: "While fiscal policy clearly is useful in combating the extremes of severe recession and demand-pull inflation, it is impossible to use fiscal policy to fine-tune the economy to the full-employment, noninflationary level of real GDP and keep the economy there indefinitely."

12. Suppose that the government engages in deficit spending to push the economy away from recession and that this spending is directed toward new "public capital" such as roads, bridges, dams, harbors, office parks, and industrial sites. How might this spending increase the expected rate of return on some types of potential private investment projects? What are the implications for the crowding-out effect?

13. Use Figure 12.4a to explain why the deliberate increase of the full-employment budget (resulting from the tax cut) will reduce the size of the actual budget deficit if the fiscal policy succeeds in pushing the economy to its full-employment output of GDP$_3$. In requesting a tax cut in the early 1960s, President Kennedy said, "It is a paradoxical truth that tax rates are too high today and tax revenues are too low and the soundest way to raise tax revenues in the long run is to cut tax rates now." Relate this quotation to your previous answer in this question.

14. Discuss: "Mainstream economists tend to focus on the aggregate demand effects of tax-rate reductions; supply-side economists emphasize the aggregate supply effects." Identify three routes through which a tax cut might increase aggregate supply. If tax cuts are so good for the economy, why don't we cut taxes to zero?

15. **Advanced Analysis** (For students who were assigned Chapters 9 and 10). Assume that, without taxes, the consumption schedule for an economy is as shown below:

GDP, Billions	Consumption, Billions
$100	$120
200	200
300	280
400	360
500	440
600	520
700	600

   a. Graph this consumption schedule, and determine the size of the MPC.
   b. Assume that a lump-sum (regressive) tax of $10 billion is imposed at all levels of GDP. Calculate the tax rate at each level of GDP. Graph the resulting consumption schedule, and compare the MPC and the multiplier with those of the pretax consumption schedule.
   c. Now suppose a proportional tax with a 10 percent tax rate is imposed instead of the regressive tax. Calculate and graph the new consumption schedule, and note the MPC and the multiplier.
   d. Finally, impose a progressive tax such that the tax rate is 0 percent when GDP is $100, 5 percent at $200, 10 percent at $300, 15 percent at $400, and so forth. Determine and graph the new consumption schedule, noting the effect of this tax system on the MPC and the multiplier.

e. Explain why proportional and progressive taxes contribute to greater economic stability, while a regressive tax does not. Demonstrate, using a graph similar to Figure 12.3.

16. **(Last Word)** What is the index of leading economic indicators, and how does it relate to discretionary fiscal policy?

17. **Web-Based Question:** *Leading economic indicators—how goes the economy?* The Conference Board, at www.conference-board.org/index.htm, tracks the leading economic indicators. Check the summary of the index of leading indicators and its individual components for the latest month. Is the index up or down? Which specific components are up, and which are down? What has been the trend of the composite index over the past 3 months?

18. **Web-Based Question:** *Current budget projections— deficits or surpluses?* The Congressional Budget Office, at www.cbo.gov/index.html, projects future deficits or surpluses on the basis of various assumptions about spending and the growth of the economy. Go to "Current Budget Projections" to find projections based on the assumption that government discretionary spending rises at the rate of inflation. What are the CBO projections for standardized (full-employment) deficits or surpluses (on budget) as a percentage of GDP over the next 10 years? Do the projected full-employment budget deficits or surpluses represent contractionary or expansionary fiscal policy? How might congressional actions, changes in the economy, or both, alter the actual budget outcomes?

3

Money, Banking, and Monetary Policy

CHAPTER

13

Money and Banking

MONEY IS A fascinating aspect of the economy:

Money bewitches people. They fret for it, and they sweat for it. They devise most ingenious ways to get it, and most ingenuous ways to get rid of it. Money is the only commodity that is good for nothing but to be gotten rid of. It will not feed you, clothe you, shelter you, or amuse you unless you spend it or invest it. It imparts value only in parting. People will do almost anything for money, and money will do almost anything for people. Money is a captivating, circulating, masquerading puzzle.[1]

In this chapter and the two chapters that follow we want to unmask the critical role of money and the monetary system in the economy. When the monetary system is working properly, it provides the lifeblood of the circular flows of income and expenditure. A well-operating monetary system helps the economy achieve both full employment and the efficient use of resources. A malfunctioning monetary system creates severe fluctuations in the economy's levels of output, employment, and prices and distorts the allocation of resources.

[1]Federal Reserve Bank of Philadelphia, "Creeping Inflation," *Business Review*, August 1957, p. 3.

■ The Functions of Money

Just what is money? There is an old saying that "money *is* what money *does*." In a general sense, anything that performs the functions of money *is* money. Here are those functions:

■ *Medium of exchange* First and foremost, money is a **medium of exchange** that is usable for buying and selling goods and services. A bakery worker does not want to be paid 200 bagels per week. Nor does the bakery owner want to receive, say, halibut in exchange for bagels. Money, however, is readily acceptable as payment. As we saw in Chapter 4, money is a social invention with which resource suppliers and producers can be paid and that can be used to buy any of the full range of items available in the marketplace. As a medium of exchange, money allows society to escape the complications of barter. And because it provides a convenient way of exchanging goods, money enables society to gain the advantages of geographic and human specialization.

- *Unit of account* Money is also a **unit of account.** Society uses monetary units—dollars, in the United States—as a yardstick for measuring the relative worth of a wide variety of goods, services, and resources. Just as we measure distance in miles or kilometers, we gauge the value of goods in dollars.

  With money as an acceptable unit of account, the price of each item need be stated only in terms of the monetary unit. We need not state the price of cows in terms of corn, crayons, and cigars. Money aids rational decision making by enabling buyers and sellers to easily compare the prices of various goods, services, and resources. It also permits us to define debt obligations, determine taxes owed, and calculate the nation's GDP.

- *Store of value* Money also serves as a **store of value** that enables people to transfer purchasing power from the present to the future. People normally do not spend all their incomes on the day they receive them. In order to buy things later, they store some of their wealth as money. The money you place in a safe or a checking account will still be available to you a few weeks or months from now. Money is often the preferred store of value for short periods because it is the most liquid (spendable) of all assets. People can obtain their money nearly instantly and can immediately use it to buy goods or take advantage of financial investment opportunities. When inflation is nonexistent or mild, holding money is a relatively risk-free way to preserve your wealth for later use.

▪ The Supply of Money

Societies have used many items as money, including whales' teeth, circular stones, elephant-tail bristles, gold coins, furs, and pieces of paper. Anything that is widely accepted as a medium of exchange can serve as money. In the United States, certain debts of government and of financial institutions are used as money, as you will see.

Money Definition M1

The narrowest definition of the U.S. money supply is called **M1.** It consists of:

- Currency (coins and paper money) in the hands of the public.
- All checkable deposits (all deposits in commercial banks and "thrift" or savings institutions on which checks of any size can be drawn).[2]

Coins and paper money are debts of government and government agencies. Checkable deposits are debts of commercial banks and savings institutions. Table 13.1 shows the amount of each sort of money in the M1 money supply.

Currency: Coins + Paper Money From copper pennies to gold-colored dollars, coins are the "small change" of our money supply. Coins, however, constitute only 2 or 3 percent of M1.

All coins in circulation in the United States are **token money.** This means that the *intrinsic value*, or the value of the metal contained in the coin itself, is less than the face value of the coin. This is to prevent people from melting down the coins for sale as a "commodity," in this case, the metal. If 50-cent pieces each contained 75 cents' worth of silver metal, it would be profitable to melt them and sell the metal. The 50-cent pieces would disappear from circulation.

Paper money constitutes about 46 percent of the U.S. economy's M1 money supply. All this paper currency is in the form of **Federal Reserve Notes,** issued by the Federal Reserve System (the U.S. central bank) with the authorization of Congress. Every bill carries the phrase "Federal Reserve Note" on its face. ▪ 13.1

Checkable Deposits The safety and convenience of checks has made **checkable deposits** the largest component of the M1 money supply. You would not think of stuffing $4896 in bills in an envelope and dropping it in a mailbox to pay a debt. But writing and mailing a check for a large sum is commonplace. The person cashing a check must

---

[2]In the ensuing discussion, we do not discuss several of the quantitatively less significant components of the definitions of money in order to avoid a maze of details. For example, traveler's checks are included in the M1 money supply. Reference to the statistical appendix of any recent *Federal Reserve Bulletin* will provide you with more comprehensive definitions.

Table 13.1

Alternative Money Definitions for the United States: M1, M2, and M3

Definition	Absolute Amount, Billions	M1	M2	M3
Currency (coins and paper money)	$ 523	48%	11%	8%
plus Checkable deposits	578*	52	12	8
equals **M1**	**$1101**	100%		
plus Savings deposits, including money market deposit accounts (MMDAs)	1812		38	26
plus Small time deposits	1024*		21	15
plus Money market mutual fund (MMMF) balances	890		18	13
equals **M2**	**$4827**		100%	
plus Large time deposits	2026*			30
equals **M3**	**$6853**			100%

The "Percentage of Total" header spans the M1, M2, and M3 columns.

*These figures include other quantitatively smaller components.

Source: *Federal Reserve Release*, Oct. 19, 2000 (www.federalreserve.gov). Data are for August 2000.

endorse it (sign it on the reverse side); the writer of the check subsequently receives a record of the canceled check as a receipt attesting to the fulfillment of the obligation. Similarly, because the writing of a check requires endorsement, the theft or loss of your checkbook is not nearly as calamitous as losing an identical amount of currency. Finally, it is more convenient to write a check than to transport and count out a large sum of currency. For all these reasons, checkable deposits (checkbook money) are a large component of the stock of money in the United States. About 52 percent of $M1$ is in the form of checkable deposits, on which checks can be drawn.

It might seem strange that checking accounts are regarded as part of the money supply. But the reason is clear: Checks are nothing more than a way to transfer the ownership of deposits in banks and other financial institutions and are generally acceptable as a medium of exchange. Although checks are less generally accepted than currency for small purchases, for major purchases most sellers willingly accept checks as payment. Moreover, people can convert checkable deposits into paper money and coins on demand; checks drawn on those deposits are thus the equivalent of currency.

To summarize:

Money, $M1$ = currency + checkable deposits

Institutions That Offer Checkable Deposits

In the United States, several types of financial institutions allow customers to write checks in any

amount on the funds they have deposited. **Commercial banks** are the primary depository institutions. They accept the deposits of households and businesses, keep the money safe until it is demanded via checks, and in the meantime use it to make available a wide variety of loans. Commercial bank loans provide short-term financial capital to businesses, and they finance consumer purchases of automobiles and other durable goods.

Savings and loan associations (S&Ls), mutual savings banks, and credit unions supplement the commercial banks and are known collectively as savings or **thrift institutions,** or simply "thrifts." *Savings and loan associations* and *mutual savings banks* accept the deposits of households and businesses and then use the funds to finance housing mortgages and to provide other loans. *Credit unions* accept deposits from and lend to "members," who usually are a group of people who work for the same company.

The checkable deposits of banks and thrifts are known variously as demand deposits, NOW (negotiable order of withdrawal) accounts, ATS (automatic transfer service) accounts, and share draft accounts. Their commonality is that depositors can write checks on them whenever, and in whatever amount, they choose.

A Qualification   We must qualify our discussion in an important way. Currency and checkable deposits owned by the government (the U.S. Treasury) and by Federal Reserve Banks, commercial banks, or other financial institutions are *excluded* from *M*1 and other measures of the money supply.

A paper dollar in the hands of, say, Emma Buck obviously constitutes just $1 of the money supply. But if we counted dollars held by banks as part of the money supply, the same $1 would count for $2 when it was deposited in a bank. It would count for a $1 demand deposit owned by Buck and also for $1 of currency resting in the bank's till or vault. By excluding currency resting in banks in determining the total money supply, we avoid this problem of double counting.

Excluding currency held by, and checkable deposits owned by, the government is more arbitrary. This exclusion permits economists to better gauge the money supply and the rate of spending in the private sector of the economy as distinct from spending initiated by government policy.

Money Definition M2

A second and broader definition of money includes *M*1 plus several near-monies. **Near-monies** are certain highly liquid financial assets that do not function directly or fully as a medium of exchange but can be readily converted into currency or checkable deposits. There are three categories of near-monies included in the *M2* definition of money:

- *Savings deposits, including money market deposit accounts* A depositor can easily withdraw funds from a **savings account** at a bank or thrift or simply request that the funds be transferred from a savings account to a checkable account. A person can also withdraw funds from a **money market deposit account (MMDA),** which is an interest-bearing account through which banks and thrifts pool individual deposits to buy a variety of interest-bearing short-term securities. MMDA, however, have a minimum balance requirement and a limit on how often a person can withdraw funds.

- *Small (less than $100,000) time deposits* Funds from **time deposits** become available at their maturity. For example, a person can convert a 6-month time deposit ("certificate of deposit") to currency without penalty 6 months or more after it has been deposited. In return for this withdrawal limitation, the financial institution pays a higher interest rate on such deposits than it does on its MMDA. Also, a person can "cash in" a CD at any time but must pay a severe penalty.

- *Money market mutual funds* By making a telephone call, using the Internet, or writing a check for $500 or more, a depositor can redeem shares in a **money market mutual fund (MMMF)** offered by a mutual fund company. Such companies use the combined funds of individual shareholders to buy interest-bearing short-term credit instruments such as certificates of deposit and U.S. government securities. They in turn can offer interest on the money market accounts of their mutual fund customers (depositors).

All three categories of near-monies imply substantial liquidity. Thus, in equation form,

$$\text{Money, } M2 = \begin{array}{l} M1 + \text{savings deposits,} \\ \text{including MMDAs} + \text{small} \\ \text{(less than \$100,000) time deposits} \\ + \text{MMMFs} \end{array}$$

In summary, *M2* includes the immediate medium-of-exchange items (currency and checkable deposits) that constitute *M*1 plus certain near-monies that can be easily converted into currency and checkable deposits. In Table 13.1 we see that the addition of all these items yields an *M2* money supply of $4827 billion compared to the narrower *M*1 money supply of $1101 billion.

Money Definition M3

A third definition of the money supply, **M3,** includes large ($100,000 or more) time deposits, usually owned by businesses as certificates of deposit. There is a market for these certificates, and they can be sold (liquidated) at any time, although perhaps at the risk of a loss. Businesses normally use large time deposits for saving, not as "money." But since businesses can convert these deposits into checkable deposits, they also are a near-money. Adding large time deposits to *M2* yields the still broader *M3* definition of the money supply:

$$\text{Money, } M3 = \begin{array}{l} M2 + \text{large (\$100,000 or} \\ \text{more) time deposits} \end{array}$$

In Table 13.1 the *M3* money supply is $6853 billion.

Still other slightly less liquid assets, such as certain government securities (for example, Treasury bills and bonds), can be easily converted into *M*1 money. Actually, there is an entire spectrum of assets that vary slightly in terms of their liquidity or "moneyness" that are not included in *M*1, *M2*, or *M3*.

Because the simple *M*1 definition includes only items directly and immediately usable as a medium of exchange, it is usually cited in discussions of the money supply. However, for some purposes economists prefer the broader *M2* definition. For example, *M2* is used as 1 of the 10 trend variables in the index of leading indicators (Last Word, Chapter 12). *M3* and still broader definitions of money are so inclusive that many economists question their usefulness.

We will use the narrow *M1* definition of the money supply in our discussion and analysis, unless stated otherwise. The important principles we will develop relating to *M1* are also applicable to *M2* and *M3*, because *M1* is the base component of these broader measures. **(Key Question 4)**

QUICK REVIEW 13.1

◼ Money serves as a medium of exchange, a unit of account, and a store of value.

◼ The narrow *M1* definition of money includes currency held by the public plus checkable deposits in commercial banks and thrift institutions.

◼ Thrift institutions as well as commercial banks offer accounts on which checks can be written.

◼ The *M2* definition of money includes *M1* plus savings deposits, including money market deposit accounts, small (less than $100,000) time deposits, and money market mutual fund balances.

◼ Money supply *M3* consists of *M2* plus large (more than $100,000) time deposits.

Credit Cards

You may wonder why we have ignored credit cards such as Visa and MasterCard in our discussion of how the money supply is defined. After all, credit cards are a convenient way to make purchases. The answer is that a credit card is not really money but, rather, a means of obtaining a short-term loan from the commercial bank or other financial institution that issued the card.

What happens when you purchase a sweatshirt with a credit card? The bank that issued the card will reimburse the store, and later you will reimburse the bank. You may have to pay an annual fee for the services provided, and if you repay the bank in installments, you will pay a sizable interest charge on the loan. Credit cards are merely a means of deferring or postponing payment for a short period.

However, credit cards and other forms of credit allow individuals and businesses to "economize" in the use of money. Credit cards enable you to hold less currency and fewer checkable deposits for transactions. They help you coordinate your expenditures and your receipt of income, thereby reducing the cash and checkable deposits you must keep available.

◼ What "Backs" the Money Supply?

The money supply in the United States essentially is "backed" (guaranteed) by government's ability to keep the value of money relatively stable. Nothing more!

Money as Debt

The major components of the money supply—paper money and checkable deposits—are debts, or promises to pay. In the United States, paper money is the circulating debt of the Federal Reserve Banks. Checkable deposits are the debts of commercial banks and thrift institutions.

Paper currency and checkable deposits have no intrinsic value. A $5 bill is just an inscribed piece of paper. A checkable deposit is merely a bookkeeping entry. And coins, we know, have less intrinsic value than their face value. Nor will government redeem the paper money you hold for anything tangible, such as gold. In effect, the government has chosen to "manage" the nation's money supply. Its monetary authorities attempt to provide the amount of money needed for the particular volume of business activity that will promote full employment, price-level stability, and economic growth.

Most economists agree that managing the money supply is more sensible than linking it to gold or to some other commodity whose supply might change arbitrarily and capriciously. A large increase in the nation's gold stock as the result of a new gold discovery might increase the money supply too rapidly and thereby trigger rapid inflation. Or a long-lasting decline in gold production might reduce the money supply to the point where recession and unemployment resulted.

In short, people cannot convert paper money into a fixed amount of gold or any other precious commodity. Money is exchangeable only for paper money. If you ask the government to redeem $5 of your paper money, it will swap one paper $5 bill for another bearing a different serial number. That is all you can get. Similarly, checkable deposits can be redeemed not for gold but only for paper money, which, as we have just seen, the government will not redeem for anything tangible.

Value of Money

So why are currency and checkable deposits money, whereas, say, Monopoly (the game) money is not? What gives a $20 bill or a $100 checking account entry its value? The answer to these questions has three parts.

Acceptability   Currency and checkable deposits are money because people accept them as money. By virtue of long-standing business practice, currency and checkable deposits perform the basic function of money: They are acceptable as a medium of exchange. We accept paper money in exchange because we are confident it will be exchangeable for real goods, services, and resources when we spend it.

Legal Tender   Our confidence in the acceptability of paper money is strengthened because government has designated currency as **legal tender.** Specifically, each bill contains the statement "This note is legal tender for all debts, public and private." That means that paper currency must be accepted in payment of a debt, or else the creditor forfeits both the privilege of charging interest and the right to sue the debtor for nonpayment. The paper money in our economy is *fiat money*; it is money because the government has declared it so, not because it can be redeemed for precious metal.

The general acceptance of paper currency in exchange is more important than the government's decree that money is legal tender, however. The government has never decreed checks to be legal tender, and yet they serve as such in the vast bulk of the economy's exchanges of goods, services, and resources. But it is true that government agencies—the Federal Deposit Insurance Corporation (FDIC) and the National Credit Union Administration (NCUA)—insure individual deposits of up to $100,000 at commercial banks and thrifts. That fact undoubtedly enhances our willingness to use checkable deposits as a medium of exchange.

Relative Scarcity   The value of money, like the economic value of anything else, depends on its supply and demand. Money derives its value from its scarcity relative to its utility (its want-satisfying power). The utility of money lies in its capacity to be exchanged for goods and services, now or in the future. The economy's demand for money thus depends on the total dollar volume of transactions in any period plus the amount of money individuals and businesses want to hold for future transactions. With a reasonably constant demand for money, the supply of money will determine the value or "purchasing power" of the monetary unit (dollar, yen, peso, or whatever).

Money and Prices

The purchasing power of money is the amount of goods and services a unit of money will buy. When money rapidly loses its purchasing power, it loses its role as money.

The Purchasing Power of the Dollar   The amount a dollar will buy varies inversely with the price level; that is, a reciprocal relationship exists between the general price level and the purchasing power of the dollar. When the consumer price index or "cost-of-living" index goes up, the value of the dollar goes down, and vice versa. Higher prices lower the value of the dollar, because more dollars are needed to buy a particular amount of goods, services, or resources. For example, if the price level doubles, the value of the dollar declines by one-half, or 50 percent.

Conversely, lower prices increase the purchasing power of the dollar, because fewer dollars are needed to obtain a specific quantity of goods and services. If the price level falls by, say, one-half, or 50 percent, the purchasing power of the dollar doubles.

In equation form, the relationship looks like this:

$$D = 1/P$$

To find the value of the dollar D, divide 1 by the price level P expressed as an index number (in hundredths). If the price level is 1, then the value of the dollar is 1. If the price level rises to, say, 1.20, D falls to .833; a 20 percent increase in the price level reduces the value of the dollar by 16.67 percent. Check your understanding of this reciprocal relationship by determining the value of D and its percentage rise when P falls by 20 percent to .80. **(Key Question 6)**

Inflation and Acceptability   In Chapter 8 we noted situations in which a nation's currency became worthless and unacceptable in exchange. They were circumstances in which the government issued so

many pieces of paper currency that the value of each of these units of money was almost totally undermined. The infamous post-World War I inflation in Germany is an example. In December 1919 there were about 50 billion marks in circulation. Four years later there were 496,585,345,900 billion marks in circulation! The result? The German mark in 1923 was worth an infinitesimal fraction of its 1919 value.[3]

Runaway inflation may significantly depreciate the value of money between the time it is received and the time it is spent. Rapid declines in the value of a currency may cause it to cease being used as a medium of exchange. Businesses and households may refuse to accept paper money in exchange because they do not want to bear the loss in its value that will occur while it is in their possession. (All this despite the fact that the government says that paper currency is legal tender!) Without an acceptable domestic medium of exchange, the economy may try to substitute a more stable currency from another nation. Example: Many transactions in Russia now take place in dollars rather than in less stable rubles. At the extreme, the economy may simply revert to barter.

Similarly, people will use money as a store of value only as long as there is no sizable deterioration in the value of that money because of inflation. And an economy can effectively employ money as a unit of account only when its purchasing power is relatively stable. A monetary yardstick that no longer measures a yard does not permit buyers and sellers to establish the terms of trade clearly. When the value of the dollar is declining rapidly, sellers will not know what to charge, and buyers will not know what to pay, for goods and services.

Stabilization of Money's Value

Stabilization of the value of money requires (1) appropriate *fiscal policy*, as explained in Chapter 12, and (2) intelligent management or regulation of the money supply (*monetary policy*). In the United States a combination of legislation, government policy, and social practice inhibits imprudent expansion of the money supply that might jeopardize money's value in exchange.

What is true for paper money is also true for checkable deposits, which are debts of commercial banks and thrift institutions. Your checking account of

---

[3]Frank G. Graham, *Exchange, Prices and Production in Hyperinflation Germany, 1920–1923* (Princeton, N.J.: Princeton University Press, 1930), p. 13.

$200 means that your bank or thrift is indebted to you for that number of dollars. You can collect this debt in one of two ways. You can go to the bank or thrift, write out a check for cash, and obtain paper money. This amounts to swapping bank or thrift debt for government-issued debt. Or, and this is more likely, you can "collect" the debt that the bank or thrift owes you by transferring your claim by check to someone else.

For example, if you buy a $200 leather coat from a store, you can pay for it by writing a check, which transfers your bank's indebtedness from you to the store. Your bank now owes the store the $200 it previously owed you. The store accepts this transfer of indebtedness (the check) as a medium of exchange because it can convert it into currency on demand or can transfer the debt to others in making purchases of its own. Thus, checks, as means of transferring the debts of banks and thrifts, are acceptable as money because we know banks and thrifts will honor these claims.

The ability of banks and thrifts to honor claims against them depends on their not creating too many of such claims. A decentralized system of private, profit-seeking banks might not contain sufficient safeguards against the creation of too many checkable deposits. For that reason, the U.S. banking and financial system exercises substantial centralization and government control to guard against the imprudent creation of those deposits.

A nation's monetary authorities make a particular quantity of money available, such as M1 in Table 13.1. In relation to the nation's real interest rate, this quantity of money establishes the economy's supply-of-money curve. Vertical line S_m in Figure 13.1c represents one such curve.

QUICK REVIEW 13.2

■ In the United States, all money consists essentially of the debts of government, commercial banks, and thrift institutions.

■ These debts efficiently perform the functions of money as long as their value, or purchasing power, is relatively stable.

■ The value of money is rooted not in specified quantities of precious metals but in the amount of goods, services, and resources that money will purchase.

■ Government's responsibility in stabilizing the value of the monetary unit calls for (1) the application of appropriate fiscal policies and (2) effective control over the supply of money.

■ The Demand for Money

Why does the public want to hold some of its wealth as *money*? There are two main reasons: to make purchases with it and to hold it as an asset.

Transactions Demand, D_t

People hold money because, as a medium of exchange, it is convenient for purchasing goods and services. Households must have enough money on hand to buy groceries and pay mortgage and utility bills. Businesses need money to pay for labor, materials, power, and other inputs. The demand for money for such uses is called the **transactions demand** for money.

The main determinant of the amount of money demanded for transactions is the level of nominal GDP. The larger the total money value of all goods and services exchanged in the economy, the larger the amount of money needed to negotiate those transactions. The transactions demand for money varies directly with nominal GDP. We specify *nominal* GDP because households and firms will want more money for transactions if prices rise or if real output increases. In both instances there will be a need for a larger dollar volume to accomplish the desired transactions.

In **Figure 13.1a (Key Graph)** we graph the quantity of money demanded for transactions against the interest rate. For simplicity, we will assume that the amount demanded depends exclusively on the level of nominal GDP and is independent of the real interest rate. (In reality, higher interest rates are associated with slightly lower volumes of money demanded for transactions.) Our simplifying assumption allows us to graph the transactions demand, D_t, as a vertical line. The transactions demand curve is positioned at $100 billion, on the assumption that each dollar held for transactions purposes is spent on an average of three times per year and that nominal GDP is $300 billion. Thus the public needs $100 billion (= $300 billion ÷ 3) to purchase that GDP.

Asset Demand, D_a

The second reason for holding money derives from money's function as a store of value. People may hold their financial assets in many forms, including corporate stocks, private or government bonds, or money. Thus, there is an **asset demand** for money.

What determines the asset demand for money? First, we must recognize that each of the various ways of holding financial assets has advantages and disadvantages. To simplify, let's compare holding money as an asset with holding bonds. The advantages of holding money are its liquidity and lack of risk. Money is the most liquid of all assets; it is immediately usable in making purchases. Money is an attractive asset to be holding when the prices of goods, services, and other financial assets are expected to decline. But when the price of a bond falls, the bondholder who sells the bond before it matures will suffer a loss. There is no such risk in holding money.

The disadvantage of holding money as an asset is that, compared with holding bonds, it does not earn interest. Or, if it is in an interest-bearing checkable deposit account, it does not earn as much interest as do bonds or noncheckable deposits. Idle currency, of course, earns no interest at all.

Knowing this, the problem is deciding how much of your financial assets to hold as, say, bonds and how much as money. The answer depends primarily on the rate of interest. A household or a business incurs an opportunity cost when it holds money; in both cases, interest income is forgone or sacrificed. If a bond pays 6 percent interest, for example, it costs $6 per year of forgone income to hold $100 as cash or in a noninterest checkable account.

It is no surprise, then, that the asset demand for money varies inversely with the rate of interest. When the interest rate or opportunity cost of holding money as an asset is low, the public will choose to hold a large amount of money as assets. When the interest rate is high, it is costly to "be liquid" and the amount of assets held as money will be small. When it is expensive to hold money as an asset, people hold less of it; when money can be held cheaply, people hold more of it. This inverse relationship between the interest rate and the amount of money people want to hold as an asset is shown by D_a in Figure 13.1b. 🔑 13.1

Total Money Demand, D_m

As shown in Figure 13.1, we find the **total demand for money,** D_m, by horizontally adding the asset demand to the transactions demand. The resulting downward-sloping line in Figure 13.1c represents the total amount of money the public wants to hold, both for transactions and as an asset, at each possible interest rate.

KEY GRAPH

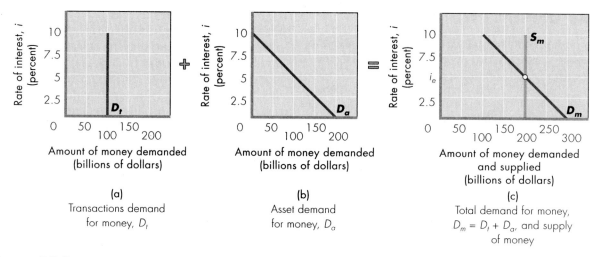

(a)
Transactions demand
for money, D_t

(b)
Asset demand
for money, D_a

(c)
Total demand for money,
$D_m = D_t + D_a$, and supply
of money

Figure 13.1

The demand for money and the money market. The total demand for money D_m is determined by horizontally adding the asset demand for money D_a to the transactions demand D_t. The transactions demand is vertical because it is assumed to depend on nominal GDP rather than on the interest rate. The asset demand varies inversely with the interest rate because of the opportunity cost involved in holding currency and checkable deposits that pay no interest or very low interest. Combining the money supply (stock) S_m with the total money demand D_m portrays the money market and determines the equilibrium interest rate i_e.

Quick Quiz 13.1

1. In this graph, at the interest rate i_e:
   a. the amount of money demanded as an asset is $50 billion.
   b. the amount of money demanded for transactions is $200 billion.
   c. bond prices will decline.
   d. $100 billion is demanded for transactions, $100 billion is demanded as an asset, and the money supply is $200 billion.

2. In this graph, at an interest rate of 10 percent:
   a. no money will be demanded as an asset.
   b. total money demanded will be $200 billion.
   c. the Federal Reserve will supply $100 billion of money.
   d. there will be a $100 billion shortage of money.

3. Curve D_a slopes downward because:
   a. lower interest rates increase the opportunity cost of holding money.

   b. lower interest rates reduce the opportunity cost of holding money.
   c. the asset demand for money varies directly (positively) with the interest rate.
   d. the transactions-demand-for-money curve is perfectly vertical.

4. Suppose the supply of money declines to $100 billion. The equilibrium interest rate would:
   a. fall, the amount of money demanded for transactions would rise, and the amount of money demanded as an asset would decline.
   b. rise, and the amounts of money demanded both for transactions and as an asset would fall.
   c. fall, and the amounts of money demanded both for transactions and as an asset would increase.
   d. rise, the amount of money demanded for transactions would be unchanged, and the amount of money demanded as an asset would decline.

Answers: 1. d; 2. a; 3. b; 4. d

Recall that the transactions demand for money depends on the nominal GDP. A change in the nominal GDP—working through the transactions demand for money—will shift the total money demand curve. Specifically, an increase in nominal GDP means that the public wants to hold a larger amount of money for transactions, and that extra demand will shift the total money demand curve to the right. In contrast, a decline in the nominal GDP will shift

the total money demand curve to the left. As an example, suppose nominal GDP increases from $300 billion to $450 billion and the average dollar held for transactions is still spent three times per year. Then the transactions demand curve will shift from $100 billion (= $300 billion ÷ 3) to $150 billion (= $450 billion ÷ 3). The total money demand curve will then lie $50 billion farther to the right at each possible interest rate.

■ The Money Market

We can combine the demand for money with the supply of money to portray the **money market** and determine the equilibrium rate of interest. In Figure 13.1c the vertical line, S_m, represents the money supply. It is a vertical line because the monetary authorities and financial institutions have provided the economy with some particular stock of money, such as the $M1$ total shown in Table 13.1.

Just as in a product market or a resource market, the intersection of demand and supply determines equilibrium price. Here, the equilibrium "price" is the interest rate (i_e), which is the price paid for the use of money.

Adjustment to a Decline in the Money Supply

A decline in the supply of money will create a temporary shortage of money and increase the equilibrium interest rate. Consider Figure 13.2, which repeats Figure 13.1c and adds two alternative supply-of-money curves.

Suppose the monetary authorities reduce the supply of money from $200 billion, S_m, to $150 billion, S_{m1}. At the initial interest rate of 5 percent, the quantity of money demanded now exceeds the quantity supplied by $50 billion. People will attempt to make up for this shortage of money by selling some of the financial assets they own (we assume for simplicity that these assets are bonds). But one person's receipt of money through the sale of a bond is another person's loss of money through the purchase of that bond. *Overall, there is only $150 billion of money available.* The collective attempt to get more money by selling bonds will increase the supply of bonds relative to the demand for bonds in the bond market, but it will not increase the amount of money available as a whole. The outcome is that the price of bonds will fall and the interest rate will rise, here to $7\frac{1}{2}$ percent.

Generalization: *Lower bond prices are associated with higher interest rates.* To clarify, suppose a bond with no expiration date pays a fixed $50 annual interest and is selling for its face value of $1000. The interest yield on this bond is 5 percent:

$$\frac{\$50}{\$1000} = 5\%$$

Now suppose the price of this bond falls to $667 because of an increased supply of bonds. The $50 fixed

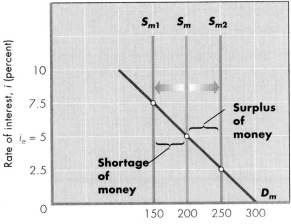

Figure 13.2

Changes in the supply of money, bond prices, and interest rates.   When a decrease in the supply of money creates a temporary shortage of money in the money market, people and institutions try to gain more money by selling bonds. The supply of bonds therefore increases, and this reduces bond prices and raises interest rates. At higher interest rates, people reduce the amount of money they want to hold. Thus, the amounts of money supplied and demanded once again are equal at the higher interest rate. An increase in the supply of money creates a temporary surplus of money, resulting in an increase in the demand for bonds and higher bond prices. Interest rates fall and equilibrium is reestablished in the money market.

annual interest payment will now yield $7\frac{1}{2}$ percent to whoever buys the bond:

$$\frac{\$50}{\$667} = 7\frac{1}{2}\%$$

Because all borrowers must compete by offering to pay lenders interest yields similar to those available on bonds, a higher general interest rate emerges. In Figure 13.2 the interest rate rises from 5 percent with the money supply at $200 billion to $7\frac{1}{2}$ percent when the money supply is $150 billion. This higher interest rate raises the opportunity cost of holding money and consequently reduces the amount of money firms and households want to hold. Here, the amount of money demanded declines from $200 billion at the 5 percent interest rate to $150 billion at the $7\frac{1}{2}$ percent interest rate. The money market has achieved a new equilibrium, now with $150 billion of money demanded and supplied at the new $7\frac{1}{2}$ percent interest rate.

Adjustment to an Increase in the Money Supply

An increase in the supply of money from $200 billion, S_m, to $250 billion, S_{m2}, in Figure 13.2 results in a surplus of $50 billion at the initial 5 percent interest rate. People will now try to get rid of money by purchasing more bonds. But one person's expenditure of money is another person's receipt of money. The collective attempt to buy more bonds will increase the demand for bonds, push bond prices upward, and lower interest rates.

Corollary: *Higher bond prices are associated with lower interest rates.* In our example, the $50 interest payment on a bond now priced at, say, $2000, will yield a bond buyer only $2\frac{1}{2}$ percent:

$$\frac{\$50}{\$2000} = 2\frac{1}{2}\%$$

The point is that interest rates in general will fall as people unsuccessfully attempt to reduce their money holdings below $250 billion by buying bonds. In this case, the interest rate will fall to a new equilibrium at $2\frac{1}{2}$ percent. Because the opportunity cost of holding money now is lower—that is, being liquid is less expensive—households and businesses will increase the amount of currency and checkable deposits they are willing to hold from $200 billion to $250 billion. Eventually, a new equilibrium in the money market will be achieved: The quantities of money demanded and supplied will each be $250 billion at an interest rate of $2\frac{1}{2}$ percent. **(Key Question 7)**

QUICK REVIEW 13.3

■ People hold money for transaction and asset purposes.

■ The total demand for money is the sum of the transactions and asset demands; it is graphed as an inverse relationship (downward-sloping line) between the interest rate and the quantity of money demanded.

■ The equilibrium interest rate is determined by money demand and supply; it occurs when people are willing to hold the exact amount of money being supplied by the monetary authorities.

■ Bond prices and interest rates are inversely related.

■ The Federal Reserve and the Banking System

In the United States, the "monetary authorities" we have been referring to are the members of the Board of Governors of the **Federal Reserve System** (the "Fed"). As shown in Figure 13.3, the Board directs the activities of the 12 Federal Reserve Banks, which in turn control the lending activity of the nation's banks and thrift institutions.

Historical Background

Early in the twentieth century, Congress decided that centralization and public control were essential for an efficient banking system. Decentralized, unregulated banking had fostered the inconvenience and confusion of numerous private bank notes being used as currency. It had also resulted in occasional episodes of monetary mismanagement such that the money supply was inappropriate to the needs of the economy: Sometimes "too much" money precipitated rapid inflation; other times "too little money" stunted the economy's growth by hindering the production and exchange of goods and services. There was no single entity charged with creating and implementing nationally consistent banking policies.

An unusually acute banking crisis in 1907 motivated Congress to appoint the National Monetary Commission to study the monetary and banking problems of the economy and to outline a course of action for Congress. The result was the Federal Reserve Act of 1913.

Let's examine the various parts of the Federal Reserve System and their relationship to one another.

Board of Governors

The central authority of the U.S. money and banking system is the **Board of Governors** of the Federal Reserve System. The U.S. president, with the confirmation of the Senate, appoints the seven Board members. Terms are 14 years and staggered so that one member is replaced every 2 years. In addition, new members are appointed when resignations occur. The president selects the chairperson and vice-chairperson of the Board from among the members. Those officers serve 4-year terms and can be reappointed to new 4-year terms by the

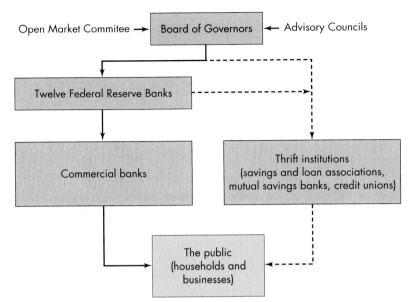

Figure 13.3

Framework of the Federal Reserve System and its relationship to the public. With the advice of the Open Market Committee and three Advisory Councils, the Board of Governors makes the basic policy decisions that provide monetary control of the U.S. money and banking systems. These decisions are implemented through the 12 Federal Reserve Banks.

president. The long-term appointments provide the Board with continuity, experienced membership, and independence from political pressures that could result in inflation.

Assistance and Advice

Several entities assist the Board of Governors in determining banking and monetary policy. The first is the most powerful.

The **Federal Open Market Committee (FOMC)** is made up of the seven members of the Board of Governors plus five of the presidents of the Federal Reserve Banks. The FOMC sets the Fed's monetary policy and directs the purchase and sale of government securities (bills, notes, and bonds) in the open market. In Chapter 15 we will discover that these aptly named *open-market operations* are the most significant technique available to the Fed for controlling the money supply.

Three *Advisory Councils* made up of private citizens meet periodically with the Board of Governors to voice their views on banking and monetary policy. The *Federal Advisory Council* is composed of 12 commercial bankers, one selected annually by each of the 12 Federal Reserve Banks. *The Thrift Institutions Advisory Council* consists of representatives from savings and loan associations, savings banks, and credit unions. The third advisory group, the 30-member *Consumer Advisory Council*, includes representatives of consumers of financial services and academic and legal specialists

in consumer matters. As their names indicate, the councils are purely advisory. They have no policy-making powers, and the Board has no obligation to heed their advice.

The 12 Federal Reserve Banks

The 12 **Federal Reserve Banks** collectively serve as the nation's "central bank." They blend private ownership and public control and mainly are so-called bankers' banks.

Central Bank   Most nations have a single central bank—for example, Britain's Bank of England or Japan's Bank of Japan. The United States' central bank consists of 12 banks whose policies are coordinated by the Fed's Board of Governors. The 12 Federal Reserve Banks accommodate the geographic size and economic diversity of the United States and the nation's large number of commercial banks and thrifts.

Figure 13.4 locates the 12 Federal Reserve Banks and indicates the district that each serves. These banks implement the basic policy of the Board of Governors. The Federal Reserve Bank in New York City conducts most of the Fed's open-market operations.

Quasi-Public Banks   The 12 Federal Reserve Banks are quasi-public banks, which blend private ownership and public control. Each Federal Reserve Bank is owned by the private commercial banks in

Figure 13.4

The 12 Federal Reserve Districts. The Federal Reserve System divides the United States into 12 districts, each having one central bank and in some instances one or more branches of the central bank. Hawaii and Alaska are included in the twelfth district. *Source: Federal Reserve Bulletin.*

its district. (Commercial banks are required to purchase shares of stock in the Federal Reserve Bank in their district.) But a government body, the Board of Governors, sets the basic policies that the Federal Reserve Banks pursue. The owners of these central banks thus control neither the central bank officials nor their policies.

Despite their private ownership, the Federal Reserve Banks are in practice public institutions. Unlike private firms, they are not motivated by profit. The policies they follow are designed by the Board of Governors to promote the well-being of the economy as a whole. Thus, the activities of the Federal Reserve Banks are frequently at odds with the profit motive.[4] Also, the Federal Reserve Banks do not compete with commercial banks. In general, they do not deal with the public; rather, they interact with the government and commercial banks and thrifts.

Bankers' Banks   The Federal Reserve Banks are "bankers' banks." They perform essentially the same functions for banks and thrifts as those institutions perform for the public. Just as banks and thrifts accept the deposits of and make loans to the public, so the central banks accept the deposits of and make loans to banks and thrifts. But the Federal Reserve

Banks have a third function, which banks and thrifts do not perform: They issue currency when they are directed to do so by the Federal Reserve Board. Congress has authorized the Federal Reserve Banks to put into circulation Federal Reserve Notes, which constitute the economy's paper money supply.

Commercial Banks and Thrifts

There are about 8600 commercial banks. Roughly three-fourths are state banks. These are private banks chartered (authorized) by the individual states to operate within those states. One-fourth are private banks chartered by the Federal government to operate nationally; these are national banks. Some of the U.S. national banks are very large, ranking among the world's largest private banks (see Global Perspective 13.1).

The 12,500 thrift institutions—11,000 of which are credit unions—are regulated by agencies separate and apart from the Board of Governors and the Federal Reserve Banks. For example, the operation of savings and loan associations is regulated and monitored by the Treasury Department's Office of Thrift Supervision. But the thrifts *are* subject to monetary control by the Federal Reserve System. In particular, like the banks, thrifts are required to keep a certain percentage of their checkable deposits as "reserves." In Figure 13.3 we use dashed arrows to indicate that the thrift institutions are partially subject to the control of the Board of Governors and the central banks. Decisions concerning monetary policy affect the thrifts along with the commercial banks.

[4]Although it is not their goal, the Federal Reserve Banks have actually operated profitably, largely as a result of the Treasury debts they hold. Part of the profit is used to pay dividends to the commercial banks that hold stock in the Federal Reserve Banks; the remaining profit is usually turned over to the U.S. Treasury.

GLOBAL PERSPECTIVE 13.1

The World's 10 Largest Commercial Banks

The world's 10 largest banks are headquartered in Europe, Japan, and the United States (1999 data).

Assets (billions of U.S. dollars)

Deutsche Bank (Germany)	$955,579
Bank of Tokyo-Mitsubishi (Japan)	726,286
Citigroup (U.S.)	716,937
BNP Paribas (France)	703,091
Bank of America (U.S.)	632,574
UBS (Switzerland)	616,798
HSBC Holdings (U.K./Hong Kong)	601,847
Fuji Bank (Japan)	561,345
Bayerische Hypo Bank (Germany)	559,860
Sumitomo Bank (Japan)	519,153

Source: Wall Street Journal, Sept. 25, 2000, p. R25.

Fed Functions and the Money Supply

The Fed performs several functions, some of which we have already identified but they are worth repeating:

- **Issuing currency** The Federal Reserve Banks issue Federal Reserve Notes, the paper currency used in the U.S. monetary system. (The Federal Reserve Bank that issued a particular bill is identified in black in the upper left of the front of the newly designed bills. "A1," for example, identifies the Boston bank, "B2" the New York bank, and so on.)
- **Setting reserve requirements and holding reserves** The Fed sets reserve requirements, which are the fractions of checking account balances that banks must maintain as currency reserves. The central banks accept as deposits from the banks and thrifts any portion of their mandated reserves not held as vault cash.
- **Lending money to banks and thrifts** From time to time the Fed lends money to banks and thrifts and charges them an interest rate called the *discount rate.*
- **Providing for check collection** The Fed provides the banking system with a means for collecting checks. If Sue writes a check on her Miami bank or thrift to Joe, who deposits it in his Dallas bank or thrift, how does the Dallas bank collect the money represented by the check drawn against the Miami bank? Answer: The Fed handles it in 2 or 3 days by adjusting the reserves (deposits) of the two banks.
- **Acting as fiscal agent** The Fed acts as the fiscal agent (provider of financial services) for the Federal government. The government collects huge sums through taxation, spends equally large amounts, and sells and redeems bonds. To carry out these activities, government uses the Fed's facilities.
- **Supervising banks** The Fed supervises the operation of banks. It makes periodic examinations to assess bank profitability, to ascertain that banks perform in accordance with the many regulations to which they are subject, and to uncover questionable practices or fraud.[5]
- **Controlling the money supply** Finally, and most important, the Fed has ultimate responsibility for regulating the supply of money, and this in turn enables it to influence interest rates. The major task of the Fed is to manage the money supply (and thus interest rates) according to the needs of the economy. This involves making an amount of money available that is consistent with high and rising levels of output and employment and a relatively constant price level. While all the other functions of the Fed are routine activities or have a service nature, managing the nation's money supply requires making basic, but unique, policy decisions. (We discuss those decisions in detail in Chapter 15.)

Federal Reserve Independence

Congress purposely established the Fed as an independent agency of government. The objective was to protect the Fed from political pressures so that it could effectively control the money supply and maintain price stability. Political pressures on Congress

---

[5]The Fed is not alone in this task of supervision. The individual states supervise all banks that they charter. The Comptroller of the Currency supervises all national banks, and the Office of Thrift Supervision supervises all thrifts. Also, the Federal Deposit Insurance Corporation supervises all banks and thrifts whose deposits it insures.

and the executive branch may at times result in inflationary fiscal policies, including tax cuts and special-interest spending. If Congress and the executive branch also controlled the nation's monetary policy, citizens and lobbying groups undoubtedly would pressure elected officials to keep interest rates low even though at times high interest rates are necessary to reduce aggregate demand and thus control inflation. An independent monetary authority (the Fed) can take actions to increase interest rates when higher rates are needed to stem inflation. Studies show that countries that have independent central banks like the Fed have lower rates of inflation, on average, than countries that have little or no central bank independence.

▮ Recent Developments in Money and Banking

The banking industry is undergoing a series of sweeping changes, spurred by competition from other financial institutions, the globalization of banking, and advances in information technology.

The Relative Decline of Banks and Thrifts

Banks and thrifts are just two of several types of firms that offer financial services. Table 13.2 lists the major categories of firms within the U.S. **financial services industry** and gives examples of firms in

Table 13.2
Major U.S. Financial Institutions

Institution	Description	Examples
Commercial banks	State and national banks that provide checking and savings accounts, sell certificates of deposit, and make loans. The Federal Deposit Insurance Corporation (FDIC) insures checking and savings accounts up to $100,000.	Chase Manhattan, Citicorp, BankAmerica, Wells Fargo
Thrifts	Savings and loan associations (S&Ls), mutual saving banks, and credit unions that offer checking and savings accounts and make loans. Historically, S&Ls made mortgage loans for houses while mutual savings banks and credit unions made small personal loans, such as automobile loans. Today, major thrifts offer the same range of banking services as commercial banks. The Federal Deposit Insurance Corporation and the National Credit Union Administration insure checking and savings deposits up to $100,000.	Home Savings of America, Washington Mutual
Insurance companies	Firms that offer policies (contracts) through which individuals pay premiums to insure against some loss, say, disability or death. In some life insurance policies and annuities, the funds ae invested for the client in stocks and bonds and paid back after a specified number of years. Thus, insurance sometimes has a saving or financial-investment element.	Prudential, New York Life, Massachusetts Mutual
Mutual fund companies	Firms that pool deposits by customers to purchase stocks or bonds (or both). Customers thus own a part of a particular set of stocks or bonds, say stocks in companies expected to grow rapidly (a growth fund) or bonds issued by state governments (a municipal bond fund).	Fidelity, Putnam, Dreyfus, Kemper
Pension funds	For-profit or nonprofit institutions that collect savings from workers (or from employers on their behalf) throughout their working years and then buy stocks and bonds with the proceeds and make monthly retirement payments.	Teachers Insurance and Annuity Association—College Retirement Equity Fund, Teamsters' Union
Securities firms	Firms that offer security advice and buy and sell stocks and bonds for clients. More generally known as *stock brokerage firms.*	Merrill-Lynch, Solomon, Leyman Brothers, Charles Schwab

each category. Although banks and thrifts remain the only institutions that offer checkable deposits that have no restrictions on either the number or size of checks, their shares of total financial assets (value of things owned) are declining. In 1980 banks and thrifts together held nearly 60 percent of financial assets in the United States. By 2000 that percentage had declined to about 30 percent.

Where did the declining shares of the banks and thrifts go? Pension funds, insurance firms, and particularly securities firms and mutual fund companies expanded their shares of financial assets. (Mutual fund companies offer shares of a wide array of stock and bond funds, as well as the previously mentioned money market funds.) Clearly, between 1980 and 2000, U.S. households and businesses channeled relatively more saving away from banks and thrifts and toward other financial institutions. Those other institutions generally offered higher rates of return on funds than did banks and thrifts, largely because they could participate more fully in national and international stock and bond markets.

Consolidation among Banks and Thrifts

During the past two decades, many banks have purchased bankrupt thrifts or have merged with other banks. Major savings and loans have also merged. The purpose of such mergers is to create large regional or national banks or thrifts that can compete more effectively in the financial services industry. Consolidation of traditional banking is expected to continue; there are 5000 fewer banks today than there were in 1990. Today, the 10 largest U.S. banks hold one-third of total bank deposits.

Convergence of Services Provided by Financial Institutions

In 1996 Congress greatly loosened the Depression-era prohibition against banks selling stocks, bonds, and mutual funds, and it ended the prohibition altogether in the Financial Services Modernization Act of 1999. Banks, thrifts, pension companies, insurance companies, and securities firms can now merge with one another and sell each other's products. Thus, the lines between the subsets of the financial industry are beginning to blur. Many banks have acquired stock brokerage firms and, in a few cases, insurance companies. For example, Citibank now owns Salomon Smith Barney, a securities firm, and Travelers Group, a large insurance company. Many large banks (for example, Wells Fargo) and pension funds (for example, TIAA-CREF) now provide mutual funds, including money market funds that pay relatively high interest and on which checks of $500 or more can be written.

The lifting of restraints against banks and thrifts should work to their advantage because they can now provide their customers with "one-stop shopping" for financial services. In general, the reform will likely intensify competition and encourage financial innovation. The downside is that financial losses in securities subsidiaries—such as could occur during a major recession—could increase the number of bank failures. Such failures might undermine confidence in the entire banking system and complicate the Fed's task of maintaining an appropriate money supply.

Globalization of Financial Markets

Another significant banking development is the increasing integration of world financial markets. Major foreign financial institutions now have operations in the United States, and U.S. financial institutions do business abroad. For example, Visa, MasterCard, and American Express offer worldwide credit card services. Moreover, U.S. mutual fund companies now offer a variety of international stock and bond funds. Globally, financial capital increasingly flows in search of the highest risk-adjusted returns. As a result, U.S. banks increasingly compete with foreign banks for both deposits and loan customers.

Recent advances in computer and communications technology are likely to speed up the trend toward international financial integration. Yet studies indicate that the bulk of investment in the major nations is still financed through domestic saving within each nation.

Electronic Transactions

Finally, the rapid advance of Internet commerce and "banking" is potentially of great significance to financial institutions and central banks. Consumers have increasingly used the Internet for such **electronic transactions** as buying goods (using credit cards), buying and selling stock and mutual fund shares, transferring bank funds between accounts, and paying bills.

Some experts believe the next step will be the widespread use of electronic money, which is simply an entry in an electronic file stored in a computer. Electronic money will be deposited, or "loaded," into an account through Internet payments such as a paycheck, retirement benefit, or stock dividend. The owner of the account will withdraw, or "unload," the money from his or her account through Internet payments to others for a wide variety of goods and services.

In the future, account holders may be able to insert so-called stored-value cards into slots in their computers and load electronic money onto the card. These plastic "smart cards" contain computer chips that store information, including the amount of electronic money the consumer has loaded. When purchases or payments are made, their amounts are automatically deducted from the balance in the card's memory. Consumers will be able to transfer traditional money to their smart cards through computers or cell phones or at automatic teller machines. Thus, it will be possible for nearly all payments to be made through the Internet or a smart card.

Chase Manhattan, Citibank, Visa, and Master-Card have already teamed up to test a "first-generation" smart-card system in various parts of the country. American Express launched its Blue Card in late 1999 and had more than 5 million accountholders at the end of 2000. Thus far, however, there has been resistance to using smart cards in the United States (although not in Europe). Americans are heavy users of credit cards, which provide interest-free loans between the time of purchase and the due date on the credit card statement. Smart cards provide for instant payment and thus do not offer this so-called interest-free float. It simply is too soon to tell whether electronic money will become the norm in the United States. If it does, however, it will present special problems for the Federal Reserve System. Unlike currency, electronic money can be "issued" by private firms rather than by the government. To control the money supply, the Federal Reserve System may need to implement new ways of maintaining control over the total amount of electronic money in the economy.

QUICK REVIEW 13.4

- The Federal Reserve System consists of the Board of Governors, 12 Federal Reserve Banks, commercial banks, and thrift institutions.

- The 12 Federal Reserve Banks are publicly controlled central banks that deal with banks and thrifts rather than with the public.

- The Federal Reserve's major role is to regulate the supply of money in the economy.

- Recent developments in banking are the (a) relative decline in traditional banking; (b) consolidation within the banking industry; (c) convergence of services offered by banks, thrifts, insurance companies, pension funds, and mutual funds; (d) globalization of banking; and (e) widespread emergence of electronic transactions.

The Global Greenback

A Large Amount of U.S. Currency Is Circulating Abroad.

Russians use American currency. So do Argentineans, Brazilians, Poles, Vietnamese, Chinese, and even Cubans. Like commercial aircraft, computer software, and movie videos, American currency has become a major U.S. "export." Russians hold about $40 billion of U.S. currency, and Argentineans hold $7 billion. The Polish government estimates that $6 billion of U.S. dollars is circulating in Poland. In all, perhaps as much as two-thirds of all U.S. currency is circulating abroad.

Dollars leave the United States when Americans buy imports, travel in other countries, or send dollars to relatives living abroad. The United States profits when the dollars stay in other countries. It costs the government about 4 cents to print a dollar. For someone abroad to obtain that new dollar, $1 worth of resources, goods, or services must be sold to Americans. These commodities are U.S. gains. The dollar goes abroad and, assuming it stays there, presents no claim on U.S. resources or goods or services. Americans in effect make 96 cents on the dollar (= $1 gain in resources, goods, or services − the 4-cent printing cost). It's like American Express selling traveler's checks that never get cashed.

Black markets and other illegal activity undoubtedly fuel some of the demand for U.S. cash abroad. The dollar is king in covert trading in diamonds, weapons, and pirated software. Billions of cash dollars are involved in the narcotics trade. But the illegal use of dollars is only a small part of the story. The massive volume of dollars in other nations reflects a global search for monetary stability. On the basis of past experience, foreign citizens are confident that the dollar's purchasing power will remain relatively steady.

Argentina has pegged its peso directly to the dollar, with the central bank issuing new pesos only when it has more dollars or gold on hand than before. The result has been a remarkable decline in inflation. In Russia and the newly independent countries of eastern Europe, the U.S. dollar has retained its buying power while that of domestic currencies has plummeted. As a result, many Russians hold their savings in dollars. In Brazil, where inflation rates above 1000 percent annually were once common, people have long sought the stability of dollars. In the shopping districts of Beijing and Shanghai, Chinese consumers trade their domestic currency for dollars. In Bolivia half of all bank accounts are denominated in dollars. There is a thriving "dollar economy" in Vietnam, and even Cuba has partially legalized the use of U.S. dollars. The U.S. dollar is the official currency in Panama, Ecuador, and Liberia.

There is little risk to the United States in satisfying the world's demand for dollars. If all the dollars came rushing back to the United States at once, the nation's money supply would surge, possibly causing demand-pull inflation. But there is not much chance of that happening. Overall, the global greenback is a positive economic force. It is a reliable medium of exchange, unit of account, and store of value that facilitates transactions that might not otherwise occur. Dollar holdings have helped buyers and sellers abroad overcome special monetary problems. The result has been increased output in those countries and thus greater output and income globally.

SUMMARY

1. Anything that is accepted as (a) a medium of exchange, (b) a unit of monetary account, and (c) a store of value can be used as money.

2. The Federal Reserve System recognizes three "official" definitions of the money supply. *M*1 consists of currency and checkable deposits; *M*2 consists of *M*1 plus savings deposits, including money market deposit accounts, small (less than $100,000) time deposits, and money market mutual fund balances; and *M*3 consists of *M*2 plus large ($100,000 or more) time deposits.

3. Money represents the debts of government and institutions offering checkable deposits (commercial banks and thrift institutions) and has value because of the goods, services, and resources it will command in the market. Maintaining the purchasing power of money depends largely on the government's effectiveness in managing the money supply.

4. The total demand for money consists of the transactions demand and the asset demand for money. The transactions demand varies directly with the nominal GDP; the asset demand varies inversely with the interest rate. The money market combines the total demand for money with the money supply to determine the equilibrium interest rate.

5. Other things equal, decreases in the supply of money raise interest rates, whereas increases in the supply of money decrease them. Interest rates and bond prices move in the opposite direction. At the equilibrium interest rate, bond prices tend to be stable and the amounts of money demanded and supplied are equal.

6. The U.S. banking system consists of (a) the Board of Governors of the Federal Reserve System, (b) the 12 Federal Reserve Banks, and (c) some 8600 commercial banks and 12,500 thrift institutions (mainly credit unions). The Board of Governors is the basic policy-making body for the entire banking system. The directives of the Board are made effective through the 12 Federal Reserve Banks, which are simultaneously (a) central banks, (b) quasi-public banks, and (c) bankers' banks.

7. The major functions of the Fed are to (a) issue Federal Reserve Notes, (b) set reserve requirements and hold reserves deposited by banks and thrifts, (c) lend money to banks and thrifts, (d) provide for the rapid collection of checks, (e) act as the fiscal agent for the Federal government, (f) supervise the operations of the banks, and (g) regulate the supply of money in the best interests of the economy.

8. The Fed is essentially an independent institution, controlled neither by the president of the United States nor by Congress. This independence shields the Fed from political pressure and allows it to raise and lower interest rates (via changes in the money supply) as needed to promote full employment, price stability, and economic growth.

9. Between 1980 and 2000, banks and thrifts lost considerable market share of the financial services industry to pension funds, insurance companies, mutual funds, and securities firms. Other recent banking developments of significance include the consolidation of the banking and thrift industry; the convergence of services offered by banks, thrifts, mutual funds, securities firms, and pension companies; the globalization of banking services; and the emergence of the Internet and electronic money, including smart cards.

TERMS AND CONCEPTS

medium of exchange
unit of account
store of value
$M1$, $M2$, $M3$
token money
Federal Reserve Notes
checkable deposits

commercial banks
thrift institutions
near-monies
savings account
money market deposit account (MMDA)
time deposits

money market mutual fund (MMMF)
legal tender
transactions demand
asset demand
total demand for money
money market

Federal Reserve System
Board of Governors
Federal Open Market Committee (FOMC)
Federal Reserve Banks
financial services industry
electronic transactions

STUDY QUESTIONS

1. What are the three basic functions of money? Describe how rapid inflation can undermine money's ability to perform each of the three functions.

2. Which two of the following financial institutions offer checkable deposits included within the $M1$ money supply: mutual fund companies; insurance companies; commercial banks; securities firms; thrift institutions? Which of the following is not included in either $M1$ or $M2$: currency held by the public; checkable deposits; money market mutual fund balances; small (less than $10,000) deposits; currency held by banks; savings deposits.

3. Explain and evaluate the following statements:
   a. The invention of money is one of the great achievements of humankind, for without it the enrichment that comes from broadening trade would have been impossible.
   b. Money is whatever society says it is.

c. In most economies of the world, the debts of government and commercial banks are used as money.

d. People often say they would like to have more money, but what they usually mean is that they would like to have more goods and services.

e. When the price of everything goes up, it is not because everything is worth more but because the currency is worth less.

f. Any central bank can create money; the trick is to create enough, but not too much, of it.

4. **Key Question** What are the components of the *M1* money supply? What is the largest component? Which of the components of *M1* is *legal tender?* Why is the face value of a coin greater than its intrinsic value? What near-monies are included in the *M2* money supply? What distinguishes the *M2* and *M3* money supplies.

5. What "backs" the money supply in the United States? What determines the value (domestic purchasing power) of money? How does the value of money relate to the price level? Who in the United States is responsible for maintaining money's value?

6. **Key Question** Suppose the price level and value of the dollar in year 1 are 1 and $1, respectively. If the price level rises to 1.25 in year 2, what is the new value of the dollar? If, instead, the price level falls to .50, what is the value of the dollar? What generalization can you draw from your answers?

7. **Key Question** What is the basic determinant of (*a*) the transactions demand and (*b*) the asset demand for money? Explain how these two demands can be combined graphically to determine total money demand. How is the equilibrium interest rate in the money market determined? How might (*a*) the expanded use of credit cards, (*b*) a shortening of worker pay periods, and (*c*) an increase in nominal GDP each independently affect the transactions demand for money, the total demand for money, and the equilibrium interest rate?

8. Assume that the following data characterize a hypothetical economy: money supply = $200 billion; quantity of money demanded for transactions = $150 billion; quantity of money demanded as an asset = $10 billion at 12 percent interest, increasing by $10 billion for each 2-percentage-point fall in the interest rate.

    a. What is the equilibrium interest rate? Explain.

    b. At the equilibrium interest rate, what are the quantity of money supplied, the total quantity of money demanded, the amount of money demanded for transactions, and the amount of money demanded as an asset?

9. Suppose a bond with no expiration date has a face value of $10,000 and annually pays a fixed amount of interest of $800. Compute and enter in the spaces provided below either the interest rate that the bond would yield to a bond buyer at each of the bond prices listed or the bond price at each of the interest yields shown. What generalization can be drawn from the completed table?

Bond Price	Interest Yield, %
$ 8,000	_____
_____	8.9
$10,000	_____
$11,000	_____
_____	6.2

10. Assume that the money market is initially in equilibrium and that the money supply is then increased. Explain the adjustments toward a new equilibrium interest rate. Will bond prices be higher or lower at the new equilibrium rate of interest? What effects would you expect the interest-rate change to have on the levels of output, employment, and prices? Answer the same questions for a *decrease* in the money supply.

11. How is the chairperson of the Federal Reserve System selected? Describe the relationship between the Board of Governors of the Federal Reserve System and the 12 Federal Reserve Banks. What is meant when economists say that the Federal Reserve Banks are central banks, quasi-public banks, and bankers' banks? What are the seven basic functions of the Federal Reserve System?

12. Following are two hypothetical ways in which the Federal Reserve Board might be appointed. Would you favor either of these two methods over the present method? Why or why not?

    a. Upon taking office, the U.S. president appoints seven people to the Federal Reserve Board, including a chair. Each appointee must be confirmed by a majority vote of the Senate, and each serves the same 4-year term as the president.

    b. Congress selects seven members from its ranks (four from the House of Representatives and three from the Senate) to serve at its pleasure as the Board of Governors of the Federal Reserve System.

13. What are the major categories of firms that make up the U.S. financial services industry? Did the bank and thrift share of the financial services market rise, fall, or stay the same between 1980 and 2000? Are there

more or fewer bank firms today than a decade ago? Why are the lines between the categories of financial firms becoming more blurred than in the past?

14. In what way are electronic money and smart cards potentially related? Do you think electronic money and smart cards will dominate transactions some time within the next 20 years? Why or why not?

15. **(Last Word)** Over the years, the Federal Reserve Banks have printed many billions of dollars more in currency than U.S. households, businesses, and financial institutions now hold. Where is this "missing" money? Why is it there?

16. **Web-Based Question:** *Who are the members of the Federal Reserve Board?* The Federal Reserve Board website, www.federalreserve.gov/BIOS/, provides a detailed biography of the seven members of the Board of Governors. What is the composition of the Board with regard to age, gender, education, previous employment, and ethnic background? Which Board members are near the ends of their terms?

17. **Web-Based Question:** *Currency trivia* Visit the website of the Federal Reserve Bank of Atlanta, www.frbatlanta.org/publica/brochure/fundfac/money.htm, to answer the following questions: What are the denominations of Federal Reserve Notes now being printed? What was the largest-denomination Federal Reserve Note ever printed and circulated, and when was it last printed? What are some tips for spotting counterfeit currency? When was the last silver dollar minted? What have been the largest and smallest U.S. coin denominations since the Coinage Act of 1792?

CHAPTER 14

How Banks and Thrifts Create Money

WE HAVE SEEN THAT the $M1$ money supply consists of currency (Federal Reserve Notes and coins) and checkable deposits. The U.S. Bureau of Engraving creates the Federal Reserve Notes and the U.S. Mint creates the coins. So who creates the checkable deposits that make up more than half the nation's $M1$ money supply? Surprisingly, it is loan officers! Although that may sound like something a congressional committee should investigate, the monetary authorities are well aware that banks and thrifts create checkable deposits. In fact, the Federal Reserve relies on these institutions to create this vital component of the nation's money supply. ■ This chapter explains how commercial banks and thrifts can create checkable deposits by issuing loans. Our examples will involve commercial banks, but remember that thrift institutions also provide checkable deposits. So the analysis applies to banks and thrifts alike.

■ The Balance Sheet of a Commercial Bank

We will analyze the workings of the U.S. monetary system by considering certain items on a commercial bank's balance sheet and the way various transactions alter those items.

The **balance sheet** of a commercial bank (or thrift) is a statement of assets and claims on assets that summarizes the financial position of the bank at a certain time. Every balance sheet must balance; this means that the value of *assets* must equal the amount of claims against those assets. The claims shown on a balance sheet are divided into two groups: the claims of nonowners against the firm's assets, called *liabilities*, and the claims of the owners of the firm against the firm's assets, called *net worth*. A balance sheet is balanced because

Assets = liabilities + net worth

■ Prologue: The Goldsmiths

The United States, like most other countries today, has a **fractional reserve banking system** *in which only a fraction of the total money supply is held in reserve as currency*. Here is the history behind the idea.

When early traders began to use gold in making transactions, they soon realized that it was both unsafe and inconvenient to carry gold and to have it weighed and assayed (judged for purity) every time they negotiated a transaction. So by the sixteenth century they had begun to deposit their gold with goldsmiths, who would store it in vaults for a fee. On receiving a gold deposit, the goldsmith would issue a receipt to the depositor. Soon people were paying for goods with goldsmiths' receipts, which served as the first kind of paper money.

At this point the goldsmiths—embryonic bankers—used a 100 percent reserve system; they backed their circulating paper money receipts fully with the gold that they held "in reserve" in their vaults. But because of the public's acceptance of the goldsmiths' receipts as paper money, the goldsmiths soon realized that owners rarely redeemed the gold they had in storage. In fact, the goldsmiths observed that the amount of gold being deposited with them in any week or month was likely to exceed the amount that was being withdrawn.

Then some clever goldsmith hit on the idea that paper "receipts" could be issued in excess of the amount of gold held. Goldsmiths would put these receipts, which were redeemable in gold, into circulation by making interest-earning loans to merchants, producers, and consumers. Borrowers were willing to accept loans in the form of gold receipts because the receipts were accepted as a medium of exchange in the marketplace.

This was the beginning of the fractional reserve system of banking, in which reserves in bank vaults are a fraction of the total money supply. If, for example, the goldsmith issued $1 million in receipts for actual gold in storage and another $1 million in receipts as loans, then the total value of paper money in circulation would be $2 million—twice the value of the gold. Gold reserves would be a fraction (one-half) of outstanding paper money.

Fractional reserve banking has two significant characteristics:

■ ***Money creation and reserves***   Banks can create money through lending. In fact, goldsmiths created money when they made loans by giving borrowers paper money that was not fully backed by gold reserves. The quantity of such money goldsmiths could create depended on the amount of reserves they deemed prudent to have available. The smaller the amount of reserves thought necessary, the larger the amount of paper money the goldsmiths could create. Today, gold is no longer used as bank reserves. Instead, the creation of checkable deposit money by banks (via their lending) is limited by the amount of *currency reserves* that the banks feel obligated, or are required by law, to keep.

■ ***Bank panics and regulation***   Banks that operate on the basis of fractional reserves are vulnerable to "panics" or "runs." A goldsmith who issued paper money equal to twice the value of his gold reserves would be unable to convert all that paper money into gold in the event that all the holders of that money appeared at his door at the same time demanding their gold. In fact, many European and U.S. banks were once ruined by this unfortunate circumstance. However, a bank panic is highly unlikely if the banker's reserve and lending policies are prudent. Indeed, one reason why banking systems are highly regulated industries is to prevent runs on banks. This is also the reason why the United States has a system of deposit insurance.   ▇ 14.1

▌A Single Commercial Bank

How can a commercial bank (or thrift) create money? If it can create money, can it destroy money too? What factors govern how a bank creates money?

Formation of a Commercial Bank

To answer these questions we must understand the items a bank carries on its balance sheet and how certain transactions affect the balance sheet. We begin with the organization of a local commercial bank.

Transaction 1: Creating a Bank   Suppose some farsighted citizens of the town of Wahoo, Nebraska (yes, there is such a place), decide their town needs a new commercial bank to provide banking services for that growing community. Once they have secured a state or national charter for their bank, they turn to the task of selling, say, $250,000 worth of capital stock (equity shares) to buyers, both in and out of the community. Their efforts meet with success and the Bank of Wahoo comes into existence—at least on paper. What does its balance sheet look like at this stage?

The founders of the bank have sold $250,000 worth of shares of stock in the bank—some to themselves, some to other people. As a result, the bank now has $250,000 in cash on hand and $250,000 worth of capital stock outstanding. The cash is an asset to the bank. Cash held by a bank is sometimes called **vault cash** or till money. The shares of stock outstanding constitute an equal amount of claims that the owners have against the bank's assets. Those shares of stock constitute the net worth of the bank. The bank's balance sheet reads:

Creating a Bank
Balance Sheet 1: Wahoo Bank

Assets		Liabilities and net worth	
Cash	$250,000	Capital stock	$250,000

Each item listed in a balance sheet such as this is called an *account*.

Transaction 2: Acquiring Property and Equipment

The board of directors (who represent the bank's owners) must now get the new bank off the drawing board and make it a reality. First, property and equipment must be acquired. Suppose the directors, confident of the success of their venture, purchase a building for $220,000 and pay $20,000 for office equipment. This simple transaction changes the composition of the bank's assets. The bank now has $240,000 less in cash and $240,000 of new property assets. Using blue to denote accounts affected by each transaction, we find that the bank's balance sheet at the end of transaction 2 appears as follows:

Acquiring Property and Equipment
Balance Sheet 2: Wahoo Bank

Assets		Liabilities and net worth	
Cash	$ 10,000	Capital stock	$250,000
Property	240,000		

Note that the balance sheet still balances, as it must.

Transaction 3: Accepting Deposits

Commercial banks have two basic functions: to accept deposits of money and to make loans. Now that the bank is operating, suppose that the citizens and businesses of Wahoo decide to deposit $100,000 in the Wahoo bank. What happens to the bank's balance sheet?

The bank receives cash, which is an asset to the bank. Suppose this money is deposited in the bank as checkable deposits (checking account entries), rather than as savings accounts or time deposits. These newly created *checkable deposits* constitute claims that the depositors have against the assets of the Wahoo bank and thus are a new liability account.

The bank's balance sheet now looks like this:

Accepting Deposits
Balance Sheet 3: Wahoo Bank

Assets		Liabilities and net worth	
Cash	$110,000	Checkable deposits	$100,000
Property	240,000	Capital stock	250,000

There has been no change in the economy's total supply of money as a result of transaction 3, but a change has occurred in the composition of the money supply. Bank money, or checkable deposits, has increased by $100,000, and currency held by the public has decreased by $100,000. Currency held by a bank, you will recall, is not part of the economy's money supply.

A withdrawal of cash will reduce the bank's checkable-deposit liabilities and its holdings of cash by the amount of the withdrawal. This, too, changes the composition, but not the total supply, of money in the economy.

Transaction 4: Depositing Reserves in a Federal Reserve Bank

All commercial banks and thrift institutions that provide checkable deposits must by law keep **required reserves.** Required reserves are an amount of funds equal to a specified percentage of the bank's own deposit liabilities. A member bank must keep these reserves on deposit with the Federal Reserve Bank in its district or as cash in the bank's vault. To simplify, we suppose the Bank of Wahoo keeps its required reserves entirely as deposits in the Federal Reserve Bank of its district. But remember that vault cash is counted as reserves and real-world banks keep a significant portion of their own reserves in their vaults.

The "specified percentage" of checkable-deposit liabilities that a commercial bank must keep as reserves is known as the **reserve ratio**—the ratio of the required reserves the commercial bank must keep to the bank's own outstanding checkable-deposit liabilities:

$$\text{Reserve ratio} = \frac{\text{commercial bank's required reserves}}{\text{commercial bank's checkable-deposit liabilities}}$$

If the reserve ratio is $\frac{1}{10}$, or 10 percent, the Wahoo bank, having accepted $100,000 in deposits from the public, would have to keep $10,000 as reserves. If the ratio is $\frac{1}{5}$, or 20 percent, $20,000 of reserves would be required. If $\frac{1}{2}$, or 50 percent, $50,000 would be required.

The Fed has the authority to establish and vary the reserve ratio within limits legislated by Congress. The limits now prevailing are shown in Table 14.1. The first $5.5 million of checkable deposits held by a commercial bank or thrift is exempt from reserve requirements. A 3 percent reserve is required on checkable deposits of between $5.5 million and $42.8 million. A 10 percent reserve is required on checkable deposits over $42.8 million, although the Fed can vary that percentage between 8 and 14 percent. Currently, no reserves are required against noncheckable nonpersonal (business) savings or time deposits, although up to 9 percent can be required. Also, after consultation with appropriate congressional committees, the Fed for 180 days may impose reserve requirements in excess of the requirements specified in Table 14.1.

In order to simplify, we will suppose that the reserve ratio for checkable deposits in commercial banks is $\frac{1}{5}$, or 20 percent. Although 20 percent obviously is higher than the requirement really is, the figure is convenient for calculations. Because we are concerned only with checkable (spendable) deposits, we ignore reserves on noncheckable savings and time deposits. The main point is that reserve requirements are fractional, meaning that they are less than 100 percent. This point is critical in our analysis of the lending ability of the banking system.

By depositing $20,000 in the Federal Reserve Bank, the Wahoo bank will just be meeting the required 20 percent ratio between its reserves and its own deposit liabilities. We will use "reserves" to mean the funds commercial banks deposit in the Federal Reserve Banks, to distinguish those funds from the public's deposits in commercial banks.

But suppose the Wahoo bank anticipates that its holdings of the checkable deposits will grow in the future. Then, instead of sending just the minimum amount, $20,000, it sends an extra $90,000, for a total of $110,000. In so doing, the bank will avoid the inconvenience of sending additional reserves to the Federal Reserve Bank each time its own checkable-deposit liabilities increase. And, as you will see, it is these extra reserves that enable banks to lend money and earn interest income.

Actually, the bank would not deposit *all* its cash in the Federal Reserve Bank. However, because (1) banks as a rule hold vault cash only in the amount of $1\frac{1}{2}$ or 2 percent of their total assets and (2) vault cash can be counted as reserves, we can assume that all the bank's cash is deposited in the Federal Reserve Bank and therefore constitutes the commercial bank's total reserves. Then we do not need to bother adding two assets—"cash" and "deposits in the Federal Reserve Bank"—to determine "reserves."

After the Wahoo bank deposits $110,000 of reserves at the Fed, its balance sheet becomes:

Depositing Reserves at the Fed			
Balance Sheet 4: Wahoo Bank			
Assets		Liabilities and net worth	
Cash	$ 0	Checkable	
Reserves	110,000	deposits	$100,000
Property	240,000	Capital stock	250,000

There are three things to note about this latest transaction.

Excess Reserves   A bank's **excess reserves** are found by subtracting its *required reserves* from its **actual reserves:**

Excess reserves = actual reserves −
required reserves

In this case,

Actual reserves	$110,000
Required reserves	−20,000
Excess reserves	$ 90,000

The only reliable way of computing excess reserves is to multiply the bank's checkable-deposit liabilities by the reserve ratio to obtain required reserves ($100,000 × 20 percent = $20,000) and then to

Table 14.1

Reserve Requirements (Reserve Ratios) for Banks and Thrifts, 2001

Type of Deposit	Current Requirement	Statutory Limits
Checkable deposits:		
$0–$5.5 million	0%	3%
$5.5–$42.8 million	3	3
Over $42.8 million	10	8–14
Noncheckable nonpersonal savings and time deposits	0	0–9

Source: Federal Reserve, Regulation D (www.federalreserve.gov). Data are for 2001.

subtract the required reserves from the actual reserves listed on the asset side of the bank's balance sheet.

To test your understanding, compute the bank's excess reserves from balance sheet 4, assuming that the reserve ratio is (1) 10 percent, (2) $33\frac{1}{3}$ percent, and (3) 50 percent.

We will soon demonstrate that the ability of a commercial bank to make loans depends on the existence of excess reserves. Understanding this concept is crucial in seeing how the banking system creates money.

Control You might think the basic purpose of reserves is to enhance the liquidity of a bank and protect commercial bank depositors from losses. Reserves would constitute a ready source of funds from which commercial banks could meet large, unexpected cash withdrawals by depositors.

But this reasoning breaks down under scrutiny. Although historically reserves have been seen as a source of liquidity and therefore as protection for depositors, a bank's required reserves are not great enough to meet sudden, massive cash withdrawals. If the banker's nightmare should materialize—everyone with checkable deposits appearing at once to demand those deposits in cash—the legal reserves held as vault cash or at the Federal Reserve Bank would be insufficient. The banker simply could not meet this "bank panic." Because reserves are fractional, checkable deposits may be much greater than a bank's required reserves.

So commercial bank deposits must be protected by other means. Periodic bank examinations are one way of promoting prudent commercial banking practices. And banking laws limit the kinds of assets banks may acquire; for example, banks are generally prohibited from buying common stocks. Furthermore, insurance funds administered by the Federal Deposit Insurance Corporation (FDIC) and the National Credit Union Administration (NCUA) insure individual deposits in banks and thrifts up to $100,000.

If it is not the purpose of reserves to provide for commercial bank liquidity, then what is their function? *Control* is the answer. Required reserves help the Fed control the lending ability of commercial banks. The Fed can take certain actions that either increase or decrease commercial bank reserves and affect the ability of banks to grant credit. The objective is to prevent banks from overextending or underextending bank credit. To the degree that these policies successfully influence the volume of commercial bank credit, the Fed can help the economy avoid business fluctuations. Another function of reserves is to facilitate the collection or "clearing" of checks. **(Key Question 2)**

Asset and Liability Transaction 4 brings up another matter. Specifically, the reserves created in transaction 4 are an asset to the depositing commercial bank because they are a claim this bank has against the assets of another institution—the Federal Reserve Bank. The checkable deposit you get by depositing money in a commercial bank is an asset to you and a liability to the bank. In the same way, the reserves that a commercial bank establishes by depositing money in a bankers' bank are an asset to that bank and a liability to the Federal Reserve Bank.

Transaction 5: Clearing a Check Drawn against the Bank
Assume that Clem Bradshaw, a Wahoo farmer, deposited a substantial portion of the $100,000 in checkable deposits that the Wahoo bank received in transaction 3. Now suppose that Clem buys $50,000 of farm machinery from the Ajax Farm Implement Company of Surprise, Nebraska. Bradshaw pays for this machinery by writing a $50,000 check, against his deposit in the Wahoo bank, to the Ajax Company. (1) How is this check collected or cleared, and (2) what effect does the collection of the check have on the balance sheets of the banks involved in the transaction?

To answer these questions, we must consider the Wahoo bank (Bradshaw's bank), the Surprise bank (the Ajax Company's bank), and the Federal Reserve Bank of Kansas City. For simplicity, we deal only with changes that occur in the specific accounts affected by this transaction. We trace the transaction in three steps, keyed by letters to Figure 14.1.

(a) Bradshaw gives his $50,000 check, drawn against the Wahoo bank, to the Ajax Company. Ajax deposits the check in its account with the Surprise bank. The Surprise bank increases Ajax's checkable deposits by $50,000 when the check is deposited. Ajax is now paid in full. Bradshaw is pleased with his new machinery.

(b) Now the Surprise bank has Bradshaw's check. This check is simply a claim against the assets of the Wahoo bank. The Surprise bank will collect this claim by sending the check (along with checks drawn on other banks) to the Federal Reserve Bank of Kansas City. Here a clerk will clear, or collect, the check for the Surprise bank by increasing Surprise's reserve in the Federal Reserve Bank by $50,000 and decreasing the Wahoo bank's reserve by that same amount. The

Federal Reserve Bank of Kansas City

Assets	Liabilities and net worth
	Reserves of Wahoo bank −$50,000 (b)
	Reserves of Surprise bank +$50,000 (b)

(c) Cleared check is returned to Wahoo bank

(b) Beaver Crossing bank sends check for collection

Wahoo Bank

Assets	Liabilities and net worth
Reserves −$50,000 (b)	Checkable deposits −$50,000 (c)

Surprise Bank

Assets	Liabilities and net worth
Reserves +$50,000 (b)	Checkable deposits +$50,000 (a)

(a) Bradshaw pays Ajax Company by check

Figure 14.1

The collection of a check through a Federal Reserve Bank.   The bank against which a check is drawn and cleared (Wahoo bank) loses both reserves and deposits; the bank in which the check is deposited (Surprise bank) acquires both reserves and deposits.

check is "collected" merely by making book-keeping notations to the effect that Wahoo's claim against the Federal Reserve Bank is reduced by $50,000 and Surprise's claim is increased by $50,000. Note these changes on the balance sheets in Figure 14.1.

(c) Finally, the Federal Reserve Bank sends the cleared check back to the Wahoo bank, and for the first time the Wahoo bank discovers that one of its depositors has drawn a check for $50,000 against his checkable deposit. Accordingly, the Wahoo bank reduces Bradshaw's checkable deposit by $50,000 and notes that the collection of this check has caused a $50,000 decline in its reserves at the Federal Reserve Bank. Observe that the balance statements of all three banks balance. The Wahoo bank has reduced both its assets and its liabilities by $50,000. The Surprise bank has $50,000 more in reserves and in checkable deposits. Ownership of reserves at the Federal Reserve Bank has changed—with Wahoo owning $50,000 less, and Surprise owning $50,000 more—but total reserves stay the same.

Whenever a check is drawn against one bank and deposited in another bank, collection of that check will reduce both the reserves and the checkable deposits of the bank on which the check is drawn. Conversely, if a bank receives a check drawn on another bank, the bank receiving the check will, in the process of collecting it, have its reserves and deposits increased by the amount of the check. In our example, the Wahoo bank loses $50,000 in both reserves and deposits to the Surprise bank. But there is no loss of reserves or deposits for the banking system as a whole. What one bank loses, another bank gains.

If we bring all the other assets and liabilities back into the picture, the Wahoo bank's balance sheet looks like this at the end of transaction 5:

Clearing a Check Balance Sheet 5: Wahoo Bank		
Assets		Liabilities and net worth
Reserves	$ 60,000	Checkable
Property	240,000	deposits $ 50,000
		Capital stock 250,000

Verify that with a 20 percent reserve requirement, the bank's excess reserves now stand at $50,000.

Money-Creating Transactions of a Commercial Bank

The next three transactions are crucial because they explain (1) how a commercial bank can literally create money by making loans, (2) how money is destroyed when loans are repaid, and (3) how banks create money by purchasing government bonds from the public.

Transaction 6: Granting a Loan
In addition to accepting deposits, commercial banks grant loans to borrowers. What effect does lending by a commercial bank have on its balance sheet?

Suppose the Gristly Meat Packing Company of Wahoo decides it is time to expand its facilities. Suppose, too, that the company needs exactly $50,000—which just happens to be equal to the Wahoo bank's excess reserves to finance this project.

Gristly goes to the Wahoo bank and requests a loan for this amount. The Wahoo bank knows the Gristly Company's fine reputation and financial soundness and is convinced of its ability to repay the loan. So the loan is granted. In return, the president of Gristly hands a promissory note—a fancy IOU— to the Wahoo bank. Gristly wants the convenience and safety of paying its obligations by check. So, instead of receiving a bushel basket full of currency from the bank, Gristly gets a $50,000 increase in its checkable-deposit account in the Wahoo bank.

The Wahoo bank has acquired an interest-earning asset (the promissory note, which it files under "Loans") and has created checkable deposits (a liability) to "pay" for this asset. Gristly has swapped an IOU for the right to draw an additional $50,000 worth of checks against its checkable deposit in the Wahoo bank. Both parties are pleased.

At the moment the loan is completed, the Wahoo bank's position is shown by balance sheet 6a:

When a Loan Is Negotiated Balance Sheet 6a: Wahoo Bank			
Assets		Liabilities and net worth	
Reserves	$ 60,000	Checkable	
Loans	50,000	deposits	$100,000
Property	240,000	Capital stock	250,000

All this looks simple enough. But a close examination of the Wahoo bank's balance statement reveals a startling fact: *When a bank makes loans, it creates money*. The president of Gristly went to the bank with something that is *not* money—her IOU—and walked out with something that *is* money—a checkable deposit.

Contrast transaction 6a with transaction 3, in which checkable deposits were created but only as a result of currency having been taken out of circulation. There was a change in the *composition* of the money supply in that situation but no change in the *total supply* of money. But when banks lend, they create checkable deposits that *are* money. By extending credit, the Wahoo bank has "monetized" an IOU. Gristly and the Wahoo bank have created and then swapped claims. The claim created by Gristly and given to the bank is not money; an individual's IOU is not acceptable as a medium of exchange. But the claim created by the bank and given to Gristly *is* money; checks drawn against a checkable deposit are acceptable as a medium of exchange.

The bulk of the money we use in our economy is created through the extension of credit by commercial banks. This checkable-deposit money may be thought of as "debts" of commercial banks and thrift institutions. Checks are bank debts in the sense that they are claims that banks and thrifts promise to pay "on demand."

But there are factors limiting the ability of a commercial bank to create checkable deposits ("bank money") by lending. The Wahoo bank can expect the newly created checkable deposit of $50,000 to be a very active account. Gristly would not borrow $50,000 at, say, 7, 10, or 12 percent interest for the sheer joy of knowing that funds were available if needed.

Assume that Gristly awards a $50,000 building contract to the Quickbuck Construction Company of Omaha. Quickbuck, true to its name, completes the expansion promptly and is paid with a check for $50,000 drawn by Gristly against its checkable deposit in the Wahoo bank. Quickbuck, with headquarters in Omaha, does not deposit this check in the Wahoo bank but instead deposits it in the Fourth National Bank of Omaha. Fourth National now has a $50,000 claim against the Wahoo bank. The check is collected in the manner described in transaction 5. As a result, the Wahoo bank loses both reserves and deposits equal to the amount of the check; Fourth National acquires $50,000 of reserves and deposits.

In summary, assuming a check is drawn by the borrower for the entire amount of the loan ($50,000) and is given to a firm that deposits it in some other bank, the Wahoo bank's balance sheet will read as follows *after the check has been cleared against it:*

After a Check Is Drawn on the Loan Balance Sheet 6b: Wahoo Bank			
Assets		Liabilities and net worth	
Reserves	$ 10,000	Checkable	
Loans	50,000	deposits	$ 50,000
Property	240,000	Capital stock	250,000

After the check has been collected, the Wahoo bank just meets the required reserve ratio of 20 percent (= $10,000 ÷ $50,000). The bank has *no* excess reserves. This poses a question: Could the Wahoo bank have lent more than $50,000—an amount greater than its excess reserves—and still have met the 20 percent reserve requirement when a check for the full amount of the loan was cleared against it? The answer is no; the bank is "fully loaned up."

Here is why: Suppose the Wahoo bank had lent $55,000 to the Gristly company. Collection of the check against the Wahoo bank would have lowered its reserves to $5,000 (= $60,000 − $55,000), and checkable deposits would once again stand at $50,000 (= $105,000 − $55,000). The ratio of actual reserves to checkable deposits would then be $5,000/$50,000, or only 10 percent. The Wahoo bank could thus not have lent $55,000.

By experimenting with other amounts over $50,000, you will find that the maximum amount the

Wahoo bank could lend at the outset of transaction 6 is $50,000. This amount is identical to the amount of excess reserves the bank had available when the loan was negotiated. *A single commercial bank in a multibank banking system can lend only an amount equal to its initial preloan excess reserves.* When it lends, the lending bank faces the possibility that checks for the entire amount of the loan will be drawn and cleared against it. If that happens, the lending bank will lose (to other banks) reserves equal to the amount it lends. So, to be safe, it limits its lending to the amount of its excess reserves.

Transaction 7: Repaying a Loan

If commercial banks create money in the form of checkable deposits when they make loans, is money destroyed when loans are repaid? Yes. Let's see what happens when Gristly repays the $50,000 it borrowed.

To simplify, we (1) suppose the loan is repaid not in installments but in one lump sum 2 years after it was made and (2) ignore interest charges on the loan. Gristly simply writes a check for $50,000 against its checkable deposit, which we assume was $50,000 before the Gristly loan was negotiated. As a result, the Wahoo bank's checkable-deposit liabilities decline by $50,000; Gristly has given up $50,000 worth of its claim against the bank's assets. In turn, the bank will surrender Gristly's IOU, which it has been holding these many months. The bank and the company have reswapped claims. But the claim given up by Gristly is money; the claim it is repurchasing—its IOU—is not. The supply of money has therefore been reduced by $50,000; that amount of checkable deposits has been destroyed, unaccompanied by an increase in the money supply elsewhere in the economy.

The Gristly Company's IOU has been "demonetized," as shown in balance sheet 7. The Wahoo bank's checkable deposits and loans have each returned to zero. The decline in checkable deposits lowers the bank's required reserves to zero and gives it new excess reserves (= its reserves of $10,000); this provides the basis for making new loans. (**Key Questions 4 and 8**)

Repaying a Loan Balance Sheet 7: Wahoo Bank			
Assets		Liabilities and net worth	
Reserves	$ 10,000	Checkable	
Loans	0	deposits	$ 0
Property	240,000	Capital stock	250,000

In the unlikely event that Gristly repays the loan with cash, the money supply will still decline by $50,000. In this case, Gristly would repurchase its IOU by handing over $50,000 in cash to the bank. Loan balances decline in the bank's asset column by $50,000, and cash increases by $50,000. Remember, we exclude from the money supply currency held by banks, because to include such cash would be double-counting; it is apparent that this constitutes a $50,000 reduction in the supply of money.

Transaction 8: Buying Government Securities   When a commercial bank buys government bonds from the public, the effect is substantially the same as lending. New money is created.

Assume that the Wahoo bank's balance sheet initially stands as it did at the end of transaction 5. Now suppose that instead of making a $50,000 loan, the bank buys $50,000 of government securities from a securities dealer. The bank receives the interest-bearing bonds, which appear on its balance statement as the asset "Securities," and gives the dealer an increase in its checkable-deposit account. The Wahoo bank's balance sheet appears as follows:

Buying Government Securities Balance Sheet 8: Wahoo Bank			
Assets		Liabilities and net worth	
Reserves	$ 60,000	Checkable	
Securities	50,000	deposits	$100,000
Property	240,000	Capital stock	250,000

Checkable deposits, that is, the supply of money, have been increased by $50,000, as in transaction 6. *Bond purchases from the public by commercial banks increase the supply of money in the same way as lending to the public does.* The bank accepts government bonds (which are not money) and gives the securities dealer an increase in its checkable deposits (which *are* money).

Of course, when the securities dealer draws and clears a check for $50,000 against the Wahoo bank, the bank loses both reserves and deposits in that amount and then just meets the legal reserve requirement. Its balance sheet now reads precisely as in 6b except that "Securities" is substituted for "Loans" on the asset side.

Finally, the selling of government bonds to the public by a commercial bank—like the repayment of a loan—reduces the supply of money. The securities buyer pays by check, and both "Securities" and "Checkable deposits" (the latter being money) decline by the amount of the sale.

Profits, Liquidity, and the Federal Funds Market

The asset items on a commercial bank's balance sheet reflect the banker's pursuit of two conflicting goals:

- *Profit*   One goal is profit. Commercial banks, like any other businesses, seek profits, which is why the bank makes loans and buys securities—the two major earning assets of commercial banks.

- *Liquidity*   The other goal is safety. For a bank, safety lies in liquidity, specifically such liquid assets as cash and excess reserves. A bank must be on guard for depositors who want to transform their checkable deposits into cash. Similarly, it must guard against more checks clearing against it than are cleared in its favor, causing a net outflow of reserves. Bankers thus seek a balance between prudence and profit. The compromise is between assets that earn higher returns and highly liquid assets that earn no returns.

An interesting way in which banks can partly reconcile the goals of profit and liquidity is to lend temporary excess reserves held at the Federal Reserve Banks to other commercial banks. Normal day-to-day flows of funds to banks rarely leave all banks with their exact levels of legally required reserves. Also, funds held at the Federal Reserve Banks are highly liquid, but they do not draw interest. Banks therefore lend these excess reserves to other banks on an overnight basis as a way of earning additional interest without sacrificing long-term liquidity. Banks that borrow in this Federal funds market—the market for immediately available reserve balances at the Federal Reserve—do so because they are temporarily short of required reserves. The interest rate paid on these overnight loans is called the **Federal funds rate.**

In Figure 14.1, we would show an overnight loan of reserves from the Surprise bank to the Wahoo bank as a decrease in reserves at the Surprise bank and an increase in reserves at the Wahoo bank. Ownership of reserves at the Federal Reserve Bank of Kansas City would change, but total reserves would not be affected. Exercise: Determine what other changes would be required on the Wahoo and Surprise banks' balance sheets as a result of the overnight loan.

■ The Banking System: Multiple-Deposit Expansion

Thus far we have seen that a single bank in a banking system can lend one dollar for each dollar of its excess reserves. The situation is different for all commercial banks as a group. We will find that the commercial banking system can lend—that is, can create money—by a multiple of its excess reserves. This multiple lending is accomplished even though each bank in the system can lend only "dollar for dollar" with its excess reserves.

How do these seemingly paradoxical results come about? To answer this question, we must keep our analysis uncluttered and rely on three simplifying assumptions:

■ The reserve ratio for all commercial banks is 20 percent.

■ Initially all banks are meeting this 20 percent reserve requirement exactly. No excess reserves exist; or, in the parlance of banking, they are "loaned up" (or "loaned out") fully in terms of the reserve requirement.

■ If any bank can increase its loans as a result of acquiring excess reserves, an amount equal to those excess reserves will be lent to one borrower, who will write a check for the entire amount of the loan and give it to someone else, who will deposit the check in another bank. This third assumption means that the worst thing possible happens to every lending bank—a check for the entire amount of the loan is drawn and cleared against it in favor of another bank.

The Banking System's Lending Potential

Suppose a junkyard owner finds a $100 bill while dismantling a car that has been on the lot for years. He deposits the $100 in bank A, which adds the $100 to its reserves. We will record only changes in the balance sheets of the various commercial banks. The deposit changes bank A's balance sheet as shown by entries (a_1):

Multiple-Deposit Expansion Process			
Balance Sheet: Commercial Bank A			
Assets		Liabilities and net worth	
Reserves	$+100 ($a_1$) − 80 ($a_3$)	Checkable deposits	$+100 ($a_1$) + 80 ($a_2$) − 80 ($a_3$)
Loans	+ 80 (a_2)		

Recall from transaction 3 that this $100 deposit of currency does not alter the money supply. While $100 of checkable-deposit money comes into being, it is offset by the $100 of currency no longer in the hands of the public (the junkyard owner). But bank A *has* acquired excess reserves of $80. Of the newly acquired $100 in currency, 20 percent, or $20, must be earmarked for the required reserves on the new $100 checkable deposit, and the remaining $80 goes to excess reserves. Remembering that a single commercial bank can lend only an amount equal to its excess reserves, we conclude that bank A can lend a maximum of $80. When a loan for this amount is made, bank A's loans increase by $80 and the borrower gets an $80 checkable deposit. We add these figures—entries (a_2)—to bank A's balance sheet.

But now we make our third assumption: The borrower draws a check ($80) for the entire amount of the loan, and gives it to someone who deposits it in bank B, a different bank. As we saw in transaction 6, bank A loses both reserves and deposits equal to the amount of the loan, as indicated in entries (a_3). The net result of these transactions is that bank A's reserves now stand at +$20 (= $100 − $80), loans at +$80, and checkable deposits at +$100 (= $100 + $80 − $80). When the dust has settled, bank A is just meeting the 20 percent reserve ratio.

Recalling transaction 5, we know that bank B acquires both the reserves and the deposits that bank

A has lost. Bank B's balance sheet is changed as in entries (b_1):

Multiple-Deposit Expansion Process
Balance Sheet: Commercial Bank B

Assets		Liabilities and net worth	
Reserves	$+80 ($b_1$)	Checkable	
	−64 (b_3)	deposits	$+80 ($b_1$)
Loans	+64 (b_2)		+64 (b_2)
			−64 (b_3)

When the borrower's check is drawn and cleared, bank A loses $80 in reserves and deposits and bank B gains $80 in reserves and deposits. But 20 percent, or $16, of bank B's new reserves must be kept as required reserves against the new $80 in checkable deposits. This means that bank B has $64 (= $80 − $16) in excess reserves. It can therefore lend $64 [entries ($b_2$)]. When the new borrower draws a check for the entire amount and deposits it in bank C, the reserves and deposits of bank B both fall by the $64 [entries ($b_3$)]. As a result of these transactions, bank B's reserves now stand at +$16 (= $80 − $64), loans at +$64, and checkable deposits at +$80 (= $80 + $64 − $64). After all this, bank B is just meeting the 20 percent reserve requirement.

We are off and running again. Bank C acquires the $64 in reserves and deposits lost by bank B. Its balance sheet changes as in entries (c_1):

Multiple-Deposit Expansion Process
Balance Sheet: Commercial Bank C

Assets		Liabilities and net worth	
Reserves	$+64.00 ($c_1$)	Checkable	
	−51.20 (c_3)	deposits	$+64.00 ($c_1$)
Loans	+51.20 (c_2)		+51.20 (c_2)
			−51.20 (c_3)

Exactly 20 percent, or $12.80, of these new reserves will be required reserves, the remaining $51.20 being excess reserves. Hence, bank C can safely lend a maximum of $51.20. Suppose it does [entries (c_2)]. And suppose the borrower draws a check for the entire amount and gives it to someone who deposits it in another bank [entries (c_3)].

Bank D—the bank receiving the $51.20 in reserves and deposits—now notes these changes on its balance sheet [entries (d_1)]:

Multiple-Deposit Expansion Process
Balance Sheet: Commercial Bank D

Assets		Liabilities and net worth	
Reserves	$+51.20 ($d_1$)	Demand	
	−40.96 (d_3)	deposits	$+51.20 ($d_1$)
Loans	+40.96 (d_2)		+40.96 (d_2)
			−40.96 (d_3)

It can now lend $40.96 [entries ($d_2$)]. The newest borrower draws a check for the full amount and deposits it in still another bank [entries (d_3)].

We could go ahead with this procedure by bringing banks E, F, G, H, . . . , N into the picture. But we suggest that you work through the computations for banks E, F, and G to be sure you understand the procedure.

The entire analysis is summarized in Table 14.2. Data for banks E through N are supplied so that you may check your computations. Our conclusion is startling: On the basis of only $80 in excess reserves (acquired by the banking system when someone deposited $100 of currency in bank A), the entire commercial banking system is able to lend $400, the sum of the amounts in column 4. The banking system can lend excess reserves by a multiple of 5 when the reserve ratio is 20 percent. Yet each single bank in the banking system is lending only an amount equal to its own excess reserves. How do we explain this? How can the banking system lend by a multiple of its excess reserves, when each individual bank can lend only dollar for dollar with its excess reserves?

The answer is that reserves lost by a single bank are not lost to the banking system as a whole. The reserves lost by bank A are acquired by bank B. Those lost by B are gained by C. C loses to D, D to E, E to F, and so forth. Although reserves can be, and are, lost by individual banks in the banking system, there is no loss of reserves for the banking system as a whole.

An individual bank can safely lend only an amount equal to its excess reserves, but the commercial banking system can lend by a multiple of its excess reserves. This contrast, incidentally, is an illustration of why it is imperative that we keep the fallacy of composition (Chapter 1) firmly in mind. Commercial banks as a group can create money by lending in a manner much different from that of the individual banks in the group.

Table 14.2

Expansion of the Money Supply by the Commercial Banking System

Bank	(1) Acquired Reserves and Deposits	(2) Required Reserves (Reserve Ratio = .2)	(3) Excess Reserves, (1) − (2)	(4) Amount Bank Can Lend; New Money Created = (3)
Bank A	$100.00 (a_1)	$20.00	**$80.00**	$ 80.00 (a_2)
Bank B	80.00 (a_3, b_1)	16.00	64.00	64.00 (b_2)
Bank C	64.00 (b_3, c_1)	12.80	51.20	51.20 (c_2)
Bank D	51.20 (c_3, d_1)	10.24	40.96	40.96 (d_2)
Bank E	40.96	8.19	32.77	32.77
Bank F	32.77	6.55	26.21	26.21
Bank G	26.21	5.24	20.97	20.97
Bank H	20.97	4.20	16.78	16.78
Bank I	16.78	3.36	13.42	13.42
Bank J	13.42	2.68	10.74	10.74
Bank K	10.74	2.15	8.59	8.59
Bank L	8.59	1.72	6.87	6.87
Bank M	6.87	1.37	5.50	5.50
Bank N	5.50	1.10	4.40	4.40
Other banks	21.99	4.40	17.59	17.59
Total amount of money created (sum of the amounts in column 4)				**$400.00**

The Monetary Multiplier

The banking system magnifies any original excess reserves into a larger amount of newly created checkable-deposit money. The *checkable-deposit multiplier*, or **monetary multiplier,** is similar in concept to the spending-income multiplier in Chapter 10. That multiplier exists because the expenditures of one household become some other household's income; the multiplier magnifies a change in initial spending into a larger change in GDP. The spending-income multiplier is the reciprocal of the MPS (the leakage into saving that occurs at each round of spending).

In contrast, the monetary multiplier exists because the reserves and deposits lost by one bank are received by another bank. It magnifies excess reserves into a larger creation of checkable-deposit money. The monetary multiplier m is the reciprocal of the required reserve ratio R (the leakage into required reserves that occurs at each step in the lending process). In short,

$$\text{Monetary multiplier} = \frac{1}{\text{required reserve ratio}}$$

or, in symbols,

$$m = \frac{1}{R}$$

In this formula, m represents the maximum amount of new checkable-deposit money that can be created by a single dollar of excess reserves, given the value of R. By multiplying the excess reserves E by m, we can find the maximum amount of new checkable-deposit money, D, that can be created by the banking system. That is,

$$\begin{array}{l}\text{Maximum} \\ \text{checkable-deposit} \\ \text{creation}\end{array} = \begin{array}{l}\text{excess} \\ \text{reserves}\end{array} \times \begin{array}{l}\text{monetary} \\ \text{multiplier}\end{array}$$

or, more simply,

$$D = E \times m$$

In our example in Table 14.2, R is .20, so m is 5 (= 1/.20). Then

$$D = \$400 = \$80 \times 5$$

Higher reserve ratios mean lower monetary multipliers and therefore less creation of new checkable-deposit money via loans; smaller reserve ratios mean higher monetary multipliers and thus more creation of new checkable-deposit money via loans. With a high reserve ratio, say, 50 percent, the monetary multiplier would be 2 (= 1/.5), and in our example the banking system could create only $160 (= $80 of excess reserves × 2) of new checkable deposits. With a low reserve ratio, say, 5 percent, the monetary multiplier would be 20 (= 1/.05), and the banking system could create $1600 (= $80 of excess reserves × 20) of new checkable deposits. Again, note the similarities with the spending-income multiplier, in which higher MPSs mean lower multipliers and lower MPSs mean higher multipliers. Also, like the spending-income multiplier, the monetary multiplier works in both directions. The monetary multiplier applies to money destruction as well as to money creation.

But keep in mind that despite the similar rationales underlying the spending-income multiplier and the monetary multiplier, the former has to do with changes in income and output and the latter with changes in the supply of money.

Figure 14.2 depicts the final outcome of our example of a multiple-deposit expansion of the money supply. The initial deposit of $100 of currency into

the bank (lower right-hand box) creates new reserves of an equal amount (upper box). With a 20 percent reserve ratio, however, only $20 of currency reserves is needed to "back up" this $100 checkable deposit. The excess reserves of $80 permit the creation of $400 of new checkable deposits via the making of loans, confirming a monetary multiplier of 5. The $100 of new reserves supports a total supply of money of $500, consisting of the $100 initial checkable deposit plus $400 of checkable deposits created through lending.

You might experiment with the following two brainteasers to test your understanding of multiple credit expansion by the banking system:

■ Rework the analysis in Table 14.2 (at least three or four steps of it) assuming the reserve ratio is 10 percent. What is the maximum amount of money the banking system can create upon acquiring $100 in new reserves and deposits? (The answer is not $800!)

■ Suppose the banking system is loaned up and faces a 20 percent reserve ratio. Explain how it might have to reduce its outstanding loans by $400 when a $100 cash withdrawal from a checkable-deposit account forces one bank to draw down its reserves by $100. **(Key Question 13)**

Some Modifications

There are certain complications that might modify the preciseness of our analysis.

Other Leakages   Aside from the leakage of required reserves at each step of the lending process, two other leakages of money from commercial banks might dampen the money-creating potential of the banking system:

■ *Currency drains*   A borrower might request that part of his or her loan be paid in currency. Or the recipient of a check drawn by a borrower might ask the bank to redeem it partially or wholly in currency rather than add it to the recipient's account. If the person who borrowed the $80 from bank A in our illustration asked for $16 of it in cash and the remaining $64 as a checkable deposit, bank B would later receive only $64 in new reserves (of which only $51.20 would be excess) rather than $80 (of which $64 was excess). This decline in excess reserves would reduce the lending potential of the banking system accordingly. In fact, if the first borrower had taken the entire $80 in cash and if this

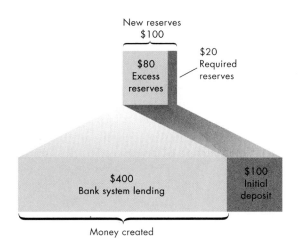

Figure 14.2
The outcome of the money expansion process.   A deposit of $100 of currency into a checking account creates an initial checkable deposit of $100. If the reserve ratio is 20 percent, only $20 of reserves is legally required to support the $100 checkable deposit. The $80 of excess reserves allows the banking system to create $400 of checkable deposits through making loans. The $100 of reserves supports a total of $500 of money ($100 + $400).

currency remained in circulation, the multiple expansion process would have stopped then and there. But the convenience and safety of checkable deposits make this unlikely.

■ *Excess reserves*   Our analysis of the commercial banking system's ability to expand the money supply by lending is based on the supposition that commercial banks are willing to meet precisely the legal reserve requirement. To the extent that bankers hold excess reserves, the overall credit expansion potential of the banking system will be reduced. For example, suppose bank A, upon receiving $100 in new cash, decided to add $25, rather than the legal minimum of $20, to its reserves. Then it would lend only $75, rather than $80, and the monetary multiplier would be diminished accordingly.[1] In fact, the amount of excess reserves that banks have held in recent years has been minimal. The explanation is simple: Excess reserves earn no interest income for a bank; loans and investments do. Hence, our assumption that a bank will lend an amount equal to its excess reserves is reasonable and generally accurate.

Need for Monetary Control

Our illustration of the banking system's ability to create money rests on the assumption that commercial banks are willing to create money by lending and that households and businesses are willing to borrow. In reality, the willingness of banks to lend on the basis of excess reserves varies cyclically, and therein lies the rationale for government control of the money supply to promote economic stability.

When prosperity reigns, banks will expand credit to the maximum of their ability. Loans are interest-earning assets, and in good economic times

there is little fear of borrowers defaulting. But, as you will find in Chapter 15, the money supply has an effect on aggregate demand. By lending and thereby creating money to the maximum of their ability during prosperity, commercial banks may contribute to excessive aggregate demand and therefore to inflation.

If recession appears on the economic horizon, bankers may hastily withdraw their invitations to borrow, seeking the safety of liquidity (excess reserves) even if this means sacrificing potential interest income. They may fear large-scale withdrawal of deposits by a panicky public and simultaneously doubt the ability of borrowers to repay. It is not surprising that during some years of the Great Depression of the 1930s banks had excess reserves but lending was at low ebb. The point is that during recession banks may decrease the money supply by cutting back on lending. This contraction of the money supply will restrain aggregate demand and intensify the recession. A rapid shrinkage of the money supply did indeed contribute to the Great Depression, as this chapter's Last Word indicates.

We thus conclude that profit-motivated bankers can be expected to vary the money supply in a way that reinforces cyclical fluctuations. For this reason the Federal Reserve System has at its disposal certain monetary tools to alter the money supply in a *countercyclical*, rather than *pro-cyclical*, fashion. We turn to an analysis of these tools in Chapter 15.

---

[1]Specifically, in our $m = 1/R$ monetary multiplier, we now add to R, the required reserve ratio, the additional excess reserves that bankers choose to keep. For example, if banks want to hold additional excess reserves equal to 5 percent of any newly acquired checkable deposits, then the denominator becomes .25 (equal to the .20 reserve ratio plus the .05 addition to excess reserves). The monetary multiplier is reduced from 5 to 1/.25, or 4.

> **QUICK REVIEW 14.3**
>
> ■   Whereas a single bank in a multibank system can safely lend (create money) by an amount equal to its excess reserves, the banking system can lend (create money) by a multiple of its excess reserves.
>
> ■   The monetary multiplier is the reciprocal of the required reserve ratio; it is the multiple by which the banking system can expand the money supply for each dollar of excess reserves.
>
> ■   Currency drains and a desire by banks to hold excess reserves may reduce the size of the monetary multiplier.

The Bank Panics of 1930 to 1933

A Series of Bank Panics in the Early 1930s Resulted in a Multiple Contraction of the Money Supply.

In the early months of the Great Depression, before there was deposit insurance, several financially weak banks became insolvent. As word spread that customers of those banks had lost their deposits, a general concern arose that something similar could happen at other banks. Depositors became frightened that their banks did not, in fact, still have all the money they had deposited. And, of course, in a fractional reserve banking system, that is the reality. Acting on their fears, people en masse tried to withdraw currency—that is, to "cash out" their accounts—from their banks. They wanted to get their money before it was all gone. This "run on the banks" caused many previously financially sound banks to declare bankruptcy. More than 9000 banks failed within 3 years.

The massive conversion of checkable deposits to currency during 1930 to 1933 reduced the nation's money supply. This might seem strange, since a check written for "cash" reduces checkable-deposit money and increases currency in the hands of the public by the same amount. So how does the money supply decline? Our discussion of the money-creation process provides the answer, but now the story becomes one of money destruction.

Suppose that people collectively cash out $10 billion from their checking accounts. As an immediate result, checkable-deposit money declines by $10 billion, while currency held by the public increases by $10 billion. But here is the catch: Assuming a reserve ratio of 20 percent, the $10 billion of currency in the banks had been supporting $50 billion of deposit money, the $10 billion of deposits plus $40 billion created through loans. The $10 billion withdrawal of currency forces banks to reduce loans (and thus checkable-deposit money) by $40 billion to continue to meet their reserve requirement. In short, a $40 billion destruction of deposit money occurs. This is the scenario that occurred in the early years of the 1930s.

Accompanying this multiple contraction of checkable deposits was the banks' "scramble for liquidity" to try to meet further withdrawals of currency. To obtain more currency, they sold many of their holdings of government securities to the public. You know from this chapter that a bank's sale of government securities to the public, like a reduction in loans, reduces the money supply. People write checks for the securities, reducing their checkable deposits, and the bank uses the currency it obtains to meet the ongoing bank run. In short, the loss of reserves from the banking system, in conjunction with the scramble for security, reduced the amount of checkable-deposit money by far more than the increase in currency in the hands of the public. Thus, the money supply collapsed.

In 1933, President Franklin Roosevelt ended the bank panics by declaring a "national bank holiday," which closed all national banks for 1 week and resulted in the federally insured deposit program. Meanwhile, the nation's money supply had plummeted by 25 percent, the largest such drop in U.S. history. This decline in the money supply contributed to the nation's deepest and longest depression.

Today, a multiple contraction of the money supply of the 1930–1933 magnitude is unthinkable. FDIC insurance has kept individual bank failures from becoming general panics. Also, while the Fed stood idly by during the bank panics of 1930 to 1933, today it would take immediate and dramatic actions to maintain the banking system's reserves and the nation's money supply. Those actions are the subject of Chapter 15.

SUMMARY

1. The operation of a commercial bank can be understood through its balance sheet, where assets equal liabilities plus net worth.

2. Modern banking systems are fractional reserve systems: Only a fraction of checkable deposits is backed by currency.

3. Commercial banks keep required reserves on deposit in a Federal Reserve Bank or as vault cash. These required reserves are equal to a specified percentage of the commercial bank's checkable-deposit liabilities. Excess reserves are equal to actual reserves minus required reserves.

4. Banks lose both reserves and checkable deposits when checks are drawn against them.

5. Commercial banks create money—checkable deposits, or checkable-deposit money—when they make loans. The creation of checkable deposits by bank lending is the most important source of money in the U.S. economy. Money is destroyed when lenders repay bank loans.

6. The ability of a single commercial bank to create money by lending depends on the size of its excess reserves. Generally speaking, a commercial bank can lend only an amount equal to its excess reserves. Money creation is thus limited because, in all likelihood, checks drawn by borrowers will be deposited in other banks, causing a loss of reserves and deposits to the lending bank equal to the amount of money that it has lent.

7. Rather than making loans, banks may decide to use excess reserves to buy bonds from the public. In doing so, banks merely credit the checkable-deposit accounts of the bond sellers, thus creating checkable-deposit money. Money vanishes when banks sell bonds

to the public, because bond buyers must draw down their checkable-deposit balances to pay for the bonds.

8. Banks earn interest by making loans and by purchasing bonds; they maintain liquidity by holding cash and excess reserves. Banks having temporary excess reserves often lend them overnight to banks that are short of required reserves. The interest rate paid on loans in this Federal funds market is called the Federal funds rate.

9. The commercial banking system as a whole can lend by a multiple of its excess reserves because the system as a whole cannot lose reserves. Individual banks, however, can lose reserves to other banks in the system.

10. The multiple by which the banking system can lend on the basis of each dollar of excess reserves is the reciprocal of the reserve ratio. This multiple credit expansion process is reversible.

11. The fact that profit-seeking banks would alter the money supply in a pro-cyclical direction underlies the need for the Federal Reserve System to control the money supply.

TERMS AND CONCEPTS

balance sheet

fractional reserve system

vault cash

required reserves

reserve ratio

excess reserves

actual reserves

Federal funds rate

monetary multiplier

STUDY QUESTIONS

1. Why must a balance sheet always balance? What are the major assets and claims on a commercial bank's balance sheet?

2. **Key Question** Why are commercial banks required to have reserves? Explain why reserves are an asset to commercial banks but a liability to the Federal Reserve Banks. What are excess reserves? How do you calculate the amount of excess reserves held by a bank? What is the significance of excess reserves?

3. "Whenever currency is deposited in a commercial bank, cash goes out of circulation and, as a result, the supply of money is reduced." Do you agree? Explain why or why not.

4. **Key Question** "When a commercial bank makes loans, it creates money; when loans are repaid, money is destroyed." Explain.

5. Explain why a single commercial bank can safely lend only an amount equal to its excess reserves but the commercial banking system as a whole can lend by a multiple of its excess reserves. What is the monetary multiplier, and how does it relate to the reserve ratio?

6. Assume that Jones deposits $500 in currency into her checkable-deposit account in First National Bank. A half-hour later Smith obtains a loan for $750 at this bank. By how much and in what direction has the money supply changed? Explain.

7. Suppose the National Bank of Commerce has excess reserves of $8000 and outstanding checkable deposits of $150,000. If the reserve ratio is 20 percent, what is the size of the bank's actual reserves?

8. **Key Question** Suppose that Continental Bank has the simplified balance sheet shown at the top of page 281 and that the reserve ratio is 20 percent:
   a.   What is the maximum amount of new loans that this bank can make? Show in column 1 how the bank's balance sheet will appear after the bank has lent this additional amount.
   b.   By how much has the supply of money changed? Explain.
   c.   How will the bank's balance sheet appear after checks drawn for the entire amount of the new loans have been cleared against the bank? Show the new balance sheet in column 2.

Assets		(1)	(2)	Liabilities and net worth		(1)	(2)
Reserves	$22,000	___	___	Checkable			
Securities	38,000	___	___	deposits	$100,000	___	___
Loans	40,000	___	___				

d.   Answer questions *a*, *b*, and *c* on the assumption that the reserve ratio is 15 percent.

9. The Third National Bank has reserves of $20,000 and checkable deposits of $100,000. The reserve ratio is 20 percent. Households deposit $5000 in currency into the bank that is added to reserves. What level of excess reserves does the bank now have?

10. Suppose again that the Third National Bank has reserves of $20,000 and checkable deposits of $100,000. The reserve ratio is 20 percent. The bank now sells $5000 in securities to the Federal Reserve Bank in its district, receiving a $5000 increase in reserves in return. What level of excess reserves does the bank now have? Why does your answer differ (yes, it does!) from the answer to question 9?

11. Suppose a bank discovers that its reserves will temporarily fall slightly short of those legally required. How might it remedy this situation through the Federal funds market? Now assume the bank finds that its reserves will be substantially and permanently deficient. What remedy is available to this bank? (Hint: Recall your answer to question 4.)

12. Suppose that Bob withdraws $100 of cash from his checking account at Security Bank and uses it to buy a camera from Joe, who deposits the $100 in his checking account in Serenity Bank. Assuming a reserve ratio of 10 percent and no initial excess reserves, determine the extent to which (*a*) Security Bank must reduce its loans and checkable deposits because of the cash withdrawal and (*b*) Serenity Bank can safely increase its loans and checkable deposits because of the cash deposit. Have the cash withdrawal and deposit changed the money supply?

13. **Key Question** Suppose the simplified consolidated balance sheet shown below is for the entire commercial banking system. All figures are in billions. The reserve ratio is 25 percent.

Assets		(1)	Liabilities and net worth		(1)
Reserves	$ 52	___	Checkable		
Securities	48	___	deposits	$200	___
Loans	100	___			

a.   What amount of excess reserves does the commercial banking system have? What is the maximum amount the banking system might lend? Show in column 1 how the consolidated balance sheet would look after this amount has been lent. What is the monetary multiplier?

b.   Answer the questions in part *a* assuming the reserve ratio is 20 percent. Explain the resulting difference in the lending ability of the commercial banking system.

14. What are banking leakages? How might they affect the money-creating potential of the banking system?

15. Explain why there is a need for the Federal Reserve System to control the money supply.

16. **(Last Word)** Explain how the bank panics of 1930 to 1933 produced a decline in the nation's money supply. Why are such panics highly unlikely today?

17. **Web-Based Question: *How's your own bank doing?*** Go to the FDIC's website, www.fdic.gov, and select Individual Banks. The FDIC's "Institution Directory" provides demographic data and financial profiles for each FDIC-insured institution. Use the directory to look up the financial statement of your personal bank or one in your community. How has it performed over the past year in the following categories: net worth, total assets, total liabilities, short-term liabilities, net income, number of employees, and number of branches?

18. **Web-Based Question: *Assets and liabilities of all commercial banks in the United States*** The Federal Reserve, at www.federalreserve.gov/releases/h8/about. htm, provides an aggregate balance sheet for commercial banks in the United States. Check the current release, and look in the asset column for "Loans and leases." Rank the following components of loans and leases in terms of size: commercial and industrial, real estate, consumer, security, and other. Over the past 12 months, which component has increased by the largest percentage? By the largest absolute amount? Has the net worth (assets less liabilities) of all commercial banks in the United States increased, decreased, or remained constant during the past year?

Monetary Policy

S OME NEWSPAPER COMMENTATORS have stated that the chairperson of the Federal Reserve Board (currently Alan Greenspan) is the second most powerful person in the United States, after the U.S. president. That is undoubtedly an exaggeration because the chair has only a single vote on the 7-person Federal Reserve Board and 12-person Federal Open Market Committee. But there can be no doubt about the chair's influence, the overall importance of the Federal Reserve, and the **monetary policy** that it conducts. Such policy consists of deliberate changes in the money supply to influence interest rates and thus the total level of spending in the economy. The goal is to achieve and maintain price-level stability, full employment, and economic growth. ■ As indicated in Chapter 13, the 12 Federal Reserve Banks together constitute the U.S. "central bank" (nicknamed the "Fed"). In Global Perspective 15.1 we list some of the other central banks in the world, along with their nicknames.

■ Consolidated Balance Sheet of the Federal Reserve Banks

The Fed's balance sheet helps us consider how the Fed conducts monetary policy. Table 15.1 consolidates the pertinent assets and liabilities of the 12 Federal Reserve Banks as of January 24, 2001. You will see that some of the Fed's assets and liabilities differ from those found on the balance sheet of a commercial bank.

Assets

The two main assets of the Federal Reserve Banks are securities and loans to commercial banks. (Again, we will simplify by referring only to *commercial banks*, even though the analysis also applies to *thrifts*—savings and loans, mutual savings banks, and credit unions.)

Securities   The securities shown in Table 15.1 are government bonds that have been purchased by the

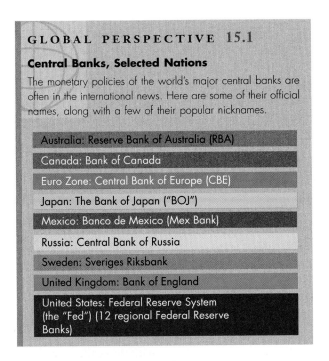

serves and, therefore, the ability of those banks to create money by lending.

Loans to Commercial Banks For reasons that will soon become clear, commercial banks occasionally borrow from Federal Reserve Banks. The IOUs that commercial banks give these "bankers' banks" in return for loans are listed on the Federal Reserve balance sheet as "Loans to commercial banks." They are assets to the Fed because they are claims against the commercial banks. To commercial banks, of course, these loans are liabilities in that they must be repaid. Through borrowing in this way, commercial banks can increase their reserves.

Liabilities

On the liability side of the Fed's consolidated balance sheet, we find three items: reserves, Treasury deposits, and Federal Reserve Notes.

Reserves of Commercial Banks The Fed requires that the commercial banks hold reserves against their checkable deposits. When held in the Federal Reserve Banks, these reserves are listed as a liability on the Fed's balance sheet. They are assets on the books of the commercial banks, which still own them even though they are deposited at the Federal Reserve Banks.

Treasury Deposits The U.S. Treasury keeps deposits in the Federal Reserve Banks and draws checks on them to pay its obligations. To the Treasury these deposits are assets; to the Federal Reserve Banks they are liabilities. The Treasury creates and replenishes these deposits by depositing tax receipts and

Federal Reserve Banks. They consist largely of Treasury bills (short-term securities) and Treasury bonds (long-term securities) issued by the U.S. government to finance past budget deficits. These securities are part of the public debt—the money borrowed by the Federal government. The Federal Reserve Banks bought some of these securities directly from the Treasury but acquired most of them from commercial banks and the public. Although they are an important source of interest income to the Federal Reserve Banks, they are mainly bought and sold to influence the size of commercial bank re-

Table 15.1

Consolidating Balance Sheet of the 12 Federal Reserve Banks, January 24, 2001 (in Millions)

Assets		Liabilities and net worth	
Securities	$518,441	Reserves of commercial banks	$ 28,678
Loans to commercial banks	28	Treasury deposits	7,357
All other assets	93,237	Federal Reserve Notes (outstanding)	549,711
		All other liabilities and net worth	25,960
Total	$611,706	Total	$611,706

Source: Federal Reserve Statistical Release, H.4.1, Jan. 24, 2001, (www.federalreserve.gov/).

money borrowed from the public or from the commercial banks through the sale of bonds.

Federal Reserve Notes Outstanding
As we have seen, the supply of paper money in the United States consists of Federal Reserve Notes issued by the Federal Reserve Banks. When this money is circulating outside the Federal Reserve Banks it constitutes claims against the assets of the Federal Reserve Banks. The Fed thus treats these notes as a liability.

■ Tools of Monetary Policy

With this look at the Federal Reserve Banks' consolidated balance sheet, we can now explore how the Fed can influence the money-creating abilities of the commercial banking system. The Fed has three tools of monetary control it can use to alter the reserves of commercial banks:
- Open-market operations
- The reserve ratio
- The discount rate 🔑 **15.1**

Open-Market Operations

Bond markets are "open" to all buyers and sellers of corporate and government bonds (securities). The Fed's **open-market operations** consist of the buying of bonds from, or the selling of bonds to, commercial banks and the general public. Open-market operations are the Fed's most important instrument for influencing the money supply.

Buying Securities
Suppose that the Fed decides to have the Federal Reserve Banks buy government bonds. They can purchase these bonds either from commercial banks or from the public. In both cases the reserves of the commercial banks will increase.

From Commercial Banks
When Federal Reserve Banks buy government bonds *from commercial banks,*
(a) The commercial banks give up part of their holdings of securities (the government bonds) to the Federal Reserve Banks.
(b) When the Federal Reserve Banks pay for those securities, they increase the reserves of the commercial banks by the amount of the purchase.
We show these outcomes as (a) and (b) on the following consolidated balance sheets of the commercial banks and the Federal Reserve Banks.

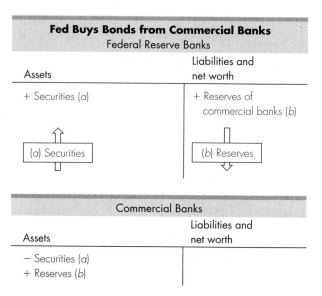

The upward arrow shows that securities have moved from the commercial banks to the Federal Reserve Banks. So we enter "− Securities" (minus securities) in the asset column of the balance sheet of the commercial banks. For the same reason, we enter " + Securities" in the asset column of the balance sheet of the Federal Reserve Banks.

The downward arrow indicates that the Federal Reserve Banks have provided reserves to the commercial banks. So we enter " + Reserves" in the asset column of the balance sheet for the commercial banks. In the liability column of the balance sheet of the Federal Reserve Banks, the plus sign indicates that although commercial bank reserves have increased, they are a liability to the Federal Reserve Banks because the reserves are owned by the commercial banks.

What is most important about this transaction is that when Federal Reserve Banks purchase securities from commercial banks, they increase the reserves in the banking system, which then increases the lending ability of the commercial banks.

From the Public
The effect on commercial bank reserves is much the same when Federal Reserve Banks purchase securities from the general public. Suppose the Gristly Meat Packing Company has government bonds that it sells in the open market to the Federal Reserve Banks. The transaction has several elements:
(a) Gristly gives up securities to the Federal Reserve Banks and gets in payment a check drawn by the Federal Reserve Banks on themselves.

(*b*) Gristly promptly deposits the check in its account with the Wahoo bank.

(*c*) The Wahoo bank sends this check against the Federal Reserve Banks to a Federal Reserve Bank for collection. As a result, the Wahoo bank enjoys an increase in its reserves.

The balance-sheet changes, labeled to correspond with the elements of the transaction, are as follows:

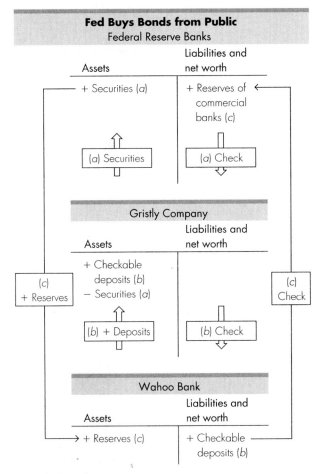

Two aspects of this transaction are particularly important. First, as with Federal Reserve purchases of securities directly from commercial banks, the purchases of securities from the public increases the lending ability of the commercial banking system. This is indicated by the " + Reserves," showing an increase in the assets of the Wahoo bank. Second, the supply of money is directly increased by the Federal Reserve Banks' purchase of government bonds (aside from any expansion of the money supply that may occur from the increase in commercial bank reserves). This direct increase in the money supply has taken the form of an increased amount of

checkable deposits in the economy as a result of Gristly's deposit; thus the " + Checkable deposits" in the Wahoo bank's balance sheet. Because these checkable deposits are an asset as viewed by Gristly, checkable deposits have increased (plus sign) on Gristly's balance sheet.

There is a slight difference between the Federal Reserve Banks' purchases of securities from the commercial banking system and their purchases of securities from the public. If we assume that all commercial banks are loaned up initially, Federal Reserve bond purchases *from commercial banks* increase the actual reserves and excess reserves of commercial banks by the entire amount of the bond purchases. As shown in the left panel in Figure 15.1, a $1000 bond purchase from a commercial bank increases both the actual and the excess reserves of the commercial bank by $1000.

In contrast, Federal Reserve Bank purchases of bonds from the public increase actual reserves but also increase checkable deposits when the sellers place the Fed's check into their personal checking accounts. Thus, a $1000 bond purchase from the public would increase checkable deposits by $1000 and hence the actual reserves of the loaned-up banking system by the same amount. But with a 20 percent reserve ratio applied to the $1000 checkable deposit, the excess reserves of the banking system would be only $800 since $200 of the $1000 would have to be held as reserves.

However, in both transactions the end result is the same: *When Federal Reserve Banks buy securities in the open market, commercial banks' reserves are increased.* When the banks lend out their excess reserves, the nation's money supply will rise. Observe in Figure 15.1 that a $1000 purchase of bonds by the Federal Reserve results in $5000 of additional money, regardless of whether the purchase was made from commercial banks or from the general public.

Selling Securities

As you may suspect, when the Federal Reserve Banks sell government bonds, commercial banks' reserves are reduced. Let's see why.

To Commercial Banks

When the Federal Reserve Banks sell securities in the open market to commercial banks,

(*a*) The Federal Reserve Banks give up securities that the commercial banks acquire.

(b) The commercial banks pay for those securities by drawing checks against their deposits—that is, against their reserves—in Federal Reserve Banks. The Fed collects those checks by reducing the commercial banks' reserves accordingly. The balance-sheet changes—again identified by (a) and (b)—appear as shown below. The reduction in commercial bank reserves is indicated by the minus signs before the appropriate entries.

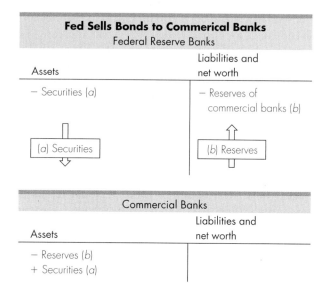

To the Public   When the Federal Reserve Banks sell securities to the public, the outcome is the same. Let's put the Gristly Company on the buying end of government bonds that the Federal Reserve Banks are selling:

(a) The Federal Reserve Banks sell government bonds to Gristly, which pays with a check drawn on the Wahoo bank.

(b) The Federal Reserve Banks clear this check against the Wahoo bank by reducing Wahoo's reserves.

(c) The Wahoo bank returns the canceled check to Gristly, reducing Gristly's checkable deposit accordingly.

We show these balance sheet changes at the top of the next page.

Federal Reserve bond sales of $1000 to the commercial banking system reduce the system's actual and excess reserves by $1000. But a $1000 bond sale to the public reduces excess reserves by $800, because the public's checkable-deposit money is also reduced by $1000 by the sale. Since the commercial banking system's outstanding checkable deposits are reduced by $1000, banks need keep $200 less in reserves.

Whether the Fed sells bonds to the public or to commercial banks, the result is the same: *When Federal Reserve Banks sell securities in the open market,*

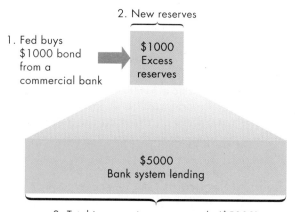

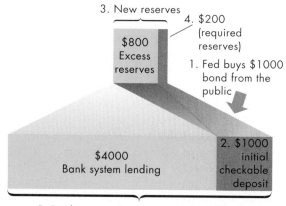

Figure 15.1

The Federal Reserve's purchase of bonds and the expansion of the money supply.   Assuming all banks are loaned up initially, a Federal Reserve purchase of a $1000 bond from either a commercial bank or the public can increase the money supply by $5000 when the reserve ratio is 20 percent. In the left panel of the diagram, the purchase of a $1000 bond from a commercial bank creates $1000 of excess reserves that support a $5000 expansion of checkable deposits through loans. In the right panel, the purchase of a $1000 bond from the public creates a $1000 checkable deposit but only $800 of excess reserves, because $200 of reserves is required to "back up" the $1000 new checkable deposit. The commercial banks can therefore expand the money supply by only $4000 by making loans. This $4000 of checkable-deposit money plus the new checkable deposit of $1000 equals $5000 of new money.

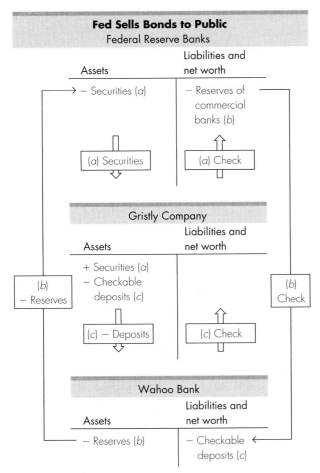

Fed Sells Bonds to Public

commercial bank reserves are reduced. If all excess reserves are already lent out, this decline in commercial bank reserves produces a decline in the nation's money supply. In our example, a $1000 sale of government securities results in a $5000 decline in the money supply whether the sale is made to commercial banks or to the general public. You can verify this by reexamining Figure 15.1 and tracing the effects of a *sale* of a $1000 bond by the Fed either to commercial banks or to the public.

What makes commercial banks and the public willing to sell government securities to, or buy them from, Federal Reserve Banks? The answer lies in the price of bonds and their interest rates. We know from Chapter 13 that bond prices and interest rates are inversely related. When the Fed buys government bonds, the demand for them increases. Government bond prices rise, and their interest rates decline. The higher bond prices and their lower interest rates prompt banks, securities firms, and individual holders of government bonds to sell them to the Federal Reserve Banks.

When the Fed sells government bonds, the additional supply of bonds in the bond market lowers bond prices and raises their interest rates, making government bonds attractive purchases for banks and the public.

The Reserve Ratio

The Fed can also manipulate the **reserve ratio** in order to influence the ability of commercial banks to lend. Suppose a commercial bank's balance sheet shows that reserves are $5000 and checkable deposits are $20,000. If the legal reserve ratio is 20 percent (row 2, Table 15.2), the bank's required reserves are $4000. Since actual reserves are $5000, the excess reserves of this bank are $1000. On the basis of $1000 of excess reserves, this one bank can lend $1000; however, the banking system as a whole can create a maximum of $5000 of new checkable-deposit money by lending (column 7).

Raising the Reserve Ratio Now, what if the Fed raised the reserve ratio from 20 to 25 percent? (See row 3.) Required reserves would jump from $4000 to $5000, shrinking excess reserves from $1000 to zero. Raising the reserve ratio increases the amount of required reserves banks must keep. As a

Table 15.2

The Effects of Changes in the Reserve Ratio on the Lending Ability of Commercial Banks

(1) Reserve Ratio, %	(2) Checkable Deposits	(3) Actual Reserves	(4) Required Reserves	(5) Excess Reserves, (3)−(4)	(6) Money-Creating Potential of Single Bank, =(5)	(7) Money-Creating Potential of Banking System
(1) 10	$20,000	$5000	$2000	$ 3000	$ 3000	$30,000
(2) 20	20,000	5000	4000	1000	1000	5,000
(3) 25	20,000	5000	5000	0	0	0
(4) 30	20,000	5000	6000	−1000	−1000	−3,333

consequence, either banks lose excess reserves, diminishing their ability to create money by lending, or they find their reserves deficient and are forced to contract checkable deposits and therefore the money supply. In the example in Table 15.2, excess reserves are transformed into required reserves, and the money-creating potential of our single bank is reduced from $1000 to zero (column 6). Moreover, the banking system's money-creating capacity declines from $5000 to zero (column 7).

What if the Fed increases the reserve requirement to 30 percent? (See row 4.) The commercial bank, to protect itself against the prospect of failing to meet this requirement, would be forced to lower its checkable deposits and at the same time increase its reserves. To reduce its checkable deposits, the bank could let outstanding loans mature and be repaid without extending new credit. To increase reserves, the bank might sell some of its bonds, adding the proceeds to its reserves. Both actions would reduce the supply of money (to clarify this, see Chapter 14, transactions 6 and 8).

Lowering the Reserve Ratio   What would happen if the Fed lowered the reserve ratio from the original 20 percent to 10 percent? (See row 1.) In this case, required reserves would decline from $4000 to $2000, and excess reserves would jump from $1000 to $3000. The single bank's lending (money-creating) ability would increase from $1000 to $3000 (column 6), and the banking system's money-creating potential would expand from $5000 to $30,000 (column 7). *Lowering the reserve ratio transforms required reserves into excess reserves and enhances the ability of banks to create new money by lending.*

The examples in Table 15.2 show that a change in the reserve ratio affects the money-creating ability of the *banking system* in two ways:

■   It changes the amount of excess reserves.
■   It changes the size of the monetary multiplier.

For example, when the legal reserve ratio is raised from 10 to 20 percent, excess reserves are reduced from $3000 to $1000 and the checkable-deposit multiplier is reduced from 10 to 5. The money-creating potential of the banking system declines from $30,000 (= $3000 × 10) to $5000 (= $1000 × 5). *Raising the reserve ratio forces banks to reduce the amount of checkable deposits they create through lending.*

Although changing the reserve ratio is a powerful technique of monetary control, it is infrequently used. The last such change was in 1992, when the Fed lowered the reserve ratio from 12 percent to 10 percent.

The Discount Rate

One of the functions of a central bank is to be a "lender of last resort." Occasionally, commercial banks have unexpected and immediate needs for additional funds. In such cases, each Federal Reserve Bank will make short-term loans to commercial banks in its district.

When a commercial bank borrows, it gives the Federal Reserve Bank a promissory note (IOU) drawn against itself and secured by acceptable collateral—typically U.S. government securities. Just as commercial banks charge interest on their loans, so too Federal Reserve Banks charge interest on loans they grant to commercial banks. The interest rate they charge is called the **discount rate.**

As a claim against the commercial bank, the borrowing bank's promissory note is an asset to the lending Federal Reserve Bank and appears on its balance sheet as "Loans to commercial banks." To the commercial bank the IOU is a liability, appearing as "Loans from the Federal Reserve Banks" on the commercial bank's balance sheet. [See entries (*a*) on the balance sheets below.]

| **Commercial Bank Borrowing from the Fed** | |
| Federal Reserve Banks | |
Assets	Liabilities and net worth
+ Loans to commercial banks (*a*) ⇧ IOUs	+ Reserves of commercial banks (*b*) + Reserves ⇩

| Commercial Banks | |
Assets	Liabilities and net worth
+ Reserves (*b*)	+ Loans from the Federal reserve Banks (*a*)

In providing the loan, the Federal Reserve Bank increases the reserves of the borrowing commercial bank. Since no required reserves need be kept against loans from Federal Reserve Banks, all new reserves acquired by borrowing from Federal Reserve Banks are excess reserves. [These changes are reflected in entries (*b*) on the balance sheets.]

In short, *borrowing from the Federal Reserve Banks by commercial banks increases the reserves of the commercial banks and enhances their ability to extend credit.*

The Fed has the power to set the discount rate at which commercial banks borrow from Federal Reserve Banks. From the commercial banks' point of view, the discount rate is a cost of acquiring reserves. A lowering of the discount rate encourages commercial banks to obtain additional reserves by borrowing from Federal Reserve Banks. When the commercial banks lend new reserves, the money supply increases.

An increase in the discount rate discourages commercial banks from obtaining additional reserves through borrowing from the Federal Reserve Banks. So the Fed raises the discount rate when it wants to restrict the money supply. **(Key Question 2)**

Easy Money and Tight Money

Suppose the economy faces recession and unemployment. The Fed decides that an increase in the supply of money is needed to increase aggregate demand so as to employ idle resources. To increase the supply of money, the Fed must increase the excess reserves of commercial banks. How can it do that?

- **Buy securities** By purchasing securities in the open market, the Fed can increase commercial bank reserves. When the Fed's checks for the securities are cleared against it, the commercial banks discover that they have more reserves.
- **Lower the reserve ratio** By lowering the reserve ratio, the Fed changes required reserves into excess reserves and increases the size of the monetary multiplier.
- **Lower the discount rate** By lowering the discount rate, the Fed may entice commercial banks to borrow more reserves from the Fed.

These actions are called an **easy money policy** (or *expansionary monetary policy*). Its purpose is to make bank loans less expensive and more available and thereby increase aggregate demand, output, and employment.

Suppose, on the other hand, excessive spending is pushing the economy into an inflationary spiral. Then the Fed should try to reduce aggregate demand by limiting or contracting the supply of money. That means reducing the reserves of commercial banks. How is that done?

- **Sell securities** By selling government bonds in the open market, the Federal Reserve Banks can reduce commercial bank reserves.
- **Increase the reserve ratio** An increase in the reserve ratio will automatically strip commercial banks of their excess reserves and decrease the size of the monetary multiplier.
- **Raise the discount rate** A boost in the discount rate will discourage commercial banks from borrowing from Federal Reserve Banks in order to build up their reserves.

These actions are called a **tight money policy** (or *restrictive monetary policy*). The objective is to tighten the supply of money in order to reduce spending and control inflation.

Relative Importance

Of the three instruments of monetary control, *buying and selling securities in the open market is the most important.* This technique has the advantage of flexibility—government securities can be purchased or sold in large or small amounts—and the impact on bank reserves is prompt. And, compared with reserve-requirement changes, open-market operations work subtly and less directly. Furthermore, there is virtually no question about the ability of the Federal Reserve Banks to affect commercial bank reserves through the purchase and sale of bonds. A glance at the consolidated balance sheet for the Federal Reserve Banks (Table 15.1) reveals very large holdings of government securities ($518 billion). The sale of those securities could theoretically reduce commercial bank reserves from $29 billion to zero.

Changing the reserve requirement is a less important instrument of monetary control, and the Fed has used this technique only sparingly. Normally, it can accomplish its monetary goals easier through open-market operations. The limited use of changes in the reserve ratio undoubtedly relates to the fact that reserves earn no interest. Consequently, raising or lowering reserve requirements has a substantial effect on bank profits.

The Fed often lowers or raises the discount rate, but this tool is much less important than open-market operations. On average, only 2 or 3 percent of commercial bank reserves are acquired from the Federal Reserve Banks. Indeed, open-market operations often lead the banks to borrow from Federal Reserve Banks. That is, if Fed sales of bonds to the

KEY GRAPH

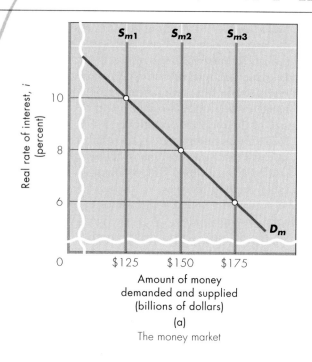

(a)

The money market

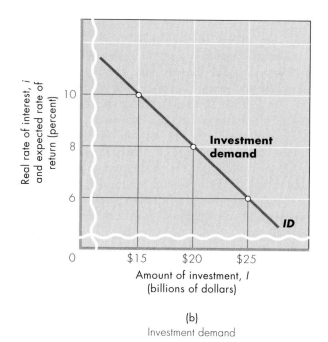

(b)

Investment demand

Quick Quiz 15.2

1. The ultimate objective of an easy money policy is depicted by:
a. a decrease in the money supply from S_{m3} to S_{m2}.
b. a reduction of the interest rate from 8 to 6 percent.
c. an increase in investment from $20 billion to $25 billion.
d. an increase in real GDP from Q_1 to Q_f.

2. A successful tight money policy is evidenced by a shift in the money supply curve from:

a. S_{m3} to S_{m2}, an increase in investment from $20 billion to $25 billion, and a decline in aggregate demand from AD_3 to AD_2.

b. S_{m1} to S_{m2}, an increase in investment from $20 billion to $25 billion, and an increase in real GDP from Q_1 to Q_f.

c. S_{m3} to S_{m2}, a decrease in investment from $25 billion to $20 billion, and a decline in the price level from P_3 to P_2.

public leave commercial banks temporarily short of reserves, commercial banks may seek loans from the Federal Reserve Banks. Commercial banks borrow from the Fed largely in response to open-market operations rather than in response to changes in the discount rate.

At best, the discount rate has an "announcement effect"; it is a clear and explicit way for the Fed to communicate to the financial community and the general economy the intended direction of monetary policy. But more likely, the discount rate is "passive." The Fed changes it simply to keep it in line with other short-term interest rates such as the Federal funds rate, rather than to implement monetary policy.

QUICK REVIEW 15.1

■ The objective of monetary policy is to help the economy achieve full employment, price-level stability, and economic growth.

■ The Fed has three main tools of monetary control, each of which works by changing the amount of excess reserves in the banking system: (a) conducting open-market operations (the Fed's buying and selling of government bonds to the banks and the public); (b) changing the reserve ratio (the percentage of commercial bank deposit liabilities required as reserves); and (c) changing the discount rate (the interest rate the Federal Reserve Banks charge on loans to banks and thrifts).

■ Open-market operations are the Fed's most important monetary control mechanism.

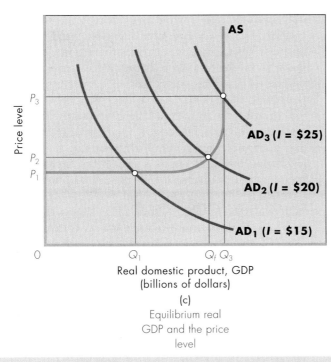

Figure 15.2

Monetary policy and equilibrium GDP. An easy money policy that shifts the money supply curve rightward from S_{m1} to S_{m2} lowers the interest rate from 10 to 8 percent. As a result, investment spending increases from \$15 billion to \$20 billion, shifting the aggregate demand curve rightward from AD_1 to AD_2, and real output rises from the recessionary level Q_1 to the full-employment level Q_f. A tight money policy that shifts the money supply curve leftward from S_{m3} to S_{m2} increases the interest rate from 6 to 8 percent. Investment spending thus falls from \$25 billion to \$20 billion, and the aggregate demand curve shifts leftward from AD_3 to AD_2, curtailing inflation.

---

    d. S_{m3} to S_{m2}, a decrease in investment from \$25 billion to \$20 billion, and an increase in aggregate demand from AD_2 to AD_3.

3. The Federal Reserve could increase the money supply from S_{m1} to S_{m2} by:

    a. increasing the discount rate.

    b. reducing taxes.

    c. buying government securities in the open market.

    d. increasing the reserve requirement.

4. If the spending-income multiplier is 4 in the economy depicted, an increase in the money supply from \$125 billion to \$150 billion will:

    a. shift the aggregate demand curve rightward by \$20 billion.

    b. increase real GDP by \$25 billion.

    c. increase real GDP by \$100 billion.

    d. shift the aggregate demand curve leftward by \$5 billion.

Answers: 1. d; 2. c; 3. c; 4. a

■ Monetary Policy, Real GDP, and the Price Level

So far we have explained only how the Fed can change the money supply. Now we need to link up the money supply, the interest rate, investment spending, and aggregate demand to see how monetary policy affects the economy. How does monetary policy work? 🗹 15.1

Cause-Effect Chain

The three diagrams in **Figure 15.2 (Key Graph)** will help you understand how monetary policy works toward achieving its goals.

Money Market Figure 15.2a represents the money market, in which the demand curve for money and the supply curve of money are brought together. Recall from Chapter 13 that the total demand for money is made up of the transactions and asset demands. The transactions demand is directly related to the nominal GDP. The asset demand is inversely related to the interest rate. The interest rate is the opportunity cost of holding money as an asset; the higher that cost, the smaller the amount of money the public wants to hold. The total demand for money D_m is thus inversely related to the interest rate, as is indicated in Figure 15.2a. Also, recall that an increase in nominal GDP will shift D_m to the right, and a decline in nominal GDP will shift D_m to the left.

This figure also shows three potential money supply curves, S_{m1}, S_{m2}, and S_{m3}. In each case the money supply is shown as a vertical line representing some fixed amount of money determined by the Fed. While monetary policy (specifically, the supply of money) helps determine the interest rate, the interest rate does not determine the location of the money supply curve.

The equilibrium interest rate is the rate at which the amount of money demanded and the amount supplied are equal. With money demand D_m in Figure 15.2a, if the supply of money is $125 billion ($S_{m1}$), the equilibrium interest rate is 10 percent. With a money supply of $150 ($S_{m2}$), the equilibrium interest rate is 8 percent; with a money supply of $175 billion ($S_{m3}$), it is 6 percent.

You know from Chapter 10 that the real, not the nominal, rate of interest is critical for investment decisions. So here we assume that Figure 15.2a portrays real interest rates.

Investment
These 10, 8, and 6 percent real interest rates are carried rightward to the investment demand curve in Figure 15.2b. This curve shows the inverse relationship between the interest rate—the cost of borrowing to invest—and the amount of investment spending. At the 10 percent interest rate it will be profitable for the nation's businesses to invest $15 billion; at 8 percent, $20 billion; at 6 percent, $25 billion.

Changes in the interest rate mainly affect the investment component of total spending, although they also affect spending on durable consumer goods (such as autos) that are purchased on credit. The impact of changing interest rates on investment spending is great because of the large cost and long-term nature of capital purchases. Capital equipment, factory buildings, and warehouses are tremendously expensive. In absolute terms, interest charges on funds borrowed for these purchases are considerable.

Similarly, the interest cost on a house purchased on a long-term contract is very large: A $\frac{1}{2}$-percentage-point change in the interest rate could amount to thousands of dollars in the total cost of a home.

Also, changes in the interest rate may affect investment spending by changing the relative attractiveness of purchases of capital equipment versus purchases of bonds. In purchasing capital goods, the interest rate is the cost of borrowing the funds to make the investment. In purchasing bonds, the interest rate is the return on the financial investment. If the interest rate increases, the cost of buying cap-

ital goods increases while the return on bonds increases. Businesses are then more inclined to use business savings to buy securities than to buy equipment. Conversely, a drop in the interest rate makes purchases of capital goods relatively more attractive than bond ownership.

In brief, the impact of changing interest rates is mainly on investment (and, through that, on aggregate demand, output, employment, and the price level). Moreover, as Figure 15.2b shows, investment spending varies inversely with the interest rate.

Equilibrium GDP
Figure 15.2c shows the impact of our three interest rates and corresponding levels of investment spending on aggregate demand. As noted, aggregate demand curve AD_1 is associated with the $15 billion level of investment, AD_2 with investment of $20 billion, and AD_3 with investment of $25 billion. That is, investment spending is one of the determinants of aggregate demand. Other things equal, the greater the investment spending, the farther to the right lies the aggregate demand curve.

Suppose the money supply in Figure 15.2a is $125 billion ($S_{m1}$), producing an equilibrium interest rate of 10 percent. In Figure 15.2b we see that this 10 percent interest rate will bring forth $15 billion of investment spending. This $15 billion of investment spending joins with consumption spending, net exports, and government spending to yield aggregate demand curve AD_1 in Figure 15.2c. The equilibrium levels of real output and prices are Q_1 and P_1, as determined by the intersection of AD_1 and the aggregate supply curve AS.

To test your understanding of these relationships, explain why each of the other two levels of money supply in Figure 15.2a results in a different interest rate, level of investment, aggregate demand curve, and equilibrium real output and price level.

Effects of an Easy Money Policy

We have assumed that the money supply is $125 billion ($S_{m1}$) in Figure 15.2a. Because the resulting real output Q_1 in Figure 15.2c is far below the full-employment output, Q_f, the economy must be experiencing substantial unemployment. The Fed therefore should institute an easy money policy.

To increase the money supply, the Federal Reserve Banks will take some combination of the following actions: (1) Buy government securities from banks and the public in the open market, (2) lower the legal reserve ratio, and (3) lower the discount rate. The intended outcome will be an increase in excess reserves in the commercial banking system. Because excess reserves are the basis on which commercial banks and thrifts can earn profit by lending and thus creating checkable-deposit money, the nation's money supply probably will rise. An increase in the money supply will lower the interest rate, increasing investment, aggregate demand, and equilibrium GDP.

For example, an increase in the money supply from $125 billion to $150 billion ($S_{m1}$ to S_{m2}) will reduce the interest rate from 10 to 8 percent, as indicated in Figure 15.2a, and will boost investment from $15 billion to $20 billion, as shown in Figure 15.2b. This $5 billion increase in investment will shift the aggregate demand curve rightward by more than the increase in investment because of the multiplier effect. If the economy's MPC is .75, the multiplier will be 4, meaning that the $5 billion increase in investment will shift the AD curve rightward by $20 billion ($= 4 \times \$5$) at each price level. Specifically, aggregate demand will shift from AD_1 to AD_2, as shown in Figure 15.2c. This rightward shift in the aggregate demand curve will increase GDP from Q_1 to the desired full-employment GDP of Q_f.[1]

Column 1 in Table 15.3 summarizes the chain of events associated with an easy money policy.

Effects of a Tight Money Policy

Now let's assume that the money supply is $175 billion ($S_{m3}$) in Figure 15.2a. This results in an interest rate of 6 percent, investment spending of $25 billion, and aggregate demand AD_3. As you can see in Figure 15.2c, we have depicted severe demand-pull inflation. Aggregate demand AD_3 is excessive relative to the economy's full-employment level of real output Q_f. To rein in spending, the Fed will institute a tight money policy.

The Federal Reserve Board will direct Federal Reserve Banks to undertake some combination of the following actions: (1) Sell government securities to banks and the public in the open market, (2) increase the legal reserve ratio, and (3) increase the discount rate. Banks then will discover that their reserves are below those required. So they will need to

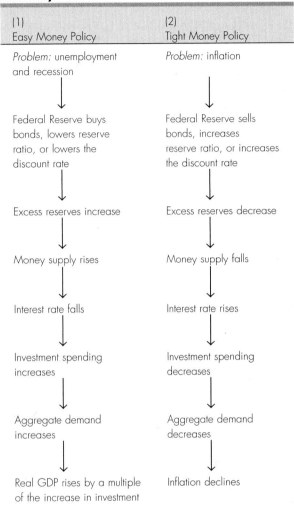

Table 15.3

Monetary Policies for Recession and Inflation

(1) Easy Money Policy	(2) Tight Money Policy
Problem: unemployment and recession	*Problem:* inflation
↓	↓
Federal Reserve buys bonds, lowers reserve ratio, or lowers the discount rate	Federal Reserve sells bonds, increases reserve ratio, or increases the discount rate
↓	↓
Excess reserves increase	Excess reserves decrease
↓	↓
Money supply rises	Money supply falls
↓	↓
Interest rate falls	Interest rate rises
↓	↓
Investment spending increases	Investment spending decreases
↓	↓
Aggregate demand increases	Aggregate demand decreases
↓	↓
Real GDP rises by a multiple of the increase in investment	Inflation declines

reduce their checkable deposits by refraining from issuing new loans as old loans are paid back. This will shrink the money supply and increase the interest rate. The higher interest rate will discourage investment, lowering aggregate demand and restraining demand-pull inflation.

If the Fed reduces the money supply from $175 billion to $150 billion ($S_{m3}$ to S_{m2} in Figure 15.2a), the interest rate will rise from 6 to 8 percent and investment will decline from $25 billion to $20 billion (Figure 15.2b). This $5 billion decrease in investment, bolstered by the multiplier process, will shift the aggregate demand curve leftward from AD_3 to AD_2. For example, if the MPC is .75, the multiplier will be 4 and the aggregate demand curve will shift leftward by

---

[1]To keep things simple we assume that the increase in real GDP does not increase the demand for money. In reality, the transactions demand for money would rise, slightly dampening the decline in the interest rate shown in Figure 15.2a.

$20 billion (= 4 × $5 billion of investment) at each price level. This leftward shift of the aggregate demand curve will eliminate the excessive spending and thus the demand-pull inflation. In the real world, of course, the goal will be to stop inflation—that is, to halt further increases in the price level—rather than to actually drive down the price level.[2]

Column 2 in Table 15.3 summarizes the cause-effect chain of a tight money policy. **(Key Question 3)**

Monetary Policy and Aggregate Supply

The effect of a specific monetary policy depends on where the initial and subsequent equilibrium points are located on the aggregate supply curve. In Figure 15.2c, if the economy is initially at a leftward point in the horizontal range of AS, then an easy money policy that shifts the aggregate demand curve rightward from AD_1 to AD_2 will have a large impact on real GDP and little or no impact on the price level.

But if the economy is already near, at, or beyond full employment, an increase in aggregate demand will have little or no effect on real output and employment. It will, however, substantially raise the price level. To see this, observe in Figure 15.2c that an increase in the aggregate demand curve from AD_2 to AD_3 would occur mainly in the vertical range of the aggregate supply curve. Needless to say, an easy money policy would be inappropriate when the economy is already achieving full employment. Figure 15.2c makes clear the reason why: It would be highly inflationary.

Similarly, a tight money policy is appropriate when the economy is fully employed and suffering demand-pull inflation but would be inappropriate when the economy is suffering substantial cyclical unemployment. In the latter case, the main impact of such a policy would be to reduce real output and deepen unemployment.

■ Effectiveness of Monetary Policy

Monetary policy has several strengths and weaknesses as a stabilization tool, as revealed by its application in the real world.

Strengths of Monetary Policy

Monetary policy is the dominant component of U.S. national stabilization policy, especially in view of the following features and evidence.

Speed and Flexibility Compared with fiscal policy, monetary policy can be quickly altered. Recall that congressional deliberations may delay the application of fiscal policy. In contrast, the Fed can buy or sell securities from day to day and thus affect the money supply and interest rates almost immediately.

Isolation from Political Pressure Because members of the Fed's Board of Governors are appointed and serve 14-year terms, they are relatively isolated from lobbying and need not worry about retaining their popularity with voters. Thus the Board, more readily than Congress, can engage in politically unpopular policies that may be necessary for the long-term health of the economy. Moreover, monetary policy itself is a subtler and more politically conservative measure than fiscal policy. Changes in government spending directly affect the allocation of resources, and changes in taxes can have extensive political ramifications. Because monetary policy works more subtly, it is more politically palatable.

Success in the 1980s and 1990s The successful use of monetary policy in the United States has bolstered the case for it effectiveness. A tight money policy helped bring the inflation rate down from 13.5 percent in 1980 to 3.2 percent 3 years later. In the early 1990s, the Fed's easy money policy helped the economy recover from the 1990–1991 recession.

The expansion of GDP that began in 1992 continued through the rest of the decade, with the unemployment rate falling to 4 percent by 2000. This was the lowest U.S. unemployment rate in 30 years. To ensure against renewed inflation during the expansion, in 1994 and 1995, and then again in early 1997, the Fed reduced reserves in the banking system to raise the interest rate and slow the growth of borrowing and spending. In 1998 the Fed temporarily reversed its course and moved to an easier monetary policy to make sure that the U.S. banking system had plenty of liquidity in the face of a severe financial crisis in Southeast Asia. The economy continued to expand briskly and in 1999 and 2000 the Fed, in a series of steps, boosted interest rates to

---

[2]Again, we assume for simplicity that the decrease in nominal GDP does not feed back to reduce the demand for money and thus the interest rate. In reality, this would occur, slightly dampening the increase in the interest rate shown in Figure 15.2a.

slow a rapidly expanding economy that threatened renewed inflation. When the economy unexpectedly and abruptly slowed in the last quarter of 2000, the Fed cut interest rates by a full percentage point in 2 increments in January 2001.

Economists credit the Fed's adroit use of monetary policy as one of a number of factors that helped the U.S. economy achieve and maintain the rare combination of full employment, price stability, and strong economic growth that occurred between 1996 and 2001.

Shortcomings and Problems

Despite its recent successes in the United States, monetary policy has certain limitations and faces real-world complications.

Less Control? Some observers believe that changes in banking practices may reduce, or make less predictable, the Fed's control of the money supply. Banking reform and the growth of electronic transactions have made it easier for people to move near-monies quickly from mutual funds and other financial investments to checking accounts, and vice versa. A particular monetary policy aimed at changing bank reserves might then be rendered less effective by movements of funds among parts of the financial services industry. For example, people might respond to a tight money policy by converting near-monies in their mutual fund accounts or other liquid financial investments to money in their checking accounts. Bank reserves would then not fall as intended by the Fed, the interest rate would not rise, and aggregate demand might not change.

Also, banking and finance are becoming increasingly global. Flows of funds to or from the United States might undermine or render inappropriate a particular domestic monetary policy. Finally, the prospects of electronic money and smart cards might complicate the measurement of money and make its issuance more difficult to control.

How legitimate are these concerns? Although they might make the Fed's exercise of monetary policy more difficult, Fed studies and experience confirm that, so far, the traditional central bank tools of monetary policy generally remain effective in moving the interest rate in the desired direction.

Changes in Velocity Total expenditures may be regarded as the money supply multiplied by the **velocity of money**—the number of times per year

the average dollar is spent on goods and services. If the money supply is $150 billion, total spending will be $600 billion if velocity is 4 but only $450 billion if velocity is 3.

In some circumstances, velocity may move counter to changes in the money supply, offsetting or frustrating monetary policy. During inflation, when the Fed restrains the money supply, velocity may increase. Conversely, during recession, when the Fed takes measures to increase the money supply, velocity may fall.

Velocity might behave this way because of the asset demand for money. An easy money policy, for example, means an increase in the supply of money relative to the demand for it and therefore a reduction in the interest rate (Figure 15.2a). But the public will hold larger money balances when the interest rate (the opportunity cost of holding money as an asset) is lower. This means dollars will move from households to businesses and back again less rapidly. That is, the velocity of money will decline. A reverse sequence of events may cause a tight money policy to induce an increase in velocity.

Cyclical Asymmetry Monetary policy may be highly effective in slowing expansions and controlling inflation but much less reliable in pushing the economy from a recession—particularly if it is severe. In short, monetary policy may suffer from **cyclical asymmetry.**

If pursued vigorously, a tight money policy could deplete commercial banking reserves to the point where banks were forced to reduce the volume of loans. That would mean a contraction of the money supply, higher interest rates, and reduced aggregate demand. The Fed can turn down the monetary spigot and eventually achieve its goal.

But it cannot be certain of achieving its goal when it turns up the monetary spigot. An easy money policy suffers from a "You can lead a horse to water, but you cannot make it drink" problem. The Fed can create excess reserves, but it cannot guarantee that the banks will actually make the loans and thus increase the supply of money. If commercial banks, seeking liquidity, are unwilling to lend, the efforts of the Fed will be of little avail. Similarly, businesses can frustrate the intentions of the Fed by deciding not to borrow excess reserves. And the public may use money pumped into the economy via open-market operations to pay off existing bank loans.

Furthermore, a severe recession may so undermine business confidence that the investment demand curve shifts to the left and frustrates an easy money policy. That is precisely what happened in Japan in the mid to late 1990s. Although its central bank drove the domestic real interest rate to below zero percent (the rate of inflation exceeded the nominal interest rate), investment spending remained low and the Japanese economy remained mired in recession. Only after prolonged recession and several rounds of expansionary fiscal policy did the Japanese economy begin to recover. The Japanese experience reminds us that monetary policy is not an ensured cure for the business cycle. ！15.1

Targeting the Federal Funds Rate

The Fed currently focuses monetary policy on altering the **Federal funds rate** as needed to stabilize the economy. Recall that this rate is the interest rate that banks charge one another on overnight loans of reserves. When the Fed announces that it will increase the Federal funds rate, it signals that it will implement a "tighter" monetary policy. When it announces that it will lower the Federal funds rate, it signals that it will implement an "easier" monetary policy. Interest rates in general rise and fall with the Federal funds rate. For example, in Figure 15.3 observe that changes in the **prime interest rate**—the interest rate banks charge their most creditworthy customers—generally parallel changes in the Federal funds rate. So, by changing the Federal funds rate, the Fed is, in effect, changing the economy's overall interest rates.

The Fed actually sets neither the Federal funds rate nor the prime rate; each is established by the interaction of lenders and borrowers. But the Fed is the monopoly supplier of bank reserves. When it reduces bank reserves, the Federal funds rate goes up; when it increases bank reserves, the Federal funds rate goes down. And since the amount of reserves in the banking system helps determine the total supply of money, changes in the supply of bank reserves affect the money supply and interest rates in general.

To increase the Federal funds interest rate, the Fed sells bonds in the open market. Such open-market operations reduce excess reserves in the banking system, lessening the supply of excess reserves available for overnight loans in the Federal funds market. The decreased supply of excess reserves in that market increases the Federal funds interest rate. In addition, reduced excess reserves decrease the amount of bank lending and hence the amount of checkable-deposit money. We know that declines in the supply of money lead to increases in interest rates in general, including the prime interest rate.

In contrast, when the Fed decides to reduce the Federal funds rate, it buys bonds from banks and the public. As a result, the supply of reserves in the Federal funds market increases and the Federal funds rate declines. The money supply rises because the increased supply of excess reserves leads to more lending and the creation of checkable-deposit money. As a result, interest rates in general fall, including the prime interest rate. **(Key Question 5)**

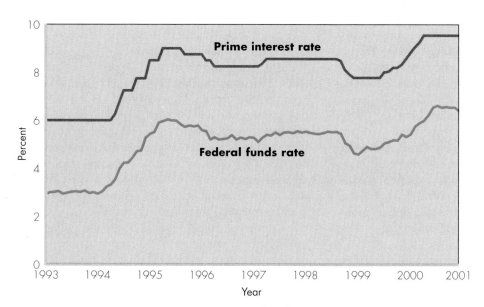

Figure 15.3

The prime interest rate and the Federal funds rate in the United States, 1993–2001. The prime interest rate rises and falls with changes in the Federal funds rate.
Source: Federal Reserve data, www.federalreserve.gov/.

Monetary Policy and the International Economy

In Chapter 12 we noted that linkages among the economies of the world complicate domestic fiscal policy. Those linkages extend to monetary policy as well.

Net Export Effect   As we saw in Chapter 12, an expansionary U.S. fiscal policy (financed by government borrowing) may increase the domestic interest rate because the government competes with the private sector in obtaining loans. The higher interest rate causes the dollar to appreciate in the foreign exchange market. So imports rise and exports fall, and the resulting decline in net exports weakens the stimulus of the expansionary fiscal policy (review Figure 12.6d). This is the so-called *net export effect* of fiscal policy.

Will an easy money policy have a similar effect? The answer is no. As outlined in column 1, Table 15.4, an easy money policy does indeed produce a net export effect, but its direction strengthens the impact of that policy. An easy money policy in the United States reduces the domestic interest rate. The lower interest rate discourages the inflow of financial capital to the United States. The demand for dollars in foreign exchange markets falls, causing the dollar to depreciate in value. It takes more dollars to buy, say, a Japanese yen or a Swiss franc. All for-

eign goods become more expensive to U.S. residents, and U.S. goods become cheaper to foreigners. U.S. imports thus fall, and U.S. exports rise; so U.S. net exports increase. As a result, aggregate expenditures and equilibrium GDP expand in the United States.

Conclusion: In contrast to an expansionary fiscal policy (which decreases net exports), an expansionary monetary policy *increases* net exports and thus strengthens monetary policy. The depreciation of the dollar that results from the lower interest rate means that net exports rise along with domestic investment. Similarly, the net export effect strengthens a tight money policy. To see the full range of effects of a tight money policy, follow through the analysis in column 2, Table 15.4.

Macro Stability and the Trade Balance

Assume that, in addition to domestic macroeconomic stability, a widely held economic goal is that the United States should balance its exports and imports. That is, U.S. net exports should be zero. In simple terms, the United States wants to "pay its own way" in international trade by earning from its exports an amount of money sufficient to finance its imports.

Table 15.4
Monetary Policy and the Net Export Effect

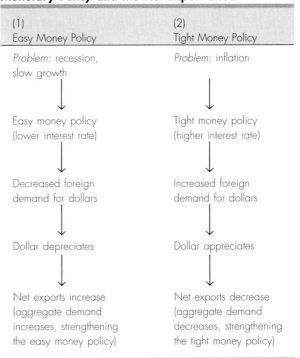

(1) Easy Money Policy	(2) Tight Money Policy
Problem: recession, slow growth	*Problem:* inflation
↓	↓
Easy money policy (lower interest rate)	Tight money policy (higher interest rate)
↓	↓
Decreased foreign demand for dollars	Increased foreign demand for dollars
↓	↓
Dollar depreciates	Dollar appreciates
↓	↓
Net exports increase (aggregate demand increases, strengthening the easy money policy)	Net exports decrease (aggregate demand decreases, strengthening the tight money policy)

Consider column 1 in Table 15.4 once again, but now suppose that the United States initially has a very large balance-of-international-trade deficit, which means its imports substantially exceed its exports and so it is not paying its way in world trade. By following through the cause-effect chain in column 1, we find that an easy money policy results in dollar depreciation and thus U.S. exports increase and U.S. imports decline. This increase in net exports eventually corrects the assumed initial balance-of-trade deficit.

Conclusion: *The easy money policy, which is appropriate for the alleviation of unemployment and sluggish growth, is compatible with the goal of correcting a balance-of-trade deficit.* Similarly, if the initial problem was a U.S. trade surplus, a tight money policy would tend to resolve it.

Now consider column 2 in Table 15.4, and assume again that the United States has a large balance-of-trade deficit. In using a tight money policy to restrain inflation, the Fed would cause net exports to decrease—U.S. exports would fall and imports would rise. That would mean a larger trade deficit.

Conclusion: *A tight money policy that is used to alleviate inflation conflicts with the goal of correcting a balance-of-trade deficit.* However, if the initial problem was a trade surplus, a tight money policy would help to resolve it.

Overall we find that an easy money policy alleviates a trade deficit and aggravates a trade surplus; a tight money policy alleviates a trade surplus and aggravates a trade deficit. The point is that certain combinations of circumstances create conflicts or tradeoffs between the use of monetary policy to achieve domestic stability and the realization of a balance in the nation's international trade. **(Key Questions 6)**

▌The "Big Picture"

Figure 15.4 (Key Graph) on pages 300 and 301 brings together the analytical and policy aspects of macroeconomics discussed in this and the eight preceding chapters. This "big picture" shows how the many concepts and principles discussed relate to one another and how they constitute a coherent theory of the price level and real output in a market economy.

Study this diagram and you will see that the levels of output, employment, income, and prices all result from the interaction of aggregate supply and aggregate demand. The items shown in red relate to public policy.

LAST WORD

For the Fed, Life Is a Metaphor

The Popular Press Often Describes the Federal Reserve Board and Its Chair (Alan Greenspan, 1987–Present) in Colorful Terms.

The Federal Reserve Board leads a very dramatic life, or so it seems when one reads journalistic accounts of its activities. It loosens or tightens reins while riding herd on a rambunctious economy, goes to the rescue of an embattled dollar, tightens spigots on credit . . . you get the picture. For the Fed, life is a metaphor.

The Fed as Mechanic The Fed sometimes must roll up its sleeves and adjust the economic machinery. The Fed spends a lot of time tightening things, loosening things, or debating about whether to tighten or loosen.

Imagine a customer taking his car into Greenspan's Garage:

Normally calm, Skeezix Greenspan took one look at the car and started to sweat. This would be hard to fix — it was an economy car:

"What's the problem?" asked Greenspan.

"It's been running beautifully for over 6 years now," said the customer. "But recently it's been acting sluggish."

"These cars are tricky," said Greenspan. "We can always loosen a few screws, as long as you don't mind the side effects."

"What side effects?" asked the customer.

"Nothing at first," said Greenspan. "We won't even know if the repairs have worked for at least a year. After that, either everything will be fine, or your car will accelerate wildly and go totally out of control."

"Just as long as it doesn't stall," said the customer. "I hate that."

The Fed as Warrior The Fed must fight inflation. But can it wage a protracted war? There are only seven Fed governors, including Greenspan—not a big army:

Gen. Greenspan sat in the war room plotting strategy. You never knew where the enemy would strike next—producer prices, retail sales, factory payrolls, manufacturing inventories.

Suddenly, one of his staff officers burst into the room:

"Straight from the Western European front, sir—the dollar is under attack by the major industrial nations."

Greenspan whirled around toward the big campaign map. "We've got to turn back this assault!" he said.

"Yes sir." The officer turned to go.

"Hold it!" Greenspan shouted. Suddenly, his mind reeled with conflicting data. A strong dollar was good for inflation, right? Yes, but it was bad for the trade deficit. Or was it the other way around? Attack? Retreat? Macroeconomic forces were closing in.

"Call out the Reserve!" he told the officer.

"Uh . . . we are the Reserve," the man answered.

The Fed as the Fall Guy Inflation isn't the only tough customer out there. The Fed must also withstand pressure from administration officials who are regularly described as "leaning heavily" on the Fed to ease up and relax. This always sounds vaguely threatening:

Alan Greenspan was walking down a deserted street late one night. Suddenly a couple of thugs wearing pinstripes and wingtips cornered him in a dark alley.

"What do you want?" Greenspan asked.

"Just relax," said one.

"How can I relax?" asked Greenspan. "I'm in a dark alley talking to thugs."

"You know what we mean," said the other. "Ease up on the federal funds rate—or else."

"Or else what?" asked Greenspan.

"Don't make us spell it out. Let's just say that if anything unfortunate happens to the gross [domestic] product, I'm holding you personally responsible."

"Yeah," added the other. "A recession could get real painful."

The Fed as Cosmic Force The Fed may be a cosmic force. After all, it does satisfy the three major criteria—power, mystery, and a New York office. Some observers even believe the Fed can control the stock market, either by action, symbolic action, anticipated action, or non-action. But saner heads realize this is ridiculous—the market has always been controlled by sunspots.

I wish we could get rid of all these romantic ideas about the Federal Reserve. If you want to talk about the Fed, keep it simple. Just say the Fed is worried about the money. This is something we all can relate to.

Source: Paul Hellman, "Greenspan and the Feds: Captains Courageous," *The Wall Street Journal*, Jan. 31, 1991, p. 18. Reprinted with permission of *The Wall Street Journal*, © 1990 Dow Jones & Company, Inc. All rights reserved.

K E Y   G R A P H

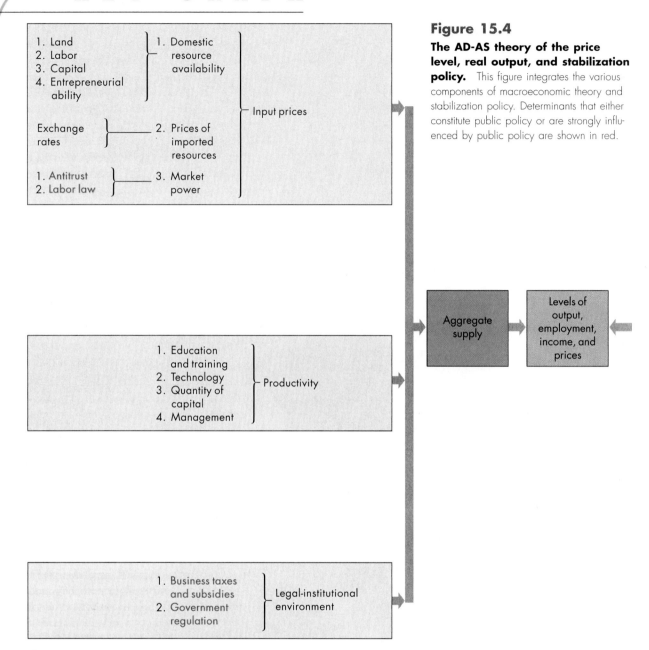

Figure 15.4

The AD-AS theory of the price level, real output, and stabilization policy. This figure integrates the various components of macroeconomic theory and stabilization policy. Determinants that either constitute public policy or are strongly influenced by public policy are shown in red.

Quick Quiz 15.4

1. All else equal, an increase in domestic resource availability will:
   a. increase input prices, reduce aggregate supply, and increase real output.
   b. raise labor productivity, reduce interest rates, and lower the international value of the dollar.
   c. increase net exports, increase investment, and reduce aggregate demand.
   d. reduce input prices, increase aggregate supply, and increase real output.

2. All else equal, an easy money policy during a recession will:
   a. lower the interest rate, increase investment, and reduce net exports.
   b. lower the interest rate, increase investment, and increase aggregate demand.
   c. increase the interest rate, increase investment, and reduce net exports.
   d. reduce productivity, aggregate supply, and real output.

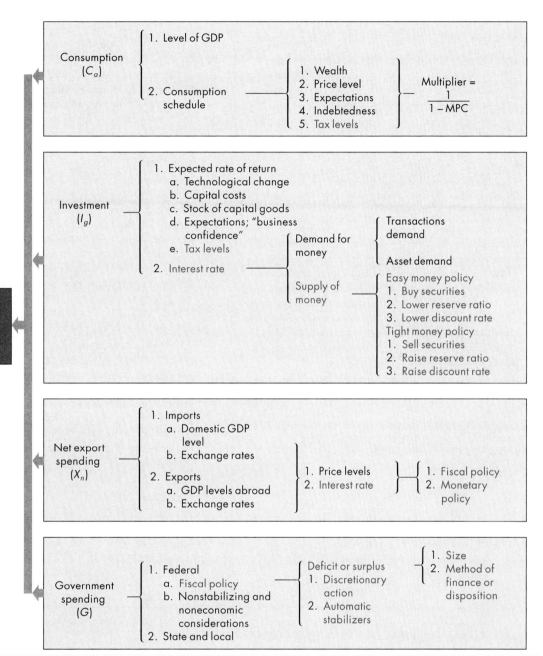

3. A personal income tax cut, combined with a reduction in corporate income and excise taxes, would:

a. increase consumption, investment, aggregate demand, and aggregate supply.

b. reduce productivity, raise input prices, and reduce aggregate supply.

c. increase government spending, reduce net exports, and increase aggregate demand.

d. increase the supply of money, reduce interest rates, increase investment, and expand real output.

4. An appreciation of the dollar would:

a. reduce the price of imported resources, lower input prices, and increase aggregate supply.

b. increase net exports and aggregate demand.

c. increase aggregate supply and aggregate demand.

d. reduce consumption, investment, net export spending, and government spending.

SUMMARY

1. As with fiscal policy, the goal of monetary policy is to help the economy achieve price stability, full employment, and economic growth.

2. In regard to monetary policy, the most important assets of the Federal Reserve Banks are securities and loans to commercial banks. Their basic liabilities are the reserves of member banks, Treasury deposits, and Federal Reserve Notes.

3. The three instruments of monetary policy are (a) open-market operations, (b) the reserve ratio, and (c) the discount rate.

4. Monetary policy operates through a complex cause-effect chain: (a) Policy decisions affect commercial bank reserves; (b) changes in reserves affect the money supply; (c) changes in the money supply alter the interest rate; (d) changes in the interest rate affect investment; (e) changes in investment affect aggregate demand; (f) changes in aggregate demand affect the equilibrium real GDP and the price level. Table 15.3 draws together all the basic notions relevant to the use of monetary policy.

5. The advantages of monetary policy include its flexibility and political acceptability. In the past two decades the Fed has successfully used monetary policy to check rapid inflation and to push the economy away from recession. Today, nearly all economists view monetary policy as a significant stabilization tool.

6. Monetary policy has some limitations and potential problems: (a) Financial innovations and global considerations have made monetary policy more difficult to administer and its impact less certain. (b) Changes in the velocity of money may partially offset policy-instigated changes in the supply of money. (c) In a severe recession, the reluctance of firms to borrow and spend on capital goods may limit the effectiveness of an expansionary monetary policy.

7. Recently, the Fed has communicated its changes in monetary policy via announcements concerning its targets for the Federal funds rate. When it deems it necessary, the Fed uses open-market operations to change that rate, which is the interest rate banks charge one another on overnight loans of excess reserves. Interest rates in general, including the prime interest rate, rise and fall with the Federal funds rate. The prime interest rate is the rate that banks charge to their most creditworthy loan customers.

8. The effect of an easy money policy on domestic GDP is strengthened by the increase in net exports that results from a lower domestic interest rate. Likewise, a tight money policy is strengthened by a decline in net exports. In some situations, there may be a tradeoff between the effect of monetary policy on the international value of a nation's currency (and thus on its trade balance) and the use of monetary policy to achieve domestic stability.

TERMS AND CONCEPTS

monetary policy	discount rate	velocity of money	prime interest rate
open-market operations	easy money policy	cyclical asymmetry	
reserve ratio	tight money policy	Federal funds rate	

STUDY QUESTIONS

1. Use commercial bank and Federal Reserve Bank balance sheets to demonstrate the impact of each of the following transactions on commercial bank reserves:

   a. Federal Reserve Banks purchase securities from private businesses and consumers.

   b. Commercial banks borrow from Federal Reserve Banks.

   c. The Fed reduces the reserve ratio.

2. **Key Question** In the table on page 303 you will find consolidated balance sheets for the commercial banking system and the 12 Federal Reserve Banks. Use columns 1 through 3 to indicate how the balance sheets would read after each of transactions *a* to *c* is completed. Do not cumulate your answers; that is, analyze each transaction separately, starting in each case from the figures provided. All accounts are in billions of dollars.

   a. A decline in the discount rate prompts commercial banks to borrow an additional $1 billion from the Federal Reserve Banks. Show the new balance-sheet figures in column 1 of each table.

   b. The Federal Reserve Banks sell $3 billion in securities to members of the public, who pay for the bonds with checks. Show the new balance-sheet figures in column 2 of each table.

   c. The Federal Reserve Banks buy $2 billion of securities from commercial banks. Show the new balance-sheet figures in column 3 of each table.

   d. Now review each of the above three transactions, asking yourself these three questions: (1) What change, if any, took place in the money supply as a direct and immediate result of each transaction? (2) What increase or decrease in the com-

	Consolidated Balance Sheet: All Commercial Banks		
	(1)	(2)	(3)
Assets:			
Reserves . . . . $ 33	_____	_____	_____
Securities 60	_____	_____	_____
Loans 60	_____	_____	_____
Liabilities and net worth:			
Checkable deposits $150	_____	_____	_____
Loans from the Federal			
Reserve Banks 3	_____	_____	_____

	Consolidated Balance Sheet: The 12 Federal Reserve Banks		
	(1)	(2)	(3)
Assets:			
Securities $60	_____	_____	_____
Loans to commercial banks . . . 3	_____	_____	_____
Liabilities and net worth:			
Reserves of commercial banks . $33	_____	_____	_____
Treasury deposits 3	_____	_____	_____
Federal Reserve Notes 27	_____	_____	_____

mercial banks' reserves took place in each transaction? (3) Assuming a reserve ratio of 20 percent, what change in the money-creating potential of the commercial banking system occurred as a result of each transaction?

3. **Key Question** Suppose that you are a member of the Board of Governors of the Federal Reserve System. The economy is experiencing a sharp and prolonged inflationary trend. What changes in (*a*) the reserve ratio, (*b*) the discount rate, and (*c*) open-market operations would you recommend? Explain in each case how the change you advocate would affect commercial bank reserves, the money supply, interest rates, and aggregate demand.

4. What is the basic objective of monetary policy? State the cause-effect chain through which monetary policy is made effective. What are the major strengths and weaknesses of monetary policy?

5. **Key Question** Distinguish between the Federal funds rate and the prime interest rate. In what way is the Federal funds rate a measure of the tightness or looseness of monetary policy? In 1999 and 2000 the Fed used open-market operations to increase the Federal funds rate. What was the logic of those actions? What was the effect on the prime interest rate?

6. **Key Question** Suppose the Fed decides to engage in a tight money policy as a way to reduce demand-pull inflation. Use the aggregate demand–aggregate supply model to show what this policy is intended to accomplish in a closed economy. Now introduce the open economy and explain how changes in the international value of the dollar might affect the location of your aggregate demand curve.

7. **(Last Word)** How do each of the following metaphors apply to the Federal Reserve's role in the economy: Fed as a mechanic; Fed as a warrior; Fed as a fall guy?

8. **Web-Based Question:** *Current U.S. interest rates* Visit the Federal Reserve's website at www.federal reserve.gov and select Research and Data, then Statistics: Releases and Historical Data, Selected Interest Rates (weekly), and Historical Data to find the most recent values for the following interest rates: the Federal funds rate, the discount rate, and the prime interest rate. Are these rates higher or lower than they were 3 years ago? Have they increased, decreased, or remained constant over the past year?

9. **Web-Based Question:** *The Federal Reserve annual report* Visit the Federal Reserve's website at www. federalreserve.gov and select Testimony and Speeches and then Monetary Policy Report to the Congress to retrieve the current annual report (in Adobe's PDF format only). Summarize the policy actions of the Board of Governors during the most recent period. In the Fed's opinion, how did the U.S. economy perform?

4

*Long-Run Perspectives
and Macroeconomic
Debates*

16

Extending the Analysis of Aggregate Supply

ECONOMIST JOHN MAYNARD Keynes once remarked, "In the long run we are all dead." If the long run is a century or more, nobody can argue with Keynes' statement. But if the long run is just a few years or even a few decades, it becomes tremendously important to households, businesses, and the economy. For that reason, macroeconomists have recently focused much attention on long-run macroeconomic adjustments and outcomes. As we will see in this and the next three chapters, that focus has produced significant insights relating to aggregate supply, economic growth, and government budgeting. We will also see that it has renewed debates over the causes of macro instability and the effectiveness of stabilization policy. ■ Our goals in this chapter are to distinguish between short-run and long-run aggregate supply, examine the inflation-unemployment relationship, and assess the effect of taxes on aggregate supply. The latter is a key concern of so-called *supply-side economics*.

■ Short-Run and Long-Run Aggregate Supply

Until now we have generally assumed that the aggregate supply curve remains stable when the aggregate demand curve shifts position. For example, we saw that an increase in aggregate demand in the upward-sloping portion of the aggregate supply curve raised both the price level and real output. That analysis is accurate and realistic for the time periods we were considering, but we need to extend the analysis of aggregate supply in order to analyze

longer periods. We begin by distinguishing between the *short run* and the *long run* as they apply to aggregate supply.

The **short run** in macroeconomics is *a period in which nominal wages (and other input prices) remain fixed as the price level increases or decreases*. There are at least two reasons why nominal wages may remain constant for a time even though the price level has changed:

■ Workers may not immediately be aware of the extent that inflation (or deflation) has changed their real wages, and thus they may not adjust their labor supply decisions and wage demands accordingly.

- Many employees are hired under fixed-wage contracts. For unionized employees, for example, nominal wages are spelled out in their collective bargaining agreements for perhaps 2 or 3 years. Also, most managers and many professionals receive set salaries established in annual contracts. For them, nominal wages remain constant for the life of the contracts, regardless of changes in the price level.

In such cases, price-level changes do not immediately give rise to changes in nominal wages. Instead, significant periods of time usually pass before such adjustments occur.

Once contracts have expired and nominal wage adjustments have been made, the economy enters the **long run.** In macroeconomics this is *the period in which nominal wages are fully responsive to previous changes in the price level.* As time passes, workers gain full information about price-level changes and how those changes affect their real wages. For example, suppose that Jessica received an hourly nominal wage of $10 when the price index was 100 (or, in decimals, 1.0) and that her real wage was also $10 (= $10 of nominal wage divided by 1.0). But when the price level rises to,

say, 120, Jessica's $10 real wage declines to $8.33 (= $10/1.2). As a result, she and other workers will adjust their labor supply and wage demands such that their nominal wages eventually will rise to restore the purchasing power of an hour of work. In our example, Jessica's nominal wage will increase from $10 to $12, returning her real wage to $10 (= $12/1.2).

Short-Run Aggregate Supply

Given these definitions of short run and long run, we can extend Chapter 11's discussion of aggregate supply.

First, consider the **short-run aggregate supply curve** AS_1 in Figure 16.1a. (Our focus now is on the intermediate range of the AS curve of Chapter 11.) Curve AS_1 is based on three assumptions: (1) The initial price level is P_1, (2) firms and workers have established nominal wages on the expectation that this price level will persist, and (3) the price level is flexible both upward and downward. Observe from point a_1 that at price level P_1 the economy is operating at its full-employment output Q_f. This output is the real production forthcoming when the economy is operating at its natural rate of unemployment (or potential output.).

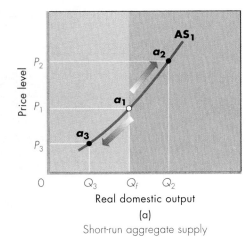

(a)

Short-run aggregate supply

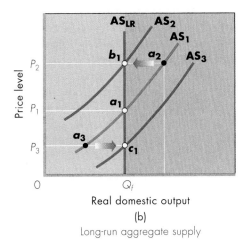

(b)

Long-run aggregate supply

Figure 16.1

Short-run and long-run aggregate supply. (a) In the short run, nominal wages are fixed and based on price level P_1 and the expectation that it will continue. An increase in the price level from P_1 to P_2 increases profits and output, moving the economy from a_1 to a_2; a decrease in the price level from P_1 to P_3 reduces profits and real output, moving the economy from a_1 to a_3. The short-run aggregate supply curve therefore slopes upward. (b) In the long run, a rise in the price level results in higher nominal wages and thus shifts the short-run aggregate supply curve to the left. Conversely, a decrease in the price level reduces nominal wages and shifts the short-run aggregate supply curve to the right. After such adjustments, the economy obtains equilibrium at points such as b_1 and c_1. Thus, the long-run aggregate supply curve is vertical.

Now let's determine the short-run effects of changes in the price level, say, from P_1 to P_2 in Figure 16.1a. The higher prices associated with price level P_2 increase firms' revenues, and because their nominal wages are fixed, their profits rise. Those higher profits lead firms to increase their output from Q_f to Q_2, and the economy moves from a_1 to a_2 on aggregate supply AS_1. At output Q_2 the economy is operating beyond its full-employment output. The firms make this possible by extending the work hours of part-time and full-time workers, enticing new workers such as homemakers and retirees into the labor force, and hiring and training the structurally unemployed. Thus, the nation's unemployment rate declines below its natural rate.

How will the firms respond when the price level *falls*, say, from P_1 to P_3 in Figure 16.1a? Because the prices they receive for their products are lower while the nominal wages they pay workers are not, firms discover that their revenues and profits have diminished or disappeared. So they reduce their production and employment, and, as shown by the movement from a_1 to a_3, real output falls to Q_3. Increased unemployment and a higher unemployment rate accompany the decline in real output. At output Q_3 the unemployment rate is greater than the natural rate of unemployment associated with output Q_f.

Long-Run Aggregate Supply

To analyze longer time periods, we need to extend the analysis of aggregate supply to account for changes in nominal wages that occur *in response to changes in the price level*. That will enable us to derive the economy's long-run aggregate supply curve.

By definition, nominal wages in the long run are fully responsive to changes in the price level. We illustrate the implications for aggregate supply in Figure 16.1b. Again, suppose that the economy is initially at point a_1 (P_1 and Q_f). As we just demonstrated, an increase in the price level from P_1 to P_2 will move the economy from point a_1 to a_2 along the short-run aggregate supply curve AS_1. In the long run, however, workers discover that their real wages (their constant nominal wages divided by the price level) have declined because of this increase in the price level. They restore their previous level of real wages by gaining nominal wage increases. Because nominal wages are one of the determinants of aggregate supply (see Figure 11.6), the short-run supply curve then shifts leftward from AS_1 to AS_2, which now reflects the higher price level P_2 and the new expectation that P_2, not P_1, will continue. The leftward shift in the short-run aggregate supply curve

to AS_2 moves the economy from a_2 to b_1. Real output falls back to its full-employment level Q_f, and the unemployment rate rises to its natural rate.

What is the long-run outcome of a *decrease* in the price level? *Assuming downward wage flexibility*, a decline in the price level from P_1 to P_3 in Figure 16.1b works in the opposite way from a price-level increase. At first the economy moves from point a_1 to a_3 on AS_1. Profits are squeezed or eliminated because prices have fallen and nominal wages have not. But this movement along AS_1 is the short-run supply response. With enough time the lower price level P_3 (which has increased real wages) results in a drop in nominal wages such that the original real wages are restored. Lower nominal wages shift the short-run aggregate supply curve rightward from AS_1 to AS_3, and real output returns to its full-employment level of Q_f at point c_1.

By tracing a line between the long-run equilibrium points b_1, a_1, and c_1, we obtain a **long-run aggregate supply curve.** Observe that it is vertical at the full-employment level of real GDP. After long-run adjustments in nominal wages, real output is Q_f regardless of the specific price level. **(Key Question 3)**

Equilibrium in the Extended AD-AS Model

Figure 16.2 shows the long-run equilibrium in the AD-AS model, now extended to include the distinction between short-run aggregate supply and long-

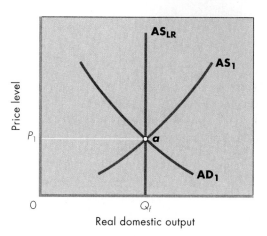

Figure 16.2

Equilibrium in the extended AD-AS model. The equilibrium price level P_1 and level of real output Q_f occur at the intersection of the aggregate demand curve AD_1, the long-run aggregate supply curve AS_{LR}, and the short-run aggregate supply curve AS_1.

run aggregate supply. (Hereafter, we will refer to this model as the *extended AD-AS model*, with "extended" referring to the inclusion of both the short-run and the long-run aggregate supply curves.) Equilibrium in the figure occurs at point *a*, where the economy's aggregate demand curve AD_1 intersects both its short-run aggregate supply curve AS_1 and the vertical long-run aggregate supply curve AS_{LR}. In long-run equilibrium, the economy's price level is P_1 and its real output is Q_f. ◹ **16.1**

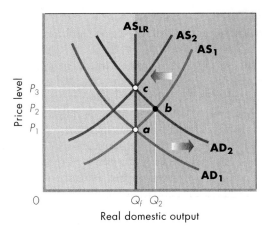

Figure 16.3

Demand-pull inflation in the extended AD-AS model. An increase in aggregate demand from AD_1 to AD_2 drives up the price level and increases real output in the short run. But in the long run, nominal wages rise and the short-run aggregate supply curve shifts leftward, as from AS_1 to AS_2. Real output then returns to its prior level, and the price level rises even more. In this scenario, the economy moves from *a* to *b* and then eventually to *c*.

> ### QUICK REVIEW 16.1
>
> ▪ The short-run aggregate supply curve has a positive slope, because nominal wages remain constant as the price level changes.
>
> ▪ The long-run aggregate supply curve is vertical, because nominal wages eventually change by the same relative amount as changes in the price level.
>
> ▪ The equilibrium GDP and price level occur at the intersection of the aggregate demand curve, the long-run aggregate supply curve, and the short-run aggregate supply curve.

▌Applying the Extended AD-AS Model

Let's see how the extended AD-AS model helps us better understand the long-run aspects of demand-pull inflation, cost-push inflation, and recession.

Demand-Pull Inflation in the Extended AD-AS Model

Recall that demand-pull inflation occurs when an increase in aggregate demand pulls up the price level. Earlier, we depicted this inflation by shifting an aggregate demand curve rightward along a stable aggregate supply curve (see Figures 11.8b and 11.8c).

In our more complex version of aggregate supply, however, an increase in the price level will eventually lead to an increase in nominal wages and thus a leftward shift of the short-run aggregate supply curve. We show this in Figure 16.3, where we initially suppose the price level is P_1 at the intersection of aggregate demand curve AD_1, short-run supply curve AS_1, and long-run aggregate supply curve AS_{LR}. Observe that the economy is achieving its full-employment real output Q_f at point *a*.

Now consider the effects of an increase in aggregate demand as represented by the rightward shift

from AD_1 to AD_2. This shift might result from any one of a number of factors, including an increase in investment spending and a rise in net exports. Whatever its cause, the increase in aggregate demand boosts the price level from P_1 to P_2 and expands real output from Q_f to Q_2 at point *b*.

So far, none of this is new to you. But now the distinction between short-run aggregate supply and long-run aggregate supply becomes important. Once workers have realized that their real wages have declined and their existing contracts have expired, nominal wages will rise. As they do, the short-run aggregate supply curve will ultimately shift leftward such that it intersects long-run aggregate supply at point *c*.[1] There, the economy has reestablished long-run equilibrium, with the price level and real output now P_3 and Q_f, respectively. Only at point *c* does the

---

[1]We say "ultimately" because the initial leftward shift in short-run aggregate supply will intersect the long-run aggregate supply curve AS_{LR} at price level P_2 (review Figure 16.1b). But the intersection of AD_2 and this new short-run aggregate supply curve (not shown) will produce a price level above P_2. (You may want to pencil this in to make sure that you understand this point.) Again nominal wages will rise, shifting the short-run aggregate supply curve farther leftward. The process will continue until the economy moves to point *c*, where the short-run aggregate supply curve is AS_2, the price level is P_3, and real output is Q_f.

new aggregate demand curve AD$_2$ intersect both the short-run aggregate supply curve AS$_2$ and the long-run aggregate supply curve AS$_{LR}$.

In the short run, demand-pull inflation drives up the price level and increases real output; in the long run, only the price level rises. In the long run, the initial increase in aggregate demand has moved the economy along its vertical aggregate supply curve AS$_{LR}$. For a while, an economy can operate beyond its full-employment level of output. But the demand-pull inflation eventually causes adjustments of nominal wages that return the economy to its full-employment output Q$_f$.

Cost-Push Inflation in the Extended AD-AS Model

Cost-push inflation arises from factors that increase the cost of production at each price level, shifting the aggregate supply curve leftward and raising the equilibrium price level. Previously (Figure 11.11), we considered cost-push inflation using only the short-run aggregate supply curve. Now we want to analyze that type of inflation in its long-run context.

Analysis   Consider Figure 16.4, in which we again assume that the economy is initially operating at price level P$_1$ and output level Q$_f$ (point a). Suppose that international oil producers agree to reduce the supply of oil to boost its price by, say, 100 percent. As a result, the per-unit production cost of producing and transporting goods and services rises substantially in the economy represented by Figure 16.4. This increase in per-unit production costs shifts the short-run aggregate supply curve to the left, as from AS$_1$ to AS$_2$, and the price level rises from P$_1$ to P$_2$ (as seen by comparing points a and b). In this case, the leftward shift of the aggregate supply curve is *not a response* to a price-level increase, as it was in our previous discussions of demand-pull inflation; it is the *initiating cause* of the price-level increase.

Policy Dilemma   Cost-push inflation creates a dilemma for policymakers. Without some expansionary stabilization policy, aggregate demand in Figure 16.4 remains in place at AD$_1$ and real output declines from Q$_f$ to Q$_2$. Government can counter this recession and the attendant rise in unemployment by using fiscal policy and monetary policy to increase aggregate demand to AD$_2$. But there is a potential policy trap here: An increase in aggregate

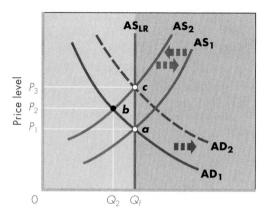

Figure 16.4

Cost-push inflation in the extended AD-AS model.   Cost-push inflation occurs when the short-run aggregate supply curve shifts leftward, as from AS$_1$ to AS$_2$. If government counters the decline in real output by increasing aggregate demand to the broken line, the price level rises even more. That is, the economy moves in steps from a to b to c. In contrast, if government allows a recession to occur, nominal wages eventually fall and the aggregate supply curve shifts back rightward to its original location. The economy moves from a to b and then eventually back to a.

demand to AD$_2$ will further raise inflation by increasing the price level from P$_2$ to P$_3$ (a move from point b to c).

Suppose the government recognizes this policy trap and decides not to increase aggregate demand from AD$_1$ to AD$_2$ (you can now disregard the dashed AD$_2$ curve) and instead decides to allow a cost-push-created recession to run its course. How will that happen? Widespread layoffs, plant shutdowns, and business failures eventually occur. At some point the demand for oil, labor, and other inputs will decline so much that oil prices and nominal wages will decline. When that happens, the initial leftward shift of the short-run aggregate supply curve will reverse itself. That is, the declining per-unit production costs caused by the recession will shift the short-run aggregate supply curve rightward from AS$_2$ to AS$_1$. The price level will return to P$_1$, and the full-employment level of output will be restored at Q$_f$ (point a on the long-run aggregate supply curve AS$_{LR}$).

This analysis yields two generalizations:

■ If the government attempts to maintain full employment when there is cost-push inflation, an inflationary spiral may occur.

■   If the government takes a hands-off approach to cost-push inflation, a recession will occur. Although the recession eventually may undo the initial rise in per-unit production costs, the economy in the meantime will experience high unemployment and a loss of real output.

Recession and the Extended AD-AS Model

By far the most controversial application of the extended AD-AS model is its application to recession (or depression) caused by decreases in aggregate demand. We will look at this controversy in detail in Chapter 19; here we simply identify the key point of contention.

Suppose in Figure 16.5 that aggregate demand initially is AD_1 and that the short-run and long-run aggregate supply curves are AS_1 and AS_{LR}, respectively. Therefore, as shown by point a, the price level is P_1 and output is Q_f. Now suppose that investment spending declines dramatically, reducing aggregate demand to AD_2. Observe that real output declines from Q_f to Q_1, indicating that a recession has occurred. But if we make the controversial assumption that prices and wages are flexible downward, the price level falls from P_1 to P_2. The lower price level

increases real wages for people who are still working, since each dollar of nominal wage has greater purchasing power. Eventually, nominal wages themselves fall to restore the previous real wage; when that happens, the short-run aggregate supply curve shifts rightward from AS_1 to AS_2. The recession ends, without the need for expansionary fiscal or monetary policy, since real output expands from Q_1 (point b) back to Q_f (point c). The economy is again located on its long-run aggregate supply curve AS_{LR}, but now at lower price level P_3.

There is much disagreement about this hypothetical scenario. The key point of dispute is how long it would take in the real world for the necessary downward price and wage adjustments to occur to regain the full-employment level of output. For now, suffice it to say that most economists believe that if such adjustments are forthcoming, they will occur only after the economy has experienced a relatively long-lasting recession with its accompanying high unemployment and large loss of output. **(Key Question 4)**

> ### QUICK REVIEW 16.2
>
> ■ In the short run, demand-pull inflation raises both the price level and real output; in the long run, nominal wages rise, the short-run aggregate supply curve shifts to the left, and only the price level increases.
>
> ■ Cost-push inflation creates a policy dilemma for the government: If it engages in an expansionary policy to increase output, an inflationary spiral may occur; if it does nothing, a recession will occur.
>
> ■ In the short run, a decline in aggregate demand reduces real output (creates a recession); in the long run, prices and nominal wages presumably fall, the short-run aggregate supply curve shifts to the right, and real output returns to its full-employment level.

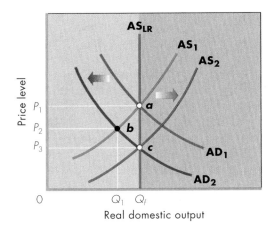

Figure 16.5

Recession in the extended AD-AS model. A recession occurs when aggregate demand shifts leftward, as from AD_1 to AD_2. If prices and wages are downwardly flexible, the price level falls from P_1 to P_2. That decline in the price level reduces nominal wages, and this eventually shifts the aggregate supply curve from AS_1 to AS_2. The price level declines to P_3, and real output increases back to Q_f. The economy moves from point a to b and then eventually to c.

▌ The Inflation-Unemployment Relationship

Because both low inflation rates and low unemployment rates are major economic goals, economists are vitally interested in their relationship. Are low unemployment and low inflation compatible goals or conflicting goals? What explains situations in which high unemployment and high inflation coexist?

The extended AD-AS model supports three significant generalizations relating to these questions:

- Under normal circumstances, there is a short-run tradeoff between the rate of inflation and the rate of unemployment.
- Aggregate supply shocks can cause both higher rates of inflation and higher rates of unemployment.
- There is no significant tradeoff between inflation and unemployment over long periods of time.

Let's examine each of these generalizations.

The Phillips Curve

We can demonstrate the short-run tradeoff between the rate of inflation and the rate of unemployment through the **Phillips Curve,** named after A. W. Phillips, who developed the idea in Great Britain. This curve, generalized later in Figure 16.7, suggests an inverse relationship between the rate of inflation and the rate of unemployment. Lower unemployment rates (measured as leftward movements on the horizontal axis) are associated with higher rates of inflation (measured as upward movements on the vertical axis). 🔎 **16.1**

The underlying rationale of the Phillips Curve becomes apparent when we view the short-run aggregate supply curve in Figure 16.6 and perform a simple mental experiment. Suppose that in some period aggregate demand expands from AD_0 to AD_2, either because firms decided to buy more capital goods or the government decided to increase its expenditures. Whatever the cause, in the short run the price level rises from P_0 to P_2 and real output rises from Q_0 to Q_2. A decline in the unemployment rate accompanies the increase in real output.

Now let's compare what would have happened if the increase in aggregate demand had been larger, say, from AD_0 to AD_3. The new equilibrium tells us that the amount of inflation and the growth of real output would both have been greater (and that the unemployment rate would have been lower). Similarly, suppose aggregate demand during the year had increased only modestly, from AD_0 to AD_1. Compared with our shift from AD_0 to AD_2, the amount of inflation and the growth of real output would have been smaller (and the unemployment rate higher).

The generalization we draw from this mental experiment is this: Assuming a constant short-run aggregate supply curve, high rates of inflation are

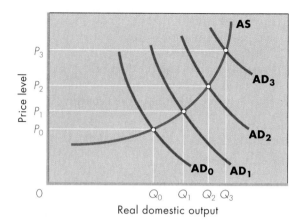

Figure 16.6

The effect of changes in aggregate demand on real output and the price level. Comparing the effects of various possible increases in aggregate demand leads to the conclusion that the larger the increase in aggregate demand, the higher the rate of inflation and the greater the increase in real output. Because real output and the unemployment rate move in opposite directions, we can generalize that, given short-run aggregate supply, high rates of inflation should be accompanied by low rates of unemployment.

accompanied by low rates of unemployment, and low rates of inflation are accompanied by high rates of unemployment. Figure 16.7a shows how the expected relationship should look, other things equal.

Figure 16.7b reveals that the facts for the 1960s nicely fit the theory. On the basis of that evidence and evidence from other countries, most economists concluded there was a stable, predictable tradeoff between unemployment and inflation. Moreover, U.S. economic policy was built on that supposed tradeoff. According to this thinking, it was impossible to achieve "full employment without inflation": Manipulation of aggregate demand through fiscal and monetary measures would simply move the economy along the Phillips Curve. An expansionary fiscal and monetary policy that boosted aggregate demand and lowered the unemployment rate would simultaneously increase inflation. A restrictive fiscal and monetary policy could be used to reduce the rate of inflation but only at the cost of a higher unemployment rate and more forgone production. Society had to choose between the incompatible goals of price stability and full employment; it had to decide where to locate on its Phillips Curve.

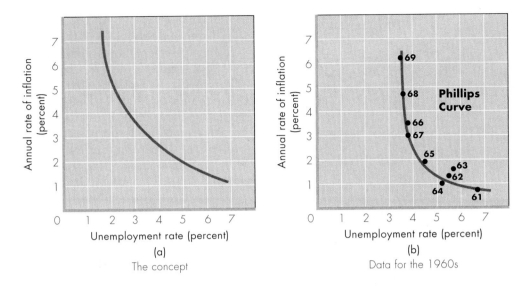

Figure 16.7

The Phillips Curve: concept and empirical data. (a) The Phillips Curve relates annual rates of inflation and annual rates of unemployment for a series of years. Because this is an inverse relationship, there presumably is a tradeoff between unemployment and inflation. (b) Data points for the 1960s seemed to confirm the Phillips Curve concept. (Note: Inflation rates are on a December-to-December basis.)

For reasons we will soon see, modern economists reject the idea of a stable, predictable Phillips Curve. Nevertheless, they agree there is a short-run tradeoff between unemployment and inflation. Given aggregate supply, increases in aggregate demand increase real output and reduce the unemployment rate. As the unemployment rate falls and dips below the natural rate, the excessive spending produces demand-pull inflation. Conversely, when recession sets in and the unemployment rate increases, the weak aggregate demand that caused the recession also leads to lower inflation rates.

Periods of exceptionally low unemployment rates and inflation rates do occur, but only under special sets of economic circumstances. One such period was the late 1990s, when faster productivity growth increased aggregate supply and fully blunted the inflationary impact of rapidly rising aggregate demand (review Figure 11.12).

Aggregate Supply Shocks and the Phillips Curve

The unemployment-inflation experience of the 1970s and early 1980s demolished the idea of an always-stable Phillips Curve. In Figure 16.8 we

show the Phillips Curve for the 1960s in green and then add the data points for 1970 through 2000. Observe that in most of the years of the 1970s and early 1980s the economy experienced both higher inflation rates and higher unemployment rates than it did in the 1960s. In fact, inflation and unemployment rose simultaneously in some of those years. This condition is called **stagflation**—a term that combines the words "stagnation" and "inflation." If there still was any such thing as a Phillips Curve, it had clearly shifted outward, perhaps as shown.

Adverse Aggregate Supply Shocks

The Phillips data points for the 1970s and early 1980s support our second generalization: *Aggregate supply shocks can cause both higher rates of inflation and higher rates of unemployment.* A series of adverse **aggregate supply shocks**—sudden, large increases in resource costs that jolt an economy's short-run aggregate supply curve leftward—hit the economy in the 1970s and early 1980s. The most significant of these shocks was a quadrupling of oil prices by the Organization of Petroleum Exporting Countries (OPEC). Consequently, the cost of producing and distributing virtually every product and service rose

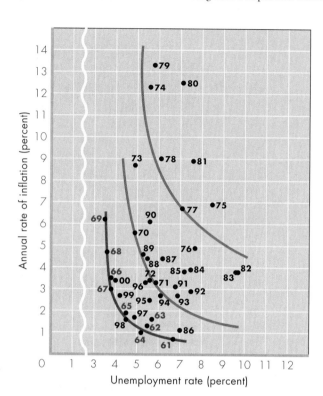

Figure 16.8

Inflation rates and unemployment rates, 1961–2000. A series of aggregate supply shocks in the 1970s resulted in higher rates of inflation and higher rates of unemployment. So data points for the 1970s and 1980s tended to be above and to the right of the Phillips Curve for the 1960s. In the 1990s the inflation-unemployment data points slowly moved back toward the original Phillips Curve. Points for the late 1990s are similar to those from the earlier era. (Note: Inflation rates are on a December-to-December basis.)

rapidly. (Other factors working to increase U.S. costs during this period included major agricultural shortfalls, a greatly depreciated dollar, wage hikes previously held down by wage-price controls, and declining productivity.)

These shocks shifted the aggregate supply curve to the left and distorted the usual inflation-unemployment relationship. Remember that we derived the inverse relationship between the rate of inflation and the unemployment rate shown in Figure 16.7 by shifting the aggregate demand curve along a stable short-run aggregate supply curve (Figure 16.6). But the cost-push inflation model shown in Figure 16.4 tells us that a *leftward shift* of the short-run aggregate supply curve increases the price level and reduces real output (and increases the

unemployment rate). This, say most economists, is what happened in two periods in the 1970s. The U.S. unemployment rate shot up from 4.9 percent in 1973 to 8.3 percent in 1975, contributing to a significant decline in real GDP. In the same period, the U.S. price level rose by 21 percent. The stagflation scenario recurred in 1978, when OPEC increased oil prices by more than 100 percent. The U.S. price level rose by 26 percent over the 1978–1980 period, while unemployment increased from 6.1 to 7.1 percent.

Stagflation's Demise Another look at Figure 16.8 reveals a generally inward movement of the inflation-unemployment points between 1982 and 1989. By 1989 the lingering effects of the early period had subsided. One precursor to this favorable trend was the deep recession of 1981–1982, largely caused by a tight money policy aimed at reducing double-digit inflation. The recession upped the unemployment rate to 9.5 percent in 1982. With so many workers unemployed, those who were working accepted smaller increases in their nominal wages—or, in some cases, wage reductions—in order to preserve their jobs. Firms, in turn, restrained their price increases to try to retain their relative shares of a greatly diminished market.

Other factors were at work. Foreign competition throughout this period held down wage and price hikes in several basic industries such as automobiles and steel. Deregulation of the airline and trucking industries also resulted in wage reductions or so-called wage givebacks. A significant decline in OPEC's monopoly power and a greatly reduced reliance on oil in the production process produced a stunning fall in the price of oil and its derivative products, such as gasoline.

All these factors combined to reduce per-unit production costs and to shift the short-run aggregate supply curve rightward (as from AS_2 to AS_1 in Figure 16.4). Employment and output expanded, and the unemployment rate fell from 9.6 percent in 1983 to 5.3 percent in 1989. Figure 16.8 reveals that the inflation-unemployment points for recent years are closer to the points associated with the Phillips Curve of the 1960s than to the points in the late 1970s and early 1980s. The points for 1997–2000, in fact, are very close to points on the 1960s curve. (The very low inflation and unemployment rates in this later period produced an exceptionally low value of the so-called *misery index*, as shown in Global Perspective 16.1.)

GLOBAL PERSPECTIVE 16.1

The Misery Index, Selected Nations, 1990–2000

The misery index adds together a nation's unemployment rate and its inflation rate to get a measure of national economic discomfort. For example, a nation with a 5 percent rate of unemployment and a 5 percent inflation rate would have a misery index number of 10, as would a nation with an 8 percent unemployment rate and a 2 percent inflation rate.

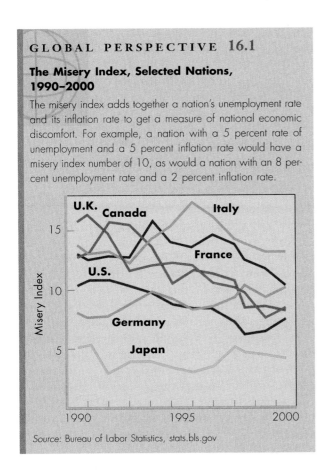

Source: Bureau of Labor Statistics, stats.bls.gov

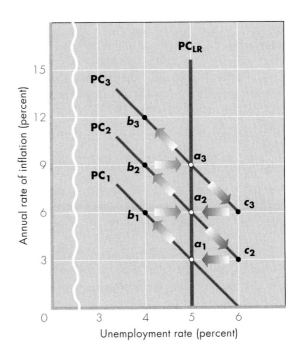

Figure 16.9

The long-run vertical Phillips Curve. Increases in aggregate demand beyond those consistent with full-employment output may temporarily boost profits, output, and employment (as from a_1 to b_1). But nominal wages eventually will catch up so as to sustain real wages. When they do, profits will fall, negating the previous short-run stimulus to production and employment (the economy now moves from b_1 to a_2). Consequently, there is no tradeoff between the rates of inflation and unemployment in the long run; that is, the long-run Phillips Curve is roughly a vertical line at the economy's natural rate of unemployment.

▌ The Long-Run Phillips Curve

The overall set of data points in Figure 16.8 supports our third generalization relating to the inflation-unemployment relationship: There is no apparent *long-run* tradeoff between inflation and unemployment. Economists point out that when decades as opposed to a few years are considered, any rate of inflation is consistent with the natural rate of unemployment prevailing at that time. We know from Chapter 8 that the natural rate of unemployment is the rate of unemployment that occurs when cyclical unemployment is zero; it is the full-employment rate of unemployment, or the rate of unemployment when the economy achieves it potential output.

How can there be a short-run inflation-unemployment tradeoff but not a long-run tradeoff? Figure 16.9 provides the answer.

Short-Run Phillips Curve

Consider Phillips Curve PC_1 in Figure 16.9. Suppose the economy initially is experiencing a 3 percent rate of inflation and a 5 percent natural rate of

unemployment. Such short-term curves as PC_1, PC_2, and PC_3 (drawn as straight lines for simplicity) exist because the actual rate of inflation is not always the same as the expected rate.

Establishing an additional point on Phillips Curve PC_1 will clarify this. We begin at a_1, where we assume nominal wages are set on the assumption that the 3 percent rate of inflation will continue. But suppose that aggregate demand increases such that the rate of inflation rises to 6 percent. With a nominal wage rate set on the expectation that the 3 percent rate of inflation will continue, the higher product prices raise business profits. Firms respond to the higher profits by hiring more workers and increasing output. In the short run, the economy moves to b_1, which, in contrast to a_1, involves a lower rate of unemployment (4 percent) and a higher rate of inflation (6 percent). The move from a_1 to b_1 is consistent both with an upward-sloping aggregate supply curve and with the inflation-unemployment tradeoff implied by the Phillips Curve analysis. But this short-run Phillips Curve simply is a manifestation of the following principle: *When the actual rate of inflation is higher than expected, profits temporarily rise and the unemployment rate temporarily falls.*

Long-Run Vertical Phillips Curve

But point b_1 is not a stable equilibrium. Workers will recognize that their nominal wages have not increased as fast as inflation and will therefore obtain nominal wage increases to restore their lost purchasing power. But as nominal wages rise to restore the level of real wages that previously existed at a_1, business profits will fall to their prior level. The reduction in profits means that the original motivation to employ more workers and increase output has disappeared.

Unemployment then returns to its natural level at point a_2. Note, however, that the economy now faces a higher actual and expected rate of inflation—6 percent rather than 3 percent. The higher level of aggregate demand that originally moved the economy from a_1 to b_1 still exists, so the inflation it created persists.

In view of the higher 6 percent expected rate of inflation, the short-run Phillips Curve shifts upward from PC_1 to PC_2 in Figure 16.9. An "along-the-Phillips-Curve" kind of move from a_1 to b_1 on PC_1 is merely a short-run or transient occurrence. In the long run, after nominal wages catch up with price-level increases, unemployment returns to its natural rate at a_2, and there is a new short-run Phillips Curve PC_2 at the higher expected rate of inflation.

The scenario repeats if aggregate demand continues to increase. Prices rise momentarily ahead of nominal wages, profits expand, and employment and output increase (as implied by the move from a_2 to b_2). But, in time, nominal wages increase so as to restore real wages. Profits then fall to their original level, pushing employment back to the normal rate at a_3. The economy's "reward" for lowering the unemployment rate below the natural rate is a still higher (9 percent) rate of inflation.

Movements along the short-run Phillips curve (a_1 to b_1 on PC_1) cause the curve to shift to a less favorable position (PC_2, then PC_3, and so on). A stable Phillips Curve with the dependable series of unemployment-rate–inflation-rate tradeoffs simply

does not exist in the long run. The economy is characterized by a **long-run vertical Phillips Curve.**

The vertical line through a_1, a_2, and a_3 shows the long-run relationship between unemployment and inflation. Any rate of inflation is consistent with the 5 percent natural rate of unemployment. So, in this view, society ought to choose a low rate of inflation rather than a high one. 🔑 16.2

Disinflation

The distinction between the short-run Phillips Curve and the long-run Phillips Curve also helps explain **disinflation**—reductions in the inflation rate from year to year. Suppose that in Figure 16.9 the economy is at a_3, where the inflation rate is 9 percent. And suppose that a decline in aggregate demand (such as that occurring in the 1981–1982 recession) reduces inflation below the 9 percent expected rate, say, to 6 percent. Business profits fall, because prices are rising less rapidly than wages. The nominal wage increases, remember, were set on the assumption that the 9 percent rate of inflation would continue. In response to the decline in profits, firms reduce their employment and consequently the unemployment rate rises. The economy temporarily slides downward from point a_3 to c_3 along the short-run Phillips Curve PC_3. *When the actual rate of inflation is lower than the expected rate, profits temporarily fall and the unemployment rate temporarily rises.*

Firms and workers eventually adjust their expectations to the new 6 percent rate of inflation, and thus newly negotiated wage increases decline. Profits are restored, employment rises, and the unemployment rate falls back to its natural rate of 6 percent at a_2. Because the expected rate of inflation is now 6 percent, the short-run Phillips Curve PC_3 shifts leftward to PC_2.

If aggregate demand declines more, the scenario will continue. Inflation declines from 6 percent to, say, 3 percent, moving the economy from a_2 to c_2 along PC_2. The lower-than-expected rate of inflation (lower prices) squeezes profits and reduces employment. But, in the long run, firms respond to the lower profits by reducing their nominal wage increases. Profits are restored and unemployment returns to its natural rate at a_1 as the short-run Phillips Curve moves from PC_2 to PC_1. Once again, the long-run Phillips Curve is vertical at the 5 percent natural rate of unemployment. **(Key Question 6)**

As implied by the upward-sloping short-run aggregate supply curve, there may be a short-run tradeoff between the rate of inflation and the rate of unemployment. This tradeoff is reflected in the Phillips Curve, which shows that lower rates of inflation are associated with higher rates of unemployment.

Aggregate supply shocks that produce severe cost-push inflation can cause stagflation—simultaneous increases in the inflation rate and the unemployment rate. Such stagflation occurred from 1973 to 1975 and recurred from 1978 to 1980, producing Phillips Curve data points above and to the right of the Phillips Curve for the 1960s.

After all nominal wage adjustments to increases and decreases in the rate of inflation have occurred, the economy ends up back at its full-employment level of output and its natural rate of unemployment. The long-run Phillips Curve therefore is vertical at the natural rate of unemployment.

Taxation and Aggregate Supply

A final topic in our discussion of aggregate supply is taxation, a key aspect of **supply-side economics.** "Supply-side economists" or "supply-siders" stress that changes in aggregate supply are an active force in determining the levels of inflation, unemployment, and economic growth. Government policies can either impede or promote rightward shifts of the short-run and long-run aggregate supply curves shown in Figure 16.2. One such policy is taxation.

These economists say that the enlargement of the U.S. tax system has impaired incentives to work, save, and invest. In this view, high tax rates impede productivity growth and hence slow the expansion of long-run aggregate supply. By reducing the after-tax rewards of workers and producers, high tax rates reduce the financial attractiveness of work, saving, and investing.

Supply-siders focus their attention on *marginal tax rates*—the rates on extra dollars of income—because those rates affect the benefits from working, saving, or investing more. In 2001 the marginal tax rates varied from 15 to 39.6 percent in the United States (See Table 5.2 for details.)

Taxes and Incentives to Work

Supply-siders believe that how long and how hard people work depends on the amounts of additional after-tax earnings they derive from their efforts. They say that government should reduce marginal tax rates on earned incomes to induce more work, and therefore increase aggregate inputs of labor. Lower marginal tax rates in a sense would make leisure more expensive and thus work more attractive. The higher opportunity cost of leisure would encourage people to substitute work for leisure. This increase in productive effort could be achieved in many ways: by increasing the number of hours worked per day or week, by encouraging workers to postpone retirement, by inducing more people to enter the labor force, by motivating people to work harder, and by avoiding long periods of unemployment.

Incentives to Save and Invest

The rewards for saving and investing have also been reduced by high marginal tax rates. For example, suppose that Tony saves $10,000 at 8 percent, bringing him $800 of interest per year. If his marginal tax rate is 40 percent, his after-tax interest earnings will be $480, not $800, and his after-tax interest rate will fall to 4.8 percent. While Tony might be willing to save (forgo current consumption) for an 8 percent return on his saving, he might rather consume when the return is only 4.8 percent.

Saving, remember, is the prerequisite of investment. Thus supply-side economists recommend lower marginal tax rates on interest earned from saving. They also call for lower taxes on income from capital to ensure that there are ready investment outlets for the economy's enhanced pool of saving. A critical determinant of investment spending is the expected after-tax return on that spending.

To summarize: Lower marginal tax rates encourage saving and investing. Workers therefore find themselves equipped with more and technologically superior machinery and equipment. Labor productivity rises, and that expands aggregate supply, which in turn keeps unemployment rates and inflation low.

The Laffer Curve

In the supply-side view, reductions in marginal tax rates increase the nation's aggregate supply and can leave the nation's tax revenues unchanged or even enlarge them. Thus, supply-side tax cuts need not produce Federal budget deficits.

This idea is based on the **Laffer Curve,** named after Arthur Laffer, who developed it. As Figure 16.10 shows, the Laffer Curve depicts the relationship between tax rates and tax revenues. As tax rates increase from 0 to 100 percent, tax revenues increase from zero to some maximum level (at *m*) and then fall to zero. Tax revenues decline beyond some point because higher tax rates discourage economic activity, thereby shrinking the tax base (domestic output and income). This is easiest to see at the extreme, where the tax rate is 100 percent. Tax revenues here are, in theory, reduced to zero because the 100 percent confiscatory tax rate has halted production. A 100 percent tax rate applied to a tax base of zero yields no revenue. ▮ 16.1

In the early 1980s Laffer suggested that the United States was at a point such as *n* on the curve in Figure 16.10. There, tax rates are so high that production is discouraged to the extent that tax revenues are below the maximum at *m*. If the economy is at *n*, then lower tax rates can either increase tax revenues or leave them unchanged. For example, lowering the tax rate point *n* to point *l* would bolster the economy such that the government would bring in the same total amount of tax revenue as before.

Laffer's reasoning was that lower tax rates stimulate incentives to work, save and invest, innovate, and accept business risks, thus triggering an expansion of real output and income. That enlarged tax base sustains tax revenues even though tax rates are lowered. Indeed, between *n* and *m* lower tax rates result in increased tax revenue.

Also, when taxes are lowered, tax avoidance (which is legal) and tax evasion (which is not) decline. High marginal tax rates prompt taxpayers to avoid taxes through various tax shelters, such as buying municipal bonds, on which the interest earned is tax-free. High rates also encourage some taxpayers to conceal income from the Internal Revenue Service. Lower tax rates reduce the inclination to engage in either tax avoidance or tax evasion. **(Key Question 8)**

Criticisms of the Laffer Curve

The Laffer Curve and its supply-side implications have been subject to severe criticism.

Taxes, Incentives, and Time A fundamental criticism relates to the degree to which economic incentives are sensitive to changes in tax rates. Skeptics say there is ample empirical evidence showing that the impact of a tax cut on incentives is small, of uncertain direction, and relatively slow to emerge. For example, with respect to work incentives, studies indicate that decreases in tax rates lead some people to work more but lead others to work less. Those who work more are enticed by the higher after-tax pay; they substitute work for leisure because the opportunity cost of leisure has increased. But other people work less because the higher after-tax pay enables them to "buy more leisure." With the tax cut, they can earn the same level of after-tax income as before with fewer work hours.

Inflation Most economists think that the demand-side effects of a tax cut exceed the supply-side effects. Thus, tax cuts undertaken when the economy is at or near its full-employment level of output may produce increases in aggregate demand that overwhelm any increase in aggregate supply. Demand-pull inflation is the likely result.

Position on the Curve Skeptics say that the Laffer Curve is merely a logical proposition and assert that there must be some level of tax rates be-

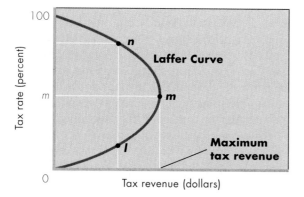

Figure 16.10

The Laffer Curve. The Laffer Curve suggests that up to point *m* higher tax rates will result in larger tax revenues. But higher tax rates will adversely affect incentives to work and produce, reducing the size of the tax base (output and income) to the extent that tax revenues will decline. It follows that if tax rates are above *m*, reductions in tax rates will produce increases in tax revenues.

Has the Impact of Oil Prices Diminished?

Significant Changes in Oil Prices Historically Have Had Major Impacts on the U.S. Economy. Have the Effects of Such Changes Weakened?

The United States and other industrial countries have experienced several aggregate supply shocks caused by significant changes in oil prices. Major increases in oil prices occurred in the mid-1970s and then again in the late 1970s. In the late 1980s and through most of the 1990s oil prices fell, hitting a low of $11 per barrel in late 1998. This decline created a "reverse" aggregate supply shock beneficial to the U.S. economy. In response to the low oil prices, OPEC and a few other major oil producers (Mexico, Norway, and Russia) restricted oil output in late 1999 to boost prices. That action, along with a rapidly growing demand for oil, sent oil prices rocketing upward once again. By March of 2000 they had reached $34 a barrel.

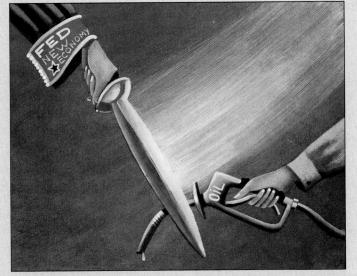

The increased oil prices were immediately felt at the gasoline pump, as gasoline prices rose significantly. Some economists feared that the rising price of oil would so increase energy prices as to shift the U.S. aggregate supply curve to the left, creating cost-push inflation and slowing the U.S. economy. But inflation in the United States remained modest, and the economy continued to grow. Why did changes in oil prices seemingly lose their punch?

First, we must acknowledge that it could be premature to declare that changes in oil price are relatively benign. It is possible that most American producers believed that the price increase was temporary, just as had been the preceding abrupt price decline. Indeed, under heavy pressure from the buying nations, OPEC agreed in 2000 to boost output. By the end of 2000, oil prices had declined to about $25 a barrel. Under the initial correct expectation of soon-to-be-lower oil prices, many manufacturers may

have decided to retain their current production plans and pricing levels. So an aggregate supply shock did not manifest itself from the boost in oil prices. Also, even if higher oil prices are permanent, it will take considerable time for the full range of energy prices (natural gas, coal, electricity, and so on) to rise and negatively affect the economy.

More likely, however, other aggregate supply determinants simply swamped the potential inflationary and negative output impacts of the oil price increases of early 2000. The overall trend of lower costs resulting from the technologically driven New Economy (the subject of the next chapter) more than compensated for the rise in oil prices. So aggregate supply did not decline as it had in earlier periods.

This was possible because oil prices are now a less significant factor in the U.S. economy than they were before. Recent research reveals that since 1980 oil price changes have had little effect on *core inflation* (the inflation rate after changes in the prices of food and energy have been subtracted). Prior to 1980, however, changes in oil prices greatly affected core inflation.* Why the difference?

One possible reason is that the Federal Reserve has become more adept, more vigilant, or both at maintaining price stability through monetary policy. So far, the Fed has not let increases in oil prices become generalized as core inflation. The second, and perhaps more important, reason is that the amount of energy consumed in producing each dollar of GDP has greatly declined. Part of this decline was fostered by the high oil and energy prices during the 1970s. But equally important has been the changing relative composition of the GDP from larger, heavier items (such as earthmoving equipment) that are energy-intensive to make and transport toward smaller, lighter items (such as microchips and software). Experts on energy economics estimate that the U.S. economy is about one-third less sensitive to oil price fluctuations than it was in the early 1980s and one-half less sensitive than in the mid-1970s.**

*Mark Hooker, "Are Oil Shocks Inflationary? Asymmetric and Nonlinear Specifications," paper presented at the Western Economic Association Conference, July 2, 2000.

**Stephen P. A. Brown and Mine K. Yücel, "Oil Prices and the Economy," Federal Reserve Bank of Dallas, *Southwest Economy*, July–August 2000, pp. 1–6.

tween 0 and 100 percent at which tax revenues will be at their maximum. Economists of all persuasions can agree with this. But the issue of where a particular economy is located on its Laffer Curve is an

empirical question. If we assume that we are at point *n* in Figure 16.10, then tax cuts will increase tax revenues. But critics say that the economy's location on the Laffer Curve is undocumented and unknown.

If the economy is at any point below *m* on the curve, then tax reductions will reduce tax revenues and possibly create budget deficits. That, say critics, is exactly what happened when the Reagan administration cut Federal income tax rates by about 25 percent over a 3-year period in the early 1980s. And, in fact, the sizable increases in marginal tax rates imposed by the Federal government in 1993 have generated large *increases* in tax revenues. The resulting budget surpluses led the Bush administration to propose reductions in marginal tax rates in 2001.

SUMMARY

1. In macroeconomics, the short run is a period in which nominal wages are fixed; they do not change in response to changes in the price level. In contrast, the long run is a period in which nominal wages are fully responsive to changes in the price level.

2. The short-run aggregate supply curve is upward-sloping. Because nominal wages are fixed, increases in the price level (prices received by firms) increase profits and real output. Conversely, decreases in the price level reduce profits and real output. However, the long-run aggregate supply curve is vertical. With sufficient time for adjustment, nominal wages rise and fall with the price level, moving the economy along a vertical aggregate supply curve at the economy's full-employment output.

3. In the short run, demand-pull inflation raises the price level and real output. Once nominal wages have increased, the temporary increase in real output is reversed.

4. In the short run, cost-push inflation raises the price level and lowers real output. Unless the government expands aggregate demand, nominal wages eventually will decline under conditions of recession and the short-run aggregate supply curve will shift back to its initial location. Prices and real output will eventually return to their original levels.

5. If prices and wages are flexible downward, a decline in aggregate demand will lower output and the price level. The decline in the price level will eventually lower nominal wages and shift the short-run aggregate supply curve rightward. Full-employment output will thus be restored.

6. Assuming a stable, upward-sloping aggregate supply curve, rightward shifts of the aggregate demand curve of various sizes yield the generalization that high rates of inflation are associated with low rates of unemployment, and vice versa. This inverse relationship is known as the Phillips Curve, and empirical data for the 1960s seemed to be consistent with it.

7. In the 1970s and early 1980s the Phillips Curve apparently shifted rightward, reflecting stagflation—simultaneously rising inflation rates and unemployment rates. The higher unemployment rates and inflation rates resulted mainly from huge oil price increases that caused large leftward shifts in the short-run aggregate supply curve (so-called aggregate supply shocks). The Phillips Curve shifted inward toward its original position in the 1980s. By 1989 stagflation had subsided, and the data points for the late 1990s were similar to those of the 1960s.

8. Although there is a short-run tradeoff between inflation and unemployment, there is no long-run tradeoff. Workers will adapt their expectations to new inflation realities, and when they do, the unemployment rate will return to the natural rate. The long-run Phillips Curve is therefore vertical at the natural rate, meaning that higher rates of inflation do not "buy" the economy less unemployment.

9. Supply-side economists focus attention on government policies such as high taxation that impede the expansion of aggregate supply. The Laffer Curve relates tax rates to levels of tax revenue and suggests that, under some circumstances, cuts in tax rates will expand the tax base (output and income) and increase tax revenues. Most economists, however, believe that the United States is operating in the range of the Laffer Curve where tax rates and tax revenues move in the same, not opposite, directions.

TERMS AND CONCEPTS

short run

long run

short-run aggregate supply curve

long-run aggregate supply curve

Phillips Curve

stagflation

aggregate supply shocks

long-run vertical Phillips Curve

disinflation

supply-side economics

Laffer Curve

STUDY QUESTIONS

1. Distinguish between the short run and the long run as they relate to macroeconomics.

2. Which of the following statements are true? Which are false? Explain why the false statements are untrue.
   a. Short-run aggregate supply curves reflect an inverse relationship between the price level and the level of real output.
   b. The long-run aggregate supply curve assumes that nominal wages are fixed.
   c. In the long run, an increase in the price level will result in an increase in nominal wages.

3. **Key Question** Suppose the full-employment level of real output (Q) for a hypothetical economy is $250 and the price level (P) initially is 100. Use the short-run aggregate supply schedules below to answer the questions that follow:

AS (P$_{100}$)		AS (P$_{125}$)		AS (P$_{75}$)	
P	Q	P	Q	P	Q
125	280	125	250	125	310
100	250	100	220	100	280
75	220	75	190	75	250

   a. What will be the level of real output in the short run if the price level unexpectedly rises from 100 to 125 because of an increase in aggregate demand? What if the price level unexpectedly falls from 100 to 75 because of a decrease in aggregate demand? Explain each situation, using figures from the table.
   b. What will be the level of real output in the long run when the price level rises from 100 to 125? When it falls from 100 to 75? Explain each situation.
   c. Show the circumstances described in parts a and b on graph paper, and derive the long-run aggregate supply curve.

4. **Key Question** Use graphical analysis to show how each of the following would affect the economy first in the short run and then in the long run. Assume that the United States is initially operating at its full-employment level of output, that prices and wages are eventually flexible both upward and downward, and that there is no counteracting fiscal or monetary policy.
   a. Because of a war abroad, the oil supply to the United States is disrupted, sending oil prices rocketing upward.
   b. Construction spending on new homes rises dramatically, greatly increasing total U.S. investment spending.

   c. Economic recession occurs abroad, significantly reducing foreign purchases of U.S. exports.

5. Assume that a particular short-run aggregate supply curve exists for an economy and that the curve is relevant for several years. Use the AD-AS analysis to show graphically why higher rates of inflation over this period would be associated with lower rates of unemployment, and vice versa. What is this inverse relationship called?

6. **Key Question** Suppose the government misjudges the natural rate of unemployment to be much lower than it actually is, and thus undertakes expansionary fiscal and monetary policies to try to achieve the lower rate. Use the concept of the short-run Phillips Curve to explain why these policies might at first succeed. Use the concept of the long-run Phillips Curve to explain the long-run outcome of these policies.

7. What do the distinctions between short-run aggregate supply and long-run aggregate supply have in common with the distinction between the short-run Phillips Curve and the long-run Phillips Curve? Explain.

8. **Key Question** What is the Laffer Curve, and how does it relate to supply-side economics? Why is determining the economy's location on the curve so important in assessing tax policy?

9. Why might one person work more, earn more, and pay more income tax when his or her tax rate is cut, while another person will work less, earn less, and pay less income tax under the same circumstance?

10. **(Last Word)** Do oil prices play a smaller role or a larger role in the U.S. economy today compared to the 1970s and 1980s? Explain why or why not.

11. **Web-Based Question:** *Phillips Curve—do the data fit the pattern for the past 5 years?* The Phillips Curve purports to show a stable short-run relationship between the rate of inflation and the unemployment rate. Plot the inflation-unemployment data points for the latest 5 years in the following manner: For inflation data, use the consumer price index—all urban consumers. For unemployment data, use the unemployment rate—civilian labor force. Do any of your plots of data points seem to confirm the Phillips Curve concept for these 5 years? Retrieve unemployment data from the Bureau of Labor Statistics website, stats.bls.gov/cpshome.htm, and select most requested series. For inflation data, go to stats.bls.gov/ cpihome.htm and select most requested series.

12. **Web-Based Question:** *The Laffer Curve—does it shift?* Congress did not substantially change Federal income tax rates between 1993 and 2000. Visit the

Bureau of Economic Analysis website, www.bea.
doc.gov/, and use the interactive feature for national
income and product accounts tables to find Table 3.2
on Federal government current receipts and expenditures. Find the annual revenues from the Federal income tax from 1993 to 2000. What happened to those
revenues over those years? Given constant tax rates,
what do the changes in tax revenues suggest about
changes in the *location* of the Laffer Curve? If lower
(or higher) tax rates do not explain the changes in tax
revenues, what do you think does?

17

Economic Growth and the New Economy

THE WORLD'S CAPITALIST countries experienced impressive growth of real GDP and real GDP per capita during the last half of the twentieth century. In the United States, real GDP increased by 450 percent between 1950 and 2000, while population increased by only 80 percent. In 2000 the value of goods and services available to the average U.S. resident was three times greater than that of 50 years earlier. This expansion of real output—this **economic growth**—greatly increased material abundance and lifted the standard of living of most Americans. ■ In Chapter 8 we explained how economic growth is measured, briefly looked at economic growth in the United States, and compared growth rates among the major nations. In this chapter we want to explore economic growth in considerably more depth.

■ Ingredients of Growth

There are six main ingredients in economic growth. We can group them as supply, demand, and efficiency factors.

Supply Factors

Four of the ingredients of economic growth relate to the physical ability of the economy to expand. They are:

■ Increases in the quantity and quality of natural resources.

■ Increases in the quantity and quality of human resources.

■ Increases in the supply (or stock) of capital goods.

■ Improvements in technology.

These **supply factors**—changes in the physical and technical agents of production—enable an economy to expand its potential GDP.

Demand Factor

The fifth ingredient of economic growth is the **demand factor:**

■ To achieve the higher production potential created by the supply factors, households, businesses, and government must *purchase* the economy's expanding output of goods and services.

When that occurs, there will be no unplanned increases in inventories and resources will remain fully employed. Economic growth requires increases in total spending to realize the output gains made available by increased production capacity.

Efficiency Factor

The sixth ingredient of economic growth is the **efficiency factor:**

- To reach its production potential, an economy must achieve economic efficiency as well as full employment.

The economy must use its resources in the least costly way (productive efficiency) to produce the specific mix of goods and services that maximizes people's well-being (allocative efficiency). The ability to expand production, together with the full use of available resources, is not sufficient for achieving maximum possible growth. Also required is the efficient use of those resources.

The supply, demand, and efficiency factors in economic growth are related. Unemployment caused by insufficient total spending (the demand factor) may lower the rate of new capital accumulation (a supply factor) and delay expenditures on research (also a supply factor). Conversely, low spending on investment (a supply factor) may cause insufficient spending (the demand factor) and unemployment. Widespread inefficiency in the use of resources (the efficiency factor) may translate into higher costs of goods and services and thus lower profits, which in turn may slow innovation and reduce the accumulation of capital (supply factors). Economic growth is a dynamic process in which the supply, demand, and efficiency factors all interact.

▮ Production Possibilities Analysis

To put the six factors underlying economic growth in proper perspective, let's first use the production possibilities analysis introduced in Chapter 2.

Growth and Production Possibilities

Recall that a curve like *AB* in Figure 17.1 is a production possibilities curve. It indicates the various *maximum* combinations of products an economy can produce with its fixed quantity and quality of nat-

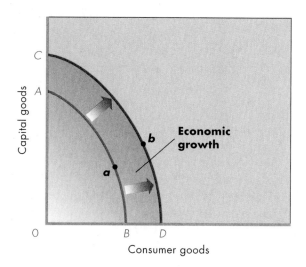

Figure 17.1

Economic growth and the production possibilities curve. Economic growth is made possible by the four supply factors that shift the production possibilities curve outward, as from *AB* to *CD*. Economic growth is realized when the demand factor and the efficiency factor move the economy from point *a* to *b*.

ural, human, and capital resources and its stock of technological knowledge. An improvement in any of the supply factors will push the production possibilities curve outward, as from *AB* to *CD*.

But the demand and efficiency factors remind us that the economy may not automatically attain its maximum production potential. The curve may shift outward but leave the economy behind at some level of operation such as *a* on *AB*. Because *a* is inside the new production possibilities curve *CD*, the economy has not achieved its growth potential. That potential will be realized only if (1) total spending increases enough to sustain full employment and (2) the additional resources that pushed the curve outward are employed efficiently so that they make the maximum possible dollar contribution to output.

An increase in total spending is needed to move the economy from point *a* to a point on *CD*. And for the economy to achieve the maximum increase in the monetary value of its output—its greatest growth of real GDP—that location on *CD* must be optimal. You will recall from Chapter 2 that this "best allocation" is determined by expanding production of each good until its marginal benefit equals its marginal cost. Here, we assume that this optimal combination of capital and consumer goods occurs at point *b*.

Example: The net increase in the size of the labor force in the United States in recent years has been roughly 2 million workers per year. That increment raises the economy's production capacity. But obtaining the extra output that these added workers could produce depends on their success in finding jobs. It also depends on whether or not the jobs are in firms and industries where the workers' talents are fully and optimally used. Society does not want new labor-force entrants to be unemployed. Nor does it want pediatricians working as plumbers or pediatricians producing services for which marginal costs exceed marginal benefits. **(Key Question 1)**

Labor and Productivity

Although demand and efficiency factors are important, discussions of economic growth focus primarily on supply factors. Society can increase its real output and income in two fundamental ways: (1) by increasing its inputs of resources, and (2) by raising the productivity of those inputs. Figure 17.2 focuses on the input of *labor* and provides a useful framework for discussing the role of supply factors in growth. A nation's real GDP in any year depends on the input of labor (measured in worker-hours) multiplied by **labor productivity** (measured as real output per worker per hour):

Real GDP = worker-hours × labor productivity

So, thought of this way, a nation's economic growth from one year to the next depends on its *increase* in labor inputs (if any) and its *increase* in labor productivity (if any).

Illustration: Assume that the hypothetical economy of Ziam has 10 workers in year 1, each working 2000 hours per year (50 weeks at 40 hours per week). The total input of labor therefore is 20,000 hours. If productivity (average real output per worker-hour) is $10, then real GDP in Ziam will be $200,000 (= 20,000 × $10). If worker-hours rise to 20,200 and labor productivity rises to $10.40, Ziam's real GDP will increase to $210,080 in year 2. Ziam's rate of economic growth will be about 5 percent [= ($210,080 − $200,000)/$200,000] for the year.

Worker-Hours
What determines the number of hours worked each year? As shown in Figure 17.2,

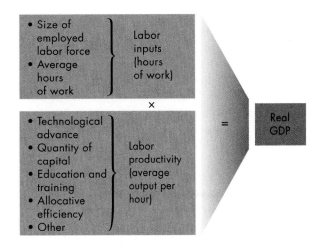

Figure 17.2

The supply determinants of real output. Real GDP is usefully viewed as the product of the quantity of labor inputs (worker-hours) multiplied by labor productivity.

the hours of labor input depend on the size of the employed labor force and the length of the average workweek. Labor-force size depends on the size of the working-age population and the **labor-force participation rate**—the percentage of the working-age population actually in the labor force. The length of the average workweek is governed by legal and institutional considerations and by collective bargaining.

Labor Productivity
Figure 17.2 tells us that labor productivity is determined by technological progress, the quantity of capital goods available to workers, the quality of the labor itself, and the efficiency with which inputs are allocated, combined, and managed. Productivity rises when the health, training, education, and motivation of workers improve, when workers have more and better machinery and natural resources with which to work, when production is better organized and managed, and when labor is reallocated from less efficient industries to more efficient industries.

Growth in the AD-AS Model

Let's now link the production possibilities analysis to long-run aggregate supply so that we can show the process of economic growth through the extended aggregate demand–aggregate supply model developed in Chapter 16.

Production Possibilities and Aggregate Supply

The supply factors that shift the economy's production possibilities curve outward also shift its long-run aggregate supply curve rightward. As shown in Figure 17.3, the outward shift of the production possibilities curve from *AB* to *CD* in graph (a) is equivalent to the rightward shift of the economy's long-run aggregate supply curve from AS_{LR1} to AS_{LR2} in graph (b). The long-run AS curves are vertical because an economy's potential output—its full-employment output—is determined by the supply and efficiency factors, not by its price level. Whatever the price level, the economy's potential output remains the same. Moreover, just as price-level changes do not shift an economy's production possibilities curve, they do not shift an economy's long-run aggregate supply curve.

Extended AD-AS Model

In Figure 17.4 we use the extended aggregate demand–aggregate supply model to depict the economic growth process. (The model is extended to include the distinction between short- and long-run aggregate supply. See Chapter 16.)

Suppose that an economy's aggregate demand curve, long-run aggregate supply curve, and short-run aggregate supply curve initially are AD_1, AS_{LR1}, and AS_1, as shown. The equilibrium price level and level of real output are P_1 and Q_1. At price level P_1, the short-run aggregate supply is AS_1; it slopes upward because, in the short run, changes in the price level cause firms to adjust their output. In the long run, however, price-level changes do not affect the economy's real output, leaving the long-run aggregate supply curve vertical at the economy's potential level of output, here Q_1. This potential level of output depends on the supply and efficiency factors previously discussed.

Now let's assume that changes in the supply factors (quantity and quality of resources and technology) shift the long-run aggregate supply curve rightward from AS_{LR1} to AS_{LR2}. The economy's potential output has increased, as reflected in the shift of the long-run aggregate supply curve from AS_{LR1} to AS_{LR2}.

If prices and wages are inflexible downward, the economy can realize its greater production potential

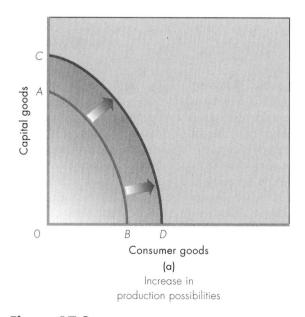

(a)
Increase in
production possibilities

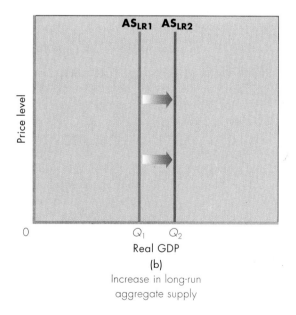

(b)
Increase in long-run
aggregate supply

Figure 17.3

Production possibilities and long-run aggregate supply. (a) Supply factors shift an economy's production possibilities curve outward, as from *AB* to *CD*. (b) The same factors (along with the efficiency factor) shift the economy's long-run aggregate supply curve to the right, as from AS_{LR1} to AS_{LR2}.

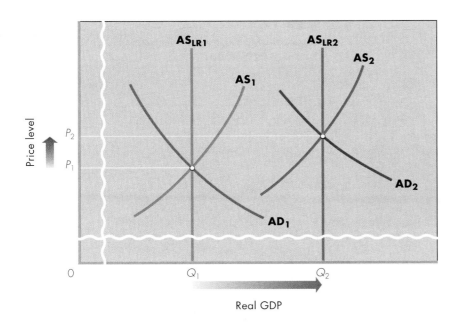

Figure 17.4

Economic growth in the extended AD-AS model. Long-run aggregate supply and short-run aggregate supply have increased over time, as from AS_{LR1} to AS_{LR2} and AS_1 to AS_2. Simultaneously, aggregate demand has shifted rightward, as from AD_1 to AD_2. The actual outcome of these combined shifts has been economic growth, shown as the increase in real output from Q_1 to Q_2, accompanied by inflation, shown as the rise in the price level from P_1 to P_2.

only through an increase in aggregate demand. Under usual circumstances, such an increase is forthcoming because the production of additional output produces additional income to households and businesses. In Figure 17.4, suppose that this additional income results in increases in consumption and investment spending such that the aggregate demand curve shifts from AD_1 to AD_2. Also suppose that the economy continues to use its resources efficiently.

The increases of aggregate supply and aggregate demand in Figure 17.4 have increased real output from Q_1 to Q_2 and have boosted the price level from P_1 to P_2. At the higher price level P_2, the economy confronts a new short-run aggregate supply curve AS_2. The result of the dynamics described in Figure 17.4 is economic growth, accompanied by mild inflation.

In brief, economic growth results from increases in aggregate supply and aggregate demand. Whether zero, mild, or rapid inflation accompanies economic growth depends on the extent to which aggregate demand increases relative to aggregate supply. (**Key Question 5**) 🔑 17.1

▌ U.S. Economic Growth Rates

Figure 17.5 shows the average annual growth rates of real GDP and real per capita GDP in the United States for the past five decades. *Over the full 50 years, real GDP grew by about 3.5 percent annually, whereas*

real GDP per capita grew by about 2.3 percent annually. Economic growth was particularly strong in the 1960s but declined during the 1970s and 1980s. Although the average annual growth rate for the 1990s only slightly exceeded that of the 1980s, real GDP surged between 1996 and 1999. Specifically, it grew by 3.6 percent in 1996, 4.4 percent in 1997, 4.4 percent in 1998, and 4.2 percent in 1999. These

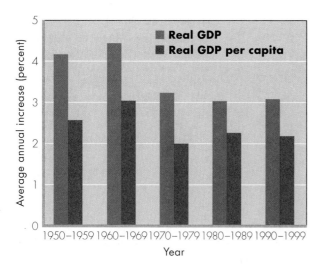

Figure 17.5

U.S. economic growth, annual averages for five decades.   Growth of real GDP has averaged about 3.5 percent annually in the last half century and annual growth of real GDP per capita averaged about 2.3 percent. Growth rates in the 1970s and 1980s were less than those in the 1960s, but the rates rebounded in the last half of the 1990s.

recent rates were not only higher than previous rates but higher than those in most other advanced industrial nations during this period. (We will defer discussion of this recent growth surge to later in this chapter.) ▮ 17.1

▮ Accounting for Growth

Table 17.1, based on the research of economist Edward Denison (1915–1992), provides estimates of the relative contributions of various factors to U.S. economic growth between 1929 and 2000.

Inputs versus Productivity

We see from Table 17.1 that the increase in labor productivity (output per hour of work) has been the single most important source of economic growth. Increases in the quantity of labor (item 1) account for only about one-third of the increase in real output since 1929; two-thirds are attributable to rising labor productivity (item 2).

Quantity of Labor

The U.S. population and the size of the labor force have both expanded significantly. Between 1929 and 2000, total population grew from 122 million to 275

Table 17.1

The Estimated Sources of Growth of U.S. Real Output, 1929–2000

Source of Growth	Percentage of Total Growth
1. Increase in quantity of labor	33
2. Increase in labor productivity	67
a. Technological advance	26
b. Quantity of capital	18
c. Education and training	11
d. Economies of scale	6
e. Improved resource allocation	6
	100

Source: Edward F. Denison, *Trends in American Economic Growth, 1929–1982* (Washington, D.C.: Brookings Institution, 1985), p. 30; *Economic Report of the President,* various years; authors' revisions and estimates.

million, and the labor force increased from 49 million to 141 million workers. Reductions in the length of the workweek reduced the growth of labor inputs before the Second World War, but the workweek has remained relatively stable since then. Falling birthrates over the past 30 years have slowed the growth of the native population, but increased immigration has partly offset that slowdown. Of greatest significance has been a surge of women's participation in the labor force. Partly because of that increased participation, U.S. labor force growth has averaged 2 million workers per year during the past 25 years.

Technological Advance

Technological advance (item *2a* in Table 17.1) is a critical engine of productivity growth and has accounted for 26 percent of the increase in real output since 1929.

Technological advance includes not only innovative production techniques but new managerial methods and new forms of business organization that improve the process of production. Generally, technological advance is generated by the discovery of new knowledge, which allows for resources to be combined in improved ways that increase output. Once discovered and implemented, new knowledge soon becomes available to entrepreneurs and firms at relatively low cost. Technological advance therefore eventually spreads through the entire economy, boosting productivity and economic growth.

Technological advance and capital formation (investment) are closely related, since technological advance usually promotes investment in new machinery and equipment. In fact, technological advance is often *embodied* within new capital. For example, the purchase of new computers brings to industry speedier, more powerful computers that incorporate new technology.

Technological advance has been both rapid and profound. Gas and diesel engines, conveyor belts, and assembly lines are significant developments of the past. So, too, are fuel-efficient commercial aircraft, integrated microcircuits, personal computers, xerography, and containerized shipping. More recently, technological advance has exploded, particularly in the areas of medicine, wireless communication, biotechnology, and the Internet. **17.2**

Quantity of Capital

Eighteen percent of the annual growth of real output since 1929 is attributed to increases in the quantity of capital (item *2b* in Table 17.1). More and better plants and equipment make workers more productive. And a nation acquires more capital by saving some of its income and using that saving to invest in plant and equipment.

A key determinant of labor productivity is the amount of capital goods available per worker. If both the aggregate stock of capital goods and the size of the labor force increase over a given period, the individual worker is not necessarily better equipped and productivity will not necessarily rise. But the quantity of capital equipment available per U.S. worker has increased greatly over time. (It is currently about $75,000 per worker.)

Public investment in the U.S. **infrastructure** (highways and bridges, public transit systems, wastewater treatment facilities, water systems, airports, educational facilities, and so on) has also grown since 1929. This public capital (infrastructure) complements private capital. Investments in new highways promote private investment in new factories and retail stores along their routes. Industrial parks developed by local governments attract manufacturing and distribution firms.

Education and Training

Ben Franklin once said: "He that hath a trade hath an estate," meaning that education and training contribute to a worker's stock of **human capital**—*the*

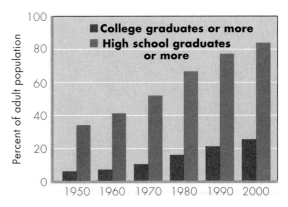

Figure 17.6

Changes in the educational attainment of the U.S. adult population. The percentage of the U.S. adult population, age 25 or more, completing high school and college has been rising in recent decades.

Source: U.S. Census Bureau, www.census.gov.

knowledge and skills that make for a productive worker. Investment in human capital includes not only formal education but also on-the-job training. Like investment in physical capital, investment in human capital is an important means of increasing labor productivity and earnings. As Table 17.1 shows, 11 percent of the growth of U.S. real GDP since 1929 owes to such investment in people's education and skills (item *2c*).

One measure of a nation's quality of labor is its level of educational attainment. Figure 17.6 shows large gains in educational attainment over the past several decades. In 1960 only 41 percent of the U.S. population age 25 or more had at least a high school education, and only 8 percent had a college education or more. By 2000, those numbers had increased to 84 percent and 26 percent, respectively. Clearly, education has become accessible to more people in the United States during the recent past.

But all is not upbeat with education in the United States. Many observers think that the quality of education in the United States has declined. Average scores on standardized college admission tests are lower than they were a few decades ago. U.S. students in science and mathematics do not do as well as students in many other nations (see Global Perspective 17.1). The United States has been producing fewer engineers and scientists, a problem that may trace back to inadequate training in math and science in elementary and high schools. And it is

Average Test Scores of Eighth-Grade Students in Math and Science, Top 10 Countries and the United States

The test performance of U.S. eighth-grade students did not rank favorably with that of eighth-graders in several other nations in the Third International Math and Science Study (1999).

Mathematics

Rank		Score
1	Singapore	604
2	South Korea	587
3	Taiwan	585
4	Hong Kong (China)	582
5	Japan	579
6	Belgium	558
7	Netherlands	540
8	Slovak Republic	534
9	Hungary	532
10	Canada	531
19	United States	502

Science

Rank		Score
1	Taiwan	569
2	Singapore	568
3	Hungary	552
4	Japan	550
5	South Korea	549
6	Netherlands	545
7	Australia	540
8	Czech Republic	539
9	United Kingdom	538
10	Finland	535
18	United States	515

argued that on-the-job training programs (apprenticeship programs) in several European nations are superior to those in the United States. For these reasons, much recent public policy discussion and legislation has been directed toward improving the quality of the U.S. education and training system.

Resource Allocation and Economies of Scale

Table 17.1 also tells us that economies of scale (item 2*d*) and improved resource allocation (item 2*e*) together explain 12 percent of U.S. growth.

Economies of Scale Reductions in per-unit cost that result from increases in the size of markets and firms are called **economies of scale.** Markets have increased in size over time, allowing firms to achieve production advantages associated with greater size. As firms expand, they use more efficient plant and equipment and methods of manufacturing and delivery that result in greater productivity. They also are better able to recoup substantial investments in developing new products and production methods. Examples: A large manufacturer of autos can use elaborate assembly lines with computerization and robotics, while smaller producers must settle for less advanced technologies using more labor inputs. Large pharmaceutical firms greatly reduce the average amount of labor (researchers, production workers) needed to produce each pill as they increase the number of pills produced. Accordingly, economies of scale result in greater real GDP and thus contribute to economic growth.

Improved Resource Allocation Improved resource allocation means that workers over time have moved from low-productivity employment to high-productivity employment. Historically, much labor has shifted from agriculture, where labor productivity is low, to manufacturing, where it is quite high. More recently, labor has shifted away from some manufacturing industries to even higher productivity industries such as computer software, business consulting, and pharmaceuticals. As a result of such shifts, the average productivity of U.S. workers has increased.

Also, discrimination in education and the labor market has historically deterred some women and minorities from entering high-productivity jobs. With the decline of such discrimination, over time many members of those groups have shifted from low-productivity jobs to higher-productivity jobs. The result has been higher overall labor productivity and real GDP.

Finally, we know from discussions in Chapter 6 that tariffs, import quotas, and other barriers to international trade tend to relegate resources to relatively unproductive pursuits. The long-run movement toward liberalized international trade through international agreements has improved the allocation of resources, increased labor productivity, and expanded real output, both here and abroad. **(Key Question 6)**

Other Factors

Several difficult-to-measure factors influence a nation's rate of economic growth. The overall social-cultural-political environment of the United States, for example, has facilitated economic growth. The market system that has prevailed in the United States since its founding has fostered many personal and corporate incentives that promote growth. The United States has also had a stable political system characterized by democratic principles, internal order, the right of property ownership, the legal status of enterprise, and the enforcement of contracts. Economic freedom and political freedom have been "growth-friendly."

Unlike the case in some nations, there are virtually no social or moral taboos on production and material progress in the United States. The nation's social philosophy has embraced material advance as an attainable and desirable economic goal. The inventor, the innovator, and the businessperson are accorded high degrees of prestige and respect in American society.

Moreover, Americans have had positive attitudes toward work and risk taking, resulting in an ample supply of willing workers and innovative entrepreneurs. A flow of energetic immigrants has greatly augmented that supply.

QUICK REVIEW 17.2

■ Improvements in labor productivity account for about two-thirds of the increases in U.S. real GDP; the use of more labor inputs accounts for the remaining one-third.

■ Improved technology, more capital, greater education and training, economies of scale, and better resource allocation have been the main contributors to U.S. productivity growth and thus to U.S. economic growth.

■ Other factors that have been favorable to U.S. growth include reliance on the market system, a stable political system, a social philosophy that embraces material progress, and an abundant supply of willing workers and entrepreneurs.

▪ Productivity Growth and the New Economy

Real output, real income, and real wages are linked to labor productivity. To see why, suppose you are alone on an uninhabited island. The number of fish you can catch or coconuts you can pick per hour—your productivity—is your real wage (or real income) per hour. By *increasing* your productivity, you can improve your standard of living because greater output per hour means there are more fish and coconuts (goods) available to consume.

So it is for the economy as a whole: Over long periods, the economy's labor productivity determines its average real hourly wage. The economy's income per hour is equal to its output per hour. Productivity growth therefore is its main route for increasing its standard of living. It allows firms to pay higher wages without lowering their business profits. Even a seemingly small percentage change in productivity growth, if sustained over several years, can make a substantial difference as to how fast a nation's standard of living rises. We know from the *rule of 70* (Chapter 8) that if a nation's productivity grows by 2.5 percent annually rather than 1.5, its standard of living will double in 28 years rather than 47 years.

Figure 17.7 shows the growth of labor productivity (as measured by changes in the index of labor productivity) in the United States from 1973 to 2000, along with separate trend lines for 1973–1995 and 1995–2000. Labor productivity grew by an average of only 1.4 percent yearly over the 1973–1995 period. But between 1995 and 2000 productivity growth averaged 3.1 percent annually. Many economists believe that this higher productivity growth resulted from a significant new wave of technological advance, coupled with global competition. They assert that the United States has achieved a **New Economy**—one that has faster productivity growth and therefore faster economic growth.

Characteristics of the New Economy

What are the characteristics of this New Economy? What, according to its advocates, distinguishes it from the economy that it superseded?

The Microchip and Information Technology

The core element of the New Economy is an explosion of entrepreneurship and innovation based on the microprocessor, or *microchip*, which bundles

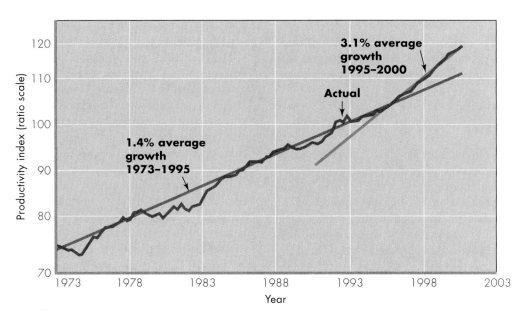

Figure 17.7

Growth of labor productivity in the United States, 1973–2000. U.S. labor productivity increased at an average annual rate of only 1.4 percent from 1973 to 1995. But between 1995 and 2000 it accelerated to an annual rate of 3.1 percent. (A ratio scale plots equal percentage changes as equal vertical distances.)
Source: Economic Report of the President, 2000; updated.

transistors on a piece of silicon. Advocates of the New Economy liken the invention of the microchip to that of electricity, the automobile, air travel, the telephone, and television in importance and scope.

The microchip has found its way into thousands of applications. It has helped create a wide array of new products and services and new ways of doing business. Its immediate result was the pocket calculator, the bar-code scanner, the personal computer, the laptop computer, and more powerful business computers. But the miniaturization of electronic circuits also advanced the development of other products such as the cell phone and pager, computer-guided lasers, deciphered genetic codes, global positioning equipment, energy conservation systems, Doppler radar, digital cameras, and many more.

Perhaps of greatest significance, the widespread availability of personal and laptop computers stimulated the desire to tie them together. That desire promoted rapid development of the Internet and all its many manifestations, such as business-to-household and business-to-business electronic commerce (e-commerce). The combination of the computer, fiber-optic cable, wireless technology, and the Internet constitutes a spectacular advance in

information technology, which has been used to connect all parts of the world.

New Firms and Increasing Returns   Hundreds of new **start-up firms** advanced various aspects of the new information technology. Some of the most successful of these firms include Intel (microchip); Apple, Dell, and Gateway (personal computers); Microsoft and Oracle (computer software); Cisco Systems (Internet switching systems); American Online (Internet service provision); Yahoo (Internet search engine); and Amazon.com (electronic commerce). There are hundreds more! Most of these firms were either "not on the radar" or "a small blip on the radar" 25 years ago. Today they each have billions of annual revenue and employ thousands of workers.

Successful new firms often experience **increasing returns,** which occur *when a firm's output increases by a larger percentage than the increase in its inputs (resources).* For example, suppose that Ima.com decides to double the size of its operations to meet the growing demand for its services. After doubling its plant and equipment and doubling its workforce, say, from 100 workers to 200 workers, it finds that its total output has tripled from 8000 units to 24,000 units. Ima.com has experienced increasing returns; its output has increased by 200 percent while its inputs have increased by only 100 percent. Consequently, its labor productivity has gone up from 80 (= 8000 units/100 workers) to 120 (= 24,000 units/200 workers). Increasing returns boost labor productivity, and this, other things equal, lowers per-unit costs of production. These reductions in costs resulting from larger firm size are *economies of scale* (Table 17.1).

There are a number of sources of increasing returns and economies of scale within the New Economy:

- *More specialized inputs*   Firms can use more specialized and thus more productive capital and workers as they expand their operations. A growing new e-commerce business, for example, can purchase highly specialized inventory management systems and hire specialized personnel such as accountants, marketing managers, and system maintenance experts.

- *Spreading of development costs*   Firms can spread high product-development costs over greater output. For example, suppose that a new software product costs $100,000 to develop and only $2 per unit to manufacture and sell. If the firm sells 1000 units of the software, its per-unit cost will be $102 [= ($100,000 + $2000)/1000], but if it sells 500,000 units, the cost will drop to only $2.20 [= ($100,000 + $1 million)/500,000].

- *Simultaneous consumption*   Many of the products and services of the New Economy can satisfy many customers at the same time. Unlike a gallon of gas that needs to be produced for each buyer, a software program needs to be produced only once. It then becomes available at very low expense to thousands or even millions of buyers. The same is true of entertainment delivered on CDs, movies distributed on film, and information disseminated through the Internet.

- *Network effects*   Software and Internet service becomes more beneficial to a buyer the greater the number of households and businesses that buy them. When others have Internet service, you can send e-mail messages to them. When they also have software that allows display of documents and photos, you can attach those items to your e-mail messages. These system advantages are called **network effects,** which are *increases in the value of the product to each user, including existing users, as the total number of users*

rises. The domestic and global expansion of the Internet, in particular, has produced network effects, as have cell phones, pagers, hand-held computers, and other aspects of wireless communication. Network effects magnify the value of output well beyond the costs of inputs.

- *Learning by doing*   Finally, firms that produce new products or pioneer new ways of doing business experience increasing returns through **learning by doing.** Tasks that initially may have taken them hours may take them only minutes once the methods are perfected.

Whatever the particular source of increasing returns, the result is higher productivity, which tends to reduce the per-unit cost of producing and delivering products. Table 17.2 lists a number of specific examples of cost reduction from technology in the New Economy.

Global Competition   The New Economy is characterized not only by information technology and increasing returns but also by heightened global competition. The collapse of the socialist economies in the

Table 17.2

Examples of Cost Reductions from Technology in the New Economy

- The cost of storing one megabit of information—enough for a 320-page book—fell from $5257 in 1975 to 17 cents in 1999.
- Prototyping each part of a car once took Ford weeks and cost $20,000 on average. Using an advanced 3-D object printer, it cut the time to just hours and the cost to less than $20.
- Studies show that telecommuting saves businesses about $20,000 annually for a worker earning $44,000—a saving in lost work time and employee retention costs, plus gains in worker productivity.
- Using scanners and computers, Weyerhaeuser increased the lumber yield and value from each log by 30 percent.
- Amoco has used 3-D seismic exploration technology to cut the cost of finding oil from nearly $10 per barrel in 1991 to under $1 per barrel today.
- Wal-Mart reduced the operating cost of its delivery trucks by 20 percent through installing computers, global positioning gear, and cell phones in 4300 vehicles.
- Banking transactions on the Internet cost 1 cent each, compared with $1.14 for face-to-face, pen-and-paper communication.

Source: Compiled and directly quoted from W. Michael Cox and Richard Alm, "The New Paradigm," Federal Reserve Bank of Dallas Annual Report, May 2000, various pages.

late 1980s and early 1990s, together with the success of market systems, has led to a reawakening of capitalism throughout the world. The new information technologies have "shrunk the globe" and made it imperative for all firms to lower their costs and prices and to innovate in order to remain competitive. Free-trade zones such as NAFTA and the European Union (EU), along with trade liberalization through the World Trade Organization (WTO), have heightened competition internationally by removing trade protection from domestic firms. The larger geographic markets, in turn, have enabled the firms of the New Economy to expand beyond their national borders.

Macroeconomic Implications

The New Economy has a number of important implications for the macroeconomy. Chief among them is that the higher productivity growth allows the economy to achieve a higher rate of economic growth. A glance back at Figure 17.3 will help make this point. If the shifts of the curves reflect annual changes in the old economy, then the New Economy would be depicted by an outward shift of the production possibilities curve beyond CD in Figure 17.3a and a shift of the long-run aggregate supply curve farther to the right than AS_{LR2} in Figure 17.3b. When coupled with economic efficiency and increased total spending, the economy's real GDP would rise by more than that shown. That is, the economy would achieve a higher rate of economic growth.

Faster Noninflationary Growth
In this view, the New Economy has a higher "safe speed limit" than the old economy because production capacity rises more rapidly. The New Economy can grow by, say, 4 percent, rather than 2 or 3 percent, each year without igniting demand-pull inflation. Increases in aggregate demand that in the past would have caused inflation do not cause inflation in the New Economy.

In the old economy prices rose as the economy approached its capacity because increased output produced decreasing returns and higher per-unit production costs. But in the New Economy proportionately more spending is for goods and services whose per-unit costs decline as output increases. Even when wage increases rise to match the productivity increases, per-unit production costs and therefore prices remain stable. Global competition in the New Economy also contributes to price stability. Proponents of the New Economy say that increasing returns and global competition explain why

inflation remained mild as real GDP rapidly increased between 1995 and 2000.

Low Natural Rate of Unemployment
A low natural rate of unemployment (NRU) such as that of 1995–2000 (4 to 5 percent) is also consistent with the New Economy. The information technology reduces frictional unemployment by enabling workers and employers to quickly find each other. And the strong demand for high-tech workers means that high-tech firms are willing to hire and train workers. Thus the transition from old economy to New Economy jobs occurs without creating significant structural unemployment.

Growing Tax Revenues
Finally, the faster economic growth in the New Economy means larger increases in personal income and therefore larger increases in government tax revenues. The quick and unexpected elimination of the Federal budget deficit during the last half of the 1990s owed much to the higher growth rate of the New Economy. The Federal government had a budget *deficit* of $160 billion in 1995; in 2000 it had a budget *surplus* of $167 billion!

A caution: Those who champion the idea of a New Economy emphasize that it does not mean that the business cycle is dead. The New Economy is simply one for which the *trend line* of economic growth is steeper than it was in the preceding two decades. Real output may periodically deviate below and above that trend line.

Skepticism about the New Economy

Sound too good to be true? Maybe so! Although most macroeconomists have revised their forecasts for long-term productivity growth upward, others are skeptical about the New Economy and urge a "wait-and-see" approach. Skeptics acknowledge that the economy has experienced a rapid advance of new technology, that many new firms have experienced increasing returns, and that global competition has increased. But they doubt that these factors are sufficiently profound to produce a 10- to 15-year period of substantially higher rates of productivity growth and real GDP growth.

The higher rates of productivity and real GDP growth between 1995 and 2000 *are* consistent with a long-lived New Economy. Unfortunately, they are also consistent with a rapid short-run economic expansion fueled by an extraordinarily brisk rise in consumption and investment spending. Such *economic booms* raise productivity by increasing real output faster than employment (labor inputs), but they are unsustainable over longer periods. Skeptics point out that productivity surged between 1975 and 1978 and between 1983 and 1986, but in each case soon reverted to its lower long-run trend.

For a time, economic expansions need not create inflation, as long as wage growth does not exceed the growth of productivity. But economic booms eventually create shortages, which produce inflationary pressures. Even industries that have decreasing or constant costs can begin to experience rising costs when the pool of available workers dries up. The excessive demand that is causing the boom eventually raises all prices, including the price of labor. Rising inflation or the threat of rising inflation prompts the Federal Reserve to engineer increases in interest rates. For example, the Fed raised rates in a series of steps in 1999 and 2000.

By reducing investment spending, the higher interest rates dampen some of the inflationary pressure but may inadvertently slow the economy too much, causing recession. In any event, productivity and output growth stall. The higher trend line of productivity inferred from the short-run spurt of productivity proves to be an illusion. Only by looking backward over long periods can economists distinguish the start of a new long-secular trend from a shorter-term boost in productivity related to the business cycle.

Given the different views on the New Economy, what should we conclude? Perhaps the safest conclusions are these:

■ We should be pleased with the exceptional performance of the economy between 1995 and 2000, *for its own sake*, whether or not it represents a New Economy (see Global Perspective 17.2). These were remarkable times for the U.S. economy. Although the prospects for a long-lived New Economy are good, it will be several more years before we will be able to declare it a reality.

■ We should also remember that economic expansions, no matter how prolonged, are prone to end eventually. In fact, the U.S. economy stalled in early 2001, leading to concerns about recession. In response, the Fed reduced interest rates by a full percentage point in two steps in January 2001. But even a recession does not negate the potential of a New Economy, which is defined in terms of long-run trends of productivity advance and economic growth, not in terms of stability. **(Key Question 9)**

GLOBAL PERSPECTIVE 17.2

Growth Competitiveness Index

The World Economic Forum annually compiles a growth competitiveness index, which uses various factors (such as innovativeness, effective transfer of technology among sectors, efficiency of the financial system, rates of investment, and degree of integration with the rest of the world) to measure the ability of a country to achieve economic growth over time. Here is its latest top 10 list:

Country	Growth Competitiveness Ranking, 2000
United States	1
Singapore	2
Luxembourg	3
Netherlands	4
Ireland	5
Finland	6
Canada	7
Hong Kong, China	8
United Kingdom	9
Switzerland	10

Source: World Economic Forum, www.weforum.org/.

QUICK REVIEW 17.3

■ Over long time periods, labor productivity growth determines an economy's growth of real wages and its standard of living.

■ Many economists believe that the United States has achieved a New Economy of faster productivity growth and higher rates of economic growth.

■ The New Economy is based on rapid technological change in the form of the microchip and information technology, increasing returns and lower per-unit costs, and heightened global competition that helps hold down prices.

■ The New Economy has a higher "economic speed limit": It can grow more rapidly than the old economy without producing inflation; it can lower the NRU; and it generates large increases in tax revenues. Nonetheless, many economists caution that it is too early to determine whether the New Economy is a lasting long-run trend or a short-lived occurrence.

▪ Is Growth Desirable and Sustainable?

Economists usually take for granted that economic growth is desirable and sustainable. But not everyone agrees.

The Antigrowth View

Critics of growth say industrialization and growth result in pollution, global warming, ozone depletion, and other environmental problems. These adverse spillover costs occur because inputs in the production process reenter the environment as some form of waste. The more rapid our growth and the higher our standard of living, the more waste the environment must absorb—or attempt to absorb. In an already wealthy society, further growth usually means satisfying increasingly trivial wants at the cost of mounting threats to the ecological system.

Critics of growth also argue that there is little compelling evidence that economic growth has solved sociological problems such as poverty, homelessness, and discrimination. Consider poverty: In the antigrowth view, American poverty is a problem of distribution, not production. The requisite for solving the problem is commitment and political courage to redistribute wealth and income, not further increases in output.

Antigrowth sentiment also says that while growth may permit us to "make a better living," it does not give us "the good life." We may be producing more and enjoying it less. Growth means frantic paces on jobs, worker burnout, and alienated employees who have little or no control over decisions affecting their lives. The changing technology at the core of growth poses new anxieties and new sources of insecurity for workers. Both high-level and low-level workers face the prospect of having their hard-earned skills and experience rendered obsolete by an onrushing technology. High-growth economies are high-stress economies, which may impair our physical and mental health.

Finally, critics of high rates of growth doubt that they are sustainable. The planet Earth has finite amounts of natural resources available, and they are being consumed at alarming rates. Higher rates of economic growth simply speed up the degradation and exhaustion of the earth's resources. In this view, slower economic growth that is sustainable is preferable to faster growth.

In Defense of Economic Growth

The primary defense of growth is that it is the path to the greater material abundance and higher living standards desired by the vast majority of people. Rising output and incomes allow people to buy:

> more education, recreation, and travel, more medical care, closer communications, more skilled personal and professional services, and better-designed as well as more numerous products. It also means more art, music, and poetry, theater, and drama. It can even mean more time and resources devoted to spiritual growth and human development.[1]

Growth also enables society to improve the nation's infrastructure, enhance the care of the sick and elderly, provide greater access for the disabled, and provide more police and fire protection. Economic growth may be the only realistic way to reduce poverty, since there is little political support for greater redistribution of income. The way to improve the economic position of the poor is to increase household incomes through higher productivity and economic growth. Also, a no-growth policy among industrial nations might severely limit growth in poor nations. Foreign investment and development assistance in those nations would fall, keeping the world's poor in poverty longer.

Economic growth has not made labor more unpleasant or hazardous, as critics suggest. New machinery is usually less taxing and less dangerous than the machinery it replaces. Air-conditioned workplaces are more pleasant than steamy workshops. Furthermore, why would an end to economic growth reduce materialism or alienation? The loudest protests against materialism are heard in those nations and groups that now enjoy the highest levels of material abundance! The high standard of living that growth provides has increased our leisure and given us more time for reflection and self-fulfillment.

Does growth threaten the environment? The connection between growth and environment is tenuous, say growth proponents. Increases in economic growth need not mean increases in pollution. Pollution is not so much a by-product of growth as it is a "problem of the commons." Much of the environment—streams, lakes, oceans, and the air—is treated as "common property," with no restrictions on its use. The commons have become our dumping

---

[1]Alice M. Rivlin, *Reviving the American Dream* (Washington, D.C.: Brookings Institution, 1992), p. 36.

grounds; we have overused and debased them. Environmental pollution is a case of spillover or external costs, and correcting this problem involves regulatory legislation, specific taxes ("effluent charges"), or market-based incentives to remedy misuse of the environment.

Those who support growth admit there are serious environmental problems. But they say that limiting growth is the wrong solution. Growth has allowed economies to reduce pollution, be more sensitive to environmental considerations, set aside wilderness, create national parks and monuments, and clean up hazardous waste, while still enabling rising household incomes.

Is growth sustainable? Yes, say the proponents of growth. If we were depleting natural resources faster than their discovery, we would see the prices of those resources rise. That has not been the case for most natural resources; in fact, the prices of most of them have declined. And if one natural resource becomes too expensive, another resource will be substituted for it. Moreover, say economists, economic growth has more to do with the expansion and application of human knowledge and information, not of extractable natural resources. In this view, economic growth is limited only by human imagination.

Some Pleasant Side Effects of the New Economy

According to Economists Jason L. Saving and W. Michael Cox, the New Economy Has Done Much More Than Simply Lift the Standard of Living of Americans.

Saving and Cox contend that the New Economy has reduced crime rates, trimmed welfare rolls, increased charitable contributions, and enhanced minority well-being. Here is their evidence.

Crime Rates Crime rates per 100,000 people clearly plummeted in the 1990s. Between 1990 and 1999, the robbery rate declined by 46 percent, the murder rate by 45 percent, the burglary rate by 41 percent, the motor vehicle theft rate by 39 percent, and the larceny-theft rate by 23 percent.

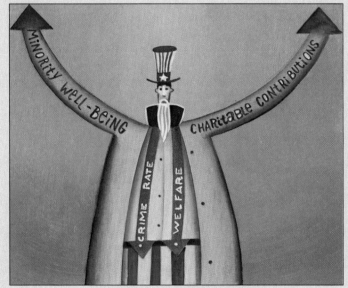

Although changes in the age composition of the population and increases in the percentage of the population incarcerated explain a substantial portion of the declining crime rate, the strong economy also has significantly contributed. People's job and income prospects influence their decisions to commit crimes. Those who expect a good future by working to earn income are less likely than others to engage in illegal activities. Also, those working full time have less time and energy for participating in illegal activities.

Welfare Rolls In 1994 the number of Americans receiving cash welfare payments (now called Temporary Assistance for Needy Families) reached an all-time high of 5.5 percent of the U.S. population. By 1999 the percentage had declined by more than one-half to 2.5 percent. The landmark Welfare Reform Act of 1996, which set time limits for welfare and established work requirements, explains much of the sharp decline. But an equally substantial part is explained by the strong economic growth and low unemployment rates of the late 1990s. With the buoyant economy, more families were able to extricate themselves from poverty.

Charitable Contributions Increases in charitable giving have also been a pleasant side effect of the expanding economy. Between 1970 and 1980, per capita contributions to charity declined at an average annual rate of .2 percent. During the expansion of the 1980s, such contributions increased at an annual average rate of 1.2 percent. In the 1990s they increased at an average annual rate of 4 percent. In fact, between 1995 and 2000 charitable giving increased by an average of 9 percent annually. The fast economic growth and new wealth associated with the New Economy explain much of this increase in charitable giving.

Minority Well-Being Saving and Cox contend that the strong economic growth and full employment of the past several years has benefited all Americans, including racial and ethnic minorities. For example, between 1993 and 1999 the poverty rate for black families declined from 31.3 to 23.6 percent. Over the same years, the rate for Hispanic families declined from 27.3 to 22.8 percent. In both cases, the percentage declines were larger than the decline for whites.

The unemployment rate also dropped more substantially for blacks and Hispanics than for whites. For blacks, it fell from 13.0 percent in 1993 to 7.6 percent in 2000; for Hispanics, it fell from 10.8 percent to 5.7 percent over those years.

Source: Jason L. Saving and W. Michael Cox, "Some Pleasant Side Effects," Federal Reserve Bank of Dallas, *Southwest Economy,* July–August 2000, pp. 7–12; updated.

SUMMARY

1. Economic growth—measured as either an increase in real output or an increase in real output per capita—increases material abundance and raises a nation's standard of living.

2. The supply factors in economic growth are (a) the quantity and quality of a nation's natural resources, (b) the quantity and quality of its human resources, (c) its stock of capital facilities, and (d) its technology. Two other factors—a sufficient level of aggregate demand and economic efficiency—are necessary for the economy to realize its growth potential.

3. The growth of production capacity is shown graphically as an outward shift of a nation's production possibilities curve or as a rightward shift of its long-run aggregate supply curve. Growth is realized when total spending rises sufficiently to match the growth of production capacity.

4. Since 1950 the annual growth rate of real GDP for the United States has averaged about 3.5 percent; the annual growth rate of real GDP per capita has been about 2.3 percent.

5. U.S. real GDP has grown partly because of increased inputs of labor and primarily because of increases in the productivity of labor. The increases in productivity have resulted mainly from technological progress, increases in the quantity of capital per worker, improvements in the quality of labor, economies of scale, and an improved allocation of labor.

6. Over long time periods, the growth of labor productivity underlies an economy's growth of real wages and its standard of living. Many economists believe that the United States has achieved a New Economy of faster productivity growth and higher rates of economic growth.

7. The New Economy is based on (a) rapid technological change in the form of the microchip and information technology, (b) increasing returns and lower per-unit costs, and (c) heightened global competition that holds down prices.

8. The main sources of increasing returns in the New Economy are (a) use of more specialized inputs as firms grow, (b) the spreading of development costs, (c) simultaneous consumption by consumers, (d) network effects, and (e) learning by doing. Increasing returns mean higher productivity and lower per-unit production costs.

9. Those who champion the New Economy say that it has a lower natural rate of unemployment than did the old economy, can grow more rapidly without producing inflation, and generates higher tax revenues because of faster growth of personal income.

10. Skeptics of the New Economy urge a wait-and-see approach. They point out that surges in productivity and real GDP growth have previously occurred during vigorous economic expansions but do not necessarily represent long-lived trends.

11. Critics of rapid growth say that it adds to environmental degradation, increases human stress, and exhausts the earth's finite supply of natural resources. Defenders of rapid growth say that it is the primary path to the rising living standards nearly universally desired by people, that it need not debase the environment, and that there are no indications that we are running out of resources. Growth is based on the expansion and application of human knowledge, which is limited only by human imagination.

TERMS AND CONCEPTS

economic growth	labor productivity	human capital	start-up firms
supply factors	labor-force participation rate	economies of scale	increasing returns
demand factor		New Economy	network effects
efficiency factor	infrastructure	information technology	learning by doing

STUDY QUESTIONS

1. **Key Question** What are the four supply factors of economic growth? What is the demand factor? What is the efficiency factor? Illustrate these factors in terms of the production possibilities curve.

2. Suppose that Alpha and Omega have identically sized working-age populations but that annual work hours are much greater in Alpha than in Omega. Provide two possible explanations.

3. Suppose that work hours in New Zombie are 200 in year 1 and productivity is $8. What is New Zombie's real GDP? If work hours increase to 210 in year 2 and productivity rises to $10, what is New Zombie's rate of economic growth?

4. What is the relationship between a nation's production possibilities curve and its long-run aggregate supply curve? How does each relate to the idea of a New Economy?

5. **Key Question** Between 1990 and 1999 the U.S. price level rose by about 20 percent while real output increased by about 33 percent. Use the aggregate demand–aggregate supply model to illustrate these outcomes graphically.

6. **Key Question** To what extent have increases in U.S. real GDP resulted from more labor inputs? From higher labor productivity? Rearrange the following contributors to the growth of real GDP in order of their quantitative importance: economies of scale, quantity of capital, improved resource allocation, education and training, technological advance.

7. True or false? If false, explain why.
    a. Technological advance, which to date has played a relatively small role in U.S. economic growth, is destined to play a more important role in the future.
    b. Many public capital goods are complementary to private capital goods.
    c. Immigration has slowed economic growth in the United States.

8. Explain why there is such a close relationship between changes in a nation's rate of productivity growth and changes in its average real hourly wage.

9. **Key Question** Relate each of the following to the New Economy:
    a. The rate of productivity growth
    b. Information technology
    c. Increasing returns
    d. Network effects
    e. Global competition

10. Provide three examples of products or services that can be simultaneously consumed by many people. Explain why labor productivity greatly rises as the firm sells more units of the product or service. Explain why the higher level of sales greatly reduces the per-unit cost of the product.

11. What is meant when economists say that the U.S. economy has "a higher safe speed limit" than it had previously? If the New Economy has a higher safe speed limit, what explains the series of interest-rate hikes engineered by the Federal Reserve in 1999 and 2000?

12. Productivity often rises during economic expansions and falls during economic recessions. Can you think of reasons why? Briefly explain. (Hint: Remember that the level of productivity involves both levels of output and levels of labor input.)

13. **(Last Word)** Explain how rapid U.S. economic growth can reduce crime rates, trim welfare rolls, increase charitable giving, and enhance the well-being of racial and ethnic minorities.

14. **Web-Based Question:** *Current GDP growth rates and per capita incomes* The Organization for Economic Cooperation and Development (OECD), at www.oecd.org/std/nahome.htm, via "On-Line Statistics" provides quarterly growth rates of real GDP for OECD member countries and an annual comparison of levels of GDP per capita based on exchange rates and purchasing power parities (PPPs). Which countries have the highest and lowest current GDP growth rates? Which have the highest and lowest per capita incomes? Does there seem to be a relationship? In your comparison, does it matter if you use per capita income based on exchange rates or that based on PPPs? Which is more reliable?

15. **Web-Based Question:** *Productivity and technology—examples of innovations in computers and communications* Recent innovations in computers and communications technologies are increasing productivity. Lucent Technologies (formerly Bell Labs), at www.lucent.com/minds/discoveries, provides a timeline of company innovations over the past 80 years. Cite five technological "home runs" (for example, the transistor in 1947) and five technological "singles" (for example, free space optical switching in 1990). Which single innovation do you think has increased productivity the most? List two innovations during the past decade. How might they boost productivity?

18

C H A P T E R

Deficits, Surpluses, and the Public Debt

BY THE YEAR 2000, the United States had amassed $5.6 trillion of public debt. How large is $5.6 trillion? We can put it into perspective this way: "One million seconds have ticked by in the past 12 days. One billion seconds took more than 31 years to elapse. One trillion seconds ago, it was around 30,000 B.C.— the Ice Age—and much of America was buried by glaciers."[1] So a debt of $5.6 trillion is a huge amount! This is a stunning number. Should we be concerned about it? ■ In this chapter we examine the public debt, budget deficits, and budget surpluses. What are the economic impacts of the public debt? Now that the United States is incurring large budget surpluses, should it use them to reduce the public debt, cut personal taxes, or strengthen social security and other social programs?

[1]Marcia Stepanek, "The National Debt: Red Ink Rising," *Seattle Post-Intelligencer* (Hearst Newspapers), Apr. 13, 1994, p. 1.

■ Deficits, Surpluses, and Debt: Definitions

A *budget deficit* is the amount by which government expenditures exceed government revenues in a given year. For example, in 1997 the Federal government spent $1601 billion while taking in revenues of $1579 billion, resulting in a $22 billion deficit. In contrast, a *budget surplus* is the amount by which government revenues exceed government expenditures in a given year. For example, in 2000 Federal revenues of $2025 billion exceeded Federal expenditures of $1789 billion, resulting in a $236 billion budget surplus.

The national or **public debt** is the total accumulation of the deficits (minus the surpluses) the Federal government has incurred through time. It represents the total amount of money owed by the Federal government to the holders of **U.S. securities:** Treasury bills, Treasury notes, Treasury bonds, and U.S. saving bonds. In 2000 that amount was $5.6 trillion.

■ Budget Philosophies

Is it good or bad to incur deficits or surpluses? Should the budget be balanced annually, if necessary by constitutional amendment? As we saw in Chapter 12, countercyclical fiscal policy should move the Federal budget toward a deficit during recession and toward a surplus during expansion. This means that discretionary fiscal policy is unlikely to result in a balanced budget in any given year. Is that a matter of concern?

Let's approach this question by examining the economic implications of several contrasting budget philosophies.

Annually Balanced Budget

Until the Great Depression of the 1930s, an **annually balanced budget** was viewed as the goal of public finance. On examination, however, it becomes clear that an annually balanced budget is not compatible with government fiscal activity viewed as a countercyclical, stabilizing force. Worse yet, an annually balanced budget intensifies the business cycle.

Illustration: Suppose the economy experiences the onset of unemployment and falling incomes. In such circumstances tax receipts automatically decline. To balance its budget, government must (1) increase tax rates, (2) reduce government expenditures, or (3) do both. But all three actions are *contractionary*; each further dampens, rather than expands, aggregate demand.

Similarly, an annually balanced budget will intensify inflation. As nominal incomes rise during the course of inflation, tax receipts automatically increase. To avoid the impending surplus, government must (1) cut tax rates, (2) increase government expenditures, or (3) do both. But each of these policies intensifies inflationary pressures.

An annually balanced budget is not economically neutral; the pursuit of such a policy intensifies the business cycle, not dampens it. Despite this problem, there is some support for a constitutional amendment requiring an annually balanced budget.

Some economists have advocated an annually balanced budget not because of a fear of deficits and a mounting public debt but because they feel that an annually balanced budget is needed to curtail the expansion of the public sector. They believe that government has a tendency to grow larger than it should because there is less popular opposition to such growth when it is financed by deficits rather than by taxes. And when budget surpluses do occur, the tendency is for government to spend down the surpluses on new government programs, rather than cut taxes. These economists, along with some politicians, want a constitutional amendment to force a balanced budget in order to slow government growth.

Cyclically Balanced Budget

Other economists contend that a **cyclically balanced budget** would enable the government to exert a countercyclical influence and at the same time balance its budget. They believe that the budget does not have to be balanced annually—there is nothing sacred about 12 months as an accounting period—but, rather, should be balanced over the course of the business cycle.

That rationale is simple, plausible, and appealing. To offset recession, the government should lower taxes and increase spending, purposely incurring a deficit. During the ensuing inflationary upswing, the government would raise taxes and slash spending. It would use the resulting surplus to retire the Federal debt incurred while financing the recession. Then government fiscal operations would exert a positive countercyclical force, and the government could still balance its budget over a period of years.

The problem with this budget philosophy is that the upswings and downswings of the business cycle are not always of equal magnitude and duration. A long severe slump followed by a modest, short period of prosperity would mean a large deficit during the slump, little or no surplus during prosperity, and a cyclical deficit in the budget.

Functional Finance

With **functional finance**, an annually or cyclically balanced budget is of secondary concern. The primary purpose of Federal finance is to provide for noninflationary full employment to balance the economy rather than the budget. If that objective causes either persistent deficits or persistent surpluses, so be it. In this philosophy, the problems of government deficits or surpluses are minor compared with prolonged recession or persistent inflation. The Federal budget is an instrument for achieving and maintaining macroeconomic stability. Government should not hesitate to incur deficits and surpluses to achieve macroeconomic stability and growth. **(Key Question 1)** 🔑 18.1

■ The Public Debt: Facts and Figures

Over the years, budget deficits have greatly exceeded budget surpluses, leading to a large public debt. As column 2 in Table 18.1 shows, in nominal terms the

Table 18.1

Quantitative Significance of the Public Debt: The Public Debt and Interest Payments in Relation to GDP, Selected Fiscal Years, 1940–2000*

(1) Year	(2) Public Debt, Billions**	(3) Gross Domestic Product, Billions**	(4) Interest Payments, Billions**	(5) Public Debt as Percentage of GDP, (2) ÷ (3)	(6) Interest Payments as Percentage of GDP, (4) ÷ (3)	(7) Per Capita Public Debt**
1940	$ 50.7	$ 96.5	$ 0.9	53%	0.9%	$ 384
1950	256.9	273.6	4.8	94	1.8	1667
1960	290.5	519.8	6.9	56	1.3	1610
1970	380.9	1013.7	14.4	38	1.4	1858
1975	541.9	1559.2	23.2	35	1.5	2507
1980	909.1	2731.8	52.5	33	1.9	3992
1985	1817.5	4141.6	129.5	44	3.1	7622
1990	3206.6	5738.4	184.4	56	3.2	12,829
1995	4921.0	7265.4	232.2	68	3.2	18,708
2000	5629.0	9962.7	222.8	57	2.2	20,441

*Fiscal years are 12-month periods ending September 30 of each year, rather than December 31 as in calendar years.
**In nominal terms.
Source: Compiled from Bureau of Economic Analysis data.

public debt was considerably higher in 2000 than it was 60 years earlier. (Not shown: It is also considerably higher in real terms.)

Causes

The main sources of large budget deficits and thus the public debt have been wars, recessions, and tax-rate cuts.

Wars Some of the public debt has resulted from the deficit financing of wars. The public debt increased substantially during the First World War and grew more than fivefold during the Second World War.

Consider the Second World War and the options it posed. The task was to reallocate a substantial portion of the economy's resources from the production of civilian goods to the production of war goods. Government expenditures for armaments and military personnel soared. To finance those expenditures, three options were available: increase taxes, print the needed money, or borrow the funds. The government feared that financing by increasing taxes would require tax rates so high that they would impair the incentive to work. The national interest required attracting more people into the labor force

and encouraging those already in it to work longer hours. Very high tax rates were felt to interfere with those goals. Printing and spending the needed money would be highly inflationary. Thus, much of the Second World War was financed by selling bonds to the public, thereby draining off spendable income and freeing resources from civilian production to make them available for defense industries.

Recessions Another cause of the public debt is recessions and the direct relationship between national income and tax revenues. In periods when the national income declines, tax collections automatically fall and budget deficits arise. Thus the public debt rose during the Great Depression of the 1930s and, more recently, during the recessions of 1974 to 1975, 1980 to 1982, and 1990 to 1991. Annual deficits, and thus the public debt, also rose between 1991 and 1993 because the Federal government incurred massive expenses in bailing out savings and loan associations that failed during the recession.

Tax Cuts Tax cuts accounted for much of the large growth in the deficit in the 1980s and early 1990s. The Economic Recovery Tax Act of 1981 provided for substantial cuts in both individual and corporate income taxes. The Reagan administration and Congress failed, however, to make offsetting reductions in government spending. Therefore, a large deficit was built into the Federal budget—one that would not balance even if the economy were operating at full employment.

Unfortunately, the economy was not at full employment during the first half of the 1980s. The 1981 tax cuts, combined with the severe 1980–1982 recession, generated rapidly rising annual deficits, which were $128 billion in 1982 and had accelerated to $221 billion by 1986. Although annual budget deficits declined between 1986 and 1989, they remained historically high even though the economy reached full employment. The annual deficits between 1982 and 1990 added $1.3 trillion to the public debt. And high annual deficits continued through the first half of the 1990s.

In 1993 the Clinton administration and Congress passed a deficit-reduction package. With the package of higher tax rates and spending limits in place, and strong economic growth, the annual deficit shrank from $255 billion in 1993 to $22 billion in 1997. As the economy continued to expand vigorously, a budget *surplus* emerged in 1998. By 2000 the annual surplus had increased to $236 billion.

Quantitative Aspects

In 2000 the U.S. debt was $5.6 trillion, up from $3.2 trillion 10 years before. But these large, seemingly incomprehensible numbers are misleading.

Debt and GDP A simple statement of the absolute size of the debt ignores the fact that the wealth and productive ability of the U.S. economy is also vast. A wealthy, highly productive nation can incur and carry a large public debt more easily than a poor nation can. It is more meaningful to measure the public debt in relation to an economy's GDP, as shown in column 5 in Table 18.1. Instead of the many-fold increase in the public debt between 1950 and 2000 shown in column 2, observe that the relative size of the debt was considerably less in 2000 than in 1950. However, our data do show that the relative size of the debt doubled between 1980 and 1995. Since 1995, that percentage has again declined.

International Comparisons As shown in Global Perspective 18.1, public debts of many other industrial nations are greater than the debt in the United States as a percentage of GDP.

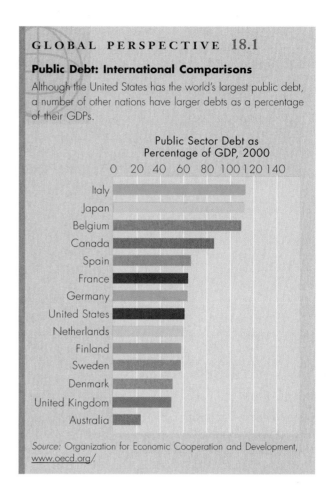

GLOBAL PERSPECTIVE 18.1

Public Debt: International Comparisons

Although the United States has the world's largest public debt, a number of other nations have larger debts as a percentage of their GDPs.

Public Sector Debt as Percentage of GDP, 2000

Source: Organization for Economic Cooperation and Development, www.oecd.org/.

Interest Charges Many economists conclude that the primary burden of the debt is the annual interest charge accruing on the bonds sold to finance the debt. We show the size of the interest payments in column 4 of Table 18.1. Interest payments began to increase sharply in the 1970s, reflecting not only increases in the debt but also periods of very high interest rates. Interest on the debt is now the fourth-largest item in the Federal budget (see Figure 5.8, page 86).

Interest payments as a percentage of GDP, however, declined from 3.2 percent to 2.2 between 1995 and 2000, as shown in column 6 in Table 18.1. That percentage reflects the level of taxation (the average tax rate) required to pay the interest on the public debt. That is, in 2000 the Federal government had to collect taxes equal to 2.2 percent of GDP to service the public debt.

Ownership Figure 18.1 shows that 63 percent of the public debt in 2000 was "held by the public" and that Federal government agencies and the Federal

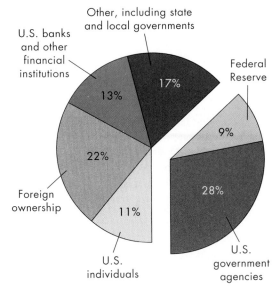

Debt held outside the Federal government and Federal Reserve (63%)

Debt held by the Federal government and Federal Reserve (37%)

Other, including state and local governments

U.S. banks and other financial institutions

13%

17%

Federal Reserve

9%

22%

28%

Foreign ownership

11%

U.S. individuals

U.S. government agencies

Total debt: $5.6 trillion

Figure 18.1

Ownership of the public debt, 2000. The total public debt can be divided into the proportion held by the public (63 percent) and the proportion held by Federal agencies and the Federal Reserve System (37 percent). Twenty-two percent of the debt is foreign-owned.

Reserve held the other 37 percent. In this case the "public" consists of individuals here and abroad, state and local governments, and U.S. financial institutions. People and institutions abroad held about 22 percent of the total debt. The vast majority of the debt is thus internally held, not externally held.

Social Security Considerations

Social security is basically a "pay-as-you-go plan" in which the mandated benefits paid out each year are financed by the payroll tax revenues received each year. But current tax rates currently bring in more revenue than current payouts, in partial preparation for the opposite circumstance when the baby boomers retire in the next two or three decades. The Federal government saves the excess revenues by purchasing U.S. securities and holding them in the **social security trust fund.**

Some economists argue that these present social security surpluses should be excluded when calculat-

ing present Federal deficits or surpluses because they represent future government obligations on a dollar-for-dollar basis. In this view the social security surplus should not be considered as an offset to current government spending. For example, without the social security surplus, the total budget surplus in 2000 would have been $152 billion less than the $236 billion reported.

> ### QUICK REVIEW 18.1
>
> ▪ A budget deficit is an excess of government expenditures over tax revenues in a given year; a budget surplus is an excess of tax revenues over government expenditures in a given year; the public debt is the total accumulation of budget deficits minus surpluses over time.
>
> ▪ The three major budget philosophies are (a) an annually balanced budget, (b) a budget balanced over the business cycle, and (c) functional finance.
>
> ▪ Wartime financing, recessions, and tax cuts (unaccompanied by expenditures cuts) are the main sources of the $5.6 trillion public debt in the United States.
>
> ▪ The U.S. public debt as a percentage of GDP was lower in 2000 than five years earlier and is in the middle range of such debt among major industrial nations.

▪ False Concerns

You may wonder if the large public debt might bankrupt the United States or at least place a tremendous burden on your children and grandchildren. Fortunately, these are false concerns.

Bankruptcy

The large U.S. public debt does not threaten to bankrupt the Federal government, leaving it unable to meet its financial obligations. There are two main reasons:

▪ ***Refinancing*** The public debt is easily refinanced. As portions of the debt come due on maturing Treasury bills, notes, and bonds each month, the government does not cut expenditures or raise taxes to provide the funds required. Rather, it refinances the debt by selling new bonds and using the proceeds to pay off holders of the maturing bonds. The new bonds are in strong demand, because lenders can obtain a relatively good interest return with no risk of default by the Federal government.

■ *Taxation* The Federal government has the constitutional authority to levy and collect taxes. A tax increase is a government option for gaining sufficient revenue to pay interest and principal on the public debt. Financially distressed private households and corporations cannot extract themselves from their financial difficulties by taxing the public. If their incomes or sales revenues fall short of their expenses, they can indeed go bankrupt. But the Federal government does have the option to impose new taxes or increase existing tax rates if necessary to finance its debt.

Burdening Future Generations

In 2000 public debt per capita was $20,441. Was each child born in 2000 handed a $20,441 bill from the Federal government? Not really! The public debt does not impose as much of a burden on future generations as generally thought.

The United States owes a substantial portion of the public debt to itself. U.S. citizens and institutions (banks, businesses, insurance companies, governmental agencies, and trust funds) own about 78 percent of the U.S. government securities. While that part of the public debt is a liability to Americans (as taxpayers), it is simultaneously an asset to Americans (as holders of Treasury bills, Treasury notes, Treasury bonds, and U.S. savings bonds).

To eliminate the American-owned part of the public debt would require a gigantic transfer payment from Americans to Americans. Taxpayers would pay higher taxes, and holders of the debt would receive an equal amount for their U.S. securities. Purchasing power in the United States would not change. Only the repayment of the 22 percent of the public debt owned by foreigners would negatively impact U.S. purchasing power.

We noted earlier that the public debt increased sharply during the Second World War. But the decision to finance military purchases through the sale of government bonds did not shift the economic burden of the war to future generations. The economic cost of the Second World War consisted of the civilian goods society had to forgo in shifting scarce resources to war goods production (recall production possibilities analysis). Regardless of whether society financed this reallocation through higher taxes or through borrowing, the real economic bur-

den of the war would have been the same. That burden was borne almost entirely by those who lived during the war. They were the ones who did without a multitude of consumer goods to enable the United States to arm itself and its allies. The next generation inherited the debt from the war but also an equal amount of government bonds.

> **QUICK REVIEW 18.2**
>
> ■ There is no danger of the Federal government's going bankrupt because it need only refinance (not retire) the public debt and it can raise revenues, if needed, through higher taxes.
>
> ■ Usually, the public debt is not a means of shifting economic burdens to future generations.

■ Substantive Issues

Although the above issues are of false concern, there are a number of substantive issues relating to the public debt. Economists, however, attach varying importance to them.

Income Distribution

The distribution of ownership of government securities is highly uneven. Some people own much more than the $20,441 per capita portion of government securities; other people own less or none at all. In general, the ownership of the public debt is concentrated among wealthier groups who own a large percentage of all stocks and bonds. Because the overall Federal tax system is only mildly progressive, payment of interest on the public debt probably increases income inequality. Income is transferred from people who, on average, have lower incomes to the higher-income bondholders. If greater income equality is one of society's goals, then this redistribution is undesirable.

Incentives

Table 18.1 indicates that the current public debt necessitates annual interest payments of $223 billion. With no increase in the size of the debt, that interest charge must be paid out of tax revenues. Higher taxes may dampen incentives to bear risk, to innovate, to invest, and to work. So, in this indirect way, a large public debt may impair economic growth. As noted earlier, the ratio of interest payments to GDP indicates the level of taxation needed to pay interest on the debt. Some economists are concerned that this ratio is higher than it was in earlier periods of U.S. history (column 6, Table 18.1).

Foreign-Owned Public Debt

The 22 percent of the U.S. debt held by citizens and institutions of foreign countries *is* an economic burden to Americans. Because we do not owe that portion of the debt "to ourselves," the payment of interest and principal on this **external public debt** enables foreigners to buy some of our output. In return for the benefits derived from the borrowed funds, the United States transfers goods and services to foreign lenders. Of course, Americans also own debt issued by foreign governments, so payment of principal and interest by those governments transfers some of their goods and services to Americans. **(Key Question 3)**

Crowding Out and the Stock of Capital

There is a potentially more serious problem. The financing (and continual refinancing) of the large public debt can transfer a real economic burden to future generations by passing on a smaller stock of capital goods. This possibility involves the *crowding-out effect:* the idea that a large public debt results in higher real interest rates, which reduce private investment spending. When crowding out is extensive, future generations will inherit an economy with a smaller production capacity and, other things equal, a lower standard of living.

Consider the investment demand curve ID_1 in Figure 18.2. (Ignore curve ID_2 for now.) If government borrowing increases the real interest rate from 6 percent to 10 percent, investment spending will fall from $25 billion to $15 billion. That is, the deficit financing will crowd out $10 billion of private investment.

Qualifications   But even with crowding out, there are two factors that could reduce the net economic burden shifted to future generations.

■ *Public Investment*   Just as private goods may involve either consumption or investment, so it is with public goods. Part of the government spending enabled by the public debt is for public investment outlays (for example, highways, mass transit systems, and electric power facili-

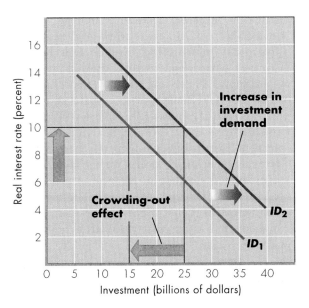

Figure 18.2

The investment demand curve and the crowding-out effect.   If the investment demand curve (ID_1) is fixed, the increase in the interest rate from 6 percent to 10 percent caused by financing a large public debt will crowd out $10 billion of private investment and decrease the size of the capital stock inherited by future generations. However, if the government spending enabled by the debt improves the profit expectations of businesses, the private investment demand curve will shift rightward, as from ID_1 to ID_2. That shift may offset the crowding-out effect wholly or in part.

ties) and "human capital" (for example, investments in education, job training, and health). Like private expenditures on machinery and equipment, those **public investments** increase the economy's future production capacity. Because of the deficit financing, the stock of public capital passed on to future generations may be higher than otherwise. That greater stock of public capital may offset the diminished stock of private capital resulting from the crowding out effect, leaving overall production capacity unimpaired.

■ *Public-Private Complementarities*   Some public and private investments are complementary. Thus, the public investment financed through the debt could spur some private sector investment by increasing its expected rate of return. For example, a Federal building in a city may encourage private investment in the form of nearby office buildings, shops, and restaurants. Through its complementary effect, the spending on public capital may shift the private investment demand curve to the right, as from ID_1 to ID_2 in Figure 18.2. Even though the government borrowing boosts the interest rate from 6 percent to 10 percent, total private investment need not fall. In the extreme case shown in Figure 18.2, it remains at $25 billion. Of course, the increase in investment demand might be smaller than that shown. If it were smaller, the crowding-out effect would not be fully offset. But the point is that an increase in private investment demand may counter the decline in investment that would otherwise result from the higher interest rate. **(Key Question 7)**

▌Deficits and Surpluses: 1990–2010

Federal deficits and the growing public debt were the main focus of fiscal policy during the first half of the 1990s. As Figure 18.3 makes clear, the absolute sizes of annual Federal deficits were enormous during that period. The budget deficit jumped from $221 billion in 1990 to $290 billion in 1992, mainly

because of the recession of 1990–1991 and a weak recovery, which slowed the inflow of tax revenues. The government's expensive bailout of the savings and loan associations also contributed to the huge deficits in those years.

Fiscal policy turned to reducing the deficits in order to promote a *reverse* crowding-out effect—that is, to lower interest rates and boost private investment spending. Spurred by the Clinton administration, in 1993 Congress passed the Deficit Reduction Act, designed to increase tax revenues by $250 billion over the following 5 years and to reduce Federal spending by the same amount.

Specifically, this legislation (1) increased the top marginal tax rate on personal income from 31 to 39.6 percent, (2) raised the corporate income tax from 34 to 35 percent, and (3) added 4.3 cents per gallon to the Federal excise tax on gasoline. The largest spending "cut" resulted from holding all discretionary spending—spending not mandated by law—to 1993 nominal levels. Normally, this spending would have increased at least as fast as inflation. Congress reaffirmed its commitment to holding down spending in 1996 by pledging in a

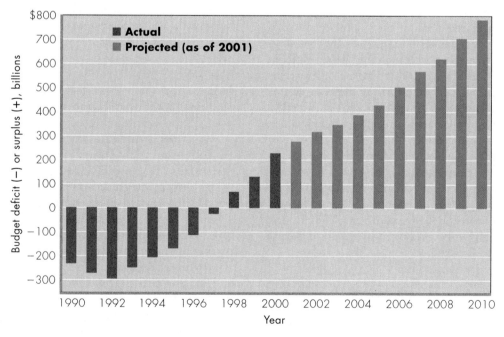

Figure 18.3

Federal budget deficits and surpluses, actual and projected, fiscal years 1990–2010 (in billions of nominal dollars). Annual budget deficits between 1990 and 1997 gave way to budget surpluses in the late 1990s and early 2000s. Barring recession and without explicit policies to reduce them, the budget surpluses are projected to grow throughout the 2000s.

Source: Economic Report of the President, 2001; Congressional Budget Office, www.cbo.gov/.

"contract with America" to eliminate budget deficits by 2002.

Aided by strong economic growth, the congressional actions reduced the deficit to $22 billion in 1997. Since 1997 rapid growth of personal and corporate income has swelled tax collections, producing a series of growing budget surpluses. The remarkableness of this turnaround cannot be overstressed. Prior to 1998, the last Federal budget surplus was in 1969. And between 1969 and 1997, about $4.5 trillion was added to the public debt.

The public debate over the Federal budget has turned 180 degrees from how to reduce large budget deficits to what should be done with huge budget surpluses. Without actions to reduce them, and assuming no recession, these surpluses are projected to accumulate to $5 trillion between 2000 and 2010. Even if the social security surpluses are excluded, the budget surpluses will amount to about $3 trillion.

■ Options for the Surpluses

There are four main options for these surpluses, along with combinations of each. The main options are:

- Pay down the public debt.
- Reduce taxes.
- Increase government expenditures.
- Bolster the social security trust fund.

Pay Down the Public Debt

The Federal government could use its surpluses to pay down the public debt. As government bonds come due, the Federal government can pay them off and not reissue new bonds. Also, because Treasury bills, notes, and bonds are bought and sold daily in financial markets, the Federal government can reduce the public debt by simply purchasing government securities and retiring them.

Those who advocate using budget surpluses to pay down the public debt say that these actions will increase U.S. economic growth over the long run. The primary economic benefit from paying down the public debt is the reverse crowding-out effect, as previously mentioned. Assuming no change in the nation's supply of money, less government borrowing in the money market would reduce the real interest rate. This in turn would boost private investment spending and thus increase the stock of private capital in the economy. As we know, increases in capital per worker contribute to eco-

nomic growth. (Also, as explained in this chapter's Last Word, paying off the debt is likely to reduce the U.S. international trade deficit, which was $369 billion in 2000.)

Many economists, however, are less enthused about paying down the public debt. They doubt the alleged strength of the reverse crowding-out effect, arguing that government borrowing is just one of many determinants of interest rates. In this view, there is no particular urgency to pay down the public debt each year because with annual budget deficits in check, the debt and the interest payment on the public debt will both decline *as percentages of GDP.*

Critics of paying down the public debt also point out that the public debt plays a positive role in the economy. Government securities—Treasury bills, notes, and bonds and U.S. savings bonds—are important components of financial holdings of individuals, businesses, and state governments. When these securities are held to maturity (the date on which the principle is paid back), they are risk-free, and all but saving bonds can be bought and sold. Moreover, the social security trust fund exclusively holds U.S. securities. Finally, the critics remind us that the main instrument of monetary policy (open-market operations) is based on buying and selling U.S. securities. As currently constituted, those operations require that the Federal Reserve, commercial banks, and the non-bank public have U.S. securities available to buy and sell.

Reduce Taxes

A second option for dealing with budget surpluses is to cut tax rates. Proponents of this approach say that the surplus revenues came from taxpayers and should be returned to them. The most direct way to return this money is to reduce tax rates or eliminate certain taxes altogether. The Bush administration strongly advocates cutting income tax rates. Others suggest increasing tax deductions and tax credits to reduce the expense of elder care, child care, and so on. Still others want to repeal the Federal estate and capital gain taxes.

Those who support tax cuts fear that without such cuts the Federal government will spend the surpluses on new social and military programs. Tax cuts, they say, will "starve the Leviathan" and thus ensure that Federal government spending does not balloon along with the excess revenues. Also, tax reduction will increase disposable income, thereby ensuring that consumption spending will remain strong through the coming years. That will help protect the economy against recession.

Critics believe that a permanent reduction of tax rates or elimination of certain taxes is an inappropriate response to a potentially temporary increase in tax revenues. If prosperity gives way to recession, the surpluses may disappear. Moreover, say the critics, there are much better ways to use the surpluses, such as paying down the debt or bolstering the social security trust fund. They also point out that tax cuts may be premature from a fiscal policy perspective. Recent budget surpluses have escalated precisely because the economy has been growing so vigorously. Those surpluses therefore have served quite appropriately as automatic stabilizers. Although the economy has recently slowed, that slowing may be temporary. In the view of the critics, it would be prudent to wait and see where the economy is headed before rushing to cut taxes. Cutting taxes in the midst of a strong rebound in the economy would invite demand-pull inflation.

Increase Government Expenditures

People who support using the surpluses to increase Federal expenditures say there are a number of possible uses for the funds that would greatly benefit society and strengthen the economy over the long run. For example, one proposal is to spend part of the surpluses to add prescription drug coverage to Medicare. Another proposal is to undertake a massive effort to restore and upgrade a deteriorating infrastructure of such public capital as highways, bridges, air traffic control facilities, rail transit, school buildings, and textbooks. And, of course, there are many other proposals—about as many as the number of groups who would benefit from increased government spending.

Critics of using the surpluses to increase government spending say that, like tax cuts, increased spending would be inflationary. Moreover, such increases would tilt the allocation of resources away from the high-tech, high-productivity private sector and toward the less productive public sector, blunting the very economic growth that generated the surpluses in the first place. And because higher spending levels tend to get "institutionalized" into Federal budgets, the enlarged government spending would continue even if tax revenues later declined as the economy slowed or receded.

Bolster the Social Security Trust Fund

Social Security is currently sound, collecting more revenues from 135 million workers than it pays to 45 million beneficiaries. But the self-financing will end and the social security trust fund will be totally depleted in 2038 because of growing social security payments to retiring baby boomers. As shown in Figure 18.4, the problem is one of demographics. The percentage of the American population age 62 or over is rapidly rising. In 2000 there were three workers for each social security beneficiary; by 2040 there will be about two workers for every beneficiary.

The large budget surpluses projected over the 2000s could help solve the problem. It is argued that the Federal government should pay off a large part of the public debt and use the annual interest savings to boost the size of the social security trust fund. That way, no major social security tax hikes or benefit reductions would be needed during the period in which the number of retirees reaches its peak.

Combinations of Policies

There are, of course, endless combinations of these options. For example, the Federal government could use one-third of the budget surpluses for repayment

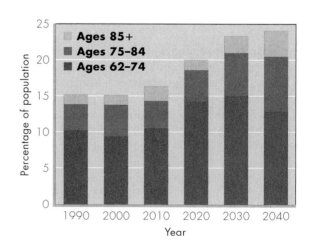

Figure 18.4

Percentage of the U.S. population age 62 or over.

The percentage of the population age 62 and over is projected to rise substantially over the next several decades, with the greatest increases occurring for those age 75 and older. This increase will strain the U.S. social security system.

Debt Reduction and the U.S. Trade Deficit

By Lowering Interest Rates, Paying Down the Public Debt Might Reduce the U.S. Trade Deficit.

In the past several years, the United States has had record high annual international trade (goods and services) deficits, both in absolute terms and as percentages of its GDP. For example, in 2000, the U.S. trade deficit was $369 billion, or 3.5 percent of GDP. To correct such trade deficits, the United States needs to boost its exports or decrease its imports.

Paying down all or part of the public debt might help do just that. Here's how: By paying down the public debt, the government would be refinancing less total debt each year. So it would not need to enter the money market to compete with the private sector for funds to the same extent as before. Real interest rates on both U.S. government and private securities therefore would fall, making financial investment in the United States less attractive to foreigners.

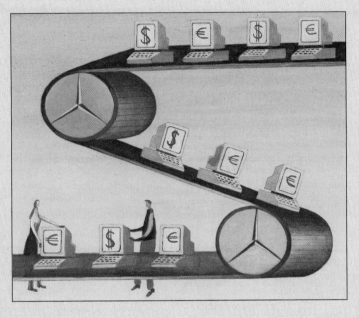

In selling their lower-yielding U.S. securities, foreigners receive U.S. dollars. This increases the worldwide supply of dollars, and the dollar depreciates. That depreciation of the dollar will eventually increase U.S. exports and decrease U.S. imports, leading to a "more favorable" balance of trade.

Let's see how this comes about. We know that exchange rates link the price levels of the world's nations. When the value of the dollar falls—that is, as dollars become less expensive to foreigners—all U.S. goods become less expensive to foreign buyers. For example, a decrease in the value of the dollar from $1 = 1 euro to $1 = .8 euro reduces prices to Europeans (in the Euro Zone) of all U.S. goods by 20 percent. The U.S. product that formerly cost 1 euro now costs .8 euro. The Europeans will react by buying more U.S. goods, and U.S. exports will rise. Conversely, at the lower exchange rate Americans get .8 rather than 1 euro for a dollar, so European goods are more expensive to people in the United States. They buy fewer Euro Zone goods, and U.S. imports fall. Bringing these together, U.S. net exports (exports minus imports) rise and the U.S. trade deficit shrinks.

There are a number of additional effects. First, the outflow of foreign funds diminishes available funds in the United States and prevents U.S. real interest rates from falling as much as they would otherwise. This dampens the effects just discussed.

Second, lower real interest rates in the United States reduce the burden on heavily indebted developing countries such as Mexico and Russia. Their dollar-denominated debts to banks and international agencies, in effect, go down, since the dollar depreciation that results means they need a smaller amount of their own currencies (pesos, rubles) to pay interest and principal on their debts. Also, any refinancing of their debts means lower real interest rates.

A trade deficit means that a nation is not exporting enough to pay for its imports. The difference can be paid for either by borrowing from abroad or by selling assets. By paying down its pubic debt and lowering real interest rates, the United States would have to do less of both. Because of reduced trade deficits, its debt from abroad would shrink, and it would have to sell off fewer assets such as factories, shopping centers, and farms to foreign investors.

Finally, real interest rates are but one of a number of independent determinants of exchange rates, and exchange rates are but one of several independent determinants of trade flows. So unforeseen changes in other factors could easily overwhelm the effects of lower real interest rates on the U.S. trade deficit.

of the debt, one-third to increase government expenditures, and one-third to reduce taxes. Or half could be used to cut taxes and half used to add to the social security trust fund. Different perspectives on what is best for society—or best for one's political constituents—will play a prominent role in the final decisions. In any event, the "problem" of deciding what to do with large budget surpluses is a more pleasant problem for society than was the problem of coping with large budget deficits.

QUICK REVIEW 18.3

▪ The borrowing and interest payments associated with the public debt may (a) increase income inequality, (b) require higher taxes, which dampen incentives, and (c) impede the growth of the nation's capital stock through crowding out of private investment.

▪ Over the past decade, the Federal budget has moved from high annual deficits to high annual surpluses.

▪ The main options for using the budget surpluses are to (a) pay down the public debt, (b) cut tax rates or eliminate certain taxes, (c) increase government expenditures, and (d) bolster the social security trust fund.

SUMMARY

1. A budget deficit is the excess of government expenditures over receipts. A budget surplus is an excess of government revenues over expenditures. The public debt is the total accumulation of the government's deficits (minus surpluses) over time and consists of Treasury bills, Treasury notes, Treasury bonds, and U.S. savings bonds.

2. Among the various budget philosophies are the annually balanced budget, the cyclically balanced budget, and functional finance. The basic problem with an annually balanced budget is that it promotes swings in the business cycle rather than counters them. Similarly, it may be difficult to balance the budget over the course of the business cycle if upswings and downswings are not of roughly comparable magnitude. Functional finance is the view that the primary purpose of Federal finance is to stabilize the economy and that problems associated with consequent deficits or surpluses are of secondary importance.

3. Historically, the growth of the public debt has resulted from deficit financing of wars; revenue declines during recessions; and tax-rate reductions, unaccompanied by reduced government spending.

4. In 2000 the U.S. public debt was $5.6 trillion, or $20,441 per person. The public (here including banks and state and local governments) holds 63 percent of that debt, while the Federal Reserve and Federal agencies hold the other 37 percent. In the 1980s and early 1990s, the public debt increased sharply as a percentage of GDP. In more recent years, that percentage has substantially declined. Interest payments as a percentage of GDP were about 2.2 percent in 2000.

5. The concern that a large public debt may bankrupt the government is a false worry because (a) the debt needs only be refinanced rather than refunded and (b) the Federal government has the power to increase taxes to make interest payments on the debt.

6. The crowding-out effect aside, the public debt is not a vehicle for shifting economic burdens to future generations. In general, Americans inherit not only the public debt (a liability) but also the U.S. securities (an asset) that finance the debt.

7. More substantive problems associated with public debt include the following: (a) Payment of interest on the debt may increase income inequality. (b) Interest payments on the debt require higher taxes, which may impair incentives. (c) Paying interest or principal on the portion of the debt held by foreigners means a transfer of real output to abroad. (d) Government borrowing to refinance or pay interest on the debt may increase interest rates and crowd out private investment spending, leaving future generations with a smaller stock of capital than they would have otherwise.

8. The increase in investment in public capital that may result from debt financing may partly or wholly offset the crowding-out effect of the public debt on private investment. Also, the added public investment may stimulate private investment, if the two are complements.

9. The large Federal budget deficits of the 1980s and early 1990s prompted Congress in 1993 to increase tax rates and limit government spending. As a result of these policies, along with a very rapid and pro-

longed economic expansion, the deficits dwindled to $22 billion in 1997. Large budget surpluses occurred in 1999, 2000, and 2001. In 2001 the Congressional Budget Office projected that $5 trillion of annual budget surpluses would accumulate between 2000 and 2010.

10. The large actual and projected budget surpluses of the 2000s set off a policy debate over what to do with them. The main options are (a) pay down the public debt, (b) reduce tax rates or eliminate some taxes altogether, (c) increase government spending, and (d) bolster the social security trust fund. Various combinations of these policies also are options.

TERMS AND CONCEPTS

public debt
U.S. securities
annually balanced budget

cyclically balanced
budget

functional finance
social security trust fund

external public debt
public investments

STUDY QUESTIONS

1. **Key Question** Assess the leeway for using fiscal policy as a stabilization tool under (a) an annually balanced budget, (b) a cyclically balanced budget, and (c) functional finance.

2. What have been the three major sources of the public debt historically? Why were annual deficits so large in the 1980s? Why did the deficit rise sharply in 1991 and 1992? What explains the large budget surpluses of the late 1990s and early 2000s?

3. **Key Question** What are the two main ways the size of the public debt is measured? Distinguish between refinancing the debt and retiring the debt. How does an internally held public debt differ from an externally held public debt? Contrast the effects of retiring an internally held debt and retiring an externally held debt.

4. True or false? If the statement is false, explain why:
   a. An internally held public debt is like a debt of the left hand to the right hand.
   b. The Federal Reserve and Federal government agencies hold more than half the public debt.
   c. The U.S. public debt was smaller in percentage terms in 2000 than it was in 1990.
   d. In recent years, social security payments have exceeded social security tax revenues.

5. Why might economists be quite concerned if the annual interest payments on the debt sharply increased as a percentage of GDP?

6. Do you think that paying off the public debt would increase or decrease income inequality? Explain.

7. **Key Question** Trace the cause-and-effect chain through which financing and refinancing of the

public debt might affect real interest rates, private investment, the stock of capital, and economic growth. How might investment in public capital and complementarities between public capital and private capital alter the outcome of the cause-effect chain?

8. Relate the Laffer Curve (Figure 16.10, page 318) to the Deficit Reduction Act of 1993 and its effect on U.S. budget deficits.

9. What role do the components of the public debt play in the day-to-day conduct of monetary policy?

10. What are the broad policy options for eliminating the large budget surpluses projected for the 2000s? If you were forced to choose only one of the options, which would it be? Explain your choice.

11. **(Last Word)** Explain how a substantial reduction of the public debt could greatly reduce the U.S. trade deficit.

12. **Web-Based Question: *The debt—to the penny*** Go to the website of the Department of Treasury, Bureau of the Public Debt, at www.publicdebt.treas. gov/opd/opdpenny.htm and find the amount of the public debt, to the penny, as of the latest date. How does it compare to the debt of 10 years ago? What has been the trend over the past 12 months?

13. **Web-Based Question: *Frequently asked questions about the public debt*** Visit the U.S. Treasury's "Public Debt Frequently Asked Questions" (FAQ) site, www.publicdebt.treas.gov/opd/opdfaq.htm, and answer the following questions: Why does the public debt sometimes go down? Why does the public debt change only once a day? As of today, who owns the public debt?

CHAPTER 19

Disputes over Macro Theory and Policy

A S   A N Y   A C A D E M I C discipline evolves, it naturally evokes a number of internal disagreements. Economics is no exception. In this chapter we examine a few alternative perspectives on macro theory and policy. After contrasting classical and Keynesian theories, we turn to recent disagreements on three inter-related questions: (1) What causes instability in the economy? (2) Is the economy self-correcting? (3) Should government adhere to *rules* or use *discretion* in setting economic policy?

▌Some History: Classical Economics and Keynes

Classical economics began with Adam Smith in 1776 and dominated economic thinking until the 1930s. It holds that full employment is the norm in a market economy and therefore a laissez-faire ("let it be") policy by government is best. Then, in the 1930s, John Maynard Keynes asserted that laissez-faire cap-italism is subject to recurring recessions that bring widespread unemployment. In the Keynesian view, active government policy is required to stabilize the economy and to prevent valuable resources from standing idle.

Let's compare these two views through modern aggregate demand and aggregate supply analysis.

The Classical View

In the **classical view,** the aggregate supply curve is vertical and is the sole determinant of the level of real output. The downsloping aggregate demand curve is stable and is the sole determinant of the price level.

Vertical Aggregate Supply Curve   Accord-ing to the classical perspective, the aggregate supply curve is a vertical line, as shown in Figure 19.1a. This line is located at the full-employment level of real output, which in this designation is also the full-capacity real GDP. According to the classical economists, the economy will operate at its full-employ-ment level of output, Q_f, because of (1) Say's law

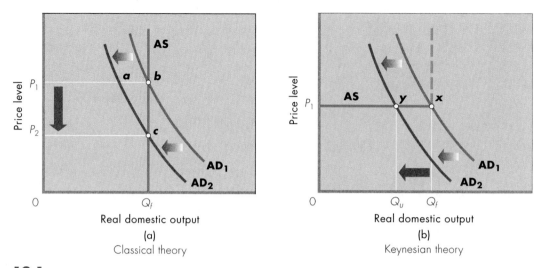

Figure 19.1

Classical and Keynesian views of the macroeconomy. (a) In classical theory, aggregate supply determines the full-employment level of real output, while aggregate demand establishes the price level. Aggregate demand normally is stable, but if it should decline, say, from AD_1 to AD_2, the price level will quickly fall from P_1 to P_2 to eliminate the temporary excess supply of ab and to restore full employment at c. (b) The Keynesian view is that aggregate demand is unstable and that prices and wages are downwardly inflexible. An AD_1 to AD_2 decline in aggregate demand has no effect on the price level. Instead, the economy moves from point x to y and real output falls to Q_u, where it can remain indefinitely.

(Last Word, Chapter 9) and (2) responsive, flexible prices and wages.

We stress that classical economists believed that Q_f does not change in response to changes in the price level. Observe that as the price level falls from P_1 to P_2 in Figure 19.1a, real output remains anchored at Q_f.

But this stability of output is at odds with the upsloping supply curves for individual products that we discussed in Chapter 3. There we found that lower prices would make production less profitable and would cause producers to offer less output and employ fewer workers. The classical response to this view is that input costs would fall along with product prices and leave real profits and output unchanged.

Consider a one-firm economy in which the firm's owner must receive a real profit of $20 in order to produce the full-employment output of 100 units. You know from Chapter 8 that what ultimately counts is the real reward the owner receives and not the level of prices. Assume that the owner's only input (aside from entrepreneurial talent) is 10 units of labor hired at $8 per worker for a total wage cost of $80 (= 10 × $8). Also assume that the 100 units of output sell for $1 per unit. So total revenue is $100 (= 100 × $1). Now the firm's nominal profit is $20 (= $100 − $80), and, using the $1 price to designate

the base price index of 100 percent, its real profit is also $20 (= $20 ÷ 1.00). Well and good; full employment is achieved. But suppose the price level declines by one-half. Would the owner still earn the $20 of real profit needed to support production of a 100-unit full-employment output?

The classical answer is yes. Once the product price has dropped to 50 cents, total revenue will be only $50 (= 100 × 50¢). But the cost of 10 units of labor will be reduced to $40 (= 10 × $4) because the wage rate will be halved. Although nominal profit falls to $10 (= $50 − $40), real profit remains at $20. By dividing the money profit of $10 by the new price index (expressed as a decimal), we obtain real profit of $20 (= $10 ÷ .50).

With perfectly flexible wages there would be no change in the real rewards and therefore in the production decisions of businesses. A change in the price level will not cause the economy to stray from full employment.

Stable Aggregate Demand   Classical economists theorize that money underlies aggregate demand. The amount of real output that can be purchased depends on (1) the quantity of money households and businesses possess and (2) the purchasing power of that money as determined by the price level. The purchasing power of the dollar refers to the real quantity of goods and services a dollar will buy. Thus, as we move down the vertical axis of Figure 19.1a, the price level is falling. This means that the purchasing power of each dollar is rising. If the price level were to fall by one-half, a certain quantity of money would then purchase a real output twice as large. With a fixed money supply, the price level and real output are inversely related.

What about the location of the aggregate demand curve? According to the classical economists, aggregate demand will be stable as long as the nation's monetary authorities maintain a constant supply of money. With a fixed aggregate supply of output, increases in the supply of money will shift the aggregate demand curve rightward and spark demand-pull inflation. Reductions in the supply of money will shift the curve leftward and trigger deflation. The key to price-level stability, then, is to control the nation's money supply to prevent unwarranted shifts in aggregate demand.

Even if there are declines in the money supply and therefore in aggregate demand, the economy depicted in Figure 19.1a will not experience unemployment. Admittedly, the immediate effect of a decline in aggregate demand from AD_1 to AD_2 is an excess supply of output, since the aggregate output of goods and services exceeds aggregate spending by the amount ab. But, with the presumed downward flexibility of product and resource prices, that excess supply will reduce product prices along with workers' wages and the prices of other inputs. As a result, the price level will quickly decline from P_1 to P_2 until the amounts of output demanded and supplied are brought once again into equilibrium, this time at c. While the price level has fallen from P_1 to P_2, real output remains at the full-employment level.

The Keynesian View

The heart of the **Keynesian view** is that product prices and wages are downwardly inflexible over very long time periods. The result is graphically represented as a horizontal aggregate supply curve. Also, aggregate demand is subject to periodic changes caused by changes in the determinants of aggregate demand.

Horizontal Aggregate Supply Curve (to Full-Employment Output)

The downward inflexibility of prices and wages presumed by the Keynesians translates to a horizontal aggregate supply curve, as shown in Figure 19.1b. Here, a decline

in real output from Q_f to Q_u will have no impact on the price level. Nor will an increase in real output from Q_u to Q_f. The aggregate supply curve therefore extends from zero real output rightward to point x, where real output is at its full-employment level, Q_f. Once full employment is reached, the aggregate supply curve becomes vertical. The dashed line extending upward from the horizontal aggregate supply curve at x shows this.

Unstable Aggregate Demand Keynesian economists view aggregate demand as unstable from one period to the next, even without changes in the money supply. In particular, the investment component of aggregate demand fluctuates, altering the location of the aggregate demand curve. Suppose aggregate demand in Figure 19.1b declines from AD_1 to AD_2. The sole impact is on output and employment. Real output falls from Q_f to Q_u, but the price level remains unchanged at P_1. Moreover, Keynesians believe that unless there is an offsetting increase in aggregate demand, real output may remain at Q_u, which is below the full-employment level Q_f. Active government policies to increase aggregate demand are essential to move the economy from point y to point x. Otherwise, the economy will suffer the wastes of recession and depression. **(Key Question 1)**

QUICK REVIEW 19.1

■ In classical macroeconomics, the aggregate supply curve is vertical at the full-employment level of real output, and the aggregate demand curve is stable as long as the money supply is constant.

■ In Keynesian macroeconomics, the aggregate supply curve is horizontal up to the full-employment level of output; then it becomes vertical. The aggregate demand curve is unstable largely because of the volatility of investment spending; such shifts cause either recession or demand-pull inflation.

▌ What Causes Macro Instability?

As earlier chapters have indicated, capitalist economies experienced considerable instability during the twentieth century. The United States, for example, experienced the Great Depression, numerous recessions, and periods of inflation. Contemporary economists have different perspectives on why this instability occurs.

Mainstream View

For simplicity, we will use the term "mainstream view" to characterize the prevailing macroeconomic perspective of the majority of economists. According to that view, which retains a Keynesian flavor, instability in the economy arises from two sources: (1) significant changes in investment spending, which change aggregate demand, and, occasionally, (2) adverse aggregate supply shocks, which change aggregate supply. Although these factors are not new to you, let's quickly review them.

Changes in Investment Spending

Mainstream macroeconomics focuses on aggregate spending and its components. Recall that the basic equation underlying aggregate expenditures is

$$C_a + I_g + X_n + G = \text{GDP}$$

That is, the aggregate amount of after-tax consumption, gross investment, net exports, and government spending determines the total amount of goods and services produced and sold. In equilibrium, $C_a + I_g + X_n + G$ (aggregate expenditures) is equal to GDP (real output). A decrease in the price level increases equilibrium GDP and thus allows us to trace out a downsloping aggregate demand curve for the economy. Any change in one of the spending components in the aggregate expenditures equation shifts the aggregate demand curve. This, in turn, changes equilibrium real output, the price level, or both.

Investment spending, in particular, is subject to wide "booms" and "busts." Significant increases in investment spending get multiplied into even greater increases in aggregate demand and thus can produce demand-pull inflation. In contrast, significant declines in investment spending get multiplied into even greater decreases in aggregate demand and thus can cause recessions.

Adverse Aggregate Supply Shocks

In the mainstream view, the second source of macroeconomic instability arises on the supply side. Occasionally, such external events as wars or an artificial supply restriction of a key resource can boost resource prices and significantly raise per-unit production costs. The result is a sizable decline in a nation's aggregate supply, which destabilizes the economy by simultaneously causing cost-push inflation and recession.

Monetarist View

Classical economics has emerged in several modern forms. One is **monetarism,** which (1) focuses on the money supply, (2) holds that markets are highly competitive, and (3) says that a competitive market system gives the economy a high degree of macroeconomic stability. Like classical economists, monetarists argue that the price and wage flexibility provided by competitive markets would cause fluctuations in aggregate demand to alter product and resource prices rather than output and employment. Thus the market system would provide substantial macroeconomic stability *were it not for government interference in the economy.* 🔑 **19.1**

The problem, as monetarists see it, is that government has promoted downward wage inflexibility through the minimum-wage law, pro-union legislation, guaranteed prices for certain farm products, pro-business monopoly legislation, and so forth. The free-market system is capable of providing macroeconomic stability, but, despite good intentions, government interference has undermined that capability. Moreover, monetarists say that government has contributed to the economy's business cycles through its clumsy and mistaken attempts to achieve greater stability through its monetary policies.

Equation of Exchange

The fundamental equation of monetarism is the **equation of exchange:**

$$MV = PQ$$

where M is the supply of money; V is the **velocity** of money, that is, *the average number of times per year a dollar is spent on final goods and services;* P is the price level or, more specifically, the average price at which each unit of physical output is sold; and Q is the physical volume of all goods and services produced.

The left side of the equation of exchange, MV, represents the total amount spent by purchasers of output, while the right side, PQ, represents the total amount received by sellers of that output. The nation's money supply (M) multiplied by the number of times it is spent each year (V) must equal the nation's nominal GDP ($= P \times Q$). The dollar value of total spending has to equal the dollar value of total output. 🔑 **19.2**

Stable Velocity

Monetarists say that velocity, V, in the equation of exchange is stable. To them, "stable" is not synonymous with "constant," however.

Monetarists are aware that velocity is higher today than it was several decades ago. Shorter pay periods, widespread use of credit cards, and faster means of making payments enable people to hold less money and to turn it over more rapidly than was possible in earlier times. These factors have enabled people to reduce their holdings of cash and checkbook money relative to the size of the nation's nominal GDP.

When monetarists say that velocity is stable, they mean that the factors altering velocity change gradually and predictably and that changes in velocity from one year to the next can be readily anticipated. Moreover, they hold that velocity does not change in response to changes in the money supply itself. Instead, people have a stable desire to hold money relative to holding other financial assets, holding real assets, and buying current output. The factors that determine the amount of money the public wants to hold depend mainly on the level of nominal GDP.

Example: Assume that when the level of nominal GDP is $400 billion, the public desires $100 billion of money to purchase that output. That means that V is 4 (= $400 billion of nominal GDP/$100 billion of money). If we further assume that the actual supply of money is $100 billion, the economy is in equilibrium with respect to money; the actual amount of money supplied equals the amount the public wants to hold.

If velocity is stable, the equation of exchange suggests that there is a predictable relationship between the money supply and nominal GDP (= PQ). An increase in the money supply of, say, $10 billion would upset equilibrium in our example, since the public would find itself holding more money or liquidity than it wants. That is, the actual amount of money held ($110 billion) would exceed the amount of holdings desired ($100 billion). In that case, the reaction of the public (households and businesses) is to restore its desired balance of money relative to other items, such as stocks and bonds, factories and equipment, houses and automobiles, and clothing and toys. But the spending of money by individual households and businesses would leave more cash in the checkable deposits or billfolds of other households and firms. And they too would try to "spend down" their excess cash balances. But, overall, the $110 billion supply of money cannot be spent down because a dollar spent is a dollar received.

Instead, the collective attempt to reduce cash balances increases aggregate demand, thereby boosting nominal GDP. Because velocity in our example is 4—that is, the dollar is spent, on average, four times per year—nominal GDP rises from $400 billion to $440 billion. At that higher nominal GDP, the money supply of $110 billion equals the amount of money desired ($440 billion/4 = $110 billion), and equilibrium is reestablished.

The $10 billion increase in the money supply thus eventually increases nominal GDP by $40 billion. Spending on goods, services, and assets expands until nominal GDP has gone up enough to restore the original 4-to-1 equilibrium relationship between nominal GDP and the money supply.

Note that the relationship GDP/M defines V. A stable relationship between nominal GDP and M means a stable V. And a change in M causes a proportionate change in nominal GDP. Thus, changes in the money supply allegedly have a predictable effect on nominal GDP (= $P \times Q$). An increase in M increases P or Q, or some combination of both; a decrease in M reduces P or Q, or some combination of both. **(Key Question 4)**

Monetary Causes of Instability

Monetarists say that inappropriate monetary policy is the single most important cause of macroeconomic instability. An increase in the money supply directly increases aggregate demand. Under conditions of full employment, that rise in aggregate demand raises the price level. For a time, higher prices cause firms to increase their real output, and the rate of unemployment falls below its natural rate. But once nominal wages rise to reflect the higher prices and thus to restore real wages, real output moves back to its full-employment level and the unemployment rate returns to its natural rate. The inappropriate increase in the money supply leads to inflation, together with instability of real output and employment.

Conversely, a decrease in the money supply reduces aggregate demand. Real output temporarily falls, and the unemployment rate rises above its natural rate. Eventually, nominal wages fall and real output returns to its full-employment level. The inappropriate decline in the money supply leads to deflation, together with instability of real GDP and employment.

The contrast between mainstream macroeconomics and monetarism on the causes of instability thus comes into sharp focus. Mainstream economists view the instability of investment as the main cause of the economy's instability. They see monetary policy as a stabilizing factor. Changes in the money supply raise or lower interest rates as needed, smooth out swings in investment, and thus reduce macroeconomic instability. In contrast, monetarists view changes in the money supply as the main cause of instability in the economy. For example, they say that the Great Depression occurred largely because the Fed allowed the money supply to fall by nearly 40 percent during that period. According to Milton Friedman, a prominent monetarist:

> And [the money supply] fell not because there were no willing borrowers—not because the horse would not drink. It fell because the Federal Reserve System forced or permitted a sharp reduction in the [money supply], because it failed to exercise the responsibilities assigned to it in the Federal Reserve Act to provide liquidity to the banking system. The Great Contraction is tragic testimony to the power of monetary policy—not, as Keynes and so many of his contemporaries believed, evidence of its impotence.[1]

Real-Business-Cycle View

A third modern view of the cause of macroeconomic instability is that business cycles are caused by real factors that affect aggregate supply rather than by monetary, or spending, factors that cause fluctuations in aggregate demand. In the **real-business-cycle theory,** business fluctuations result from significant changes in technology and resource availability. Those changes affect productivity and thus the long-run growth trend of aggregate supply.

An example focusing on recession will clarify this thinking. Suppose productivity (output per worker) declines sharply because of a large increase in oil prices, which makes it prohibitively expensive to operate certain types of machinery. That decline in productivity implies a reduction in the economy's ability to produce real output. The result would be a decrease in the economy's long-run aggregate supply curve, as represented by the leftward shift from AS_{LR1} to AS_{LR2} in Figure 19.2.

As real output falls from Q_1 to Q_2, the public needs less money to buy the reduced volume of goods and services. So the demand for money falls. Moreover, the slowdown in business activity means that businesses need to borrow less from banks, reducing the part of the money supply created by banks through their lending. Thus, the supply of

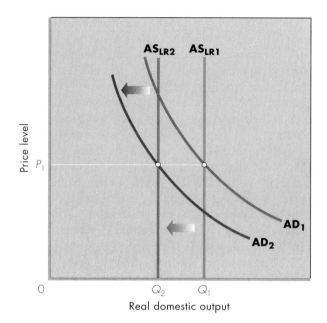

Figure 19.2

The real-business-cycle theory.   In the real-business-cycle theory, a decline in resource availability shifts the nation's long-run aggregate supply curve to the left from AS_{LR1} to AS_{LR2}. The decline in real output from Q_1 to Q_2, in turn, reduces money demand (less is needed) and money supply (fewer loans are taken out) such that aggregate demand shifts leftward from AD_1 to AD_2. The result is a recession in which the price level remains constant.

money also falls. In this controversial scenario, changes in the supply of money respond to changes in the demand for money. The decline in the money supply then reduces aggregate demand, as from AD_1 to AD_2 in Figure 19.2. The outcome is a decline in real output from Q_1 to Q_2, with no change in the price level.

Conversely, a large increase in aggregate supply (not shown) caused by, say, major innovations in the production process would shift the long-run aggregate supply curve rightward. Real output would increase, and money demand and money supply would both increase. Aggregate demand would shift rightward by an amount equal to the rightward shift of long-run aggregate supply. Real output would increase, without driving up the price level.

Conclusion: In the real-business-cycle theory, macro instability arises on the aggregate supply side of the economy, not on the aggregate demand side, as mainstream economists and monetarists usually claim.

[1]Milton Friedman, *The Optimum Quantity of Money and Other Essays* (Chicago: Aldine, 1969), p. 97.

Coordination Failures

A fourth and final modern view of macroeconomic instability relates to so-called **coordination failures.** Such failures occur when people fail to reach a mutually beneficial equilibrium because they lack a way to coordinate their actions.

Noneconomic Example   Consider first a noneconomic example. Suppose you learn of an impending informal party at a nearby beach, although it looks as though it might rain. If you expect others to be there, you will decide to go. If you expect that others will not go, you will decide to stay home. There are several possible equilibrium outcomes, depending on the mix of people's expectations. Let's consider just two. If each person assumes that all the others will be at the party, all will go. The party will occur and presumably everyone will have a good time. But if each person assumes that everyone else will stay home, all will stay home and there will be no party. When the party does not take place, even though all would be better off if it did take place, a coordination failure has occurred.

Macroeconomic Example   Now let's apply this example to macroeconomic instability, specifically recession. Suppose that individual firms and households expect other firms and consumers to cut back their investment and consumption spending. As a result, each firm and household will anticipate a reduction of aggregate demand. Firms therefore will cut back their own investment spending, since they will anticipate that their future production capacity will be excessive. Households will also reduce their own spending (increase their saving), because they anticipate that they will experience reduced work hours, possible layoffs, and falling incomes in the future.

Aggregate demand will indeed decline and the economy will indeed experience a recession in response to what amounts to a self-fulfilling prophecy. Moreover, the economy will stay at a below-full-employment level of output because, once there, producers and households have no individual incentive to increase spending. If all producers and households would agree to increase their investment and consumption spending simultaneously, then aggregate demand would rise, and real output and real income would increase. Each producer and each consumer would be better off. However, this outcome does not occur because there is no mechanism for

firms and households to agree on such a joint spending increase.

In this case, the economy is stuck in an *unemployment equilibrium* because of a coordination failure. With a different set of expectations, a coordination failure might leave the economy in an *inflation equilibrium.* In this view, there are a number of such potential equilibrium positions in the economy, some good and some bad, depending on people's mix of expectations. Macroeconomic instability, then, reflects the movement of the economy from one such equilibrium position to another as expectations change.

■ Does the Economy "Self-Correct"?

Just as there are disputes over the causes of macroeconomic instability, there are disputes over whether or not the economy will correct itself when instability does occur. And economists also disagree on how long it will take for any such self-correction to take place.

New Classical View of Self-Correction

New classical economists tend to be either monetarists or adherents of **rational expectations theory:** *the idea that businesses, consumers, and workers expect changes in policies or circumstances to have certain effects* *on the economy and, in pursuing their own self-interest, take actions to make sure those changes affect them as little as possible.* The **new classical economics** holds that when the economy occasionally diverges from its full-employment output, internal mechanisms within the economy will automatically move it back to that output. Policymakers should stand back and let the automatic correction occur, rather than engaging in active fiscal and monetary policy. This perspective is that associated with the vertical long-run Phillips Curve, which we discussed in Chapter 16. 🔑 **19.3**

Graphical Analysis Figure 19.3a relates the new classical analysis to the question of self-correction. Specifically, an increase in aggregate demand, say, from AD_1 to AD_2, moves the economy upward along its short-run aggregate supply curve AS_1 from a to b. The price level rises and real output increases. In the long run, however, nominal wages rise to restore real wages. Per-unit production costs then increase, and the short-run aggregate supply curve shifts leftward, eventually from AS_1 to AS_2. The economy moves from b to c, and real output returns to its full-employment level, Q_1. This level of output is dictated by the economy's vertical long-run aggregate supply curve, AS_{LR}.

Conversely, a decrease in aggregate demand from AD_1 to AD_3 in Figure 19.3b first moves the economy downward along its short-run aggregate supply curve AS_1 from point a to d. The price level declines, as does the level of real output. But in the long run, nominal wages decline such that real wages fall to their previous levels. When that happens, per-unit production costs decline and the short-run aggregate supply curve shifts to the right, eventually from AS_1 to AS_3. The economy moves back to e, where it again achieves its full-employment level, Q_1. As in Figure 19.3a, the economy in Figure 19.3b has automatically self-corrected to its full-employment output and its natural rate of unemployment.

Speed of Adjustment There is some disagreement among new classical economists on how long it will take for self-correction to occur. Monetarists usually hold the *adaptive* expectations view that people form their expectations on the basis of present realities and only gradually change their expectations as experience unfolds. This means that the shifts in the short-run aggregate supply curves shown in Figure 19.3 may not occur for 2 or 3 years or even longer. Other new classical economists, however, accept the rational expectations assumption that workers anticipate some future outcomes before they oc-

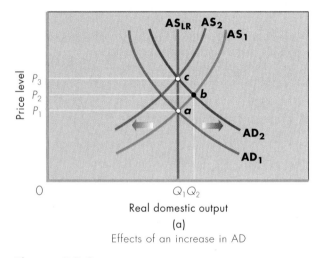

(a)
Effects of an increase in AD

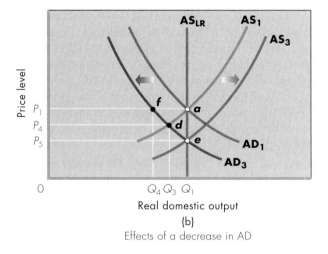

(b)
Effects of a decrease in AD

Figure 19.3

New classical view of self-correction. (a) An unanticipated increase in aggregate demand from AD_1 to AD_2 first moves the economy from a to b. The economy then self-corrects to c. An anticipated increase in aggregate demand moves the economy directly from a to c. (b) An unanticipated decrease in aggregate demand from AD_1 to AD_3 moves the economy from a to d. The economy then self-corrects to e. An anticipated decrease in aggregate demand moves the economy directly from a to e. (Mainstream economists, however, say that if the price level remains at P_1, the economy will move from a to f, and even if the price level falls to P_2, the economy may remain at d because of downward wage inflexibility.)

cur. When price-level changes are fully anticipated, adjustments of nominal wages are very quick or even instantaneous. Let's see why.

Although several new theories, including Keynesian ones, incorporate rational expectations, our interest here is the new classical version of the rational expectations theory (hereafter, RET). RET is based on two assumptions:

- People behave rationally, gathering and intelligently processing information to form expectations about things that are economically important to them. They adjust those expectations quickly as new developments affecting future economic outcomes occur. Where there is adequate information, people's beliefs about future economic outcomes accurately reflect the likelihood that those outcomes will occur. For example, if it is clear that a certain policy will cause inflation, people will recognize that fact and adjust their economic behavior in anticipation of inflation.

- Like classical economists, RET economists assume that all product and resource markets are highly competitive and that prices and wages are flexible both upward and downward. But the RET economists go further, assuming that new information is quickly (in some cases, instantaneously) taken into account in the demand and supply curves of such markets. The upshot is that equilibrium prices and quantities adjust rapidly to unforeseen events—say, technological change or aggregate supply shocks. They adjust instantaneously to events that have known outcomes—for example, changes in fiscal or monetary policy.

Unanticipated Price-Level Changes The implication of RET is not only that the economy is self-correcting but that self-correction occurs quickly. In this thinking, unanticipated changes in the price level—so-called **price-level surprises**—do cause temporary changes in real output. Suppose, for example, that an unanticipated increase in foreign demand for U.S. goods increases U.S. aggregate demand from AD_1 to AD_2 in Figure 19.3a. The immediate result is an unexpected increase in the price level from P_1 to P_2.

But now an interesting question arises. If wages and prices are flexible, as assumed in RET, why doesn't the higher price level immediately cause nominal wages to rise, such that there is no increase in real output at all? Why does the economy temporar-

ily move from point a to b along AS_1? In RET, firms increase output from Q_1 to Q_2 because of misperceptions about rising prices of their own products relative to the prices of other products (and to the prices of labor). They mistakenly think the higher prices of their own products have resulted from increased demand for those products relative to the demands for other products. Expecting higher profits, they increase their own production. But in fact *all* prices, including the price of labor (nominal wages), are rising because of the general increase in aggregate demand. Once firms see that *all* prices and wages are rising, they decrease their production to previous levels.

In terms of Figure 19.3a, the increase in nominal wages shifts the short-run aggregate supply curve leftward, ultimately from AS_1 to AS_2, and the economy moves from b to c. Thus, the increase in real output caused by the price-level surprise corrects itself.

The same analysis in reverse applies to an unanticipated price-level decrease. In the economy represented by Figure 19.3b, firms misperceive that the prices of their own products are falling due to decreases in the demand for those products relative to other products. They anticipate declines in profit and cut production. As a result of their collective actions, real output in the economy falls. But seeing that all prices and wages are dropping, firms increase their output to prior levels. The short-run aggregate supply curve in Figure 19.3b shifts rightward from AS_1 to AS_3, and the economy "self-corrects" by moving from d to e.

Fully Anticipated Price-Level Changes In RET, fully *anticipated* price-level changes do not change real output, even for short periods. In Figure 19.3a, again consider the increase in aggregate demand from AD_1 to AD_2. Businesses immediately recognize that the higher prices being paid for their products are part of the inflation they had anticipated. They understand that the same forces that are causing the inflation result in higher nominal wages, leaving their profits unchanged. The economy therefore moves directly from a to c. The price level rises as expected, and output remains at its full-employment level Q_1.

Similarly, a fully *anticipated* price-level decrease will leave real output unchanged. Firms conclude that nominal wages are declining by the same percentage amount as the declining price level, leaving profits unchanged. The economy represented by Figure 19.3b therefore moves directly from a to e.

Deflation occurs, but the economy continues to produce its full-employment output Q_1. The anticipated decline in aggregate demand causes no change in real output. **!** 19.1

Mainstream View of Self-Correction

Almost all economists acknowledge that the new classical economists have made significant contributions to the theory of aggregate supply. In fact, mainstream economists have incorporated some aspects of RET into their own more detailed models. However, most economists strongly disagree with RET on the question of downward price and wage flexibility. While the stock market, foreign exchange market, and certain commodity markets experience day-to-day or minute-to-minute price changes, including price declines, that is not true of many product markets and most labor markets. There is ample evidence, say mainstream economists, that many prices and wages are inflexible downward for long periods. As a result, it may take years for the economy to move from recession back to full-employment output, unless it gets help from fiscal and monetary policy.

Graphical Analysis

To understand this mainstream view, again examine Figure 19.3b. Suppose aggregate demand declines from AD_1 to AD_3 because of a significant decline in investment spending. If the price level remains at P_1, the economy will not move from a to d to e, as suggested by RET. Instead, the economy will move from a to f, as if it were moving along a horizontal aggregate supply curve between those two points. Real output will decline from its full-employment level, Q_1, to the recessionary level, Q_4.

But let's assume that surpluses in product markets eventually cause the price level to fall to P_4. Will this lead to the decline in nominal wages needed to shift aggregate supply from AS_1 to AS_2, as suggested by the new classical economists? "Highly unlikely" say mainstream economists. Even more so than prices, nominal wages tend to be inflexible downward. If nominal wages do not decline in response to the decline in the price level, then the short-run aggregate supply curve will not shift rightward. The self-correction mechanism assumed by RET and new classical economists will break down. Instead, the economy will remain at d, experiencing less-than-full-employment output and a high rate of unemployment.

Downward Wage Inflexibility

In Chapter 11 we discussed several reasons why firms may not be able to, or may not want to, lower nominal wages. Firms may not be able to cut wages because of wage contracts and the legal minimum wage. And firms may not want to lower wages if they fear potential problems with morale, effort, and efficiency.

While contracts are thought to be the main cause of wage rigidity, so-called efficiency wages and insider-outsider relationships may also play a role. Let's explore both.

Efficiency Wage Theory

Recall from Chapter 11 that an **efficiency wage** is a wage that minimizes the firm's labor cost per unit of output. Normally, we would think that the market wage is the efficiency wage since it is the lowest wage at which a firm can obtain a particular type of labor. But where the cost of supervising workers is high or where worker turnover is great, firms may discover that paying a wage that is higher than the market wage will lower their wage cost per unit of output.

Example: Suppose a firm's workers, on average, produce 8 units of output at a $9 market wage but 10 units of output at a $10 above-market wage. The efficiency wage is $10, not the $9 market wage. At the $10 wage, the labor cost per unit of output is only $1 (= $10 wage/10 units of output), compared with $1.12 (= $9 wage/8 units of output) at the $9 wage.

How can a higher wage result in greater efficiency?

- **Greater work effort** The above-market wage, in effect, raises the cost to workers of losing their jobs as a result of poor performance. Because workers have a strong incentive to retain their relatively high-paying jobs, they are more likely to provide greater work effort. Looked at differently, workers are more reluctant to shirk (neglect or avoid work) because the higher wage makes job loss more costly to them. Consequently, the above-market wage can be the efficient wage; it can enhance worker productivity so much that the higher wage more than pays for itself.

- **Lower supervision costs** With less incentive among workers to shirk, the firm needs fewer supervisory personnel to monitor work performance. This, too, can lower the firm's overall wage cost per unit of output.

- **Reduced job turnover** The above-market pay discourages workers from voluntarily leaving their jobs. The lower turnover rate reduces the firm's cost of hiring and training workers. It also gives the firm a more experienced, more productive workforce.

The key implication for macroeconomic instability is that efficiency wages add to the downward inflexibility of wages. Firms that pay efficiency wages will be reluctant to cut wages when aggregate demand declines, since such cuts may encourage shirking, require more supervisory personnel, and increase turnover. In other words, wage cuts that reduce productivity and raise per-unit labor costs are self-defeating. 🔎 **19.4**

Insider-Outsider Relationships

Other economists theorize that downward wage inflexibility may relate to relationships between "insiders" and "outsiders." Insiders are workers who retain employment even during recession. Outsiders are workers who have been laid off from a firm and unemployed workers who would like to work at that firm.

When recession produces layoffs and widespread unemployment, we might expect outsiders to offer to work for less than the current wage rate, in effect, bidding down wage rates. We might also expect firms to hire such workers in order to reduce their costs. But, according to the **insider-outsider theory,** outsiders may not be able to underbid existing wages because employers may view the nonwage cost of hiring them to be prohibitive. Employers might fear that insiders would view acceptance of such underbidding as undermining years of effort to increase wages or, worse, as "stealing" jobs. So insiders may refuse to cooperate with new workers who have undercut their pay. Where teamwork is critical for production, such lack of cooperation will reduce overall productivity and thereby lower the firms' profits.

Even if firms are willing to employ outsiders at less than the current wage, those workers might refuse to work for less than the existing wage. To do so might invite harassment from the insiders whose pay they have undercut. Thus, outsiders may remain unemployed, relying on past saving, unemployment compensation, and other social programs to make ends meet.

As in the efficiency wage theory, the insider-outsider theory implies that wages will be inflexible downward when aggregate demand declines. Self-correction may eventually occur but not nearly as rapidly as the new classical economists contend. (**Key Question 7**)

> ### QUICK REVIEW 19.3
>
> ▪ New classical economists believe that the economy "self-corrects" when unanticipated events divert it from its full-employment level of real output.
>
> ▪ In RET, unanticipated price-level changes cause changes in real output in the short run but not in the long run.
>
> ▪ According to RET, market participants immediately change their actions in response to anticipated price-level changes such that no change in real output occurs.
>
> ▪ Mainstream economists say that the economy can get mired in recession for long periods because of downward price and wage inflexibility.
>
> ▪ Sources of downward wage inflexibility include contracts, efficiency wages, and insider-outsider relationships.

▪ Rules or Discretion?

These different views on the causes of instability and on the speed of self-correction have led to vigorous debate on macro policy. Should the government adhere to policy rules that prohibit it from causing instability in an economy that is otherwise stable? Or should it use discretionary fiscal and monetary policy, when needed, to stabilize a sometimes-unstable economy? ⚠ **19.2**

In Support of Policy Rules

Monetarists and other new classical economists believe policy rules would reduce instability in the economy. They believe that such rules would prevent government from trying to "manage" aggregate demand. That would be a desirable trend, because in their view such management is misguided and thus is likely to *cause* more instability than it cures.

Monetary Rule   Since inappropriate monetary policy is the major source of macroeconomic instability, say monetarists, the enactment of a **monetary rule** would make sense. One such rule would be a requirement that the Fed expand the money supply each year at the same annual rate as the typical growth of the economy's production capacity. (We will examine a more complex monetary rule in this chapter's Last Word.) That fixed-rate expansion of the money supply would occur year after year

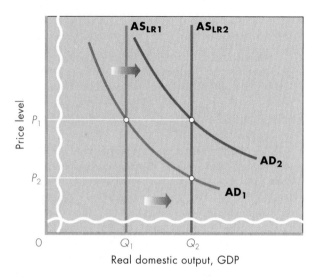

Figure 19.4

Rationale for a monetary rule.   A monetary rule that required the Fed to increase the money supply at an annual rate
linked to the long-run increase in potential GDP would shift aggregate demand rightward, as from AD_1 to AD_2, at the same
pace as the shift in long-run aggregate supply, here AS_{LR1} to
AS_{LR2}. Thus the economy would experience growth without inflation or deflation.

regardless of the state of the economy. The Fed's
sole monetary role would then be to use its tools
(open-market operations, discount-rate changes, and
changes in reserve requirements) to ensure that the
nation's money supply grew steadily by, say, 3 to 5
percent a year. According to Milton Friedman,

> Such a rule . . . would eliminate . . . the major cause
> of instability in the economy—the capricious and un-
> predictable impact of countercyclical monetary pol-
> icy. As long as the money supply grows at a constant
> rate each year, be it 3, 4, or 5 percent, any decline
> into recession will be temporary. The liquidity pro-
> vided by a constantly growing money supply will cause
> aggregate demand to expand. Similarly, if the supply
> of money does not rise at a more than average rate,
> any inflationary increase in spending will burn itself
> out for lack of fuel.[2]

Figure 19.4 illustrates the rationale for a monetary rule. Suppose the economy represented there is
operating at its full-employment real output, Q_1.
Also suppose the nation's long-run aggregate supply
curve shifts rightward, as from AS_{LR1} to AS_{LR2}, each

year, signifying the average annual potential increase
in real output. As you saw in earlier chapters, such
annual increases in "potential GDP" result from
added resources, improved resources, and improved
technology.

Monetarists argue that a monetary rule would tie
increases in the money supply to the typical rightward shift of long-run aggregate supply. In view of
the direct link between changes in the money supply
and aggregate demand, this would ensure that the
AD curve would shift rightward, as from AD_1 to AD_2,
each year. As a result, real GDP would rise from Q_1
to Q_2 and the price level would remain constant at
P_1. A monetary rule, then, would promote steady
growth of real output along with price stability.

Generally, RET economists also support a monetary rule. They conclude that an easy or tight money
policy would alter the rate of inflation but not real
output. Suppose, for example, the Fed implements
an easy money policy to reduce interest rates, expand investment spending, and boost real GDP. On
the basis of past experience and economic knowledge, the public would anticipate that this policy is
inflationary and would take protective actions.
Workers would press for higher nominal wages; firms
would raise their product prices; and lenders would
lift their nominal interest rates on loans.

All these responses are designed to prevent inflation from having adverse effects on the real income of workers, businesses, and lenders. But collectively they would immediately raise wage and
price levels. So the increase in aggregate demand
brought about by the easy money policy would be
completely dissipated in higher prices and wages.
Real output and employment would not expand.

In this view, the combination of rational expectations and instantaneous market adjustments dooms
discretionary monetary policy to ineffectiveness. If
discretionary monetary policy produces only inflation (or deflation), say the RET economists, then it
makes sense to limit the Fed's discretion and to require that Congress enact a monetary rule consistent
with price stability at all times.

Balanced Budget   Monetarists and new classical
economists question the effectiveness of fiscal policy.
At the extreme, a few of them favor a constitutional
amendment requiring that the Federal government
balance its budget annually. Others simply suggest
that government be "passive" in its fiscal policy, not
intentionally creating budget deficits or surpluses.
They believe that deficits and surpluses caused by

recession or inflationary expansion will eventually correct themselves as the economy self-corrects to its full-employment output.

Monetarists are particularly strong in their opposition to expansionary fiscal policy. They believe that the deficit spending accompanying such a policy has a strong tendency to crowd out private investment. Suppose government runs a budget deficit by printing and selling U.S. securities—that is, by borrowing from the public. By engaging in such borrowing, the government is competing with private businesses for funds. The borrowing increases the demand for money, which then raises the interest rate and crowds out a substantial amount of private investment that would otherwise have been profitable. The net effect of a budget deficit on aggregate demand therefore is unpredictable and, at best, modest.

RET economists reject discretionary fiscal policy for the same reason they reject active monetary policy: They don't think it works. Business and labor will immediately adjust their behavior in anticipation of the price-level effects of a change in fiscal policy. The economy will move directly to the anticipated new price level. Like monetary policy, say the RET theorists, fiscal policy can move the economy along its vertical long-run aggregate supply curve. But because its effects on inflation are fully anticipated, fiscal policy cannot alter real GDP even in the short run. The best course of action for government is to balance its budget.

In Defense of Discretionary Stabilization Policy

Mainstream economists oppose both a monetary rule and a balanced-budget requirement. They believe that monetary policy and fiscal policy are important tools for achieving and maintaining full employment, price stability, and economic growth.

Discretionary Monetary Policy

In supporting discretionary monetary policy, mainstream economists argue that the rationale for a monetary rule is flawed. While there is indeed a close relationship between the money supply and nominal GDP over long periods, in shorter periods this relationship breaks down. The reason is that the velocity of money has proved to be more variable and unpredictable than monetarists contend. Arguing that velocity is variable both cyclically and over time, mainstream economists contend that a constant annual rate of increase

in the money supply might not eliminate fluctuations in aggregate demand. In terms of the equation of exchange, a steady rise of M does not guarantee a steady expansion of aggregate demand because V—the rate at which money is spent—can change.

Look again at Figure 19.4, in which we demonstrated the monetary rule: Expand the money supply annually by a fixed percentage, regardless of the state of the economy. During the period in question, optimistic business expectations might create a boom in investment spending and thus shift the aggregate demand curve to some location to the right of AD_2. (You may want to pencil in a new AD curve, labeling it AD_3.) The price level would then rise above P_1; that is, demand-pull inflation would occur. In this case, the monetary rule will not accomplish its goal of maintaining price stability. Mainstream economists say that the Fed can use a tight money policy to reduce the excessive investment spending and thereby hold the rightward shift of aggregate demand to AD_2, thus avoiding inflation.

Similarly, suppose instead that investment declines because of pessimistic business expectations. Aggregate demand will then increase by some amount less than the increase from AD_1 to AD_2 in Figure 19.4. Again, the monetary rule fails the stability test: The price level sinks below P_1 (deflation occurs). Or if the price level is inflexible downward at P_1, the economy will not achieve its full-employment output (unemployment rises). An easy money policy can help avoid each outcome.

Mainstream economists quip that the trouble with the monetary rule is that it tells the policymaker: "Don't do something, just stand there."

Discretionary Fiscal Policy

Mainstream economists support the use of fiscal policy to keep recessions from deepening or to keep mild inflation from becoming severe inflation. They recognize the possibility of crowding out but do not think it is a serious problem when business borrowing is depressed, as is usually the case in recession. Because politicians can abuse fiscal policy, most economists feel that it should be held in reserve for situations where monetary policy appears to be ineffective or working too slowly.

As indicated earlier, mainstream economists oppose requirements to balance the budget annually. Tax revenues fall sharply during recessions and rise briskly during periods of demand-pull inflation. Therefore, a law or a constitutional amendment mandating an annually balanced budget would require that the government increase tax rates and reduce government spending during recession and reduce tax rates and increase government spending during economic booms. The first set of actions would worsen recession, and the second set would fuel inflation.

Increased Macro Stability

Finally, mainstream economists point out that the U.S. economy has been much more stable in the last half-century than it had been in earlier periods. It is not a coincidence, they say, that use of discretionary fiscal and monetary policies characterized the latter period but not the former. These policies have helped tame the business cycle. Moreover, mainstream economists point out several specific policy successes in the past two decades:

- A tight money policy dropped inflation from 13.5 percent in 1980 to 3.2 percent in 1983.
- An expansionary fiscal policy reduced the unemployment rate from 9.7 percent in 1982 to 5.5 percent in 1988.
- An easy money policy helped the economy recover from the 1990–1991 recession.
- Judicious tightening of monetary policy in the mid-1990s, and then again in the late 1990s, helped the economy remain on a noninflationary, full-employment growth path. **(Key Question 13)**

▌ Summary of Alternative Views

In Table 19.1 we summarize the central ideas and policy implications of three macroeconomic theories: mainstream macroeconomics, monetarism, and rational expectations theory. Note that we have broadly defined new classical economics to include both monetarism and the rational expectations theory, since both adhere to the view that the economy tends automatically to achieve equilibrium at its full-employment output. Also note that "mainstream macroeconomics" remains based on Keynesian ideas.

These different perspectives have obliged mainstream economists to rethink some of their fundamental principles and to revise many of their positions. Although considerable disagreement remains, mainstream macroeconomists agree with monetarists that "money matters" and that excessive growth of the money supply is the major cause of long-lasting, rapid inflation. They also agree with RET proponents and theorists of coordination failures that expectations matter. If government can create expectations of price stability, full employment, and economic growth, households and firms will tend to act in ways to make them happen. In short, thanks to ongoing challenges to conventional wisdom, macroeconomics continues to evolve.

Table 19.1
Summary of Alternative Macroeconomic Views

Issue	Mainstream Macroeconomics (Keynesian based)	New Classical Economics	
		Monetarism	Rational Expectations
View of the private economy	Potentially unstable	Stable in long run at natural rate of unemployment	Stable in long run at natural rate of unemployment
Cause of the observed instability of the private economy	Investment plans unequal to saving plans (changes in AD); AS shocks	Inappropriate monetary policy	Unanticipated AD and AS shocks in the short run
Appropriate macro policies	Active fiscal and monetary policy	Monetary rule	Monetary rule
How changes in the money supply affect the economy	By changing the interest rate, which changes investment and real GDP	By directly changing AD, which changes GDP	No effect on output because price-level changes are anticipated
View of the velocity of money	Unstable	Stable	No consensus
How fiscal policy affects the economy	Changes AD and GDP via the multiplier process	No effect unless money supply changes	No effect because price-level changes are anticipated
View of cost-push inflation	Possible (AS shock)	Impossible in the long run in the absence of excessive money supply growth	Impossible in the long run in the absence of excessive money supply growth

The Taylor Rule: Could a Robot Replace Alan Greenspan?

Macroeconomist John Taylor of Stanford University Calls for a New Monetary Rule That Would Institutionalize Appropriate Fed Policy Responses to Changes in Real Output and Inflation.

In our discussion of rules versus discretion, "rules" were associated with a *passive* monetary policy—one in which the monetary rule required that the Fed expand the money supply at a fixed annual rate regardless of the state of the economy. "Discretion," on the other hand, was associated with an *active* monetary policy in which the Fed changed interest rates in response to actual or anticipated changes in the economy.

Economist John Taylor has put a new twist on the rules-versus-discretion debate by suggesting a hybrid policy rule that dictates the precise active monetary actions the Fed should take when changes in the economy occur. This so-called *Taylor rule* combines traditional monetarism, with its emphasis on a monetary rule, and the more mainstream view that active monetary policy is a useful tool for taming inflation and limiting recession. Unlike the Friedman monetary rule, the Taylor rule holds, for example, that monetary policy should respond to changes in both real GDP and inflation, not simply inflation. The key adjustment instrument is the interest rate, not the money supply.

The Taylor rule has three parts:

- If real GDP rises 1 percent above potential GDP, the Fed should raise the Federal funds rate (the interbank interest rate of overnight loans), relative to the current inflation rate, by .5 percent.
- If inflation rises by 1 percent above its target of 2 percent, then the Fed should raise the Federal funds rate by .5 percent relative to the inflation rate.
- When real GDP is equal to potential GDP and inflation is equal to its target rate of 2 percent, the Federal funds rate should remain at about 4 percent, which would imply a real interest rate of 2 percent.*

Taylor has neither suggested nor implied that a robot, programmed with the Taylor rule, should replace Alan Greenspan, chairman of the Federal Reserve System. The Fed's discretion to override the rule (or "contingency plan for policy") would be retained, but the Fed would have to explain why its policies diverged from the rule. So the rule would remove the "mystery" associated with monetary policy and increase the Fed's accountability. Also, says Taylor, if used consistently, the rule would enable market participants to predict Fed behavior, and this would increase Fed credibility and reduce uncertainty.

Critics of the Taylor rule admit it is more in tune with countercyclical Fed policy than with Friedman's simple monetary rule. But they see no reason to limit the Fed's discretion in adjusting interest rates as it sees fit to achieve stabilization and growth. Monetary policy may be more art than science. The critics also point out that the Fed has done a remarkable job of promoting price stability, full employment, and economic growth over the past decade. In view of this success, they ask, "Why saddle the Fed with a highly mechanical monetary rule?"

---

*John Taylor, *Inflation, Unemployment, and Monetary Policy* (Cambridge, Mass.: MIT Press, 1998), pp. 44–47. The Dismal Scientist, at www. dismal.com/toolbox/taylor.asp, provides a "Taylor Rule Calculator" that allows you to determine the "correct" Federal funds rate by choosing among various natural rates of unemployment and targeted rates of inflation. For a hands-on experience with the rule, you may want to give it a try.

SUMMARY

1. In classical economics the aggregate supply curve is vertical and establishes the level of real output, while the aggregate demand curve tends to be stable and establishes the price level. So the economy is relatively stable.

2. In Keynesian economics the aggregate supply curve is horizontal at less-than-full-employment levels of real output, while the aggregate demand curve is inherently unstable. So the economy is relatively unstable.

3. The mainstream view is that macro instability is caused by the volatility of investment spending, which shifts the aggregate demand curve. If aggregate demand increases too rapidly, demand-pull inflation may occur; if aggregate demand decreases, recession may occur. Occasionally, adverse supply shocks also cause instability.

4. Monetarism focuses on the equation of exchange: $MV = PQ$. Because velocity is thought to be stable, changes in M create changes in nominal GDP ($= PQ$). Monetarists believe that the most significant cause of macroeconomic instability has been inappropriate monetary policy. Rapid increases in M cause inflation; insufficient growth of M causes recession. In this view, a major cause of the Great Depression was inappropriate monetary policy, which allowed the money supply to decline by nearly 40 percent.

5. Real-business-cycle theory views changes in resource availability and technology (real factors), which alter productivity, as the main causes of macroeconomic instability. In this theory, shifts in the economy's long-run aggregate supply curve change real output. In turn, money demand and money supply change, shifting the aggregate demand curve in the same direction as the initial change in long-run aggregate supply. Real output thus can change without a change in the price level.

6. A coordination failure is said to occur when people lack a way to coordinate their actions in order to achieve a mutually beneficial equilibrium. Depending on people's expectations, the economy can come to rest at either a good equilibrium (noninflationary full-employment output) or a bad equilibrium (less-than-full-employment output or de-

mand-pull inflation). A bad equilibrium is a result of a coordination failure.

7. The rational expectations theory (RET) rests on two assumptions: (1) With sufficient information, people's beliefs about future economic outcomes accurately reflect the likelihood that those outcomes will occur; and (2) markets are highly competitive, and prices and wages are flexible both upward and downward.

8. New classical economists (monetarists and rational expectations theorists) see the economy as automatically correcting itself when disturbed from its full-employment level of real output. In RET, unanticipated changes in aggregate demand change the price level, and in the short run this leads firms to change output. But once the firms realize that all prices are changing (including nominal wages) as part of general inflation or deflation, they restore their output to the previous level. Anticipated changes in aggregate demand produce only changes in the price level, not changes in real output.

9. Mainstream economists reject the new classical view that all prices and wages are flexible downward. They contend that nominal wages, in particular, are inflexible downward because of several factors, including labor contracts, efficiency wages, and insider-outsider relationships. This means that declines in aggregate demand lower real output, not only wages and prices.

10. Monetarist and RET economists recommend a monetary rule according to which the Fed is directed to increase the money supply at a fixed annual rate equal to the long-run growth of potential GDP. They also support maintaining a "neutral" fiscal policy, as opposed to using discretionary fiscal policy to create budget deficits or budget surpluses. A few monetarists and RET economists favor a constitutional amendment requiring that the Federal government balance its budget annually.

11. Mainstream economists oppose a monetary rule and a balanced-budget requirement and vigorously defend discretionary monetary and fiscal policies. They say that both theory and evidence suggest that such policies are helpful in achieving full employment, price stability, and economic growth.

TERMS AND CONCEPTS

classical view
Keynesian view
monetarism
equation of exchange

velocity
real-business-cycle theory
coordination failures

rational expectations theory
new classical economics
price-level surprises

efficiency wage
insider-outsider theory
monetary rule

STUDY QUESTIONS

1. **Key Question** Use the aggregate demand–aggregate supply model to compare the "old" classical and the Keynesian interpretations of (*a*) the aggregate supply curve and (*b*) the stability of the aggregate demand curve. Which of these interpretations seems more consistent with the realities of the Great Depression?

2. According to mainstream economists, what is the usual cause of macroeconomic instability? What role does the spending-income multiplier play in creating instability? How might adverse aggregate supply factors cause instability, according to mainstream economists?

3. State and explain the basic equation of monetarism. What is the major cause of macroeconomic instability, as viewed by monetarists?

4. **Key Question** Suppose that the money supply and the nominal GDP for a hypothetical economy are $96 billion and $336 billion, respectively. What is the velocity of money? How will households and businesses react if the central bank reduces the money supply by $20 billion? By how much will nominal GDP have to fall to restore equilibrium, according to the monetarist perspective?

5. Briefly describe the difference between a so-called real business cycle and a more traditional "spending" business cycle.

6. Craig and Kris were walking directly toward each other in a congested store aisle. Craig moved to his left to avoid Kris, and at the same time Kris moved to his right to avoid Craig. They bumped into each other. What concept does this example illustrate? How does this idea relate to macroeconomic instability?

7. **Key Question** Use an AD-AS graph to demonstrate and explain the price-level and real-output outcome of an anticipated decline in aggregate demand, as viewed by RET economists. (Assume that the economy initially is operating at its full-employment level of output.) Then demonstrate and explain on the same graph the outcome as viewed by mainstream economists.

8. What is an efficiency wage? How might payment of an above-market wage reduce shirking by employees and reduce worker turnover? How might efficiency wages contribute to downward wage inflexibility, at least for a time, when aggregate demand declines?

9. How might relationships between so-called insiders and outsiders contribute to downward wage inflexibility?

10. Use the equation of exchange to explain the rationale for a monetary rule. Why will such a rule run into trouble if *V* unexpectedly falls because of, say, a drop in investment spending by businesses?

11. Answer parts *a* and *b*, below, on the basis of the following information for a hypothetical economy in year 1: money supply = $400 billion; long-term annual growth of potential GDP = 3 percent; velocity = 4. Assume that the banking system initially has no excess reserves and that the reserve requirement is 10 percent. Also assume that velocity is constant and that the economy initially is operating at its full-employment real output.
    a. What is the level of nominal GDP in year 1?
    b. Suppose the Fed adheres to a monetary rule through open-market operations. What amount of U.S. securities will it have to sell to, or buy from, banks or the public between years 1 and 2 to meet its monetary rule?

12. Explain the difference between "active" discretionary fiscal policy advocated by mainstream economists and "passive" fiscal policy advocated by new classical economists. Explain: "The problem with a balanced-budget amendment is that it would, in a sense, require active fiscal policy—but in the wrong direction—as the economy slides into recession."

13. **Key Question** Place "MON," "RET," or "MAIN" beside the statements that most closely reflect monetarist, rational expectations, or mainstream views, respectively:
    a. Anticipated changes in aggregate demand affect only the price level; they have no effect on real output.
    b. Downward wage inflexibility means that declines in aggregate demand can cause long-lasting recession.
    c. Changes in the money supply *M* increase *PQ*; at first only *Q* rises because nominal wages are fixed, but once workers adapt their expectations to new realities, *P* rises and *Q* returns to its former level.
    d. Fiscal and monetary policies smooth out the business cycle.
    e. The Fed should increase the money supply at a fixed annual rate.

14. You have just been elected president of the United States, and the present chairperson of the Federal Reserve Board has resigned. You need to appoint a new person to this position, as well as a person to chair your Council of Economic Advisers. Using Table 19.1 and your knowledge of macroeconomics, identify the views on macro theory and policy you would want your appointees to hold. Remember, the economic health of the entire nation—and your chances for reelection—may depend on your selections.

15. **(Last Word)** Compare and contrast the Taylor rule for monetary policy with the older, simpler monetary rule advocated by Milton Friedman.

16. **Web-Based Question:** *The equation of exchange— what is the current velocity of money?* The fundamental equation of monetarism is the equation of exchange: $MV = PQ = $ GDP. The velocity of money, V, can be found by dividing GDP by M, the money supply. Calculate the velocity of money for the past few years. Which GDP data should be used: real or nominal GDP? Why? How stable is V during this time? Is V increasing or decreasing? Get GDP data from the "GDP and Related Data" section at the Bureau of Economic Analysis website, www.bea.doc.gov/. Money supply data can be found at the website of the Federal Reserve, www.federalreserve.gov/, by selecting in sequence: Research and Data, Statistics: Releases and Historical Data, and Money Stock—Historical Data.

17. **Web-Based Question:** *Comparative stability of real GDP—how does the United States fare?* Visit the OECD Internet site, www.oecd.org/std/nahome.htm, and select On-line Statistics. Then examine "Quarterly Growth Rates in GDP at Constant Prices." Which three OECD countries have had the greatest stability of real GDP growth in the past 5 years? Which three the least?

5

International Economics and the World Economy

CHAPTER 20

International Trade

THE **WTO**, TRADE deficits, dumping. Exchange rates, the EU, the G-7 nations. The IMF, official reserves, currency interventions. Capital flight, special economic zones, the ruble. This is the language of international economics, the subject of Part 5. To understand the increasingly integrated world economy, we need to learn more about this language and the ideas that it conveys. ■ In this chapter we build on Chapter 6 by providing both a deeper analysis of the benefits of international trade and a fuller appraisal of the arguments for protectionism. Then in Chapter 21 we examine exchange rates and the balance of payments. Chapter 22 looks at the special problems of developing economies. A "bonus" Internet chapter at our website examines the transition economies of Russia and China.

▮ Some Key Facts

In Chapter 6 we dealt with a number of facts about international trade. Let's briefly review them and add a few more:

- Exports of goods and services make up about 12 percent of total U.S. output. That percentage is much lower than the percentage in many other nations. Examples: Netherlands, 56 percent; Canada, 41 percent; New Zealand, 29 percent; the United Kingdom, 29 percent.
- The United States leads the world in the volume of exports and imports, as measured in dollars. Currently, the United States provides about one-eighth of the world's exports. Germany, Japan, Britain, and France follow in the list of the top five exporters by dollar volume.

- Since 1975, U.S. exports have doubled as a percentage of GDP.
- In 2000 the United States imported $450 billion more goods than it exported. But in that year U.S. exports of services exceeded imports of services by $81 billion. So the combined trade deficit of goods and services was $369 billion.
- The principal commodities among U.S. exports are semiconductors, computers, chemicals, consumer durables, and generating equipment. The principle imports are automobiles, computers, petroleum, and clothing.
- Like other advanced industrial nations, the United States imports some of the same categories of goods that it exports. Examples: automobiles, computers, chemicals, semiconductors, and telecommunications equipment.

- Most of U.S. export and import trade takes place with other industrially advanced nations, specifically Canada, nations of western Europe, and Japan.

- Although the United States, Japan, and western European nations dominate world trade (Global Perspective 20.1), several other nations have increased their roles significantly. Collectively, the southeast Asian economies of South Korea, Taiwan, Singapore, and Hong Kong (which is part of China), have expanded their share of world trade from 3 percent in 1972 to more than 10 percent today. Russia, the eastern European nations, and mainland China have also increased their international trade.

- International trade (and finance) link world economies (review Figure 6.1, page 94.) Through trade, changes in economic conditions in one place on the globe can quickly affect other places. Examples: In 1998 economic problems in the southeast Asian countries of South Korea, Indonesia, Malaysia, and the Philippines reduced demand for Japanese imports and negatively affected Japan's economy. In 2000, hikes in world oil prices threatened to slow economic growth in Europe and the United States.

- International trade and finance is often at the center of economic policy. Examples: The U.S. Congress often grapples with international trade issues such as trade relations with China. The World Trade Organization (WTO) and the International Monetary Fund (IMF) regularly meet to establish rules relating to international trade and finance. Such meetings often attract protestors who oppose global capitalism.

With these facts in mind, we now look more closely at the economics of international trade.

The Economic Basis for Trade

In Chapter 6 we found that international trade enables nations to specialize their production, enhance their resource productivity, and acquire more goods and services. Sovereign nations, like individuals and the regions of a nation, can gain by specializing in the products they can produce with greatest relative efficiency and by trading for the goods they cannot produce as efficiently. A more complete answer to the question "Why do nations trade?" hinges on three facts:

- The distribution of natural, human, and capital resources among nations is uneven; nations differ in their endowments of economic resources.

- Efficient production of various goods requires different technologies or combinations of resources.

- Products are differentiated as to quality and other nonprice attributes. A few or many people may prefer certain imported goods to similar goods made domestically.

To recognize the character and interaction of these three facts, think of Japan, for example, which has a large, well-educated labor force and abundant, and therefore inexpensive, skilled labor. As a result, Japan can produce efficiently (at low cost) a variety of **labor-intensive goods** such as cameras, portable CD players, video game players, and video recorders whose design and production require much skilled labor.

In contrast, Australia has vast amounts of land and can inexpensively produce such **land-intensive goods** as wheat, wool, and meat. Brazil has the soil, tropical climate, rainfall, and ready supply of unskilled labor that are needed for the efficient, low-cost production of coffee.

Industrially advanced economies with relatively large amounts of capital can inexpensively produce goods whose production requires much capital, including such **capital-intensive goods** as automobiles, agricultural equipment, machinery, and chemicals.

GLOBAL PERSPECTIVE 20.1

Shares of World Exports, Selected Nations

The United States has the largest share of world exports, followed closely by Germany and Japan. The seven largest export nations account for nearly 50 percent of world exports.

Percentage Share of World Exports, 1999

United States	
Germany	
Japan	
France	
United Kingdom	
Canada	
Italy	

Source: World Trade Organization, www.wto.org.

All nations, regardless of their labor, land, or capital intensity, can find special niches for individual products that are in demand worldwide because of their special qualities. Examples: fashions from Italy, luxury automobiles from Germany, software from the United States, and watches from Switzerland.

The distribution of resources, technology, and product distinctiveness among nations, however, is not forever fixed. When that distribution changes, the relative efficiency and success with which nations produce and sell goods also changes. For example, in the past few decades South Korea has upgraded the quality of its labor force and has greatly expanded its stock of capital. Although South Korea was primarily an exporter of agricultural products and raw materials a half-century ago, it now exports large quantities of manufactured goods. Similarly, the new technologies that gave us synthetic fibers and synthetic rubber drastically altered the resource mix needed to produce these goods and changed the relative efficiency of nations in manufacturing them.

As national economies evolve, the size and quality of their labor forces may change, the volume and composition of their capital stocks may shift, new technologies may develop, and even the quality of land and the quantity of natural resources may be altered. As such changes occur, the relative efficiency with which a nation can produce specific goods will also change.

■ Comparative Advantage: Graphical Analysis

Implicit in what we have been saying is the principle of comparative advantage, described through production possibilities tables in Chapter 6. We look again at that idea, now using graphical analysis. ◹ 20.1

Two Isolated Nations

Suppose the world economy is composed of just two nations: the United States and Brazil. Each nation can produce both wheat and coffee, but at different levels of economic efficiency. Suppose the U.S. and Brazilian domestic production possibilities curves for coffee and wheat are as shown in Figure 20.1a and 20.1b. Note especially two characteristics of these production possibilities curves:

- **Constant costs**   The "curves" are drawn as straight lines, in contrast to the concave-to-the-origin production possibilities frontiers we examined in Chapter 2. This means that we have replaced the law of increasing opportunity costs with the assumption of constant costs. This substitution simplifies our discussion but does not impair the validity of our analysis and conclusions. Later we will consider the effects of increasing opportunity costs.

- **Different costs**   The production possibilities curves of the United States and Brazil reflect different resource mixes and differing levels of

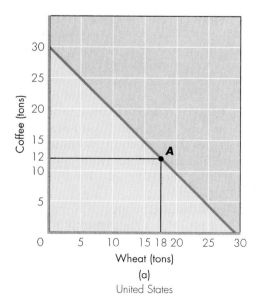

(a)
United States

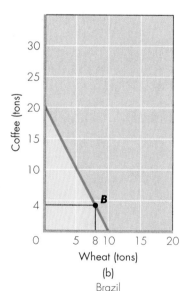

(b)
Brazil

Figure 20.1

Production possibilities for the United States and Brazil. The two production possibilities curves show the combinations of coffee and wheat that (a) the United States and (b) Brazil can produce domestically. The curves for both countries are straight lines because we are assuming constant opportunity costs. The different cost ratios, 1 coffee ≡ 1 wheat for the United States, and 2 coffee ≡ 1 wheat for Brazil, are reflected in the different slopes of the two lines.

technological progress. Specifically, they tell us that the opportunity costs of producing wheat and coffee differ between the two nations.

United States

In Figure 20.1a, with full employment, the United States will operate on its production possibilities curve. On that curve, it can increase its output of wheat from 0 tons to 30 tons by forgoing 30 tons of coffee output. This means that the slope of the production possibilities curve is -1 ($= -30$ coffee$/+30$ wheat), implying that 1 ton of coffee must be sacrificed for each extra ton of wheat. In the United States the domestic exchange ratio or **cost ratio** for the two products is 1 ton of coffee for 1 ton of wheat, or $1C \equiv 1W$. Said differently, the United States can "exchange" a ton of coffee for a ton of wheat. Our constant-cost assumption means that this exchange or opportunity-cost equation prevails for all possible moves from one point to another along the U.S. production possibilities curve.

Brazil

Brazil's production possibilities curve in Figure 20.1b represents a different full-employment opportunity-cost ratio. In Brazil, 20 tons of coffee must be given up to get 10 tons of wheat. The slope of the production possibilities curve is -2 ($= -20$ coffee$/+10$ wheat). This means that in Brazil the opportunity-cost ratio for the two goods is 2 tons of coffee for 1 ton of wheat, or $2C \equiv 1W$.

Self-Sufficiency Output Mix

If the United States and Brazil are isolated and are to be self-sufficient, then each country must choose some output mix on its production possibilities curve. It will choose the mix that provides the greatest total utility, or satisfaction. Assume that point A in Figure 20.1a is the optimal mix in the United States;

that is, society deems the combination of 18 tons of wheat and 12 tons of coffee preferable to any other combination of the goods available along the production possibilities curve. Suppose Brazil's optimal product mix is 8 tons of wheat and 4 tons of coffee, indicated by point B in Figure 20.1b. These choices are reflected in column 1 of Table 20.1.

Specializing Based on Comparative Advantage

We can determine the products in which the United States and Brazil should specialize as follows: The **principle of comparative advantage** says that total output will be greatest when each good is produced by the nation that has the lowest domestic opportunity cost for that good. In our two-nation illustration, the United States has the lower domestic opportunity cost for wheat; the United States need forgo only 1 ton of coffee to produce 1 ton of wheat, whereas Brazil must forgo 2 tons of coffee for 1 ton of wheat. The United States has a comparative (cost) advantage in wheat and should specialize in wheat production. The "world" (that is, the United States and Brazil) in our example would clearly not be economizing in the use of its resources if a high-cost producer (Brazil) produced a specific product (wheat) when a low-cost producer (the United States) could have produced it. Having Brazil produce wheat would mean that the world economy would have to give up more coffee than is necessary to obtain a ton of wheat.

Brazil has the lower domestic opportunity cost for coffee; it must sacrifice only $\frac{1}{2}$ ton of wheat in producing 1 ton of coffee, while the United States must forgo 1 ton of wheat in producing a ton of coffee. Brazil has a comparative advantage in coffee and should specialize in coffee production. Again, the world would not be employing its resources

Table 20.1

International Specialization According to Comparative Advantage and the Gains from Trade

Country	(1) Outputs before Specialization	(2) Outputs after Specialization	(3) Amounts Exported (−) and Imported (+)	(4) Outputs Available after Trade	(5) Gains from Specialization and Trade, (4) − (1)
United States	18 wheat 12 coffee	30 wheat 0 coffee	−10 wheat +15 coffee	20 wheat 15 coffee	2 wheat 3 coffee
Brazil	8 wheat 4 coffee	0 wheat 20 coffee	+10 wheat −15 coffee	10 wheat 5 coffee	2 wheat 1 coffee

economically if coffee were produced by a high-cost producer (the United States) rather than by a low-cost producer (Brazil). If the United States produced coffee, the world would be giving up more wheat than necessary to obtain each ton of coffee. Economizing requires that any particular good be produced by the nation having the lowest domestic opportunity cost, or the comparative advantage for that good. The United States should produce wheat, and Brazil should produce coffee.

In column 2 of Table 20.1 we verify that specialized production enables the world to get more output from its fixed amount of resources. By specializing completely in wheat, the United States can produce 30 tons of wheat and no coffee. Brazil, by specializing completely in coffee, can produce 20 tons of coffee and no wheat. The world ends up with 4 more tons of wheat (30 tons compared with 26) *and* 4 more tons of coffee (20 tons compared with 16) than it would if there were self-sufficiency or unspecialized production.

Terms of Trade

But consumers of each nation want both wheat *and* coffee. They can have both if the two nations trade the two products. But what will be the **terms of trade?** At what exchange ratio will the United States and Brazil trade wheat and coffee?

Because $1W \equiv 1C$ in the United States, the United States must get *more than* 1 ton of coffee for each ton of wheat exported; otherwise, it will not benefit from exporting wheat in exchange for Brazilian coffee. The United States must get a better "price" (more coffee) for its wheat in the world market than it can get domestically; otherwise, there is no gain from trade and it will not occur.

Similarly, because $1W \equiv 2C$ in Brazil, Brazil must get 1 ton of wheat by exporting some amount *less than* 2 tons of coffee. Brazil must be able to pay a lower "price" for wheat in the world market than it must pay domestically, or else it will not want to trade. The international exchange ratio or terms of trade must lie somewhere between

$1W \equiv 1C$ (United States' cost conditions)

and

$1W \equiv 2C$ (Brazil's cost conditions)

But where between these limits will the world exchange ratio fall? The United States will prefer a rate close to $1W \equiv 2C$, say, $1W \equiv 1\frac{3}{4}C$. The United

States wants to get as much coffee as possible for each ton of wheat it exports. Similarly, Brazil wants a rate near $1W \equiv 1C$, say, $1W \equiv 1\frac{1}{4}C$. Brazil wants to export as little coffee as possible for each ton of wheat it receives in exchange. The exchange ratio or terms of trade determine how the gains from international specialization and trade are divided between the two nations.

The actual exchange ratio depends on world supply and demand for the two products. If overall world demand for coffee is weak relative to its supply and if the demand for wheat is strong relative to its supply, the price of coffee will be lower and the price of wheat higher. The exchange ratio will settle nearer the $1W \equiv 2C$ figure the United States prefers. If overall world demand for coffee is great relative to its supply and if the demand for wheat is weak relative to its supply, the ratio will settle nearer the $1W \equiv 1C$ level favorable to Brazil. (We discuss equilibrium world prices later in this chapter.)

Gains from Trade

Suppose the international terms of trade are $1W \equiv 1\frac{1}{2}C$. The possibility of trading on these terms permits each nation to supplement its domestic production possibilities curve with a **trading possibilities line** (or curve), as shown in **Figure 20.2 (Key Graph).** Just as a production possibilities curve shows the amounts of these products a full-employment economy can obtain by shifting resources from one to the other, a trading possibilities line shows the amounts of two products a nation can obtain by specializing in one product and trading for the other. The trading possibilities lines in Figure 20.2 reflect the assumption that both nations specialize on the basis of comparative advantage: The United States specializes completely in wheat (at point W in Figure 20.2a), and Brazil specializes completely in coffee (at point c in Figure 20.2b).

Improved Options   Now the United States is not constrained by its domestic production possibilities line, which requires it to give up 1 ton of wheat for every ton of coffee it wants as it moves up its domestic production possibilities line from, say, point W. Instead, the United States, through trade with Brazil, can get $1\frac{1}{2}$ tons of coffee for every ton of wheat it exports to Brazil, as long as Brazil has coffee to export. Trading possibilities line WC' thus represents the $1W \equiv 1\frac{1}{2}C$ trading ratio.

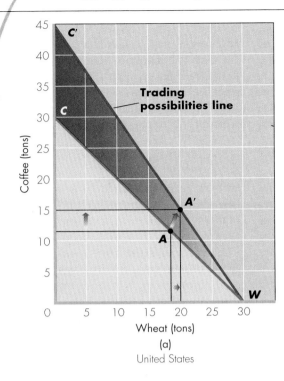

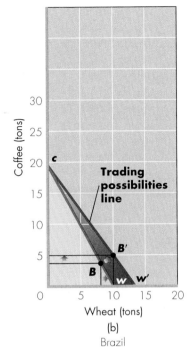

Figure 20.2

Trading possibility lines and the gains from trade.

As a result of specialization and trade, both the United States and Brazil can have higher levels of output than the levels attainable on their domestic production possibilities curves. (a) The United States can move from point A on its domestic production possibilities curve to, say, A' on its trading possibilities line. (b) Brazil can move from B to B'.

Quick Quiz 20.2

1. The production possiblities curves in graphs (a) and (b) imply:
   a. increasing domestic opportunity costs.
   b. decreasing domestic opportunity costs.
   c. constant domestic opportunity costs.
   d. first decreasing, then increasing, domestic opportunity costs.

2. Before specialization, the domestic opportunity cost of producing 1 unit of wheat is:
   a. 1 unit of coffee in both the United States and Brazil.
   b. 1 unit of coffee in the United States and 2 units of coffee in Brazil.
   c. 2 units of coffee in the United States and 1 unit of coffee in Brazil.
   d. 1 unit of coffee in the United States and $\frac{1}{2}$ unit of coffee in Brazil.

3. After specialization and international trade, the world output of wheat and coffee is:
   a. 20 tons of wheat and 20 tons of coffee.
   b. 45 tons of wheat and 15 tons of coffee.
   c. 30 tons of wheat and 20 tons of coffee.
   d. 10 tons of wheat and 30 tons of coffee.

4. After specialization and international trade:
   a. the United States can obtain units of coffee at less cost than it could before trade.
   b. Brazil can obtain more than 20 tons of coffee, if it so chooses.
   c. the United States no longer has a comparative advantage in producing wheat.
   d. Brazil can benefit by prohibiting coffee imports from the United States.

Answers: 1. c; 2. b; 3. c; 4. a

Similarly, Brazil, starting at, say, point *c*, no longer has to move down its domestic production possibilities curve, giving up 2 tons of coffee for each ton of wheat it wants. It can now export just $1\frac{1}{2}$ tons of coffee for each ton of wheat it wants by moving down its trading possibilities line *cw'*.

Specialization and trade create a new exchange ratio between wheat and coffee, reflected in each nation's trading possibilities line. This exchange ratio is superior for both nations to the unspecialized exchange ratio embodied in their production possibilities curves. By specializing in wheat and trading for

Brazil's coffee, the United States can obtain more than 1 ton of coffee for 1 ton of wheat. By specializing in coffee and trading for U.S. wheat, Brazil can get 1 ton of wheat for less than 2 tons of coffee. In both cases, self-sufficiency is undesirable.

Added Output   By specializing on the basis of comparative advantage and by trading for goods that are produced in the nation with greater domestic efficiency, the United States and Brazil can realize combinations of wheat and coffee beyond their production possibilities curves. *Specialization according to comparative advantage results in a more efficient allocation of world resources, and larger outputs of both products are therefore available to both nations.*

Suppose that at the $1W \equiv 1\frac{1}{2}C$ terms of trade, the United States exports 10 tons of wheat to Brazil and in return Brazil exports 15 tons of coffee to the United States. How do the new quantities of wheat and coffee available to the two nations compare with the optimal product mixes that existed before specialization and trade? Point A in Figure 20.2a reminds us that the United States chose 18 tons of wheat and 12 tons of coffee originally. But by producing 30 tons of wheat and no coffee and by trading 10 tons of wheat for 15 tons of coffee, the United States can obtain 20 tons of wheat and 15 tons of coffee. This new, superior combination of wheat and coffee is indicated by point A' in Figure 20.2a. Compared with the no-trade amounts of 18 tons of wheat and 12 tons of coffee, the United States' **gains from trade** are 2 tons of wheat and 3 tons of coffee.

Similarly, recall that Brazil's optimal product mix was 4 tons of coffee and 8 tons of wheat (point B) before specialization and trade. Now, after specializing in coffee and trading, Brazil can have 5 tons of coffee and 10 tons of wheat. It accomplishes that by producing 20 tons of coffee and no wheat and exporting 15 tons of its coffee in exchange for 10 tons of American wheat. This new position is indicated by point B' in Figure 20.2b. Brazil's gains from trade are 1 ton of coffee and 2 tons of wheat.

As a result of specialization and trade, both countries have more of both products. Table 20.1, which summarizes the transactions and outcomes, merits careful study.

The fact that points A' and B' are economic positions superior to A and B is enormously important. We know that a nation can expand its production possibilities boundary by (1) expanding the quantity and improving the quality of its resources or (2) re-

alizing technological progress. We have now established that international trade can enable a nation to circumvent the output constraint illustrated by its production possibilities curve. The outcome of international specialization and trade is equivalent to having more and better resources or discovering improved production techniques.

Trade with Increasing Costs

To explain the basic principles underlying international trade, we simplified our analysis in several ways. For example, we limited discussion to two products and two nations. But multiproduct and multinational analysis yields the same conclusions. We also assumed constant opportunity costs (linear production possibilities curves), which is a more substantive simplification. Let's consider the effect of allowing increasing opportunity costs (concave-to-the-origin production possibilities curves) to enter the picture.

Suppose that the United States and Brazil initially are at positions on their concave production possibilities curves where their domestic cost ratios are $1W \equiv 1C$ and $1W \equiv 2C$, as they were in our constant-cost analysis. As before, comparative advantage indicates that the United States should specialize in wheat and Brazil in coffee. But now, as the United States begins to expand wheat production, its cost of wheat will rise; it will have to sacrifice more than 1 ton of coffee to get 1 additional ton of wheat. Resources are no longer perfectly substitutable between alternative uses, as the constant-cost assumption implied. Resources less and less suitable to wheat production must be allocated to the U.S. wheat industry in expanding wheat output, and that means increasing costs—the sacrifice of larger and larger amounts of coffee for each additional ton of wheat.

Similarly, Brazil, starting from its $1W \equiv 2C$ cost ratio position, expands coffee production. But as it does, it will find that its $1W \equiv 2C$ cost ratio begins to rise. Sacrificing a ton of wheat will free resources that are capable of producing only something less than 2 tons of coffee, because those transferred resources are less suitable to coffee production.

As the U.S. cost ratio falls from $1W \equiv 1C$ and the Brazilian ratio rises from $1W \equiv 2C$, a point will be reached where the cost ratios are equal in the two nations, perhaps at $1W \equiv 1\frac{3}{4}C$. At this point the underlying basis for further specialization and trade—differing cost ratios—has disappeared, and further specialization is therefore uneconomical. And, most importantly, this point of equal cost ratios may be reached while the United States is still producing some coffee along with its wheat and Brazil is producing some wheat along with its coffee. The primary effect of increasing opportunity costs is less-than-complete specialization. For this reason we often find domestically produced products competing directly against identical or similar imported products within a particular economy. (**Key Question 4**)

The Case for Free Trade

The case for free trade reduces to one compelling argument: *Through free trade based on the principle of comparative advantage, the world economy can achieve a more efficient allocation of resources and a higher level of material well-being than it can without free trade.*

Since the resource mixes and technological knowledge of the world's nations are all somewhat different, each nation can produce particular commodities at different real costs. Each nation should produce goods for which its domestic opportunity costs are lower than the domestic opportunity costs of other nations and exchange those goods for products for which its domestic opportunity costs are high relative to those of other nations. If each nation does this, the world will realize the advantages of geographic and human specialization. The world and each free-trading nation can obtain a larger real income from the fixed supplies of resources available to it. Government trade barriers lessen or eliminate gains from specialization. If nations cannot trade freely, they must shift resources from efficient (low-cost) to inefficient (high-cost) uses in order to satisfy their diverse wants.

One side benefit of free trade is that it promotes competition and deters monopoly. The increased competition from foreign firms forces domestic firms to find and use the lowest-cost production techniques. It also compels them to be innovative with respect to both product quality and production methods, thereby contributing to economic growth. And free trade gives consumers a wider range of product choices. The reasons to favor free trade are the same as the reasons to endorse competition.

A second side benefit of free trade is that it links national interests and breaks down national animosities. Confronted with political disagreements, trading partners tend to negotiate rather than make war.

Supply and Demand Analysis of Exports and Imports

Supply and demand analysis reveals how equilibrium prices and quantities of exports and imports are determined. The amount of a good or a service a nation will export or import depends on differences between the equilibrium world price and the equilibrium domestic price. The interaction of *world* supply and demand determines the equilibrium **world price**—the price that equates the quantities supplied and demanded globally. *Domestic* supply and demand determine the equilibrium **domestic price**—the price that would prevail in a closed economy that does not engage in international trade. The domestic price equates quantity supplied and quantity demanded domestically.

In the absence of trade, the domestic prices in a closed economy may or may not equal the world equilibrium prices. When economies are opened for international trade, differences between world and domestic prices encourage exports or imports. To see how, consider the international effects of such price differences in a simple two-nation world, consisting of the United States and Canada, that are both producing aluminum. We assume there are no trade barriers, such as tariffs and quotas, and no international transportation costs.

Supply and Demand in the United States

Figure 20.3a shows the domestic supply curve S_d and the domestic demand curve D_d for aluminum in the United States, which for now is a closed economy.

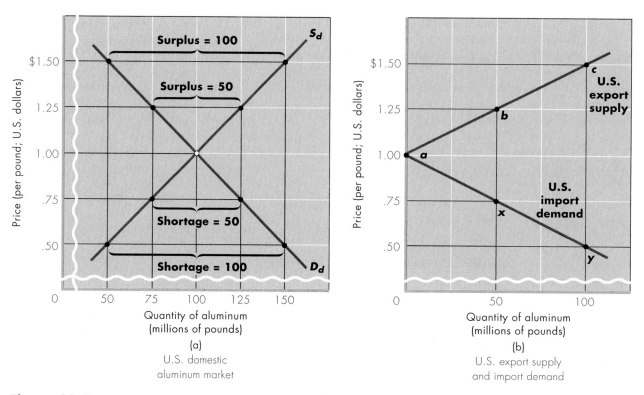

Figure 20.3

U.S. export supply and import demand. (a) Domestic supply S_d and demand D_d set the domestic equilibrium price of aluminum at $1 per pound. At world prices above $1 there are domestic surpluses of aluminum. At prices below $1 there are domestic shortages. (b) Surpluses are exported (top curve), and shortages are met by importing aluminum (lower curve). The export supply curve shows the direct relationship between world prices and U.S. exports; the import demand curve portrays the inverse relationship between world prices and U.S. imports.

The intersection of S_d and D_d determines the equilibrium domestic price of $1 per pound and the equilibrium domestic quantity of 100 million pounds. Domestic suppliers produce 100 million pounds and sell them all at $1 a pound. So there are no domestic surpluses or shortages of aluminum.

But what if the U.S. economy were opened to trade and the world price of aluminum were above or below this $1 domestic price?

U.S. Export Supply

If the aluminum price in the rest of the world (that is, Canada) exceeds $1, U.S. firms will produce more than 100 million pounds and will export the excess domestic output. First, consider a world price of $1.25. We see from the supply curve S_d that U.S. aluminum firms will produce 125 million pounds of aluminum at that price. The demand curve D_d tells us that the United States will purchase only 75 million pounds at $1.25. The outcome is a domestic surplus of 50 million

pounds of aluminum. U.S. producers will export those 50 million pounds at the $1.25 world price.

What if the world price were $1.50? The supply curve shows that U.S. firms will produce 150 million pounds of aluminum, while the demand curve tells us that U.S. consumers will buy only 50 million pounds. So U.S. producers will export the domestic surplus of 100 million pounds.

Toward the top of Figure 20.3b we plot the domestic surpluses—the U.S. exports—that occur at world prices above the $1 domestic equilibrium price. When the world and domestic prices are equal (= $1), the quantity of exports supplied is zero (point *a*). There is no surplus of domestic output to export. But when the world price is $1.25, U.S. firms export 50 million pounds of surplus aluminum (point *b*). At a $1.50 world price, the domestic surplus of 100 million pounds is exported (point *c*).

The U.S. **export supply curve,** found by connecting points *a*, *b*, and *c*, shows the amount of aluminum U.S. producers will export at each world price above $1. This curve *slopes upward*, indicating a direct or positive relationship between the world price and the amount of U.S. exports. *As world prices increase relative to domestic prices, U.S. exports rise.*

U.S. Import Demand

If the world price is below the domestic $1 price, the United States will import aluminum. Consider a $.75 world price. The supply curve in Figure 20.3a reveals that at that price U.S. firms produce only 75 million pounds of aluminum. But the demand curve shows that the United States wants to buy 125 million pounds at that price. The result is a domestic shortage of 50 million pounds. To satisfy that shortage, the United States will import 50 million pounds of aluminum.

At an even lower world price, $.50, U.S. producers will supply only 50 million pounds. Because U.S. consumers want to buy 150 million pounds at that price, there is a domestic shortage of 100 million pounds. Imports will flow to the United States to make up the difference. That is, at a $.50 world

price U.S. firms will supply 50 million pounds and 100 million pounds will be imported.

In Figure 20.3b we plot the U.S. **import demand curve** from these data. This *downsloping curve* shows the amounts of aluminum that will be imported at world prices below the $1 U.S. domestic price. The relationship between world prices and imported amounts is inverse or negative. At a world price of $1, domestic output will satisfy U.S. demand; imports will be zero (point *a*). But at $.75 the United States will import 50 million pounds of aluminum (point *x*); at $.50, the United States will import 100 million pounds (point *y*). Connecting points *a*, *x*, and *y* yields the *downsloping* U.S. import demand curve. *It reveals that as world prices fall relative to U.S. domestic prices, U.S. imports increase.*

Supply and Demand in Canada

We repeat our analysis in Figure 20.4, this time from the viewpoint Canada. (We have converted Canadian dollar prices to U.S. dollar prices via the exchange

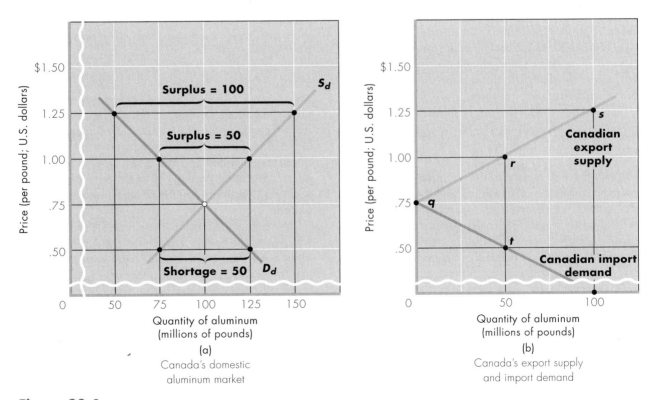

Figure 20.4

Canadian export supply and import demand. (a) At world prices above the $.75 domestic price, production in Canada exceeds domestic consumption. At world prices below $.75, domestic shortages occur. (b) Surpluses result in exports, and shortages result in imports. The Canadian export supply curve and import demand curve depict the relationships between world prices and exports or imports.

rate.) Note that the domestic supply curve S_d and the domestic demand curve D_d for aluminum in Canada yield a domestic price of $.75, which is $.25 lower than the $1 U.S. domestic price.

The analysis proceeds exactly as above except that the domestic price is now the Canadian price. If the world price is $.75, Canadians will neither export nor import aluminum (giving us point q in Figure 20.4b.) At world prices above $.75, Canadian firms will produce more aluminum than Canadian consumers will buy. Canadian firms will export the surplus. At a $1 world price, Figure 20.4a tells us that Canada will have and export a domestic surplus of 50 million pounds (yielding point r). At $1.25, it will have and will export a domestic surplus of 100 million pounds (point s). Connecting these points yields the upsloping Canadian export supply curve, which reflects the domestic surpluses (and hence the exports) that occur when the world price exceeds the $.75 Canadian domestic price.

At world prices below $.75, domestic shortages occur in Canada. At a $.50 world price, Figure 20.4a shows that Canadian consumers want to buy 125 million pounds of aluminum but Canadian firms will produce only 75 million pounds. The shortage will bring 50 million pounds of imports to Canada (point t in Figure 20.4b.) The Canadian import demand curve in that figure shows the Canadian imports that will occur at all world aluminum prices below the $.75 Canadian domestic price.

Equilibrium World Price, Exports, and Imports

We now have the tools for determining the **equilibrium world price** of aluminum and the equilibrium world levels of exports and imports when the world is opened to trade. Figure 20.5 combines the U.S. export supply curve and import demand curve in Figure 20.3b and the Canadian export supply curve and import demand curve in Figure 20.4b. The two U.S. curves proceed rightward from the $1 U.S. domestic price; the two Canadian curves proceed rightward from the $.75 Canadian domestic price.

International equilibrium occurs in this two-nation model where one nation's import demand curve intersects another nation's export supply curve. In this case the U.S. import demand curve intersects Canada's export supply curve at e. There, the world price of aluminum is $.88. The Canadian export supply curve indicates that Canada will export 25 million pounds of aluminum at this price. Also at this

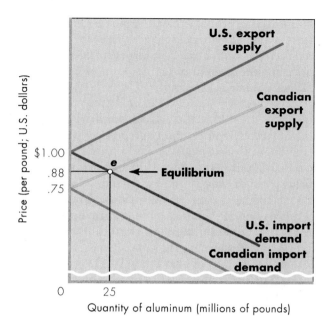

Figure 20.5

Equilibrium world price and quantity of exports and imports. In a two-nation world, the equilibrium world price (= $.88) is determined by the intersection of one nation's export supply curve and the other nation's import demand curve. This intersection also decides the equilibrium volume of exports and imports. Here, Canada exports 25 million pounds of aluminum to the United States.

price the United States will import 25 million pounds from Canada, indicated by the U.S. import demand curve. The $.88 world price equates the quantity of imports demanded and the quantity of exports supplied (25 million pounds). Thus there will be world trade of 25 million pounds of aluminum at $.88 per pound.

Note that after trade, the single $.88 world price will prevail in both Canada and the United States. Only one price for a standardized commodity can persist in a highly competitive world market. With trade, all consumers can buy a pound of aluminum for $.88, and all producers can sell it for that price. This world price means that Canadians will pay more for aluminum with trade ($.88) than without it ($.75). The increased Canadian output caused by trade raises Canadian per-unit production costs and therefore raises the price of aluminum in Canada. The United States, however, pays less for aluminum with trade ($.88) than without it ($1). The U.S. gain comes from Canada's comparative cost advantage in producing aluminum.

Why would Canada willingly send 25 million pounds of its aluminum output to the United States for U.S. consumption? After all, producing this output uses up scarce Canadian resources and drives up the price of aluminum for Canadians. Canadians are willing to export aluminum to the United States because Canadians gain the means—the U.S. dollars—to import other goods, say, computer software, from the United States. Canadian exports enable Canadians to acquire imports that have greater value to Canadians than the exported aluminum. Canadian exports to the United States finance Canadian imports from the United States. **(Key Question 6)**

▌Trade Barriers

No matter how compelling the case for free trade, barriers to free trade *do* exist. Let's expand Chapter 6's discussion of trade barriers.

Excise taxes on imported goods are called **tariffs**; they may be imposed to obtain revenue or to protect domestic firms. A **revenue tariff** is usually applied to a product that is not being produced domestically, for example, tin, coffee, or bananas in the case of the United States. Rates on revenue tariffs are modest; their purpose is to provide the Federal government with revenue. A **protective tariff** is designed to shield domestic producers from foreign competition. Although protective tariffs are usually not high enough to stop the importation of foreign goods, they put foreign producers at a competitive disadvantage in selling in domestic markets.

An **import quota** specifies the maximum amount of a commodity that may be imported in any period. Import quotas can more effectively retard international commerce than tariffs. A product might be imported in large quantities despite high tariffs; low import quotas completely prohibit imports once quotas have been filled.

A **nontariff barrier (NTB)** is a licensing requirement that specifies unreasonable standards pertaining to product quality and safety, or unnecessary bureaucratic red tape that is used to restrict imports. Japan and the European countries frequently require that their domestic importers of foreign goods obtain licenses. By restricting the issuance of licenses, imports can be restricted. Great Britain uses this barrier to bar the importation of coal.

A **voluntary export restriction (VER)** is a trade barrier by which foreign firms "voluntarily" limit the amount of their exports to a particular country.

VERs, which have the effect of import quotas, are agreed to by exporters in the hope of avoiding more stringent trade barriers. Japanese auto manufacturers agreed to a VER on exports to the United States under the threat of higher U.S. tariffs or the imposition of low import quotas. Later in this chapter we will consider the arguments and appeals that are made to justify protection. 🔎 20.1

Economic Impact of Tariffs

Once again we turn to supply and demand analysis—now to examine the economic effects of protective tariffs. Curves D_d and S_d in Figure 20.6 show domestic demand and supply for a product in which a nation, say, the United States, has a comparative disadvantage—for example, video cassette recorders (VCRs). (Disregard curve $S_d + Q$ for now.) Without world trade, the domestic price and output would be P_d and q, respectively.

Assume now that the domestic economy is opened to world trade and that the Japanese, who

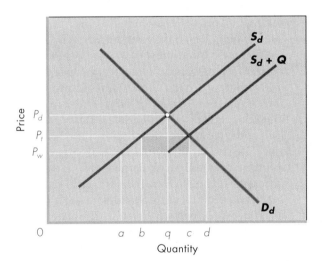

Figure 20.6

The economic effects of a protective tariff or an import quota. A tariff that increases the price of a good from P_w to P_t will reduce domestic consumption from d to c. Domestic producers will be able to sell more output (b rather than a) at a higher price (P_t rather than P_w). Foreign exporters are injured because they sell less output (bc rather than ad). The orange area indicates the amount of tariff paid by domestic consumers. An import quota of bc units has the same effect as the tariff, with one exception: The amount represented by the orange area will go to foreign producers rather than to the domestic government.

have a comparative advantage in VCRs, begin to sell their recorders in the United States. We assume that with free trade the domestic price cannot differ from the world price, which here is P_w. At P_w domestic consumption is d and domestic production is a. The horizontal distance between the domestic supply and demand curves at P_w represents imports of ad. Thus far, our analysis is similar to the analysis of world prices in Figure 20.3.

Direct Effects

Suppose now that the United States imposes a tariff on each imported VCR. The tariff, which raises the price of imported VCRs from P_w to P_t, has four effects:

- *Decline in consumption* Consumption of video recorders in the United States declines from d to c as the higher price moves buyers up and to the left along their demand curve. The tariff prompts consumers to buy fewer recorders; they reallocate a portion of their expenditures to less desired substitute products. U.S. consumers are clearly injured by the tariff, since they pay P_wP_t more for each of the c units they buy at price P_t.
- *Increased domestic production* U.S. producers—who are not subject to the tariff—receive the higher price P_t per unit. Because this new price is higher than the pretariff world price P_w, the domestic VCR industry moves up and to the right along its supply curve S_d, increasing domestic output from a to b. Domestic producers thus enjoy both a higher price and expanded sales; this explains why domestic producers lobby for protective tariffs. But from a social point of view, the greater domestic production from a to b means that the tariff permits domestic producers of recorders to bid resources away from other, more efficient, U.S. industries.
- *Decline in imports* Japanese producers are hurt. Although the sales price of each recorder is higher by P_wP_t, that amount accrues to the U.S. government, not to Japanese producers. The after-tariff world price, or the per-unit revenue to Japanese producers, remains at P_w, but the volume of U.S. imports (Japanese exports) falls from ad to bc.
- *Tariff revenue* The orange rectangle represents the amount of revenue the tariff yields. Total revenue from the tariff is determined by multiplying the tariff, P_wP_t per unit, by the number of recorders imported, bc. This tariff revenue is a transfer of income from consumers to government and does not represent any net change

in the nation's economic well-being. The result is that government gains this portion of what consumers lose by paying more for VCRs.

Indirect Effect

Tariffs have a subtle effect beyond what our supply and demand diagram can show. Because Japan sells fewer VCRs in the United States, it earns fewer dollars and so must buy fewer U.S. exports. U.S. export industries must then cut production and release resources. These are highly efficient industries, as we know from their comparative advantage and their ability to sell goods in world markets.

Tariffs directly promote the expansion of inefficient industries that do not have a comparative advantage; they also indirectly cause the contraction of relatively efficient industries that do have a comparative advantage. Put bluntly, tariffs cause resources to be shifted in the wrong direction—and that is not surprising. We know that specialization and world trade lead to more efficient use of world resources and greater world output. But protective tariffs reduce world trade. Therefore, tariffs also reduce efficiency and the world's real output.

Economic Impact of Quotas

We noted earlier that an import quota is a legal limit placed on the amount of some product that can be imported in a given year. Quotas have the same economic impact as a tariff, with one big difference: While tariffs generate revenue for the domestic government, a quota transfers that revenue to foreign producers.

Suppose in Figure 20.6 that, instead of imposing a tariff, the United States prohibits any imports of Japanese VCRs in excess of bc units. In other words, an import quota of bc recorders is imposed on Japan. We deliberately chose the size of this quota to be the same amount as imports would be under a P_wP_t tariff so that we can compare "equivalent" situations. As a consequence of the quota, the supply of recorders is $S_d + Q$ in the United States. This supply consists of the domestic supply plus the fixed amount bc ($= Q$) that importers will provide at each domestic price. The supply curve $S_d + Q$ does not extend below price P_w, because Japanese producers would not export recorders to the United States at any price below P_w; instead, they would sell them to other countries at the world market price of P_w.

Most of the economic results are the same as those with a tariff. VCR prices are higher (P_t instead of P_w) because imports have been reduced from *ad* to *bc*. Domestic consumption of VCRs is down from *d* to *c*. U.S. producers enjoy both a higher price (P_t rather than P_w) and increased sales (*b* rather than *a*).

The difference is that the price increase of $P_w P_t$ paid by U.S. consumers on imports of *bc*—the orange area—no longer goes to the U.S. Treasury as tariff (tax) revenue but flows to the Japanese firms that have acquired the rights to sell VCRs in the United States. For consumers in the United States, a tariff produces a better economic outcome than a quota, other things being the same. A tariff generates government revenue that can be used to cut other taxes or to finance public goods and services that benefit the United States. In contrast, the higher price created by quotas results in additional revenue for foreign producers. **(Key Question 7)**

Net Costs of Tariffs and Quotas

Figure 20.6 shows that tariffs and quotas impose costs on domestic consumers but provide gains to domestic producers and, in the case of tariffs, revenue to the Federal government. The consumer costs of trade restrictions are calculated by determining the effect the restrictions have on consumer prices. Protection raises the price of a product in three ways: (1) The price of the imported product goes up; (2) the higher price of imports causes some consumers to shift their purchases to higher-priced domestically produced goods; and (3) the prices of domestically produced goods rise because import competition has declined.

Study after study finds that the costs to consumers substantially exceed the gains to producers and government. A sizable net cost or efficiency loss to society arises from trade protection. Furthermore, industries employ large amounts of economic resources to influence Congress to pass and retain protectionist laws. Because these rent-seeking efforts divert resources away from more socially desirable purposes, trade restrictions impose that cost on society.

Conclusion: The gains that U.S. trade barriers create for protected industries and their workers come at the expense of much greater losses for the entire economy. The result is economic inefficiency.

Impact on Income Distribution

Tariffs and quotas affect low-income families proportionately more than high-income families. Because they act much like sales or excise taxes, these trade restrictions are highly regressive. That is, the "overcharge" associated with trade protection falls as a percentage of income as income increases. For example, a family with an annual income of $10,000 may pay an overcharge of $100 per year because of the trade restrictions on apparel, while a family with an income of $100,000 may pay a $500 overcharge. As a percentage of income, the lower-income family pays 1 percent (= $100 of overcharge/$10,000 of income); the higher-income family, only .5 percent (= $500/$100,000).

■ The Case for Protection: A Critical Review

Despite the logic of specialization and trade, there are still protectionists in some union halls, corporate boardrooms, and the halls of Congress. What arguments do protectionists make to justify trade barriers? How valid are those arguments?

Military Self-Sufficiency Argument

The argument here is not economic but political-military: Protective tariffs are needed to preserve or strengthen industries that produce the materials essential for national defense. In an uncertain world, the political-military objectives (self-sufficiency) sometimes must take precedence over economic goals (efficiency in the use of world resources).

Unfortunately, it is difficult to measure and compare the benefit of increased national security against the cost of economic inefficiency when protective tariffs are imposed. The economist can only point out that there are economic costs when a nation levies tariffs to increase military self-sufficiency.

All people in the United States would agree that it is not a good idea to import missile guidance systems from Iraq, yet the self-sufficiency argument is open to serious abuse. Nearly every industry can claim that it makes direct or indirect contributions to national security and hence deserves protection from imports.

Are there not better ways than tariffs to provide needed strength in strategic industries? When it is achieved through tariffs, this self-sufficiency increases the domestic prices of the products of the protected industry. Thus only those consumers who buy the industry's products shoulder the cost of greater military security. A direct subsidy to strategic industries, financed out of general tax revenues, would distribute those costs more equitably.

Increased Domestic Employment Argument

Arguing for a tariff to "save U.S. jobs" becomes fashionable as an economy encounters a recession. In an economy that engages in international trade, exports involve spending on domestic output and imports reflect spending to obtain part of another nation's output. So, in this argument, reducing imports will divert spending on another nation's output to spending on domestic output. Thus domestic output and employment will rise. But this argument has several shortcomings:

- *Job creation from imports* While imports may eliminate some U.S. jobs, they create others. Imports may have eliminated the jobs of some U.S. steel and textile workers in recent years, but other workers have gained jobs unloading ships and selling imported cars and imported electronic equipment. Import restrictions alter the composition of employment, but they may have little or no effect on the volume of employment.
- *Fallacy of composition* All nations cannot simultaneously succeed in restricting imports while maintaining their exports; what is true for one nation is not true for all nations. The exports of one nation must be the imports of another nation. To the extent that one country is able to expand its economy through an excess of exports over imports, the resulting excess of imports over exports worsens another economy's unemployment problem. It is no wonder that tariffs and import quotas meant to achieve domestic full employment are called "beggar my neighbor" policies: They achieve short-run domestic goals by making trading partners poorer.
- *Possibility of retaliation* Nations adversely affected by tariffs and quotas are likely to retaliate, causing a "trade-barrier war" that will choke off trade and make all nations worse off. The Smoot-Hawley Tariff Act of 1930, which imposed the highest tariffs ever enacted in the United States, backfired miserably. Rather than increasing U.S. output, this tariff act only led to retaliatory restrictions by affected nations. That trade war caused a further contraction of international trade and lowered the income and employment levels of all nations. As stated by a U.S. international trade expert:

A trade war in which countries restrict each other's exports in pursuit of some illusory advantage is not much like a real war. On the one hand, nobody gets killed. On the other, unlike real wars, it is almost impossible for anyone to win, since the main losers when a country imposes barriers to trade are not foreign exporters but domestic residents. In effect, a trade war is a conflict in which each country uses most of its ammunition to shoot itself in the foot.[1]   20.1

- *Long-run feedbacks* In the long run, forcing an excess of exports over imports cannot succeed in raising domestic employment. It is through U.S. imports that foreign nations earn dollars for buying U.S. exports. In the long run a nation must import in order to export. The long-run impact of tariffs is not an increase in domestic employment but, at best, a reallocation of workers away from export industries and to protected domestic industries. This shift implies a less efficient allocation of resources.

Diversification-for-Stability Argument

Highly specialized economies such as Saudi Arabia (based on oil) and Cuba (based on sugar) are dependent on international markets for their income. In these economies, wars, international political developments, recessions abroad, and random fluctuations in world supply and demand for one or two particular goods can cause deep declines in export revenues and therefore in domestic income. Tariff and quota protection are allegedly needed in such nations to enable greater industrial diversification. That way, these economies will not be so dependent on exporting one or two products to obtain the other goods they need. Such goods will be available domestically, thereby providing greater domestic stability.

There is some truth in this diversification-for-stability argument. There are also two serious shortcomings:

- The argument has little or no relevance to the United States and other advanced economies.
- The economic costs of diversification may be great; for example, one-crop economies may be highly inefficient at manufacturing.

[1]Paul Krugman, *Peddling Prosperity* (New York: Norton, 1994), p. 287.

Infant Industry Argument

The infant industry argument contends that protective tariffs are needed to allow new domestic industries to establish themselves. Temporarily shielding young domestic firms from the severe competition of more mature and more efficient foreign firms will give infant industries a chance to develop and become efficient producers.

This argument for protection rests on an alleged exception to the case for free trade. The exception is that young industries have not had, and if they face mature foreign competition will never have, the chance to make the long-run adjustments needed for larger scale and greater efficiency in production. In this view, tariff protection for such infant industries will correct a misallocation of world resources perpetuated by historically different levels of economic development between domestic and foreign industries.

Counterarguments   There are some logical problems with the infant industry argument:

- In the developing nations it is difficult to determine which industries are the infants that are capable of achieving economic maturity and therefore deserving protection.
- Protective tariffs may persist even after industrial maturity has been realized.
- Most economists feel that if infant industries are to be subsidized, there are better means than tariffs for doing so. Direct subsidies, for example, have the advantage of making explicit which industries are being aided and to what degree.

Strategic Trade Policy   In recent years the infant industry argument has taken a modified form in advanced economies. Now proponents contend that government should use trade barriers to reduce the risk of investing in product development by domestic firms, particularly where advanced technology is involved. Firms protected from foreign competition can grow more rapidly and achieve greater economies of scale than unprotected foreign competitors. The protected firms can eventually dominate world markets because of their lower costs. Supposedly, dominance of world markets will enable the domestic firms to return high profits to the home nation. These profits will exceed the domestic sacrifices caused by trade barriers. Also, advances in high-technology industries are deemed benefi-

cial, because the advances achieved in one domestic industry often can be transferred to other domestic industries.

Japan and South Korea, in particular, have been accused of using this form of **strategic trade policy.** The problem with this strategy and therefore with this argument for tariffs is that the nations put at a disadvantage by strategic trade policies tend to retaliate with tariffs of their own. The outcome may be higher tariffs worldwide, reduction of world trade, and the loss of potential gains from technological advances.

Protection-against-Dumping Argument

This argument contends that tariffs are needed to protect domestic firms from "dumping" by foreign producers. **Dumping** is the selling of excess goods in a foreign market at a price below cost. Economists cite two plausible reasons for this behavior. First, firms may use dumping abroad to drive out domestic competitors there, thus obtaining monopoly power and monopoly prices and profits for the importing firm. The long-term economic profits resulting from this strategy may more than offset the earlier losses that accompany the below-cost sales.

Second, dumping may be a form of price discrimination, which is charging different prices to different customers even though costs are the same. The foreign seller may find it can maximize its profit by charging a high price in its monopolized domestic market while unloading its surplus output at a lower price in the United States. The surplus output may be needed so that the firm can obtain the overall per-unit cost saving associated with large-scale production. The higher profit in the home market more than makes up for the losses incurred on sales abroad.

Because dumping is a legitimate concern, many nations prohibit it. For example, where dumping is shown to injure U.S. firms, the Federal government imposes tariffs called "antidumping duties" on the specific goods. But there are relatively few documented cases of dumping each year, and those few cases do not justify widespread, permanent tariffs.

In fact, foreign producers argue that the United States uses dumping allegations and antidumping duties to restrict legitimate trade. Some foreign firms clearly can produce certain goods at substantially less per-unit cost than U.S. competitors. So what may seem to be dumping actually is comparative advantage at work. If antidumping laws are abused, they might increase the price of imports and restrict competition in the U.S. market. Such reduced competition might enable U.S. firms to raise prices at consumers' expense. And even where true dumping does occur, U.S. consumers gain from the lower-priced product, at least in the short run, much as they gain from a price war among U.S. producers.

Cheap Foreign Labor Argument

The cheap foreign labor argument says that domestic firms and workers must be shielded from the ruinous competition of countries where wages are low. If protection is not provided, cheap imports will flood U.S. markets and the prices of U.S. goods—along with the wages of U.S. workers—will be pulled down. That is, the domestic living standards in the United States will be reduced.

This argument can be rebutted at several levels. The logic of the argument suggests that it is not mutually beneficial for rich and poor persons to trade with one another. However, that is not the case. A low-income farmworker may pick lettuce or tomatoes for a rich landowner, and both may benefit from the transaction. And U.S. consumers gain when they buy a Taiwanese-made pocket radio for $12 as opposed to a similar U.S.-made radio selling for $20.

Also, recall that gains from trade are based on comparative advantage, not on absolute advantage. Look back at Figure 20.1, and suppose that the United States and Brazil have labor forces of exactly the same size. Noting the positions of the production possibilities curves, observe that U.S. labor can produce more of either good. Thus, it is more productive. Because of this greater productivity, we can expect wages and living standards to be higher for U.S. labor. Brazil's less productive labor will receive lower wages.

The cheap foreign labor argument suggests that, to maintain our standard of living, the United States should not trade with low-wage Brazil. Suppose it does not. Will wages and living standards rise in the United States as a result? No. To obtain coffee, the United States will have to reallocate a portion of its labor from its efficient wheat industry to its inefficient coffee industry. As a re-

sult, the average productivity of U.S. labor will fall, as will real wages and living standards. The labor forces of both countries will have diminished standards of living because without specialization and trade they will have less output available to them. Compare column 4 with column 1 in Table 20.1 or points A' and B' with A and B in Figure 20.2 to confirm this point.

A Summing Up

The many arguments for protection are not weighty. Under proper conditions, the infant industry argument stands as a valid exception, justifiable on economic grounds. And on political-military grounds, the self-sufficiency argument can be used to validate some protection. But both arguments are open to severe overuse, and both neglect other ways of promoting industrial development and military self-sufficiency. Most of the other arguments are emotional appeals—half-truths and fallacies. They see only the immediate, direct consequences of protective tariffs, but ignore the fact that in the long run a nation must import in order to export.

There is also compelling historical evidence suggesting that free trade has led to prosperity and growth and that protectionism has had the opposite effects. Here are several examples:

- The U.S. Constitution forbids individual states from levying tariffs, and that makes the United States itself a huge free-trade area. Economic historians cite this as a positive factor in the economic development of the United States.
- The creation of the Common Market in Europe after the Second World War eliminated tariffs among member nations. Economists agree that the creation of this free-trade area, now the European Union, was a major ingredient in western European prosperity.
- The trend toward tariff reduction since the mid-1930s stimulated expansion of the world economy after the Second World War.
- The high tariffs imposed by the Smoot-Hawley Act of 1930 and the retaliation that it engendered worsened the Great Depression of the 1930s.
- In general, developing countries that have relied on import restrictions to protect their domestic industries have had slow growth compared to those that have pursued more open economic policies.

▮ The World Trade Organization

As indicated in Chapter 6, the inefficiencies of trade protectionism have led nations to seek various ways to reduce tariffs and quotas. In 1994 more than 120 of the world's nations, which together constituted the **World Trade Organization (WTO),** agreed to several trade liberalizations to be fully implemented by 2005. These liberalizations include:

■ Reductions in tariffs worldwide.
■ New rules to promote trade in services.
■ Reductions in agricultural subsidies that have distorted the global pattern of trade in agricultural goods.

■ New protections for intellectual property (copyrights, patents, trademarks).
■ The phasing out of quotas on textiles and apparel, replacing them with gradually declining tariffs.

When they are fully implemented in 2005, economists predict that these trade liberalizations will have boosted the world's GDP by $6 trillion, or 8 percent.

The 1994 agreement created the WTO to oversee the provisions of the agreement, resolve any disputes under the trade rules, and meet periodically to consider further trade liberalization. In 2001 some 140 nations belonged to the WTO. As a symbol of trade liberalization and global capitalism, the WTO has become a target of protest groups such as some labor unions (which fear loss of jobs and labor protections), environmental groups (which fear environmental degradation), socialists (who dislike capitalism and multinational corporations), and anarchists (who dislike government of any kind).

Economists agree that labor protections such as workplace safety, enforcement of child labor laws, and collective bargaining rights, as well as environmental concerns such as protection of forests and fisheries, are legitimate issues. But most economists believe these causes should not be used to slow or reverse trade liberalization. Trade liberalization increases world efficiency and world output. Rising standards of living enable developing and developed nations alike to "buy" more protections for labor and the environment. In this view, protestors should direct their political efforts toward changing the labor and environmental laws within the nations that they deem lacking in such protections. Trade liberalization is too important in its own right to be linked to a host of other, sometimes conflicting, political and economic causes.

Petition of the Candlemakers, 1845

French Economist Frédéric Bastiat (1801–1850) Devastated the Proponents of Protectionism by Satirically Extending Their Reasoning to Its Logical and Absurd Conclusions.

Petition of the Manufacturers of Candles, Waxlights, Lamps, Candlesticks, Street Lamps, Snuffers, Extinguishers, and of the Producers of Oil Tallow, Rosin, Alcohol, and, Generally, of Everything Connected with Lighting.

TO MESSIEURS THE MEMBERS OF THE CHAMBER OF DEPUTIES.

Gentlemen—You are on the right road. You reject abstract theories, and have little consideration for cheapness and plenty. Your chief care is the interest of the producer. You desire to emancipate him from external competition, and reserve the national market for national industry.

We are about to offer you an admirable opportunity of applying your—what shall we call it? your theory? No; nothing is more deceptive than theory; your doctrine? your system? your principle? but you dislike doctrines, you abhor systems, and as for principles, you deny that there are any in social economy: we shall say, then, your practice, your practice without theory and without principle.

We are suffering from the intolerable competition of a foreign rival, placed, it would seem, in a condition so far superior to ours

for the production of light, that he absolutely inundates our national market with it at a price fabulously reduced. The moment he shows himself, our trade leaves us—all consumers apply to him; and a branch of native industry, having countless ramifications, is all at once rendered completely stagnant. This rival . . . is no other than the Sun.

What we pray for is, that it may please you to pass a law ordering the shutting up of all windows, skylights, dormer windows, outside and inside shutters, curtains, blinds, bull's-eyes; in a word, of all openings, holes, chinks, clefts, and fissures, by or through which the light of the sun has been in use to enter houses, to the prejudice of the meritorious manufacturers with which we flatter ourselves we have accommodated our country,—a country which, in gratitude, ought not to abandon us now to a strife so unequal.

If you shut up as much as possible all access to natural light, and create a demand for artificial light, which of our French manufacturers will not be encouraged by it?

If more tallow is consumed, then there must be more oxen and sheep; and, consequently, we shall behold the multiplication of artificial meadows, meat, wool, hides, and, above all, manure, which is the basis and foundation of all agricultural wealth.

The same remark applies to navigation. Thousands of vessels will proceed to the whale fishery; and, in a short time, we shall possess a navy capable of maintaining the honor of France, and gratifying the patriotic aspirations of your petitioners, the undersigned candlemakers and others.

Only have the goodness to reflect, Gentlemen, and you will be convinced that there is, perhaps, no Frenchman, from the wealthy coalmaster to the humblest vender of lucifer matches, whose lot will not be ameliorated by the success of this our petition.

Source: Frédéric Bastiat, *Economic Sophisms* (Edinburgh: Oliver and Boyd, Tweeddale Court, 1873), pp. 49–53, abridged.

SUMMARY

1. The United States leads the world in the volume of international trade. Since 1975 U.S. exports and imports have more than doubled as a percentage of GDP. Other major trading nations are Germany, Japan, the western European nations, and the southeast Asian economies of Hong Kong (part of China), South Korea, Taiwan, and Singapore.

2. World trade is based on three considerations: the uneven distribution of economic resources among nations, the fact that efficient production of various goods requires particular techniques or combinations of resources, and the differentiated products produced among nations.

3. Mutually advantageous specialization and trade are possible between any two nations if they have different domestic opportunity-cost ratios for any two products. By specializing on the basis of comparative advantage, nations can obtain larger real incomes with fixed amounts of resources. The terms of trade determine how this increase in world output is shared by the trading nations. Increasing (rather than constant) opportunity costs limit specialization and trade.

4. A nation's export supply curve shows the quantities of a product the nation will export at world prices that exceed the domestic price (the price in a closed, no-international-trade economy). A nation's import demand curve reveals the quantities of a product it will import at world prices below the domestic price. In a two-nation model, the equilibrium world price and the equilibrium quantities of exports and imports occur where one nation's export supply curve intersects the other nation's import demand curve.

5. Trade barriers take the form of protective tariffs, quotas, nontariff barriers, and "voluntary" export restrictions. Supply and demand analysis reveals that protective tariffs and quotas increase the prices and reduce the quantities demanded of the affected goods.

Sales by foreign exporters diminish; domestic producers, however, gain higher prices and enlarged sales. Consumer losses from trade restrictions greatly exceed producer and government gains, creating an efficiency loss to society.

6. The strongest arguments for protection are the infant industry and military self-sufficiency arguments. Most other arguments for protection are half-truths, emotional appeals, or fallacies that emphasize the immediate effects of trade barriers while ignoring long-run consequences. Numerous historical examples suggest that free trade promotes economic growth; protectionism does not.

7. In 2001 the World Trade Organization (WTO) consisted of 140 member nations. It oversees trade agreements among the nations, resolves disputes over the rules, and periodically meets to discuss and negotiate further trade liberalization. Recently, the WTO has become a focus of protests by labor groups, environmental groups, socialists, and anarchists. Most economists believe that trade liberalization is too important to be tied to other political and economic causes, which should be pursued independently of trade rules.

TERMS AND CONCEPTS

labor-intensive goods	trading possibilities line	tariffs	strategic trade policy
land-intensive goods	gains from trade	revenue tariff	dumping
capital-intensive goods	world price	protective tariff	World Trade
cost ratio	domestic price	import quota	Organization (WTO)
principle of comparative advantage	export supply curve	nontariff barrier (NTB)	
terms of trade	import demand curve	voluntary export restriction (VER)	
	equilibrium world price		

STUDY QUESTIONS

1. Quantitatively, how important is international trade to the United States relative to other nations?

2. Distinguish among land-, labor-, and capital-intensive commodities, citing one nontextbook example of each. What role do these distinctions play in explaining international trade? What role do distinctive products, unrelated to cost advantages, play in international trade?

3. Suppose nation A can produce 80 units of X by using all its resources to produce X or 60 units of Y by de-

voting all its resources to Y. Comparable figures for nation B are 60 units of X and 60 units of Y. Assuming constant costs, in which product should each nation specialize? Why? What are the limits of the terms of trade?

4. **Key Question** At the top of the next page are hypothetical production possibilities tables for New Zealand and Spain.

**New Zealand's Production Possibilities Table
(Millions of Bushels)**

Product	Production Alternatives			
	A	B	C	D
Apples	0	20	40	60
Plums	15	10	5	0

**Spain's Production Possibilities Table
(Millions of Bushels)**

Product	Production Alternatives			
	R	S	T	U
Apples	0	20	40	60
Plums	60	40	20	0

Plot the production possibilities data for each of the two countries separately. Referring to your graphs, answer the following:

a.   What is each country's cost ratio of producing plums and apples.

b.   Which nation should specialize in which product?

c.   Show the trading possibilities lines for each nation if the actual terms of trade are 1 plum for 2 apples. (Plot these lines on your graph.)

d.   Suppose the optimum product mixes before specialization and trade were alternative B in New Zealand and alternative S in Spain. What would be the gains from specialization and trade?

5.   "The United States can produce X more efficiently than can Great Britain. Yet we import X from Great Britain." Explain.

6.   **Key Question** Refer to Figure 3.5, page 51. Assume that the graph depicts the U.S. domestic market for corn. How many bushels of corn, if any, will the United States export or import at a world price of $1, $2, $3, $4, and $5? Use this information to construct the U.S. export supply curve and import demand curve for corn. Suppose the only other corn-producing nation is France, where the domestic price is $4. Which country will export corn; which will import it?

7.   **Key Question** Draw a domestic supply and demand diagram for a product in which the United States does not have a comparative advantage. What impact do foreign imports have on domestic price and quantity? On your diagram show a protective tariff that eliminates approximately one-half of the assumed imports. What are the price-quantity effects of this tariff on (a) domestic consumers, (b) domestic produc-

ers, and (c) foreign exporters? How would the effects of a quota that creates the same amount of imports differ?

8.   "The potentially valid arguments for tariff protection are also the most easily abused." What are those arguments? Why are they susceptible to abuse? Evaluate the use of artificial trade barriers, such as tariffs and import quotas, as a means of achieving and maintaining full employment.

9.   Evaluate the following statements:

a.   Protective tariffs reduce both the imports and the exports of the nation that levies tariffs.

b.   The extensive application of protective tariffs destroys the ability of the international market system to allocate resources efficiently.

c.   Unemployment in some industries can often be reduced through tariff protection, but by the same token inefficiency typically increases.

d.   Foreign firms that "dump" their products onto the U.S. market are in effect providing bargains to the country's citizens.

e.   In view of the rapidity with which technological advance is dispersed around the world, free trade will inevitably yield structural maladjustments, unemployment, and balance-of-payments problems for industrially advanced nations.

f.   Free trade can improve the composition and efficiency of domestic output. Competition from Volkswagen, Toyota, and Honda forced Detroit to make a compact car, and foreign success with the oxygen process forced American steel firms to modernize.

g.   In the long run, foreign trade is neutral with respect to total employment.

10.   Between 1981 and 1985 the Japanese agreed to a voluntary export restriction that reduced U.S. imports of Japanese automobiles by about 10 percent. What would you expect the short-run effects of that restriction to be on the U.S. and Japanese automobile industries? If this restriction were permanent, what would be its long-run effects in the two nations on (a) the allocation of resources, (b) the volume of employment, (c) the price level, and (d) the standard of living?

11.   What is the WTO, and how does it relate to international trade? What problems, if any, arise when too many extraneous issues are tied to efforts to liberalize trade?

12.   **(Last Word)** What point is Bastiat trying to make with his petition of the candlemakers?

13.   **Web-Based Question:** *Trade liberalization—the WTO* Go to the website of the World Trade Organization (www.wto.org/) to retrieve the latest

news from the WTO. List and summarize three recent news items relating to the WTO. Search the sections Trade Topics and Resources to find information on both international trade and the environment and international trade and poverty. Summarize the WTO's major conclusions on these two topics.

14. **Web-Based Question:** *The U.S. International Trade Commission—what is it and what does it do?* Go to www.usitc.gov to determine the duties of the U.S. International Trade Commission (USITC). How does this organization differ from the World Trade Organization (question 13)? From the site map, find Sunset Reviews to determine what they are and how they relate to the Uruguay Round agreement of the WTO. Go to New Releases and identify and briefly describe three USITC rulings relating to charges of unfair international trade practices that harm U.S. producers.

Exchange Rates, the Balance of Payments, and Trade Deficits

I F Y O U T A K E a U.S. dollar to the bank and ask to exchange it for U.S. currency, you will get a puzzled look. If you persist, you may get a dollar's worth of change: One U.S. dollar can buy exactly one U.S. dollar. But on March 6, 2001, for example, 1 U.S. dollar could buy 885,000 Turkish lira, 1.93 Australian dollars, .68 British pounds, 1.54 Canadian dollars, 1.07 European euros, 118.88 Japanese yen, or 9.66 Mexican pesos. What explains this seemingly haphazard array of exchange rates? ■ In Chapter 20 we examined comparative advantage as the underlying economic basis of world trade and discussed the effects of barriers to free trade. Now we introduce the monetary or financial aspects of international trade: How are currencies of different nations exchanged when import and export transactions occur? What is meant by a "favorable" or an "unfavorable" balance of payments? What is the difference between flexible exchange rates and fixed exchange rates? What are the causes and consequences of the large U.S. trade deficits?

■ Financing International Trade

One factor that makes international trade different from domestic trade is the involvement of different national currencies. When a U.S. firm exports goods to a Mexican firm, the U.S. exporter wants to be paid in dollars. But the Mexican importer possesses pesos. The importer must exchange pesos for dollars before the U.S. export transaction can occur.

This problem is resolved in foreign exchange markets, in which dollars can purchase Mexican pesos, European euros, South Korean won, British pounds, Japanese yen, or any other currency, and

vice versa. Sponsored by major banks in New York, London, Zurich, Tokyo, and elsewhere, foreign exchange markets facilitate exports and imports.

U.S. Export Transaction

Suppose a U.S. exporter agrees to sell $300,000 of computers to a British firm. Assume, for simplicity, that the rate of exchange—the rate at which pounds can be exchanged for, or converted into, dollars, and vice versa—is $2 for £1 (the actual exchange rate is about $1.50 = 1 pound). This means the British importer must pay the equivalent of £150,000 to the

U.S. exporter to obtain the $300,000 worth of computers. Also assume that all buyers of pounds and dollars are in the United States and Great Britain. Let's follow the steps in the transaction:

■ To pay for the computers, the British buyer draws a check for £150,000 on its checking account in a London bank and sends it to the U.S. exporter.

■ But the U.S. exporting firm must pay its bills in dollars, not pounds. So the exporter sells the £150,000 check on the London bank to its bank in, say, New York City, which is a dealer in foreign exchange. The bank adds $300,000 to the U.S. exporter's checking account for the £150,000 check.

■ The New York bank deposits the £150,000 in a correspondent London bank for future sale to some U.S. buyer who needs pounds.

Note this important point: *U.S. exports create a foreign demand for dollars, and the fulfillment of that demand increases the supply of foreign currencies (pounds, in this case) owned by U.S. banks and available to U.S. buyers.*

U.S. Import Transaction

Why would the New York bank be willing to buy pounds for dollars? As just indicated, the New York bank is a dealer in foreign exchange; it is in the business of buying (for a fee) and selling (also for a fee) one currency for another.

Let's now examine how the New York bank would sell pounds for dollars to finance a U.S. import (British export) transaction. Suppose a U.S. retail firm wants to import £150,000 of compact discs produced in Britain by a hot new musical group. Again, let's track the steps in the transaction:

■ The U.S. importer purchases £150,000 at the $2 = £1 exchange rate by writing a check for $300,000 on its New York bank. Because the British exporting firm wants to be paid in pounds rather than dollars, the U.S. importer must exchange dollars for pounds, which it does by going to the New York bank and purchasing £150,000 for $300,000. (Perhaps the U.S. importer purchases the same £150,000 that the New York bank acquired from the U.S. exporter.)

■ The U.S. importer sends its newly purchased check for £150,000 to the British firm, which deposits it in the London bank.

Here we see that *U.S. imports create a domestic demand for foreign currencies (pounds, in this case), and the fulfillment of that demand reduces the supplies of foreign currencies (again, pounds) held by U.S. banks and available to U.S. consumers.*

The combined export and import transactions bring one more point into focus. U.S. exports (the computers) make available, or "earn," a supply of foreign currencies for U.S. banks, and U.S. imports (the compact discs) create a demand for those currencies. In a broad sense, any nation's exports finance or "pay for" its imports. Exports provide the foreign currencies needed to pay for imports.

Postscript: Although our examples are confined to exporting and importing goods, demand for and supplies of pounds also arise from transactions involving services and the payment of interest and dividends on foreign investments. The United States demands pounds not only to buy imports but also to buy insurance and transportation services from the British, to vacation in London, to pay dividends and interest on British investments in the United States, and to make new financial and real investments in Britain. **(Key Question 2)**

■ The Balance of Payments

A nation's **balance of payments** is the sum of all the transactions that take place between its residents and the residents of all foreign nations. Those transactions include exports and imports of goods, exports and imports of services, tourist expenditures, interest and dividends received or paid abroad, and purchases and sales of financial or real assets abroad. The U.S. Commerce Department's Bureau of Economic Analysis compiles the balance-of-payments statement each year. *The statement shows all the payments a nation receives from foreign countries and all the payments it makes to them.*

Table 21.1 is a simplified balance-of-payments statement for the United States in 1999. Let's take a close look at this accounting statement to see what it reveals about U.S. international trade and finance. To help our explanation, we divide the single balance-of-payments account into three of its components: the *current account*, the *capital account*, and the *official reserves account*.

Current Account

The top portion of Table 21.1 summarizes U.S. trade in currently produced goods and services and is called the **current account.** Items 1 and 2 show U.S. exports and imports of goods (merchandise) in 1999. U.S. exports have a *plus* (+) sign because they

Table 21.1
The U.S. Balance of Payments, 1999 (in Billions)

Current account		
(1) U.S. goods exports	$+ 684	
(2) U.S. goods imports	−1030	
(3) *Balance on goods*		$− 346
(4) U.S. exports of services	+ 272	
(5) U.S. imports of services	− 191	
(6) *Balance on services*		+ 81
(7) *Balance on goods and services*		− 265
(8) Net investment income	− 18	
(9) Net transfers	− 48	
(10) **Balance on current account**		**−331**
Capital account		
(11) Foreign purchases of assets in the United States .	+ 760*	
(12) U.S. purchases of assets abroad	− 438*	
(13) **Balance on capital account**		**+322**
Official reserves account		
(14) **Official reserves**		**+ 9**
		$ 0

*Includes one-half of a $12 billion statistical discrepancy that is listed in the capital account.
Source: Survey of Current Business, October 2000 (www.bea.doc.gov).

are a *credit*; they earn and make available foreign exchange in the United States. As you saw in the preceding section, any export-type transaction that obligates foreigners to make "inpayments" to the United States generates supplies of foreign currencies in the U.S. banks.

U.S. imports have a *minus* (−) sign because they are a *debit*; they reduce the stock of foreign currencies in the United States. Our earlier discussion of trade financing indicated that U.S. imports obligate the United States to make "outpayments" to the rest of the world that reduce available supplies of foreign currencies held by U.S. banks.

Balance on Goods   Items 1 and 2 in Table 21.1 reveal that in 1999 U.S. goods exports of $684 billion did not earn enough foreign currencies to finance U.S. goods imports of $1030 billion. A country's *balance of trade on goods* is the difference between its exports and its imports of goods. If exports exceed imports, the result is a surplus on the balance of goods. If imports exceed exports, there is a trade deficit on the balance of goods. We note in item 3 that in 1999 the United States incurred a trade deficit on goods of $346 billion. (Global Perspective 21.1 shows U.S. trade deficits and surpluses relative to selected nations.)

GLOBAL PERSPECTIVE 21.1

U.S. Trade Balances in Goods, Selected Nations, 1999

The United States has large trade deficits in goods with several nations, in particular, Japan and China.

Source: Department of Commerce, Bureau of Economic Analysis, www.bea.doc.gov/.

Balance on Services   The United States exports not only goods, such as airplanes and computer software, but also services, such as insurance, consulting, travel, and brokerage services, to residents of foreign nations. Item 4 in Table 21.1 shows that these service "exports" totaled $272 billion in 1999 and are a credit (thus the + sign). Item 5 indicates that the United States "imports" similar services from foreigners; those service imports were $191 billion in 1999 and are a debit (thus the − sign). So the balance on services (item 6) in 1999 was $81 billion.

The **balance on goods and services** shown as item 7 is the difference between U.S. exports of goods and services (items 1 and 4) and U.S. imports of goods and services (items 2 and 5). In 1999, U.S. imports of goods and services exceeded U.S. exports of goods and services by $265 billion. So a **trade deficit** (or "unfavorable balance of trade") occurred. In contrast, a **trade surplus** (or "favorable balance of trade") occurs when exports of goods and services exceed imports of goods and services.

Balance on Current Account   Item 8, *net investment income*, represents the difference between (1) the interest and dividend payments foreigners paid the United States for the use of exported U.S. capital and (2) the interest and dividends the United States paid for the use of foreign capital invested in the United States. Observe that in 1999 U.S. net investment income was a negative $18 billion worth of foreign currencies.

Item 9 shows net transfers, both public and private, between the United States and the rest of the world. Included here is foreign aid, pensions paid to U.S. citizens living abroad, and remittances by immigrants to relatives abroad. These $48 billion of transfers are net U.S. outpayments that decrease available supplies of foreign exchange. They are, in a sense, the exporting of goodwill and the importing of "thank-you notes."

By adding all transactions in the current account, we obtain the **balance on current account** shown in item 10. In 1999 the United States had a current account deficit of $331 billion. This means that the U.S. current account transactions (items 2, 5, 8, and 9) created outpayments of foreign currencies from the United States greater than the inpayments of foreign currencies to the United States.

Capital Account

The second account within the overall balance-of-trade account is the **capital account,** which summarizes the purchase or sale of real or financial assets and the corresponding flows of monetary payments that accompany them. For example, a foreign firm may buy a real asset, say, an office building in the United States, or a financial asset, for instance, a U.S. government security. Both kinds of transaction involve the "export" of the ownership of U.S. assets from the United States in return for inpayments of foreign currency. As indicated in line 11, these "exports" of ownership of assets are designated *foreign purchases of assets in the United States*. They have a + sign because, like exports of U.S. goods and services, they represent inpayments of foreign currencies.

Conversely, a U.S. firm may buy, say, a hotel chain (real asset) in a foreign country or some of the common stock (financial asset) of a foreign firm. Both transactions involve the "import" of the ownership of the real or financial assets to the United States and are paid for by outpayments of foreign currencies. These "imports" are designated *U.S. purchases of assets abroad* and, as shown in line 12, have a − sign; like U.S. imports of goods and services, they represent outpayments of foreign currencies from the United States.

Items 11 and 12 combined yield a **balance on capital account** of +$322 billion for 1999 (line 13). In 1999 the United States "exported" $760 billion of ownership of its real and financial assets and "imported" $438 billion. This capital account surplus brought in $322 billion of foreign currencies to the United States.

Official Reserves Account

The third account in the overall balance of payments is the official reserves account. The central banks of nations hold quantities of foreign currencies called **official reserves.** These reserves can be drawn on to make up any net deficit in the combined current and capital accounts (much as you would draw on your savings to pay for a special purchase). In 1999 the United States had a $9 billion deficit in the combined current and capital accounts (line 10 minus line 13). This balance in the U.S. international payments required that the U.S. government deplete its official reserves of foreign currencies by $9 billion (item 14). The + sign indicates that this drawing down and exporting of reserves is a credit—an inpayment from official reserves that was needed to balance the overall balance-of-payments account.

In some years, the current and capital accounts balances are positive, meaning that the United States earned more foreign currencies than it needed. The surplus would create outpayments, not to other countries, but to the stock of official reserves. As such, item 13 would have a − sign because it is a debit.

The three components of the balance of payments (the current account, the capital account, and the official reserves account) must together equal zero. Every unit of foreign exchange used (as reflected in a minus outpayment or debit transaction) must have a source (a plus inpayment or credit transaction).

Payments Deficits and Surpluses

Although the balance of payments must always sum to zero, economists and political officials speak of **balance-of-payments deficits and surpluses;** they are referring to imbalances between the current and capital accounts (line 10 minus line 13) that cause a drawing down or a building up of foreign currencies. A drawing down of official reserves (to create a positive official reserves entry in Table 21.1) measures a nation's balance-of-payments deficit; a building up of official reserves (which is shown as a negative official reserves entry) measures a nation's balance-of-payments surplus.

A balance-of-payments deficit is not necessarily bad, nor is a balance-of-payments surplus necessarily good. Both simply happen. However, any nation's official reserves are limited. Persistent payments deficits, which must be financed by drawing down those reserves, would ultimately deplete the reserves. That nation would have to adopt policies to correct its balance of payments. Such policies might require painful macroeconomic adjustments, trade barriers and similar restrictions, or a major depreciation of its currency. For this reason, nations seek to achieve payments balance, at least over several-year periods.

It is clear from Table 21.1 that in 1999 the United States had a large current account deficit, a large capital account surplus, and a relatively small payments deficit. Large current account deficits have been the norm for the United States in recent years. We need to examine the causes and consequences of trade deficits but will defer that discussion until later in this chapter. **(Key Question 3)**

■ Flexible Exchange Rates

Both the size and the persistence of a nation's balance-of-payments deficits and surpluses and the adjustments it must make to correct those imbalances depend on the system of exchange rates being used. There are two "pure" types of exchange-rate systems:

■ **A flexible- or floating-exchange-rate system** through which demand and supply determine exchange rates and in which no government intervention occurs.

■ **A fixed-exchange-rate system** through which governments determine exchange rates and make necessary adjustments in their economies to maintain those rates.

We begin by looking at flexible exchange rates. Let's examine the rate, or price, at which U.S. dollars might be exchanged for British pounds. In **Figure 21.1 (Key Graph)** we show demand D_1 and supply S_1 of pounds in the currency market. ◢ **21.1**

The *demand-for-pounds curve* is downward-sloping because all British goods and services will be cheaper to the United States if pounds become less expensive to the United States. That is, at lower dollar prices for pounds, the United States can get more pounds and therefore more British goods and services per dollar. To buy those cheaper British goods, U.S. consumers will increase the quantity of pounds they demand.

KEY GRAPH

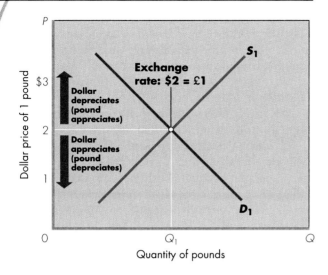

Quantity of pounds

Figure 21.1

The market for foreign currency (pounds). The intersection of the demand-for-pounds curve D_1 and the supply-of-pounds curve S_1 determines the equilibrium dollar price of pounds, here, $2. That means that the exchange rate is $2 = £1. The upward green arrow is a reminder that a higher dollar price of pounds (say, $3 = £1, caused by a shift in either the demand or the supply curve) means that the dollar has depreciated (the pound has appreciated). The downward green arrow tells us that a lower dollar price of pounds (say, $1 = £1, again caused by a shift in either the demand or the supply curve) means that the dollar has appreciated (the pound has depreciated).

Quick Quiz 21.3

1. Which of the following statements is true?
   a. The quantity of pounds demanded falls when the dollar appreciates.
   b. The quantity of pounds supplied declines as the dollar price of the pound rises.
   c. At the equilibrium exchange rate, the pound price of $1 is ½ pound.
   d. The dollar appreciates if the demand for pounds increases.

2. At the price of $2 for 1 pound in this figure:
   a. the dollar-pound exchange rate is unstable.
   b. the quantity of pounds supplied equals the quantity demanded.
   c. the dollar price of 1 pound equals the pound price of $1.
   d. U.S. goods exports to Britain must equal U.S. goods imports from Britain.

3. Other things equal, a leftward shift of the demand curve in this figure:
   a. would depreciate the dollar.
   b. would create a shortage of pounds at the previous price of $2 for 1 pound.
   c. might be caused by a major recession in the United States.
   d. might be caused by a significant rise of real interest rates in Britain.

4. Other things equal, a rightward shift of the supply curve in this figure would:
   a. depreciate the dollar and might be caused by a significant rise of real interest rates in Britain.
   b. depreciate the dollar and might be caused by a significant fall of real interest rates in Britain.
   c. appreciate the dollar and might be caused by a significant rise of real interest rates in the United States.
   d. appreciate the dollar and might be caused by a significant fall of interest rates in the United States.

Answers: 1. c; 2. b; 3. c; 4. c

The *supply-of-pounds* curve is upward-sloping because the British will purchase more U.S. goods when the dollar price of pounds rises (that is, as the pound price of dollars falls). When the British buy more U.S. goods, they supply a greater quantity of pounds to the foreign exchange market. In other words, they must exchange pounds for dollars to purchase U.S. goods. So, when the dollar price of pounds rises, the quantity of pounds supplied goes up.

The intersection of the supply curve and the demand curve will determine the dollar price of pounds. Here, that price (exchange rate) is $2 for £1.

Depreciation and Appreciation

An exchange rate determined by market forces can, and often does, change daily like stock and bond prices. When the dollar price of pounds *rises*, for example, from $2 = £1 to $3 = £1, the dollar has *depreciated* relative to the pound (and the pound has appreciated relative to the dollar). When a currency depreciates, more units of it (dollars) are needed to buy a single unit of some other currency (a pound).

When the dollar price of pounds *falls*, for example, from $2 = £1 to $1 = £1, the dollar has *appreciated* relative to the pound. When a currency appreciates, fewer units of it (dollars) are needed to buy a single unit of some other currency (pounds).

In our U.S.-Britain illustrations, depreciation of the dollar means an appreciation of the pound, and vice versa. When the dollar price of a pound jumps from $2 = £1 to $3 = £1, the pound has appreciated relative to the dollar because it takes fewer pounds to buy $1. At $2 = £1, it took £$\frac{1}{2}$ to buy $1; at $3 = £1, it takes only £$\frac{1}{3}$ to buy $1. Conversely, when the dollar appreciated relative to the pound, the pound depreciated relative to the dollar. More pounds were needed to buy a dollar.

Determinants of Exchange Rates

What factors would cause a nation's currency to appreciate or depreciate in the market for foreign exchange? Here are three generalizations:

■ If the demand for a nation's currency increases (all else equal), that currency will appreciate; if the demand declines, that currency will depreciate.

■ If the supply of a nation's currency increases, that currency will depreciate; if the supply decreases, that currency will appreciate.

■ If a nation's currency appreciates, some foreign currency depreciates relative to it.

With these generalizations in mind, let's examine the determinants of exchange rates—the factors that shift the demand or supply curve for a certain currency.

Changes in Tastes   Any change in consumer tastes or preferences for the products of a foreign country may alter the demand for that nation's currency and change its exchange rate. If technological advances in U.S. wireless phones make them more attractive to British consumers and businesses, then the British will supply more pounds in the exchange market in order to purchase more U.S. wireless phones. The supply-of-pounds curve will shift to the right, causing the pound to depreciate and the dollar to appreciate.

In contrast, the U.S. demand-for-pounds curve will shift to the right if British woolen apparel becomes more fashionable in the United States. So the pound will appreciate and the dollar will depreciate.

Relative Income Changes   A nation's currency is likely to depreciate if its growth of national income is more rapid than that of other countries. Here's why: A country's imports vary directly with its income level. As total income rises in the United States, people there buy both more domestic goods and more foreign goods. If the U.S. economy is expanding rapidly and the British economy is stagnant, U.S. imports of British goods, and therefore U.S. demands for pounds, will increase. The dollar price of pounds will rise, so the dollar will depreciate.

Relative Price-Level Changes   Changes in the relative price levels of two nations may change the demand and supply of currencies and alter the exchange rate between the two nations' currencies.

The **purchasing-power-parity theory** holds that exchange rates equate the purchasing power of various currencies. That is, the exchange rates among national currencies adjust to match the ratios of the nations' price levels: If a certain market basket of goods costs $10,000 in the United States and £5,000 in Great Britain, according to this theory the exchange rate will be $2 = £1. That way, a dollar spent on goods sold in Britain, Japan, Turkey, and other nations will have equal purchasing power.   ▣ **21.1**

In practice, however, exchange rates depart from purchasing power parity, even over long periods. Nevertheless, changes in relative price levels are a determinant of exchange rates. If, for example, the domestic price level rises rapidly in the United States and remains constant in Great Britain, U.S. consumers will seek out low-priced British goods, increasing the demand for pounds. The British will purchase fewer U.S. goods, reducing the supply of pounds. This combination of demand and supply changes will cause the pound to appreciate and the dollar to depreciate.

Relative Interest Rates   Changes in relative interest rates between two countries may alter their exchange rate. Suppose that real interest rates rise in the United States but stay constant in Great Britain. British citizens will then find the United States an attractive place in which to make financial investments. To undertake these investments, they will have to supply pounds in the foreign exchange market to obtain dollars. The increase in the supply of pounds results in depreciation of the pound and appreciation of the dollar.

Speculation   Currency speculators are people who buy and sell currencies with an eye toward reselling or repurchasing them at a profit. Suppose speculators expect the U.S. economy to (1) grow more rapidly than the British economy and (2) experience a more rapid rise in its price level than will Britain. These expectations translate into an anticipation that the pound will appreciate and the dollar will depreciate. Speculators who are holding dollars will therefore try to convert them into pounds. This effort will increase the demand for pounds and cause the dollar price of pounds to rise (that is, cause the dollar to depreciate). A self-fulfilling prophecy occurs: The pound appreciates and the dollar depreciates because speculators act on the belief that these changes will in fact take place. In this way, speculation can cause changes in exchange rates. (We deal with currency speculation in more detail in this chapter's Last Word.)

Table 21.2 has more illustrations of the determinants of exchange rates; the table is worth careful study.

Flexible Rates and the Balance of Payments

Proponents of flexible exchange rates say they have an important feature: They automatically adjust and eventually eliminate balance-of-payments deficits or surpluses. We can explain this idea through Figure 21.2, in which S_1 and D_1 are the supply and demand curves for pounds from Figure 21.1. The equilibrium exchange rate of $2 = £1 means that there is no balance-of-payments deficit or surplus between the United States and Britain. At that exchange rate, the quantity of pounds demanded by U.S. consumers to import British goods, buy British transportation and insurance services, and pay interest and dividends on British investments in the United States equals the amount of pounds supplied by the British in buying U.S. exports, purchasing services from the United States, and making interest and dividend payments on U.S. investments in Britain. The United States would have no need to either draw down or build up its official reserves to balance its payments.

Suppose tastes change and U.S. consumers buy more British automobiles; the U.S. price level increases relative to Britain's; or interest rates fall in the United States compared to those in Britain. Any or all of these changes will increase the U.S. demand

Table 21.2

Determinants of Exchange Rates: Factors That Change the Demand for or the Supply of a Particular Currency and Thus Alter the Exchange Rate

Determinant	Examples
Change in tastes	Japanese autos decline in popularity in the United States (Japanese yen depreciates; U.S. dollar appreciates).
	European tourists flock to the United States (U.S. dollar appreciates; European euro depreciates).
Change in relative incomes	England encounters a recession, reducing its imports, while U.S. real output and real income surge, increasing U.S. imports (British pound appreciates; U.S. dollar depreciates).
Change in relative prices	Switzerland experiences a 3% inflation rate compared to Canada's 10% rate (Swiss franc appreciates; Canadian dollar depreciates).
Change in relative real interest rates	The Federal Reserve drives up interest rates in the United States, while the Bank of England takes no such action (U.S. dollar appreciates; British pound depreciates).
Speculation	Currency traders believe South Korea will have much greater inflation than Taiwan (South Korean won depreciates; Taiwan dollar appreciates).
	Currency traders think Finland's interest rates will plummet relative to Denmark's rates (Finland's markka depreciates; Denmark's krone appreciates).

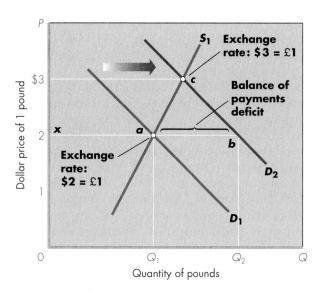

Figure 21.2

Adjustments under flexible exchange rates and fixed exchange rates. Under flexible exchange rates, a shift in the demand for pounds from D_1 to D_2, other things equal, would cause a U.S. balance-of-payments deficit *ab*. That deficit would be corrected by a change in the exchange rate from $2 = £1 to $3 = £1. Under fixed exchange rates, the United States would cover the shortage of pounds *ab* by using international monetary reserves, restricting trade, implementing exchange controls, or enacting a contractionary stabilization policy.

for British pounds, for example, from D_1 to D_2 in Figure 21.2.

If the exchange rate remains at the initial $2 = £1, a U.S. balance-of-payments deficit will occur in the amount of *ab*. At the $2 = £1 rate, U.S. consumers will demand the quantity of pounds shown by point *b* but Britain will supply only the amount shown by *a*. There will be a shortage of pounds. But this shortage will not last because this is a competitive market. Instead, the dollar price of pounds will rise (the dollar will depreciate) until the balance-of-payments deficit is eliminated. That occurs at the new equilibrium exchange rate of $3 = £1, where the quantities of pounds demanded and supplied are again equal.

To explain why this occurred, we reemphasize that the exchange rate links all domestic (U.S.) prices with all foreign (British) prices. The dollar price of a foreign good is found by multiplying the foreign price by the exchange rate (in dollars per unit of the foreign currency). At an exchange rate of $2 = £1, a British automobile priced at £15,000 will cost a U.S. consumer $30,000 (= 15,000 × $2).

A change in the exchange rate alters the prices of all British goods to U.S. consumers and all U.S.

goods to British buyers. The shift in the exchange rate (here from $2 = £1 to $3 = £1) changes the relative attractiveness of U.S. imports and exports and restores equilibrium in the U.S. (and British) balance of payments. From the U.S. view, as the dollar price of pounds changes from $2 to $3, the British auto priced at £15,000, which formerly cost a U.S. consumer $30,000, now costs $45,000 (= 15,000 × $3). Other British goods will also cost U.S. consumers more, and U.S. imports of British goods will decline. A movement from point *b* toward point *c* in Figure 21.2 graphically illustrates this concept.

From Britain's standpoint, the exchange rate (the pound price of dollars) has fallen (from $£\frac{1}{2}$ to $£\frac{1}{3}$ for $1). The international value of the pound has appreciated. The British previously got only $2 for £1; now they get $3 for £1. U.S. goods are therefore cheaper to the British, and U.S. exports to Britain will rise. In Figure 21.2, this is shown by a movement from point *a* toward point *c*.

The two adjustments—a decrease in U.S. imports from Britain and an increase in U.S. exports to Britain—are just what are needed to correct the U.S. balance-of-payments deficit. These changes end when, at point *c*, the quantities of British pounds demanded and supplied are equal. **(Key Questions 6 and 9)**

Disadvantages of Flexible Exchange Rates

Even though flexible exchange rates automatically work to eliminate payment imbalances, they may cause several significant problems.

Uncertainty and Diminished Trade

The risks and uncertainties associated with flexible exchange rates may discourage the flow of trade. Suppose a U.S. automobile dealer contracts to purchase 10 British cars for £150,000. At the current exchange rate of, say, $2 for £1, the U.S. importer expects to pay $300,000 for these automobiles. But if during the 3-month delivery period the rate of exchange shifts to $3 for £1, the £150,000 payment contracted by the U.S. importer will be $450,000.

That increase in the dollar price of pounds may thus turn the U.S. importer's anticipated profit into substantial loss. Aware of the possibility of an adverse change in the exchange rate, the U.S. importer may not be willing to assume the risks involved. The U.S. firm may confine its operations to domestic automobiles, so international trade in this product will not occur.

The same thing can happen with investments. Assume that when the exchange rate is $3 to £1, a U.S. firm invests $30,000 (or £10,000) in a British enterprise. It estimates a return of 10 percent; that is, it anticipates annual earnings of $3000 or £1000. Suppose these expectations prove correct in that the British firm earns £1000 in the first year on the £10,000 investment. But suppose that during the year, the value of the dollar appreciates to $2 = £1. The absolute return is now only $2000 (rather than $3000), and the rate of return falls from the anticipated 10 percent to only $6\frac{2}{3}$ percent (= $2000/$30,000). Investment is risky in any case. The added risk of changing exchange rates may persuade the U.S. investor not to venture overseas.[1]

Terms-of-Trade Changes   A decline in the international value of its currency will worsen a nation's terms of trade. For example, an increase in the dollar price of a pound will mean that the United States must export more goods and services to finance a specific level of imports from Britain.

Instability   Flexible exchange rates may destabilize the domestic economy, because wide fluctuations stimulate and then depress industries producing exported goods. If the U.S. economy is operating at full employment and its currency depreciates, as in our illustration, the results will be inflationary, for two reasons. (1) Foreign demand for U.S. goods may rise, increasing total spending and pulling up U.S. prices. Also, the prices of all U.S. imports will increase. (2) Conversely, appreciation of the dollar will lower U.S. exports and increase imports, possibly causing unemployment.

Flexible or floating exchange rates may also complicate the use of domestic stabilization policies in seeking full employment and price stability. This is especially true for nations whose exports and imports are large relative to their total domestic output.

▌Fixed Exchange Rates

To circumvent the disadvantages of flexible exchange rates, at times nations have fixed or "pegged" their exchange rates. For our analysis of fixed exchange

rates, we assume that the United States and Britain agree to maintain a $2 = £1 exchange rate.

The problem is that such a government agreement cannot keep from changing the demand for and the supply of pounds. With the rate fixed, a shift in demand or supply will threaten the fixed-exchange-rate system, and government must intervene to ensure that the exchange rate is maintained.

In Figure 21.2, suppose the U.S. demand for pounds increases from D_1 to D_2 and a U.S. payment deficit *ab* arises. Now, the new equilibrium exchange rate ($3 = £1) is below the fixed exchange rate ($2 = £1). How can the United States prevent the shortage of pounds from driving the exchange rate up to the new equilibrium level? How can it maintain the fixed exchange rate? The answer is by altering market demand or market supply or both so that they will intersect at the $2 = £1 rate. There are several ways to do this.

Use of Reserves

One way to maintain a fixed exchange rate is to manipulate the market through the use of official reserves. Such manipulations are called **currency interventions.** By selling part of its reserves of pounds, the U.S. government could increase the supply of pounds, shifting supply curve S_1 to the right so that it intersects D_2 at *b* in Figure 21.2 and thereby maintains the exchange rate at $2 = £1.

How do official reserves originate? Perhaps a balance-of-payments surplus occurred in the past. The U.S. government would have purchased that surplus. That is, at some earlier time the U.S. government may have spent dollars to buy the surplus pounds that were threatening to reduce the exchange rate to below the $2 = £1 fixed rate. Those purchases would have bolstered the U.S. official reserves of pounds.

Nations have also used gold as "international money" to obtain official reserves. In our example, the U.S. government could sell some of its gold to Britain to obtain pounds. It could then sell pounds for dollars. That would shift the supply-of-pounds curve to the right, and the $2 = £1 exchange rate could be maintained.

It is critical that the amount of reserves and gold be enough to accomplish the required increase in the supply of pounds. There is no problem if deficits and surpluses occur more or less randomly and are of similar size. Then, last year's balance-of-payments surplus with Britain will increase the U.S. reserve of

---

[1]You will see in this chapter's Last Word, however, that a trader can circumvent part of the risk of unfavorable exchange-rate fluctuations by "hedging" in the "futures market" or "forward market" for foreign exchange.

pounds, and that reserve can be used to "finance" this year's deficit. But if the United States encounters persistent and sizable deficits for an extended period, it may exhaust its reserves, and thus be forced to abandon fixed exchange rates. Or, at the least, a nation whose reserves are inadequate must use less appealing options to maintain exchange rates. Let's consider some of those options.

Trade Policies

To maintain fixed exchange rates, a nation can try to control the flow of trade and finance directly. The United States could try to maintain the $2 = £1$ exchange rate in the face of a shortage of pounds by discouraging imports (thereby reducing the demand for pounds) and encouraging exports (thus increasing the supply of pounds). Imports could be reduced by means of new tariffs or import quotas; special taxes could be levied on the interest and dividends U.S. financial investors receive from foreign investments. Also, the U.S. government could subsidize certain U.S. exports to increase the supply of pounds.

The fundamental problem is that these policies reduce the volume of world trade and change its makeup from what is economically desirable. When nations impose tariffs, quotas, and the like, they lose some of the economic benefits of a free flow of world trade. That loss should not be underestimated: Trade barriers by one nation lead to retaliatory responses from other nations, multiplying the loss.

Exchange Controls and Rationing

Another option is to adopt exchange controls and rationing. Under **exchange controls** the U.S. government could handle the problem of a pound shortage by requiring that all pounds obtained by U.S. exporters be sold to the Federal government. Then the government would allocate or ration this short supply of pounds (represented by xa in Figure 21.2) among various U.S. importers, who actually demand the quantity xb. In effect, this policy would restrict the value of U.S. imports to the amount of foreign exchange earned by U.S. exports. Assuming balance in the capital account, there would then be no balance-of-payments deficit. U.S. demand for British imports with the value ab would simply not be fulfilled.

There are major objections to exchange controls:

- **Distorted trade**   Like tariffs, quotas, and export subsidies (trade controls), exchange controls would distort the pattern of international trade away from the pattern suggested by comparative advantage.

- **Favoritism**   The process of rationing scarce foreign exchange might lead to government favoritism toward selected importers (big contributors to reelection campaigns, for example).

- **Restricted choice**   Controls would limit freedom of consumer choice. The U.S. consumers who prefer Volkswagens might have to buy Chevrolets. The business opportunities for some U.S. importers might be impaired if the government were to limit imports.

- **Black markets**   Enforcement problems are likely under exchange controls. U.S. importers might want foreign exchange badly enough to pay more than the $2 = £1$ official rate, setting the stage for black-market dealings between importers and illegal sellers of foreign exchange.

Domestic Macroeconomic Adjustments

A final way to maintain a fixed exchange rate would be to use domestic stabilization policies (monetary policy and fiscal policy) to eliminate the shortage of foreign currency. Tax hikes, reductions in government spending, and a high-interest-rate policy would reduce total spending in the U.S. economy and, consequently, domestic income. Because the volume of imports varies directly with domestic income, demand for British goods, and therefore for pounds, would be restrained.

If these "contractionary" policies served to reduce the domestic price level relative to Britain's, U.S. buyers of consumer and capital goods would divert their demands from British goods to U.S. goods, reducing the demand for pounds. Moreover, the high-interest-rate policy would lift U.S. interest rates relative to those in Britain.

Lower prices on U.S. goods and higher U.S. interest rates would increase British imports of U.S. goods and would increase British financial investment in the United States. Both developments would increase the supply of pounds. The combination of a decrease in the demand for and an increase in the supply of pounds would reduce or eliminate the original U.S. balance-of-payments deficit. In Figure 21.2 the new supply and demand curves would intersect at some new equilibrium point on line ab, where the exchange rate remains at $2 = £1$.

Maintaining fixed exchange rates by such means is hardly appealing. The "price" of exchange-rate stability for the United States would be a decline in output, employment, and price levels—in other words, a recession. Eliminating a balance-of-payments deficit and achieving domestic stability are both important national economic goals, but to sacrifice stability to balance payments would be to let the tail wag the dog.

QUICK REVIEW 21.2

■ In a system in which exchange rates are flexible (meaning that they are free to float), the rates are determined by the demand for and supply of individual national currencies in the foreign-exchange market.

■ Determinants of flexible exchange rates (factors that shift currency supply and demand curves) include changes in (a) tastes, (b) relative national incomes, (c) relative price levels, (d) real interest rates, and (e) speculation.

■ Under a system of fixed exchange rates, nations set their exchange rates and then maintain them by buying or selling reserves of currencies, establishing trade barriers, employing exchange controls, or incurring inflation or recession.

International Exchange-Rate Systems

In recent times the world's nations have used three different exchange-rate systems: a fixed-rate system, a modified fixed-rate system, and a modified flexible-rate system.

The Gold Standard: Fixed Exchange Rates

Between 1879 and 1934 the major nations of the world adhered to a fixed-rate system called the **gold standard.** Under this system, each nation must:

■ Define its currency in terms of a quantity of gold.

■ Maintain a fixed relationship between its stock of gold and its money supply.

■ Allow gold to be freely exported and imported.

If each nation defines its currency in terms of gold, the various national currencies will have fixed relationships to one another. For example, if the United States defines $1 as worth 25 grains of gold, and Britain defines £1 as worth 50 grains of gold, then a British pound is worth 2 × 25 grains, or $2. This exchange rate was fixed under the gold standard. The exchange rate did not change in response to changes in currency demand and supply.

Gold Flows If we ignore the costs of packing, insuring, and shipping gold between countries, under the gold standard the rate of exchange would not vary from this $2 = £1 rate. No one in the United States would pay more than $2 = £1 because 50 grains of gold could always be bought for $2 in the United States and sold for £1 in Britain. Nor would the British pay more than £1 for $2. Why should they when they could buy 50 grains of gold in Britain for £1 and sell it in the United States for $2?

Under the gold standard, the potential free flow of gold between nations resulted in fixed exchange rates.

Domestic Macroeconomic Adjustments When currency demand or supply changes, the gold standard requires domestic macroeconomic adjustments to maintain the fixed exchange rate. To see why, suppose that U.S. tastes change such that U.S. consumers want to buy more British goods. The resulting increase in the demand for pounds creates a shortage of pounds in the United States (recall Figure 21.2), implying a U.S. balance-of-payments deficit.

What will happen? Remember that the rules of the gold standard prohibit the exchange rate from moving from the fixed $2 = £1 rate. The rate cannot move to, say, a new equilibrium at $3 = £1 to correct the imbalance. Instead, gold will flow from the United States to Britain to correct the payments imbalance.

But recall that the gold standard requires that participants maintain a fixed relationship between their domestic money supplies and their quantities of gold. The flow of gold from the United States to Britain will require a reduction of the money supply in the United States. Other things equal, that will reduce total spending in the United States and lower U.S. real domestic output, employment, income, and, perhaps, prices. Also, the decline in the money supply will boost U.S. interest rates.

The opposite will occur in Britain. The inflow of gold will increase the money supply, and this will increase total spending in Britain. Domestic output, employment, income, and, perhaps, prices will rise. The British interest rate will fall.

Declining U.S. incomes and prices will reduce the U.S. demand for British goods and therefore reduce the U.S. demand for pounds. Lower interest rates in Britain will make it less attractive for U.S. investors to make financial investments there, also lessening the demand for pounds. For all these reasons, the demand for pounds in the United States will decline. In Britain, higher incomes, prices, and interest rates will make U.S. imports and U.S. financial investments more attractive. In buying these imports and making these financial investments, British citizens will supply more pounds in the exchange market.

In short, domestic macroeconomic adjustments in the United States and Britain, triggered by the international flow of gold, will produce new demand and supply conditions for pounds such that the $2 = £1 exchange rate is maintained. After all the adjustments are made, the United States will not have a payments deficit and Britain will not have a payments surplus.

So the gold standard has the advantage of maintaining stable exchange rates and correcting balance-of-payments deficits and surpluses automatically. However, its critical drawback is that nations must accept domestic adjustments in such distasteful forms as unemployment and falling incomes, on the one hand, or inflation, on the other hand. Under the gold standard, a nation's money supply is altered by changes in supply and demand in currency markets, and nations cannot establish their own monetary policy in their own national interest. If the United States, for example, were to experience declining output and income, the loss of gold under the gold standard would reduce the U.S. money supply. That would increase interest rates, retard borrowing and spending, and produce further declines in output and income.

Collapse of the Gold Standard

The gold standard collapsed under the weight of the world-wide Depression of the 1930s. As domestic output and employment fell worldwide, the restoration of prosperity became the primary goal of afflicted nations. They responded by enacting protectionist measures to reduce imports. The idea was to get their economies moving again by promoting consumption of domestically produced goods. To make their exports less expensive abroad, many nations redefined their currencies at lower levels in terms of gold. For example, a country that had previously defined the value of its currency at 1 unit = 25 ounces of gold might redefine it as 1 unit = 10 ounces of gold. Such redefining is an example of **devaluation**—a deliberate action by government to reduce the international value of its currency. A series of such devaluations in the 1930s meant that exchange rates were no longer fixed. That violated a major tenet of the gold standard, and the system broke down.

The Bretton Woods System

The Great Depression and the Second World War left world trade and the world monetary system in shambles. To lay the groundwork for a new international monetary system, in 1944 major nations held an international conference at Bretton Woods, New Hampshire. The conference produced a commitment to a modified fixed-exchange-rate system called an *adjustable-peg system*, or, simply, the **Bretton Woods system.** The new system sought to capture the advantages of the old gold standard (fixed exchange rate) while avoiding its disadvantages (painful domestic macroeconomic adjustments).

Furthermore, the conference created the **International Monetary Fund (IMF)** to make the new exchange-rate system feasible and workable. The new international monetary system managed through the IMF prevailed with modifications until 1971. (The IMF still plays a basic role in international finance; in recent years it has performed a major role in providing loans to developing countries, nations experiencing financial crises, and nations making the transition from communism to capitalism.)

IMF and Pegged Exchange Rates How did the adjustable-peg system of exchange rates work? First, as with the gold standard, each IMF member had to define its currency in terms of gold (or dollars), thus establishing rates of exchange between its currency and the currencies of all other members. In addition, each nation was obligated to keep its exchange rate stable with respect to every other currency. To do so, nations would have to use their official currency reserves to intervene in foreign exchange markets.

Assume again that the U.S. dollar and the British pound were "pegged" to each other at $2 = £1. And suppose again that the demand for pounds temporarily increases so that a shortage of pounds occurs in the United States (the United States has a balance-of-payments deficit). How can the United States keep its pledge to maintain a $2 = £1 exchange rate when the new equilibrium rate is, say, $3 = £1? As we noted previously, the United States can supply additional pounds to the exchange market, increasing the supply of pounds such that the equilibrium exchange rate falls back to $2 = £1.

Under the Bretton Woods system there were three main sources of the needed pounds:

- *Official reserves* The United States might currently possess pounds in its official reserves as the result of past actions against a payments surplus.
- *Gold sales* The U.S. government might sell some of its gold to Britain for pounds. The proceeds would then be offered in the exchange market to augment the supply of pounds.
- *IMF borrowing* The needed pounds might be borrowed from the IMF. Nations participating in the Bretton Woods system were required to make contributions to the IMF based on the size of their national income, population, and volume of trade. If necessary, the United States could borrow pounds on a short-term basis from the IMF by supplying its own currency as collateral.

Fundamental Imbalances: Adjusting the Peg

The Bretton Woods system recognized that from time to time a nation may be confronted with persistent and sizable balance-of-payments problems that cannot be corrected through the means listed above. In such cases, the nation would eventually run out of official reserves and be unable to maintain its fixed-exchange-rate system. The Bretton Woods remedy was correction by devaluation, that is, by an "orderly" reduction of the nation's pegged exchange rate. Also, the IMF allowed each member nation to alter the value of its currency by 10 percent, on its own, to correct a so-called fundamental (persistent and continuing) balance-of-payments deficit. Larger exchange-rate changes required the permission of the Fund's board of directors.

By requiring approval of significant rate changes, the Fund guarded against arbitrary and competitive currency devaluations by nations seeking only to boost output in their own countries at the expense of other countries. In our example, devaluation of the dollar would increase U.S. exports and lower U.S. imports, correcting its persistent payments deficit.

Demise of the Bretton Woods System

Under this adjustable-peg system, nations came to accept gold and the dollar as international reserves. The acceptability of gold as an international medium of exchange derived from its earlier use under the gold standard. Other nations accepted the dollar as international money because the United States had accumulated large quantities of gold, and between 1934 and 1971 it maintained a policy of buying gold from, and selling gold to, foreign governments at a fixed price of $35 per ounce. The dollar was convertible into gold on demand, so the dollar came to be regarded as a substitute for gold, or "as good as gold." And since the discovery of new gold was limited, the growing volume of dollars helped provide a medium of exchange for the expanding world trade.

But a major problem arose. The United States had persistent payments deficits throughout the 1950s and 1960s. Those deficits were financed in part by U.S. gold reserves but mostly by payment of U.S. dollars. As the amount of dollars held by foreigners soared and the U.S. gold reserves dwindled, other nations began to question whether the dollar was really "as good as gold." The ability of the United States to continue to convert dollars into gold at $35 per ounce became increasingly doubtful, as did the role of dollars as international monetary reserves. Thus the dilemma was: To maintain the dollar as a reserve medium, the U.S. payments deficit had to be eliminated. But elimination of the payments deficit would remove the source of additional dollar reserves and thus limit the growth of international trade and finance.

The problem culminated in 1971 when the United States ended its 37-year-old policy of exchanging gold for dollars at $35 per ounce. It severed the link between gold and the international value of the dollar, thereby "floating" the dollar and letting market forces determine its value. The floating of the dollar withdrew U.S. support from the Bretton Woods system of fixed exchange rates and, in effect, ended the system.

The Current System: The Managed Float

The current international exchange-rate system (1971–present) is an "almost" flexible system called **managed floating exchange rates.** Exchange rates among major currencies are free to float to their equilibrium market levels, but nations occasionally use currency interventions in the foreign exchange market to stabilize or alter market exchange rates.

Normally, the major trading nations allow their exchange rates to float up or down to equilibrium levels based on supply and demand in the foreign exchange market. They recognize that changing economic conditions among nations require continuing changes in equilibrium exchange rates to avoid persistent payments deficits or surpluses. They rely on freely operating foreign exchange markets to accomplish the necessary adjustments. The result has been considerably more volatile exchange rates than those during the Bretton Woods era.

But nations also recognize that certain trends in the movement of equilibrium exchange rates may be at odds with national or international objectives. On occasion, nations therefore intervene in the foreign exchange market by buying or selling large amounts of specific currencies. This way, they can "manage" or stabilize exchange rates by influencing currency demand and supply.

For example, in 1987 the Group of Seven industrial nations (G-7 nations)—the United States, Germany, Japan, Britain, France, Italy, and Canada—agreed to stabilize the value of the dollar. During the previous 2 years the dollar had declined rapidly because of large U.S. trade deficits. Although the U.S. trade deficits remained sizable, the G-7 nations concluded that further dollar depreciation might disrupt economic growth in member nations (other than the United States). The G-7 nations therefore purchased large amounts of dollars to boost the dollar's value. Since 1987 the G-7 nations (now G-8 with the addition of Russia) have periodically intervened in foreign exchange markets to stabilize currency values.

In 2000, the United States and the European nations sold dollars and bought euros in an effort to stabilize the falling value of the euro relative to the dollar. In the previous year the euro (€) had depreciated from $1 = €1.17 to $1 = €.87.

The current exchange-rate system is thus an "almost" flexible exchange-rate system. The "almost" refers mainly to the periodic currency interventions by governments; it also refers to the fact that the actual system is more complicated than described. While the major currencies such as dollars, euros, pounds, and yen fluctuate in response to changing supply and demand, some developing nations peg their currencies to the dollar and allow their currencies to fluctuate with it against other currencies. Also, some nations peg the value of their currencies to a "basket" or group of other currencies.

How well has the managed float worked? It has both proponents and critics.

In Support of the Managed Float

Proponents of the managed-float system argue that is has functioned far better than many experts anticipated. Skeptics had predicted that fluctuating exchange rates would reduce world trade and finance. But in real terms world trade under the managed float has grown tremendously over the past several decades. Moreover, as supporters are quick to point out, currency crises such as those in Mexico and southeast Asia in the last half of the 1990s were not the result of the floating-exchange-rate system itself. Rather, the abrupt currency devaluations and depreciations resulted from internal problems in those nations, in conjunction with the nations' tendency to peg their currencies to the dollar or to a basket of currencies. In some cases, flexible exchange rates would have made these adjustments far more gradual.

Proponents also point out that the managed float has weathered severe economic turbulence that might have caused a fixed-rate system to break down. Such events as extraordinary oil price increases in 1973–1974 and again in 1981–1983, inflationary recessions in several nations in the mid-1970s, major national recessions in the early 1980s, and large U.S. budget deficits in the 1980s and the first half of the 1990s all caused substantial imbalances in international trade and finance. Flexible rates enabled the system to adjust to those events, whereas the same events would have put unbearable pressures on a fixed-rate system.

Concerns with the Managed Float

There is still much sentiment in favor of greater exchange-rate stability. Those favoring more stable exchange rates see problems with the current system. They argue that the excessive volatility of exchange rates under the managed float threatens the prosperity of economies that rely heavily on exports. Several financial crises in individual nations (for example, Mexico, South Korea, Indonesia, Thailand, Russia, and Brazil) have resulted from abrupt changes in exchange rates. These crises have led to massive "bailouts" of those economies via IMF loans. The IMF bailouts, in turn, may encourage nations to undertake risky and inappropriate economic policies since they know that, if need be, the IMF will come to the rescue. Moreover, some exchange-rate volatility has occurred even when underlying economic and financial conditions were relatively stable, suggesting that speculation plays too large a role in determining exchange rates.

Perhaps more importantly, assert the critics, the managed float has not eliminated trade imbalances, as flexible rates are supposed to do. Thus, the United States has run persistent trade deficits for many years, while Japan has run persistent surpluses. Changes in exchange rates between dollars and yen have not yet corrected these imbalances, as is supposed to be the case under flexible exchange rates.

Skeptics say the managed float is basically a "nonsystem"; the guidelines concerning what each nation may or may not do with its exchange rates are not specific enough to keep the system working in the long run. Nations inevitably will be tempted to intervene in the foreign exchange market, not merely to smooth out short-term fluctuations in exchange rates but to prop up their currency if it is chronically weak or to manipulate the exchange rate to achieve domestic stabilization goals.

So what are we to conclude? Flexible exchange rates have not worked perfectly, but they have not failed miserably. Thus far they have survived, and no doubt have eased, several major shocks to the international trading system. Meanwhile, the "managed" part of the float has given nations some sense of control over their collective economic destinies. On balance, most economists favor continuation of the present system of "almost" flexible exchange rates.

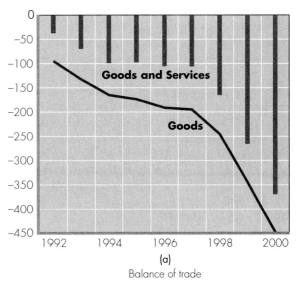

Billions of Dollars

(a)
Balance of trade

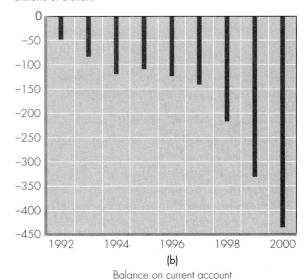

Billions of Dollars

(b)
Balance on current account

Figure 21.3

Recent U.S. trade deficits. U.S. trade deficits in (a) "goods" and "goods and services" and (b) the current account recently have been very large.

Source: U.S. Department of Commerce, Bureau of Economic Analysis, www.bea.doc.gov/.

> **QUICK REVIEW 21.3**
>
> ▪ Under the gold standard (1879–1934), nations fixed exchange rates by valuing their currencies in terms of gold, by tying their stocks of money to gold, and by allowing gold to flow between nations when balance-of-payments deficits and surpluses occurred.
>
> ▪ The Bretton Woods exchange-rate system (1944–1971) fixed or pegged exchange rates but permitted orderly adjustments of the pegs under special circumstances.
>
> ▪ The managed floating system of exchange rates (1971–present) relies on foreign exchange markets to establish equilibrium exchange rates. The system permits nations to buy and sell foreign currency to stabilize short-term changes in exchange rates or to correct exchange-rate imbalances that are negatively affecting the world economy.

▪ Recent U.S. Trade Deficits

Figure 21.3 reveals that U.S. trade and current account deficits over the past several years were large and persistent. For example, the trade deficit on goods for 2000 was $450 billion. That year, the trade deficit on goods and services was $369 billion, and the current account deficit was $435 billion.

Causes of the Trade Deficits

There are several reasons for these persistent trade deficits. First, since 1992 the U.S. economy has grown more rapidly than the economies of several major trading nations. This growth of income has boosted U.S. purchases of foreign goods (U.S. imports). In contrast, Japan, some European nations, and Canada have suffered either recession or slower income growth during this period. Thus, their purchases of U.S. goods (U.S. exports) have not kept pace with the rise of U.S. imports. Persistent U.S. trade imbalances with Japan are particularly noteworthy.

Second, a declining saving rate in the United States has contributed to U.S. trade deficits. The saving rate (saving/total income) in the United States has declined at the same time that the investment rate (investment/total income) has remained stable or even increased. The gap has been met through foreign purchases of U.S. real and financial assets, creating a large capital account surplus. Because foreigners are financing more of U.S. investment, U.S. citizens are able to save less and consume more, including consumption of imported goods. That is, the capital account surplus may partly cause the trade deficit, not simply result from it.

Implications of U.S. Trade Deficits

There is disagreement on whether the large trade deficits should concern the United States. Most economists see both benefits and costs to trade deficits.

Increased Current Consumption

At the time a trade deficit or a current account deficit is occurring, American consumers benefit. A trade deficit means that the United States is receiving more goods and services as imports from abroad than it is sending out as exports. Taken alone, a trade deficit allows the United States to consume outside its production possibilities curve. It augments the domestic standard of living. But there is a catch: The gain in present consumption may come at the expense of reduced future consumption.

Increased U.S. Indebtedness

A trade deficit is considered "unfavorable" because it must be financed by borrowing from the rest of the world, selling off assets, or dipping into foreign currency reserves. Recall that current account deficits are financed primarily by net inpayments of foreign currencies to the United States. When U.S. exports are insufficient to finance U.S. imports, the United States increases both its debt to people abroad and the value of foreign claims against assets in the United States. Financing of the U.S. trade deficit has resulted in a larger foreign accumulation of claims against U.S. financial and real assets than the U.S. claim against foreign assets. Today, the United States is the world's largest debtor nation. In 1999, foreigners owned $1.5 billion more of U.S. assets (corporations, land, stocks, bonds, loan notes) than the United States owned in foreign assets.

If the United States wants to regain ownership of these domestic assets, at some future time it will have to export more than it imports. At that time, domestic consumption will be lower because the United States will need to send more of its output abroad than it receives as imports. Therefore, the current consumption gains delivered by U.S. current account deficits may mean permanent debt, permanent foreign ownership, or large sacrifices of future consumption.

We say "may mean" above because the foreign lending to U.S. firms and foreign investment in the United States increases the U.S. capital stock. U.S. production capacity therefore might increase more rapidly than otherwise because of a large surplus on the capital account. Faster increases in production capacity and real GDP enhance the economy's ability to service foreign debt and buy back real capital, if that is desired.

In short, U.S. trade deficits are a mixed blessing. Their long-term impacts are largely unknown.

Speculation in Currency Markets

Are Speculators a Negative or a Positive Influence in Currency Markets and International Trade?

Most people buy foreign currency to facilitate the purchase of goods or services from another country. A U.S. importer buys Japanese yen to purchase Japanese autos. A Hong Kong financial investor purchases Australian dollars to invest in the Australian stock market. But there is another group of participants in the currency market—speculators—that buys and sells foreign currencies in the hope of reselling or rebuying them later at a profit.

Contributing to Exchange-Rate Fluctuations Speculators were much in the news in late 1997 and 1998 when they were widely accused of driving down the values of the South Korean won, Thailand baht, Malaysian ringgit, and Indonesian rupiah. The value of these currencies fell by as much as 50 percent within 1 month, and speculators undoubtedly contributed to the swiftness of those declines. The expectation of currency depreciation (or appreciation) can be self-fulfilling. If speculators, for example, expect the Indonesian rupiah to be devalued or to depreciate, they quickly sell rupiah and buy currencies that they think will increase in relative value. The sharp increase in the supply of rupiah indeed reduces its value; this reduction then may trigger further selling of rupiah in expectation of further declines in its value.

But changed economic realities, not speculation, are normally the underlying causes of changes in currency values. That was largely the case with the southeast Asian countries in which actual and threatened bankruptcies in the financial and manufacturing sectors undermined confidence in the strength of the currencies. Anticipating the eventual declines in currency values, speculators simply hastened those declines. That is, the declines in value probably would have occurred with or without speculators.

Moreover, on a daily basis, speculation clearly has positive effects in foreign exchange markets.

Smoothing Out Short-Term Fluctuations in Currency Prices When temporarily weak demand or strong supply reduces a currency's value, speculators quickly buy the currency, adding to its demand and strengthening its value. When temporarily strong demand or weak supply increases a currency's value, speculators sell the currency. That selling increases the supply of the currency and

reduces its value. In this way speculators smooth out supply and demand, and thus exchange rates, over short time periods. This day-to-day exchange-rate stabilization aids international trade.

Absorbing Risk Speculators also absorb risk that others do not want to bear. Because of potential adverse changes in exchange rates, international transactions are riskier than domestic transactions. Suppose AnyTime, a hypothetical retailer, signs a contract with a Swiss manufacturer to buy 10,000 Swatch watches to be delivered in 3 months. The stipulated price is 75 Swiss francs per watch, which in dollars is $50 per watch at the present exchange rate of, say, $1 = 1.5 francs. AnyTime's total bill for the 10,000 watches will be $500,000 (= 750,000 francs).

But if the Swiss franc were to appreciate, say, to $1 = 1 franc, the dollar price per watch would rise from $50 to $75 and AnyTime would owe $750,000 for the watches (= 750,000 francs). AnyTime may reduce the risk of such an unfavorable exchange-rate fluctuation by hedging in the futures market. Hedging is an action by a buyer or a seller to protect against a change in future prices. The futures market is a market in which currencies are bought and sold at prices fixed now, for delivery at a specified date in the future.

AnyTime can purchase the needed 750,000 francs at the current $1 = 1.5 francs exchange rate, but with delivery in 3 months when the Swiss watches are delivered. And here is where speculators come in. For a price determined in the futures market, they agree to deliver the 750,000 francs to AnyTime in 3 months at the $1 = 1.5 francs exchange rate, regardless of the exchange rate then. The speculators need not own francs when the agreement is made. If the Swiss franc depreciates to, say, $1 = 2 francs in this period, the speculators profit. They can buy the 750,000 francs stipulated in the contract for $375,000, pocketing the difference between that amount and the $500,000 AnyTime has agreed to pay for the 750,000 francs. If the Swiss franc appreciates, the speculators, but not AnyTime, suffer a loss.

The amount AnyTime must pay for this "exchange-rate insurance" will depend on how the market views the likelihood of the franc depreciating, appreciating, or staying constant over the 3-month period. As in all competitive markets, supply and demand determine the price of the futures contract.

The futures market thus eliminates much of the exchange-rate risk associated with buying foreign goods for future delivery. Without it, AnyTime might have decided against importing Swiss watches. But the futures market and currency speculators greatly increase the likelihood that the transaction will occur. Operating through the futures market, speculation promotes international trade.

In short, although speculators in currency markets occasionally contribute to swings in exchange rates, on a day-to-day basis they play a positive role in currency markets.

SUMMARY

1. U.S. exports create a foreign demand for dollars and make a supply of foreign exchange available to the United States. Conversely, U.S. imports create a demand for foreign exchange and make a supply of dollars available to foreigners. Generally, a nation's exports earn the foreign currencies needed to pay for its imports.

2. The balance of payments records all international trade and financial transactions taking place between a given nation and the rest of the world. The balance on goods and services (the trade balance) compares exports and imports of both goods and services. The current account balance includes not only goods and services transactions but also net investment income and net transfers.

3. A deficit in the current account may be offset by a surplus in the capital account. Conversely, a surplus in the current account may be offset by a deficit in the capital account. A balance-of-payments deficit occurs when the sum of the current and capital accounts is negative. Such a deficit is financed with official reserves. A balance-of-payments surplus occurs when the sum of the current and capital accounts is positive. A payments surplus results in an increase in official reserves. The desirability of a balance-of-payments deficit or surplus depends on its size and its persistence.

4. Flexible or floating exchange rates between international currencies are determined by the demand for and supply of those currencies. Under flexible rates a currency will depreciate or appreciate as a result of changes in tastes, relative income changes, relative price changes, relative changes in real interest rates, and speculation.

5. The maintenance of fixed exchange rates requires adequate reserves to accommodate periodic payments deficits. If reserves are inadequate, nations must invoke protectionist trade policies, engage in exchange controls, or endure undesirable domestic macroeconomic adjustments.

6. The gold standard, a fixed-rate system, provided exchange-rate stability until its disintegration during the 1930s. Under this system, gold flows between nations precipitated sometimes painful changes in price, income, and employment levels in bringing about international equilibrium.

7. Under the Bretton Woods system, exchange rates were pegged to one another and were stable. Participating nations were obligated to maintain these rates by using stabilization funds, gold, or loans from the IMF. Persistent or "fundamental" payments deficits could be resolved by IMF-sanctioned currency devaluations.

8. Since 1971 the world's major nations have used a system of managed floating exchange rates. Market forces generally set rates, although governments intervene with varying frequency to alter their exchange rates.

9. Over the past several years the United States experienced large trade deficits. Causes include (a) faster growth of income in the United States than in some European nations, Canada, and Japan, resulting in expanding U.S. imports, and (b) a declining U.S. saving rate, which has produced a large capital account surplus and has freed U.S. income for spending on imports.

10. U.S. trade deficits have produced current increases in the living standards of U.S. consumers. The accompanying surpluses on the capital account have increased U.S. debt to the rest of the world and increased foreign ownership of assets in the United States. This greater foreign investment in the United States, however, has undoubtedly increased U.S. production possibilities.

TERMS AND CONCEPTS

balance of payments

current account

balance on goods and services

trade deficit

trade surplus

balance on current account

capital account

balance on capital account

official reserves

balance-of-payments deficits and surpluses

flexible- or floating-exchange-rate system

fixed exchange-rate system

purchasing-power-parity theory

currency interventions

exchange controls

gold standard

devaluation

Bretton Woods system

International Monetary Fund (IMF)

managed floating exchange rates

STUDY QUESTIONS

1. Explain how a U.S. automobile importer might finance a shipment of Toyotas from Japan. Trace the steps as to how a U.S. export of machinery to Italy might be financed. Explain: "U.S. exports earn supplies of foreign currencies that Americans can use to finance imports."

2. **Key Question** Indicate whether each of the following creates a demand for or a supply of European euros in foreign exchange markets:
    a. A U.S. airline firm purchases several Airbus planes assembled in France.
    b. A German automobile firm decides to build an assembly plant in South Carolina.
    c. A U.S. college student decides to spend a year studying at the Sorbonne in Paris.
    d. An Italian manufacturer ships machinery from one Italian port to another on a Liberian freighter.
    e. The U.S. economy grows faster than the French economy.
    f. A U.S. government bond held by a Spanish citizen matures, and the loan amount is paid back to that person.
    g. It is widely believed that the euro will depreciate in the near future.

3. **Key Question** Alpha's balance-of-payments data for 2001 are shown below. All figures are in billions of dollars. What are (a) the balance of trade, (b) the balance on goods and services, (c) the balance on current account, and (d) the balance on capital account? Does Alpha have a balance-of-payments deficit or surplus? Explain.

Goods exports	+ $40	Net transfers	+ $10
Goods imports	− 30	Foreign purchases	
Service exports	+ 15	of assets in the	
Service imports	− 10	United States	+ 10
Net investment income	− 5	U.S. purchases of	
		assets abroad	− 40
		Official reserves	+ 10

4. "A rise in the dollar price of yen necessarily means a fall in the yen price of dollars." Do you agree? Illustrate and elaborate: "The critical thing about exchange rates is that they provide a direct link between the prices of goods and services produced in all trading nations of the world." Explain the purchasing-power-parity theory of exchange rates.

5. Suppose that a Swiss watchmaker imports watch components from Sweden and exports watches to the United States. Also suppose the dollar depreciates, and the Swedish krona appreciates, relative to the Swiss franc. Speculate as to how each would hurt the Swiss watchmaker.

6. **Key Question** Explain why the U.S. demand for Mexican pesos is downward-sloping and the supply of pesos to Americans is upward-sloping. Assuming a system of flexible exchange rates between Mexico and the United States, indicate whether each of the following would cause the Mexican peso to appreciate or depreciate:
    a. The United States unilaterally reduces tariffs on Mexican products.
    b. Mexico encounters severe inflation.
    c. Deteriorating political relations reduce American tourism in Mexico.
    d. The U.S. economy moves into a severe recession.
    e. The United States engages in a high-interest-rate monetary policy.
    f. Mexican products become more fashionable to U.S. consumers.
    g. The Mexican government encourages U.S. firms to invest in Mexican oil fields.
    h. The rate of productivity growth in the United States diminishes sharply.

7. Explain why you agree or disagree with the following statements:
    a. A country that grows faster than its major trading partners can expect the international value of its currency to depreciate.
    b. A nation whose interest rate is rising more rapidly than interest rates in other nations can expect the international value of its currency to appreciate.
    c. A country's currency will appreciate if its inflation rate is less than that of the rest of the world.

8. "Exports pay for imports. Yet in 2000 the nations of the world exported about $369 billion more worth of goods and services to the United States than they imported from the United States." Resolve the apparent inconsistency of these two statements.

9. **Key Question** Diagram a market in which the equilibrium dollar price of 1 unit of fictitious currency zee (Z) is $5 (the exchange rate is $5 = Z1). Then show on your diagram a decline in the demand for zee.
    a. Referring to your diagram, discuss the adjustment options the United States would have in maintaining the exchange rate at $5 = Z1 under a fixed-exchange-rate system.
    b. How would the U.S. balance-of-payments surplus that is created (by the decline in demand) get resolved under a system of flexible exchange rates?

10. Compare and contrast the Bretton Woods system of exchange rates with that of the gold standard. What caused the collapse of the gold standard? What caused the demise of the Bretton Woods system?

11. Describe what is meant by the term "managed float." Did the managed-float system precede or follow the adjustable-peg system? Explain.

12. What have been the major causes of the large U.S. trade deficits since 1992? What are the major benefits and costs associated with trade deficits? Explain: "A trade deficit means that a nation is receiving more goods and services from abroad than it is sending abroad." How can that be called "unfavorable"?

13. **(Last Word)** Suppose Winter Sports—a hypothetical French retailer of snowboards—wants to order 5000 snowboards made in the United States. The price per board is $200, the present exchange rate is 1 euro = $1, and payment is due in dollars when the boards are delivered in 3 months. Use a numerical example to explain why exchange-rate risk might make the French retailer hesitant to place the order. How might speculators absorb some of Winter Sports' risk?

14. **Web-Based Question:** *The U.S. balance on goods and services—what are the latest figures?* The U.S. Census Bureau reports the latest data on U.S. trade in goods and services at its website www.census.gov/indicator/www/ustrade.html. Over the past month, has the trade balance in goods and services improved (that is, yielded a smaller deficit or a larger surplus) or deteriorated? Is the relative trade strength of the United States compared to the rest of the world in goods or in services? Which product groups had the largest increases in exports? Which had the largest increases in imports?

15. **Web-Based Question:** *The yen-dollar exchange rate* The Federal Reserve Board of Governors provides exchange rates for various currencies for the last decade at www.federalreserve.gov/releases (Foreign Exchange Rates; Historical Data). Has the dollar appreciated, depreciated, or remained constant relative to the Canadian dollar, the European euro, the Japanese yen, the Swedish krona, and the Swiss franc over the past 5 years?

22

The Economics of Developing Countries

I T I S D I F F I C U L T for those of us in the United States, where per capita GDP in 2000 was nearly $34,000 to grasp the fact that about 2.8 billion people, or nearly half the world population, live on $2 or less a day. And about 1.2 billion live on less than $1 a day. Hunger, squalor, and disease are the norm in many nations of the world. ■ In this chapter we identify the developing countries, discuss their characteristics, and explore the obstacles that have impeded their growth. We also examine the appropriate roles of the private sector and government in economic development. Finally, we look at policies that might help developing countries increase their growth rates.

■ The Rich and the Poor

Just as there is considerable income inequality among families within a nation, so too is there great income inequality among the family of nations. According to the United Nations, the richest 20 percent of the world's population receives more than 80 percent of the world's income; the poorest 20 percent receives less than 2 percent. The poorest 60 percent receives less than 6 percent of the world's income.

Classifications

The World Bank classifies countries into high-income, medium-income, and low-income countries on the basis of GDP per capita, as shown in Figure 22.1. The *high-income nations*, shown in gold, are known as the **industrially advanced countries (IACs);** they include the United States, Japan, Canada, Australia, New Zealand, and most of the nations of western Europe. In general, these nations have well-developed market economies based on large stocks of capital goods, advanced production technologies, and well-educated workers. In 1999 these economies had a per capita GDP of $25,730.

The remaining nations of the world are called **developing countries (DVCs).** They have wide variations of income per capita and are mainly located in Africa, Asia, and Latin America. The DVCs are a diverse group that can be subdivided into two groups:

■ The *middle-income nations*, shown in green in Figure 22.1, include such countries as Brazil, Iran, Poland, Russia, South Africa, and Thailand. Per capita output of these middle-income nations ranged from $756 to $9265 in 1999 and averaged $2000.

■ The *low-income nations*, shown in red-orange,

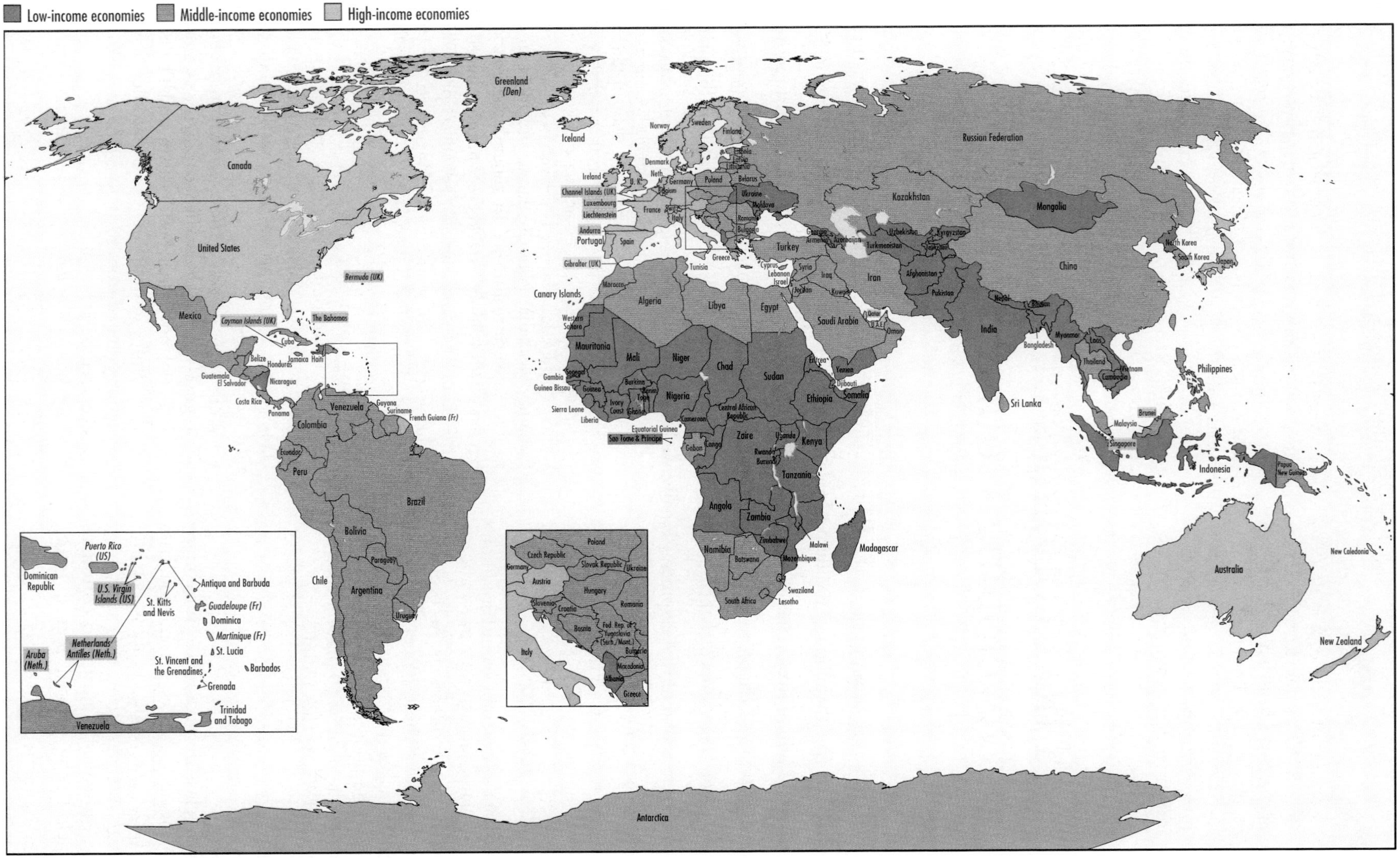

Figure 22.1

Groups of economies. The world's nations are grouped into industrially advanced countries (IACs) and developing countries (DVCs). The IACs (shown in gold) are high-income countries. The DVCs are middle-income and low-income countries (shown respectively in green and in red-orange.)
(Source: World Bank data, www.worldbank.com/.)

Low-income economies   Middle-income economies   High-income economies had a per capita output of $755 or less in 1999 and averaged only $410 of output per person. India, Indonesia, and the sub-Saharan nations of Africa dominate this group. These DVCs have relatively low levels of industrialization. In general, literacy rates are low, unemployment is high, population growth is rapid, and exports consist largely of agricultural produce (such as cocoa, bananas, sugar, raw cotton) and raw materials (such as copper, iron ore, natural rubber). Capital equipment is minimal, production technologies are simple, and labor productivity is very low. About 40 percent of the world's population lives in these nations, all of which suffer widespread poverty.

Comparisons

Several comparisons will bring the differences in world income into sharper focus:

- In 1999, U.S. total GDP was approximately $8.4 trillion; the combined GDPs of the DVCs in that year came to only $6.3 trillion.
- The United States, with only 5 percent of the world's population, produces 27 percent of the world's output.
- Per capita GDP of the United States is 235 times greater than per capita GDP in Sierra Leone, one of the world's poorest nations.
- The annual sales of the world's largest corporations exceed the GDPs of many of the DVCs. General Motors' annual world revenues are greater than the GDPs of all but 22 nations.
- In 1999, the assets of the world's three wealthiest people exceeded the combined GDPs of the world's 48 poorest countries.

Growth, Decline, and Income Gaps

Two other points relating to the nations shown in Figure 22.1 should be noted. First, the various nations have demonstrated considerable differences in their ability to improve circumstances over time. On the one hand, DVCs such as China, Malaysia, Chile, and Thailand achieved high annual growth rates in their GDPs in recent decades. Consequently, their real output per capita increased several fold. Several former DVCs, such as Singapore, Greece, and Hong Kong (now part of China), have achieved IAC status. In contrast, a number of DVCs in sub-Saharan Africa have recently been experiencing declining per capita GDPs.

Second, the absolute income gap between rich and poor nations has been widening. Suppose the per capita incomes of the advanced and developing countries were growing at about 2 percent per year. Because the income base in the advanced countries is initially much higher, the absolute income gap grows. If per capita income is $400 a year in a DVC, a 2 percent growth rate means an $8 increase in income. Where per capita income is $20,000 per year in an IAC, the same 2 percent growth rate translates into a $400 increase in income. Thus the absolute income gap will have increased from $19,600 (= $20,000 − $400) to $19,992 (= $20,400 − $408). The DVCs must grow faster than the IACs for the gap to be narrowed. **(Key Question 3)**

The Human Realities

Mere statistics conceal the human implications of the extreme poverty characterizing so much of our planet:

> Let us examine a typical "extended" family in rural Asia. The Asian household is likely to comprise ten or more people, including parents, five to seven children, two grandparents, and some aunts and uncles. They have a combined annual income, both in money and in "kind" (i.e., they consume a share of the food they grow), of $250 to $300. Together they live in a poorly constructed one-room house as tenant farmers on a large agricultural estate owned by an absentee landlord who lives in the nearby city. The father, mother, uncle, and the older children must work all day on the land. None of the adults can read or write; of the five school-age children, only one attends school regularly; and he cannot expect to proceed beyond three or four years of primary education. There is only one meal a day; it rarely changes and it is rarely sufficient to alleviate the childrens' constant hunger pains. The house has no electricity, sanitation, or fresh water supply. There is much sickness, but qualified doctors and medical practitioners are far away in the cities attending to the needs of wealthier families. The work is hard, the sun is hot and aspirations for a better life are constantly being snuffed out. In this part of the world the only relief from the daily struggle for physical survival lies in the spiritual traditions of the people.[1]

---

[1]Michael P. Todaro, *Economic Development in the Third World*, 7th ed. (New York: Addison Wesley Longman, 2000), p. 4.

Table 22.1
Selected Socioeconomic Indicators of Development

Country	(1) Per Capita Output, 1999	(2) Life Expectancy at Birth, 1998	(3) Infant Mortality per 1000 Live Births, 1998	(4) Adult Illiteracy Rate, Percent, 1998	(5) Percent of Labor Force in Agriculture, 1990	(6) Per Capita Energy Consumption, 1997*
Japan	$32,230	80 years	4	1	7	4084
United States	30,600	77	7	1	3	8076
Brazil	4,420	67	33	16	23	1051
Mauritania	380	54	90	59	55	103
China	780	70	31	17	72	907
India	450	63	70	44	64	479
Bangladesh	370	59	73	60	65	197
Ethiopia	206	43	107	64	86	287
Mozambique	230	44	134	58	83	461

*Kilograms of oil equivalent.
Source: World Development Indicators, 2000; Human Development Report, 2000; World Development Report, 2000–2001.

Table 22.1 contrasts various socioeconomic indicators for selected DVCs with those for the United States and Japan. Note that these data confirm the major points stressed in the quotation from Todaro.

■ Obstacles to Economic Development

The paths to economic development are essentially the same for developing countries as for the industrially advanced economies:

■ The DVCs must use their existing supplies of resources more efficiently. This means that they must eliminate unemployment and underemployment and also combine labor and capital resources in a way that will achieve lowest-cost production. They must also direct their scarce resources so that they will achieve allocative efficiency.

■ The DVCs must expand their available supplies of resources. By achieving greater supplies of raw materials, capital equipment, and productive labor, and by advancing its technological knowledge, a DVC can push its production possibilities curve outward.

All DVCs are aware of these two paths to economic development. Why, then, have some of them traveled those paths while others have lagged far behind? The difference lies in the physical, human, and socioeconomic environments of the various nations.

Natural Resources

No simple generalization is possible as to the role of natural resources in the economic development of DVCs because the distribution of natural resources among them is so uneven. Some DVCs have valuable deposits of bauxite, tin, copper, tungsten, nitrates, and petroleum and have been able to use their natural resource endowments to achieve rapid growth and a significant redistribution of income from the rich to the poor nations. The Organization of Petroleum Exporting Countries (OPEC) is a standard example. In other instances, natural resources are owned or controlled by the multinational corporations of industrially advanced countries, with the economic benefits from these resources largely diverted abroad. Furthermore, world markets for many of the farm products and raw materials that the DVCs export are subject to large price fluctuations that contribute to instability in their economies.

Other DVCs lack mineral deposits, have little arable land, and have few sources of power. Moreover, most of the poor countries are situated in Central and South America, Africa, the Indian subcontinent, and southeast Asia, where tropical climates prevail. The heat and humidity hinder productive labor; human, crop, and livestock diseases are widespread; and weed and insect infestations plague agriculture.

A weak resource base can be a serious obstacle to growth. Real capital can be accumulated and the quality of the labor force improved through education and training. But it is not as easy to augment the natural resource base. It may be unrealistic for many of the DVCs to envision an economic destiny comparable with that of, say, the United States or Canada. But we must be careful in generalizing: Japan, for example, has achieved a high level of living despite a limited natural resource base. It simply imports the large quantities of natural resources that it needs to produce goods for consumption at home and export abroad.

Human Resources

Three statements describe many of the poorest DVCs with respect to human resources:

■ They are overpopulated.
■ Unemployment and underemployment are widespread.
■ Labor productivity is low.

Overpopulation Many of the DVCs with the most meager natural and capital resources have the largest populations to support. Table 22.2 shows the high population densities and population growth rates of a few selected nations compared with those of the United States and of the world.

Most important in the long run is the contrast in population growth rates. The DVCs are currently experiencing a 1.8 percent annual increase in population compared with a .7 percent annual rate for IACs. Since such a large percentage of the world's current population already lives in DVCs, this per-

centage difference in population growth rates is highly significant: During the next 15 years, 9 out of every 10 people added to the world population will be born in developing nations. This fact is dramatically reflected in the population realities and projections shown in Figure 22.2.

Population statistics help explain why the per capita income gap between the DVCs and the IACs has widened. In some of the poorest DVCs, rapid population growth actually strains the food supply so severely that per capita food consumption falls to or below the biological subsistence level. In the worst instances, only malnutrition and disease, and the high death rate they cause, keep incomes near subsistence.

It would seem at first glance that, since

$$\text{Standard of living} = \frac{\text{consumer goods (food) production}}{\text{population}}$$

the standard of living could be raised by boosting the production of consumer goods such as food. But the problem is more complex, because any increase in the output of consumer goods that initially raises the standard of living may eventually induce a population increase. This increase, if sufficiently large, will dissipate the improvement in living standards, and subsistence living levels will again prevail.

Table 22.2

Population Statistics, Selected Countries

Country	Population per Square Mile, 2000	Annual Rate of Population Increase, 1990–1999
United States	78	1.0%
Pakistan	461	2.5
Bangladesh	2499	1.6
Venezuela	69	2.2
India	883	1.8
China	350	1.1
Kenya	136	2.7
Philippines	690	2.3
World	**120**	**1.0%**

Sources: Statistical Abstract of the United States, 2000; World Development Report, 2000–2001.

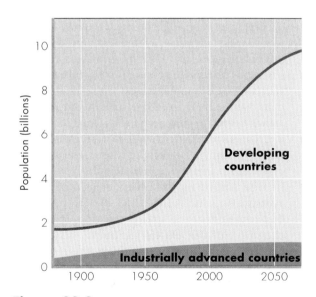

Figure 22.2

Population growth in developing countries and advanced industrial countries, 1900–2050. The majority of the world's population lives in the developing nations, and those nations will account for most of the rapid increase in population over the next half-century.

Source: Population Reference Bureau, www.prb.org/.

Why might population growth in DVCs accompany increases in food production? First, the nation's death rate will decline. That decline is the result of (1) a higher level of per capita food consumption and (2) the basic medical and sanitation programs that accompany the initial phases of economic development.

Second, the birthrate will remain high or may rise, particularly as medical and sanitation programs cut infant mortality. The cliché that "the rich get richer and the poor get children" is uncomfortably accurate for many of the poorest DVCs. An increase in the per capita standard of living may lead to a population upsurge that will cease only when the standard of living has again been reduced to the level of bare subsistence.

In addition to the fact that rapid population growth may convert an expanding GDP into a stagnant or slow-growing GDP per capita, there are four other reasons why population expansion is often an obstacle to development:

- **Saving and investment**   Large families reduce the capacity of households to save, thereby restricting the economy's ability to accumulate capital.
- **Productivity**   As population grows, more investment is required to maintain the amount of real capital per person. If investment fails to keep pace, each worker will have fewer tools and equipment, and that will reduce worker productivity (output per worker). Declining productivity implies stagnating or declining per capita incomes.
- **Resource overuse**   Because most developing countries are heavily dependent on agriculture, rapid population growth may result in the overuse of limited natural resources, such as land. The much-publicized African famines are partly the result of overgrazing and overplanting of land caused by the pressing need to feed a growing population.
- **Urban problems**   Rapid population growth in the cities of the DVCs, accompanied by unprecedented inflows of rural migrants, generates massive urban problems. Rapid population growth aggravates problems such as substandard housing, poor public services, congestion, pollution, and crime. The resolution or lessening of these difficulties necessitates a diversion of resources from growth-oriented uses.

Most authorities advocate birth control as the most effective means for breaking out of the population dilemma. And breakthroughs in contraceptive technology in recent decades have made this solution increasingly relevant. But obstacles to population control are great. Low literacy rates make it difficult to disseminate information about contraceptive devices. In peasant agriculture, large families are a major source of labor. Adults may regard having many children as a kind of informal social security system: The more children, the greater the probability of the parents' having a relative to care for them in old age. Finally, many nations that stand to gain the most through birth control are often the least willing, for religious reasons, to embrace contraception programs. For example, population growth in Latin America (which has a high proportion of Catholics) is among the most rapid in the world.

China, which has about one-fifth of the world's population, began its harsh "one-child" program in 1980. The government advocates late marriages and one child per family. Couples having more than one child are fined or lose various social benefits. Even though the rate of population growth has diminished under this program, China's population continues to expand. Between 1980 and 1999 it increased by 267 million people. India, the world's second most populous nation, had a 310 million, or 45 percent, population increase in the 1980–1999 period. With a total population of 998 million, India has 17 percent of the world's population but less than 2.5 percent of the world's landmass.

Qualifications   We need to qualify our focus on population growth as a major cause of low incomes, however. As with natural resources, the relationship between population and economic growth is less clear than one might expect. High population density and rapid population growth do not necessarily mean poverty. China and India have immense populations and are poor, but Japan, Singapore, and Hong Kong are densely populated and are wealthy.

Also, the population growth rate for the DVCs as a group has declined significantly in recent decades. Between 1980 and 1999, the annual population growth rate was about 1.6 percent; for 1999–2015 it is expected to fall to 1.2 percent (compared to .3 percent in the IACs).

Finally, not everyone agrees that reducing population growth is the key to increasing per capita GDP in the developing countries. The **demographic transition view** holds that rising income transforms the population dynamics of a nation by reducing birthrates. In this view, large populations are a consequence of poverty, not a cause. The task is to increase income; declining birth rates will then follow.

This view observes there are both marginal benefits and marginal costs of having another child. In DVCs the marginal benefits are relatively large because the extra child becomes an extra worker who can help support the family. Extra children can provide financial support and security for parents in their old age, so people in poor countries have high birthrates. But in wealthy IACs the marginal cost of having another child is relatively high. Care of children may require that one of the parents sacrifice high earnings or that the parents purchase expensive child care. Also, children require extended and expensive education for the highly skilled jobs characteristic of the IAC economies. Finally, the wealth of the IACs results in "social safety nets" (such as retirement and disability benefits) that protect adults from the insecurity associated with old age and the inability to work. According to this view, people in the IACs recognize that high birthrates are not in the family's short-term or long-term interest. So many of them choose to have fewer children.

Note the differences in causation between the traditional view and the demographic transition view. The traditional view is that reduced birthrates must come first and then higher per capita income will follow. Lower birthrates *cause* the per capita income growth. The demographic transition view says that higher incomes must first be achieved and then lower rates of population growth will follow. Higher incomes *cause* slower population growth. **(Key Question 6)**

Unemployment and Underemployment

Employment-related data for many DVCs are either nonexistent or highly unreliable. But observation suggests that unemployment is high. There is also significant **underemployment,** which means that a large number of people are employed fewer hours per week than they want, work at jobs unrelated to their training, or spend much of the time on their jobs unproductively.

Many economists contend that unemployment may be as high as 15 to 20 percent in the rapidly growing urban areas of the DVCs. There has been substantial migration in most developing countries from rural to urban areas, motivated by the expectation of finding jobs with higher wage rates than are available in agricultural and other rural employment. But this huge migration to the cities reduces a migrant's chance of obtaining a job. In many cases, migration to the cities has greatly exceeded the growth of urban job opportunities, resulting in very high urban unemployment rates. Thus, rapid rural-urban migration has given rise to urban unemployment rates that are two or three times as great as rural rates.

Underemployment is widespread and characteristic of most DVCs. In many of the poorer DVCs, rural agricultural labor is so abundant relative to capital and natural resources that a significant percentage of the labor contributes little or nothing to agricultural output. Similarly, many DVC workers are self-employed as proprietors of small shops, in handicrafts, or as street vendors. A lack of demand means that small shop owners or vendors spend their idle time in the shop or on the street. While they are not unemployed, they are clearly underemployed.

Low Labor Productivity   Labor productivity tends to be low in DVCs. As we will see, developing nations have found it difficult to invest in physical capital. As a result, their workers are poorly equipped with machinery and tools and therefore are relatively unproductive. Remember that rapid population growth tends to reduce the amount of physical capital available per worker, and that reduction erodes labor productivity and decreases real incomes.

Moreover, most poor countries have not been able to invest adequately in their human capital (see Table 22.1, columns 3 and 4); consequently, expenditures on health and education have been meager. Low levels of literacy, malnutrition, lack of proper medical care, and insufficient educational facilities all contribute to populations that are ill equipped for industrialization and economic expansion. Attitudes may also play a role: In countries where hard work is associated with slavery and inferiority, many people try to avoid it. Also, by denying educational and work opportunities to women, many of the poorest DVCs forgo vast amounts of productive human capital.

Particularly vital is the absence of a vigorous entrepreneurial class willing to bear risks, accumulate capital, and provide the organizational requisites essential to economic growth. Closely related is the lack of labor trained to handle the routine supervisory functions basic to any program of development. Ironically, the higher-education systems of some DVCs emphasize the humanities and offer fewer courses in business, engineering, and the sciences. Some DVCs are characterized by an authoritarian view of human relations, sometimes fostered by repressive governments, that creates an environment hostile to thinking independently, taking initiatives, and assuming economic risks. Authoritarianism discourages experimentation and change, which are the essence of entrepreneurship.

While migration from the DVCs has modestly offset rapid population growth, it has also deprived some DVCs of highly productive workers. Often the best-trained and most highly motivated workers, such as physicians, engineers, teachers, and nurses, leave the DVCs to better their circumstances in the IACs. This so-called **brain drain** contributes to the deterioration in the overall skill level and productivity of the labor force.

Capital Accumulation

The accumulation of capital goods is an important focal point of economic development. All DVCs have a relative dearth of capital goods such as factories, machinery and equipment, and public utilities. Better-equipped labor forces would greatly enhance productivity and would help boost per capita output. There is a close relationship between output per worker (labor productivity) and real income per worker. A nation must produce more goods and services per worker in order to enjoy more goods and services per worker as income. One way of increasing labor productivity is to provide each worker with more tools and equipment.

Increasing the stock of capital goods is crucial, because the possibility of augmenting the supply of arable land is slight. An alternative is to supply the available agricultural workforce with more and better capital equipment. And, once initiated, the process of capital accumulation may be cumulative. If capital accumulation increases output faster than the growth in population, a margin of saving may arise that permits further capital formation. In a sense, capital accumulation feeds on itself.

Let's first consider the possibility that developing nations will manage to accumulate capital domestically. Then we will consider the possibility that foreign funds will flow into developing nations to support capital expansion.

Domestic Capital Formation A developing nation, like any other nation, accumulates capital through saving and investing. A nation must save (refrain from consumption) to free some of its re-

sources from the production of consumer goods. Investment spending must then absorb those released resources in the production of capital goods. But impediments to saving and investing are much greater in a low-income nation than they are in an advanced economy.

Savings Potential Consider first the savings side of the picture. The situation here is mixed and varies greatly between countries. Some of the very poor countries, such as Chad, Ghana, Ethiopia, Madagascar, Sierra Leone, and Uganda, had negative saving or save only 0 to 6 percent of their GDPs. The people are simply too poor to save a significant portion of their incomes. Interestingly, however, other developing countries save as large a percentage of their domestic outputs as do advanced industrial countries. In 1999 India and China saved 20 and 42 percent of their domestic outputs, respectively, compared to 30 percent for Japan, 23 percent for Germany, and 15 percent for the United States. The problem is that the domestic outputs of the DVCs are so low that even when saving rates are comparable to those of advanced nations, the total volume of saving is not large.

Capital Flight Some of the developing countries have suffered **capital flight,** the transfer of private DVC savings to accounts held in the IACs. (In this usage, "capital" is simply "money," "money capital," or "financial capital.") Many wealthy citizens of DVCs have used their savings to invest in the more economically advanced nations, enabling them to avoid the high investment risks at home, such as loss of savings or real capital from government expropriation, abrupt changes in taxation, potential hyperinflation, or high volatility of exchange rates. If a DVC's political climate is unsettled, savers may shift their funds overseas to a "safe haven" in fear that a new government might confiscate their wealth. Rapid or skyrocketing inflation in a DVC would have similar detrimental effects. The transfer of savings overseas may also be a means of evading high domestic taxes on interest income or capital gains. Finally, money capital may flow to the IACs to achieve higher interest rates or a greater variety of investment opportunities.

Whatever the motivation, the amount of capital flight from some DVCs is significant and offsets much of the IACs' lending and granting of other financial aid to the developing nations.

Investment Obstacles   There are as many obstacles on the investment side of capital formation in DVCs as on the saving side. Those obstacles include a lack of investors and a lack of incentives to invest.

In some developing nations, the major obstacle to investment is the lack of entrepreneurs who are willing to assume the risks associated with investment. This is a special case of the human capital limitations of the labor force mentioned above.

But the incentive to invest may be weak even in the presence of substantial savings and a large number of willing entrepreneurs. Several factors may combine in a DVC to reduce investment incentives, including political instability, high rates of inflation, and lack of economies of scale. Similarly, very low incomes in a DVC result in a lack of buying power and thus weak demand for all but agricultural goods. This factor is crucial, because the chances of competing successfully with mature industries in the international market are slim. Then, too, lack of trained administrative personnel may be a factor in retarding investment.

Finally, the **infrastructure** (stock of public capital goods) in many DVCs is insufficient to enable private firms to achieve adequate returns on their investments. Poor roads and bridges, inadequate railways, little gas and electricity production, poor communications, unsatisfactory housing, and inadequate educational and public health facilities create an inhospitable environment for private investment. A substantial portion of any new private investment would have to be used to create the infrastructure needed by all firms. Rarely can firms provide an investment in infrastructure themselves and still earn a positive return on their overall investment.

For all these reasons, investment incentives in many DVCs are lacking. It is significant that four-fifths of the overseas investments of multinational firms go to the IACs and only one-fifth to the DVCs. If the multinationals are reluctant to invest in the DVCs, we can hardly blame local entrepreneurs for being reluctant too.

How then can developing nations build up the infrastructure needed to attract investment? The higher-income DVCs may be able to accomplish this through taxation and public spending. But in the poorest DVCs there is little income to tax. Nevertheless, with leadership and a willingness to cooperate, a poor DVC can accumulate capital by transferring surplus agricultural labor to the improvement of the infrastructure. If each agricultural village allocated its surplus labor to the construction of irrigation canals, wells, schools, sanitary facilities, and roads, significant amounts of capital might be accumulated at no significant sacrifice of consumer goods production. Such investment bypasses the problems inherent in the financial aspects of the capital accumulation process. It does not require that consumers save portions of their money income, nor does it presume the presence of an entrepreneurial class anxious to invest. When leadership and cooperative spirit are present, this "in-kind" investment is a promising avenue for accumulation of basic capital goods. **(Key Question 7)**

Technological Advance

Technological advance and capital formation are frequently part of the same process. Yet there are advantages in discussing technological advance separately.

Given the rudimentary state of technology in the DVCs, they are far from the frontiers of technological advance. But the IACs have accumulated an enormous body of technological knowledge that the developing countries might adopt and apply without expensive research. Crop rotation and contour plowing require no additional capital equipment and would contribute significantly to productivity. By raising grain storage bins a few inches aboveground, a large amount of grain spoilage could be avoided. Although such changes may sound trivial to people of advanced nations, the resulting gains in productivity might mean the difference between subsistence and starvation in some poverty-ridden nations.

The application of either existing or new technological knowledge often requires the use of new and different capital goods. But, within limits, a nation can obtain at least part of that capital without an increase in the rate of capital formation. If a DVC channels the annual flow of replacement investment from technologically inferior to technologically superior capital equipment, it can increase productivity even with a constant level of investment spending. Actually, it can achieve some advances through **capital-saving technology** rather than **capital-using technology.** A new fertilizer, better adapted to a nation's topography and climate, might be cheaper than the fertilizer currently being used. A seemingly high-priced metal plow that will last 10 years may be cheaper in the long run than an inexpensive but technologically inferior wooden plow that has to be replaced every year.

To what extent have DVCs adopted and effectively used available IAC technological knowledge? The picture is mixed. There is no doubt that such technological borrowing has been instrumental in the rapid growth of such Pacific Rim countries as Japan, South Korea, Taiwan, and Singapore. Similarly, the OPEC nations have benefited significantly from IAC knowledge of oil exploration, production, and refining. Recently Russia, the nations of eastern Europe, and China have adopted western technology to hasten their conversion to market-based economies.

Still, the transfer of advanced technologies to the poorest DVCs is not an easy matter. In IACs technological advances usually depend on the availability of highly skilled labor and abundant capital. Such advances tend to be capital-using or, to put it another way, labor-saving. Developing economies require technologies appropriate to quite different resource endowments: abundant unskilled labor and very limited quantities of capital goods. Although labor-using and capital-saving technologies are appropriate to DVCs, much of the highly advanced technology of advanced nations is inappropriate to them. They must develop their own appropriate technologies. Moreover, many DVCs have "traditional economies" and are not highly receptive to change. That is particularly true of peasant agriculture, which dominates the economies of most of the poorer DVCs. Since technological change that fails may well mean hunger and malnutrition, there is a strong tendency to retain traditional production techniques.

Sociocultural and Institutional Factors

Economic considerations alone do not explain why an economy does or does not grow. Substantial sociocultural and institutional readjustments are usually an integral part of the growth process. Economic development means not only changes in a nation's physical environment (new transportation and communications facilities, new schools, new housing, new plants and equipment) but also changes in the way people think, behave, and associate with one another. Emancipation from custom and tradition is frequently a prerequisite of economic development. A critical but intangible ingredient in that development is **the will to develop.** Economic growth may hinge on what individuals within DVCs want for themselves and their children. Do they want more

material abundance? If so, are they willing to make the necessary changes in their institutions and old ways of doing things?

Sociocultural Obstacles
Sociocultural impediments to growth are numerous and varied. Some of the very low income countries have failed to achieve the preconditions for a national economic entity. Tribal and ethnic allegiances take precedence over national allegiance. Each tribe confines its economic activity to the tribal unit, eliminating any possibility for production-increasing specialization and trade. The desperate economic circumstances in Somalia, Sudan, Liberia, Zaire, Rawanda, and other African nations are due in no small measure to martial and political conflicts among rival groups.

In countries with a formal or informal caste system, labor is allocated to occupations on the basis of status or tradition rather than on the basis of skill or merit. The result is a misallocation of human resources.

Religious beliefs and observances may seriously restrict the length of the workday and divert to ceremonial uses resources that might have been used for investment. Some religious and philosophical beliefs are dominated by the fatalistic view that the universe is capricious, the idea that there is little or no correlation between an individual's activities and endeavors and the outcomes or experiences that person encounters. The **capricious universe view** leads to a fatalistic attitude. If "providence" rather than hard work, saving, and investing is the cause of one's lot in life, why save, work hard, and invest? Why engage in family planning? Why innovate?

Other attitudes and cultural factors may impede economic activity and growth: emphasis on the performance of duties rather than on individual initiative; focus on the group rather than on individual achievement; and the belief in reincarnation, which reduces the importance of one's current life.

Institutional Obstacles
Political corruption and bribery are common in many DVCs. School systems and public service agencies are often ineptly administered, and their functioning is frequently impaired by petty politics. Tax systems are frequently arbitrary, unjust, cumbersome, and detrimental to incentives to work and invest. Political decisions are often motivated by a desire to enhance the nation's international prestige rather than to foster development.

Because of the predominance of farming in DVCs, the problem of achieving an optimal institutional environment in agriculture is a vital consideration in any growth program. Specifically, the institutional problem of **land reform** demands attention in many DVCs. But the reform that is needed may vary tremendously from nation to nation. In some DVCs the problem is excessive concentration of land ownership in the hands of a few wealthy families. This situation is demoralizing for tenants, weakens their incentive to produce, and typically does not promote capital improvements. At the other extreme is the situation in which each family owns and farms a piece of land far too small for the use of modern agricultural technology. An important complication to the problem of land reform is that political considerations sometimes push reform in the direction of farms that are too small to achieve economies of scale. For many nations, land reform is the most acute institutional problem to be resolved in initiating economic development.

Examples: Land reform in South Korea weakened the political control of the landed aristocracy and opened the way for the emergence of strong commercial and industrial middle classes, all to the benefit of the country's economic development. In contrast, the prolonged dominance of the landed aristocracy in the Philippines may have stifled economic development in that nation.

QUICK REVIEW 22.1

■ About 40 percent of the world's population lives in the low-income DVCs.

■ Scarce natural resources and inhospitable climates restrict economic growth in many DVCs.

■ Most of the poorest DVCs are characterized by overpopulation, high unemployment rates, underemployment, and low labor productivity.

■ Low saving rates, capital flight, weak infrastructures, and lack of investors impair capital accumulation in many DVCs.

■ Sociocultural and institutional factors are often serious impediments to economic growth in DVCs.

■ The Vicious Circle

Many of the characteristics of DVCs just described are both causes and consequences of their poverty. These countries are caught in a **vicious circle of poverty.** They stay poor because they are poor! Consider Figure 22.3. Common to most DVCs is low per capita income. A family that is poor has

little ability or incentive to save. Furthermore, low incomes mean low levels of product demand. Thus, there are few available resources, on the one hand, and no strong incentives, on the other hand, for investment in physical or human capital. Consequently, labor productivity is low. And since output per person is real income per person, it follows that per capita income is low.

Many economists think that the key to breaking out of this vicious circle is to increase the rate of capital accumulation, to achieve a level of investment of, say, 10 percent of the national income. But Figure 22.3 reminds us that rapid population growth may partially or entirely undo the potentially beneficial effects of a higher rate of capital accumulation. Suppose that initially a DVC is realizing no growth in its real GDP but somehow manages to increase saving and investment to 10 percent of its GDP. As a result, real GDP begins to grow at, say, 2.5 percent per year. With a stable population, real GDP per capita will also grow at 2.5 percent per year. If that growth persists, the standard of living will double in about 28 years. But what if population also grows at the rate of 2.5 percent per year, as it does in parts of the Middle East, northern Africa, and sub-Saharan Africa? Then real income per person will remain unchanged and the vicious circle will persist.

But if population can be kept constant or limited to some growth rate significantly below 2.5 percent, real income per person will rise. Then the possibility arises of further enlargement of the flows of saving and investment, continuing advances in productivity, and the continued growth of per capita real income. If a process of self-sustaining expansion of income, saving, investment, and productivity can be achieved, the self-perpetuating vicious circle of poverty can be transformed into a self-regenerating, beneficent circle of economic progress. The challenge is to make effective the policies and strategies that will accomplish that transition. **(Key Question 13)** 🔑 **22.1**

■ Role of Government

Economists do not agree on the appropriate role of government in fostering DVC growth.

A Positive Role

One view is that, at least during initial stages of development, government should play a major role because of the types of obstacles facing DVCs.

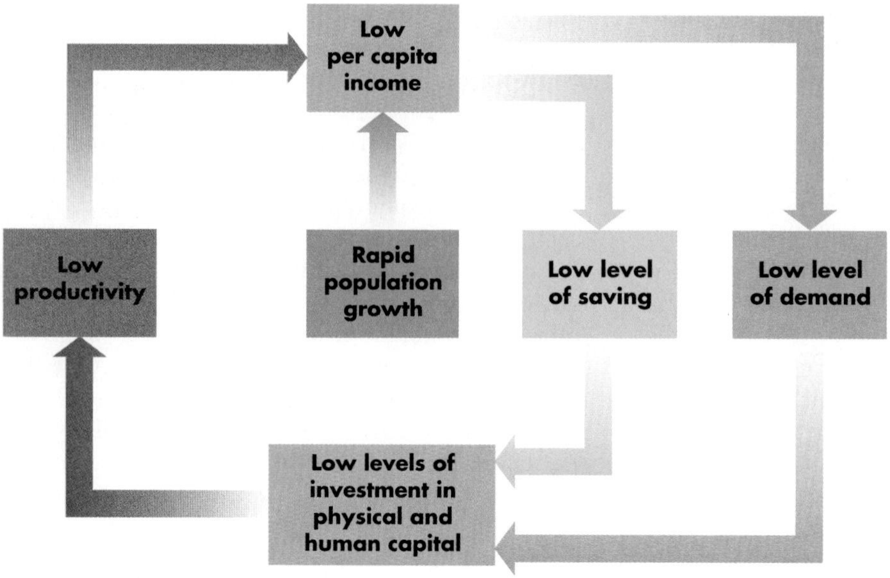

Figure 22.3

The vicious circle of poverty.
Low per capita incomes make it difficult for poor nations to save and invest, a condition that perpetuates low productivity and low incomes. Furthermore, rapid population growth may quickly absorb increases in per capita real income and thereby destroy the possibility of breaking out of the poverty circle.

Law and Order

Some of the poorest countries of the world are plagued by banditry and intertribal warfare that divert attention and resources from the task of development. A strong, stable national government is needed to establish domestic law and order and to achieve peace and unity. Research demonstrates that political instability (as measured by the number of revolutions and coups per decade) and slow growth go hand in hand.

Lack of Entrepreneurship

The lack of a sizable and vigorous entrepreneurial class, ready and willing to accumulate capital and initiate production, indicates that in some DVCs private enterprise is not capable of spearheading the growth process. Government may have to take the lead, at least at first.

Infrastructure

Many obstacles to economic growth are related to an inadequate infrastructure. Sanitation and basic medical programs, education, irrigation and soil conservation projects, and construction of highways and transportation-communication facilities are all essentially nonmarketable goods and services that yield widespread spillover benefits. Government is the only institution that is in a position to provide these public goods and services in required quantities.

Forced Saving and Investment

Government action may also be required to break through the saving and investment shortfalls that impede capital formation in DVCs.

It is possible that only government fiscal action can force the economy to accumulate capital. There are two alternatives. One is to force the economy to save by raising taxes and then to channel the tax revenues into priority investment projects. However, honestly and efficiently administering the tax system and achieving a high degree of compliance with tax laws may present grave problems.

The other alternative is to force the economy to save through inflation. Government can finance capital accumulation by creating and spending new money or by selling bonds to banks and spending the proceeds. The resulting inflation is the equivalent of an arbitrary tax on the economy.

There are serious arguments against forcing the economy to save through inflation, however. First, inflation often diverts investment away from productive facilities to such targets as luxury housing, precious metals and jewels, or foreign securities, which provide a better hedge against rising prices. Also, significant inflation may erode voluntary private saving because would-be savers are reluctant to accumulate depreciating money or securities payable in money of declining value. Often, too, inflation induces capital flight. Finally, inflation may boost the nation's imports and retard its flow of exports, thereby creating balance-of-payments difficulties.

Social-Institutional Problems Government is in the best position to deal with the social-institutional obstacles to growth. Controlling population growth and promoting land reform are problems that call for the broad approach that only government can provide. And government is in a position to nurture the will to develop, to change a philosophy of "Heaven and faith will determine the course of events" to one of "God helps those who help themselves."

Public Sector Problems

Still, serious problems and disadvantages may arise with a government-directed development program. If entrepreneurial talent is lacking in the private sector, is it likely that quality leaders will surface in the ranks of government? Is there not a real danger that government bureaucracy will impede, not stimulate, social and economic change? And what of the tendency of some political leaders to favor spectacular "showpiece" projects at the expense of less showy but more productive programs? Might not political objectives take precedence over the economic goals of a governmentally directed development program?

Development experts are less enthusiastic about the role of government in the growth process than they were 30 years ago. Unfortunately, government misadministration and **corruption** are common in many DVCs, and government officials sometimes line their own pockets with foreign-aid funds. Moreover, political leaders often confer monopoly privileges on relatives, friends, and political supporters and grant exclusive rights to relatives or friends to produce, import, or export certain products. Such monopoly privileges lead to higher domestic prices and diminish the DVC's ability to compete in world markets.

Similarly, managers of state-owned enterprises are often appointed on the basis of cronyism rather than competence. Many DVC governments, particularly in Africa, have created "marketing boards" as the sole purchaser of agricultural products from local farmers. The boards buy farm products at artificially low prices and sell them at higher world prices; the "profit" ends up in the pockets of

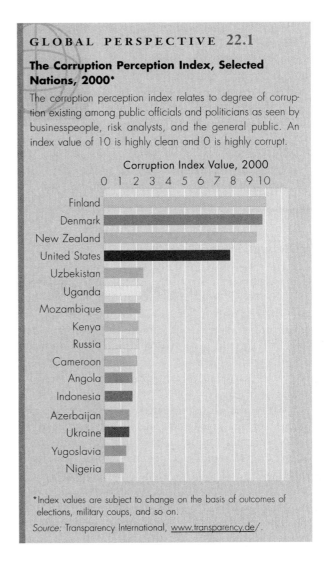

GLOBAL PERSPECTIVE 22.1

The Corruption Perception Index, Selected Nations, 2000*

The corruption perception index relates to degree of corruption existing among public officials and politicians as seen by businesspeople, risk analysts, and the general public. An index value of 10 is highly clean and 0 is highly corrupt.

Corruption Index Value, 2000

0 1 2 3 4 5 6 7 8 9 10

Finland
Denmark
New Zealand
United States
Uzbekistan
Uganda
Mozambique
Kenya
Russia
Cameroon
Angola
Indonesia
Azerbaijan
Ukraine
Yugoslavia
Nigeria

*Index values are subject to change on the basis of outcomes of elections, military coups, and so on.

Source: Transparency International, www.transparency.de/.

government officials. In recent years the perception of government has shifted from that of catalyst and promoter of growth to that of a potential impediment to development. According to a recent ranking of 90 nations based on perceived corruption, the 40 nations at the bottom of the list (most corrupt) were DVCs. Global Perspective 22.1 shows the 3 least corrupt nations, the United States, and the 12 most corrupt nations according to the index.

▪ Role of Advanced Nations

How can the IACs help developing countries in their pursuit of economic growth? To what degree have IACs provided assistance?

Generally, IACs can aid developing nations through (1) expanding trade with the DVCs, (2) providing foreign aid in the form of government grants and loans, and (3) providing transfers of technology and flows of private capital.

Expanding Trade

Some authorities maintain that the simplest and most effective way for the United States and other industrially advanced nations to aid developing nations is to lower international trade barriers. Such action would enable DVCs to elevate their national incomes through increased trade.

Although there is some truth in this view, lowering trade barriers is not a panacea. Some poor nations do need only large foreign markets for their raw materials in order to achieve growth. But the problem for many poor nations is not to obtain markets in which to sell existing products or relatively abundant raw materials but to get the capital and technical assistance they need to produce something worthy for export.

Moreover, close trade ties with advanced nations entail certain disadvantages. Dependence on the IACs' demand for imports would leave the DVCs vulnerable to temporary declines in the IACs' production. By reducing the demand for exports, recessions in the IACs might have disastrous consequences for the prices of raw materials from and the export earnings of the DVCs. For example, during the recession in the IACs in the early 1990s, the world price of zinc fell from $.82 per pound to $.46 per pound, and the world price of tin fell from $5.20 per pound to $3.50 per pound. Because mineral exports are a major source of DVC income, stability and growth in IACs are important to economic progress in the developing nations.

Foreign Aid: Public Loans and Grants

Foreign capital—either public or private—can play a crucial role in breaking an emerging country's circle of poverty by supplementing its saving and investment. As previously noted, many DVCs lack the infrastructure needed to attract either domestic or foreign private capital. The infusion of foreign aid that strengthens infrastructure could enhance the flow of private capital to the DVCs.

Direct Aid The United States and other IACs have assisted DVCs directly through a variety of programs and through participation in international bodies designed to stimulate economic development. Over the past decade, U.S. loans and grants to the DVCs totaled $10 billion to $14 billion per year. The U.S. Agency for International Development (USAID) administers most of this aid. Some of it, however, consists of grants of surplus food under the Food for Peace program. Other advanced nations also have substantial foreign aid programs. In recent years foreign aid from all IACs has totaled between $40 billion and $60 billion per year.

Such aid is typically distributed on the basis of political and military rather than economic considerations, however. Israel, Turkey, Egypt, and Greece, for example, are major recipients of U.S. aid. Asian, Latin American, and African nations with much lower standards of living receive less. Aid from the IACs themselves amounts to only about one-third of 1 percent of the IACs' collective GDP (see Global Perspective 22.2). Finally, the shift of Russia and eastern Europe toward more democratic, market-oriented systems has made those nations "new play-

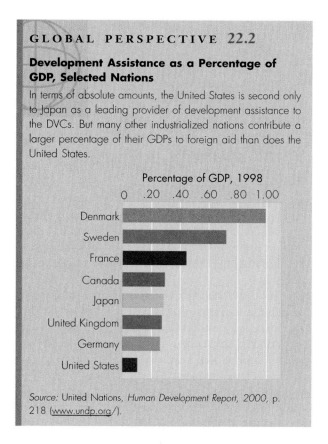

GLOBAL PERSPECTIVE 22.2

Development Assistance as a Percentage of GDP, Selected Nations

In terms of absolute amounts, the United States is second only to Japan as a leading provider of development assistance to the DVCs. But many other industrialized nations contribute a larger percentage of their GDPs to foreign aid than does the United States.

Percentage of GDP, 1998

Denmark
Sweden
France
Canada
Japan
United Kingdom
Germany
United States

Source: United Nations, *Human Development Report, 2000,* p. 218 (www.undp.org/).

ers" among foreign aid recipients. The DVCs are concerned that IAC aid that formerly flowed to Latin America, Asia, and Africa has been redirected to Poland, Hungary, and Russia. Moreover, there is a likelihood that substantially larger aid will flow to the Middle East if the PLO-Israeli peace process is eventually successful.

The World Bank Group   The United States is a participant in the **World Bank,** whose major objective is helping DVCs achieve economic growth. [The World Bank was established in 1945, along with the International Monetary Fund (IMF).] Supported by about 180 member nations, the World Bank not only lends out of its capital funds but also sells bonds and lends the proceeds and guarantees and insures private loans:

- The World Bank is a "last-resort" lending agency; its loans are limited to economic projects for which private funds are not readily available.
- Many World Bank loans have been for basic development projects—dams, irrigation projects, health and sanitation programs, communications and transportation facilities. Consequently, the Bank has helped finance the infrastructure needed to encourage the flow of private capital.
- The Bank has provided technical assistance to the DVCs by helping them determine what avenues of growth seem appropriate for their economic development.

Affiliates of the World Bank function in areas where the World Bank has proved weak. The *International Finance Corporation (IFC),* for example, invests in private enterprises in the DVCs. The *International Development Association (IDA)* makes "soft loans" (which may not be self-liquidating) to the poorest DVCs on more liberal terms than does the World Bank.

Foreign Harm?   Nevertheless, foreign aid to the DVCs has met with several criticisms.

Dependency and Incentives   A basic criticism is that foreign aid may promote dependency rather than self-sustaining growth. Critics argue that injections of funds from the IACs encourage the DVCs to ignore the painful economic decisions, the institutional and cultural reforms, and the changes in attitudes toward thrift, industry, hard work, and self-reliance that are needed for economic growth. They say that, after some five decades of foreign aid, the

DVCs' demand for foreign aid has increased rather than decreased. These aid programs should have withered away if they had been successful in promoting sustainable growth.

Bureaucracy and Centralized Government   IAC aid is given to the governments of the DVCs, not to their residents or businesses. The consequence is that the aid typically generates massive, ineffective government bureaucracies and centralizes government power over the economy. The stagnation and collapse of the Soviet Union and communist countries of eastern Europe is evidence that highly bureaucratized economies are not very conducive to economic growth and development. Furthermore, not only does the bureaucratization of the DVCs divert valuable human resources from the private to the public sector, but it often shifts the nation's focus from producing more output to bickering over how unearned "income" should be distributed.

Corruption and Misuse   Critics also allege that foreign aid is being used ineffectively. As we noted previously, corruption is a major problem in many DVCs, and some estimates suggest that from 10 to 20 percent of the aid is diverted to government officials. Also, IAC-based aid consultants and multinational corporations are major beneficiaries of aid programs. Some economists contend that as much as one-fourth of each year's aid is spent on expert consultants. Furthermore, because IAC corporations manage many of the aid projects, they are major beneficiaries of, and lobbyists for, foreign aid.

The Decline of Foreign Aid   Foreign aid to developing countries is on the decline. In 1990 IACs provided $58 billion of foreign aid; by 1999 that aid had dropped to $40 billion. The various criticisms of foreign aid are undoubtedly one reason for the decline. Another reason is the end of the Cold War, in which the United States and the former Soviet Union vied for the political and military allegiance of developing nations. Nations such as Cuba, Ethiopia, and North Korea, which adhered to communist principles, received substantial foreign aid from the Soviet Union. And the United States lavished aid on developing nations such as Egypt, Mexico, Thailand, Turkey, and Chile, which tended to support U.S. policies. But with the disintegration of the former Soviet Union, the political-military rationale for foreign aid lost much of its force.

Flows of Private Capital

The IACs also send substantial amounts of private capital to the DVCs. Among the private investors are corporations, commercial banks, and, more recently, financial investment companies. General Motors or Ford might finance construction of plants in Mexico or Brazil to assemble autos or produce auto parts. Chase Manhattan or Bank of America might make loans to private firms operating in Argentina or China or directly to the governments of Thailand and Malaysia. And the financial investment companies Fidelity or Putnam might purchase stock of promising Hungarian and Chilean firms as part of their "emerging markets" mutual funds, which then could be purchased by individual investors in the IACs.

The flow of private capital to the DVCs increased briskly in the 1990s, jumping from $50 billion in 1990 to $250 billion in 1999. The major reason for the increased flow of private capital is that many DVCs have reformed their economies to promote growth and thus are better credit risks. At the macro level, many DVCs have reduced budget deficits and controlled inflation. At the micro level, some governments have privatized state-owned businesses and deregulated industry. Some DVCs have reduced tariffs and have adjusted unrealistically fixed exchange rates. In general, the DVCs have reduced the economic role of government and increased the role of free markets in their economies. Those reforms have made the DVCs more attractive to foreign lenders.

The makeup of the private capital flow to the DVCs, however, is now different from what it was in prior decades. First, private IAC firms and individuals, rather than commercial banks, are the primary lenders. Second, a greater proportion of the flow now consists of **direct foreign investment** in DVCs, rather than loans to DVC governments. Such direct investment includes the building of new factories in DVCs by multinational firms and the purchase of DVC firms (or parts of them). Whereas DVCs once viewed direct foreign investment as "exploitation," many of them now seek out direct foreign investment as a way to expand their capital stock and improve their citizens' job opportunities and wages. Those wages are often very low by IAC standards but high by DVC standards. Another benefit of direct investment in DVCs is that management skills and technological knowledge often accompany the capital.

Two words of caution: The strong flow of private capital to the DVCs is highly selective. Recently, most of the flow has been directed toward China, Mexico, southeast Asian nations, and eastern European nations. Relatively little IAC capital is flowing toward such extremely impoverished DVCs as those in Africa.

In fact, many impoverished countries face staggering debt burdens from previous government and private loans. Payment of interest and principle on this external debt is diverting expenditures away from maintenance of infrastructure, new infrastructure, education, and private investment.

> **QUICK REVIEW 22.2**
>
> ■ DVC governments may encourage economic growth by (a) providing law and order, (b) taking the lead in establishing enterprises, (c) improving the infrastructure, (d) forcing higher levels of saving and investing, and (e) resolving social-institutional problems.
>
> ■ The IACs can assist the DVCs through expanded trade, foreign aid, and flows of private capital.
>
> ■ Many of the poorest DVCs have large external debts that pose an additional obstacle to economic growth.
>
> ■ In the 1990s the flow of foreign aid to DVCs declined, whereas the flow of private capital (particularly direct investment) increased.

■ Where from Here?

The developing nations face daunting tasks. There simply are no magic methods for achieving quick economic development. Moreover, the developing nations are not homogeneous. Some DVCs are far ahead of others in achieving economic development. Nevertheless, our discussion has directly suggested or implied a set of policies that would promote the growth process in the DVCs. We conclude the chapter by listing and briefly summarizing those policies.

DVC Policies for Promoting Growth

Economists suggest that developing nations have several ways of fostering their economic growth:

■ *Establishing and implementing the rule of law* Clearly defined and regularly enforced property rights bolster economic growth by ensuring that individuals receive and retain the fruits of their labor. Since legal protections reduce investment risk, the rule of law encourages direct investments by firms in the IACs. Government itself must live by the law. The presence of corruption in the government sanctions criminality throughout the economic system. Such criminality undermines the growth of output by diverting scarce resources toward activities that "transfer" income away from activities that produce goods and services.

- *Opening economies to international trade* Other things equal, open economies grow as much as 1.2 percentage points per year faster than closed economies.
- *Controlling population growth* Slower population growth converts increases in real output and income to increases in real *per capita* output and income. Families with fewer children consume less and save more; they also free up time for women to participate in the labor market.
- *Encouraging foreign direct investment* DVCs that welcome direct foreign investment enjoy greater growth rates than DVCs that view such investment suspiciously and put severe obstacles in its way.
- *Building human capital* Programs that encourage literacy, education, and labor market skills enhance economic growth. Higher-education loans and grants should contain strong incentives for recipients to remain in the home country (or to return to the home country) after receiving their degrees.
- *Making peace with neighbors* Countries at war or in fear of war with neighboring nations divert scarce resources to armaments, rather than to private capital or public infrastructure. Sustained peace among neighboring nations eventually leads to economic cooperation and integration, broadened markets, and stronger growth.
- *Establishing independent central banks* High rates of inflation are not conducive to economic investment and growth. DVCs can help keep inflation in check by establishing independent central banks to maintain proper control over their money supplies. Studies indicate that DVCs that control inflation enjoy higher growth rates than those that do not.
- *Establishing realistic exchange-rate policies* Exchange rates that are fixed at unrealistic levels invite balance-of-payments problems and speculative trading in currencies. Often, such trading forces a nation into an abrupt reevaluation

of its currency, sending shock waves throughout its economy. More flexible exchange rates enable more gradual adjustments and thus less susceptibility to major currency shocks and the domestic disruption they cause.

- *Privatizing state industries* Many DVCs would benefit by converting state enterprises into private firms. State enterprises often are inefficient, more concerned with appeasing labor unions than with introducing modern technology and delivering goods and services at minimum per-unit cost. Moreover, state enterprises are poor "incubators" for the development of profit-focused, entrepreneurial persons who leave the firm to set up their own businesses.

IAC Policies for Fostering DVC Growth

What can the IACs do to improve living conditions and promote growth in the developing nations? Here there is more disagreement among the experts. Economists offer a variety of suggestions, some of which we have already mentioned:

- *Directing foreign aid to the poorest DVCs* Much of the foreign aid emanating from the IACs is strongly influenced by political and military consideration rather than on the basis of their economic needs or degree of destitution. Only one-fourth of foreign aid goes to the 10 countries in which 70 percent of the world's poorest people live. The most affluent 40 percent of the DVC population receives over twice as much aid as the poorest 40 percent. Many economists argue that the IACs should shift foreign aid away from the middle-income DVCs and toward the poorest DVCs.
- *Reducing tariffs and import quotas* Trade barriers instituted by the IACs are often highest for labor-intensive manufactured goods such as textiles, clothing, footwear, and processed agricultural products. These are precisely the sorts of products for which the DVCs have a comparative advantage. Also, many IACs tariffs rise as the degree of product processing increases; for example, tariffs on chocolates are higher than those on cocoa. This practice discourages the DVCs from developing processing industries of their own.
- *Providing debt forgiveness to the poorest DVCs* The current debt of the poorest DVCs is so

large that it serves as a severe roadblock to DVC growth. Many economists support debt forgiveness for the poorest DVCs on loans provided by IAC governments. And, in fact, the process of debt forgiveness has begun. In 1999 the G-8 nations agreed to $29 billion of debt relief for highly indebted poor nations over 5 years. The World Bank has also agreed to an additional $50 billion of debt relief.

■ ***Admitting in temporary workers and discouraging brain drains*** Economists recommend that the IACs help the DVCs by accepting more temporary workers from the DVCs. Temporary migration provides an outlet for surplus DVC labor. Moreover, migrant remittances to families in the home country serve as a sorely needed source of income. Further, IACs should discourage brain drains from the DVCs, in which the brightest and best-educated workers in the DVCs are recruited to the IACs. As you might imagine, such proposals command more support in the DVCs than in the IACs.

■ ***Discouraging arms sales to the DVCs*** Finally, the IACs should discourage the sale of military equipment to the DVCs. Such purchases by the DVCs divert public expenditures from infrastructure and education.

Famine in Africa

The Roots of Africa's Persistent Famines Lie in Both Natural and Human Causes.

A number of sub-Saharan African nations are periodically threatened by famine. For example, in the early 1990s about 300,000 children under the age of 5 died from famine in Somalia. In 2000 famine threatened the lives of an estimated 12 million people in 10 African nations (Ethiopia, Kenya, Eritrea, Djibouti, Uganda, Somalia, Rwanda, Burundi, Tanzania, and Sudan). Although most African countries were self-sufficient in food at the time they became independent nations, they are now heavily dependent on imported foodstuffs for survival.

The immediate cause of famine often is drought. For example, in Kenya drought and crop failures in 1999 and 2000 killed much of the nation's livestock, leaving an estimated 3.5 million people at risk of starvation. But the ultimate causes of sub-Saharan Africa's inability to feed itself are rooted in a complex interplay of natural and human conditions. Lack of rainfall, chronic civil strife, rapid population growth, widespread soil erosion, and counterproductive public policies all contribute to Africa's famines.

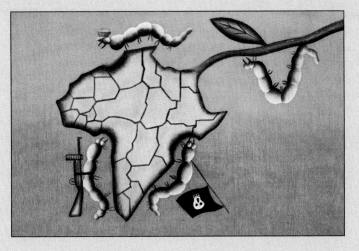

Civil Strife Regional rebellions, prolonged civil wars, and wars between nations have devastated several African nations. Ethiopia, Sudan, and Rawanda, for example, have been plagued by decades of civil strife. As another example, Ethiopia has recently been at war with its neighbor Eritrea. Not only do these conflicts divert precious resources from civilian uses, but they seriously complicate the ability of wealthy nations to provide famine and developmental aid. Governments frequently divert donated food to the army and deny it to starving civilians. In Somalia, factional feuding destroyed most of the existing schools, factories, and government ministries and reduced the country to anarchy. Armed gangs stole water pumps, tractors, and livestock from farms and looted ports of donated foodstuffs.

Population Growth Although slowing from previous growth rates, the population of sub-Saharan Africa is still growing very rapidly. Population is projected to grow by 2.2 percent annually from 2000 to 2015, compared to .6 percent in the industrially advanced economies. When crops are abundant, the sub-Saharan nations are able to feed their growing population. But when war and famine hit, hunger and malnutrition quickly follow.

Ecological Degradation Population growth has also contributed to the ecological degradation of Africa. With population pressures and the increasing need for food, marginal land has been deforested and put into crop production. In many cases trees that have served as a barrier to the encroachment of the desert have been cut down for fuel, allowing the fragile topsoil to be blown away by desert winds. The scarcity of wood that has accompanied deforestation has forced the use of animal dung for fuel, thereby denying its traditional use as fertilizer.

Furthermore, traditional fallow periods have been shortened, resulting in overplanting and overgrazing and a wearing out of the soil. Deforestation and land overuse have reduced the capacity of the land to absorb moisture, diminishing its productivity and its ability to resist drought. All this is complicated by the fact that there are few facilities for crop storage, making it difficult, even when crops are good, to accumulate a surplus for future lean years. A large percentage of domestic farm output in some parts of Africa is lost to rats, insects, and spoilage.

Public Policies Ill-advised public policies have contributed to Africa's famines. First, many African governments generally have neglected investment in agriculture in favor of industrial development and military strength. It is estimated that African governments on the average spend four times as much on armaments as they do on agriculture. Second, many African governments have adopted a policy of setting the prices of agricultural commodities at low levels to provide cheap food for growing urban populations. That policy has diminished the incentives of farmers to increase production. While foreign aid has helped ease the effects of Africa's food-population problems, most experts reject aid as a long-term solution. Experience suggests that aid in the form of food can provide only temporary relief and may undermine the achievement of long-run local self-sufficiency. Foreign food aid, it is contended, treats symptoms, not causes.

External Debt All this is made more complex by the fact that the sub-Saharan nations are burdened with large external debts. The World Bank reports that the aggregate external debt of these nations was $84 billion in 1980 and grew to $230 billion by 1999. As a condition of further aid, these nations have had to invoke austerity programs that have contributed to declines in their per capita incomes. One tragic consequence is that many of these nations have cut back on social service programs such as health care for children. For that reason, in 2000 the major industrial nations and the World Bank initiated a program to forgive the debts of some of these nations, on the condition that they end warfare and use the savings in interest and principal to ease the plight of their populations.

SUMMARY

1. The majority of the world's nations are developing countries (low- and middle-income nations). While some DVCs have been realizing rapid growth rates in recent years, others have experienced little or no growth.

2. Scarcities of natural resources make it more challenging for a nation to develop.

3. The large and rapidly growing populations in many DVCs contribute to low per capita incomes. Increases in per capita incomes frequently induce greater population growth, often reducing per capita incomes to near-subsistence levels. The demographic transition view, however, suggests that rising living standards must precede declining birthrates.

4. Most DVCs suffer from unemployment and underemployment. Labor productivity is low because of insufficient investment in physical and human capital.

5. In many DVCs, formidable obstacles impede both saving and investment. In some of the poorest DVCs, the savings potential is very low, and many savers transfer their funds to the IACs rather than invest them domestically. The lack of a vigorous entrepreneurial class and the weakness of investment incentives also impede capital accumulation.

6. Appropriate social and institutional changes and, in particular, the presence of "the will to develop" are essential ingredients in economic development.

7. The vicious circle of poverty brings together many of the obstacles to growth, supporting the view that poor countries stay poor because of their poverty. Low incomes inhibit saving and the accumulation of physical and human capital, making it difficult to increase productivity and incomes. Overly rapid population growth, however, may offset promising attempts to break the vicious circle.

8. The nature of the obstacles to growth—the absence of an entrepreneurial class, the dearth of infrastructure, the saving-investment dilemma, and the presence of social-institutional obstacles to growth—suggests that government should play a major role in initiating growth. However, the corruption and maladministration that are common to the public sectors of many DVCs suggest that government may not be very effective in instigating growth.

9. Advanced nations can encourage development in the DVCs by reducing IAC trade barriers and by providing both public and private capital. Critics of foreign aid, however, say that it (a) creates DVC dependency, (b) contributes to the growth of bureaucracies and centralized economic control, and (c) is rendered ineffective by corruption and mismanagement.

10. In the 1990s the IACs reduced foreign aid to the DVCs but increased direct investment and other private capital flows to the DVCs.

11. Economists suggest that DVCs could make further progress by establishing and enforcing the rule of law, opening their economies to international trade, controlling population growth, encouraging direct foreign investment, building human capital, maintaining peace with neighbors, establishing independent central banks, setting realistic exchange rates, and privatizing state industries. The IACs can help in this process by directing foreign aid to the neediest nations, reducing tariffs and import quotas, providing debt forgiveness to the poorest DVCs, allowing more low-skilled immigration from the DVCs, and discouraging arms sales to the DVCs.

TERMS AND CONCEPTS

industrially advanced countries (IACs)	underemployment	capital-using technology	corruption
developing countries (DVCs)	brain drain	the will to develop	World Bank
	capital flight	capricious universe view	direct foreign investment
demographic transition view	infrastructure	land reform	
	capital-saving technology	vicious circle of poverty	

STUDY QUESTIONS

1. What are the characteristics of a developing nation? List the two basic avenues of economic growth available to such a nation. State and explain the obstacles that DVCs face in breaking the poverty barrier. Use the "vicious circle of poverty" concept to outline steps a DVC might take to initiate economic development.

2. Explain how the absolute per capita income gap between rich and poor nations might increase, even though per capita income (or output) is growing faster in DVCs than in IACs.

3. **Key Question** Assume a DVC and an IAC presently have real per capita outputs of $500 and $5000, respectively. If both nations have a 3 percent increase in their real per capita outputs, by how much will the per capita output gap change?

4. Discuss and evaluate:
   a. The path to economic development has been blazed by American capitalism. It is up to the DVCs to follow that trail.
   b. The problem with the DVCs is that income is too equally distributed. Economic inequality promotes saving, and saving is a prerequisite of investment. Therefore, greater inequality in the income distribution of the DVCs would be a spur to capital accumulation and growth.
   c. The core of economic development involves changing human beings more than it does altering a nation's physical environment.
   d. The U.S. "foreign aid" program is a sham. In reality it represents neocolonialism—a means by which the DVCs can be nominally free in a political sense but remain totally subservient in an economic sense.
   e. The biggest obstacle facing poor nations in their quest for development is the lack of capital goods.

5. Studies indicate that, in general, landlocked countries tend to have lower per capita income levels than surrounding nations that border on oceans and seas. Why do you think that is the case? Use Global Perspective 22.1 to identify a major exception to this generalization. Why do you think this country is an exception?

6. **Key Question** Contrast the demographic transition view of population growth with the traditional view that slower population growth is a prerequisite for rising living standards in the DVCs.

7. **Key Question** Because real capital is supposed to earn a higher return where it is scarce, how do you explain the fact that most international investment flows to the IACs (where capital is relatively abundant) rather than to the DVCs (where capital is very scarce)?

8. Do you think that the nature of the problems the DVCs face requires government-directed as opposed to a private-enterprise-directed development process? Explain why or why not.

9. What were the trends in government-provided foreign aid versus private capital flows to the DVCs in the 1990s? Why do you think those trends occurred?

10. Do you favor debt forgiveness to all the DVCs, just the poorest ones, or none at all? What incentive problem might debt relief create? Would you be willing to pay $20 a year more in personal income taxes for debt forgiveness? How about $200 dollars? How about $2000 dollars?

11. What types of products do the DVCs typically export? How do those exports relate to the law of comparative advantage? How do tariffs by IACs reduce the standard of living of DVCs?

12. Do you think that IACs such as the United States should open their doors wider to the immigration of low-skilled DVC workers in order to help the DVCs develop? Do you think that it is appropriate for students from DVC nations to stay in IAC nations to work and build careers?

13. **Key Question** Use Figure 22.2 (changing the box labels as necessary) to explain rapid economic growth in a country such as South Korea or Chile. What factors other than those contained in the figure might contribute to that growth?

14. **(Last Word)** Explain how civil wars, population growth, and public policy decisions have contributed to periodic famines in Africa.

15. **Web-Based Question: *Group of 77—promoting the developing world*** The Group of 77 (G-77) was established in 1964 by 77 developing countries. The group promotes the collective economic interests of the developing world. Go to its website at www.g77.org/. What are the group's current developmental activities? What are the highlights in the latest *Group of 77 Journal?*

16. **Web-Based Question: *The World Bank Group— what's new in development economics?*** The major objective of the World Bank Group (www.world bank.org/) is to assist developing countries to achieve economic growth. What are three legs of the World Bank's development stool? What are the five agencies that make up the World Bank Group? Which is the most influential? Go to the "Development Economics" section of the "Topics in Development" area and read the current research findings in "What's Hot in Development Economics?" What are the problems or opportunities, and what is the World Bank doing about them?

GLOSSARY

Note: Terms set in *italic* type are defined separately in this glossary.

abstraction Elimination of irrelevant and noneconomic facts to obtain an *economic principle*.

actual investment The amount that *firms* do invest; equal to *planned investment* plus *unplanned investment*.

actual reserves The funds that a bank has on deposit at the *Federal Reserve Bank* of its district (plus its *vault cash*).

adjustable pegs The device used in the *Bretton Woods system* to alter *exchange rates* in an orderly way to eliminate persistent payments deficits and surpluses. Each nation defined its monetary unit in terms of (pegged it to) gold or the dollar, kept the *rate of exchange* for its money stable in the short run, and adjusted its rate in the long run when faced with international payments disequilibrium.

aggregate demand A schedule or curve that shows the total quantity of goods and services demanded (purchased) at different *price levels*.

aggregate demand–aggregate supply model The macroeconomic model that uses *aggregate demand* and *aggregate supply* to determine and explain the *price level* and the real *domestic output*.

aggregate expenditures The total amount spent for final goods and services in an economy.

aggregate expenditures–domestic output approach Determination of the equilibrium *gross domestic product* by finding the real GDP at which *aggregate expenditures* equal *domestic output*.

aggregate expenditures schedule A schedule or curve showing the total amount spent for final goods and services at different levels of *real GDP*.

aggregate supply A schedule or curve showing the total quantity of goods and services supplied (produced) at different *price levels*.

aggregate supply shocks Sudden, large changes in resource costs that shift an economy's aggregate supply curve.

aggregation The combining of individual units or data into one unit or number. For example, all prices of individual goods and services are combined into a *price level* or all units of output are aggregated into *real gross domestic product*.

allocative efficiency The apportionment of resources among firms and industries to obtain the production of the products most wanted by society (consumers); the output of each product at which its *marginal cost* and *price* or *marginal benefit* are equal.

annually balanced budget A budget in which government expenditures and tax collections are equal each year.

anticipated inflation Increases in the price level (*inflation*) that occur at the expected rate.

appreciation (of the dollar) An increase in the value of the dollar relative to the currency of another nation, so a dollar buys a larger amount of the foreign currency and thus of foreign goods.

asset Anything of monetary value owned by a firm or individual.

asset demand for money The amount of *money* people want to hold as a *store of value*; this amount varies inversely with the *interest rate*.

average propensity to consume Fraction (or percentage) of *disposable income* that households plan to spend for consumer goods and services; consumption divided by *disposable income*.

average propensity to save Fraction (or percentage) of *disposable income* that households save; *saving* divided by *disposable income*.

average tax rate Total tax paid divided by total (taxable) income, as a percentage.

balanced-budget multiplier The extent to which an equal change in government spending and taxes changes equilibrium *gross domestic product*; always has a value of 1, since it is equal to the amount of the equal changes in *G* and *T*.

balance of payments (See *international balance of payments*.)

balance-of-payments deficit The amount by which the sum of the *balance on current account* and the *balance on capital account* is negative in a year.

balance-of-payments surplus The amount by which the sum of the *balance on current account* and the *balance on capital account* is positive in a year.

balance on capital account The foreign purchases of assets in the United States less American purchases of assets abroad in a year.

balance on current account The exports of goods and services of a nation less its imports of goods and services plus its *net investment income* and *net transfers* in a year.

balance on goods and services The exports of goods and services of a nation less its imports of goods and services in a year.

balance sheet   A statement of the *assets, liabilities,* and *net worth* of a firm or individual at some given time.

bank deposits   The deposits that individuals or firms have at banks (or thrifts) or that banks have at the *Federal Reserve Banks*.

bankers' bank   A bank that accepts the deposits of and makes loans to *depository institutions;* in the United States, a *Federal Reserve Bank*.

bank reserves   The deposits of commercial banks and thrifts at *Federal Reserve Banks* plus bank and thrift *vault cash*.

barter   The exchange of one good or service for another good or service.

base year   The year with which other years are compared when an index is constructed; for example, the base year for a *price index*.

Board of Governors   The seven-member group that supervises and controls the money and banking system of the United States; the Board of Governors of the Federal Reserve System; the Federal Reserve Board.

bond   A financial device through which a borrower (a firm or government) is obligated to pay the principal and interest on a loan at a specific date in the future.

brain drain   The emigration of highly educated, highly skilled workers from a country.

break-even income   The level of *disposable income* at which *households* plan to consume (spend) all their income and to save none of it; also, in an income transfer program, the level of earned income at which subsidy payments become zero.

Bretton Woods system   The international monetary system developed after the Second World War in which *adjustable pegs* were employed, the *International Monetary Fund* helped stabilize foreign exchange rates, and gold and the dollar were used as *international monetary reserves*.

budget deficit   The amount by which the expenditures of the Federal government exceed its revenues in any year.

budget surplus   The amount by which the revenues of the Federal government exceed its expenditures in any year.

built-in stabilizer   A mechanism that increases government's budget deficit (or reduces its surplus) during a recession and increases government's budget surplus (or reduces its deficit) during inflation without any action by policymakers. The tax system is one such mechanism.

Bureau of Economic Analysis (BEA)   An agency of the U.S. Department of Commerce that compiles the national product and income accounts.

business cycle   Recurring increases and decreases in the level of economic activity over periods of years; consists of peak, recession, trough, and recovery phases.

business firm   (See *firm*.)

capital   Human-made resources (buildings, machinery, and equipment) used to produce goods and services; goods that do not directly satisfy human wants; also called capital goods.

capital account   The section of a nation's *international balance-of-payments* statement that records the foreign purchases of assets in the United States (creating monetary inflows) and U.S. purchases of assets abroad (creating monetary outflows).

capital account deficit   A negative *balance on capital account*.

capital account surplus   A positive *balance on capital account*.

capital flight   The transfer of savings from *developing countries* to industrially advanced countries to avoid government expropriation, taxation, and high rates of inflation or to realize better investment opportunities.

capital gain   The gain realized when securities or properties are sold for a price greater than the price paid for them.

capital goods   (See *capital*.)

capital-intensive commodity   A product that requires a relatively large amount of *capital* to be produced.

capitalism   An economic system in which property resources are privately owned and markets and prices are used to direct and coordinate economic activities.

capital-saving technological advance   An improvement in *technology* that permits a greater quantity of a product to be produced with a specific amount of *capital* (or permits the same amount of the product to be produced with a smaller amount of capital).

capital stock   The total available *capital* in a nation.

capital-using technological advance   An improvement in *technology* that requires the use of a greater amount of *capital* to produce a specific quantity of a product.

cartel   A formal agreement among firms (or countries) in an industry to set the price of a product and establish the outputs of the individual firms (or countries) or to divide the market for the product geographically.

causation   A relationship in which the occurrence of one or more events brings about another event.

CEA   (See *Council of Economic Advisers*.)

central bank   A bank whose chief function is the control of the nation's *money supply;* in the United States, the Federal Reserve System.

central economic planning   Government determination of the objectives of the economy and how resources will be directed to attain those goals.

ceteris paribus **assumption**   (See *other-things-equal assumption*.)

change in demand A change in the *quantity demanded* of a good or service at every price; a shift of the *demand curve* to the left or right.

change in supply A change in the *quantity supplied* of a good or service at every price; a shift of the *supply curve* to the left or right.

checkable deposit Any deposit in a *commercial bank* or *thrift institution* against which a check may be written.

checkable-deposit multiplier (See *monetary multiplier.*)

checking account A *checkable deposit* in a *commercial bank* or *thrift institution*.

check clearing The process by which funds are transferred from the checking accounts of the writers of checks to the checking accounts of the recipients of the checks.

circular flow model The flow of resources from *households* to *firms* and of products from firms to households. These flows are accompanied by reverse flows of money from firms to households and from households to firms.

classical economics The macroeconomic generalizations accepted by most economists before the 1930s that led to the conclusion that a capitalistic economy was self-regulating and therefore would usually employ its resources fully.

closed economy An economy that neither exports nor imports goods and services.

coincidence of wants A situation in which the good or service that one trader desires to obtain is the same as that which another trader desires to give up and an item that the second trader wishes to acquire is the same as that which the first trader desires to surrender.

COLA (See *cost-of-living adjustment.*)

command system A method of organizing an economy in which property resources are publicly owned and government uses *central economic planning* to direct and coordinate economic activities; command economy.

commercial bank A firm that engages in the business of banking (accepts deposits, offers checking accounts, and makes loans).

commercial banking system All *commercial banks* and *thrift institutions* as a group.

communism (See *command system.*)

comparative advantage A lower relative or comparative cost than that of another producer.

compensation to employees *Wages* and salaries plus wage and salary supplements paid by employers to workers.

competing goods (See *substitute goods.*)

competition The presence in a market of independent buyers and sellers competing with one another and the freedom of buyers and sellers to enter and leave the market.

complementary goods Products and services that are used together. When the price of one falls, the demand for the other increases (and conversely).

complex multiplier The *multiplier* that exists when changes in the *gross domestic product* change *net taxes* and *imports*, as well as *saving*.

conglomerates Firms that produce goods and services in two or more separate industries.

consumer goods Products and services that satisfy human wants directly.

consumer price index (CPI) An index that measures the prices of a fixed "market basket" of some 300 goods and services bought by a "typical" consumer.

consumer sovereignty Determination by consumers of the types and quantities of goods and services that will be produced with the scarce resources of the economy; consumers' direction of production through their dollar votes.

consumption of fixed capital An estimate of the amount of *capital* worn out or used up (consumed) in producing the *gross domestic product*; also called depreciation.

consumption schedule A schedule showing the amounts *households* plan to spend for *consumer goods* at different levels of *disposable income*.

contractionary fiscal policy A decrease in *government purchases* for goods and services, an increase in *net taxes*, or some combination of the two, for the purpose of decreasing *aggregate demand* and thus controlling inflation.

coordination failure A situation in which people do not reach a mutually beneficial outcome because they lack some way to jointly coordinate their actions; a possible cause of macroeconomic instability.

corporate income tax A tax levied on the net income (profit) of corporations.

corporation A legal entity ("person") chartered by a state or the Federal government that is distinct and separate from the individuals who own it.

correlation A systematic and dependable association between two sets of data (two kinds of events); does not necessarily indicate causation.

cost-of-living adjustment (COLA) An automatic increase in the incomes (wages) of workers when inflation occurs; guaranteed by a collective bargaining contract between firms and workers.

cost-push inflation Increases in the price level (inflation) resulting from an increase in resource costs (for example, raw-material prices) and hence in *per-unit production costs*; inflation caused by reductions in *aggregate supply*.

cost ratio An equality showing the number of units of two products that can be produced with the same resources; the cost ratio 1 corn $\equiv$ 3 olives shows that the resources required to produce 3 units of olives must be shifted to corn production to produce a unit of corn.

Council of Economic Advisers (CEA) A group of three persons that advises and assists the president of the United States on economic matters (including the preparation of the annual *Economic Report of the President*).

creative destruction The hypothesis that the creation of new products and production methods simultaneously destroys the market power of existing monopolies.

credit An accounting item that increases the value of an asset (such as the foreign money owned by the residents of a nation).

credit union An association of persons who have a common tie (such as being employees of the same firm or members of the same labor union) that sells shares to (accepts deposits from) its members and makes loans to them.

crowding-out effect A rise in interest rates and a resulting decrease in *planned investment* caused by the Federal government's increased borrowing in the money market.

currency Coins and paper money.

currency appreciation (See *exchange-rate appreciation*.)

currency depreciation (See *exchange-rate depreciation*.)

currency intervention A government's buying and selling of its own currency or foreign currencies to alter international exchange rates.

current account The section in a nation's *international balance of payments* that records its exports and imports of goods and services, its *net investment income*, and its *net transfers*.

cyclical deficit A Federal *budget deficit* that is caused by a recession and the consequent decline in tax revenues.

cyclically balanced budget The equality of government expenditures and net tax collections over the course of a *business cycle*; deficits incurred during periods of recession are offset by surpluses obtained during periods of prosperity (inflation).

cyclical unemployment A type of *unemployment* caused by insufficient total spending (or by insufficient *aggregate demand*).

debit An accounting item that decreases the value of an asset (such as the foreign money owned by the residents of a nation).

deflating Finding the *real gross domestic product* by decreasing the dollar value of the GDP for a year in which prices were higher than in the *base year*.

deflation A decline in the economy's *price level*.

demand A schedule showing the amounts of a good or service that buyers (or a buyer) wish to purchase at various prices during some time period.

demand curve A curve illustrating *demand*.

demand factor (in growth) The increase in the level of *aggregate demand* that brings about the *economic growth* made possible by an increase in the production potential of the economy.

demand management The use of *fiscal policy* and *monetary policy* to increase or decrease *aggregate demand*.

demand-pull inflation Increases in the price level (inflation) resulting from an excess of demand over output at the existing price level, caused by an increase in *aggregate demand*.

dependent variable A variable that changes as a consequence of a change in some other (independent) variable; the "effect" or outcome.

depository institutions Firms that accept deposits of *money* from the public (businesses and persons); *commercial banks, savings and loan associations, mutual savings banks*, and *credit unions*.

depreciation (See *consumption of fixed capital*.)

depreciation (of the dollar) A decrease in the value of the dollar relative to another currency, so a dollar buys a smaller amount of the foreign currency and therefore of foreign goods.

derived demand The demand for a resource that depends on the demand for the products it helps to produce.

determinants of aggregate demand Factors such as consumption spending, *investment*, government spending, and *net exports* that, if they change, shift the aggregate demand curve.

determinants of aggregate supply Factors such as input prices, *productivity*, and the legal-institutional environment that, if they change, shift the aggregate supply curve.

determinants of demand Factors other than price that determine the quantities demanded of a good or service.

determinants of supply Factors other than price that determine the quantities supplied of a good or service.

devaluation A decrease in the governmentally defined value of a currency.

developing countries (DVCs) Many countries of Africa, Asia, and Latin America that are characterized by lack of capital goods, use of nonadvanced technologies, low literacy rates, high unemployment, rapid population growth, and labor forces heavily committed to agriculture.

direct foreign investment The building of new factories (or the purchase of existing capital) in a particular nation by corporations of other nations.

direct relationship The relationship between two variables that change in the same direction, for example, product price and quantity supplied.

discount rate The interest rate that the *Federal Reserve Banks* charge on the loans they make to *commercial banks* and *thrift institutions*.

discouraged workers Employees who have left the *labor force* because they have not been able to find employment.

discretionary fiscal policy Deliberate changes in taxes (tax rates) and government spending by Congress to promote full employment, price stability, and economic growth.

discrimination The practice of according individuals or groups inferior treatment in hiring, occupational access, education and training, promotion, wage rates, or working conditions even though they have the same abilities, education and skills, and work experience as other workers.

disinflation A reduction in the rate of *inflation*.

disposable income *Personal income* less personal taxes; income available for *personal consumption expenditures* and *personal saving*.

dissaving Spending for consumer goods and services in excess of *disposable income;* the amount by which *personal consumption expenditures* exceed disposable income.

dividends Payments by a corporation of all or part of its profit to its stockholders (the corporate owners).

division of labor The separation of the work required to produce a product into a number of different tasks that are performed by different workers; *specialization* of workers.

dollar votes The "votes" that consumers and entrepreneurs cast for the production of consumer and capital goods, respectively, when they purchase those goods in product and resource markets.

domestic capital formation The process of adding to a nation's stock of *capital* by saving and investing part of its own domestic output.

domestic output *Gross* (or net) *domestic product;* the total output of final goods and services produced in the economy.

domestic price The price of a good or service within a country, determined by domestic demand and supply.

double taxation The taxation of both corporate net income (profits) and the *dividends* paid from this net income when they become the personal income of households.

dumping The sale of products below cost in a foreign country or below the prices charged at home.

durable good A consumer good with an expected life (use) of 3 or more years.

earnings The money income received by a worker; equal to the *wage* (rate) multiplied by the amount of time worked.

easy money policy Federal Reserve System actions to increase the *money supply* to lower interest rates and expand *real GDP*.

e-cash Electronic money; an entry (usable as money) stored in a computer or a stored-value card ("smart card").

economic analysis The process of deriving *economic principles* from relevant economic facts.

economic cost A payment that must be made to obtain and retain the services of a *resource;* the income a firm must provide to a resource supplier to attract the resource away from an alternative use; equal to the quantity of other products that cannot be produced when resources are instead used to make a particular product.

economic efficiency The use of the minimum necessary resources to obtain the socially optimal amounts of goods and services; entails both *productive efficiency* and *allocative efficiency*.

economic growth (1) An outward shift in the *production possibilities curve* that results from an increase in resource supplies or quality or an improvement in *technology;* (2) an increase of real output *(gross domestic product)* or real output per capita.

economic law An *economic principle* that has been tested and retested and has stood the test of time.

economic model A simplified picture of economic reality; an abstract generalization.

economic perspective A viewpoint that envisions individuals and institutions making rational decisions by comparing the marginal benefits and marginal costs associated with their actions.

economic policy A course of action intended to correct or avoid a problem.

economic principles Widely accepted generalizations about the economic behavior of individuals and institutions.

economic profit The *total revenue* of a firm less its *economic costs* (which include both payments to resource suppliers and the opportunity costs of firm-owned resources); also called "pure profit" and "above-normal profit."

economic resources The *land, labor, capital,* and *entrepreneurial ability* that are used in the production of goods and services; productive agents; factors of production.

economics The social science dealing with the use of scarce resources to obtain the maximum satisfaction of society's virtually unlimited economic wants.

economic system A particular set of institutional arrangements and a coordinating mechanism for solving the economizing problem; a method of organizing an economy, of which the *market system* and the *command system* are the two general types.

economic theory A statement of a cause-effect relationship; when accepted by all economists, an *economic principle*.

economies of scale   Reductions in the *per-unit cost* of producing a product as the firm expands the size of plant (its output) in the *long run;* the economies of mass production.

economizing problem   The choices necessitated because society's economic wants for goods and services are unlimited but the *resources* available to satisfy these wants are limited (scarce).

efficiency factors (in growth)   The capacity of an economy to combine resources effectively to achieve growth of real output that the *supply factors* (of growth) make possible.

efficiency wage   A wage that minimizes wage costs per unit of output by encouraging greater effort or reducing turnover.

efficient allocation of resources   The allocation of an economy's resources among the production of different products that leads to the maximum satisfaction of consumers' wants, thus producing the socially optimal mix of output with society's scarce resources.

Employment Act of 1946   Federal legislation that committed the Federal government to the maintenance of economic stability (a high level of employment, a stable price level, and economic growth); established the *Council of Economic Advisers* and the *Joint Economic Committee;* and required an annual economic report by the president to Congress.

employment rate   The percentage of the *labor force* employed at any time.

entrepreneurial ability   The human resource that combines the other resources to produce a product, makes nonroutine decisions, innovates, and bears risks.

equation of exchange $MV = PQ$, in which M is the supply of money, V is the *velocity* of money, P is the *price level*, and Q is the physical volume of *final goods and services* produced.

equilibrium price   The *price* in a competitive market at which the *quantity demanded* and the *quantity supplied* are equal, there is neither a shortage nor a surplus, and there is no tendency for price to rise or fall.

equilibrium price level   The price level at which the aggregate demand curve intersects the aggregate supply curve.

equilibrium quantity   (1) The quantity demanded and supplied at the equilibrium price in a competitive market; (2) the profit-maximizing output of a firm.

equilibrium real domestic output   The *gross domestic product* at which the total quantity of final goods and services purchased (*aggregate expenditures*) is equal to the total quantity of final goods and services produced (the real domestic output); the real domestic output at which the aggregate demand curve intersects the aggregate supply curve.

euro   The common currency unit used by 12 European nations in the Euro Zone, which includes all nations of the *European Union* except Great Britain, Denmark, and Sweden.

European Union (EU)   An association of 15 European nations that has eliminated tariffs and import quotas among them, established common tariffs for goods imported from outside the member nations, allowed the free movement of labor and capital among them, and created other common economic policies. Includes Austria, Belgium, Denmark, Finland, France, Germany, Great Britain, Greece, Ireland, Italy, Luxembourg, the Netherlands, Portugal, Spain, and Sweden.

excess reserves   The amount by which a bank's or thrift's *actual reserves* exceed its *required reserves;* actual reserves minus required reserves.

exchange control   (See *foreign exchange control.*)

exchange rate   The *rate of exchange* of one nation's currency for another nation's currency.

exchange-rate appreciation   An increase in the value of a nation's currency in foreign exchange markets; an increase in the *rate of exchange* for foreign currencies.

exchange-rate depreciation   A decrease in the value of a nation's currency in foreign exchange markets; a decrease in the *rate of exchange* for foreign currencies.

exchange-rate determinant   Any factor other than the *rate of exchange* that determines a currency's demand and supply in the *foreign exchange market.*

excise tax   A tax levied on the production of a specific product or on the quantity of the product purchased.

exclusion principle   The ability to exclude those who do not pay for a product from receiving its benefits.

exhaustive expenditure   An expenditure by government resulting directly in the employment of *economic resources* and in the absorption by government of the goods and services those resources produce; a *government purchase.*

expansionary fiscal policy   An increase in *government purchases* of goods and services, a decrease in *net taxes*, or some combination of the two for the purpose of increasing *aggregate demand* and expanding real output.

expectations   The anticipations of consumers, firms, and others about future economic conditions.

expected rate of return   The increase in profit a firm anticipates it will obtain by purchasing capital (or engaging in research and development); expressed as a percentage of the total cost of the investment (or R&D) activity.

expenditures approach   The method that adds all expenditures made for *final goods and services* to measure the *gross domestic product.*

expenditures-output approach   (See *aggregate expenditures–domestic output approach.*)

exports Goods and services produced in a nation and sold to buyers in other nations.

export subsidies Government payments to domestic producers to enable them to reduce the *price* of a good or service to foreign buyers.

export supply curve An upward-sloping curve that shows the amount of a product that domestic firms will export at each *world price* that is above the *domestic price*.

export transaction A sale of a good or service that increases the amount of foreign currency flowing to a nation's citizens, firms, and government.

external debt Private or public debt owed to foreign citizens, firms, and institutions.

externality (See *spillover*.)

face value The dollar or cents value stamped on a U.S. coin.

factors of production *Economic resources: land, capital, labor,* and *entrepreneurial ability.*

fallacy of composition The false notion that what is true for the individual (or part) is necessarily true for the group (or whole).

FDIC (See *Federal Deposit Insurance Corporation*.)

Federal Advisory Committee The group of 12 commercial bankers that advises the Board of Governors on banking policy.

Federal Deposit Insurance Corporation (FDIC) The federally chartered corporation that insures deposit liabilities (up to $100,000 per account) of *commercial banks* and *thrift institutions* (excluding *credit unions*, whose deposits are insured by the *National Credit Union Administration*).

Federal funds rate The interest rate banks and other depository institutions charge one another on overnight loans made out of their *excess reserves*.

Federal government The government of the United States, as distinct from the state and local governments.

Federal Open Market Committee (FOMC) The 12-member group that determines the purchase and sale policies of the *Federal Reserve Banks* in the market for U.S. government securities.

Federal Reserve Banks The 12 banks chartered by the U.S. government to control the *money supply* and perform other functions. (See *central bank, quasi-public bank,* and *bankers' bank*.)

Federal Reserve Note Paper money issued by the *Federal Reserve Banks*.

fiat money Anything that is *money* because government has decreed it to be money.

final goods and services Goods and services that have been purchased for final use and not for resale or further processing or manufacturing.

financial capital (See *money capital*.)

firm An organization that employs resources to produce a good or service for profit and owns and operates one or more *plants*.

fiscal federalism The system of transfers (grants) by which the Federal government shares its revenues with state and local governments.

fiscal policy Changes in government spending and tax collections designed to achieve a full-employment and noninflationary domestic output; also called *discretionary fiscal policy*.

fixed exchange rate A *rate of exchange* that is set in some way and therefore prevented from rising or falling with changes in currency supply and demand.

flexible exchange rate A *rate of exchange* determined by the international demand for and supply of a nation's money; a rate free to rise or fall (to float).

floating exchange rate (See *flexible exchange rate*.)

foreign competition (See *import competition*.)

foreign exchange control The control a government may exercise over the quantity of foreign currency demanded by its citizens and firms and over the *rates of exchange* in order to limit its *outpayments* to its *inpayments* (to eliminate a *payments deficit*).

foreign exchange market A market in which the money (currency) of one nation can be used to purchase (can be exchanged for) the money of another nation.

foreign exchange rate (See *rate of exchange*.)

foreign purchase effect The inverse relationship between the *net exports* of an economy and its price level relative to foreign price levels.

Four Fundamental Questions (of economics) The four questions that every economy must answer: what to produce, how to produce it, how to divide the total output, and how to ensure economic flexibility.

45° line A line along which the value of *GDP* (measured horizontally) is equal to the value of *aggregate expenditures* (measured vertically).

fractional reserve A *reserve requirement* that is less than 100 percent of the checkable-deposit liabilities of a *commercial bank* or *thrift institution*.

freedom of choice The freedom of owners of property resources to employ or dispose of them as they see fit, of workers to enter any line of work for which they are qualified, and of consumers to spend their incomes in a manner that they think is appropriate.

freedom of enterprise The freedom of *firms* to obtain economic resources, to use those resources to produce products of the firm's own choosing, and to sell their products in markets of their choice.

free-rider problem The inability of potential providers of an economically desirable but indivisible good or service to obtain payment from those who benefit, because the *exclusion principle* is not applicable.

free trade The absence of artificial (government-imposed) barriers to trade among individuals and firms in different nations.

frictional unemployment A type of unemployment caused by workers voluntarily changing jobs and by temporary layoffs; unemployed workers between jobs.

full employment (1) The use of all available resources to produce want-satisfying goods and services; (2) the situation in which the *unemployment rate* is equal to the *full-employment unemployment rate* and there is *frictional* and *structural* but no *cyclical unemployment* (and the *real GDP* of the economy equals its *potential output*).

full-employment budget A comparison of the government expenditures and tax collections that would occur if the economy operated at *full employment* throughout the year.

full-employment unemployment rate The *unemployment rate* at which there is no *cyclical unemployment* of the *labor force*; equal to between 4 and 5 percent in the United States because some *frictional* and *structural unemployment* is unavoidable.

full production Employment of available resources so that the maximum amount of (or total value of) goods and services is produced; occurs when both *productive efficiency* and *allocative efficiency* are realized.

functional distribution of income The manner in which *national income* is divided among the functions performed to earn it (or the kinds of resources provided to earn it); the division of national income into wages and salaries, proprietors' income, corporate profits, interest, and rent.

functional finance The use of *fiscal policy* to achieve a noninflationary full-employment *gross domestic product* without regard to the effect on the *public debt*.

gains from trade The extra output that trading partners obtain through specialization of production and exchange of goods and services.

GDP (See *gross domestic product*.)

GDP deflator The *price index* found by dividing *nominal GDP* by *real GDP*; a price index used to adjust money (or nominal) GDP to real GDP.

GDP gap The amount by which actual *gross domestic product* falls below potential gross domestic product.

General Agreement on Tariffs and Trade (GATT) The international agreement reached in 1947 in which 23 nations agreed to give equal and nondiscriminatory treatment to one another, to reduce tariff rates by multinational negotiations, and to eliminate *import quotas*. It now includes most nations and has become the *World Trade Organization*.

generalization Statement of the nature of the relation between two or more sets of facts.

gold standard A historical system of fixed exchange rates in which nations defined their currencies in terms of gold, maintained a fixed relationship between their stocks of gold and their money supplies, and allowed gold to be freely exported and imported.

government purchases Expenditures by government for goods and services that government consumes in providing public goods and for public (or social) capital that has a long lifetime; the expenditures of all governments in the economy for those *final goods and services*.

government transfer payment The disbursement of money (or goods and services) by government for which government receives no currently produced good or service in return.

gross domestic product (GDP) The total market value of all *final goods and services* produced annually within the boundaries of the United States, whether by U.S. or foreign-supplied resources.

gross private domestic investment Expenditures for newly produced *capital goods* (such as machinery, equipment, tools, and buildings) and for additions to inventories.

G-7 nations A group of seven major industrial nations (the United States, Japan, Germany, United Kingdom, France, Italy, and Canada) whose leaders meet regularly to discuss common economic problems and try to coordinate economic policies (recently has also included Russia, making it unofficially the G-8).

guiding function of prices The ability of price changes to bring about changes in the quantities of products and resources demanded and supplied.

horizontal axis The "left-right" or "west-east" axis on a graph or grid.

horizontal range The horizontal segment of the aggregate supply curve along which the price level is constant as real domestic output changes.

household An economic unit (of one or more persons) that provides the economy with resources and uses the income received to purchase goods and services that satisfy economic wants.

human capital The accumulation of prior investments in education, training, health, and other factors that increase productivity.

human capital investment Any expenditure undertaken to improve the education, skills, health, or mobility of workers, with an expectation of greater productivity and thus a positive return on the investment.

hyperinflation A very rapid rise in the price level; an extremely high rate of inflation.

hypothesis A tentative explanation of cause and effect that requires testing.

IMF (See *International Monetary Fund*.)

import competition The competition that domestic firms encounter from the products and services of foreign producers.

import demand curve A downsloping curve showing the amount of a product that an economy will import at each *world price* below the *domestic price*.

import quota A limit imposed by a nation on the quantity (or total value) of a good that may be imported during some period of time.

imports Spending by individuals, *firms*, and governments for goods and services produced in foreign nations.

import transaction The purchase of a good or service that decreases the amount of foreign money held by citizens, firms, and governments of a nation.

income A flow of dollars (or purchasing power) per unit of time derived from the use of human or property resources.

income approach The method that adds all the income generated by the production of *final goods and services* to measure the *gross domestic product*.

income effect A change in the quantity demanded of a product that results from the change in *real income (purchasing power)* produced by a change in the product's price.

income inequality The unequal distribution of an economy's total income among households or families.

increase in demand An increase in the *quantity demanded* of a good or service at every price; a shift of the *demand curve* to the right.

increase in supply An increase in the *quantity supplied* of a good or service at every price; a shift in the *supply curve* to the right.

increasing returns An increase in a firm's output by a larger percentage than the percentage increase in its inputs.

independent goods Products or services for which there is no relationship between the price of one and the demand for the other. When the price of one rises or falls, the demand for the other remains constant.

independent variable The variable causing a change in some other (dependent) variable.

indirect business taxes Such taxes as *sales*, *excise*, and business *property taxes*, license fees, and *tariffs* that firms treat as costs of producing a product and pass on (in whole or in part) to buyers by charging higher prices.

individual demand The demand schedule or *demand curve* of a single buyer.

individual supply The supply schedule or *supply curve* of a single seller.

industrially advanced countries (IACs) High-income countries such as the United States, Canada, Japan, and the nations of western Europe that have highly developed *market economies* based on large stocks of technologically advanced capital goods and skilled labor forces.

industry A group of (one or more) *firms* that produce identical or similar products.

inferior good A good or service whose consumption declines as income rises (and conversely), price remaining constant.

inflating Determining *real gross domestic product* by increasing the dollar value of the *nominal gross domestic product* produced in a year in which prices are lower than those in a *base year*.

inflation A rise in the general level of prices in an economy.

inflationary expectations The belief of workers, firms, and consumers that substantial inflation will occur in the future.

inflationary gap The amount by which the *aggregate expenditures schedule* must shift downward to decrease the *nominal GDP* to its full-employment noninflationary level.

inflation premium The component of the *nominal interest rate* that reflects anticipated inflation.

information technology New and more efficient methods of delivering and receiving information through use of computers, fax machines, wireless phones, and the Internet.

infrastructure The capital goods usually provided by the *public sector* for the use of its citizens and firms (for example, highways, bridges, transit systems, wastewater treatment facilities, municipal water systems, and airports).

injection An addition of spending to the income-expenditure stream: *investment*, *government purchases*, and *net exports*.

in-kind investment (See *nonfinancial investment*.)

innovation The first commercially successful introduction of a new product, the use of a new method of production, or the creation of a new form of business organization.

inpayments   The receipts of domestic or foreign money that individuals, firms, and governments of one nation obtain from the sale of goods and services abroad, as investment income and remittances, and from foreign purchases of its assets.

insider-outsider theory   The hypothesis that nominal wages are inflexible downward because firms are aware that workers ("insiders") who retain employment during recession may refuse to work cooperatively with previously unemployed workers ("outsiders") who offer to work for less than the current wage.

interest   The payment made for the use of money (of borrowed funds).

interest income   Payments of income to those who supply the economy with *capital*.

interest rate   The annual rate at which interest is paid; a percentage of the borrowed amount.

interest-rate effect   The tendency for increases in the *price level* to increase the demand for money, raise interest rates, and, as a result, reduce total spending and real output in the economy (and the reverse for price-level decreases).

intermediate goods   Products that are purchased for resale or further processing or manufacturing.

intermediate range   The upward-sloping segment of the aggregate supply curve lying between the *horizontal range* and the *vertical range*.

internally held public debt   *Public debt* owed to citizens, firms, and institutions of the same nation that issued the debt.

international balance of payments   A summary of all the transactions that took place between the individuals, firms, and government units of one nation and those of all other nations during a year.

international balance-of-payments deficit   (See *balance-of-payments deficit*.)

international balance-of-payments surplus   (See *balance-of-payments surplus*.)

international gold standard   (See *gold standard*.)

International Monetary Fund (IMF)   The international association of nations that was formed after World War II to make loans of foreign monies to nations with temporary *payments deficits* and, until the early 1970s, to administer the *adjustable pegs*. It now mainly makes loans to nations facing possible defaults on private and government loans.

international monetary reserves   The foreign currencies and other assets such as gold that a nation can use to settle a *payments deficit*.

international value of the dollar   The price that must be paid in foreign currency (money) to obtain one U.S. dollar.

intrinsic value   The market value of the metal within a coin.

inventories   Goods that have been produced but remain unsold.

inverse relationship   The relationship between two variables that change in opposite directions, for example, product price and quantity demanded.

investment   Spending for the production and accumulation of *capital* and additions to inventories.

investment demand curve   A curve that shows the amounts of *investment* demanded by an economy at a series of *real interest rates*.

investment goods   Same as *capital* or capital goods.

investment in human capital   (See *human capital investment*.)

investment schedule   A curve or schedule that shows the amounts firms plan to invest at various possible values of *real gross domestic product*.

invisible hand   The tendency of firms and resource suppliers that seek to further their own self-interests in competitive markets to also promote the interest of society.

Joint Economic Committee (JEC)   Committee of senators and representatives that investigates economic problems of national interest.

Keynesian economics   The macroeconomic generalizations that lead to the conclusion that a capitalistic economy is characterized by macroeconomic instability and that *fiscal policy* and *monetary policy* can be used to promote *full employment*, *price-level stability*, and *economic growth*.

Keynesianism   The philosophical, ideological, and analytical views pertaining to *Keynesian economics*.

labor   People's physical and mental talents and efforts that are used to help produce goods and services.

labor force   Persons 16 years of age and older who are not in institutions and who are employed or are unemployed (and seeking work).

labor-force participation rate   The percentage of the working-age population that is actually in the *labor force*.

labor-intensive commodity   A product requiring a relatively large amount of *labor* to be produced.

labor productivity   Total output divided by the quantity of labor employed to produce it.

labor theory of value   (Web chapter) The Marxian idea that the economic value of any commodity is determined solely by the amount of labor that is required to produce it.

labor union A group of workers organized to advance the interests of the group (to increase wages, shorten the hours worked, improve working conditions, and so on).

Laffer Curve A curve relating government tax rates and tax revenues and on which a particular tax rate (between zero and 100 percent) maximizes tax revenues.

laissez-faire capitalism (See *capitalism*.)

land Natural resources ("free gifts of nature") used to produce goods and services.

land-intensive commodity A product requiring a relatively large amount of land to be produced.

law of demand The principle that, other things equal, an increase in a product's price will reduce the quantity of it demanded, and conversely for a decrease in price.

law of increasing opportunity costs The principle that as the production of a good increases, the *opportunity cost* of producing an additional unit rises.

law of supply The principle that, other things equal, an increase in the price of a product will increase the quantity of it supplied, and conversely for a price decrease.

leakage (1) A withdrawal of potential spending from the income-expenditures stream via *saving*, tax payments, or *imports*; (2) a withdrawal that reduces the lending potential of the banking system.

learning by doing Achieving greater *productivity* and lower *average total cost* through gains in knowledge and skill that accompany repetition of a task; a source of *economies of scale*.

legal reserves The minimum amount a *depository institution* must keep on deposit with the *Federal Reserve Bank* in its district or must hold as *vault cash*.

legal tender Anything that government says must be accepted in payment of a debt.

lending potential of an individual commercial bank The amount by which a single bank can safely increase the *money supply* by making new loans to (or buying securities from) the public; equal to the bank's excess reserves.

lending potential of the banking system The amount by which the banking system can increase the *money supply* by making new loans to (or buying securities from) the public; equal to the *excess reserves* of the banking system multiplied by the *monetary multiplier*.

liability A debt with a monetary value; an amount owed by a firm or an individual.

limited liability Restriction of the maximum loss to a predetermined amount for the owners (stockholders) of a *corporation*. The maximum loss is the amount they paid for their shares of stock.

limited-liability company An unincorporated business whose owners are protected by *limited liability*.

liquidity The ease with which an asset can be converted quickly into cash with little or no loss of purchasing power. Money is said to be perfectly liquid, whereas other assets have a lesser degree of liquidity.

long run (1) In *microeconomics*, a period of time long enough to enable producers of a product to change the quantities of all the resources they employ; period in which all resources and costs are variable and no resources or costs are fixed. (2) In *macroeconomics*, a period sufficiently long for *nominal wages* and other input prices to change in response to a change in the nation's *price level*.

long-run aggregate supply curve The aggregate supply curve associated with a time period in which input prices (especially *nominal wages*) are fully responsive to changes in the *price level*.

lump-sum tax A tax that is a constant amount (the tax revenue of government is the same) at all levels of GDP.

M1 The most narrowly defined *money supply*, equal to *currency* in the hands of the public and the *checkable deposits* of commercial banks and thrift institutions.

M2 A more broadly defined *money supply*, equal to M1 plus *noncheckable savings accounts* (including *money market deposit accounts*), small *time deposits* (deposits of less than $100,000), and individual *money market mutual fund* balances.

M3 A very broadly defined *money supply*, equal to M2 plus large *time deposits* (deposits of $100,000 or more).

macroeconomics The part of economics concerned with the economy as a whole; with such major aggregates as the household, business, and government sectors; and with measures of the total economy.

managed floating exchange rate An *exchange rate* that is allowed to change (float) as a result of changes in currency supply and demand but at times is altered (managed) by governments via their buying and selling of particular currencies.

marginal analysis The comparison of marginal ("extra" or "additional") benefits and marginal costs, usually for decision making.

marginal benefit The extra (additional) benefit of consuming 1 more unit of some good or service; the change in total benefit when 1 more unit is consumed.

marginal cost The extra (additional) cost of producing 1 more unit of output; equal to the change in total cost divided by the change in output.

marginal propensity to consume The fraction of any change in *disposable income* spent for *consumer goods*; equal to the change in consumption divided by the change in disposable income.

marginal propensity to save   The fraction of any change in *disposable income* that households save; equal to the change in *saving* divided by the change in disposable income.

marginal tax rate   The tax rate paid on each additional dollar of income.

marginal utility   The extra *utility* a consumer obtains from the consumption of 1 additional unit of a good or service; equal to the change in total utility divided by the change in the quantity consumed.

market   Any institution or mechanism that brings together buyers (demanders) and sellers (suppliers) of a particular good or service.

market demand   (See *total demand*.)

market economy   An economy in which only the private decisions of consumers, resource suppliers, and firms determine how resources are allocated; the *market system*.

market failure   The inability of a market to bring about the allocation of resources that best satisfies the wants of society; in particular, the overallocation or underallocation of resources to the production of a particular good or service because of *spillovers* or informational problems or because markets do not provide desired *public goods*.

market system   All the product and resource markets of a *market economy* and the relationships among them; a method that allows the prices determined in those markets to allocate the economy's scarce resources and to communicate and coordinate the decisions made by consumers, firms, and resource suppliers.

Medicaid   A Federal program that helps finance the medical expenses of low-income individuals and families.

Medicare   A Federal program that is financed by *payroll taxes* and provides for (1) compulsory hospital insurance for senior citizens and (2) low-cost voluntary insurance to help older Americans pay physicians' fees.

medium of exchange   Any item sellers generally accept and buyers generally use to pay for a good or service; *money*; a convenient means of exchanging goods and services without engaging in *barter*.

microeconomics   The part of economics concerned with such individual units as *industries*, *firms*, and *households* and with individual markets, specific goods and services, and product and resource prices.

minimum wage   The lowest *wage* employers may legally pay for an hour of work.

monetarism   The macroeconomic view that the main cause of changes in aggregate output and the price level is fluctuations in the *money supply*; espoused by advocates of a *monetary rule*.

monetary multiplier   The multiple of its *excess reserves* by which the banking system can expand *checkable deposits* and thus the *money supply* by making new loans (or buying securities); equal to 1 divided by the *reserve requirement*.

monetary policy   A central bank's changing of the *money supply* to influence interest rates and assist the economy in achieving price stability, full employment, and economic growth.

monetary rule   The rule suggested by *monetarism*. As traditionally formulated, the rule says that the *money supply* should be expanded each year at the same annual rate as the potential rate of growth of the *real gross domestic product*; the supply of money should be increased steadily between 3 and 5 percent per year. (Also see *Taylor rule*.)

money   Any item that is generally acceptable to sellers in exchange for goods and services.

money capital   Money available to purchase *capital*; simply *money*, as defined by economists.

money income   (See *nominal income*.)

money market   The market in which the demand for and the supply of money determine the *interest rate* (or the level of interest rates) in the economy.

money market deposit accounts (MMDAs)   Interest-earning accounts at banks and *thrift institutions*, which pool the funds of depositors to buy various short-term securities.

money market mutual funds (MMMFs)   Interest-bearing accounts offered by investment companies, which pool depositors' funds for the purchase of short-term securities. Depositors may write checks in minimum amounts or more against their accounts.

money supply   Narrowly defined, $M1$; more broadly defined, $M2$ and $M3$.

monopoly   A market structure in which the number of sellers is so small that each seller is able to influence the total supply and the price of the good or service.

most-favored-nation (MFN) status   An agreement by the United States to allow some other nation's *exports* into the United States at the lowest tariff level levied by the United States, then or at any later time.

multinational corporations   Firms that own production facilities in two or more countries and produce and sell their products globally.

multiple counting   Wrongly including the value of *intermediate goods* in the *gross domestic product*; counting the same good or service more than once.

multiplier   The ratio of a change in the equilibrium GDP to the change in *investment* or in any other component of *aggregate expenditures* or *aggregate demand*; the number by which a change in any component of aggregate expenditures or aggregate demand must be multiplied to find the resulting change in the equilibrium GDP.

multiplier effect   The effect on equilibrium GDP of a change in *aggregate expenditures* or *aggregate demand* (caused by a change in the *consumption schedule, investment, government purchases,* or *net exports*).

mutually exclusive goals   Two or more goals that conflict and cannot be achieved simultaneously.

mutual savings bank   A firm without stockholders that accepts deposits primarily from small individual savers and that lends primarily to individuals to finance the purchases of autos and residences.

national bank   A *commercial bank* authorized to operate by the U.S. government.

National Credit Union Administration (NCUA)   The federally chartered agency that insures deposit liabilities (up to $100,000 per account) in *credit unions.*

national income   Total income earned by resource suppliers for their contributions to *gross domestic product;* equal to the gross domestic product minus *nonincome charges,* minus *net foreign factor income.*

national income accounting   The techniques used to measure the overall production of the economy and other related variables for the nation as a whole.

natural monopoly   An industry in which *economies of scale* are so great that a single firm can produce the product at a lower average total cost than would be possible if more than one firm produced the product.

natural rate of unemployment   The *full-employment unemployment rate;* the unemployment rate occurring when there is no cyclical unemployment and the economy is achieving its potential output; the unemployment rate at which actual inflation equals expected inflation.

near-money   Financial assets, the most important of which are *noncheckable savings accounts, time deposits,* and U.S. short-term securities and savings bonds, which are not a medium of exchange but can be readily converted into money.

negative relationship   (See *inverse relationship.*)

net domestic product   *Gross domestic product* less the part of the year's output that is needed to replace the *capital goods* worn out in producing the output; the nation's total output available for consumption or additions to the *capital stock.*

net export effect   The idea that the impact of a change in *monetary policy* or *fiscal policy* will be strengthened or weakened by the consequent change in *net exports.* The change in net exports occurs because of changes in real interest rates, which affect exchange rates.

net exports   *Exports* minus *imports.*

net foreign factor income   Payments by a nation of resource income to the rest of the world minus receipts of resource income from the rest of the world.

net investment income   The interest and dividend income received by the residents of a nation from residents of other nations less the interest and dividend payments made by the residents of that nation to the residents of other nations.

net private domestic investment   *Gross private domestic investment* less *consumption of fixed capital;* the addition to the nation's stock of *capital* during a year.

net taxes   The taxes collected by government less *government transfer payments.*

net transfers   The personal and government transfer payments made by one nation to residents of foreign nations less the personal and government transfer payments received from residents of foreign nations.

network effects   Increases in the value of a product to each user, including existing users, as the total number of users rises.

net worth   The total *assets* less the total *liabilities* of a firm or an individual; for a firm, the claims of the owners against the firm's total assets; for an individual, his or her wealth.

new classical economics   The theory that, although unanticipated price-level changes may create macroeconomic instability in the short run, the economy is stable at the full-employment level of domestic output in the long run because prices and wages adjust automatically to correct movements away from the full-employment, noninflationary output.

New Economy   The label attached by some economists and the popular press to the U.S. economy since 1995. The main characteristics are substantially faster *productivity growth* and *economic growth,* caused by rapid technological advance and the emergence of the global economy.

nominal gross domestic product (GDP)   The *GDP* measured in terms of the price level at the time of measurement (unadjusted for *inflation*).

nominal income   The number of dollars received by an individual or group for its resources during some period of time.

nominal interest rate   The interest rate expressed in terms of annual amounts currently charged for interest and not adjusted for inflation.

nominal wage   The amount of money received by a worker per unit of time (hour, day, etc.); money wage.

noncheckable savings account   A savings account against which no checks can be written.

nondiscretionary fiscal policy   (See *built-in stabilizer.*)

nondurable good   A *consumer good* with an expected life (use) of less than 3 years.

nonexhaustive expenditure An expenditure by government that does not result directly in the employment of economic resources or the production of goods and services; see *government transfer payment*.

nonfinancial investment An investment that does not require that *households* save a part of their money incomes but uses surplus (unproductive) labor to build *capital goods*.

nonincome charges *Consumption of fixed capital* and *indirect business taxes*; amounts subtracted from *GDP* (along with *net foreign factor income*) in determining *national income*.

nonincome determinants of consumption and saving All influences on consumption and saving other than the level of *GDP*.

noninterest determinants of investment All influences on the level of investment spending other than the *interest rate*.

noninvestment transaction An expenditure for stocks, bonds, or secondhand *capital goods*.

nonmarket transactions The production of goods and services excluded in the measurement of the *gross domestic product* because they are not bought and sold.

nonproduction transaction The purchase and sale of any item that is not a currently produced good or service.

nontariff barriers All barriers other than *protective tariffs* that nations erect to impede international trade, including *import quotas*, licensing requirements, unreasonable product-quality standards, unnecessary bureaucratic detail in customs procedures, and so on.

normal good A good or service whose consumption increases when income increases and falls when income decreases, price remaining constant.

normal profit The payment made by a firm to obtain and retain *entrepreneurial ability*; the minimum income entrepreneurial ability must receive to induce it to perform entrepreneurial functions for a firm.

normative economics That part of economics involving value judgments about what the economy should be like; focused on which economic goals and policies should be implemented; policy economics.

North American Free Trade Agreement (NAFTA) A 1993 agreement establishing, over a 15-year period, a free-trade zone composed of Canada, Mexico, and the United States.

official reserves Foreign currencies owned by the central bank of a nation.

Okun's law The generalization that any 1-percentage-point rise in the *unemployment rate* above the *full-employment unemployment rate* will increase the GDP gap by 2 percent of the *potential output* (GDP) of the economy.

OPEC (See *Organization of Petroleum Exporting Countries*.)

open economy An economy that exports and imports goods and services.

open-market operations The buying and selling of U.S. government securities by the *Federal Reserve Banks* for purposes of carrying out *monetary policy*.

opportunity cost The amount of other products that must be forgone or sacrificed to produce a unit of a product.

Organization of Petroleum Exporting Countries (OPEC) A cartel of 11 oil-producing countries (Algeria, Indonesia, Iran, Iraq, Kuwait, Libya, Nigeria, Qatar, Saudi Arabia, Venezuela, and the UAE) that controls the quantity and price of crude oil exported by its members and that accounts for 60 percent of the world's export of oil.

other-things-equal assumption The assumption that factors other than those being considered are held constant.

outpayments The expenditures of domestic or foreign currency that the individuals, firms, and governments of one nation make to purchase goods and services, for *remittances*, to pay investment income, and for purchases of foreign assets.

paper money Pieces of paper used as a *medium of exchange*; in the United States, *Federal Reserve Notes*.

partnership An unincorporated firm owned and operated by two or more persons.

patent An exclusive right given to inventors to produce and sell a new product or machine for 20 years from the time of patent application.

payments deficit (See *balance-of-payments deficit*.)

payments surplus (See *balance-of-payments surplus*.)

payroll tax A tax levied on employers of labor equal to a percentage of all or part of the wages and salaries paid by them and on employees equal to a percentage of all or part of the wages and salaries received by them.

per capita GDP *Gross domestic product* (GDP) per person; the average GDP of a population.

per capita income A nation's total income per person; the average income of a population.

personal consumption expenditures The expenditures of *households* for *durable* and *nondurable consumer goods* and services.

personal distribution of income The manner in which the economy's *personal* or *disposable income* is divided among different income classes or different households or families.

personal income The earned and unearned income available to resource suppliers and others before the payment of personal taxes.

personal income tax A tax levied on the taxable income of individuals, households, and unincorporated firms.

personal saving The *personal income* of households less personal taxes and *personal consumption expenditures; disposable income* not spent for *consumer goods.*

per-unit production cost The average production cost of a particular level of output; total input cost divided by units of output.

Phillips Curve A curve showing the relationship between the *unemployment rate* (on the horizontal axis) and the annual rate of increase in the *price level* (on the vertical axis).

planned investment The amount that *firms* plan or intend to invest.

plant A physical establishment that performs one or more functions in the production, fabrication, and distribution of goods and services.

policy economics The formulation of courses of action to bring about desired economic outcomes or to prevent undesired occurrences.

political business cycle The alleged tendency of Congress to destabilize the economy by reducing taxes and increasing government expenditures before elections and to raise taxes and lower expenditures after elections.

positive economics The analysis of facts or data to establish scientific generalizations about economic behavior.

positive relationship A direct relationship between two variables.

post hoc, ergo propter hoc **fallacy** The false belief that when one event precedes another, the first event must have caused the second event.

potential output The real output *(GDP)* an economy can produce when it fully employs its available resources.

poverty A situation in which the basic needs of an individual or family exceed the means to satisfy them.

poverty rate The percentage of the population with incomes below the official poverty income levels that are established by the Federal government.

premature inflation A type of inflation that sometimes occurs before the economy has reached *full employment.*

price The amount of money needed to buy a particular good, service, or resource.

price index An index number that shows how the weighted-average price of a "market basket" of goods changes over time.

price level The weighted average of the prices of all the final goods and services produced in an economy.

price-level stability A steadiness of the price level from one period to the next; zero or low annual inflation; also called "price stability."

price-level surprises Unanticipated changes in the price level.

price-wage flexibility Changes in the *prices* of products and in the *wages* paid to workers; the ability of prices and wages to rise or fall.

price war Successive and continued decreases in the prices charged by firms in an oligopolistic industry. Each firm lowers its price below rivals' prices, hoping to increase its sales and revenues at its rivals' expense.

prime interest rate The *interest rate* banks charge their most creditworthy borrowers—for example, large corporations with excellent credit records.

principal-agent problem A conflict of interest that occurs when agents (workers or managers) pursue their own objectives to the detriment of the principals' (stockholders') goals.

private good A good or service that is subject to the *exclusion principle* and is provided by privately owned firms to consumers who are willing to pay for it.

private property The right of private persons and firms to obtain, own, control, employ, dispose of, and bequeath *land, capital,* and other property.

private sector The *households* and business *firms* of the economy.

production possibilities curve A curve showing the different combinations of two goods or services that can be produced in a *full-employment, full-production* economy where the available supplies of resources and technology are fixed.

productive efficiency The production of a good in the least costly way; occurs when production takes place at the output at which average cost is a minimum.

productivity A measure of average output or real output per unit of input. For example, the productivity of labor is determined by dividing real output by hours of work.

productivity growth The percentage change in *productivity* from one period to another.

product market A market in which products are sold by *firms* and bought by *households.*

profit The return to the resource *entrepreneurial ability* (see *normal profit*); *total revenue* minus total cost (see *economic profit*).

progressive tax A tax whose *average tax rate* increases as the taxpayer's income increases and decreases as the taxpayer's income decreases.

property tax A tax on the value of property (*capital, land, stocks* and *bonds,* and other *assets*) owned by *firms* and *households.*

proportional tax A tax whose *average tax rate* remains constant as the taxpayer's income increases or decreases.

protective tariff A *tariff* designed to shield domestic producers of a good or service from the competition of foreign producers.

public debt The total amount owed by the Federal government to the owners of government securities; equal to the sum of past government *budget deficits* less government *budget surpluses*.

public good A good or service that is indivisible and to which the *exclusion principle* does not apply; a good or service with these characteristics provided by government.

public investments Government expenditures on public capital (such as roads, highways, bridges, mass-transit systems, and electric power facilities) and on *human capital* (such as education, training, and health).

public sector The part of the economy that contains all government entities; government.

purchasing power The amount of goods and services that a monetary unit of income can buy.

purchasing power parity The idea that exchange rates between nations equate the purchasing power of various currencies. Exchange rates between any two nations adjust to reflect the price-level differences between the countries.

pure rate of interest An essentially risk-free, long-term interest rate that is free of the influence of market imperfections.

quantity demanded The amount of a good or service that buyers (or a buyer) desire to purchase at a particular price during some period.

quantity supplied The amount of a good or service that producers (or a producer) offer to sell at a particular price during some period.

quasi-public bank A bank that is privately owned but governmentally (publicly) controlled; each of the U.S. *Federal Reserve Banks*.

quasi-public good A good or service to which the *exclusion principle* could apply but that has such a large *spillover benefit* that government sponsors its production to prevent an underallocation of resources.

R&D Research and development activities undertaken to bring about *technological advance*.

rate of exchange The price paid in one's own money to acquire 1 unit of a foreign currency; the rate at which the money of one nation is exchanged for the money of another nation.

rate of return The gain in net revenue divided by the cost of an investment or an *R&D* expenditure; expressed as a percentage.

rational behavior Human behavior based on comparison of marginal costs and marginal benefits; behavior designed to maximize total utility.

rational expectations theory The hypothesis that firms and households expect monetary and fiscal policies to have certain effects on the economy and (in pursuit of their own self-interests) take actions that make these policies ineffective.

rationing function of prices The ability of market forces in competitive markets to equalize *quantity demanded* and *quantity supplied* and to eliminate shortages and surpluses via changes in prices.

real-balances effect The tendency for increases in the *price level* to lower the real value (or purchasing power) of financial assets with fixed money value and, as a result, to reduce total spending and *real GDP*, and conversely for decreases in the price level.

real-business-cycle theory A theory that *business cycles* result from changes in technology and resource availability, which affect *productivity* and thus shift *the long-run aggregate supply curve* either leftward or rightward.

real capital (See *capital*.)

real GDP (See *real gross domestic product*.)

real gross domestic product (GDP) *Gross domestic product* adjusted for inflation; gross domestic product in a year divided by the GDP *price index* for that year, expressed as a decimal.

real income The amount of goods and services that can be purchased with *nominal income* during some period of time; nominal income adjusted for inflation.

real interest rate The interest rate expressed in dollars of constant value (adjusted for *inflation*) and equal to the *nominal interest rate* less the expected rate of inflation.

real wage The amount of goods and services a worker can purchase with his or her *nominal wage*; the purchasing power of the nominal wage.

recession A period of declining real GDP, accompanied by lower real income and higher unemployment.

recessionary gap The amount by which the *aggregate expenditures schedule* must shift upward to increase the real GDP to its full-employment, noninflationary level.

Reciprocal Trade Agreements Act A 1934 Federal law that authorized the president to negotiate up to 50 percent lower tariffs with foreign nations that agreed to reduce their tariffs on U.S. goods. (Such agreements incorporated the *most-favored-nation* clause.)

refinancing the public debt Paying owners of maturing government securities with money obtained by selling new securities or with new securities.

regressive tax   A tax whose *average tax rate* decreases as the taxpayer's income increases and increases as the taxpayer's income decreases.

rental income   The payments (income) received by those who supply *land* to the economy.

required reserves   The funds that banks and thrifts must deposit with the *Federal Reserve Bank* (or hold as *vault cash*) to meet the legal *reserve requirement;* a fixed percentage of the bank's or thrift's checkable deposits.

reserve requirement   The specified minimum percentage of its checkable deposits that a bank or thrift must keep on deposit at the Federal Reserve Bank in its district or hold as *vault cash*.

resource   A natural, human, or manufactured item that helps produce goods and services; a productive agent or factor of production.

resource market   A market in which *households* sell and *firms* buy resources or the services of resources.

retiring the public debt   Reducing the size of the *public debt* by paying money to owners of maturing U.S. government securities.

revaluation   An increase in the governmentally defined value of the nation's currency relative to other nations' currencies.

revenue tariff   A *tariff* designed to produce income for the Federal government.

roundabout production   The construction and use of *capital* to aid in the production of *consumer goods*.

rule of 70   A method for determining the number of years it will take for some measure to double, given its annual percentage increase. Example: To determine the number of years it will take for the *price level* to double, divide 70 by the annual rate of *inflation*.

sales tax   A tax levied on the cost (at retail) of a broad group of products.

saving   Disposable income not spent for consumer goods; equal to *disposable income* minus *personal consumption expenditures*.

savings and loan association (S&L)   A firm that accepts deposits primarily from small individual savers and lends primarily to individuals to finance purchases such as autos and homes; now nearly indistinguishable from a *commercial bank*.

saving schedule   A schedule that shows the amounts *households* plan to save (plan not to spend for *consumer goods*), at different levels of *disposable income*.

savings deposit   A deposit that is interest-bearing and that the depositor can normally withdraw at any time.

savings institution   A *thrift institution*.

Say's law   The largely discredited macroeconomic generalization that the production of goods and services (supply) creates an equal *demand* for those goods and services.

scarce resources   The limited quantities of *land, capital, labor,* and *entrepreneurial ability* that are never sufficient to satisfy people's virtually unlimited economic wants.

scientific method   The procedure for the systematic pursuit of knowledge involving the observation of facts and the formulation and testing of hypotheses to obtain theories, principles, and laws.

seasonal variations   Increases and decreases in the level of economic activity within a single year, caused by a change in the season.

secular trend   A long-term tendency; a change in some variable over a very long period of years.

self-interest   That which each firm, property owner, worker, and consumer believes is best for itself and seeks to obtain.

seniority   The length of time a worker has been employed absolutely or relative to other workers; may be used to determine which workers will be laid off when there is insufficient work for them all and who will be rehired when more work becomes available.

separation of ownership and control   The fact that different groups of people own a *corporation* (the stockholders) and manage it (the directors and officers).

service   An (intangible) act or use for which a consumer, firm, or government is willing to pay.

shirking   Workers' neglecting or evading work to increase their *utility* or well-being.

shortage   The amount by which the *quantity demanded* of a product exceeds the *quantity supplied* at a particular (below-equilibrium) price.

short run   (1) In microeconomics, a period of time in which producers are able to change the quantities of some but not all of the resources they employ; a period in which some resources (usually plant) are fixed and some are variable. (2) In macroeconomics, a period in which nominal wages and other input prices do not change in response to a change in the price level.

short-run aggregate supply curve   An aggregate supply curve relevant to a time period in which input prices (particularly *nominal wages*) do not change in response to changes in the *price level*.

simple multiplier   The *multiplier* in any economy in which government collects no *net taxes*, there are no *imports*, and *investment* is independent of the level of income; equal to 1 divided by the *marginal propensity to save*.

slope of a line   The ratio of the vertical change (the rise or fall) to the horizontal change (the run) between any two points on a line. The slope of an upward-sloping line is positive, reflecting a direct relationship between two variables; the slope of a downward-sloping line is negative, reflecting an inverse relationship between two variables.

Smoot-Hawley Tariff Act   Legislation passed in 1930 that established very high tariffs. Its objective was to reduce imports and stimulate the domestic economy, but it resulted only in retaliatory tariffs by other nations.

social security trust fund   A Federal fund that saves excessive social security tax revenues received in one year to meet social security benefit obligations that exceed social security tax revenues in some subsequent year.

sole proprietorship   An unincorporated *firm* owned and operated by one person.

special economic zones   (Web chapter) Regions of China open to foreign investment, private ownership, and relatively free international trade.

specialization   The use of the resources of an individual, a firm, a region, or a nation to concentrate production on one or a small number of goods and services.

speculation   The activity of buying or selling with the motive of later reselling or rebuying for profit.

spillover   A benefit or cost from production or consumption, accruing without compensation to nonbuyers and nonsellers of the product (see *spillover benefit* and *spillover cost*).

spillover benefit   A benefit obtained without compensation by third parties from the production or consumption of sellers or buyers. Example: A beekeeper benefits when a neighboring farmer plants clover.

spillover cost   A cost imposed without compensation on third parties by the production or consumption of sellers or buyers. Example: A manufacturer dumps toxic chemicals into a river, killing the fish sought by sport fishers.

SSI   (See *Supplemental Security Income*.)

stagflation   Inflation accompanied by stagnation in the rate of growth of output and an increase in unemployment in the economy; simultaneous increases in the *price level* and the *unemployment rate*.

startup (firm)   A new firm focused on creating and introducing a particular new product or employing a specific new production or distribution method.

state bank   A *commercial bank* authorized by a state government to engage in the business of banking.

state-owned enterprises   (Web chapter) Businesses that are owned by the government; the major types of enterprises in Russia and China before their transitions to the market system.

stock (corporate)   An ownership share in a corporation.

store of value   An *asset* set aside for future use; one of the three functions of *money*.

strategic trade policy   The use of trade barriers to reduce the risk inherent in product development by domestic firms, particularly that involving advanced technology.

strike   The withholding of labor services by an organized group of workers (a *labor union*).

structural unemployment   Unemployment of workers whose skills are not demanded by employers, who lack sufficient skill to obtain employment, or who cannot easily move to locations where jobs are available.

subsidy   A payment of funds (or goods and services) by a government, firm, or household for which it receives no good or service in return. When made by a government, it is a *government transfer payment*.

substitute goods   Products or services that can be used in place of each other. When the price of one falls, the demand for the other product falls; conversely, when the price of one product rises, the demand for the other product rises.

substitution effect   (1) A change in the quantity demanded of a *consumer good* that results from a change in its relative expensiveness produced by a change in the product's price; (2) the effect of a change in the price of a *resource* on the quantity of the resource employed by a firm, assuming no change in its output.

superior good   (See *normal good*.)

supply   A schedule showing the amounts of a good or service that sellers (or a seller) will offer at various prices during some period.

supply curve   A curve illustrating *supply*.

supply factor (in growth)   An increase in the availability of a resource, an improvement in its quality, or an expansion of technological knowledge that makes it possible for an economy to produce a greater output of goods and services.

supply-side economics   A view of macroeconomics that emphasizes the role of costs and *aggregate supply* in explaining *inflation*, *unemployment*, and *economic growth*.

surplus   The amount by which the *quantity supplied* of a product exceeds the *quantity demanded* at a specific (above-equilibrium) price.

surplus value   (Web chapter) The amount by which a worker's daily output in dollar terms exceeds his or her daily wage; the amount of the worker's output appropriated by capitalists as profit; a Marxian term.

tariff   A tax imposed by a nation on an imported good.

tax   An involuntary payment of money (or goods and services) to a government by a *household* or *firm* for which the household or firm receives no good or service directly in return.

tax incidence The person or group that ends up paying a tax.

tax-transfer disincentives Decreases in the incentives to work, save, invest, innovate, and take risks that allegedly result from high *marginal tax rates* and *transfer payments*.

Taylor rule A modern monetary rule proposed by economist John Taylor that would stipulate exactly how much the Federal Reserve should change interest rates in response to divergences of real GDP from potential GDP and divergences of actual rates of inflation from a target rate of inflation.

technological advance New and better goods and services and new and better ways of producing or distributing them.

technology The body of knowledge and techniques that can be used to combine *economic resources* to produce goods and services.

terms of trade The rate at which units of one product can be exchanged for units of another product; the price of a good or service; the amount of one good or service that must be given up to obtain 1 unit of another good or service.

theoretical economics The process of deriving and applying economic theories and principles.

thrift institution A *savings and loan association, mutual savings bank,* or *credit union.*

tight money policy Federal Reserve System actions that contract, or restrict, the growth of the nation's *money supply* for the purpose of reducing or eliminating inflation.

till money (See *vault cash.*)

time deposit An interest-earning deposit in a *commercial bank* or *thrift institution* that the depositor can withdraw without penalty after the end of a specified period.

token money Coins having a *face value* greater than their *intrinsic value.*

total demand The demand schedule or the *demand curve* of all buyers of a good or service; also called market demand.

total demand for money The sum of the *transactions demand for money* and the *asset demand for money.*

total product The total output of a particular good or service produced by a firm (or a group of firms or the entire economy).

total revenue The total number of dollars received by a firm (or firms) from the sale of a product; equal to the total expenditures for the product produced by the firm (or firms); equal to the quantity sold (demanded) multiplied by the price at which it is sold.

total spending The total amount that buyers of goods and services spend or plan to spend; also called *aggregate expenditures.*

total supply The supply schedule or the *supply curve* of all sellers of a good or service; also called market supply.

township and village enterprises (Web chapter) Privately owned rural manufacturing firms in China.

trade balance The export of goods (or goods and services) of a nation less its imports of goods (or goods and services).

trade bloc A group of nations that lower or abolish trade barriers among members. Examples include the *European Union* and the nations of the *North American Free Trade Agreement.*

trade controls *Tariffs, export subsidies, import quotas,* and other means a nation may employ to reduce *imports* and expand *exports.*

trade deficit The amount by which a nation's *imports* of goods (or goods and services) exceed its *exports* of goods (or goods and services).

tradeoff The sacrifice of some or all of one economic goal, good, or service to achieve some other goal, good, or service.

trade surplus The amount by which a nation's *exports* of goods (or goods and services) exceed its *imports* of goods (or goods and services).

trading possibilities line A line that shows the different combinations of two products that an economy is able to obtain (consume) when it specializes in the production of one product and trades (exports) it to obtain the other product.

transactions demand for money The amount of money people want to hold for use as a *medium of exchange* (to make payments); varies directly with the *nominal GDP.*

transfer payment A payment of *money* (or goods and services) by a government to a *household* or *firm* for which the payer receives no good or service directly in return.

unanticipated inflation Increases in the price level (*inflation*) at a rate greater than expected.

underemployment (1) The failure to produce the maximum amount of goods and services that can be produced from the resources employed; the failure to achieve *full production;* (2) a situation in which workers are employed in positions requiring less education and skill than they have.

undistributed corporate profits After-tax corporate profits not distributed as dividends to stockholders; corporate or business saving; also called retained earnings.

unemployment   The failure to use all available *economic resources* to produce desired goods and services; the failure of the economy to fully employ its *labor force*.

unemployment compensation   (See *unemployment insurance*.)

unemployment insurance   The social insurance program that in the United States is financed by state *payroll taxes* on employers and makes income available to workers who become unemployed and are unable to find jobs.

unemployment rate   The percentage of the *labor force* unemployed at any time.

unit labor cost   Labor cost per unit of output; total labor cost divided by total output.

unit of account   A standard unit in which prices can be stated and the value of goods and services can be compared; one of the three functions of *money*.

unlimited liability   Absence of any limits on the maximum amount that an individual (usually a business owner) may become legally required to pay.

unlimited wants   The insatiable desire of consumers for goods and services that will give them satisfaction or *utility*.

unplanned changes in inventories   Changes in inventories that firms did not anticipate; changes in inventories that occur because of unexpected increases or decreases of aggregate spending (of *aggregate expenditures*).

unplanned investment   Actual investment less *planned investment*; increases or decreases in the *inventories* of firms resulting from production greater than sales.

urban collectives   (Web chapter) Chinese enterprises jointly owned by their managers and their workforces and located in urban areas.

Uruguay Round   The eighth and most recent round of trade negotiations under *GATT* (now the *World Trade Organization*).

utility   The want-satisfying power of a good or service; the satisfaction or pleasure a consumer obtains from the consumption of a good or service (or from the consumption of a collection of goods and services).

value added   The value of the product sold by a *firm* less the value of the products (materials) purchased and used by the firm to produce the product.

value judgment   Opinion of what is desirable or undesirable; belief regarding what ought or ought not to be (regarding what is right or just and wrong or unjust).

value of money   The quantity of goods and services for which a unit of money (a dollar) can be exchanged; the purchasing power of a unit of money; the reciprocal of the *price level*.

vault cash   The *currency* a bank has in its vault and cash drawers.

velocity   The number of times per year that the average dollar in the *money supply* is spent for *final goods and services*; nominal GDP divided by the money supply.

vertical axis   The "up-down" or "north-south" axis on a graph or grid.

vertical intercept   The point at which a line meets the vertical axis of a graph.

vertical range   The vertical segment of the aggregate supply curve along which the economy is at full capacity.

very long run   A period in which *technology* can change and in which *firms* can introduce new products.

vicious circle of poverty   A problem common in some *developing countries* in which their low per capita incomes are an obstacle to realizing the levels of saving and investment requisite to acceptable rates of economic growth.

voluntary export restrictions   Voluntary limitations by countries or firms of their exports to a particular foreign nation to avoid enactment of formal trade barriers by that nation.

wage`   The price paid for the use or services of *labor* per unit of time (per hour, per day, and so on).

wage rate   (See *wage*.)

wages   The income of those who supply the economy with *labor*.

wealth   Anything that has value because it produces income or could produce income. Wealth is a stock; income is a flow. Assets less liabilities; net worth.

wealth effect   The tendency for people to increase their consumption spending when the value of their financial and real assets rises and to decrease their consumption spending when the value of those assets falls.

"will to develop"   The state of wanting economic growth strongly enough to change from old to new ways of doing things.

World Bank   A bank that lends (and guarantees loans) to developing nations to assist them in increasing their *capital stock* and thus in achieving *economic growth*; formally, the International Bank for Reconstruction and Development.

world price   The international market price of a good or service, determined by world demand and supply.

World Trade Organization (WTO)   An organization established in 1994 to replace *GATT* to oversee the provisions of the *Uruguay Round* and resolve any disputes stemming from it.

WTO   (See *World Trade Organization*.)

INDEX

INDEX

National income and related statistics for selected years, 1977–2000

National income statistics in rows 1–17 are in billions of current dollars. Details may not add to totals because of rounding.

			1977	1978	1979	1980	1981	1982	1983	1984	1985	1986
THE SUM OF	1	Personal consumption expenditures	1,278.4	1,430.4	1,596.3	1,762.9	1,944.2	2,079.3	2,286.4	2,498.4	2,712.6	2,895.
	2	Gross private domestic investment	361.3	436.0	490.6	477.9	570.8	516.1	564.2	735.5	736.3	747.
	3	Government purchases	415.3	455.6	503.5	569.7	631.4	684.4	735.9	800.8	878.3	942.
	4	Net exports	−23.7	−26.1	−24.0	−14.9	−15.0	−20.5	−51.7	−102.0	−114.2	−131.
EQUALS	5	Gross domestic product	2,031.4	2,295.9	2,566.4	2,795.6	3,131.3	3,259.2	3,534.9	3,932.7	4,213.0	4,452.
LESS	6	Consumption of fixed capital	231.6	261.5	300.4	345.3	394.8	436.4	456.1	482.3	516.5	551.
EQUALS	7	Net domestic product	1,799.8	2,034.4	2,266.0	2,450.3	2,736.5	2,822.8	3,078.8	3,450.4	3,696.5	3,901.
LESS	8	Net foreign factor income earned in the U.S.	−20.7	−22.1	−32.9	−35.3	−34.7	−36.5	−36.9	−35.3	−25.3	−15.
LESS	9	Indirect business taxes	184.7	196.3	223.3	242.6	274.1	256.3	319.2	323.4	341.4	391.
EQUALS	10	National income	1,635.8	1,860.2	2,075.6	2,243.0	2,497.1	2,603.0	2,796.5	3,162.3	3,380.4	3,525.
LESS	11	Social security contributions	113.1	131.3	152.7	166.2	195.7	208.9	226.0	257.5	281.4	303.
LESS	12	Corporate income taxes	73.0	83.5	88.0	84.8	81.1	63.1	77.2	94.0	96.5	106.
LESS	13	Undistributed corporate profits	83.2	99.0	106.0	83.8	71.8	39.8	47.4	56.6	34.6	8.
PLUS	14	Transfer payments*	270.6	301.9	352.6	415.7	450.9	477.2	501.0	520.6	547.1	605.
EQUALS	15	Personal income	1,637.1	1,848.3	2,081.5	2,323.9	2,599.4	2,768.4	2,946.9	3,274.8	3,515.0	3,712.
LESS	16	Personal taxes	201.1	233.5	273.3	304.1	351.5	361.6	360.9	387.2	428.5	449.
EQUALS	17	Disposable income	1,436.0	1,614.8	1,808.2	2,019.8	2,247.9	2,406.8	2,586.0	2,887.6	3,086.5	3,262.

RELATED STATISTICS

			1977	1978	1979	1980	1981	1982	1983	1984	1985	1986
	18	Real gross domestic product (in billions of 1996 dollars)	4,511.8	4,760.6	4,912.1	4,900.9	5,021.0	4,919.3	5,132.3	5,505.2	5,717.1	5,912.
	19	Percent change in real GDP	4.6	5.5	3.2	−0.2	2.5	−2.0	4.3	7.3	3.8	3.
	20	Real disposable income per capita (in 1996 dollars)	15,256	15,845	16,120	16,063	16,265	16,328	16,673	17,799	18,229	18,641
	21	Consumer price index (1982–84 = 100)	60.6	65.2	72.6	82.4	90.9	96.5	99.6	103.9	107.6	109.
	22	Rate of inflation (%)	6.5	7.6	11.3	13.5	10.3	6.2	3.2	4.3	3.6	1.
	23	Index of industrial production (1992 = 100)	74.9	79.3	82.0	79.7	81.0	76.7	79.5	86.6	88.0	89.
	24	Supply of money, M1 (in billions of dollars)	330.5	356.9	381.4	408.1	436.2	474.3	520.8	551.2	619.3	724.2
	25	Prime interest rate (%)	6.83	9.06	12.67	15.27	18.87	14.86	10.79	12.04	9.93	8.
	26	Population (in millions)	220.2	222.6	225.1	227.7	230.0	232.2	234.3	236.3	238.5	240.
	27	Civilian labor force (in millions)	99.0	102.3	105.0	106.9	108.7	110.2	111.6	113.5	115.5	117.
	28	Unemployment (in millions)	7.0	6.2	6.1	7.6	8.3	10.7	10.7	8.5	8.3	8.
	29	Unemployment rate as % of civilian labor force	7.1	6.1	5.8	7.1	7.6	9.7	9.6	7.5	7.2	7.
	30	Index of productivity (1992 = 100)	79.8	80.7	80.7	80.4	82.0	81.7	84.6	87.0	88.7	91.
	31	Annual change in productivity (%)	1.6	1.1	0.0	−0.3	1.9	−0.4	3.6	2.8	2.0	3.
	32	Trade balance on current account (in billions of dollars)	−14.3	−15.1	−0.3	2.3	5.0	−5.5	−38.7	−94.3	−118.2	−147.2
	33	Public debt (in billions of dollars)	706.4	776.6	829.5	909.1	994.8	1,137.3	1,371.7	1,564.7	1,817.5	2,120.

Sources: Bureau of Economic Analysis, Bureau of Labor Statistics, Federal Reserve System, and *Economic Report of the President, 2001.*